Communications
in Computer and Information Science 232

Minli Dai (Ed.)

Innovative Computing and Information

International Conference, ICCIC 2011
Wuhan, China, September 17-18, 2011
Proceedings, Part II

Volume Editor

Minli Dai
Suzhou University
No. 1, Shizi Street
Suzhou City, 215006, China
E-mail: minlidai2010@126.com

ISSN 1865-0929 e-ISSN 1865-0937
ISBN 978-3-642-23997-7 e-ISBN 978-3-642-23998-4
DOI 10.1007/978-3-642-23998-4
Springer Heidelberg Dordrecht London New York

Library of Congress Control Number: Applied for

CR Subject Classification (1998): C.2, H.4, I.2, H.3, D.2, J.1, H.5

Typesetting: Camera-ready by author, data conversion by Scientific Publishing Services, Chennai, India

Printed on acid-free paper

Springer is part of Springer Science+Business Media (www.springer.com)

Preface

The present book includes extended and revised versions of a set of selected papers from the 2011 International Conference on Computing, Information and Control (ICCIC 2011) held in Wuhan, China, September 17–18, 2011.

The ICCIC is the most comprehensive conference focused on the various aspects of advances in computing, information and control providing a chance for academic and industry professionals to discuss recent progress in the area. The goal of this conference is to bring together researchers from academia and industry as well as practitioners to share ideas, problems and solutions relating to the multifaceted aspects of computing, information and control.

Being crucial for the development of this subject area, the conference encompasses a large number of related research topics and applications. In order to ensure a high-quality international conference, the reviewing course is carried out by experts from home and abroad with all low-quality papers being rejected. All accepted papers are included in the Springer LNCS CCIS proceedings.

Wuhan, the capital of the Hubei province, is a modern metropolis with unlimited possibilities, situated in the heart of China. Wuhan is an energetic city, a commercial center of finance, industry, trade and science, with many international companies located here. Having scientific, technological and educational institutions such as Laser City and the Wuhan University, the city is also an intellectual center.

Nothing would have been achieved without the help of the Program Chairs, organization staff, and the members of the Program Committees. Thank you.

We are confident that the proceedings provide detailed insight into the new trends in this area.

August 2011 Yanwen Wu

Organization

Honorary Chair

Weitao Zheng	Wuhan Institute of Physical Education, Key Laboratory of Sports Engineering of General Administration of Sport of China

General Chair

Yanwen Wu	Huazhong Normal Universtiy, China

Program Chair

Qihai Zhou	Southwestern University of Finance and Economics, China

Program Committee

Sinon Pietro Romano	Azerbaijan State Oil Academy, Azerbaijan

International Program Committee

Ming-Jyi Jang	Far-East University, Taiwan
Tzuu-Hseng S. Li	National Cheng Kung University, Taiwan
Yanwen Wu	Huazhong Normal University, China
Teh-Lu Liao	National Cheng Kung University, Taiwan
Yi-Pin Kuo	Far-East University, Taiwan
Qingtang Liu	Huazhong Normal University, China
Wei-Chang Du	I-Shou University, Taiwan
Jiuming Yang	Huazhong Normal University, China
Hui Jiang	WuHan Golden Bridgee-Network Security Technology Co., Ltd., China
Zhonghua Wang	Huazhong Normal University, China
Jun-Juh Yan	Shu-Te University, Taiwan
Dong Huang	Huazhong University of Science and Technology, China
JunQi Wu	Huazhong Normal University, China

Table of Contents – Part II

Influencing Factors of Sports Lottery Marketing—Empirical Study Based on Data from Jiangsu 1
Peng Tang, Rong Pan, and Jiayi Liu

Decision Making of Electrical Equipment Renewa: Based on Crow-AMSAA Theory 10
Hongjing Zhang and Shuyan Wang

Applying PCA to Analyze the Main Factors That Affect the Ship Market Trend 17
Xin Tang, Yuantao Jiang, and Zhifeng Xu

Internet-Based Electronic Toll Collection System Using WiFi Technology 22
Li Ru'yuan, Wang Zhi'an, Li'yan, and Wang Xuhui

A Path Out of the Management Theory Jungle: From the Perspective of Chinese Management Philosophy 26
Wu Zhaochun

The Study on Regulation Policy of International Service Trade 34
Xie Lifen

The Study on Reputation Model of Retail Enterprises Supply Chain Based on Game Theory 40
An Xinhua

The Government's Role in Venture Capital Financing of Hi-tech SMEs in China 47
Zhijian Lu and Yiwen Shen

The Research on the Informatization Issues during Chinese Medicine Industry Modernization 52
Xiong Xinzhong

A Grey Correlation Analysis on Modern Rural Logistics and Rural Finance Development 60
Hu Bangyong

An Energy Efficient-Based AODVM Routing in MANET 66
Yun Zhang

Research and Practice of Training Teaching Based on MSF Software Process 73
Xiaoyu Ke and Min Jin

Green Supply Chain Management in Construction Industry 81
Zhu Mingqiang and Zou Zuxu

Interlocking Directorate and Firm's Diversification Strategy: Perspective of Strategy Learning 87
Yue Yang and Ning Cai

A Decision Support System for Ship Concept Design Using Genetic Algorithms 95
Yuantao Jiang and Siqin Yu

Enterprise Performance Evaluation Based on BP Neural Networks 101
Lv Feng and Zhang Zhiwen

Design and Research of Traffic Accidents Simulation System 109
Yang Lei and Zhang Zhijun

The Construction of Real-Time Integrated Surveillance System in Water Conservancy 116
Qing-Xun Ma

Exploration on Oil Field Road Safety Quantificational Evaluation in the North of Shaanxi Zone 122
Qing-Xun Ma

Research of Ecological Landscape Assessment Systems of Road Based on GIS and ES 128
Fengling Wang and Yu Li

The Measurement of Coordination Degree between Manufacturing and Logistics—Based on Gray Correlation System Model 136
Jian-Liang Peng and Kuai-Juan Zhang

Studies on Prediction of Unsafe Events Caused by Human Factors in ERM 143
Yulong Zhan, Di Wu, Yitong Hao, and Yao Yu

The Design and Implementation of Streaming Video Broadcast System Based on IPV6 150
Cai Wei, Wang Huixia, and Huang Kebin

Government Audit and National Economic Security 157
Cheng Chen

A Metadata Management Model-Oriented Data Resource Planning and Application 164
Xiaojun Liu, Lianzhong Liu, and Qian Yang

The Streaming Media Based Design of VOD System 172
Wang Huixia, Liu Zhibing, He Fang, and Cai Wei

Applications of Bioinformatics Based on Websites Services in Study of Environmental Microbiology 181
Yongliang Zheng, Lifang Long, Jun Xiang, Shiwang Liu, Deli Liu, and Yuling Zhong

On the View of Criminal Legislation Model Driving Reform– A Perspective of Network Intellectual Property 187
Lu Zhen

The Research of the Meteorological Distance Education Based on Mobile Education 194
Yuan Feng, Xianzhi Zhang, Xiaoyan Gong, and Lejiang Guo

An Empirical Research on Technological Innovation Capability of Enterprises Based on Logistic Regression Model 202
Na Li and Chuiyong Zheng

Research on Channels Managerial Tactics Based on Product Life Cycle Theory 211
Rongsheng Lv and Jian Wang

Analysis of the Theory of Commercial Value in Chinese-Foreign Cooperation in Running Schools in Higher Education 218
Lihui Xie

Empirical Study on Market Efficiency in Hubei-China Automotive Industry Based on SCP Paradigm 226
Xuetao Lee and Shuxiu Yu

MapGIS-Based Research in "One Planning Map" Compilation of Township-Level Land Use – Take Nieshi Town of Linxiang City as an Example 235
Fengjuan Wei and Yanzhong Liu

Modeling and Analyzing of Farmer Specialty Co-operativesŠ Internal Movement Mechanism 244
Huifeng Zhao

Security Analysis of WAPI Access Authentication Protocol WAI 253
Zhang Ruihong and Yang Wei

Research on Econometric Model for Domestic Tourism Income Based on Rough Set 259
He Xiaoya and Jie Zhiben

Research on Exhibition Economy of Poyang Lake Ecological Economic Region 267
Xiong Guojing

Land Use Change in the Coastal Area of the Pearl River Estuary Based on GIS and RS 274
Hengyao Tang and Yuan Fang

Gravity Center Change in the Coastal Area of the Pearl River Estuary Based on GIS and RS 281
Chen Xiaolin and Zhou Fei

A Study on Conflict and Coordination between Industrial Policy and Competition Policy 287
Qiong Huang and Renfa Yang

The Key Update Algorithm Based on HIBE 294
Xiaocheng Lu and Fang Deng

Design and Implementation of Technology Data Sharing Platform with Web Services 303
Liu Dong-Ping, Chen Li, Chen Rui, and Jin Jie

A System Planning for a Coal Logistics Service Provider 312
Yang He

On the Innovation of Finance Management under the E-Commerce Environment 318
Liu Jingzhong

Evaluative Conceptualization of Risk Prevention Mechanism upon Basic Principles of Environmental Law 326
Lin Youqu and Zhang Chunhong

A Comparative Study on SMEs External Environment 331
Liu Tanming

The Control Systems Design of Budgetary Slack in Chinese Enterprise 342
Shuang-Cai Zhang and Gui-Ying Liu

Treatment of Cr (VI) Contaminated Groundwater by PRB Simulation with Ash and Iron 350
Wei Zhang, Feng Ding, and Huasheng Wang

Study on Effective Elastic Thickness of Longmenshan Fault Zone after the Wenchuan Earthquake 357
Zedan Tao and Xiwei Wu

Optimization for Mix Design of High-Performance Concrete Using Orthogonal Test 364
Li Xiaoyong and Ma Wendi

First Order Dynamic Sliding Mode Control for Wheeled Mobile Robots 373
Da Lingrong and Tian Zhixiang

Residual Strength for Concrete after Exposure to High Temperatures ... 382
Li Xiaoyong and Bu Fanjie

Control Strategy for Wind and Solar Hybrid Generation System 391
Xin Gao

Deep Heat Transfer Performance and Ratio of Length to Diameter in Shell and Tube Heat Exchangers 396
Fuhua Jiang and Xianhe Deng

Study of the Free Surface Fluctuations in a GMAW Weld Pool with Globular Transfer Model 405
Zhao Pengcheng and Li Dasen

Development of Visual Analysis System Based on Visual Basic 414
Haibo Lin, Yingqian Zhang, Yumei Luo, and Yan Shi

Research on Entropy-TOPSIS in External Environment Evaluation of Power Grid Corporation 420
Qingyou Yan, Xiaoya Wang, Siqi He, and Lili Zhu

A New Mixed Variable Step Size ELMS Algorithm and Its Application in ANC 428
Sun Li Jun, Zhang Shou_Yong, and Wang Xiang_Li

A New Variable Step-Size Constant Modulus Blind Equalization Algorithm 436
Sun Li Jun, Zhang Shou-Yong, and Dai Bin

A New Algorithm of Echo Cancellation in Mobile Applications 443
Sun Li Jun, Dai Bin, and Zhang Shou-Yong

A System Integration Approach for E-Government System Development 450
Wen-Qian Liang, Hui-Jin Wang, and Shun Long

The Effects of Goods Sorting Mechanisms on Consumer Behavior and Seller Strategy in Online Marketplaces 458
Zhuzhu He, Shanshan Wang, Yuewen Liu, and Kaiquan Xu

A Study on R-TOPSIS Method and Its Application to Web Site Building Alternatives Selection 466
Ling Zhang and De-Qun Zhou

Research on Strategic Human Resource Management Innovation-Oriented 475
Sun Bo

A Database Integration Method for Small and Medium Information System 484
Bing Wang

E-Government: An Approach to Modern Public-Service Oriented Government 493
Yong Wu, Fang Zhou, and Jun-Min Liu

An Empirical Analysis on Effecting Factor of Urban-Rural Income Disparity in Heilongjiang Province 499
Guangji Tong and Cungui Li

The Economic Disparities of Shenyang Economic Region with Cluster Analysis 510
Guangji Tong and Tiankuo Wang

An Empirical Study on Effecting Factor of Migration of Rural Labor in China 518
Guangji Tong and Jingli Lan

A Novel Real-Time Eye Detection in Human-Computer Interaction 530
Yan Chao, Wang Yuanqing, and Zhang Zhaoyang

Author Index 539

Influencing Factors of Sports Lottery Marketing—Empirical Study Based on Data from Jiangsu

Peng Tang[1], Rong Pan[1], and Jiayi Liu[2]

[1] Department of Sports, School of Business, Hohai University, Nanjing, China
[2] School of Public Administration, Hohai University, Nanjing, China
azgad11@yahoo.cn

Abstract. Methods of investigation and literature are applied and time series analysis of dynamic equilibrium is adopted in this article to discuss the relationship between sales volume of sports lottery and per capita GDP, market share rate of sports lottery as well as the Community Chest relationship in Jiangsu Province from the perspective of sports lottery market in Jiangsu province based on co-integration analysis. Variables which affect significantly sale of lottery are found out. The relationship between sales volume of sports lottery and per capita GDP, market share rate of sports lottery as well as the Community Chest relationship in Jiangsu Province is verified to be a positive correlation by Co-integration analysis. Then Granger causality test is made. Finally, some conclusions about marketing innovation of sports lottery in Jiangsu Province are put forward.

Keywords: Sports Lottery, co integration analysis, Marketing Innovation.

1 Introduction

Lottery issuing has a history of over 200 years around the world and more than 100 countries issue lottery currently. Issuing of sports lottery is considered as a powerful support for sports cause in some western countries such as U.S.A., Italy, Canada, France and British. China approved to issue Chinese sports lottery in 1994 so as to raise funds for national fitness, Olympic honor and contests holding. This is a public-spirited activity whose fund both comes from and pays for the public. At present, methods to issue and types of lottery are increasingly variable, which lays a solid foundation for dramatic growth of sales volume of sports lottery. In 2009, sports lottery cause of Jiangsu remained " three-leading"--- leading contribution rate of natioanl sports lottery (more than 12%), leading occupation rate with 58.85% market share in Jiangsu and leading amount of rewards whose bonus overtook a million yuan (126/year) in Jiangsu. It is investigated that, current types of sports lottery supplied by Jiangsu market are immediate cash-in sports lottery, 3D sports lottery, 5D sports lottery, 5/22 combination-type sports lottery as well as traditional sports lottery. Most of them don't have a direct connection with sports. With tenuity connotation, playing measures of sports lottery have a large gap with sports lottery in its true meaning. It is this, causing conflict between increasingly cirulation of sports lottery and unbalanced market development. Meanwhile, increasingly management problems are bothering public

M. Dai (Ed.): ICCIC 2011, Part II, CCIS 232, pp. 1–9, 2011.

welfare funds for sports lottery such as low money return rate and unsatisfying selling environment which impose negative influence on sports lottery market of Jiangsu. With the rapid development of sports cause in Jiangsu, marketization, socialization and legalization will be the direction for marketing management innovation of Jiangsu Province. Empirical analysis with quantitative methods will be adopted in this paper.

2 Literature Summary

Sports lottery is playing an increasingly importance role in Chinese sports cause since 1990s. However, there still remain some shortcomings in the rapid development process of marketing of Chinese sports lottery.

Zhihong Bao and Yanxia Ji profoundly studies the consumers' psychology motivations and traits of consumers. Some suggestions on the issuance are put forward, such as standard manipulation, absorbing more consumers in all kinds of age and enriching the playing method to promote and realize the maintain, rapid and stable development of Chinese sports lottery market[1]. Liegang Humade investigation on consumption behavior of sports lottery consumer in Zhejiang province by the method of questionnaire investigation and mathematical statistics. The result showed that the biggest group of consumer was the person aged at 20～30, middle and high school education background, salary below average. The main motivation was to try their luck. Those occasionally buying sports lottery occupied large proportion. They usually spend 2～20 RMB each time[2]. Gang Li studied the determinants of per capita sales of different sport and welfare lottery from the angle of vertical, horizontal and panel so as to make clear the relation among different in rules or issuing subject. With the increasing of income, per capita sales of lottery decreased. Lower income class is the main body of buying lottery[3]. Shuzhuang Chen made in on sports lottery market, consuming behavior and the consuming mind in Guangdong Province by using the method of questionnaire investigation and mathematical statistics. The result shows that the biggest group of consumer is the person aged at 18 - 45. middle and high school education background, salary average; The most of consumers have the better knowledge and motivations, their consuming mind is cooperatively mature, and the mien is right[4]. The mass sports consumption supply of Fujian province was investigated and analyzed thoroughly by methods of documents, investigation, mathematical and logical analysis by Guolong Huang. The results show that the society and economy environment of the mass sports consumption of Fujian province are fairly good; Purchasing sports clothing, exercise equipment, sports lottery ticket, etc. are mainly consumption in the structure of consumption. The exercise courses of the highest rate of selection of the mass sports consumption of Fujian province are swimming, badminton, table tennis, Wushu, tennis, etc. Each consumption under thirty yuan is a universal and acceptable standard of all or different mass group[5]. The statistic analysis on consumer behavior and structure by Lingzhu concludes that the sports lottery consumers are mainly constituted by young or middle aged males, largely involving those of low income and lack of educational background, or those with blindness in consumption[6]. Based on the input (incentive), internal, external and output (response) factors, Guangxue Li explores the formation and changes of sports lottery consumption in the southwest region by applying the methods of questionnaire and interview. He also analyzes the consumers' characteristics of composition and behavior[7]. Lingfeng Zhao learnt from the single account system in western national treasury and put forward suggestions that it is useful to strengthen the management of off-budget funds of public welfare funds of physical training lottery, try a new comprehensive fiscal budget, evaluate the use efficiency of public welfare funds of physical training lottery, establish the management committee of public welfare funds of physical training lottery and endow it with the power of management and supervision and enact the management principles of lottery to intensify the standard management of lottery[8]. With the methods of questionnaire ,personal visiting ,documentation and mathematical statistics , Aifeng Wan, from the view of consumption psychology and sociology, researches and logically analyzes the factors influencing the consumption of Nanjing consumers of sports lottery[9].

3 Co-integration Analysis

Since 1980s, the long-term equilibrium relationship of co-integration analysis to two nonstationary time series can be verified by two-step method of Engle –Granger and co-integration systematic analysis based on VAR put forward by Johansen (1988) and Johansen-Juselius (1990).

A. Data and Model

Methods of investigation and literature are adopted in research to study the following four variables: sales volume of sports lottery in Jiangsu (XS), per capita GDP (PGDP), market share rate of sports lottery (MR) and the Community Chest (GYJ). It is judged that there is certain connection between sports lottery in Jiangsu (XS) and per capita GDP (PGDP), market share rate of sports lottery (MR) and the Community Chest (GYJ). Then co-integration analysis will be conducted. In empirical analysis, data sample spacing is 1990-2009 and all data used are from << Statistical Yearbook of Jiangsu>>, <<Lottery Statistical Yearbook of Jiangsu>> and website of Jiangsu lottery. To facilitate our research, the natural logarithm of the four variables are gained to obtain new variable sequence named $LNXS$, $LNPGDP$, $LNMR$ and $LNGYJ$.

Its general regression model is:

$$LNXS = C_1 + C_2 \bullet LNPGDP$$

$$LNXS = C_1 + C_2 \bullet LNMR$$

$$LNXS = C_1 + C_2 \bullet LNGYJ$$

B. Unit Root Test

Since most economic time series are nonstationary, unit root test must be done before co- integration verification. Only when variable sequence is a unit root series of same step, co-integration regression can be conducted. Firstly, timing variables analyzed must be conducted unit root verification before using this method. If a series passed through d difference before becoming stationary sequence, then the series is called unit root with d step and denoted by $I(d)$. ADF (Augmented Dickey-Fuller) Method was adopted to verify the stability of variable and the results are as follows:

Table 1. Results of ADF Verification

Variable	Forms of Verification (C, T, K)	ADF Value	5% Critical Value	Result
LNXS	(C, T, 1)	-3.3635	-3.0299	Nonstationary
⊿LNXS	(C, 1, 2)	-2.2954	-3.6908	Stationary
LNPGDP	(C, T, 1)	-3.3787	-3.0299	Nonstationary
⊿LNPGDP	(C, 0, 1)	-1.2658	-3.0404	Stationary
LNMR	(C, T, 1)	-1.1427	-3.0299	Nonstationary
⊿LNMR	(C, 0, 2)	-3.1482	-3.0403	Stationary
LNGYJ	(C, T, 1)	-1.5055	-3.6736	Nonstationary
⊿LNGYJ	(C, 0, 3)	-2.7060	-3.6908	Stationary

Note: Results of ADF verification in Table 1 are calculated by EVIEW5.0. Forms of verification (C, T, K) represent equation of unit root test with constant term, term of time trend and lag order. Adding lag term is to make residual term become white noise. ⊿ represents difference operator.

According to Table 1, the horizontal sequences of all variables are nonstationary and their first differences are stationary. Therefore, co-integration analysis can be made.

C. *Co-integration Test*

Co-integration systematic method based on VAR put forward by Johansen-Juselius is adopted here. In line with pricing principle of AIC ($AIC = \log(\frac{\sum \varepsilon_i^2}{N} + \frac{2k}{N})$), results of test are shown in Table 2 and Table 3.

Table 2. Results of Johansen Co-integration Test

	Supposed Amount of CE(S)	Likelihood	5% Critical Value	Eigen Value
XS and PGDP	0*	5.856026	14.26460	0.6318
	at most 1	0.698828	3.841466	0.4032
XS and GYJ	0*	0.251352	15.49471	0.7521
	at most 1	0.01667	3.841466	0.5823
XS and MR	0*	0.428940	15.49471	0.2401
	at most 1	0.026002	3.841466	0.4910

Note: * represents significance more than 5%. Constant term but linear trend term is included. Results of test in table are calculated by EVIEW6.0.

Table 3. Co-integration Vector after Standardization

	LNXS	*LNPGDP*	*C*
XS and PGDP	1.000000	15.35067	-91636.53
	Likelihood	-246.2768	
XS and GYJ	1.000000	6.914402	10232.05
	Likelihood	-249.8210	
XS and MR	1.000000	4.93347	-43995.42
	Likelihood	-265.047	

Results of test indicate:

(1) Under significance level of 5%, there is only one co-integration equation between sales volume of sports lottery in Jiangsu (XS) and per capita GDP (PGDP). After standardization, the co- integration equation is: $LNXS = 15.35067 LNPGDP - 91636.53$ This co-integration equation indicates that a long-term stable equilibrium relationship exists between sales volume of sports lottery in Jiangsu (XS) and per capita GDP (PGDP). In the long run, 1% growth of per capita GDP (PGDP) will lead to 15.35067% increase of sales volume of sports lottery in Jiangsu.

(2) Under significance level of 5%, there is only one co-integration equation between sales volume of sports lottery in Jiangsu (XS) and the Community Chest (GYJ). After standardization, the co- integration equation is: $LNXS = 6.914402 LNGYJ + 10232.05$ This co-integration equation indicates that a long-term stable equilibrium relationship exists between sales volume of sports lottery in Jiangsu (XS) and the Community Chest (GYJ). In the long run, 1% growth of sales volume of sports lottery in Jiangsu (XS) will lead to 15.35067% increase of the Community Chest in Jiangsu.

(3) Under significance level of 5%, there is only one co-integration equation between sales volume of sports lottery in Jiangsu (XS) and market share rate of sports lottery (MR). After standardization, the co- integration equation is: $LNXS = 4.93347 LNMR - 43995.42$ This co-integration equation indicates that a long-term stable equilibrium relationship exists between sales volume of sports lottery in Jiangsu (XS) and market share rate of sports lottery (MR). In the long run, 1% growth of market share rate of sports lottery (MR) will lead to 15.35067% increase of market share rate of sports lottery (MR) in Jiangsu.

D. Granger Causality Test

Causality between LNXS、LNPGDP and LNGYJ is shown in Table 4.

In line with Table 4:

(1) LNXS isn't Causality cause of LNPGDP but LNPGDP is Causality cause of LNXS.
(2) LNGYJ isn't Causality cause of LNXS but LNXS is Causality cause of LNGYJ.
(3) LNMR isn't Causality cause of LNXS but LNXS is Causality cause of LNMR.

Table 4. Causality Analysis between LNXS、LNPGDP and LNGYJ

	Null Hypothesis	Optimal Lag Phase	Objective Number	F Statistics	P Value
Causality between LNXS and LNPGDP	LNXS isn't Causality cause of LNPGDP	1	18	5.97755	0.94996
	LNPGDP isn't Causality cause of LNXS	1	18	0.69294	0.5177
Causality between LNXS and LNGYJ	LNGYJ isn't Causality cause of LNXS	1	18	1.13872	0.3502
	LNXS is Causality cause of LNGYJ	1	18	16.2865	0.0003
Causality between LNXS and LNGYJ	LNMR isn't Causality cause of LNXS	1	18	1.37128	0.2882
	LNXS is Causality cause of LNMR	1	18	1.42331	0.2761

E. Variable Relationship

Judge the relationship between sales volume of sports lottery and per capita GDP, market share rate of sports lottery as well as the Community Chest in Jiangsu Province base on variables analysis. Results are calculated by software and shown as follows:

Table 5. Results of Johansen Co-integration Test

Supposed Amount of CE (S)	Likelihood	5% Critical Value	Eigen Value
0*	0.892436	47.85613	0.0000
at most 1	0.821196	29.79707	0.0075
at most 2	0.249872	15.49471	0.7645
at most 3	0.012636	3.841466	0.6323

Note: * represents significance more than 5%. Constant term but linear trend term is included. Results of test in table are calculated by EVIEW6.0.

Table 6. Co-integration Vector after Standardization

LNXS	LNPGDP	LNGYJ	LNMR	C
1.000000	4.537145	4.204551	1.54656	-68053.67
Likelihood	-239.7605			

According to test results of Table 6, under significance level of 5%, there is only one co-integration equation between sales volume of sports lottery in Jiangsu (XS) and market share rate of sports lottery. After standardization, the co- integration equation is:

$LNXS = 4.537145LNPGDP + 4.204551LNGYJ + 1.54656LNMR - 68053.67$ This co-integration equation indicates that a long-term stable equilibrium relationship exists between sales volume of sports lottery in Jiangsu and per capita GDP, market share rate of sports lottery as well as the Community Chest. Specifically, 1% growth of per capita GDP will lead to 4.5% increase of sales volume of sports lottery in Jiangsu and 1% increase of Community Chest will cause 4.2% growth of sales volume of sports lottery in Jiangsu. Likewise, 1% increase of market share rate of sports lottery will lead to 1.5 % growth of sales volume of sports lottery in Jiangsu in the long run.

F. Illustration of Model

In accordance with co-integration analysis, a long-term stable equilibrium relationship exists between sales volume of sports lottery in Jiangsu and per capita GDP, market share rate of sports lottery as well as the Community Chest. They are as follows respectively:

[1] There is a positive correlation between per capita GDP and sales volume of sports lottery in Jiangsu. In the long run, 1% growth of per capita GDP will lead to 15.35067% increase of sales volume of sports lottery in Jiangsu. LNPGDP is Causality cause of LNGYJ.

[2] There is a positive correlation between the Community Chest and sales volume of sports lottery in Jiangsu. In the long run, 1% growth of sales volume of sports lottery will lead to 15.35067% increase of the Community Chest in Jiangsu. LNXS is Causality cause of LNGYJ.

[3] There is a positive correlation between the market share rate and sales volume of sports lottery in Jiangsu. In the long run, 1% growth of market share rate of sports lottery will lead to 15.35067% increase of sales volume of sports lottery in Jiangsu. LNXS is Causality cause of LNMR.

4 Conclusion and Enlightenment

Empirical method is adopted in this paper to explore the relationship between sales volume of sports lottery in Jiangsu and per capita GDP, market share rate of sports lottery as well as the Community Chest. According to the abovementioned analysis, currently, the following aspects can be useful in advancing development of sports lottery of Jiangsu besides main factors studied in the paper.

(1) Explore actively new products of sports lottery to meet the needs of lottery buyers. Various types of lottery including guess competition should be empoldered to main current and gain more market share in lottery market. By dint of the opportunity of 2010 Shanghai Exposition, it may be a good choice for Jiangsu Sports Lottery Center to explore new kind of lottery such as Exposition Lottery. More attention should be put on types of production and structure of playing measures. In U.S.A., sports lottery of guess competition kind is very popular, which can be draw by Jiangsu Sports Lottery Center.

(2) Expand sale scale and extend marketing channel. Jiangsu Sports Lottery Center should further regulate management system in Jiangsu Province and advance self-improvement of sales network, increase number of sales network and improve the coverage rate of sales network. Meanwhile, train salespeople of sports lottery regularly or irregularly to facilitate their master of basic knowledge of sports lottery marketing so as to improve their comprehensive quality in all aspects. Moreover, mode of lottery such as on-line purchasing and purchase by cell phone should be actively improved and populous area should add sales network.

(3) Further perfect legal management system and strengthen legal construction of sports lottery. Perfect laws and regulations is the prerequisite to create sound environment for development of sports lottery market. <<Lottery Law>> is the guarantee for sound development of lottery industry. Jiangsu Sports Lottery Center can formulate local regulation based on government legislation for development of sports lottery in Jiangsu to insure sustainable, stable and rapid development of sports lottery cause in Jiangsu.

(4) Increase money return rate and strengthen propaganda work. The degree of money return rate and possibility of obtaining top prize are vital elements to attract lottery buyers and inspire their demand. At the same time, propaganda work is indispensable component in issuing process of sports lottery. Internet, TV and newspaper should be made full use.

References

1. Bao, Z., Ji, Y.: The Psychological Research on Consumers' Economic Behavior in Sports Lottery. Economy and Management 18(12), 65–67 (2004)
2. Hu, L.: Investigation on Consumption Behavior of Sports Lottery Consumer in Zhejiang Province. China Sport Science and Technology 41(6), 12–14 (2005)
3. Li, G.: The Determinants of Per Capita Sales of Lottery and the Forecast on the Developing Trend of the Lottery Market in China. China Sport Science 26(12), 30–35 (2006)
4. Chen, S.: Investigation on Current Situation of Sports Lottery Consumer in Guangdong Province. Journal of Physical Education Institute of ShanxiNormalUniversity 22(4), 21–23 (2007)
5. Huang, G.: Investigation of the mass sports consumption supply in Fujian province and consideration about the sports market development. Journal of Shandong Institute of Physical Education and Sports 24(11), 28–31 (2008)

6. Zhu, L.: Research on Behavior and Structure of Sichuan Sports Lottery Consumers. Journal of Luoyang Normal University, 173–175 (February 2008)
7. Li, G.: Investigation of Sports Lottery Consumption Market in Southwest Region. Journal of Jianghan University (Natural Sciences) 37, 105–108 (2009)
8. Zhao, L.: Problems and Suggestions When Distributing Sport Lottery Public Welfare Funds in China. Hainna Finance, 75–78 (March 2009)
9. Wang, A., Wang, Z., Chen, Y., Shi, W., Jiang, F.: Research Into the Several Factors Influencing the Consumption of Nanjing Consumers of Sports Lottery. Journal of Shandong Institute of Physical Education 20(62), 27–30 (2004)

Decision Making of Electrical Equipment Renewal: Based on Crow-AMSAA Theory

Hongjing Zhang and Shuyan Wang

School of Economics and Management
Northeast DianLi University
Jilin, China
francesca.collins1@gmail.com

Abstract. Crow-AMSAA reliability growth model is introduced into the operation process of electrical equipment according to the characteristics of electrical equipment renewal. Better reliability can achieved by considering failure occurrence as a random process. Therefore, a more accurate estimate of Life Cycle Cost of electric equipment is obtained. With an example to prove this model can provide a scientific method on decision making of electrical equipment renewal.

Keywords: Renewal Decision Making, Crow-AMSAA model, Reliability Growth, Net Present Value.

1 Introduction

A life cycle cost of electrical equipment is mainly composed by acquisition costs, operation costs, maintenance costs, failure costs and disposing costs. Because electric power devices require high reliability and higher penalty costs of failure, these characteristics make electrical equipment operation, maintenance and failure costs usually accounted for a large proportion in the total cost, and this part of the costs are uncertain, difficult to predict. Therefore, That becomes the focus of decision-making power equipment renewal to predict the reliability of electrical equipment.

2 Traditional Methods of Defect Equipment Replacement Decision

Traditionally economic life is single standard to determine whether electrical equipment need to be replaced .The traditional device management to pursue the main goal is to "extend the life of the equipment" and "maintain the equipment's normal capacity," so the main task is to do the technical management but not with economic rationality. Under the electricity market conditions, equipment management focuses on accessing to higher economic life cycle cost and overall efficiency. The goal is economic efficiency. Clearly, it can not meet the management need only with technology, it must be combined the economics elements with the technical management.

M. Dai (Ed.): ICCIC 2011, Part II, CCIS 232, pp. 10–16, 2011.

when making decisions use Life-cycle approach in operation of equipment, the cost generated by equipment failure most often is not easy to determine and higher punishment cost, which part of the costs is more difficult to predict. Therefore, we need to introduce reliability prediction model to predict the reliability of electrical equipment.

After Duane presented the concept of reliability growth testing, Crow on the growth of in-depth reliability study using the Crow-AMSAA model of the problem is formalized. This model using maximum likelihood estimation of model parameters and goodness of fit test, The basic principle is observed by all the errors on the basis of an error model to achieve restoration, which just shows that the number of error patterns that do not meet system reliability goals to support the error rate ,This paper using Crow-AMSAA model time to failure of electrical equipment to predict the number of LCC based on the use of life cycle cost of the net present value to place on the old and new equipment costs were calculated to determine whether to change on equipment replacement.

3 Equipment Renewal Decision Model

A. Equipment Renewal NPV

Equipment Selection generally follow the cost minimization of the principle that the more the costs incurred by each program to minimize the cost of the program as the final option. Therefore, the electrical equipment renewal is belonging to construction project in the investment. At present, the main methods used by the static and dynamic Investment Law Investment Law. In considering the time value of the case, the analysis of dynamic investment law is often more practical. Dynamic Investment Law, including net present value and net annual value method, in this paper, we will use the more commonly used net present value method, the NPV method. Defined as:

$$NPV(i_0) = \sum_{t}^{n} (CI - CO)_t (1 + i_0)^{-t} \tag{1}$$

The formula: $(CI - CO)_t$ is the t in net cash flow; n for the calculation period; i_0 as the benchmark discount rate [5].

Equipment renewal decision costs involved in decision-making are: CA for acquisition costs, CO for operation costs, CM for maintenance costs, CF for failure costs, CD for disposing costs (If the calculation of retirement age to the device), L for equipment residual fees.

$$NPV = CA + \sum_{i}^{n} [CO_i + CM_i + CF_i] \frac{1}{(1+I_c)^i} + CD \frac{1}{(1+I_c)^{n^*}} - L \frac{1}{(1+I_c)^n} \tag{2}$$

Where, CO_i, CM_i, CF_i respectively, the first i years of equipment operation, maintenance, fault cost, I_c as the benchmark rate of return (usually on an annualized basis), n as computing cycles, n^* as the equipment retirement age.

B. Crow-AMSAA model introduction

Life-cycle approach in the use of economic operation of equipment when making decisions, the costs arising from equipment failure is often not easy to identify with the most and the penalty cost higher characteristic, this part of the costs is more difficult to predict. Therefore, we need to introduce reliability prediction model to predict the reliability of electrical equipment.

Crow-AMSAA model (CA model) is based strictly on the basis of random process theory of system reliability evaluation of an effective statistical model. It is equivalent to a Weibull density function with non-homogeneous Poisson process (N.H.P.P.) model. The use of CA and other reliability growth model for a class change system reliability (repairable system) studies, usually during the first test data through the system failure time quantitative tests tend to observe whether the system has the reliability significantly changes in the Laplace test can be used. Crow-AMSAA reliability growth model is introduced to the use of electrical equipment the process of updating the system, through the Occurrence of equipment failure is a random process in order to better achieve the reliability of power equipment used in a good fit, on this basis the cost of power equipment failures can be more accurate estimate.

C. Crow-AMSAA model based on the improved model of the equipment replacement decision

As the Crow-AMSAA model gives a cumulative time of the cumulative events (such as the failure event) occurred on the forecast, Therefore, the future of CA model can predict the number of time periods of equipment failure is estimated to start counting time $T_0 = 0$, m total breakdown in failure number of T_n time.

$$m = (T_n - T_0)^{\beta} \lambda \tag{3}$$

Of which: λ ,β= Type parameters(λ<0,β>0)

λ is total time T in each time interval within the fault density. When 0 <β <1, the test phase of the error is in accordance with the non-homogeneous Poisson process in the wrong way in decreasing intensity.

As the forecast is usually a fairly long time continuous system or equipment costs incurred, in order to have comparable, taking into account the time value of money, combined with Crow-AMSAA model of failure predicted that this equipment updated decision model could be improved are:

$$NPV = CA + \lambda CF_i \sum_{i}^{n} [\frac{(T_i - T_0)^{\beta}}{(1+I_c)^i} - \frac{(T_{i-1} - T_0)^{\beta}}{(1+I_c)^i}] + \sum_{i}^{n} CK_i \frac{1}{(1+I_c)^i} + CD \frac{1}{(1+I_c)^{n^*}} - L \frac{1}{(1+I_c)^{n}} \tag{4}$$

In the type(4): CK_i place for the first i system during the daily operation and maintenance costs ($CK_i = CO_i + CM_i$) ,including basic energy, regulate dimensional inspection, it has nothing to do with whether the equipment normal operation; CF_i fault occurs each time the costs incurred, including the failure repair manual inspection, replacement parts cost and impact of the loss failure.

λ and β in the model parameters to be estimated, using maximum likelihood estimation can go to the $\hat{\lambda}$ and $\hat{\beta}$, when the failure to reach a predetermined number of records the number of suspension, that is, Censored test. The results are as follows:

$$\hat{\beta} = \frac{n}{(n-1)\ln T_n - \sum_{i=1}^{n-1} \ln T_i}; \hat{\lambda} = \frac{n}{T_n^{\beta}} \tag{5}$$

Where n is the total number of failures, T_n (n =1, 2, ...) is the second failure occurred at a time. For reliability prediction, using the classical Cramer-Von Mises goodness of fit test to carry out inspection [6]. Using statistics C_n^2 in the CA model:

$$C_n^2 = \frac{1}{12n} + \sum_i [\left(\frac{t_i}{t_s}\right)^{\hat{\beta}} - \frac{2i-1}{2n}]^2 \tag{6}$$

CA model is the process of modeling instead of modeling the system, so that it can be used for less data reliability growth modeling. CA model also for small samples and a variety of fault types of missing data is very useful mixed. CA is calculated with time-varying prediction failure rate and the effective number of fault. Therefore, the reliability analysis based on the CA model and in the electrical equipment based on cost modeling method has high practical value.

4 Numerical Examples

High-voltage circuit breaker (or high-voltage switch) is the main power substation control equipment, with the arc characteristics, when the system during normal operation, it cut off and all electrical equipment connected to line and no-load and load current; When the system fails, it and the Relay Protection meet, quickly cut off the fault current to prevent the expansion of the scope of the accident. So, the high voltage circuit breakers work has a direct impact on the safe operation of power systems.

Suppose a substation reconstruction project in progress, 110kV circuit breaker on whether to update the active devices to two options: Program 1, continue to use the active breaker to retire; Program II, the replacement equipment for the new circuit breaker circuit breaker serving equipment. For ease of comparison, we first do some explanation:

- Take more years to 10 years in each of the system to run on average about 324.85 days, or T_i =324.85i , （i =0,1,2,...,10） ; interest rate to 6%;
- 8 new and old equipment failures to take history as the failure prediction data, including the failure occurrence time and fault duration, see Table 1;
- The new and old equipment *CA* purchase cost is given by the Table 2, due to continued use of old equipment, the cost does not occur, so the cost of *CA* is zero;
- In normal use in the daily operation and maintenance costs (including the use of process losses) of old equipment to 3,600 Yuan / year, new equipment for 4000 Yuan / year;

- Failure punishment costs include an average of one-time fault repair costs (including labor, replacement of components, etc.) the old equipment was 1,000 Yuan / time, new equipment for the 1,200 Yuan / time; Interruption of about 16,000 Yuan / hour to maintain old and new equipment, the average time spent troubleshooting the loss of old equipment outage cost about 3,605,920,000 Yuan/time, new equipment for the 3.41 billion Yuan/time;
- As in the comparison period, the old and new equipment had not reached retirement age, the cost of equipment retired A zero;
- Equipment value calculation equipment depreciation use the annual summation model calculate annual depreciation rate:

$$\text{Annual depreciation rate}=\frac{(\text{Depreciation period}-\text{The number of years has been used})}{\text{Depreciation period}\times(\text{Depreciation period}+1)/2}$$

Expiration of the equipment in service for 30 years, the service expired equipment residual value 5400 Yuan, then the program after 10 years residual value of equipment were (updated year old equipment has been operated for 10 years):

$L_1 = 7432.26$ (Yuan) $L_2 = 11361.29$ (Yuan)

Table 1. The history file of equipment failure

		1	2	3	4	5	6	7	8
old one	Failure time (days)	253	553	972	1444	1750	2024	2175	2250
	Failure duration (hours)	19.6	22	26.3	15.8	20	27	32.2	17.4
New one	Failure time (days)	183	537	1093	1616	1933	2209	2362	2441
	Failure duration (hours)	27	23.5	20	24.4	18.3	16.8	21.5	19

Laplace test can be used. Laplace test statistic for use of U, if the system in continuous time T test failures have been recorded within the n, C statistic is:

$$U=\left\{\frac{1}{nT}\sum_{i=1}^{n}t_i-\frac{1}{2}\right\}\sqrt{12n} \tag{7}$$

Under the given level of significance, Statistic U will be calculated and compares the results with given grade check critical value u_α: ①if $U \le -u_\alpha$, significant trend of reliability growth; ②if $U \ge u_\alpha$, significantly reduce the reliability of the trend; ③if $-u_\alpha \le U \le u_\alpha$, no obvious trend of reliability.

Table 2. The item list of equipment cost unit:yuan

		old equipment	new equipment
One-time investment CA	cost of equipment	0	180000
	cost of installation debugging	0	6000
	Other costs	0	10200
operation and maintenance cost CK_i		3600	4000
Failure penalty fees CF_i	Failure repair	1000	1200
	Interruption costs	360592	341000
Cost of equipment retired CD		0	0
Equipment salvage L		7432.26	11361.29

Combined with the data in Table 1, on the old and new equipment for reliability growth trend test, using the formula (7), Statistics U calculation were:

$U_1 = 1.326$; $U_2 = 1.309$;

Take the same level of significance $\alpha = 0.20$, Look-up table was $U_\alpha = 1.282$, have $U_1 > U_2 > U_\alpha$,Can be given significance level conditions, to accept the reliability of old and new devices have significantly decreased, can use the Crow-AMSAA reliability growth model system, the reliability of the equipment fitted. The failure data in Table 1, substitution of equation (5), parameter estimation, calculated by:

$\hat{\beta}_1 = 1.5205$; $\hat{\lambda}_1 = 6.3988\text{E-}5$

$\hat{\beta}_2 = 1.4068$; $\hat{\lambda}_2 = 13.7233\text{E-}5$

Then estimated parameters and fault log data were substituted into the formula (6) for model projections of goodness of fit test, calculate statistics $C^2_{n,i}$, and are as follows:

$C^2_{n,1} = 0.0861$ $C^2_{n,2} = 0.1143$

Given the level of significance $\alpha =$ 0.10 Look-up table available $C^2_{n,1} < C^2_{n,2} < C^2_{n,\alpha} = 0.1620$, Crow-AMSAA model can be considered a good fit of the equipment failure rate.

Finally, we will table 2 in each group of data generation equipment replacement decision model equation (4), the program cost by the net present value of the two schemes are compared:

$$NPV_{old} = 1741694.53\,(yuan)$$
$$NPV_{new} = 2027526.31\,(yuan)$$

Be seen from the results $NPV_{old} < NPV_{new}$, Option One is an optional program, which continue to use existing equipment.

5 Conclusions

Based on the traditional methods of equipment renewal research, this paper proposed a new method which combined acquisition costs, operation costs, maintenance costs, failure costs and disposing costs together. Compared with the traditional method, failure costs are accounted into the cost calculations. From the results, it is concluded that when considering the failure costs, the initial acquisition cost only accounts for smaller proportion of the whole life cycle cost. The new model makes more comprehensive and conform to reality. This paper focuses on the number of equipment failures in order to accurately calculate the failure costs. Therefore, we are introduced into the CA model of reliability growth process of using electrical equipment systems, failure occurred by looking for a random process to achieve better reliability of power devices used in a good fit, achieved on this basis Power Device Life Cycle Cost of a more accurate estimate. This is the innovation of this paper. An example calculation and analysis, and concluded that for equipment investment decisions, should take into account the investment in the future the number of occurrence in order to make the right choice.

References

1. Ren, Y.L., Wang, J., Mu, G., Wang, H.Y.: CA model based on electrical equipment life cycle cost study. Industrial Engineering and Management, 63–67 (May 2008)
2. Crow, L.H.: An extended reliability growth model for managing and assessing corrective actions. Reliability and Maintainability, 73–80 (2004)
3. Elmira, P.: Basic factors to forecast maintenance cost and failure processes for nuclear power plants. Nuclear Engineering and Design, 41–47 (2006)
4. Reliability Growth Management Manual, pp. 142–151. National Defense military standard published in the Department of Work Committee, Beijing (1995)
5. Wu, T., Feng, Q., Ouyang, Z.: Technical economics, pp. 78–79. Tsinghai University Press, Beijing (2004)
6. Ian, B.M.: Modified Cameroon misses goodness-of-fit tests for spectral distribution functions. Stochastic An International Journal of Probability and Stochastic Processes 1(1-4), 53–60 (1975)
7. Zhu, Y., Weng, C.: Reliability Growth. Science Press, Beijing (1992)
8. Tian, K.: Active airborne equipment reliability growth. Electronic Product Reliability and Environmental Testing, 58–61 (January 2002)
9. Mei, W.: Using AMSAA reliability growth model to predict product. Air Force Engineering University (4-2), 81–83 (2003)

Applying PCA to Analyze the Main Factors That Affect the Ship Market Trend

Xin Tang, Yuantao Jiang, and Zhifeng Xu

School of Economics and Management
Shanghai Maritime University
Shanghai 200135, China
mbasarir1@gmail.com

Abstract. As a result of the international financial crisis, the shipbuilding industry experienced a downturn in the year of 2008. In order to promote restructuring and upgrading of the shipbuilding industry as well as to promote its development in a sustainable and stable way, new plan was put in place in order to retrieve the great loss in the shipbuilding industry last year. The thesis is mainly quoted at the data of ship market and shipbuilding industry, which is primarily from 1993-2002. PCA(Principal Component Analysis) and FA(Factor Analysis) are used to make the research of the main factors that affect the market demand in order to do some of the groundwork for the next round research in the ship market.

Keywords: shipbuilding industry, main factors, PCA, FA, ship market.

1 Introduction

The shipbuilding industry is a comprehensive industry that plays an important role in promoting the development of shipping industry [1], marine transportation and national defense Construction by providing different types of the technical equipment for them. It also occupies a vital place in the national economy.

The production of the ship would take a long cycle of time and a large amount of money mainly because the shipbuilding industry follows the principles "production on order" which the production quantities are depended on the numbers of the orders [2]. Furthermore, the shipbuilding technology acquires high integration level and profession. Therefore, the shipbuilding industry is such a comprehensive industry that if we want to make a thorough study on it, we must collect a large numbers of data and make the analysis of the key factors that affects the shipbuilding industry.

2 Review of PCA

Principal component analysis (PCA) involves a mathematical procedure that transforms a number of possibly correlated variables into a smaller number of uncorrelated variables called principal components [3]. The first principal component

M. Dai (Ed.): ICCIC 2011, Part II, CCIS 232, pp. 17–21, 2011.

accounts for as much of the variability in the data as possible, and each succeeding component accounts for as much of the remaining variability as possible. Depending on the field of application, it is also named the discrete Karhunen–Loève transform (K.L.T.), the Hotelling transform or proper orthogonal decomposition (POD).

PCA is mathematically defined as an orthogonal linear transformation that transforms the data to a new coordinate system such that the greatest variance by any projection of the data comes to lie on the first coordinate (called the first principal component) [4], the second greatest variance on the second coordinate, and so on. PCA is theoretically the optimum transform for given data in least square terms [5].

For a data matrix, $\mathbf{X}^T$, with zero empirical mean (the empirical mean of the distribution has been subtracted from the data set), where each row represents a different repetition of the experiment, and each column gives the results from a particular probe, the PCA transformation is given by:

$$\mathbf{Y}^T = \mathbf{X}^T\mathbf{W} = \mathbf{V}\mathbf{\Sigma}^T \quad (1)$$

Where the matrix Σ is an m-by-n diagonal matrix with nonnegative real numbers on the diagonal and $\mathbf{W}\ \mathbf{\Sigma}\ \mathbf{V}^T$ is the singular value decomposition (svd) of $\mathbf{X}$.

The different factors that affect the ship market determine the variability in index of assessment. The number of the factors is so large that they can't be listed detailed in such a limited space [6]. So I do the PCA mainly based on a smaller sample which includes the 11 most commonly used indexes that to widely reflect the ship market conditions. And there is some internal relationship between those indexes.

I. The PCA Model of Main Factors

Principal component analysis is a statistical method used to describe variability among observed variables in terms of a potentially lower number of unobserved variables called factors. Indexes and their code are list in Table 1 [7].

Suppose we have a set of p observable random variables, $x_1 \cdots x_p$ with means $\mu_1 \cdots \mu_p$. Suppose for some unknown constants l_{ij} and k unobserved random variables F_j, where $i \in 1, \ldots, p$ and $j \in 1, \ldots, k$, andwhere k < p, we have

$$x_i - \mu_i = l_{i1}F_1 + \cdots + l_{ik}F_k + \epsilon_i. \quad (2)$$

Table 1. Indexes and Their Cod

code	index	code	index
A	World's Economic Growth Rate	G	Shipping Efficiency Fluctuation Ratio
B	International Sea-borne Freight Traffic Growth Rate	H	Orders In Hand Change Rate
C	International Trade Growth Rate	I	The new ship completions fluctuation ratio
D	Shipping Freight Change Rate	J	Old Ship Scrapping Change Rate
E	New Ship Price Fluctuation Ratio	K	World Ship-making capacity Growth rate
F	Fleet Growth Rate		

Table 2. The data of 11 indexes

Index / Year	1993	1994	1995	1996	1997	1998	1999	2000	2001	2002
A	2.90	5.00	4.00	4.60	4.20	2.50	3.50	4.60	1.70	1.90
B	3.40	3.20	3.70	2.40	5.55	-1.09	1.86	4.67	0.98	0.04
C	-0.92	14.03	18.99	4.60	3.75	-1.41	1.64	12.32	-3.74	4.03
D	7.02	0.74	18.71	-19.13	0.69	-16.58	1.21	17.30	-4.83	-4.44
E	0.68	-6.76	2.90	-4.92	0.74	-17.16	-0.90	6.36	-7.69	-2.78
F	1.98	2.90	3.57	4.25	3.64	2.00	2.74	-0.57	2.64	4.80
G	1.48	0.36	0.02	-1.81	1.85	-2.90	-1.12	5.28	-1.43	-4.36
H	-10.68	2.62	15.27	5.42	-4.72	23.04	1.55	6.93	11.60	1.25
I	12.90	-5.71	16.16	12.46	-0.35	-2.04	7.73	14.59	8.98	18.12
J	-2.61	27.84	-34.30	30.10	-28.78	68.17	14.38	-12.75	5.34	23.07
K	10.11	4.83	4.15	17.26	3.40	4.01	3.86	4.73	5.16	3.99

Table 3. Correlation Matrix

	Zscore (×93)	**Zscore (×94)**	**Zscore (×95)**	**Zscore (×96)**	**Zscore (×97)**	**Zscore (×98)**	**Zscore (×99)**	**Zscore (×00)**	**Zscore (×01)**	**Zscore (×02)**
Zscore (×93)	1.000	-0.369	-0.210	-0.060	0.367	-0.453	0.087	0.381	-0.582	0.113
Zscore (×94)	-0.369	1.000	-0.654	0.624	-0.692	0.820	0.664	-0.655	0.455	0.538
Zscore (×95)	0.210	-0.654	1.000	-0.639	0.778	-0.767	-0.651	0.928	-0.326	-0.515
Zscore (×96)	-0.060	0.624	-0.639	1.000	-0.602	0.799	0.808	-0.683	0.433	0.833
Zscore (×97)	0.367	-0.692	0.778	-0.602	1.000	-0.883	-0.785	0.670	-0.301	-0.685
Zscore (×98)	-0.453	0.820	-0.767	0.799	-0.883	1.000	0.809	-0.790	0.622	0.717
Zscore (×99)	0.087	0.664	-0.651	0.808	-0.785	0.809	1.000	-0.566	0.201	0.947
Zscore (×00)	0.381	-0.655	0.928	-0.683	0.670	-0.790	-0.566	1.000	-0.555	-0.463
Zscore (×01)	-0.562	0.455	-0.326	0.433	-0.301	0.622	0.201	-0.555	1.000	0.078
Zscore (×02)	0.113	0.538	-0.515	0.833	-0.685	0.717	0.947	0.463	0.078	1.000

Any solution of the above set of equations following the constraints for F is defined as the factors, and L as the loading matrix.

The data from 1993 to 2002 of the 11 indexes in the Factor Analysis is collected by the author. The factors and data are shown in Table II where the data processing is in the form of percentage.

By using the SPSS to standardized the data. The SPSS FACTOR procedure saves standardized factor scores as variables and display factor score coefficient matrix in table 3 and PCA in table 4.

Table 4. Total Variance Explained

Component	Initial Eigenvalues			Extraction Sums of Squared Loadings		
	Total	% of Variance	Cumulative %	Total	% of Variance	Cumulative %
1	6.313	63.134	63.134	6.313	63.134	63.134
2	1.774	17.740	80.874	1.774	17.740	80.874
3	0.670	6.696	87.570	0.670	6.696	87.570
4	0.598	5.978	93.548	0.598	5.978	93.548
5	0.336	3.362	96.910	0.336	3.362	96.910
6	0.217	2.173	99.083	0.217	2.173	99.083
7	0.071	0.710	99.793	0.071	0.710	99.793
8	0.014	0.136	99.928	0.014	0.136	99.928
9	0.007	0.071	100.000	0.007	0.071	100.000
10	8.63E-0.06	8.63E-0.05	100.000			

Table 5. Component Matrix

	Component								
	1	2	3	4	5	6	7	8	9
Zscore (×93)	-0.333	0.835	0.007	0.351	0.158	0.204	-0.039	-0.019	0.020
Zscore (×94)	0.829	-0.122	0.010	-0.171	0.514	-0.067	-0.005	-0.016	0.002
Zscore (×95)	-0.849	0.018	0.463	-0.245	0.006	-0.027	0.039	-0.050	0.000
Zscore (×96)	0.854	0.233	0.296	0.224	-0.070	-0.224	-0.153	-0.003	-0.020
Zscore (×97)	-8.878	-0.028	0.230	0.328	0.146	-0.179	0.105	0.058	0.005
Zscore (×98)	0.977	-0.121	0.095	-0.104	-0.035	0.070	-0.020	0.056	0.046
Zscore (×99)	0.859	0.461	0.104	-0.095	0.001	0.125	0.100	0.032	-0.055
Zscore (×00)	-0.854	0.227	0.264	-0.352	0.047	0.092	-0.114	0.048	0.002
Zscore (×01)	0.526	-0.650	0.432	0.0256	-0.012	0.221	0.012	-0.014	-0.001
Zscore (×02)	0.773	0.553	0.197	-0.136	-0.131	-0.103	0.099	-0.019	0.034

As we can see from table 4, the eigenvalue of former two factors is >1 and the cumulative is up to 80.874%.It means that those 2 factors have the highest correlations with the principal component factors. So can we figure out the loading matrix of initial factors in table 5.

3 Conclusion

According to the analysis of the table 4 and table 5, we can make sure that those indexes which are commonly used in research of the ship market are somehow useful and beneficial. Otherwise, among all the factors that affect the ship market, F1(International Sea-borne Freight Traffic, International Trade, Shipping Efficiency, Fleet Growth Rate, Orders In Hand, The new ship completions, Shipping Freight, World Ship-making capacity.. etc) and F2 (World's Economic Growth Rate, Old Ship Scrapping Rate...etc)are the most important one based on the analysis. What's more, the percentage of F1 is 63.134% and the percentage of F2 is 17.74%. Therefore, we should attach more importance to those main factors when we research and analogy of the ship market.

Acknowledgment. This work was supported by the Science & Technology Program of Shanghai Maritime University.

References

1. Rosipal, R., Girolami, M., Trejo, L.J., Cichocki, A.: Kernel PCA for feature extraction and de-noising in nonlinear regression. Neural Corrzput. F9 Applic. 10, 231–243 (2001)
2. Scarsi, R.: The bulk shipping business: market cycles and shipowners' biases. Maritime Policy &Manage 34(6), 5772590 (2007)
3. Ahn, J.H., Oh, J.H.: A constrained EM algorithm for principal component analysis. Neural Comput. 15, 57–65 (2003)
4. Osuna, E., Freund, R., Girosi, F.: Training support vectormachines: An application to face detection. In: Proceedings of IEEE Conference on CVPR 1997, vol. 6, pp. 130–136 (1997)
5. Figueiredo, M.A.T., Jain, A.K.: Unsupervised learning of finite mixture models. IEEE Traps. Patt. Anal. Mach. Intell. 24, 381–396 (2002)
6. Kim, H.C., Kim, D., Bang, S.Y.: An efficient model order selection for PCA mixture model. Pattern Recognition Lett. 24, 1385–1393 (2003); Elissa, K.: Title of paper if known (unpublished)
7. Perlibakas, V.: Distance measures for PCA-based face recognition. Pattern Recognition Lett. 25, 711–724 (2004)

Internet-Based Electronic Toll Collection System Using WiFi Technology

Li Ru'yuan, Wang Zhi'an, Li'yan, and Wang Xuhui

Department of Computer Science
Handan College
Handan, Hebei Province 056005, China

Abstract. The rapid development of road network becomes the basis for economic development, while road network management system becomes the key for improving the operation-efficiency of road network. In recent years, drawing on the successful application abroad, electronic toll collection system (ETC) came to appear in China. However, unbalanced regional development and complex structure of road network in China becomes the barrier to the rapid development of ETC. This paper proposes a new internet-based ETC using WiFi technology with a less investment and widely applications.

Keywords: ETC, Electronic Toll, Highway WiFi, Toll Station, Road Network.

1 Introduction

Traditional manual toll collection (MTC) requires the complete process including vehicle decelerating, idle line up, making payment, printing pass bills, giving change and vehicle accelerating to leave the station. Toll stations are often associated with a lot of congestion and exhaust emissions. Under the method of ETC, the vehicle can pass through the gate and complete payment with a speed of about 20 km / hour , which not only saves processing time, but also reduces vehicle fuel consumption and exhaust emissions, raising the traffic capacity by 4 to 6 times. Thus ETC is an effective way to solve the highway congestion problem, a way to save land resources and an effective means of energy conservation. Considering the benefits above, ETC is recognized as an effective supplement to intelligent transportation [1].

From the late 80s, the developed countries have begun to adopt the ETC technology. From the end of 2008, Yangtze River Delta Highway Toll Collection System (ETC) has started. In 2010, Jiangsu, Zhejiang, Anhui, Jiangxi and Shanghai are expected to achieve interoperability ETC [2]. In the same time, Beijing stated to build ETC channel in highway toll stations. There are 365 ETC channels covering almost all highway toll stations until now in Beijing [3].

Despite the rapid increase of ETC channels, the high construction cost prohibits ETC's expansion in China. Since the vast land, complex structure of road network and car owners' conscious, they are the main barriers to use ETC widely. It is common to see long queues in front of manual channel and empty ETC channel with an occasional quickly-passed car in many highway toll stations [2].

M. Dai (Ed.): ICCIC 2011, Part II, CCIS 232, pp. 22–25, 2011.

Thus, taking current application problems into account, this paper proposes a new ETC system based on WiFi technology used internet with a less investment and widely applications.

2 Design Ideas

2.1 All the highway toll stations establish an information storage server internet-based for ETC system on province-based unit. The information of all vehicles passing through the toll station road will be stored by the automatic identification system.

2.2 When a vehicle approaching toll stations, car-based smart terminal connects with electronic toll system at the toll stations using WiFi technology.

2.3 Specially-designed connection system can effectively connects car-based smart terminal and car-owners' payment card database. Billing system reads information from the province-based information storage server and calculates the fees. Electronic payment subsystem charges the fee and submits to the bank. The bank completes the deal processing and reply real-time information back to car-owner.

2.4 Charging system at the toll station sends fee-charging information to lane management system, then the removes the lane bar manually or by electronic system which can identify and match the vehicle license information with its charging status.

3 Technology Support

3.1 The automatic identification and storage of passing vehicle information. When a vehicle is approaching the highway toll station, the camera setting at the gate can catch the vehicle license and vehicle characteristics instantly. Current ETC has already solved the technical problems, hence this paper will not go any further in this aspect. The crucial point is the information should be automatically updated to the province-based database.

3.2 Using WiFi to realize the information connection when the vehicle approaching the exit of highway. WiFi can build connection between two smart terminals in a few hundred meters of range. Thus, WiFi connection can be established between WiFi AP near the toll station and the car-owner's smart terminal which may be mobile phones, car computers or tablet computers, as long as terminal with WIFI Internet access, during the car passing the gate with slowing speed. To ensure the operational simplicity and safety, this paper proposes and designs a special connection program. After building the connection, it can automatically collect the vehicle license and car-owner's payment card number information, then identify the passing gate information of the specific car from the province-based passing-car information storage database and calculate the fee. Finally, this connection program can complete the payment process through CUP transfer system. Tip: The car-owner should be noticed about the charging amount vocally or in text, then he can choose automatic transfer or manual confirmation.

3.3 The charging and payment information will be sent to lane management system, and then lane management system will match identified vehicle license information with its payment status.

3.4 The car-based special connection program tailored for each specific type of vehicle can be downloaded from road network portal.

4 Comparison with ETC

The method proposed in this paper is consistent with ETC in aspects of working objectives and principles, but this new method is relying on the new WiFi technology and based on Internet, which offers the following advantages:

4.1 Cheaper, easy to design and implement. In early stages, setting up a vehicle license and characteristic identification system, an internet-connected computer and a few AP will accomplish the task.

4.2 Simultaneous use of both traditional and electronic charging methods. In traditional charging method, the toll operator can see payment status of the passing vehicle on his computer and operates the bar accordingly.

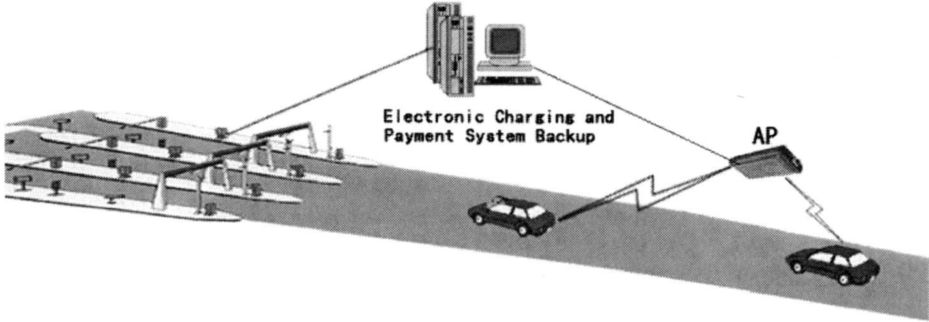

Fig. 1. Electronic Charging and Payment System

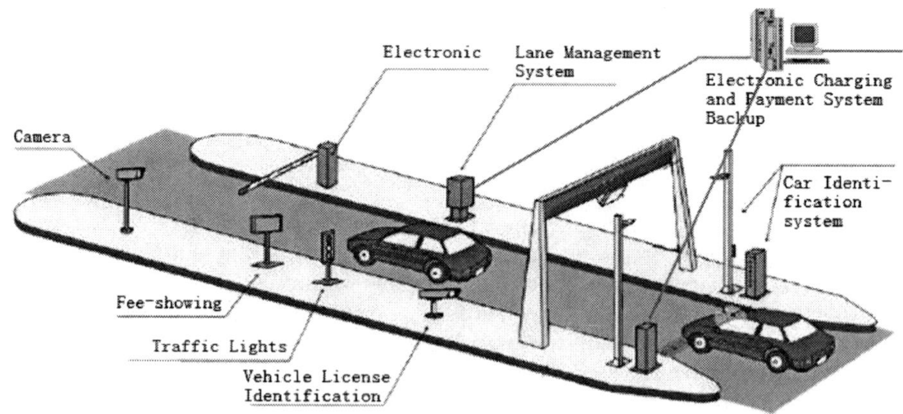

Fig. 2. Automatic identification of traffic system

4.3 There is no need to establish specific electronic toll channel at toll stations and thus car-owners do not have to bother with the choice between traditional and electronic passing channels. Electronic charging method requires the almost the same action and offers the better experience of car-owner as the traditional method.

4.4 Long-distance and several locations of payment greatly expand the charging capacity. An industrial use AP can propagate stably in the open for more than 1000 meters, so car-owners start to slow down at the notice of the toll two km ahead, then the connection between the car and the toll can be established 1000 meters in front of the toll and finally electronically payment can be made. Hence this method greatly enlarges the working capacity of the toll considering the fact that 1000 meters in front of the toll are available payment area. It relieves people the time and bother to complete the payment in front of the toll window.

5 Summary and Outlook

In the twenty-first century, information technology based on computer and Internet has penetrated into people' lives. Many seemingly complicated tasks may have simple solutions. Common-use civilian technology is not necessarily unsafe. The new electronic toll method proposed in this paper can be very flexible to use. For example, the traditionally manual toll can be transformed to automatically electronic toll. Car-owner can download the special connection program from the toll portal using 3G or internet. Then electronic payment can be accomplished though CUP. Therefore, the rapid development of the Internet can change our lives greatly.

References

1. Baidu.Com ETC
2. ETC Interconnection among Shanghai, Jiangsu, Zhejiang, Jiangxi and Anhui Highway Expected to Realize in Xinhua (June 29, 2010)
3. Huaxia Bank Overcome ETC Bottleneck in Beijing, "catfish effect" CDC (May 31, 2010) (appeared in ETC Market)
4. Tang, S.: WIFI technology and applied resarch. Fujian Computer (2009-2010)
5. Li, R., et al.: The Innovation of Urban Road Navigation by "Automobile Network". In: ICCSNA 2010, Hong kong, vol. I, pp. 417–419 (2010)

A Path Out of the Management Theory Jungle: From the Perspective of Chinese Management Philosophy

Wu Zhaochun

School of Business Guangzhou City Polytechnic Guangzhou, China

Abstract. Professor Koontz said that we were exploring the management theory jungle a half century ago. However, we are still stay in this jungle and it has brought a lot of problems to our society. This paper studies those problems from the angle of Chinese management philosophy, and gives some solutions to those problems. What's more, in China, do companies should apply western management thoughts or Chinese traditional thoughts in management? This paper can give some references.

Keywords: Management Theory Jungle, Management Thoughts, Management Philosophy, Chinese Traditional Thoughts.

1 Introduction

In recent years, many significant events happened in the western world such as the oil crisis, the events of Enron in the USA, Iraq War, financial crisis and sovereign-debt crisis. When people deal with these issues, they also think about the cause of these crises. Why is the global financial crisis originated from the UAS, one of the countries who possess the most advanced management theory? The reason lies in the obvious defects that exist in the Western corporate management thought and theory. On the one hand, however, Chinese learn from the west with its advanced management thought and theory; on the other hand, these theories including some contradictory ones which make Chinese confused. Chinese people should reexamine the capitalistic management thought and theory as well as the Chinese traditional management thought, with the later one based on the Chinese native culture and having a glorious history of five thousand years. By analyzing the evolution of western management thought and theory, we can see that Chinese traditional management thought is a good way to solve the problem of western corporations. Chinese corporation should also discard their cultural inferiority and advocate and practice Chinese traditional management idea, which can guide corporations at home and abroad to succeed.

2 Management Theory Jungle

2.1 The Management Theory Jungle

Management, in the modern sense, originated from the west. It's generally believed that Scientific Theory of Management written by Taylor symbolizes the birth of

M. Dai (Ed.): ICCIC 2011, Part II, CCIS 232, pp. 26–33, 2011.

modern management, though management practice almost has a long history as that of human being. In the last two hundred years, productive forces have developed greatly in pace with modern management. In The Academy of Management Journal published in December, 1961, however, Horold Koontz stated the management theory jungle that there are different opinions about management theory, which are still immature. (Koontz, 1961). Koontz, however, divides various management theories into six schools: management process school, experience or case study school, human behavior school, social system school, the decision theory school and mathematics school. He thought people should go out of the management theory jungle.

In fact, theoretical disorder derives from the disorder of management thinking. The west especially America is rich in management thoughts and theories, but at the same time, America lacks a culture root deep enough to nourish them. When these thoughts and theories develop beyond the sense of a skill, their cultural root could no longer nourish them. This cultural root on which management thoughts and theories depend, refers to a national ethos. The absence of this national ethos brought the mess of the management theory jungle and the global financial crisis".

2.2 The Philosophy of Management Theory Evolution

The evolution of management thoughts has a deep root in its philosophical origin. In perspective of philosophy, western management thoughts have two philosophical clues: one is rationalism, the other is irrationalism.

Rationalism is the mainstream of western philosophy and thoughts. It holes that human reasoning can be the source of knowledge. Human reasoning is logical, systematic and standardized. It's commonly believed that from the renaissance, western rationalism start to draw public concern and the replacement of God by rationalism became a landmark in history. Along with Descartes' theory, rationalism spread throughout Europe between 17th and 18th century. Rationalism can be dated back to naturalisratio, the thought "water is the origin of the earth", in ancient Greek. Then it developed into the experience rationalism, which attempts to define rationalism within the boundary of experience; then, it developed into genius rationalism and scientific rationality after the Renaissance and the Enlightenment; Finally, it developed into mechanical rationality, instrumental rationality and mathematics rationality, which believes that only those can be deduced from mathematics and geometry are science and truth. The scientific thought of rationalism is reductionism. It's a metaphysical method which reduces advanced movement, for example vital movement, to a lower rank of basic movement, for example mechanical movement, and which admits the replacement of advanced movement by basic movement. Reductionism also believes that various phenomena can be reduced to a set of basic independent elements, whose nature will not be changed by the effects of external factors. The nature of a phenomenon can be deduced through research on these basic elements. Reductionism and analytic approach supplement each other. Analytic approach is an important research method, in which axiomatic approach best represent reductionism. This kind of management theory and thoughts centers on "work", abides by rational logic to find the objective laws of management, emphasizes on the rational decision, qualified and standard management and orderly stable organizational structure, specific assignment of responsibility, subordination relations, strict rules and regulations, financial incentive and discipline control.

Rational management theory and thoughts include taylorism-scientific management and theories of bureaucracy put forward by Webber. After the Second World War, the success of operational research as well as the development of systematology, cybernetics, information theory and computer technology, provide scientific management with scientific methodology foundation and technical support. At that time, mathematical school, social system school, system management school, the decision theory school spring up, which focuses more on scientific management than human's nature. In terms of management science school, management is a pure science, which can be decided and managed by mathematical model and logical program but no toleration to a single irrational artistic ingredient.

The emergence of the western irrationalism philosophy was not only the response and introspection to capitalism, but also the call and prophesies of a new age. It changed the single development pattern of western philosophy which centered on rationalism, created a new mode of philosophical thinking and provided the broader prospect for the development of western philosophy. Although it's not the mainstream of western management thoughts, irrationalism pays the attention to humane in the west and plays important role in the development of management thoughts. Irrationalism refers to those thoughts that place the irrational elements of psychology with precedence and emphasize the role of determination, desire, emotion and intuition rather than that of ration and logic. Rationalism attaches importance to the study of external world, while irrationalism attempts to find reason internal. It can be traced back to the fairy tale of ancient Greek and show that the human succumbs to the more excellent wisdom and power; From ancient Greek to Middle Ages, theology of religions and scholasticism strictly control people's thinking and behaviors; After the conflict with the renaissance, the enlightenment, scientism and rationalism, irrationalism is taken into account again when the capitalism exhausted in modern times. Especially after the Second World War, irrational philosophy is unprecedented popular and the most representative and influential are existentialism and post-structuralism.

The management thought of western rationalism and irrationalism has not only played significant role in history, but also made big troubles so that its development faced big difficulty.

2.3 The Dilemma of Western Management Theories

In such a western world of value diversity, the disorder of management thoughts leads to the dilemma of management theory: On the one hand, different modern management tools, methods and theories occur, so that management is unprecedented prosperity; On the other hand, more and more problems and contradiction of cooperation management and social management can't be solved, because some right solutions lost their effects in the changeable world. The direct cause is the defects of western mode of management thinking and the lack of support of western philosophical thoughts, so that no rhythmical idea and theoretical innovation are made.

In terms of thinking modes, westerners are tend to view things separate, while Chinese are tend to view things as an integral whole (Luo Jining, 2005). From the angle of management theory, the basic paradox of western management theory is the paradox between human and thing and the paradox between human and matter.

Westerners view human, thing and matter separately and solve problems in a separate way. Chinese people, however, treat human, thing and matter as an integration, so that specific people will do specific thing with specific matter.

In perspective of philosophy, it can't deny the great contribution to modern society made by the western rationalism, but the cold rationalism cultivated by science, the over-confident technique with the morally neutral appearance accelerates the human's self-destruction. Social management is developing in the direction of impersonal engineering control. All these combinations lead the activity of persecution and slaughter of human being into a social collective action that closely organized by the planner, performer and sufferer.

The negative effects can be analyzed from technical level and systematic level. On technical level, it exist many paradoxes in itself. Firstly, the improvement and development of human technology need the strong support of human's intellect and thought; while what the technological development brought is the explosion and overflow of information so that human's intellect and thought can't bear on the burden. The product made by human's intellect and thought suppress its development. Secondly, because of the widespread use of technology, E-Culture as well as the artificial intelligence equipment eliminates human's creative impulse and human individuality with its industrialization, complanation, lot sizing and impersonality of intellectual production spiritual production. High technicalization and industrial monopoly of different software designs eliminates people's chance to cultivate and develop their own talents. People have no choice but to accept the various designs that made ration into technique, so that the artificial reason obliterates human's thought and soul; Thirdly, instrumental rationality developed from technology, the utilitarian rationality from market competition and value rationality from widespread of currency etc discard the human spirit . The means of life becomes the aim of life and the human becomes the means to serve. Human's value is distorted, ration is limited, thought is despised, idea of commodity fetishism makes money become the worst master and human become the saddest slave.

Besides, in the systematic level, it is commonly believed that the mode of human's development, especially the production and consuming mode walks into a dead-end drag after the industrial revolution. This kind of mode has three defects. One is the widening North-South gap, although some lucky places have developed, many more places suffered from poverty. Secondly, although it promotes the economic development and social improvement, it overly uses up the resource and destroys the ecological balance and living environment; thirdly, although it meets the recent needs of some people, it sacrifices long-term benefit of human's development in a whole.

Therefore, this mode can't bring the universal and common development as well as protect the environment. Then, excessive exuberance of western rationalism makes ethics and morality lost, destroys the home of human's spirit. The lost of this spirit is not resulted from the foreign aggression, but the certain wrong theory. All these "rationalism" such as artificial reason, instrumental rationality and pragmatic reason are popular with their simplicity and practical. However, the cost of "simplicity" and "practical" is to cut our spiritual source in our heart. The principle of "simplicity" and "practical" really helps us make success in different fields, but we should think about is there anything wrong with the life style based on this method of thinking if all these success can't give us happiness.

3 A Path Out of the Management Theory Jungle

Because of a break from reality, western management theory can't solve the complex practical problems; The disorder of management thoughts make people unable to decide which is right; From the level of management theory and thoughts, it's difficult to find the deep reason behind the predicament, so an exam on the level of management philosophy is needed.

China's excellent performance in the financial crisis has drawn the attention of the international community. China fever has been aroused throughout the world. China's secret of avoiding the crisis has been discussed throughout the world. Both academic and practical circles are diligently doing research on China's culture and its management mode in believing that Chinese management style and life style is the only solution to the world's crisis. This thesis will thus further discuss the solution of western management thoughts and theory from cultural value, way of thinking and management philosophy.

3.1 Learning China's Traditional Cultural Values

In terms of management, Chinese traditional cultural value takes emphasis on the "righteousness" but "profit" no matter to enterprise management or to social management; There was a saying "The man of honor seeks righteousness, while the man of disgrace only cares about profit." in The Analects· Righteousness; there are many similar sayings in Chinese traditional culture. Chinese traditional culture pays emphasis on comity and harmonious environment but competition; However, the western world gives up some social principles such as equity and justice, because maximizing efficiency is the most important. Emphasis on the "long-term development" rather than "short-term efficiency" shows that people pursue thrifty, accumulation, endurance and tradition and pursue the stable and high-level life and mode of producing. The fundamental contradiction of western management is the contradiction between "human" and "thing". They treat them separate rather than integrative, while Chinese culture holds that human and things is an integral whole, only through the practices of moral culture can manage family and country.

America Los Angeles on October 1st, 2009, an article published in "China Commerce" indicated that the global financial crisis has taken a light toll on the Chinese economy and Chinese people because most Chinese people live thrifty. American should change its value and life style in order to overcome the financial crisis and maintain sustainable development. That is why Chinese life style is growing popular in America. Chinese traditional cultural value can make up for the disadvantages of western cultural value. To study from Chinese traditional cultural value also can bring a new thinking space to the development of western management thoughts and theory and help to find the solution of dilemma.

3.2 Drawing on China's Traditional Way of Thinking

The basic reason of western management thoughts disorder is the defects in the mode of thinking. In terms of thinking tendency, westerners are tend to focus on parts, while Chinese are focus on the entirety (Luo Jining,2005). Chinese people know that the relationship among human, things and matter are dialectic and integrative, while western people think they are separate from each other. Chinese people know how to control their desire because they know desire, which is not like the endless matter. The GDP of China is lower than that of America, while Chinese are richer than American. Because most of Chinese people can't spend their money and deposit their money in the bank .However, most American are lack of money and need to borrow money to meet their consuming .This is why China and Japan are the biggest creditors of America.

According to the book Chinese System Thinking Modes written by Liu Changlin, Chinese traditional thinking modes can be summarized as follows: the Holism, the Super System Theory, the Theory of harmony and Tai Chi Thoughts etc. Traditional Chinese culture has three characteristics: first, the unity of heaven and humanity represents cosmology. That is to say, the subject and the object compose a unity, and human being is one part of the whole universe; nature and human are in unitary.

Second is the integration of system thinking mode, which is not a general theory of the way of thinking, but refers to a super organic system that even complex than the simple mechanical system. That truth is well elaborated in Lao-tse's Tao Te Ching in such a sentence: "Tao, the subtle reality of the universe can not be described." Western culture focuses on analysis whereas Chinese culture put emphasis on comprehensive and overall thinking on the structure and functions, without concerning about the entity or element in microscopic view. Chinese people have a dominant logic, like "Unity between Theory and Practice", "Put what you learned into practice", which indicate that human beings are making use of the knowledge of objects and striving to connect material with moral knowledge and practice instead of being driven by the outside world.

Third is the humanistic spirit with harmony as its foundation. The harmonious society is the humanistic spirit. The word "harmony" consists of the harmony between man and his mind, the harmony between man and society, the harmony between man and nature, and the reasonable way of doing things. The essence of Chinese traditional culture is people-centered, which means that knowledge is a tool for human beings. The "Tai Chi thought", which was regarded as "the fifth invention", is imbued with the same spirit of the Theory of harmony. Within the range of people's cognitive knowledge, the "Tai Chi Thought" at least includes the concepts of Yin and Yang (the relationship between contradiction and interaction), of constant flux, of eternality. Chinese profound traditional ideas, in recent years, have gained acknowledgement by some western scholars. Especially, scholars in Harvard University have translated many Chinese thinking modes into English. Because westerners realized that Chinese traditional thinking modes will help them out.

3.3 Practicing in Accordance with Chinese Traditional Philosophy of Management

By analysis of the philosophy clues of western management thoughts, it is easy to find that the concept of "rational limitation" and "irrational limitation" in western management thoughts can not be the guide principle in solving their problems, such as the problem of the growth limit, the problem of the sustainable development, the problem of the relationship between human mind and morals. In western history, tremendous material enrichment brings no real happiness to westerners. More social problems, like AIDS, suicide committing, high crime rates, prison overcrowding and gender discrimination, terrorism etc, resulting in insecurity and dangers. Thus, people live in panic. It is difficult to imagine what the happiness is if living in such a society.

The developing direction of the "Western Rationalism" is the practical rationality of Chinese tradition. Nowadays, in modern western countries, many management thoughts and theories are put up from different aspects, in order to learn the way of management. Its value dies down with the pass of time, because the final relentless reasoning based on Mathematics reason and the mechanical reason can not work soundly under moral standards. From the late financial crisis happened in 2008, we know that the logical argumentation and strict mathematical derivation is reasonable on the surface. However, the financial activity did not operate under moral bottom line, thus eventually led to the spread-out economic disaster. The advantage of Rationalism is that it is conducive to solve the low level management problem of machinery and equipment in the industrial production process, but it can not control human desires and morality. Human created tools, methods and process will finally be put into human practice, into the practical rationality of "Unity between Theory and Practice" and "Put what you've learned into practice". The derivation is hypothetical, but the management can not be impractical.

"Western irrationalism" has a long history, getting rapid development since the Renaissance period. Until now, the theory is gradually shifting from initial care for humans per se to anarchism; individualism or liberalism. The essence of the theory had changed and regarded the satisfaction of their own desires as the ways of individual liberation and publicizing individual character. Such kind of arrogance, selfishness and unfettered free spirit created a "free competition" social environment manipulated by capital. However, this "free competition environment" damages the real freedom of other people, reflecting the lacks of the care for human soul and the humanity. In historical terms, the developing direction of irrational dimension of western management thoughts tends to be humanism in East. Humanism in the East is totally different from the western selfishness, liberalism and individualism. Humanism in the East advocates that human beings and one's soul should get along in harmony, which is called "setting heart in the right place", which means people should care for soul, reasonably meet his own desires, while get alone with people around them, without destroying any harmony. According to the "Humanism in the East", the principle of dealing with interpersonal relationship is "harmony is most precious", "Reasonable and fair", "Harmony brings wealth"; when dealing with the relationship between people, nature and the surroundings, the principle is "The unity of heaven and humanity" and "Jointly balanced growth and coexistence".

In conclusion, borrowing China's traditional cultural values, drawing on China's traditional way of thinking and practicing in accordance with Chinese traditional philosophy of management could be a good way to walk out western management theory jungle and social crisis.

References

1. Koontz, H.: The management theory jungle. Academy of Management (1961)
2. Koontz, H.: The management theory jungle revisited. Academy of Management Review (1980)

3. Keys, M.: The Japanese management theory jungle. Academy of Management Review (1984)
4. Schollhammer, H.: The comparative management theory jungle. Academy of management Journal (1969)
5. Carson, Lanier, P.A., Carson, K.D., Guidry B.N.: Clearing a path through the management fashion jungle: Some preliminary trailblazing. Academy of Management (2000)

The Study on Regulation Policy of International Service Trade

Xie Lifen

School of Business Jiu Jiang Institute Jiujiang, China 332005
chunri166@163.com

Abstract. Through using the gravity model and OECD's PMR indicators, this paper has quantify the effects of outward and inward oriented regulation policy of international service trade. Further, inward oriented regulation policies of service export country have no effects for export country, but outward oriented regulation policies distinctly decrease the local services sector's export performance.

Keywords: Regulation Policy, Service Trade, International Trade e.

1 Introduction

The relationship between regulation of service industries and liberalization of trade in service has been a controversial topic in international trade field. Since services are intangible and often require that the service provider and the consumer interact directly, services are more affected by regulation than is merchandise trade. Due to market imperfections stemming from monopoly and asymmetric information, regulation is certainly justified in international trade in service; at the other hand, excessive and distorted regulation policies can constitute a cost and reduce the benefits of liberalization of international trade in service. As a result, liberalization of international trade in service should be a combination polices of decreasing regulation of foreign entry barriers of trade in service and increasing regulation of completing market competition mechanism. The opinions of defining liberalization of trade in service as de-regulation is fault, defining regulation as trade barriers is also fault, liberalization of trade in service often needs the combinations of de-regulation and intensify regulation of different policies together (Mattoo and Sauvé, 2003).With a view to distinguishing these two opposite effects, we classify the regulation of service industries as outward oriented regulation policy and inward oriented regulation policy. Through the classification, we expect to quantify these two policy effects on international trade in service.

The study is organized as follows: Section 2 is literature review, Section 3 is data analysis and regression model, Section 4 is the regression results, Section 5 is conclusions and policy implications.

M. Dai (Ed.): ICCIC 2011, Part II, CCIS 232, pp. 34–39, 2011.

2 Literature Review

The treatment of all trade barriers as tariff equivalents is the weakness of a number of empirical studies analyzing the impact of Doha round liberalization using general equilibrium modeling. These studies abstract from the fact that different regulatory policy has different trade effects (e.g. Dee and Hanslow, 2000; Dee, 2005).

There are two main reasons that the regulation policies of service industries turns into trade barriers: firstly, Regulatory heterogeneity of different countries can be an obstacle for international trade in services. Maijoor, et al. (1998) illustrative the different regulation policies of EU countries on audit service constitute the main obstacles of the trade in this sector. Also, Kox, H. and Lejour, A. (2005), Kox, L.M. and Nord°as, H.K. (2007) use econometric methods estimate the how much are the cost would be in EU. Secondly, the opaque, low efficient, too excessive and unsuitable regulation also constitute obstacles of trade in service(Nicoletti et al., 2003; Copenhagen Economics,2005).The above literatures review that fact that modulate and harmonize regulation policies of service industry between countries is necessary in the way of Liberalization of Trade in Service.

In addition, the appropriate regulation policy can correct the imperfection market failure and decreasing the trade barriers. Many researchers consider countries should perfect their local competition mechanism before open service market to the outside world, otherwise the welfare of the country may be deteriorated in the process of Liberalization of trade in service, it is caused by the local and foreign providers allied as cartel, monopolized rents are seized by the foreign providers and transfer to foreign countries as a result(Low & Mattoo,2000; Francois & Wootton,2001; Copeland,2002; Konan & Assche,2006).

These two opposite opinions illustrate the positive and negative effects of regulation of service industries on international trade in service. Base on the classification of regulation policy, we plan to use econometric method to quantify these two effects.

3 Data and Model

3.1 Product Market Regulation Indicator

The OECD Economics Department developed a detailed database with indicators of product market regulations for member states. The database is mainly formed by official government responses to the OECD Regulatory Indicators Questionnaire. The first version of the database referred to the reference year 1998 and consisted of some 1600 items of product market regulation for each country. A later version for 2003 reduced the number of items to some 805 (Conway et al., 2005).

The basic data are used to calculate composite indicators or summary indicators. The summary indicators are obtained by means of factor analysis, in which each component of the regulatory framework is weighted according to its contribution to the overall variance in the data. The methodology is described in Nicoletti, Scarpetta and Boylaud (2000). Five sub-domains of product market regulation for which summary indicators have been developed are: barriers to competition, administrative barriers for start-ups, regulatory and administrative opacity, explicit barriers to trade and investment, and state control. Details for the sub-domain indicators can be found in

Conway et al. (2005).Since the barriers to trade and investment correlate with outward oriented regulation policy; barriers to competition, administrative barriers for start-ups, regulatory and administrative opacity, and state control correlate with inward oriented regulation policy, so we can use the PMR indicator in our analysis.

3.2 Regress Model

The gravity model is the workhorse model for empirical analysis of the relation between trade costs and trade flows. The gravity model explains bilateral trade as a function of the trading partner's market size, and bilateral trade costs relative to all other trading partners. Trade costs in turn include transport, tariffs and a host of administrative costs related to crossing the border, translating information to a foreign language and cultural context and entering and enforcing contracts with foreign suppliers. Commonly used measures of such costs are the distance between the trading partners, whether or not they have a common border, whether or not they share a common language and whether or not one or both are members of a regional trade agreement. The gravity model can express as follows:

Log(Tradeij)=Cij+Log(GDPCi)+Log(GDPCj)+Log(POPi)+Log(POPj)+ Log(DISTij)+LANGUAGEij+BORDERij+Xij+uij

In the following, in order to emphasis on the variable of regulation policy, on the basis of the above equation, we construct our regression models as follows:

- Effects on import country if outward oriented regulation policy implemented by import country:

Log(IMPORTij)=Cij+Log(GDPCi)+Log(GDPCj)+Log(POPi)+Log(POPj)+ Log(DISTij)+LANGUAGEij+BORDERij+EUij+Log(OUTWARDPMRj)+uij (1)

- Effects on import country if inward oriented regulation policy implemented by import country:

Log(IMPORTij)=Cij+Log(GDPCi)+Log(GDPCj)+Log(POPi)+Log(POPj)+ Log(DISTij)+LANGUAGEij+BORDERij+EUij+Log(INWARDPMRj)+uij (2)

- Effects on export country if outward oriented regulation policy implemented by export country:

Log(EXPORTij)=Cij+Log(GDPCi)+Log(GDPCj)+Log(POPi)+Log(POPj)+ Log(DISTij)+LANGUAGEij+BORDERij+EUij+Log(OUTWARDPMRi)+uij (3)

- Effects on export country if inward oriented regulation policy implemented by export country:

Log(EXPORTij)=Cij+Log(GDPCi)+Log(GDPCj)+Log(POPi)+Log(POPj) +Log(DISTij)+LANGUAGEij+BORDERij+EUij+Log(INWARDPMRi)+ uij

The indicators' meaning in the gravity equation (1)-(4) are presented below: GDPCi: per capita gdp of country i; GDPCj: per capita gdp of country j; POPi: population of country i; POPj: population of country j; DISTij: distance between country i and country j's economic zone; LANGUAGEij: if country i and country j share a common language, then=1, else=0; EUij: If country i and country j are EU membership, then=1,else=0; BORDERij: If country i and country j have a common border, then=1, else=0; EXPORTij: service export value of country i to country i; IMPORTij: service import value of country j from country i; INWARDPMRi: Inward Oriented Regulation policy of country i; INWARDPMRj: inward oriented regulation policy of country j; OUTWARDPMRi: outward oriented regulation policy of country i; OUTWARDPMRj: outward oriented regulation policy of country j; Cij: intercept; uij: white noise.

4 Estimates Results

This section applies the gravity model for estimating the impact of regulation policy of service industries on international trade in service. According to the PMR indicator and the OECD database of trade in service, we choose 27 export countries and 30 import countries from OECD as our research sample, so we can have 810 observations. 27 export countries are Australia, Austria, Belgium, Canada, Czech Republic, Denmark, Finland, France, Greece, Hungary, Ireland, Italy, Japan, Korea, Luxembourg, Mexico, Netherlands, New Zealand, Norway, Poland, Portugal, Slovak epublic, Spain, Sweden, Turkey, United Kingdom, United States; 30 import countries are: Australia, Austria, Belgium, Canada, Czech Republic, Denmark, Finland, France, Germany, Greece, Hungary, Iceland ,Ireland, Italy, Japan, Korea, Luxembourg, Mexico, Netherlands, New Zealand, Norway, Poland, Portugal, Slovak Republic, Spain, Sweden, Switzerland, Turkey, United Kingdom, United States. In addition, per capita gdp, population data are from UN's national account database, distance and common border and language data are from Jon Haveman's international trade data, bilateral service trade data are from the OECD. Stat Extracts.

We collect all data of the year 2003 in our sample, and separately regress the above gravity equations (1)-(4) using the cross-section Generalized Least Square method, the results are presents in Table 1.

The results are presented in Table 1 by and large support our hypothesis, almost all the variable coefficients get their expected values and are significant at the 1% level: The bilateral market size and population variable, common border and language variable, both the export and import country are EU membership variable are positive correlate with the international trade in service, and the distance variable are negative correlate with the service trade volume.

As to our interested Regulation policy variable, we can conclude:

- No matter service import country implement outward or inward oriented regulation policies, they constitute an entry cost for Foreign Service providers and these two effects is almost the same. In addition, we can see the coefficient of per capita GDP variable increase from 0.699 of outward oriented regulation policy to 1.02 of inward oriented regulation policy, it means that in despite of OECD country's excessive or improper inward oriented regulation policy restraining the import of service, but it also produce the side effects of correcting the imperfection market failure, increase the bilateral service trade as a result.
- When service export country implements inward oriented regulation policies, it has no obvious effects on the service export, but when it implements

outward oriented regulation policies, it distinctly decrease the service export, suggesting that the outward oriented regulation policies at home can be a drag on local firm's international competitiveness.

- The coefficient of EU membership variable are positive, it means that when the import and export countries of service are EU members, it can increase bilateral service trade 1.75%-2.01%, and it also suggest that harmonized policy in EU, including the regulation policy of service industry, can decrease the negative effects of regulation policy on international trade in service.

Table 1. The Regression Results Of Gravity Eqution (1)-(4)

code	Import country		Export country	
	Equation1	Equation2	Equation3	Equation4
Regulation policy variable	-1.10*** (-8.980)	-1.023*** (-5.958)	-0.252* (-1.776)	-0.047 (-0.308)
Log(DISTij)	-0.566*** (-11.146)	-0.669*** (-12.544)	-0.583*** (-11.603)	-0.591*** (-11.68)
Log(GDPCj)	0.699*** (8.489)	1.02*** (13.410)	1.263*** (16.947)	1.260*** (16.989)
Log(GDPCi)	1.575*** (25.698)	1.626*** (27.05)	1.534*** (20.563)	1.612*** (25.923)
Log(POPj)	0.829*** (29.395)	0.798*** (30.587)	0.749*** (28.455)	0.751*** (28.54)
Log(POPi)	0.763*** (27.351)	0.779*** (27.922)	0.754*** (27.615)	0.755*** (27.449)
LANGUAGEij	0.426*** (5.546)	0.443*** (5.623)	0.467*** (5.739)	0.484*** (5.782)
BORDERij	0.689*** (4.728)	0.614*** (4.068)	0.644*** (4.495)	0.626*** (4.3441)
EUij	0.564*** (5.028)	0.703*** (6.581)	0.586*** (5.671)	0.603*** (5.820)
Adjusted R2	0.829	0.831	0.827	0.827
D.W.	1.597	1.593	1.598	1.613
Number of obs	546	546	546	546

Notes: The t-value are presented in parentheses. Values marked (***) and (**) are significant at the 1% and 5% levels, respectively.

5 Conclusions and Policy Implications

This paper argues that the regulatory policy of service industries affects the international trade in service. Indicators of Product Market Regulation are introduced in a gravity model to quantify these effects.

We can conclude that:

- No matter service import country implement outward or inward oriented regulation policies, they constitute an entry cost for Foreign Service providers, and these two effects are almost the same. In order to more liberalization of trade in service, it is necessary for service import country to reduce the regulation policies of service industry.

- When service export country implement inward oriented regulation policies, it has no obvious effects on the service export, but when it implement outward oriented regulation policies, it distinctly decrease the local firm's international competitiveness on service export.
- A more harmonized policies between countries should be made, it can decrease the cost of service provider's entry, consequently have a positive effects to international trade in service.

References

1. Copenhagen Economics, Economic Assessment of the Barriers to the Internal Market for Services. Copenhagen Economics (January 2005)
2. Copeland, B.: Benefits and Costs of Trade and Investment Liberalization in Services: Implications from Trade Theory. In: Curtis, J., Ciuriak, D. (eds.) Trade Policy Research 2002, pp. 107–218. Minister of Public Works and Government Service, Canada (2002)
3. Dee, P., Hanslow, K.: Multilateral Liberalization of Service Trade. Productivity Commission Staff Research Paper, Ausinfo, Canberra (2000)
4. Francois, J., Wootton, I.: Market Structure, Trade Liberalization, and the GATS. European Journal of Political Economy 17, 389–402 (2001)
5. Conway, P., Janod, V., Nicoletti, G.: Product Market Regulation in OECD Countries: 1998 to 2003. OECD Economics Department Working Papers (419) (2005)
6. Konan, D., Maskus, K.: Quantifying the Impact of Service Liberalization in a Developing Country. Journal of Development Economics (2006)
7. Kox, H., Lejour, A.: The Effects of the Service Directive on intra-EU trade and FDI. Revue Economique 57(4), 747–769 (2006)
8. Kox, H.L.M., Nordäs, H.K.: Services Trade and Domestic Regulation. OECD Trade Directorate and CPB Netherlands Bureau for Economic Policy Analysis (February 2007)
9. Low, P., Mattoo, A.: Is There a Better Way? Alternative Approaches to Liberalization under GATS. In: Sauve, P., Stern, R. (eds.) GATS 2000: New Directions in Services Trade Liberalization, pp. 449–472. Brookings Institution Press, Washington, DC (2000)
10. Kox, H., Lejour, A.: Regulatory Heterogeneity as Obstacle for International Services Trade. CPB Discussion Paper (49) (September 2005)
11. Nicoletti, G., Scarpetta, S.: Regulation, Productivity and Growth. Economic Policy 36 (2003)

The Study on Reputation Model of Retail Enterprises Supply Chain Based on Game Theory

An Xinhua

School of Economics, Wuhan University of Technology,
Nanyang Institute of Technology
azgad11@yahoo.cn

Abstract. A good retail enterprise must have the steady revenue growth and well-deserved reputation. It should offer high quality products with reasonable competitive price and respond immediately to uncertainly customer demands with good services. Therefore, the reputation and historical performance play the key role in forming long term steady customer relationship. When the cost that reduced by the establishment of reputation is greater than the maintenance cost for the catering supply chain, the game between the catering supply chain and customers will bring profit to both sides.

Keywords: Retail Enterprises, Supply Chain, Reputation Model, Game Theory.

1 Introduction

Along with the development of the medical and health system of China, people's attention and demand level on health is upgraded. On the other aspect, the complexity and uncertainty of the market are growing. The structural contradiction of supply exceeding demand gets more obvious. Therefore, keeping the competition advantage in the market, rapid response of the market change and offering satisfied products and services to customers become a key problem of the entire nodes in the supply chain. Enterprises must take customers' demands and relationships seriously. Any enterprise which only considers its own profit but ignore the communication of customers will not be successful in the market [1].

The reputation of the retail enterprise that directly faces customers is very important and influences the final customers the most. However, the judgment and evaluation of the reputation of such enterprises (usually the most downstream enterprises) by customers are not independently determined by the behavior and effort of the enterprises, which are also influenced by the reputation and its relevant factors of every enterprise in the supply chain. This means we should bring the relationship of the reputation and customers' demand from the system point of view into the research of supply chain coordination and game theory. Supply chain reputation can be defined as the trust level of customers to the entire supply chain. It is a time-accumulated variable that relies on the effort every member enterprise. Therefore, the game of all the members in the supply chain becomes a continuous dynamic game [2].

M. Dai (Ed.): ICCIC 2011, Part II, CCIS 232, pp. 40–46, 2011.

Wang [3] analyzed the competition behavior of the two-echelon decentralized supply chain partnership composed by plenty retailers and found the competition behavior existed in all retailers and suppliers. Eriksson and Lindgren [4] discussed the influence to cooperation caused by mutation factors of the multi-prisoner's dilemma. Ferreira and Dufourt [5] analyzed the source of the complexity in the cooperation competition game based on the bounded rationality of human beings. Krep [6] built the classic KMRW reputation model, and stated that if there are not enough information the equilibrium of cooperation game only can be meet when the repetition of game is sufficient. Balachandran and Radhakrishnan [7] studied the commitment-punishment contract under moral risk of one side and both sides. Branconi and Loch [8] presented that the reputation based concealed motivation system is an efficient method to coordinate the organization relationship and to prevent moral risk. In this work, we analyze the game between the supply chain and customers and present the reputation model of supply chain enterprises based on the establishment cost of supply chain reputation.

The rest of the paper is organized as follows. The game analysis of retail enterprises and customers is presented in Section 2. In Section 3, the reputation model of the supply chain enterprise is proposed. The conclusion is given in Section 4.

2 The Game of Retail Enterprises and Customers

Compared with the developed country, the industry of China has multiple circulative forms and channels which lead to a complex and scattered supply chain form (see Fig. 1). In the traditional supply chain management, there are price and profit based game relations between the node enterprises. The chain from suppliers to customers is essentially a game chain, because gain profit of one side means lose profit of the other. However, in the customer demand driven model, the supply chain requires all the node enterprises must build a trust and information sharing mechanism to connect and optimize the upstream and downstream. Then a synchronized network which provides rapid response to customer demand is built. This integrated supply chain management system can reduce the cost of supply chain operation and bring profit to all the node enterprises.

In order to gain profit, the marketing of enterprises should meet customers' demand and desire. Therefore, on one hand, the operation of enterprises requires profit; on the other hand, customers need the best service and the lowest price, which will cause cost increase and profit compression. However, the benefits of enterprises and customers are not opposite at all. The transaction of both sides is a dynamic non-zero-sum two-person game [9].

Information unbalance will occur when handling the relationship between enterprises and customers, for example, enterprises can change low quality products for high ones, whereas customers can only know the quality at time t when buying the products at time t+1. From the dynamic game with incomplete information point of view, the strategy choice during transaction process between enterprises and customers is a kind of signaling game [10].

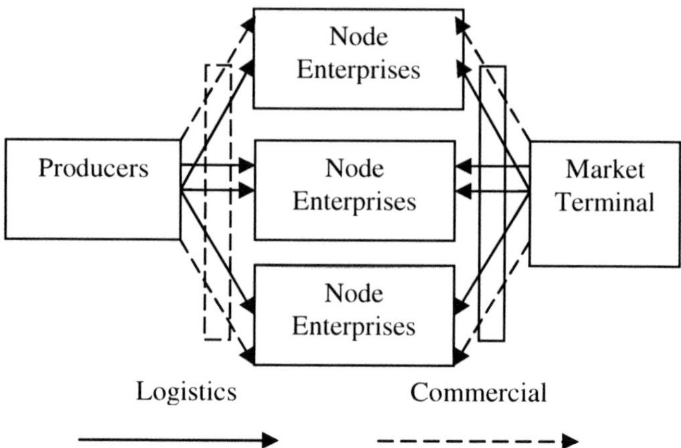

Fig. 1. The integrated chart of the commercial and the logistics channel

Define ci(t) is the supply chain reputation maintenance cost of the enterprise i, $o_i(t)$ is the production of the enterprise i at time t, $p_i(t)$ is the profit of the enterprise i at time t, P(t) is the total profit of the supply chain at time t, we have

$$P(t)=\sum_{i=1}^{n} p_i(t)=\sum_{i=1}^{n}\left[\omega_i(t)(o_i(t)-c_i(t))\right] \tag{1}$$

Where ω(t) is the proportion factor of production and profit of enterprise i, n is the total number of the enterprises.

The proportion of value and income which enterprise i offer to customers during the transaction process is $k_i \cdot \delta_i \cdot p_i(t)$, where $0 \le k_i, \delta_i \le 1$, ki and δ_i are the proportion factor and discount factor of enterprise i, respectively. If the enterprise income for now is P_0 and the total cost that customers paid during the transaction (including the currency and non-currency cost) is $C(t)=\sum_{j=1}^{m} g_j(t)$, where m is the total number of customers, $g_j(t)$ is the cost which customer j paid at time t. The net profit of the supply chain is $P_e=\sum_{i=1}^{n}[(1-k_i\delta_i)p_i(t)]$ and the total profit of customers is $P_C=\sum_{i=1}^{n}[k_i \cdot \delta_i \cdot p_i(t)]$. The equilibrium strategy during the transaction between the enterprise and customers should satisfy the following equations.

$$\begin{aligned}&\sum_{i=1}^{n}[(1-k_i\delta_i)p_i(t)]=P_e \ge P_0\\&\sum_{i=1}^{n}[k_i \cdot \delta_i \cdot p_i(t)]=P_e \ge C(t)=\sum_{j=1}^{m} g_j(t)\end{aligned} \tag{2}$$

From the above equation, we know the Bayesian equilibrium strategy of incomplete information of both sides should satisfy

$$P_0 \le P(t)-C(t)=\sum_{i=1}^{n}\left[\omega_i(t)(o_i(t)-c_i(t))\right]-\sum_{j=1}^{m} g_j(t) \tag{3}$$

Therefore, if the enterprise wants to increase the income, it needs to increase the benefit of customers and reduce the cost that customers paid during this process. In the enterprise management area, especially marketing, development of the customer value and the consideration of the customer profit and cost are key problems. There are many studies about the enterprise profit management, which present the positive influence of the good enterprise reputation to the increase of customers' demands and reduction of cost [11, 12].

3 The Reputation Model of the Supply Chain Enterprise

In the model of last section, every customer knows all the information before buying. In the infinitely repeated game, we know that driven by short term profit, enterprises provide low quality products to cheat customers. Once customers realize this, they will not buy any products from these enterprises. The expected profit by mixed strategy provides no benefit for both enterprises and customers. However, enterprises will provide high quality products for the long term benefit. The equilibrium result is (buying, high quality). Meanwhile, enterprises, in other word, the supply chain created reputation for customers, by which the transaction cost of enterprises and customers can be efficiently reduced. For enterprises in the supply chain, the cost reduced by the reputation should be larger than the reputation maintenance cost, so that enterprises will make efforts to maintain the reputation of the supply chain. We add the reputation parameter in the signal game between catering enterprises and customers. The model is as follows.

For the supply chain, good reputation always means there will be higher profit and lower cost in the future. In the two stage game between enterprises and customers, first, the supply chain enterprise has private information, for example, quality of products and services. They can be separated as two types: T=H, L, where H represents reputation type and L represents non-reputation type. In the first stage, customers do not know the enterprise type. The supply chain enterprise always takes the first action: sending signal $s_1 \geq 0$. Before signal sending, it can predict the action that customers will take. When customers received the signal, they will speculate the enterprise type and take the action $a_1 \geq 0$ according to different types [13].

The profit function of supply chain enterprise in the second stage is

$$F_2(t) = p_2 a_2 - n_2(T) s_2^2 - f s_2 + z_2 s_1 \tag{4}$$

where $a_2 > 0$ means the positive profit for the supply chain enterprise when customers take the action a_2 ; $n_2(t)$ and f means the negative profit which the L type sending is larger than the H type, $n_2(L) > n_2(H) > 0$, $f > 0$; $z_2 > 0$ means the positive profit of the second stage brought by the signal sent in the first stage.

In the first stage, signaling game happens between supply chain enterprises and customers. The result includes the only separating equilibrium [13]. The posterior inference is 1 or 0 if customers speculated the enterprise is H type. The game between the enterprise and customers is Stackelberg game, and we should use backward induction to solve [14]. The profit function of the supply chain enterprise when customers take the optimal action in the second stage is

$$F_2(T)=\frac{1}{2}p_2c(T)d^{-1}s_2-n_2(T)s_2^2-fs_2+z_2s_1 \tag{5}$$

where c(H)>c(L)>0 represents that customers prefer the H type enterprise; d>0 means the negative effect when customers take action. Considering the effect of reputation, the H type supply chain enterprise already creates reputation in the first stage and use it in the second stage. It will send signal s_1(H)in the first stage. Customers will consider it as the H type and take action $a_2(H,s_2)$. The profit function of H type supply chain enterprise is

$$F_2(H)=\frac{1}{2}p_2c(H)d^{-1}s_2-n_2(H)s_2^2-fs_2+z_2s_1 \tag{6}$$

From the above equation, we can obtain the optimal signal sent by the H type supply chain enterprise in the second stage.

$$S_2^*(H)=\frac{1}{4}p_2n_2^{-1}(H)c(H)d^{-1}-\frac{1}{2}n_2^{-1}(H)f \tag{7}$$

If the L type supply chain enterprise did not create reputation in the first stage, it can not use it in the second stage. The profit function of L type supply chain enterprise is

$$F_2(L)=\frac{1}{2}p_2c(L)d^{-1}s_2-n_2(L)s_2^2-fs_2+z_2s_1 \tag{8}$$

The optimal signal is

$$S_2^*(L)=\frac{1}{4}p_2n_2^{-1}(L)c(L)d^{-1}-\frac{1}{2}n_2^{-1}(L)f \tag{9}$$

Because n_2(L) > n_2(H) >0 and c (H) >c (L) > 0 , $S_2^*(H)>S_2^*(L)$. The optimal signal of the reputation enterprise is larger than the optimal signal without reputation, and will bring more profit.

If L type supply chain enterprise creates reputation in the first stage and use it in the second stage, it will send signal s_1 (H) in the first stage. Customers will consider it as the Htype and take action a_2 (H, s_2). The profit function of L type supply chain enterprise is

$$\overline{F}_2(L)=\frac{1}{2}p_2c(H)d^{-1}s_2-n_2(L)s_2^2-fs_2+z_2s_4 \tag{10}$$

The optimal signal is

$$\overline{S}_2^*(L)=\frac{1}{4}p_2n_2^{-1}(L)c(H)d^{-1}-\frac{1}{2}n_2^{-1}(L)f \tag{11}$$

Because c (H) >c (L) >0 , other variables in (9) and (11) are equal and larger than 0. Therefore, $\overline{S}_2^*(L)>S_2^*(L)>0$.

In the above equation, if the non-reputation enterprise creates reputation in the first stage, the optimal signal in the second stage is larger than the optimal signal without reputation, and will bring more profit.

Substituting the optimal signal into (10) and (8), and subtracting them, we can obtain the cost reduced by the existence of reputation

$$d_i(T)=\begin{cases} d_i(H)=F_2(H)-F_2(L) \\ d_i(L)=\bar{F}_2(L)-F_2(L) \end{cases} \tag{12}$$

For the entire supply chain, the cost reduced by the existence of reputation is

$$D(T)=\sum_{i=1}^{n} d_i(T) \tag{13}$$

where T is H or L considering different enterprise. When $D(T)>\sum_{i=1}^{n} c_i(T)$, the reduced cost is larger than the maintenance cost of the catering enterprise. It will bring benefit to both enterprises and customers. When the cost reduced by reputation is smaller than the production of supply chain minuses the total profit of the catering enterprises and the total cost that customers paid, the creation of reputation has no benefit to the entire supply chain.

In the reputation creation cost, except regular methods of marketing and cooperation, we should also pay attention to the benefit that new technology offers to the supply chain management, for example, the e-commerce method based on the network platform. These methods can not only efficiently coordinate the relationship of enterprises in the supply chain but also conveniently match the customer requirements and supply chain connections to obtain a further optimization of supply chain and an increase of enterprise reputation.

4 Conclusions

For retail enterprises, which provide products and services, studies on reputation of supply chain have more significance. The consumption process of service is also the production process, which needs customer participating. Therefore, the reputation of enterprises influences the customers' loyalty to a large extent. Establishing and keeping a long term reputation, the supply chain enterprise can increase their competition and profit.

References

1. Costantino, F., Di Gravio, G., Tronci, M.: Simulation model of the logistic distribution in a medical oxygen supply chain. In: Proceedings of the 19th European Conference on Modelling and Simulation, pp. 175–183 (2005)
2. Schneeweiss, C., Zimmer, K.: Hierarchical Coordination Mechanisms within the Supply Chain. European Journal of Operational Research 153, 687–703 (2004)
3. Wang, H., Guo, M., Efstathiou, J.: A game-theoretical cooperative mechanism design for a two-echelon decentralized supply chain. European Journal of Operational Research 157, 372–388 (2004)
4. Eriksson, A., Lindgren, K.: Cooperation driven by mutations in multi-person Prisoner's Dilemma. Journal of Theoretical Biology 232, 399–409 (2005)

5. Ferreira, R.D., Dufourt, F.: Free entry equilibria with positive profits: A unified approach to quantity and price competition games. International Journal of Economic Theory 3, 75 (2007)
6. Kreps, D., Milgrom, P., Roberts, J., Robert, W.: Rational cooperation in the finitely repeated prisoners' dilemma. Journal of Economic Theory 27, 245–252 (1982)
7. Balachandran, K.R., Radhakrishnan, S.: Quality implications of warranties in a supply chain. Management Science 51, 1266–1277 (2005)
8. van Branconi, C., Loch, C.H.: Contracting for major projects: eight business levers for top management. International Journal of Project Management 22, 119–130 (2004)
9. Guo, W.-j., Qi, H., Guo, Q.-j.: Reputation model of supply chain based on the game of catering enterprises and customers. In: The Second International Conference on Intelligent Computation Technology and Automation, pp. 956–958 (2009)
10. Chen, J., Tu, M., Sun, D.: Signaling game of environmental purchasing in ecological supply chain. Journal of System Engineering 19, 202–206 (2004)
11. Woodruff: Customer value: the next source for competitive advantage. Journal of the Academy of Marketing Science 25, 139–153 (1997)
12. Jian-hua, C., Shi-hua, M.: A Dynamic Reputation Incentive Model in Construction Supply Chain. In: International Conference on Management Science & Engineering, pp. 385–392 (2008)
13. Gang, Y., Zhaohan, S., Tiaojun, X.: An effective algorithm for computing equilibrium outcome of a class of signaling games. International Journal of Information Technology & Decision Making 1, 209–228 (2002)
14. He, X., Prasad, A., Sethi, S.P., Gutierrez, G.J.: A survey of Stackelberg differential game models in supply and marketing channels. Journal of Systems Science and Systems Engineering 16, 385–413 (2007)

The Government's Role in Venture Capital Financing of Hi-tech SMEs in China

Zhijian Lu and Yiwen Shen

School of Management, Zhejiang University, Hangzhou, Zhejiang Province, China
Economy and Management School
Zhejiang Normal University, Jinhua, Zhejiang Province, China
boriskgn633@gmail.com

Abstract. Hi-tech SMEs are difficult to obtain financing from banks in China, they have little or no collateral, the value of their innovation is hard to evaluate. For these reasons, entrepreneurs in the hi-tech SMEs tend to rely on venture capital, but hi-tech SMEs have two deficiencies. This paper first analyses these two deficiencies: the limited appropriability of technology innovation and asymmetric information, which lead to market failure, so venture capital investment in hi-tech SMEs isn't optimal, there exists a financing gap, then we elaborate on various kinds of effective laws and economic policies foreign governments have adopted to solve the financing gap, based on present situation in China, at last the paper proposes what policies Chinese government should adopt to bridge this gap.

Keywords: hi-tech SMEs, venture capital, financing, government.

1 Introduction

In recent years, small and medium sized enterprises (SMEs) have meet great difficulties because of revaluation of the RMB and rising of labor force cost in China, at the same time commercial banks tighten financing to control the risk. Obtaining financing become more difficult for SMEs, especially for the hi-tech SMEs, because they have several characteristics that limit their options for obtaining financing from the banks: they have little or no collateral, their assets tend to be intangible, and the value of their innovation is hard to evaluate. What policies should Chinese government at all levels adopt to resolve this financing problem? Encouraging development of venture capital industry is a good idea for the Chinese government.

Venture capital(VC) is an important source of long-term investment capital, VC can be defined as an activity by which corporate investors provide long-term equity finance, supported by business skills to enterprises with the potential to grow rapidly with the aim of making high capital gain with the high risk rather than interest income or dividend yield. VC is called hi-tech enterprises incubator and engine of economic growth, but VC cannot overcome the "financing gap" fully, because hi-tech SMEs have two deficiencies that may cause suboptimal VC financing in market economy, first: the limited appropriability of technology innovation of SMEs frequently causes private

M. Dai (Ed.): ICCIC 2011, Part II, CCIS 232, pp. 47–51, 2011.

returns to fall short of the social returns and thus leads to suboptimal financing, it is concerned with positive externalities. Second, capital market imperfection undermines an enterprise's capacity to raise the external fund, which is concerned with asymmetric information. These two reasons lead to market failure, and it is theoretical basis for government intervention.

At first the paper points out why the government intervenes venture capital financing of hi-tech SMEs, then aiming at these two questions, what policies the Chinese government at all levels should adopt to alleviate market failure, finally summarizes the major conclusions.

2 Theoretical Analysis of Government Intervention in Venture Capital Financing— Positive Externalities and Asymmetric Information

For hi-tech SMEs, VC is not only a source of financing but also a source of professional support, VC stimulates the firm's transition from technology innovation to a marketable product, Kortum and Lerner (2000) calculated that VC backed firms accounted for about 14 percent of industrial innovation in the US in 1998, although they spent only about 3 percent of all research and development funds. Innovation of hi-tech SMEs not only gives them a chance but also optimizes industry structure through technology diffusion, creates job opportunities and advances economic growth. Positive externalities of venture capital financing make it has the characteristics of public goods, according to economy theory, VC investment in hi-tech SMEs is suboptimal.

Imperfections in capital markets are the second financing-related cause of under-investment in hi-tech SMEs, Chang and Shih(2004) compare the distinct systems of China and Taiwan, they get the conclusions that mature and well developed capital markets are important for the allocation of financial resource to innovation of hi-tech SMEs. In a perfect capital market, all projects are funded according to their own merits, since riskier projects call for higher rate of interest, market can clear in equilibrium.

However, in practice, there exists asymmetric information to entrepreneur and the venture capitalist, the entrepreneur has better information about expected costs and returns, which he can't honestly communicate to the venture capitalist, who has difficulties to discriminate between good projects and bad projects, thus he gives all projects higher risk, and asks more preferential conditions in the contract, so that good projects don't get a good price, at last the venture capitalist finds that all projects are bad in VC market, it is called adverse selection. Second, moral hazard is an incentive problem, the entrepreneur may reduce his effort, pursue growth instead of returns to the venture capitalist ,when the costs of monitoring the entrepreneur become too high, the venture capitalist has to abandon financing even though the project may be profitable, especially, hi-tech SMEs have not accumulated a steady cash-flow and lack not only collateral, but also a track record establishing good reputation among venture capitalists, moreover venture capitalists must take into account the statistical fact that many SMEs fail(Kaniovski and Peneder,2008).

3 The Government's Role in Bridging the Financing Gap of Hi-tech SMEs

Positive externalities and asymmetric information of financing hi-tech SMEs lead to market failure, it means there exists a financing gap, Chinese government at all levels should exert more roles, adopt a series of appropriate policies to stimulate VC market, encourage more private funds entry, in order to fill this gap, the government's measures include direct and indirect fiscal policies.

Government's direct fiscal policies include direct VC investment and subsidy, direct VC investment has three modes: 1,the government invests in VC firms; 2,the government dedicates public money to set up own VC funds; 3,the government cooperates with private sector to set up VC funds.

Among government's supporting programmes for VC firms, the US government's Small Business Investment Company(SBIC) programme is most representative, The US Small Business Investment Act of 1958 authorized the formation of SBICs as a hybrid scheme of federally subsidized pools of VC and private funding for the purpose of investing in small firms of all types, a SBIC is a privately managed firm and acts as an intermediary between large investors and the small enterprises targeted by the scheme, It is able to borrow at preference rates from the federal government and raise additional money in the capital market. The SBIC's basic mode is that of an equity enhancement programme where the state's involvement is either through being an investor or through acting as a guarantor to other fund raisers. It allows for additional and cheaper funding to be raised and thereby creates a leverage advantage to private investors. The SBIC scheme is generally perceived to be a success, Carpentier & Suret (2005) found that SBICs had financed numerous traditional and hi-tech SMEs at a low or zero cost for the government, the SBICs helped a number of individuals to develop their investment skills and subsequently raised institutional money to become formal venture capitalists. It was an example where government involvement helped the emerging venture capitalists to become professional in their investment activities.

Other governments have applied this or comparable approaches, in 1997, the Australian government formally adopted a local equivalent of the revised SBIC scheme by creating the Innovation Investment Fund. Kenney et al. (2002) considered Israel "the most successful case of the export of Silicon Valley-style VC practice", Israel government played an important role in encouraging the growth of VC industry. Yozma was set up by the Israel government in 1993, to create the infrastructure for a domestic VC market. According to Gilson (2003), Yozma was plainly influenced by the US experience and compared to programmes elsewhere in the world came "closer to getting the incentive structure right".

Another policy is government subsidy, providing subsidy to VC firms and hi-tech SMEs is common in the world, it can lower the entry threshold of VC market, for example, European Seed Capital Scheme gives a subsidy for VC firms to cover some of the costs from running the firms, Singapore government provides 50% loss subsidy for VC firms which run under deficit for three years continuously, the German government's non-defense R&D project funding scheme (DPF) provided subsidy over 700 million euros to SMEs for R&D in 2005 (Aschhoff, 2008), Japanese government provides 50% R&D expenditure to hi-tech SMEs according to Subsidies for the Technology Development Program (TDP), limit is from JPY 5 million to JPY 20 million.

Government's indirect fiscal policy includes tax policy, guarantee and government purchase. Tax policies have a great impact on VC industry, It can determine the incentives of individuals to start up new firms and of venture capitalists to finance and advise them. Rosen (2002) produces ample evidence that once started, the decisions in new firms regarding employment, capital investment and production are markedly influenced by taxes. Gentry and Hubbard's (2000) empirical analysis demonstrates that the progressivity of the tax schedule is important for entrepreneurship, Gompers and Lerner (1998) found some evidence of a moderately negative effect of the capital gains tax on VC investments and fund raising. For example, from 1957 to 1997, the capital gains tax rate of the US change for several times, it had great impact on VC industry. New commitments to VC firms accelerated from $68 million in 1977 when the capital gains rate was 49 percent to $5.1 billion by 1983 when the rate had been dropped to 20 percent, that was a 700 percent increase in capital raised for new firms. After 1987 capital gains tax rate hiked, the number of companies receiving VC funding steadily declined. In 1986, 1,512 firms received funding. That number had fallen to 800 by 1991. It remained relatively low until it skyrocketed following the 1997 capital gains tax cut. (See http://www.nvca.org/ffax.html). New business formation dramatically increased following the 1997 cut of the top capital gains rate. Between 1997 and 2000, the amount of money raised in IPOs more than doubled.

Government guarantee: investment in hi-tech SMEs will take significant risks. Many portfolio companies fail and result in full or partial loss of the venture capitalist's investment with an adverse impact on VC fund returns. To reduce the costs of failure and to encourage private sector investors, loan and equity guarantees are often provided as financial instruments to transfer part or all of the risk of investment from investors to the government as provider of the guarantee. If a start-up fails, part of the loss is covered by the government guarantee. for example, the American Small Business Administration (SBA) had a Express program which offers a 50% loan guarantee up to $295 000. This program has become very popular, accounting for 68% of loans by number. French government offers 60% guarantee of loss which invests in technology innovation, the UK government's Small Firms Loan Guarantee Program offers 75% guarantee, maximum size of loan is $567 500, Length of loan is 10 years.

Government departments should become a major client for hi-tech Sesotho enterprises get more chance to develop through government purchase.For example, in the US, the law was passed to encourage government department to purchase from SMEs or start-up companies. Otherwise, the government should support VC ecosystem through teaching entrepreneurship, training bankers and fund-managers in the appraisal of technology based firms, protecting intellectual property and the patents and innovations of start-up firms, promoting technology transfer between universities and enterprises.

Chinese VC industry is infant and in early stage, but China is one of the fastest growing markets for VC investing in the world, it was estimated that $1.17 billion was raised by VC firms to invest in China (Balfour, 2006), the government should learn from foreign successful experience, exert more role in venture capital financing of hi-tech SMEs, try its best to bridge this financing gap.

4 Conclusion

VC financing of hi-tech SMEs exists positive externalities (spillovers) and the problem of asymmetric information (together with transaction costs), which leads to market failure, so there exists a financing gap, Chinese government should adopt direct and indirect fiscal policies including direct investment, subsidy, tax, guarantee and government purchase etc. to attract more VC investment in hi-tech SMEs, resolve their financial difficulties, close the financing gap, enlarge employment and promote economic growth.

References

1. Rin, M.D., Nicodano, G., Sembenelli, A.: Public Policy and the Creation of Active Venture Capital Markets. Journal of Public Economics (90(8-9)) (2006)
2. Lerner, J.: The Government as Venture Capitalist: The Long Run Impact of the SBIR Program. Journal of Business (72(3)) (1999)
3. Kortum, S., Lerner, J.: Assessing the contribution of venture capital to innovation. Journal of Economics 31(4) (Winter 2000)
4. Chang, P.-L., Shih, H.-Y.: The innovation systems of Taiwan and China: a comparative analysis. Technovation 24(7), 529–539 (2004)
5. Kaniovski, S., Peneder, M.: Determinants of Firm Survival: a Duration Analysis Using the Generalized Gamma Distribution Empirica. Journal of Applied Economics and Economic Policy, 0340-8744 35(1), 41–58 (2008)
6. Carpentier, C., L'Her, J.-F., Suret, J.-M.: PIPEs: A Canadian Perspective. Journal of Private Equity 8(4), 41–49 (Fall 2005)
7. Gilson, R.J.: Engineering a Venture Capital Market: Lessons from the American Experience. Stanford Law Review 55 (April 2003)
8. Aschhoff, B.: Who Gets the Money? The Dynamics of R&D Project Subsidies in Germany, Discussion Paper (8-18) (2008)
9. Rosen, H.S.: Venture Capital, Entrepreneurship and Public Policy. CESifo Seminar Series (2002), http://www.cesifo.de
10. Gentry, W.M., Hubbard, R.G.: Tax Policy and Entry into Entrepreneurship. American Economic Review 90, 283–287 (2000)
11. Kenney, M., Han, K., Tanaka, S.: The Globalization of Venture Capital: The Cases of Taiwan and Japan (2002), http://www.insme.info/documenti/kenney.pdf
12. Gompers, P.A., Lerner, J.P.: What Drives Venture Capital Fundraising? Brookings Papers on Economic Activity - Microeconomics, 149–192 (1998)
13. Xu, Y.L., Liang, J.X.: Study on venture capital and public policy. Forum on Science and Technology in China, 93–96 (August 2007)
14. Ben-Ari, G., Vonortas, N.S.: Risk financing for knowledge-based Enterprises: mechanisms and policy options. Science and Public Policy 34(7), 475–488 (2007)
15. Balfour, F.: Venture capital's new promised land. Business Week 3967, 44–44 (2006)
16. Meyer, T.: The Public Sector's Role in the Promotion of Venture Capital Markets. Working Paper 8 (2007)
17. Lei, Z.Z.: The International Experience and Enlightenment of Government's Support on the Venture Capital. Technology Economy and Management Reasearch 6, 95–98 (2009)
18. Ying, H., Bo, Z.C.: The change of government's role in venture capital. Special Zone Economy 6, 183–184 (2006)

The Research on the Informatization Issues during Chinese Medicine Industry Modernization

Xiong Xinzhong

School of Economics, Wuhan University of Technology, Wuhan, China, 430070
Nanyang Institute of Technology, Nanyang, China, 473004
junhuhk@hotmail.com

Abstract. Information Technique is technological support of traditional chinese medicine industry modernization, TCM remained stagnant in the past century, which key reason is that technology of massive information acquiring, saving, and utilizing fell behind. It is no doubt that information technology is extension of si zhen. TCM has much lagged behind times level on collecting exterior information, which is not adapt to high development of modern information technology. Construction of diagnostic information database of TCM is of particular importance.

Keywords: Informatization, Chinese Medicine, Industry Modernization.

1 Introduction

Traditional Chinese Medicine (TCM) is one of the most outstanding contributions of Chinese to the world. In long-term medical practice of the Chinese medical physicians, they realized close relationship between the external expressive form of human body and the essence of disease, and diagnose disease through 'syndrome differentiation'. The external expressive form of body can be captured through four methods of diagnosis (called si zhen in Chinese): inspection, auscultation and olfaction, inquiring, palpation. The inspection process involves examining the patient by observing his or her shape, expression, tongue, etc. The auscultation and olfaction processes involve collecting information for diagnosis by listening to the voice and smelling the odor of patient. All of these bring up the major motive in researches on modernizing TCM, which can provide accurate and opportune diagnosis. Application of modern Information Technique is a breakthrough of study on modernization of TCM diagnosis, which has practical significance to help the objective of TCM diagnosis and the modernization of diagnosis means.

Information Technique (IT) is a kind of technology that can accomplish information acquisition, information transmission, information process, information regeneration, and information utilization and so on [1], which take computer technology as research tool. The development of modern science and technology can provide a powerful support for researches on modernization of TCM diagnosis. Sensor technology, image processing technology, signal processing technology and pattern recognition technology involved in modernization of TCM diagnosis, have

M. Dai (Ed.): ICCIC 2011, Part II, CCIS 232, pp. 52–59, 2011.

obtained the great progress in recent years, which makes it to possible to carry on modernizing TCM diagnosis by integrating the technologies.

This paper is aimed to illustrate the contents and methods of modernizing TCM diagnosis using modern Information Technique, modern TCM diagnostic processes based on modern IT is illustrated in Fig. 1.

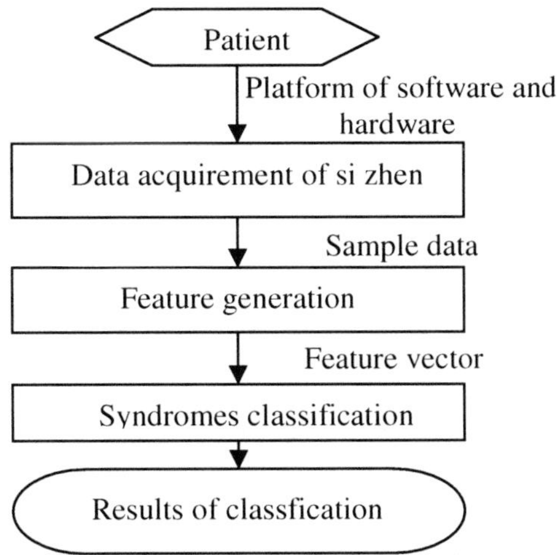

Fig. 1. Modern TCM diagnostic processes

2 Information Acquirement of TCM Diagnosis Based on Modern Information Technology

Information of si zhen should be acquired objectively, accurately and steadily, which is one of content of modern diagnosis of TCM. And, only this question is solved, the repeatability of acquirement of si zhen information can be guaranteed, on the basis of this, furthermore, information processing, feature exaction and pattern recognition of si zhen can be meaningful.

2.1 Data Acquirement of Inspection Examination Base on IT

In the diagnosis through inspection, a patient's tongue color is traditionally observed. According to TCM principle, different portions of tongue reveal the information of corresponding internal organs of a human body. The relationship between some diseases and abnormalities in the patient's tongue and tongue coating has been substantiated by clinical evidence, which has motivated the development of various tongue image processing techniques.

Digital Image Processing methods have become a mainstream technology to process and analyze tongue image, and based on these methods, corresponding tongue image analysis instrument was developed successfully. For example, a tongue image analysis instrument with type TP-1 was manufactured successfully by Shanghai University of TCM and Shanghai Jiao Tong University [2]. The tongue image acquisition hardware part of this instrument is composed of digital camera, closed and dark box, standard illuminator and computer. Tongue is firstly shot through digital camera in closed and dark box equipped with standard illuminator, and red, green, blue (RGB) model was used to represent the tongue colors, then R, G, and B value are sent to computer to process. The contents of preprocess of tongue image mainly includes: segmentations of the tongues body and calibrations of their colors.

Owing to existing difference of color domain in acquisition equipment and display equipment for tongue image, color of tongue image in display not to be consistent with tongue itself. Many researches on color reproduction have already been carried out.

2.2 Data Acquirement of Auscultation

According to the TCM theory, states of Ying and Yang which correspond to changes in the viscera function, may lead to change in voice. Owing to difference of personal auditory, the acquirement of patient's voice is lack of objectivity, which leads to mis-diagnosis for auscultation examination. With the development of modern information technology, a few studies on objective auscultation examination have been done in this area.

Basic principle of sound acquisition system is described as follows: human physiological sound is firstly transformed to electrical signals through microphone and acoustic sensor, and then electrical signals are transformed to digital signals through A/D conversion card to input microcomputer processing. The speech data were recorded in a moderately quiet room. Study on objective acquirement of patient's voice has widely developed. For example, an end –point detecting algorithm [5] was incorporated to remove the leading and trailing non-speech portions of each utterance. Weng et al. [6] applied vowels like /a/, /i/, /u/, /e/, and /o/ to distinguish normal people and patients with gastritis. The literature [7] reported that the vowel /a/ was chosen as the utterance for each patient to pronounce in this research. The reason for this is that almost everyone can pronounce /a/ without any special training even if the speaker is a patient suffering from severe disease.

2.3 Data Acquirement of Inquiring

Inquiring is asking the patient about the disease condition in order to understand the pathological process. Inquiring covers a wide range of topic. Inquiring covers chills and fever, perspiration, appetite and thirst, pain and so on.

The descriptions of inquiring have strong subjectivity and fuzziness, influencing greatly accurate of TCM diagnosis. Recently with development of study on normalization and quantization of symptom and syndrome in TCM, the scholars of TCM field have developed a few work of establishing scale related to TCM syndrome, which can assess symptom quantity and obtain better objective and comparable data. Methods of statistical and clinical epidemiologic research are employed to develop inquiring scale. Design philosophy of inquiring scale is described as following: (1) Questionnaire is formed. (2) Preliminary screening of questionnaire's items is made by Delphi after consultation and demonstration of statistics specialists, epidemiologic specialists and expert of TCM. (3) Screening of primary selected items is made once again with statistical method, meanwhile symptoms and physical sign are quantized.

2.4 Data Acquirement of Palpation

Palpation is method of diagnosis in which the pathological condition is detected by palpation, feeling, and pressing certain areas of the body. Pulse signal is usually felt by finger touching of Chinese doctors. Subjective pulse diagnosis is very difficult to learn and many times accurate subjective pulse diagnosis can only be made by TCM practitioners after years of experience [8]. Therefore a computational system to accurately diagnosis pulse waves is highly desirable; however, objective acquirement of pulse signal is absolutely necessary before analyzing the pulse wave data using computational approaches.

Measurement equipment needed to be used to record pulse data. A pulse detecting system usually consists of strain-gage sensors, amplifiers, filters, A/D translators, I/O ports and integrated digital signal processing software. Acquirement equipment of pulse data comprises input of two parts: one is to weight the pressure when the condense microphone is pressed against the patient's wrist. The other part is to measure the pulse using a condense microphone with amplifiers and filters, allowing the transmission of the pulse waves into the computer via an A/D converter.

3 Data Analysis and Feature Extraction of Si Zhen Information Base on It

Raw Data of si zhen information that is acquired through platform of hardware and software include useful feature information, which can be obtained with the method of data analysis and feature exaction. So, models and methods that reject interference effectively and mine feature information, needed to be established, which is the second key content of modern diagnosis of TCM.

3.1 Feature Extraction of Tongue Image Information

Digital image processing and computer vision technology are widely applied in the feature extraction of tongue image. Through the extraction and analysis for surface feature of tongue shape, color, edge and texture, feature data is provided for the tongue image pattern recognition and laid basis for the future tongue image recognition.

Generally, two kinds of quantitative features, chromatic and textural measures, are mainly extracted from tongue images. Xu et al [9] employed grey difference statistics according to tongue texture to quantify the tongue texture in CON, ASM, ENT and MEAN. Ding et al [10] convert RGB file format of tongue image into Lab file format to study the color feature of eight kind of tongue-fur. Su et al [11] introduced an effective method for analyzing moisture of tongue-fur based on the Dichromatic Reflection Model. The formation of the highlight areas and the influence of characters of CCD camera to the formatted color image are studied in this paper. Ying et al extracted eight characteristic variables of tongue manifestations, including color, shape, wetness-dry-ness, etc., to analyze tongue manifestations of 49 patients with cerebrovascular diseases and 39 health people respectively. The result showed that accuracy of classification according to eight characteristic variables was obviously higher than that according only to the color characteristics of tongue body or coating.

The paper [10] analyze the tongue features locally, a tongue image is divided into a number of blocks with size 36*36. The color and texture features of each block are analyzed. The feature about tongue color and thick or thin of tongue coating is extracted in CLE L*u*v* color space. Tongue textures features are analyzed using Gabor wavelet opponent color features.

3.2 Feature Extraction of Voice Information

After the acquirement of voice, voice signal is analyzed with signal processing methods to extract related characteristics. Modern signal processing method include: speech packetization algorithm, speech endpoint detection, Time-Domain analysis, spectrum analysis, analyzing linear prediction, nonlinear analysis and so on.

Some researches have been made by forerunner to extract the feature parameters. Chiu et al. [8] analyzed the vowel /a/ using time-frequency parameters, such as zero-crossing average numbers, variations on peaks and valleys, variations on formant frequencies, etc. Chiu et al. also studied objective auscultation of traditional Chinese medical diagnosis using fractal dimension analysis. Mo et al. applied seven parameters (harmonic, top frequency, amplitude, formant, cacophony, fundamental frequency, duration of top frequency) as the objective parameters of TCM acoustic diagnosis.

3.3 Feature Selection of Inquiring Information

Inquiring concludes massive information. Data mining and statistic analysis are effective knowledge discovery methods for variable reduction, which can usually find the symptoms most relating to syndrome differentiation. Generally, the methods to find the feature variable include: the principal component analysis, factor analysis, Tough Set and so on. Li et al. [18] bring 50 integrated medicine indexes into frequency analysis during establishing diagnostic criterion of acute ischemic stroke with qi efficiency and blood stasis syndrome. The variances of less frequency were deleted, and 31 variances were preserved to perform principal component analysis. Cha et al. [19] bring subjective symptoms of 467 rheumatoid arthritis patients into factor analysis, extracting disease factor, asthenia factor, chill factor, and fever. Moreover, variance analysis was made on these factors, and the result showed only three syndrome factors can well different Damp Heat Syndrome, Cold Damp Syndrome, a syndrome of intermixing of cold and heat, and syndrome of deficiency of the liver and kidney.

3.4 Feature Extraction of Palpation Information

The traditional mathematical analysis of pulse signal is a time-domain analysis. Characteristic points of pulse chat with specified physiological significance, such as chief wave, dichotic wave, height of dicrotic wave, area value etc, are extracted through time-domain transform. These characteristic points are combined with physiological factor to obtain many results of clinic medicine value. Modern tools and methods of mathematical analysis, such as wavelet transform, multiple sensors information coalescence technique, multiple scale estimation theory, time-frequency representation analysis, open a new avenue for researching pulse signal of Traditional Chinese Medicine. For example, the pulse signals were decomposed into three layers wavelet coefficients by which the pulse signals were reconstructed [20]. On the third layer wavelet signals, the energy values of eight frequency bands from low frequency to high frequency were calculated, and the energy values were used as the characters vectors of the pulse signals. Li et al. [21] transformed time-domain pulse wave to frequency-domain through discrete fast Fourier transform, and obtain corresponding pulse spectrum curve, showing amplitude spectrum and phase spectrum of different pulse condition, and differentiating characteristic of different frequency pulse.

4 Feature Generation of Si Zhen Information

Inspection, auscultation, inquiring, and palpation are the four approaches to understand the pathological conditions. They cannot be separated, but relate to and supplement on another. In the clinical situation, only by combining the four a comprehensive and systematic understanding of the condition of the disease can be gained and a correct diagnosis can be made.

After si zhen information is acquired, we can establish database of si zhen. Owing to data of si zhen are enormous, Computational methods for TCM allow researches to identify required information efficiently, discover new relationship.

Through the acquirement of si zhen information from a patient, we can obtain a sample data (x_1, x_2, and x_3... x_n). A matrix of m×n can be composed with m samples, where n is the number of symptoms and m is the number of samples. Here n value is usually very great in order to descript the disease symptom completely and detailedly, which bring large difficulty to process data. For every variable x_i ($i = 1, 2, \ldots, n$) , their contribution degrees to diagnosis should be different. Thus conspicuous feature data need to be exacted from sample data with the method of feature selection and feature exaction, which call feature generation [22]. Feature selection is that variables related most to diagnosis classification are selected from sample variable. Feature extraction is that multiple variables of sample are transformed to new variables with principle component analysis and data fusion etc. Through feature generation, the sample data was transformed into feature vector (y_1, y_2... y_k), which dimension is less than dimension of sample vector, that is $k < n$. We can make full use the theory of mathematical statistics and data mining to establish the method of data reduction and knowledge discovery, which can select and exact the data feature, and find dependence relations of data.

5 Classification of TCM Syndromes

After feature data of si zhen information has been extracted effectively, these feature data must be analyzed and judge synthetically to deduct diagnostic results. Analysis and judgment of the feature data should be implemented based on: reasonable and scientific syndrome class is established, and reasonable and scientific model and method of syndrome classification is used.

Machine learning, statistics analysis and data mining offer methodology guidance for study on diagnostic classification. Modern classification technologies of information are classified into multiple types according to data characteristics, which showing in Fig. 2.

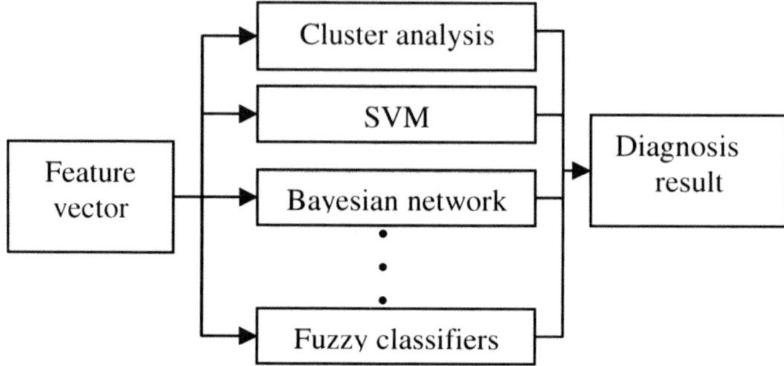

Fig. 2. Process of Differential Diagnosis

Many scholars have applied regression and discriminant analysis to quantitative diagnosis of TCM syndromes, which aims to establish quantitative relation between symptoms and syndromes. Scholars analyze sample data with statistical method to establish regression equation and discriminant function. Discriminant function is linear combination of each vector of diagnostic information vector (feature vector), where independent variables of function represent symptoms and dependent variables represent syndromes. Discriminant function is used for criterion of syndrome differentiation. But, independent variables (symptoms) of every sample is valued according to subjective judgment of expert, so discriminant function is actually summary of expert cognition, which leading to this criterion to lack for objectivity.

Some scholars have applied cluster analysis to quantitative diagnosis of TCM syndromes. Syndrome differentiation is actually to classify patients according to symptoms; patients of the same syndrome are classified into the same category; patients of the different syndrome are classified into the different category. However, simple cluster method can only process one-dimensional data, not process multidimensional data.

Latent Class Analysis (LCA) is initially proposed by Lazarsfeld in 1950, and is researched deeply by Hagenaars & McCutcheon. LCA can explain the rules among the observed variables by intruding latent variables. Prof. Zhang Lian-wen of Hong Kong University of Scientific and Technology improved on the model of LCA to Hierarchical latent Class Model (HLC). In the latent structure, the leaf nodes represent the symptoms, and the root nodes represent the syndrome type, and other hidden connection nodes represent pathology factors. The syndrome differentiation of TCM refers to the relations between the syndrome (latent variable) and symptoms (manifest variables), is a kind of latent structure theory that discusses the association of various pathology factors and relationship between the syndrome and symptom. Wang et al collected 2004 questionnaires concerning bloodstains symptoms and physical signs, and established a Latent Structure Model to analyze these data.

Support Vector Machine (SVM), a kernel based classification technique, is widely used in feature recognition. Yan et al constructed the differential diagnostic model based on multi-SVM, and made a comparison between different kernel functions for differential diagnostics. The result showed that the model based on mule-SVM presented can deal with accompanying syndromes better.

6 Conclusion

It is one of the premises of realizing modernization of TCM diagnosis to specify diagnostic operating regulations, to establish diagnostic data criterion of TCM, and to construct diagnostic information database of TCM with reliable and abundant data. Modern information processing technology is applied to TCM diagnosis to have practical significance to help the objectivity and modernization of TCM diagnosis.

Innovation and development of modernization of TCM diagnosis should be made on the basis of inherited principle of TCM diagnosis, with the help of computer analysis technology, syndrome differentiation of TCM should be deepened and extended, which is expected to realize continuous development of TCM.

References

1. Zhang, W., He, R.: Comment on extension of Information Technology to traditional Chinese medical four diagnostic information. Chinese Archives of Traditional Chinese Medicine 22, 1850 (2004)
2. Wang, Y.Q., Li, F.F., Yan, H.X., Yao, D.: A Review of Digitalized Traditional Diagnostic Techniques. World Science Age: Modernization of Traditional Chinese Medicine 9(3), 96–101 (2007)
3. Kass, M., Witkin, A., Terzopoulos, D.: Snakes: Active contour models. Int. J. Computer Vision 1(4), 321–331 (1987)
4. Wang, Y.Z., Yang, J., Zhou, Y.: Image Segmentation in Tongue Charaterization. Journal of Biomedical Engineering 22(6), 1128–1133 (2005)
5. Rabiner, L.R., Sambur, M.R.: An algorithm for determining the endpoints of isolated utterances. Bell Syst. Tech. J. 54, 297–315 (1975)
6. Weng, C.S., Shyu, L.Y., Chang, Y.H., Chiang, L.N.: A study of acoustical method in traditional Chinese medicine for the upper GI disorder patients. Chinese Journal of Medical and Biological Engineering 18(4), 245–252 (1998)
7. Shimizu, T., Furuse, N., Yamazaki, T., et al.: Chaos of Vowel /a/ in Japanese Patients with Depression: A Preliminary Study. Occup. Health. 47, 267–269 (2005)
8. Xu, J.T., Sun, Y., Zhang, Z.F.: Analysis and discrimination of tongue texture characteristic by different statistics. Journal of Shanghai University of Traditional Chinese Medicine 17(3), 55–57 (2003)
9. Ding, M., Zhang, J.Z.: Quantitative analysis and categorization of tongue-fur based on L*a*b* color pattern. Journal of Instrumentation 23(3), 328–340 (2002)
10. Su, K., Lu, X.: An Image Processing-Based Method to Analyze Moisture of Tongue-fur. Journal of Image and Graphics 4(A), 345–348 (1999)
11. Ying, J., Li, Z.X., Li, S.: Collection and analysis of characteristics of tongue manifestations in patients with cerebrovascular diseases. Journal of Beijing University of Traditional Chinese Medicine 28, 62–65 (2007)

A Grey Correlation Analysis on Modern Rural Logistics and Rural Finance Development

Hu Bangyong

School of Economics and Management, Chongqing Three Gorges University, Wanzhou, Chongqing, China
xfwan2006@163.com

Abstract. Development of rural logistics have been included in China's 10th Five-Year Plan. China's current rural financial system can not meet the needs of the construction of rural logistics. Logistics finance supply shortage has seriously hindered the construction of China's modern logistics in rural areas. This paper studies the factors affecting rural logistics development, mainly analyzes the relationship between the development of rural finance and rural logistics. At last the paper points out the measure to innovate the modern rural logistics finance system.

Keywords: Grey correlation analysis, Logistics finance, Rural logistics.

1 Introduction

The development of rural logistics has an important role in the promotion of rural economic growth, but china's modern logistics system in rural areas is not perfect, logistics infrastructure is still lagging behind, logistics finance is in short supply. It is very necessary to improve the rural financial system in order to develop modern logistics in rural areas, but also it is an important way for resolving the construction of modern logistics in rural areas.

Foreign scholars have some study on the relationship between the rural logistics and rural finance. Mckinnon and Edward. S. Shaw (1973) believe that in many developing countries, because of financial repression and financial duality, rate distortion, lack of financial instruments, Single credit instruments, loan quota and so on, all these reasons result the rural financial markets inefficient; Hugh. T. Patrick (1996), Yale University economist, who studied the relationship between the development of rural organizations and rural economic growth; Mark Drabenstott (2002), U.S. Agricultural Research Center Vice-Chairman, believes that the rural financial system must reform in order to adapt to the growth of rural economy; Meyer(2002)believes that rural financial services can promote the production and investment, but also can smooth consumption and improve food security; Mason and Basin(2003)believe that the market structure and market conduct determine the effect of the market system, they used the structure-conduct-performance analysis and linked the relationship between the value chain and rural finance; Nagarjn and Meye (2005) believe that the value chain for each business and financial sector are closely linked.

M. Dai (Ed.): ICCIC 2011, Part II, CCIS 232, pp. 60–65, 2011.

Domestic scholars also have some studies on rural Logistics Finance. FU Honglei, Yi Xiuqin (2003) believe that lower costs, brand building, online trading systems accelerate the development of rural logistics; Chen yong (2003), according to the characteristics of China's logistics development in rural areas, elaborated on the need for the development of modern logistics in rural areas, at last proposed response to the development of modern rural logistics; WANG Xinli (2005) made a special study of China's rural Logistics, which also involves the construction of rural logistics and financial support, but there is no in-depth study.

2 The Establishment of Grey Correlation Analysis

2.1 Gray Characteristics of Logistics Development in Rural Areas

The construction of modern logistics in rural areas and rural finance development are closely related. Rural finance development is a prerequisite for development of rural logistics, while the development of logistics in rural areas is the promotion of rural financial development.

Factors affecting rural logistics development are varied. Zhang Huaqin and other scholars considered that the main factors affect the development of logistics in rural areas included: (1) The level of development of rural finance; (2) The level of development of rural infrastructure; (3) The degree of development of rural education; (4) Natural disasters in rural areas; (5) The Government's policy. These five factors affect the development of logistics in rural areas, and these factors have obvious characteristics of gray. Based on gray system theory, I will analyze the above-mentioned five factors on the degree of influence the development of logistics in rural areas, distinguish which is the main factor, which is the secondary factor.

2.2 Principles and Methods

Suppose there are N determining factors, characteristics of various factors to reflect changes in the data columns are as follows: $\{x_1(t)\}$ $\{x_2(t)\}\cdots\{x_n(t)\}$, $t = 1,2,3...M$, the correlation coefficient of x_j and x_i is defined as:

$$\varepsilon_{ij}(t) = \frac{\Delta_{\min} + K\Delta_{\max}}{\Delta_{ij}(t) + K\Delta_{\max}} \quad t = 1,2,3...M \tag{1}$$

In the formula (1), $\varepsilon_{ij}(t)$ is correlation coefficient of x_j and x_i in the t moment.

$$\Delta_{ij}(t) = x_i(t) - x_j(t)$$

$$\Delta_{\max} = \max\max \Delta_{ij}(t)$$

$$\Delta_{\min} = \min\min \Delta_{ij}(t)$$

K is the range (0,1) interval of the gray scale. Clearly, $\Delta_{\min}$ is the minimum value of $\Delta_{ij}(t)$, when $\Delta_{ij}(t)$ take the minimum, the correlation coefficient $\varepsilon_{ij}(t)$ obtain the maximum $\max \varepsilon_{ij}(t) = 1$; The maximum value of $\Delta_{ij}(t)$ is $\Delta_{\max}$, when $\Delta_{ij}(t)$ take the maximum, the correlation coefficient $\varepsilon_{ij}(t)$ obtain the minimum $\min \varepsilon_{ij}(t) = [1/(1+K)] \times (K + \Delta_{\min} / \Delta_{\max})$. $\varepsilon_{ij}(t)$ is a bounded discrete function. Suppose $K = 1$, then there is:

$$0.5(1 + \frac{\Delta_{\min}}{\Delta_{\max}}) \leq \varepsilon_{ij} \leq 1$$

In the actual calculation, take $\Delta_{\min} = 0$, then there is: $0.5 \leq \varepsilon_{ij} \leq 1$ .To make $\varepsilon_{ij} = \varepsilon_{ij}(t)$ curve with the time changing, it was known as the correlation curve.

Correlation curve and the axis surrounded by an area of ε_{ij} and ε_{ii}, the correlation of x_j and x_i is defined as follows:

$$r_{ij} = \frac{s_{ij}(t)}{s_{ii}(t)}$$

Clearly, $s_{ii} = 1 \times M = M$, so $r_{ij} = \frac{s_{ij}(t)}{M}$

In the actual calculation, Commonly used $r_{ij} \approx \frac{1}{M} \sum_{i=1}^{M} \varepsilon_{ij}(t)$ instead of the formula $r_{ij} = \frac{s_{ij}(t)}{M}$. In order to eliminate the impact of dimension and enhance the comparability between the different dimension, we need all the elements of the raw data for the initial transformation, then use the transformation obtained new data for correlation calculation. Initial conversion formula is: $x'(t) = x_i(t) / x_i(1), i = 1,2,...n; t = 1,2...m$.

2.3 Data Acquisition and Description

As shown in Table 1, with the number of cars owned in rural areas to reflect the rural logistics development(x_0 / *per* 100 inhabitants); With the amount of loans in rural areas

Table 1. The Description of Main Factors Affecting Rural Logistics

Factors	Year				
	2000	2001	2002	2003	2004
x_0	1.32	1.2	1.29	1.4	1.43
x_1	10947.7	12124.5	13696.8	16072.5	17912.3
x_2	12.86	16.41	19.96	23.55	21.54
x_3	16.41	1205	1259	1328	1476
x_4	34374	31793	27319	32516	16297
x_5	1231.5	1456.7	1580.8	1754.5	2357.9

to reflect the development of rural finance(x_1); With culture and education investment in rural areas to reflect the degree of development of rural education(x_2); With the number of rural transportation practitioners to reflect the level of rural infrastructure(x_3); Natural disasters in rural areas with the disaster area to express(x_4); The Government policy is expressed as the amount of financial support for agriculture (x_5).

2.4 Calculation of Correlation

1) The sample matrix

$$\begin{pmatrix} 1.32 & 1.20 & 1.29 & 1.40 & 1.43 \\ 10947.7 & 12124.5 & 13696.84 & 16072.5 & 17912.32 \\ 12.86 & 16.41 & 19.96 & 23.55 & 21.54 \\ 1170.6 & 1205.4 & 1259.1 & 1328.2 & 1475.9 \\ 34374 & 31793 & 27319 & 32516 & 16297 \\ 1231.5 & 1456.7 & 1580.8 & 1754.5 & 2357.9 \end{pmatrix}$$

2) Dimensionless processing

$$\begin{pmatrix} 1 & 0.91 & 0.98 & 1.06 & 1.08 \\ 1 & 1.11 & 1.25 & 1.47 & 1.64 \\ 1 & 1.28 & 1.55 & 1.83 & 1.67 \\ 1 & 1.03 & 1.08 & 1.13 & 1.26 \\ 1 & 0.92 & 0.79 & 0.95 & 0.47 \\ 1 & 1.18 & 1.28 & 1.42 & 1.91 \end{pmatrix}$$

3) Differential transformation

$$\begin{pmatrix} 0 & 0.20 & 0.27 & 0.41 & 0.56 \\ 0 & 0.37 & 0.57 & 0.77 & 0.59 \\ 0 & 0.12 & 0.1 & 0.07 & 0.18 \\ 0 & 0.01 & 0.19 & 0.11 & 0.61 \\ 0 & 0.27 & 0.3 & 0.36 & 0.83 \end{pmatrix}$$

In the above matrix, the maximum and minimum values are as follows:

$M = \Delta_{max} = 0.83$, $m = m_{min} = 0$

4) Correlation coefficient matrix

$$\begin{pmatrix} 1 & 0.97 & 0.36 & 0.33 & 0.37 \\ 1 & 0.95 & 0.93 & 0.91 & 0.93 \\ 1 & 0.98 & 0.99 & 0.99 & 0.98 \\ 1 & 1.00 & 0.98 & 0.99 & 0.93 \\ 1 & 0.97 & 0.96 & 0.96 & 0.90 \end{pmatrix}$$

5) The correlation

$R_1 = 3.21$ $R_2 = 2.71$ $R_3 = 4.13$ $R_4 = 3.86$ $R_5 = 3.06$

Apparently, $R_3 > R_4 > R_1 > R_5 > R_2$

3 Conclusions

The results can be seen from the above: all the five factors have an impact on the development of logistics in rural areas, rural infrastructure development is the first factor that affects rural logistics, second, natural disasters in rural areas, rural finance development, as well as government policy conditions also affect rural logistics development, however, the degree of development of rural education in rural areas has little effect on the development of logistics. The reason may be as follows:

(1)At present the development of logistics in China's rural areas is at a preliminary stage, infrastructure construction plays a decisive role in the early stages of logistics development. Therefore, the priority of construction of rural logistics is building strong rural public infrastructure, but the infrastructure needs of rural finance development in order to provide strong financial support.

(2)The impact of natural disasters was always a major factor in China's agricultural development. Despite the developed areas of disaster prevention and resilience continue to increase, the farmers of the vast underdeveloped areas still can not do anything for natural disasters. Natural disasters in rural areas is bound to affect the development of logistics, therefore, in order to enhance disaster prevention capabilities, we should provide strong financial support to develop the rural logistics.

(3)The development of rural finance have a greater impact on rural logistics, the level of the development of rural finance restrict other factors which affect rural Logistics development. The early stages of logistics development in rural areas, need a lot of money to build logistics infrastructure in order to support and develop rural logistics enterprises. At the present, China's rural finance itself is still in a primitive state, business single, supporting for agriculture is insufficient. Rural finance does not play a full role in the development of rural logistics. So we should further reform and improve the rural financial service system in order to support the development of rural logistics.

Anyway, in the economic globalization process, in order to build a new socialist countryside in China, the government must provide strong financial support to develop the rural economy and China's rural logistics.

References

1. Besley: How do market failures justify intervention in Rural credit markets. The World Bank Research Observer 1, 27–48 (1994)
2. Towi, D.R.: Supply Chain Dynamics the-Change Engineering Challenge of the Mid 1990s, Proceedings of the Institution of Mechanical Engineers. Journal of Manufacture 206(B4), 233–245 (1992)
3. Beamon, B.M.: Supply Chain Design and Analysis: Models and methods. International Journal of Production Economics 55, 5–14 (1998)
4. Yaron, B.: Developing rural financial markets. Finance & Development 12, 40–43 (1997)
5. Fuenies: The use of village agents in rural credit delivery. The Journal of Development Studies 12, 18–20 (1996)
6. Bowersox, D.J.: Business Logistics Management (1973)

7. Blenchard, S.B.: Logistics Engineering and Management, vol. 4. Prentice Hall, Englewood Cliffs (1992)
8. Barbarosoglu, G., Yazgac, T.: An application of the analytic hierarchy process to the supplier selection problem. Production and Inventory Management Journal 38(1), 14–21 (1997)
9. Dickson, G.W.: An analysis of vendor selection systems and decisions. Journal of Purchasing 2(1), 5–17 (1996)
10. Liu, J., Ding, F.-Y., Lall, V.: Using data envelopment analysis to compare suppliers for selection and performance improvement. Supply Chain Management: an International supplier Journal 5(3), 143–150 (2000)
11. Bin, S., Wen, D.: DEA/PCA evaluation of the structures of logistics industry. Journal of Southwest Jiaotong University (5), 559–602 (2006)
12. Tian, H., Lin, G.: Evaluation of the operational efficiency for highway listed companies based on DEA. Development Research, 84–86 (2007)
13. Pischke, Adams, Donald: Rural financial markets in developing countries. The Johns Hopkins University Press (1987)
14. Van Laarhoven, P.J.M., Pedrycz, W.: A Fuzzy extension of saaty's priority theory. Fuzzy Sets and Systems 11, 229–241 (1983)
15. Facchinetti, G., Ricci, R.G., Muzziolis: Note on Ranking Fuzzy Triangular Number. International Journal of Intelligent System 13, 613–622 (1998)
16. Barney, J.B.: Gaining and Sustaining Competitive Advantage, pp. 284–313. Addison Wesley Publishing Company Inc., Reading (1996)
17. Fuenies: The use of village agent in rural credit delivery. The Journal of Development Studies 12, 188–209 (1996)
18. Jain: The international of formal and informal credit markets in developing countries: symiosis versus crowding out. Journal of Development Economies 59, 419–444 (1998)
19. Bouman, H.: Pawn broking as an instrument of rural banking in the third world. Economic Development and Cultural Change 10, 69–86 (1998)
20. Thillairajah: Development of rural financial markets in Sub-Saharan Africa, pp. 6–145. World Bank, Washington, D.C (1994)
21. Bose: Formal-informal sector interaction in rural credit markets. The Journal of Development Economies 56, 265–280 (1998)
22. Hu, B.: The Empirical Analysis of the Influence on the FDI by the Real exchange rate In China. Applications on Probability and Statistics 2, 50–53 (2010)
23. Demirguc-Kunt, L.: Regulations, market structure, institutions, and the cost of financial intermediation. Journal of Money, Credit and Banking 3, 593–622 (2004)

An Energy Efficient-Based AODVM Routing in MANET

Yun Zhang

School of Computing, Wuhan Institute of Technology, Wuhan 430074, P.R. China
mfzhou123@foxmail.com

Abstract. Mobile Ad hoc Networks (MANETs) is power constrained since mobile nodes operate with limited battery energy. So battery life is also important research issue in the routing protocol design. During packet transmission over multi-hop nodes, if a node failed, it should be caused link failure and source node will perform route recovery. It results that increases time of route recovery and packet loss rate. This paper proposes an Energy efficient-based AODVM routing algorithm in MANET (EAODV). It is typically proposed in order to increase the reliability of data transmission or to provide load balancing. In our simulation, we compare EAODV routing protocol with AODVM routing protocol, in terms of the remaining energy, the routing overhead ratio, the average end-to-end delay, the path lifetime, and power consumed when a packet is transmitted. The simulation results show that the EAODV routing protocol provide an accurate and efficient method of estimating and evaluating the route stability in dynamic MANETs.

Keywords: MANETs, Energy efficient, AODVM, routing algorithm.

1 Introduction

A Mobile Ad hoc Network (MANET) is an autonomous distributed system that consists of a set of mobile nodes that move arbitrarily and use wireless links to communicate with other nodes that reside within its transmission range [1-7]. Building such networks usually poses a significant technical challenge because of the constraints imposed by the characteristics of the MANETs. One important constraint is the scarce power resource if the nodes are operated by batteries [5-10].

Multipath routing is very useful technique to find out the multiple paths between source and destination by using a single route discovery. Multipath routing protocols can attempt to find node-disjoint, link-disjoint, or non-disjoint routes. Node-disjoint routes have no nodes or links in common. Link-disjoint routes have no links in common, but may have nodes in common. Non-disjoint routes can have nodes and links in common. The multipath routing is more effective than the single path routing because multipath can provide load balancing, fault-tolerance, and higher aggregated bandwidth [4-10].

In MANETs, energy efficiency is as important as general performance measures such as delay, remaining energy, the packet delivery ratio since it directly affects the network life time. The network under investigation is a set of intercommunicating, wireless, energy-limited transceiver-processors. Each transceiver-processor is energy-limited in

M. Dai (Ed.): ICCIC 2011, Part II, CCIS 232, pp. 66–72, 2011.

the sense that it battery operated and unattended; once its battery energy has been depleted, the transceiver-processor can no longer support date transport [8-10]. To consider power efficiency, we need a power-aware metric for gauge and compare various routing algorithms. One major metric is "the lowest total energy consumption" to route a communication session along the routes. Thus, offering effective ways for the best usage of energy in these protocols is necessary.

In this paper an effective way for energy efficient consumption has been proposed through the introduction of the Energy efficient-based AODVM routing algorithm in MANET (EAODV), which in turn it causes an increase in the networks life time which is one of the most important parameters in this type of networks. The goal of this paper is to develop a protocol to find out energy efficient-based multipath routing provisioning for load balancing, and to reduces power consumption for packet transmission and prolongs network lifetime in MANETs.

The rest of the paper is organized as follows: In section 2, we introduce multipath routing in MANETs. Section 3 we present energy efficient model in MANET. Some simulating results are provided in section 4. Finally, the paper concludes in section 5.

2 Multipath Routing in MANETs

Many routing protocols preserve a caching mechanism by which multiple routing paths to the same destination are stored. Multipath routing is essential for load balancing and offering quality of service. On-demand routing protocols are inherently attractive for multipath routing, because of faster and more efficient recovery from route failures. Multipath algorithms based on the AODV [4] protocol have also been proposed. AOMDV[5] extends the prominent AODV to discover multiple link-disjoint paths between the source and the destination in every route discovery. It uses the routing information already available in the AODV protocol as much as possible. It makes use of AODV control packets with a few extra fields in the packet header such as advertised hop count and route list which contains multiple paths. The main problem, which is called "route cutoff" in AOMDV, is that when there are one or more common intermediate nodes in a pair of link-disjoint paths, it cannot find both of the reverse paths. To reduce route discovery latency, it is necessary to find out all of the existing link-disjoint reverse paths. To improve the performance of AODV protocol, a multipath version of AODV called AODVM has been proposed in Ye et al [6]. In the AODVM protocol, a destination node selects paths that pass through more reliable nodes. In contrast to the AODV protocol, intermediate nodes are not allowed to send a route reply directly to the source. Also, duplicate RREQ packets are not discarded by intermediate nodes. Instead, all received RREQ packets are recorded in an RREQ table at the intermediate nodes. The destination sends an RREP for all the received RREQ packets. An intermediate node forwards a received RREP packet to the neighbor in the RREQ table that is along the shortest path to the source. To ensure that nodes do not participate in more than one route, whenever a node overhears one of its neighbors broadcasting an RREP packet, it deletes that neighbor from its RREQ table. Because a node cannot participate in more than one route, the discovered routes must be node-disjoint.

Aiming at maximally disjoints path maintenance for traffic distribution, the Split Multipath Routing (SMR) is proposed in [7]. SMR is used to construct maximally disjoint paths. Maximally disjoint paths have as few links or nodes in common as possible. Duplicate RREQs are not necessarily discarded. Instead, intermediate nodes forward RREQs that are received through a different incoming link, and whose hop count is not larger than the previously received RREQs. The Scalable Multipath On-demand Routing (SMORT) is proposed in [8], which establishes fail-safe paths between intermediate nodes and the destination, reducing the delay and routing overhead, while achieving higher packet delivery ratios.

3 Energy Efficient Model

It assume that the attenuation in the signal strength is inversely proportional to the square of the distance i.e., if P_t and P_r are the transmit and receiver powers respectively,

$$P_r = P_t \times d^{-\alpha} \tag{1}$$

where α is the path loss exponent and usually lies between 2 and 6, α=2 for short distance and α=6 for longer distance. d is the transmission distance.

A generic expression to calculate the energy required to transmit a packet p is: $P_t = i \times v \times t_p$ Joules, where: i is the current consumption, v is the voltage used, and t_p the time required to transmit the packet [9]. It is supposed that all mobile devices are equipped with IEEE 802.11b network interface cards (NICs). The energy consumption values were obtained by comparing commercial products with the experimental data reported in [10].

The values used for the voltage and the packet transmission time were: v = 5V and $t_p = (p_h / 6\times10^6 + p_d / 54\times10^6)$ s, where p_h and p_d are the packet header and payload size in bits, respectively. Calculated the energy required to transmit and receive a packet p by using: P_t=(280mA×v×t_p) and P_r=(240mA×v×t_p) respectively [11].

The energy to transmit and receive a single packet over the network from its source node s to its destination node d over a specific path k is given by $(P_t + P_r) \times |P_k|$, where $|P_k|$ is the number of hops from source to destination. Clearly, this energy calculation is dependent on the number of hops required to get from source to destination, but NOT the actual links used.

Using this idea, the energy to transmit and receive a single packet over the network from its source node s to its destination node d where the individual packet follows one path k, chosen with probability Pr_k, from the number of all possible paths, Paths from s to d is given by $(P_t + P_r) \times Pr_k \times |P_k|$, where $\sum_{k=1}^{Paths} Pr_k = 1$.

The energy to transmit and receive an entire date over the network from its source node s to its destination node d where the individual packet follows one path k, chosen with probability Pr_k, from a set of Paths possible paths from s to d is given by

$$(P_t + P_r) \times (\sum_{k=1}^{Paths} Pr_k \times | P_k |) \tag{2}$$

The routing probabilities result from potentially complex network behavior which depends on the network loading and other factors. The total energy required to transport a single packet from its source to its destination, P is given by:

$$P = (P_t + P_r) \times (\sum_{k=1}^{Paths} Pr_k \times |P_k|) \quad (3)$$

4 Simulation Experiments

4.1 Simulation Model

To conduct the simulation studies, we have used randomly generated networks on which the algorithms were executed [12]. This ensures that the simulation results are independent of the characteristics of any particular network topology.

To effectively evaluate EAODV's performance, we compare it with other famous multicast routing protocols AODVM [6] for cost to control information, average link-connect time, the success rate to find the path and the feature of data transmission. Our simulation modeled a network of mobile nodes placed randomly within 1000m × 1000 m area. Radio propagation range for each node was 250 meters and channel capacity of 2 Mbps is chosen. Node initial energy for each node was 80 joules. There were no network partitions throughout the simulation. Each simulation is executed for 600 seconds of simulation time. Multiple runs with different seed values were conducted for each scenario and collected data was averaged over those runs. A free space propagation model was used in our experiments. A traffic generator was developed to simulate CBR sources. The size of the data payload is 512 bytes. Data sessions with randomly selected sources and destinations were simulated. Each source transmits data packets at a minimum rate of 4 packets/sec, and maximum rate of 10 packets/sec.

4.2 Simulation Results

The results of the simulation are positive with respect to performance. We use the ns-2 simulator [13] to evaluate the EAODV protocol.

The remaining node energy of all routers at the end of simulation has been plotted in Fig. 1. The graph shows that EAODV has distributed overall energy over the entire network in a more balanced way.

The total number of packets used for the routing process is taken as the routing overhead in our study. The routing overhead ratio displays the level of transmission overhead expenses of the network with the given protocol. Fig. 2 shows a comparison of routing overhead ratio. On the average EAODV reduces the routing overhead by 10-20 % as compared to AODVM. This is because of route request pruning at the cluster level and less route discovery.

Fig. 3 depicts the comparison of average end-to-end delay under total of network nodes for both protocols. From the Fig. 3 we can see that when the total of network nodes increases, EAODV average end-to-end delay is lower than that of AODVM.

Fig. 4 shows the simulation results of path lifetime under total of network nodes for both protocols. From the results shown in Fig. 4, we can see that the path lifetime of EAODV routing protocol is longer than that of the AODVM routing protocols. The main reason is that we took into account the power saving and power saving to design the routing protocol.

With regard to the power consumed when a byte of data is transmitted, Fig. 5 shows the simulation results of EAODV routing protocol, and AODVM. From the results shown in Fig. 5, because we have taken the path lifetime into account, the power consumed in transmitting a byte of data is lower, on average, in EAODV protocol than that AODVM routing protocols.

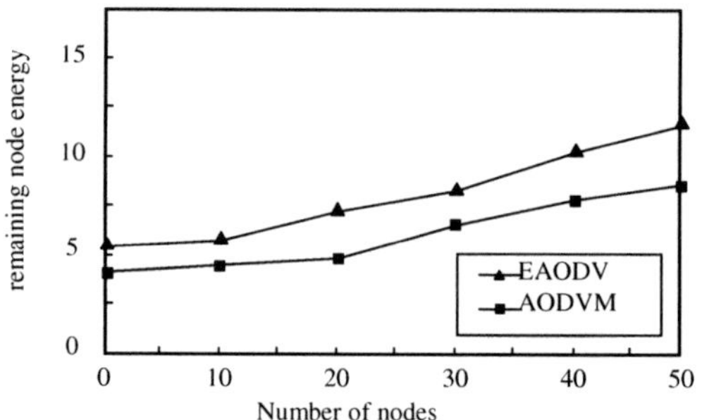

Fig. 1. Comparison of remaining energy

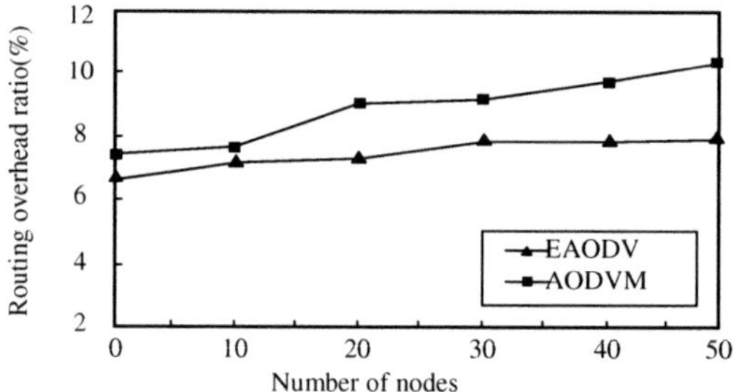

Fig. 2. Comparison of routing overhead ratio

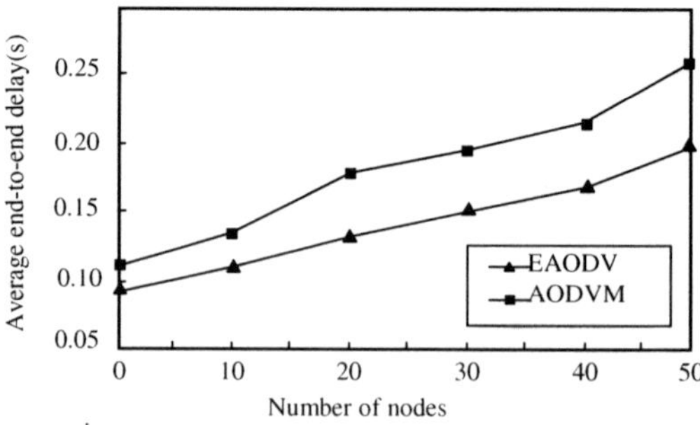

Fig. 3. Comparison of average end-to-end delay

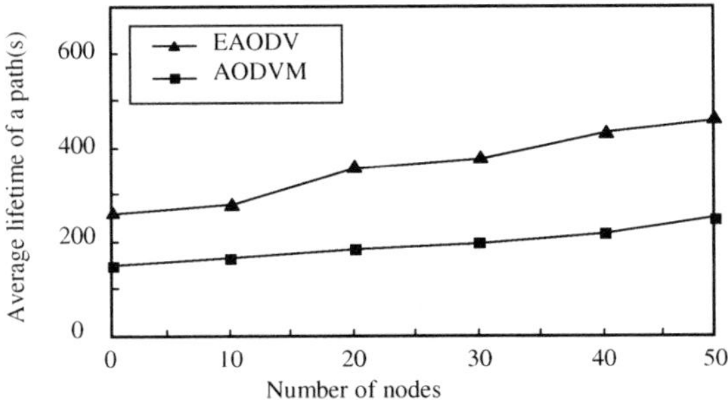

Fig. 4. Comparison of path lifetime

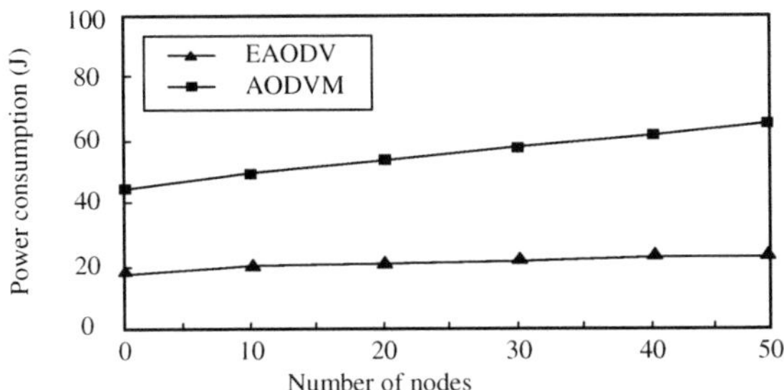

Fig. 5. Comparison of power consumed

5 Conclusion

This paper discusses multpath routing problem, which may deal with the energy entropy model for researching the MANET multpath routing problem. It presents an Energy Efficient-Based AODVM routing algorithm in MANET (EAODV). As a result, by taking remaining energy, packet delivery ratio, routing overhead ratio, average end-to-end delay, path lifetime, and power consumed into account, the EAODV routing algorithm efficienty reduces power consumption for packet transmission and prolongs network lifetime. The EAODV routing algorithm can be easily extended to other mobile networks QoS routing problems with NP complexity.

Acknowledgment. This work is supported by The Young and Middle-aged Elitists' Scientific and Technological Innovation Team Project of the Institutions of Higher Education in Hubei Province (No. T200902), Key Scientific Research Project of Hubei Education Department (D20102205, Q20102202, B20102202).

References

1. Sun, B.L., Gui, C., Zhang, Q.F., et al.: Fuzzy Controller Based QoS Routing Algorithm with a Multiclass Scheme for MANET. International Journal of Computers, Communications & Control IV(4), 427–438 (2009)

2. Sun, B.L., Pi, S.C., Gui, C., et al.: Multiple Constraints QoS Multicast Routing Optimization Algorithm in MANET based on GA. Progress in Natural Science 18(3), 331–336 (2008)
3. Sun, B.L., Gui, C., Zhang, Q.F., et al.: A Multipath on-Demand Routing with Path Selection Entropy for Ad Hoc Networks. In: The 9th International Conference for Young Computer Scientists (ICYCS 2008), Hunan, China, November 18-21, pp. 558–563 (2008)
4. Perkings, E., Belding-Royer, E.M., Das, S.R.: Ad Hoc On-Demand Distance Vector (AODV) Routing. IETF RFC (July 2003), `http://www.ietf.org/rfc/rfc3561.txt`
5. Marina, M.K., Das, S.R.: On-demand multipath distance vector routing in ad hoc networks. In: Proceedings of IEEE International Conference on Network Protocols (ICNP), Mission Inn, Riverside, California, November 11-14, pp. 14–23 (2001)
6. Ye, Z., Krishnamurthy, S.V., Tripathi, S.K.: A framework for reliable routing in mobile ad hoc networks. In: Proceedings of IEEE INFOCOM 2003, San Francisco, CA, USA, pp. 270–280 (April 2003)
7. Lee, S.J., Gerla, M.: Split multipath routing with maximally disjoint paths in ad hoc networks. In: Proceedings of IEEE International Conference on Communications, Helsinki, Finland, pp. 3201–3205 (July 2001)
8. Reddy, L.R., Raghavan, S.V.: Smort: Scalable multipath on-demand routing for mobile ad hoc networks. Ad Hoc Networks 5(2), 162–188 (2007)
9. De Rango, F., Lonetti, P., Marano, S.: MEA-DSR: A Multipath Energy-aware Routing Protocol for Wireless Ad Hoc Networks. In: IFIP International Federation for Information Processing, Advances in Ad Hoc Networking, Spain, June 25-27, vol. 265, pp. 215–225 (2008)
10. Feeney, L.M., Nilsson, M.: Investigating the Energy Consumption of a Wireless Network Interface in an Ad Hoc Networking Environment. In: Proceedings of IEEE INFOCOM, pp. 1548–1557 (April 2001)
11. Kawahigashi, H., Terashima, Y., Miyauchi, N.: A Proposal for a New Measure Analogous to Entropy for Bandwidth Constrained, Control-Based Ad-Hoc Network Design. In: Military Communications Conference, MILCOM 2006, Washington, DC, USA, October 23-25, 7 Pages (2006)
12. Waxman, B.: Routing of Multipoint Connections. IEEE Journal on Selected Areas in Communications 6(9), 1617–1622 (1988)
13. The Network Simulator - ns-2, `http://www.isi.edu/nsnam/ns/`

Research and Practice of Training Teaching Based on MSF Software Process*

Xiaoyu Ke and Min Jin

School of Software, Hunan University Software College of Fujian University of Techology China
School of Software, Hunan University ChangSha, Hunan, China
tatsuokija@foxmail.com

Abstract. Currently software training has become a compulsory course for pre-service students whose major is software or relevant to software. Aimed at the situation and main problems of software training in higher vocational schools, this paper proposes some ideas along with a mode on how to conduct software training in these schools. The main issue on this training mode is described in detail. Furthermore, an improvement strategy of software training based on software process is presented.

Keywords: Software Process Based, Case Training Teaching, Software Process Improvement, Microsoft Solutions Framework.

1 Introduction — Status and Problems of Software Vocational School's Practical Training System

With the continuous expansion of higher education scale, the number of software major graduates has increased dramatically during the last decades. However, there is an awkward situation on the job market. On one hand, software industry urgently needs a large amount of software talents for the development. On the other hand, it is very difficult for many graduates to find a suitable job [1]. This phenomenon is mainly due to the gap between college educating system and company need. In other words, the major courses and traditional teaching mode hardly keep step with the highly developing IT industry[1].

The current structure of software talents shows like "olive-shaped", a situation in which high-end and low-end talents are missing. High-end talents are those senior technical and management personnel, the international software personnel and versatile talents, and low-end talents are those programming-skilled basic programmer. Software talents mainly come from universities and research institutions, most of whom are middle-end talents, and these people do not have enough experience and ability to do systems analysts, and it will be a waste of human resources for them to be programmers.

* This research work is supported by Training Program of Key Young Teachers in Universities of Hunan Province, Provincial Natural Science Fund of Hunan under grants No. 07JJ6137 and 863 National High Technology Research and Development key Program of China under grants No. 2008AA042802.

M. Dai (Ed.): ICCIC 2011, Part II, CCIS 232, pp. 73–80, 2011.

Meanwhile, companies themselves do not pay enough attention on the software people's daily training, which leads to the front-line technicians cannot adapt to the industry's fast development. At present the contradiction between software talents training mode and the actual needs of enterprises is gradually deepening, which has restrict the development of software industry.

Higher vocational education, as a very important part of higher education, therefore, has entered into a rapid developing period. The quickened pace of national information construction and the fast development of IT industry have created a bright future for software higher vocational schools.

Higher vocational education is essentially employment-oriented, which is to fulfill the need of social economic construction and to turn out social skill-applying type talents. Therefore, the close combination of theory and practice, production and lecturing, has become the basic way of personnel training in higher vocational education. Computer software technology, as a high-new one, has developed very quickly and its speed of updating knowledge in theory, technology and tools is much faster than traditional industry, and only through the close combination and interaction between production, lecturing and science researching, can it bring up applying type talents that really adapt to the society[2].

At present some colleges or universities have some meaningful exploration, but there are still a few problems remain, such as:

1.1 Nonstandardized Process and Documentation

Even students do not follow the necessary rules in practice, and blind development is far from the actual development process. File compiling is necessary in developing projects and the process documenting is the basic requirement of project management. If there is no standardized file, it cannot fully reflect the work done by project team; cannot guarantee the smooth communication among team members; cannot promise the consistency of project development. Students often do not pay attention to file compiling, and hurry to write code.

1.2 Nonstandardized Project Management

Student project owners have few and not systematic training in project management. Project owners are lack of project management knowledge system and the reconization of some common tools and methods, so they do not have a guideline on project management knowledge. They entirely rely on their own knowledge and skills, management work largely arbitrary and blind.

1.3 Inexplicit Plan

Project owners are lack of the knowledge on the function of overall and section plans. They are arbitrary when making overall plans, disarticulated on plan and controlling management, unable to have effective process control management.

1.4 Nonstrict Testing

Many students, even advisers cannot distinguish what is unit testing, what is integration testing, and what is system testing.

At the moment, software colleges pay more and more attentions on the combination between subject lecturing and job training for talents educating mode, especially on practical training session. So we have a 2+1 mode, that is to say, the first 2 years is of theoretical study, the last year of practice or practical training, which is to say, practical training is the last class for students before entering the society.

2 Software Practical Concept Discussion

Since 2006, after undertaking the teaching mission of practical training, I have been thinking about a question: how we can guide the junior students, who are going to enter software industry, to do with their best state on their position and with their biggest potential.

Practical training is built around one or more main basic course and professional course, to apply the knowledge learnt in classes into combining actual project applying design, to carry out a comprehensive analysis of design capacity of training.

Practical training aims to train students, in the area of expertise, to initially grasp to solve real application problems when they should have access to information, the ability to integrate the knowledge they have learned, in order to lay the foundation for future professional work. The purpose is to enhance the practical ability of students, to make them be able to adapt to work, without corporate training. After 3-month practical training in practical training center, students can manage according to the company requirement to employees.

In the practical training site, students can integrate into the real operating environment of hi-tech IT companies; study and understand the IT enterprises' normativeness, specialization, standardization, and large-scale on software development and development process of system integration project; experience IT companies' requirement on employee knowledge structure, technology skills, comprehensive quality and corporate culture; participate in all software enterprises in the development of real projects, communicating with and guided by experienced technical and management personnel in various types of IT enterprises; accelerate the identity change from students to employees; strengthen students' capability and confidence of finding job.

At present, our school takes MSF(Microsoft Solutions Framework, Microsoft process) as the guiding ideology of software practical training, successfully launching practical training for many times. However, some problems are also exposed, for example, students often do not have high enthusiasm on process file writing, and they urgently need a software practical training process that is more focused and more fit for students, so as to enhance the effectiveness and level of software practical training.

Aim to solve the above problems, this paper tries to put forward a solution.

3 Software Practical Training Process Mode and Improvement

3.1 Team-Forming in Practical Training

Because of the restrictions of practical training workshop, a practical training workshop has no more than six groups, each of them has no more than six individuals (not less than three individuals), in which a team leader selected by team members, three developers, two testers. Role rotation system is used, which means in different phases, people act in different roles.

3.2 Choosing a Software Training Process Model

In the software project development process, there existing all kinds of risks, such as, the constant changing needs, the non perfect requirement specifications, rough codes, unsuitable and unscientific team models, inefficient work process, and unclear objectives and so on, which will lead to the failure of project.

For above issue, that how to do the software process management and improvement, the software industry has proposed many kinds of plans. Such as Microsoft Solutions Framework (MSF), Carnegie Mellon University's Software Capability Maturity Model (CMM), Rational Unified Process (RUP) and Agile software process and so on.

Problems also happen while guiding students in practical training. Practical training has its own feature, and we can not completely follow the software industry's experience or structure, but to cut the coat according to the cloth and have its character. After comprehensive comparison, practical training center thinks that CMM or RUP is too cumbersome, AP too light and not good for students to know about the complete software process system. And the MSF, after appropriate change, is much more suitable for students to develop practical training project and can satisfy students' need to learn the overall software process.

What MSF stressed on is the small, diverse project teams, in which team members are divided into six kinds of roles: product management role, program management role, development role, testing role, user experience role and release management role. The relations between the roles are like a ring and is equal and good for communication:

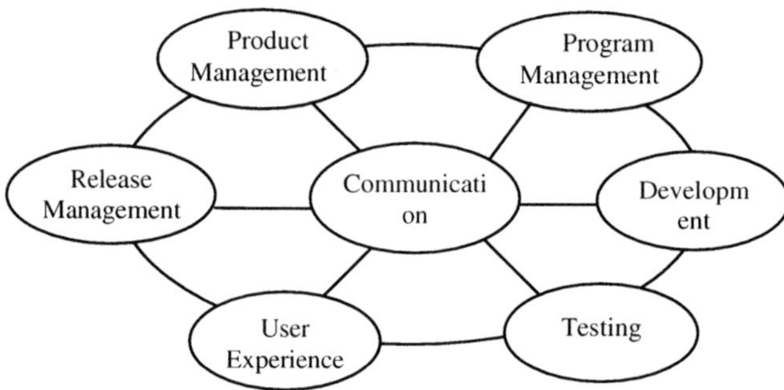

Fig. 1. The relations of Roles

In the case of limited resources, a variety of roles can be combined by a commitment to an individual, but the six kinds of roles do not mean that a project team needs at least six individuals, that is to say, a role is not necessarily undertaken by an individual. In smaller development team, some members in the team may act as many roles at the same time (that is the current domestic model of many small software companies), but the merger should follow the following principles:

Table 1. The principles of merger

	Product Management	Program Management	Development	Testing	User Experience	Release Management
Product Management		N	N	P	P	U
Program Management	N		N	U	U	P
Development	N	N		N	N	N
Testing	P	U	N		P	P
User Experience	P	U	N	P		U
Release Management	U	P	N	P	U	

Note: U — the merger is not recommended, N — can not be merged, P — could be merged.

To sum up: the smallest project team can only have three role members: product manager, program manager and development engineer. Among them, product manager does as testing and user experiencing role, program manager also as release management role.

At the same time, if we image that every role is acted by one member, which needs six team members. This kind of team-building mold is just suitable for practical training team members that required by practical training center. And they can have a flexible rotation system In different phase, different team members experience different roles.

3.3 Practical Training System Mold

At the first stage of practical training system, according to the above mentioned, practical training center take Microsoft Solutions Framework MSF process model as basis, and divide the process into conceptual phase, planning phase, development phase, stability and deployment phase.

1) Envisioning Phase

At this phase, it is mainly guided by advisors to imitate the practical training case developed by the real project, in which party A and the development members (students) have communications, make clear the project range, have early common sense on project target and the maximum, set up a baseline that can be accepted by everyone, and it is just on the baseline that the solution plan is made. At this phase, a project's prospect range file will be submitted.

2) Planning Phase

The main task of this phase is to get project information from the previous phase to conduct business modeling, and to complete the system designing and database designing job.

Documents to be submitted in this phase are: project schedule, requirements analysis specifications, and detailed design specifications.

3) Developing Phase

This phase is to create a solution, achieve the solution code, and complete unit testing. Finally the source code, executable files, and unit testing report are submitted.

This phase will go through multiple iterations of the loop: concept validation and completion->internal release 1->internal release 2 internal release n…, until it finally reach the design objectives.

4) Stabilizing Phase

This phase will focus on testing and improving work of development application, submitting functional testing plan and the final testing report. After the training, students can clearly grasp every step of the testing, understand package installation process.

5) Deploying Phase

After getting instructor's approval, they can launch the ready solution plans, mainly submitting the application process package and user manual.

Some practical training case in different phases has the following class distribution as below:

Table 2. Lessons distribution

NO.	Subject	Lessons
1	Preparation phase	8
1.1	To learn Training Materials	4
1.2	To study System Project	4
2	Envisioning Phase	64
2.1	To explain the business scenario, the project structure, needs analysis	4
2.2	To assign task - to achieve needs analysis	48
2.3	To explain the project needs analysis	4
2.4	To assessment this phase	8
3	Planning Phase	80
3.1	To explain the system design, database design, timing diagram, logic diagram, class diagram	4
3.2	To assign task - to achieve the detailed design process	64
3.3	To explain the detailed design	4
3.4	To assessment this phase	8
4	Developing Phase	250
4.1	To explain the coding standard	2
4.2	To develop code	176
4.3	To compile test cases, test code (unit test)	40
4.4	To fix bugs	16
4.5	To assessment this phase	16
5	Stabilizing and Deploying Phase	40
5.1	System test	16
5.2	To fix bugs and optimize code	8
5.3	To make installation package	8
5.4	To install and test	8
6	To hold the assessment meeting	8
Total		450

Although this practical training follow software engineering as the guiding ideology, arranged according to MSF process phase, each phase provide a corresponding template for the students for reference, and the time of document writing and code developing is about half and half. The purpose is to strengthen the knowledge of software engineering to practical training students.

But after several rounds of practical training we found: for students without any project experience, better drag controls and codes, which is more intuitionistic and fulfilled, than write packs of unintelligible documents.

Furthermore, in view of training students to be software blue-collar, combining the present students' real capability in practical training, we consider to bring agile development into the practical training system, make suitable adjustment to practical training system and blend into the MSF software process.

Table 3. Lessons distribution(revised)

NO.	Subject	Lessons
1	Preparation phase	2
1.1	To learn Training Materials	2
2	Envisioning Phase	6
2.1	To explain System Project	1
2.2	To explain the scope document	2
2.3	To explain the structure document	2
2.4	To explain the plan	1
3	Planning Phase	30
3.1	To explain the requirements list	6
3.2	To explain the requirements analysis	6
3.3	To explain the detailed design	8
3.4	To explain the database design	6
3.5	To explain the project plan, assign tasks	4
4	Developing Phase	384
4.1	To release the first internal version	96
4.1.1	To develop code	86
4.1.2	To compile test cases, test code (unit test) and fix bugs	10
4.2	To release the second internal version	96
4.2.1	To develop code	86
4.2.2	To compile test cases, test code (unit test),test functions of previous version and fix bugs	10
4.3	To release the third internal version	96
4.3.1	To develop code	86
4.3.2	To compile test cases, test code (unit test),test functions of previous version and fix bugs	10
4.4	To release the fourth internal version	96
4.4.1	To develop code	86
4.4.2	To compile test cases, test code (unit test),test functions of previous version and fix bugs	10
5	Stabilizing and Deploying Phase	24
5.1	System test	8
5.2	To fix bugs and optimize code	8
5.3	To make installation package	4
5.4	To install and test	4
6	To hold the assessment meeting	4
Total		450

Program has been adjusted, weakening the proportion of the document, but also retaining the project in several key documents in order to develop on this basis, while strengthening the code in development phase and testing training. Revised program is as above.

After program revision, it gives students more time to write codes, continue to improve their own projects, so to be more fulfilled.

4 Conclusion

This paper discussed the software practical training system based on software process, and the problems happened in the present practical training mode and plan, proposing an improving program. It is believed in the further, the practical training process will have consistant adjustment and optimization, in the hope of bringing up students as the really applying-type talents.

Acknowledgment. I thank for the supports by Training Program of Key Young Teachers in Universities of Hunan Province, Provincial Natural Science Fund of Hunan and 863 National High Technology Research and Development key Program of China, And also thank my school and my advisor.

References

1. Jian, S.J., Hai, D.L.: To explore software practical training teaching in independent Colleges. Research in Higher Education of Engineering (S1), 69 (2007)
2. Zhang, Z.Y.: Research of software training Solution based on the method of cooperation between corporation and colleges, vol. (09), p. 6 (2008)
3. He, Y.Z.: Research on the Reform of Computer Software Courses. Modern Computer (03) (2008)
4. Jiang, P., Liu, Q., Li, S.-y.: Improved and Rapid Software Component Selection Process. In: Proceedings of International Forum on Information Technology and Applications (IFITA 2009) (2009)
5. Wang, C.-h., Lin, L.-d.: The Implementation of Software Engineering's Thoughtway in Teaching of Programming Language. Higher Education Forum (01) (2010)
6. Niazi, M., Babar, M.A., Katugampola, N.M.: Demotivators of Software Process Improvement. An Empirical Investigation. Software Process Improvement and Practice 13, 249–264 (2008)
7. Sandberg, A.B., Mathiassen, L.: Managing Slowdown in Improvement Projects. IEEE Software 25(6) (2008)
8. Oktaba, H., García, F., Piattini, M., Ruiz, F., Pino, F.J.: Claudia Alquicira, vol. (10), pp. 21–28. IEEE Computer Society, Los Alamitos (2007)
9. Holmberg, L., Nilsson, A., Olsson, H.H., Sandberg, A.B.: Appreciative Inquiry in Software Process Improvement. Software Process Improvement and Practice 14(2) (2009)

Green Supply Chain Management in Construction Industry

Zhu Mingqiang and Zou Zuxu

School of Civil Engineering and Architecture, Wuhan Polytechnic University, Wu Han, China
pkrysl@yahoo.cn

Abstract. According to the definition of green supply chain management, giving its connotation in detail. Analyzing the construction industry impact on the environment protection and sustainable development, reviewing the implementation of the green supply chain management in developed countries and regions construction industry, studying on how to implement green supply chain management in the construction industry.

Keywords: green supply chain, management, construction industry, application.

1 Introduction

At present, human society has entered the era of rapid development, the construction industry has been rapid development, but led to a shortage of resources, environmental pollution. Especially in China, the economy is the development of high-speed, and large-scale construction projects are doing now, the problem of China's resources and the environment is very severe, and strive to man and nature, environmental compatibility coexistence and harmonious development is urgent. in order to achieve harmony between man and nature, green supply chain management thinking is not only necessary to the construction industry, but also is a concrete manifestation implementing the scientific concept of development.

2 Basic Principles of Green Supply Chain

2.1 The Content of Green Supply Chain Management

The so-called supply chain refers to focus on core business, through the logistics, information flow and capital flow control, from procurement of raw materials, intermediate goods and even the final product, finally from the sales network to the hands of the consumer, products will be sent to suppliers, manufacturers, distributors, retailers, end-users, and will connect the functions of a whole network structure. Supply chain management is an integrated management ideas and methods, is the entire supply chain from the perspective of the traditional business enterprises within the sector between enterprises and the functions of the system, strategic coordination, to improve supply chain and every the long-term corporate performance. In recent years academics have made an in-depth study in the supply chain strategic design, planning and

M. Dai (Ed.): ICCIC 2011, Part II, CCIS 232, pp. 81–86, 2011.

operation. Some famous multinational corporations such as Wal-Mart, P & G, have achieved tremendous results in the practice of supply chain management. Green supply chain management is based on green manufacturing and supply chain management theory of technology, involving suppliers, manufacturers, vendors and users. Its purpose is making products from raw materials acquisition, processing, packaging, warehousing, transport, use, disposal and recycling to scrap the use of the whole process, the environmental impact is the smallest and the resources is efficient.

2.2 The Features of Green Supply Chain Management

Green supply chain is the application of green manufacturing in the supply chain, but it is much more complicated than the supply chain, what in the flow of green supply chain is not just an ordinary raw materials, products, but also a"green"logistics. Large flows of green manufacturing is related to the"green"information.

2.3 The Significance of Green Supply Chain Management in China's Construction Industry

In order to maintain the sustainable development of China's construction industry, it is imperative to implement the green supply chain management of the new strategic management. Through the implementation of green supply chain management in the construction industry, not only can reduce construction activities on the consumption of natural resources, but also can effectively improve the entire construction process on the environment unfriendly act. The study shows that the implementation of green supply chain management can enhance their competitive edge, improve the enterprise's organizational performance, reduce production costs, protect the natural environment and play a very important role in the sustainable development of construction industry.

3 The Application Status of Supply Chain Management in Construction Industry

3.1 Foreign Application Situation

Green supply chain management originated in the United States, the U.S. National Science Foundation (NSF) funded 400,000 U.S. dollars in the Michigan State University Manufacturing Research Association (MRA) in 1996, The concept of green supply chain was an important content of the study. Construction industry supply chain management of the first foreign research began in the 1980s, Kossel in Stanford University formed a construction industry supply chain management theory, the official presentation of this study should be attributed to Bertelsen.William and Fischert, etc..The big contractors have realized that the implementation of supply chain management can improve production plans procurement, but the obstacles of the successful implementation of the supply chain management in construction industry can be found, such as the lack of trust managers.

In 1999, 0 'Brien, who pointed out that the construction supply chain management provided a new approach to reduce construction costs and increase the application on the construction of reliability and speed. Construction supply chain management is the independent production units of the production activities of large-scale systems for all these activities optimization. Manufacturing supply chain management technology applications has improved customer service, but also saved hundreds of millions of dollars of funds. Bertelsen, who in 1993, indicated that the adverse supply chain management may be on the increase-10 percent of the cost by some of the construction industry research, time limit was also affected. the Supply Chain Management Research Group of British construction industry points out: the importance of the function of the supply chain management internal organization, including: production planning, procurement, transport, storage, inventory. And providers of supply chain relationship factors, including: higher quality services, interest costs, streamlining the construction process, simplifying the procedures for orders; with the owners of the supply chain relationship factors, including: interest costs, streamlining the construction process, simplifying the bidding process; development of the construction supply chain collaboration of the main objectives, including: the interests of owners and improving customer service, reducing paper work, increasing profitability, improving the quality assurance; the key factors of construction supply chain, including: trust, the reliability of supply, top management support, mutual interests, information-smooth, joint business planning; the main obstacles of construction supply chain, including: the lack of top management commitment, bad communication, inadequate support systems, low commitment to the partnership, the lack of proper information technology support.

3.2 Domestic Application Situation

In China, the green supply chain management research is still in its initial stage, the focus of the study is to introduce the concept of integrated features, architecture; the main research areas, the article about the implementation of the strategy is only the strategy research, not quantitative and systematic analysis.

In short, the green supply chain management research in China's construction industry is still in the exploratory stage, we should vigorously study developed countries and regions.

4 Application Proposal of Green Supply Chain in Construction Industry Areas

4.1 The Design of the Green Supply Chain

The design of effective supply chain supply chain is a necessary prerequisite to the successful operation. It can improve customer service, achieve effective balance between cost and service, enhance corporation's competition power, increase flexibility, develop new markets and increase work efficiency. in the design of the supply chain, based on the successful supply chain in manufacturing, construction supply chain should be designed in terms of different construction corporations.

Different types of products require different supply chain design. Generally, from the broad sense, basic products can be divided into two basic types: functional products and innovative products. The so-called functional products, which refer to a lower profit margin, the demand for the products is more stable; so-called innovative products refer to higher profit margins and unstable demand products. It is easy to forecast future demand for the functional products due to their tiny changes and stable demand. In addition, these products have long life cycle and can be used to meet consumers' basic requirements. Construction products are functional products, in order to avoid fewer profit margins, construction corporations should improve current product and management mode to achieve higher profit margins by researching customer psychology and considering market demand, the existing production and management methods need to be improved. The processes of green products supply chain design of construction products are showed as follows: the construction market analysis, in order to understand the current market demand for construction products and the situation of construction products, features and development trends, While summing up the status of construction enterprises, researching direction of the supply chain development, analyzing the problems may affect the supply chain design, analyzing the necessity set up supply chain design goals ,and the access to lower unit costs, higher customer service levels and environmental benefits, analyzing the balance between objectives; analyzing the construction of the supply chain, and form the basic framework of the supply chain. The supply chain analysis of the composition of materials, including the main equipment suppliers, construction, engineers and contractors and the choice of location, if it is feasible, the programmed can be carried out following the design, otherwise, they should re-design, the main issues to be addressed include: the composition of the supply chain members, the source of raw materials, production planning, information management system design, logistics management systems design. After green supply chain design has completed, testing through certain techniques methods is necessary.

4.2 B. The Processes of Construction Green Supply Chain

Construction of green supply chain is the supply chain that fully integrated construction industry characteristics its operation model processes are as follows(1) The procurement link of green supply chain; Through fountainhead control, the awareness of the environmental pollution prevention and energy conservation can be carried out in the entire supply chain. In addition, green purchasing not only can satisfy the public demand for environmental products, but also can lower the overall cost, so the green procurement policy and practice can bring economic benefits and competitive advantage for enterprises. Corporations in green supply chain should design green purchasing in following aspects: the management and choice of green supplier, at this stage we need to take into account providers whether the material is contaminated and whether the manufacturing process is clean, the process can save energy, to reduce waste and the use of materials, we can communicate with suppliers and request their productions. implementation of collaborative procurement, collaborative procurement refers to the process, in which corporations adjust their plans and delivery according to demand-supply information that are shared by both corporations and suppliers, suppliers can adjust their own plans according to corporation's inventory and plan, and decrease the inventory without reducing service level.(2)The construction link of green supply chain; Production in green supply chain includes not only construction process, but also the process happened from engineering construction design, such as material selection, logistics design and decoration design. Green design. Green design is the entire process of life cycle, including construction concept design, construction, usage, reclaim, reuse and dispose trash. Green design examines the whole life cycle based on sustainable development, It emphasizes systematic analysis and evaluation according to life-cycle perspective in production development stage, eliminating the potential negative impact on the environment, and introducing 3 R(reduce, rescue, recycle) into production development stage directly. Green material selection. Green material is a relative concept, which is still in the continuous development and improvement process. Green materials include advanced materials, high-quality, low energy consumption material, security during the product process, low noise, no pollution, in line with modern engineering requirements.(3) Payment in Green supply chain; Green supply chain payment is actually a delivery process from suppliers to core corporations (construction companies), including six major elements: material, the transportation of production space move, storage of time pass, circulation process, packaging, handing and information. According to the analysis of non-green factors above, here are some strategies to reduce non-green factor: transport strategy, taking use of green cars, reducing the total amount of cars by changing transport, using the green channel, reducing vehicle emissions of conducting joint distribution, reducing pollution, eliminating staggered transport; simplifying the supply and distribution system, reducing the number of vehicles running by increasing efficiency of vehicles usage, improving distribution efficiency, building storage systems that can develop sustainably; concerning reasonable selection of logistics brokers. The brokers' green ability and reputation are important for corporations to implement green supply chain, therefore enterprises should strictly choose their own green supply chain links, and enhance their green image.(4) The recovery link of green supply chain; At present, 30 to 40 percent of municipal refuse are construction refuse in our country. Almost all construction refuse are shipped to suburbs or rural areas without any processing by construction companies, they are stacked in the open or buried, spent a lot of land acquisition costs, and other construction funds, and lost garbage, dust and sand-lime dust caused by cleaning, transporting and stacking garbage also cause serious environmental pollution. With the issue and implement of many laws and regulations that protect arable land and environment in our country, construction corporations and environmental protection department are facing an important subject: how to treat and discharge construction garbage. Recovery in green supply chain includes the following major areas: recovery, with payment or free of charge, salesman reclaims waste produced by final customers or downstream corporations in the process of production and sale. These salesmen may be corporations in each supply chain nodes, for example waste from the customer may return to upstream suppliers, manufacturers, they may also be returned to downstream distributors, distribution, retailers; testing and treating decisions, in accordance with the product structure and product characteristics of the viable treatment options, the plan includes selling recovery goods directly, selling goods after processing, reusing some parts and abandoning production or parts, then confirming an optimal plan based on cost-benefit analysis; Scrap treatment: for those recovery goods or parts that have no economic value or endanger the environment seriously, it is better to select a treatment such as mechanical treatment, which has no environmental pollution or pollutes environment little.

In brief, as it is not long from the establishment of the green supply chain management theory to the development, it there may be some imperfections in the application process, particularly, to apply it in the innovative development of our country's construction industry is a completely new practice. Along with the thoroughgoing research, the green supply chain management function will be manifesting more evidently. Our country's construction industry is in the essential developing stage; they have an arduous task to reform and develop it. It will have extremely beneficial reference value if we can pay attention to the model overseas advanced management concept such as the green supply chain management. Our country's construction industry can combine it with our own situation to enhance the benefit unceasingly and can make a greater contribution to our country economic and social development.

Acknowledgment. The authors will thank the support of the Project of Hubei Provincial Department of Education Humanities and Social Sciences NO. 2010q071.

References

1. Jeremy, H.: Environmental supply chain dynamics. Journal of Cleaner Production (8), 12–18 (2000)
2. Spence, R., Mulligan, H.: Sustainable development and the construction industry. Habitant INTl 25, 22–25 (2003)
3. Shen, L.Y.: Implementation of environmental management in the Hong Kong construction industry. International Journal of Project Management 5, 122–125 (2005) (in Chinese)
4. George, O.: Greening the construction supply chain in Singapore. European Journal of Purchasing & Supply Management 2, 42–45 (2006)
5. Zhou, Q., Cote, R.P.: Integrating green supply chain management into an embryonic eco-industrial development: a case study of the Guitang Group. Journal of Cleaner Production 7, 32–35 (2007) (in Chinese)
6. Joseph, S.: A strategic decision framework for green supply chain Management. Journal of Cleaner Production (11), 201–207 (2003) (in Chinese)
7. Mollenkopf, D., Closs, D.J.: The hidden value in reverse logistics. Supply Chain Management Review (6), 313–315 (2005) (in Chinese)

Interlocking Directorate and Firm's Diversification Strategy: Perspective of Strategy Learning

Yue Yang and Ning Cai

College of Public Administration
Zhejiang University
Hangzhou, China

Abstract. This study examines the influence of the social network of board interlocks on diversification strategy acknowledgement and implement. The author suggests both organizational level and individual level of interlocking directorate have an effect on board strategy decision through affecting the effects of strategy learning, and the empirical analysis proves it. Results that network density, centrality and the status of CEO Interlocks are positive related with the relationship between diversification strategy at the outside firm and the focal firm, while proportion of interlocking outside director plays negative influence. Finally, some conclusions are drawn and a discussion of future directions is given.

Keywords: Interlocking directorate, Strategy learning, Diversification strategy.

1 Introduction

Recent lots of company law, governance practitioners and many academics accept that boards of directors are being held accountable for the organizations they govern. A key aspect of this performance role is board involvement in strategy. Researchers frequently do organization research through social embeddedness theory; they claimed that the social relationship structure the organization embedded could model the strategy choice. The corporate governance has become the governance of networks relationship from the internal governance structure of single enterprise [1]. So the interlocking directorate, which is the most important social relationship form, has attached more and more attention.

Interlocking directorate theory is the most widely used environmental management strategy. It is the situation that one person hold position in two or more directorates in difference firms [2]. In China, the interlocking directorate in firms has become generalization, and the influence has been more and more important [3] [4]. Though interlocking directorate has been widely noticed by academic circles, the research in China is limited. Previous studies in China pay more attention on the description of the phenomenon itself and the network shape. The analysis on antecedents and consequences of interlocking is simple, so it could not reveal the performance of the embedded firms in interlocking directorate network. That is to say, how interlocking directorate influence strategy is still in "black box".

M. Dai (Ed.): ICCIC 2011, Part II, CCIS 232, pp. 87–94, 2011.

In the paper, the author proposes that variance among the directors who create board interlocks affects the likelihood that strategies are transmitted across them by learning strategy. We choice diversification strategy, one of the most important strategy as research object, in order to discuss the effect of interlocking network on the strategy decision. Firstly, mechanism of the influence of interlocking directorate on board diversification strategy is expressed on macroeconomic perspective (organizational level) and microeconomic perspective (individual level). Further, there are four hypothesis from characteristic of network (density and centrality) and characteristic of individual node (CEO interlocks and proportion of interlocking outside director) analyzing the relationship between interlocking and strategy decision. Then the empirical analysis is given on the sample of Chinese limited companies from 2002 to 2007. Finally, some conclusions are drawn and a discussion of future directions is given.

2 Theoretical Research and Hypotheses

Upper echelons theory focuses that top executives tend to make strategic choice under conditions of overloaded information and ambiguity [5]. Strategic decisions are the result of behavioral factors rather than the result of techno-economic. Strategic decision makers economize on search and choice processes, relying on established channels to acquire information and on external referents for insight into reasonable alternatives. Thus, interlocking directorate ties are seen as an important instrument for informational and social influences on strategy decision making. Because of bounded rationality, they look to their counterparts in an effort to draw meaning from the numerous and ambiguous indications. They construct logic for their own contexts by relying on the experiences, definitions, and interpretations on similar contexts to their counterparts.

2.1 Network Features and Strategy Learning

1) Network density

In social network analysis, density refers to the extent to which all possible relations are actually present. According to resource dependence theory, interlocking directorates provide information to be exchanged [6]. Interlocking directors have access to a firm's proprietary data, are apprised of important investment proposals, especially the diversification proposition, and are able to bring their experience to bear on strategic problems. Access to unique information and corporate experience is recognized as a benefit of interlocking directors, directors with more board seats with other important firms are more likely to use their experience to influence boardroom discussions, and signal to its stakeholders, that it is a legitimate firm worthy of support (Bigley and Wiersema, 2002)[7]. In short, I propose the following:

Hypothesis 1: Network density of interlocking directorate is positive related with the relationship between diversification strategy at the outside firm and diversification strategy at the focal firm.

2) Network centrality

Network centrality refers to an individual director's positioning within the overall interlocking directorate(burt, 1992)[8], with more central directors closer to the center of a core of a system of exchanges due to the quality and quantity of their directorships(Hoffman, Stearns, Shrader,1990)[9]. In social network analysis, a point of centrality refers to a point with "a large number of connections with the other points in its immediate environment". In this sense, the best connected points in a network can be regarded as its most central and pivotal points. A firm that is more centrally located in an interlocking network is expected to be able to accumulate significant power and influence (Mintz and Schwartz, 1985)[10]. How connected an individual director is highlights another source of power and influence within a board, following the logic that directors with experience across multiple firms are legitimized in the boardroom and better-positioned to influence board outcomes (Finkelstein, 1992) [11]. Thus,

Hypothesis 2: Network centrality of interlocking directorate is positive related with the relationship between diversification strategy at the outside firm and diversification strategy at the focal firm.

2.2 Individual Features and Strategy Learning

a) CEO Interlocks

Power has long been a topic of interest in the governance literature, whether for an individual or group, power predicts the ability to influence strategy [11]. CEO as the interlocking director, who is outside directorships or service on other firm's boards, is an important means by which be board of directors scans its business environment, and gains actual insight into other organizations' activities. The CEO's outside directorships are likely to be the most influential of external ties, given the direct involvement of the CEO both in the acquisition of information and in internal decision making. Mizruchi (1983) argues boards can "impel, impede, or exert no effect on strategic change in organizations", depending on their power and inclination for altering the strategic direction of the firm [2].

Compare to other interlocking directors, CEO interlocks can become more effective managers: (1) If firms on whose boards CEOs serve are pursuing new approaches to some aspects of business, the CEOs can adapt these approaches to their own firms. (2) Serving on the boards of certain types of institutions (such as banks, multinationals) is valuable; such directorships can provide the CEO with valuable information about trends in interest rates, international business, or major input factor prices. (3) Seeing how other CEOs run their businesses can help CEOs modify their own management styles.

Hypothesis 3: The relationship between diversification strategy at the outside firm and diversification strategy at the focal firm will be stronger if interlocking director is .the focal firm's CEO.

b) Proportion of interlocking outside director

It has been repeatedly suggested that outside directors are often inadequately prepared to participate in board discussions because their time and attention are divided and diluted by their other board appointments; serving on boards at multiple companies makes it difficult for them to gain an adequate understanding of the issues facing any one firm. At the same time, Stokman (1984) show that the vast majority of new director appointments were drawn from a relatively small number of persons with high levels of experience and expertise [12]. These directors were chosen for their individual characteristics rather than for the organizations they represent. As in the cases described by mace, it is likely that the interlocks created by these individuals are largely independent of relations between the firms themselves.

Though outside directors are not responsible for creating strategic policy, the act as advisers and counselors to senior management and thus help shape managerial thinking by bringing external information and insight to the attention of executive team member as well as outside perspectives.

Hypothesis 4: Proportion of interlocking outside director is negative related with the relationship between diversification strategy at the outside firm and diversification strategy at the focal firm.

3 Methods

3.1 Sample and Data Collection

Construction of the raw sample began with the listed companies (random sampling for 500 companies) in China. A company enters the sample by having a director join its board between 2002 and 2007. If a board has multiple interlocked directors, each new directorship is evaluated independently for inclusion based on the diversification profiles of its interlocked firms. The author reconstructs the raw data of directors in sample firms and deal with it using the network analysis software UCINET5. Details on the directors, along with company financials and other information are gathered primarily from Wind Info Database and COIN Database. The final sample consisted of 103 focal firms and included 274 firm-year observations.

3.2 Dependent Variable

Firstly, We measure the extent of diversification of each focal firm using the entropy measure (Palepu, 1985) [13]. The entropy measure captures the extent of total diversification, based on company sales in the number of reported business segments. Specifically, related diversification gauges the extent to which a company's sales are represented by similar industry segments, while unrelated diversification measures the extent to which the firm's sales are derived form different 2-digit SIC industries.

Then, the index of diversification strategic conformity is used to measure the relationship of diversification strategic between focal firm and its interlocked firms. Diversification strategic conformity is the degree to which the focal firm's diversification strategy profile adheres to interlocked firms. Following Finkelstein and Hambrick (1990) [14], we calculated the extent of diversification levels for each focal firm and its all interlocked firms (using the average level if there were two or more firms). Then we measured the conformity by standardizing, for each year of study, each diversification level (mean=1, standard deviation=1) and the calculated absolute differences of each firm's score form the average diversification level of its interlocked firms.

$$SS_{it} = norm\left|S_{it} - S_{at}\right|$$

Where DS is the strategic similarity of firm i to the interlocked firms in period t and S is the diversification of firm i in period t, S is the average level of diversification of the interlocked firms.

3.3 Independent Variables

Density: Density was measured by the total number of ties divided by the total number of possible linkages (UCINET, 1996).

Centrality: Centrality could be measured in a number of ways (Freeman,1979) [15]. In the paper we computed degree centrality, which represents the number of alternatives available to an actor and captures exchange behaviors that occur via direct interaction, such as threatening and reciprocation. Operationally, degree is given by the total number of links to other firms.

Executive status: This variable was dummy-coded with a 1 indicating the interlocking director is the CEO at an interlocked firm, and 0 otherwise.

Proportion of interlocking outside director: Proportion of outside interlocking director was measured the percentage of interlocking outside directors in all the interlocking directors.

3.4 Control Variables

There were three control variables in the model. Board size was measured as the number of directors in the focal firms. Firm age was measured as the number of years since the firm was founded. Firm size was measured as the log of total assets.

4 Results

Table 1 provides the bivariate correlations for all used to analyze predictions of interlocking directorate network to contribute to diversification strategy conformity. Table 2 reports GLS regression results with diversification strategic conformity as the dependent variable. Model 2 estimates the influence of the characteristic of interlocking directorate network on diversification strategy conformity. Model 3 estimates the influence of the characteristic of interlocked boards on diversification strategy conformity. Model 4 is the multiple regression for all the independent variables. Hypothesis 1 and 2 posited that interlocking network features would be positively related to diversification strategic conformity. The results strongly support the proposition. The number and the position of the interlocking director both increase the relationship between diversification strategic at the interlocked firm and the focal firm, and directors who are heavily interlocked are more likely to be wield greater influence and nuanced understanding of bringing their experience to boardroom discussions (Bigley and Wiersema, 2002) [7]. Density and centrality are the most important element of a network. Result supports that density and centrality are both positively associated with diversification strategy conformity. It illustrates the network of interlocking directorate is a significant channel for strategy learning.

Directors can learn about the efficacy of different practices and how to implement them properly by observing the consequences of management decisions in the interlocked firms (Haunschild, 1993) [16].

Table 1. Pearson correlation coefficients

	Independent variable	1	2	3	4	5	6	7
1	Density	1						
2	Centrality	0.23	1					
3	Executive status	0.11	-0.27	1				
4	Proportion	0.14	-0.08	0.15	1			
5	Board size	0.12	0.19	-0.05	0.24	1		
6	Firm age	0.22	0.18	-0.13	0.07	0.19	1	
7	Firm size	0.02	0.25	-0.08	0.21	0.35	0.37	1

Hypothesis 3 predicts a positive relationship between CEO interlocks on other firm's board and diversification strategic conformity, though we find little support for this in any of the models presented in the result. Theoretically speaking, CEO's discretional power is immense on the board of directors and in the executive team. CEO interlocks facilitate the interorganizational transfer of numerous practices. This king of interlock could strengthen any strategic links between the two firms. Mizruchi also indicated that CEO outside directors were chosen as individuals because firms wanted board members who were capable of providing input and advice, often on issues specific to already-identified corporate strategies[2]. It result that interlocked firms could promote reputation itself and learning the management experience form the CEO's outside directorships. That is to say, the interlocked firms could be weaker performance than focal firm, so focal firm could only have little benefit form the outside directorships. Hypothesis 4 predicts proportion of interlocking outside director

Table 2. Results of Multiple Regression Analysis

variable	Model 1	Model 2	Model 3	Model 4
Density		0.37 **		0.29 *
Centrality		0.21 **		0.13 *
Executive status			0.02 *	0.01*
Proportion			-0.11**	-0.12 *
Board size	0.14*	0.15*	0.14*	0.13*
Firm age	0.02**	0.02*	0.01*	0.01*
Firm size	0.11*	0.12**	0.11*	0.09**
constant	0.83 **	0.88 *	0.92 *	1.22 *
F	4.23	6.59	5.70	7.36
R^2	0.16	0.35	0.21	0.42

*p<0.05;**p<0.01;***p<0.001; T-tests were one-tailed for hypothesized effects, two-tailed for control variables.

is negative related with the relationship between diversification strategy at the outside firm and the focal firm, the results offer strong support for this hypothesis. There maybe two reasons to explain the phenomenon. Fist, Most part of outside director is composed of the professor in university, or officers in intermediary agency such as laws, accountants. They have not enough time to take part in interaction with the member in other firms and learn relational knowledge to contribution to the focal firm's strategy decision. Second, the corporate governance structure is not perfect in China, so the affection of outside director could not totally reflect. Their advice for strategy decision usually could not be accepted and implemented. Hypothesis 3 and 4 claim that the characteristic of interlocking directors could also influence the effect of strategy learning.

5 Discussion and Conclusions

How difference among interlocking directors impact their effect on firm strategies is an important question of corporate governance and strategic management. The research is little which explores individual directors as carriers of strategic knowledge between firms, along with how the network of interlocking directorate constrains the receptivity of the board and firm to that learning of strategy. In the paper, the result proved that interlocking directorate could promote the ability of strategy decision in board. Inter-organizational strategy imitation and diffusion are the main causation of the consequence. Interlocking directorates have great effects on strategy decision-making by taking part in diversification in other firms, accelerating knowledge, transfer and communication, reducing risk of entering new market, maintaining and improving the relationship between parent corporations and affiliated firms. When a director has more exposure to related diversification strategies from his or her outside directorships, the firm of his or her board becomes more likely to pursue a related diversification strategy as well. We found that both macro-level and micro-level of interlocking directorate had an effect on strategy choice through affecting the effects of strategy learning. On the aspect of network, the density and centrality of interlocking directorate network are positive related with the relationship between diversification strategy at the outside firm and diversification strategy at the focal firm. On the aspect of individual, the relationship between diversification strategy at the outside firm and diversification strategy at the focal firm will be stronger if interlocking director is .the focal firm's CEO, and proportion of interlocking outside director is negative related with the relationship between diversification strategy at the outside firm and diversification strategy at the focal firm. It suggests that if one company attempts to improve its board's ability of strategy acknowledgement and implement through the external ties of interlocking directorate, it should pay attention to two aspects: one is the position and power in the interlocking network; the other is the composition of the interlocking directors.

One limitation of this study is the sample in empirical analysis is not enough perfect. We should have more companies to prove the conclusion effectively. Another limitation of this study is it is still not known how interlocking directorate influence firm performance through strategy learning. We only analyze the first step of the reaction chain. Future investigations could build on our results to explore these issues further. We believe that such research, along with the results presented in this paper, can widen the understanding of this significant aspect of technology innovation model selection.

References

1. Granovetter, M.: Economic Action and Social Structure: The Problem of Embeddedness. The American Journal of Sociology 91(3), 156–174 (1985)
2. Mizruchi, M.S.: Who Controls Whom? An Examination of the Relation Between Management and Board of Directors in Large American Corporations. Academy of Management Review 8, 426–435 (1983)
3. Duan, H., Zhong, W.: An Empirical Study on the Causes of Interlocking Directorates-Based on Listed Companies in Shanghai. Science of Science and Management of S. & T. 8, 156–161 (2008)
4. Lu, C.-c., Chen, S.-h., Joachim, S.: Theories of Interlocking Directorates: An Empirical Testing Based on the Listed Companies of China. China Industrial Economy 1, 113–119 (2006)
5. Geletkanycz, Hambrick: The External Ties of Top Executives: Implications for Strategic Choice and Performance. Administrative Quarterly 42, 654–681 (1997)
6. Pfeffer, Salancik: The External Control of Organizations. Harper, New York (1978)
7. Bigley, G., Wiersema, M.: New CEOs and Corporate Strategic Refocusing: How Experience as Heir Apparent Influences the Use of Power. Administrative Science Quarterly 47, 707–727 (2008)
8. Burt, R.: Structural Holes: the Social Structure of Competition. Harvard University Press, Cambridge (1992)
9. Hoffman, A., Stearns, T., Shrader, C.: Structure, context, and centrality in interorganizational networks. Journal of Business Research 20(4), 333–354 (1990)
10. Mintz, Schwartz: The Power Structure of American Business. U. of Chicago Press, Chicago (1985)
11. Finkelstein: Power in Top Management Teams: Dimensions, Measurement, and Validation. Academy of Management Journal 35, 505–538 (1992)
12. Stokman, F.N., Van der Knoop, J., Wasseur, F.W.: Interlocks in the Netherlands: Stability and Careers in the Period 1960-1980. Soc. Netw. 10, 183–208 (1988)
13. Palepu, K.: Diversification Strategy, Profit Performance, and the Entropy Measure. Strategic Management Journal 6, 239–255 (1985)
14. Finkelstein, Sydney, Hambrick, D.C.: Top-management Team Tenure and Organizational Outcomes: the Moderating Role of Managerial Discretion. Administrative Science Quarterly 35, 484–503 (1992)
15. Freeman: Centrality in Social Networks: Conceptual Clarification. Social Networks 1, 215–239 (1979)
16. Haunschild: Interorganizational Imitation: the Impact of Interlocks on corporate acquisition activity. Administrative Science Quarterly 38, 564–592 (1993)

A Decision Support System for Ship Concept Design Using Genetic Algorithms

Yuantao Jiang and Siqin Yu

School of Economics and Management
Shanghai Maritime University
Shanghai 200135, China
Ceciliasl@yahoo.cn

Abstract. It is estimated that more than 80 percent of ship's manufacture cost is caused by concept design of ship. For a large ship, this means tens of billions of dollars. Based on the relationship between design process and DSS (Decision Support system), this paper discussed the conceptual design process of ship. A model of optimizing ship design was developed. Genetic algorithms were used to simulate the ship design. The conclusion was given finally.

Keywords: ship concept design, DSS, Genetic algorithms.

1 Introduction

The ship design is a decision process that designers will make. The decisions range in difficulty from the very simple to the very complex and in scope from the very narrow to the very broad. Simple decisions are made without much consideration of the factors affecting and affected by the decision. But, the design processes of ship is a complex decision, and designers normally give such decisions much more thought and consider more of the factors involved. Based on the complexity and scope involved in design process, the thought given may be a brief mental comparison of alternatives, or it may be a thorough analysis appropriate to a complex situation in which there are significant differences in the impacts of various factors considered and in impacts of various alternative courses of action[1].

Decision support system (DSS) could provide organizations with informative analyses to improve decision efficient. A DSS includes a model, a source of data and a user interface in which the model is very important. Research on product design and decision support system for design has been widely explored in the past decades and its application ranges from the business communities, government agencies and private individuals. The DSS of ship concept design uses the WWW technology to help designer to input demand parameters and to review suggested projects and simulated results. In Section 2 we present the design process of ship and the advantage of DSS. The optimization model of ship concept design is analyzed in section 3. The encoding of genetic algorithms to solve the optimization problem is detailed in Section 4.

M. Dai (Ed.): ICCIC 2011, Part II, CCIS 232, pp. 95–100, 2011.

2 The Process of Ship Concept Design

The conceptual design model of ship is an activity in the early design stage in which the concept of a product is formulated. The concept of ship includes ship requirements, functions, possible behaviors, form/structure (layout), and associated properties. The conceptual design activity of ship is decomposed into seven subactivities. Figure 1 shows subactivities A1 to A7. The concept design model describes functions and their input and output data in conceptual design.

As in fig1, the concept design of ship is a continuous process that is central to the successful management of all design units[2]. It is also a decision process of selecting one right project from two or more alternative ones. All decisions will involve some risk and uncertainty because designers cannot grasp the units that constitute the whole ship. Since designers cannot find or control everything, they must base their decisions on those units that they can easily know and learn. While designers cannot always guarantee right decision, experience hade proved that well-thought-out decisions must be more likely to yield right project than are choices made haphazardly. So, building and using computer based decision support system can help designers to identify right projects to avoid risk and uncertainty.

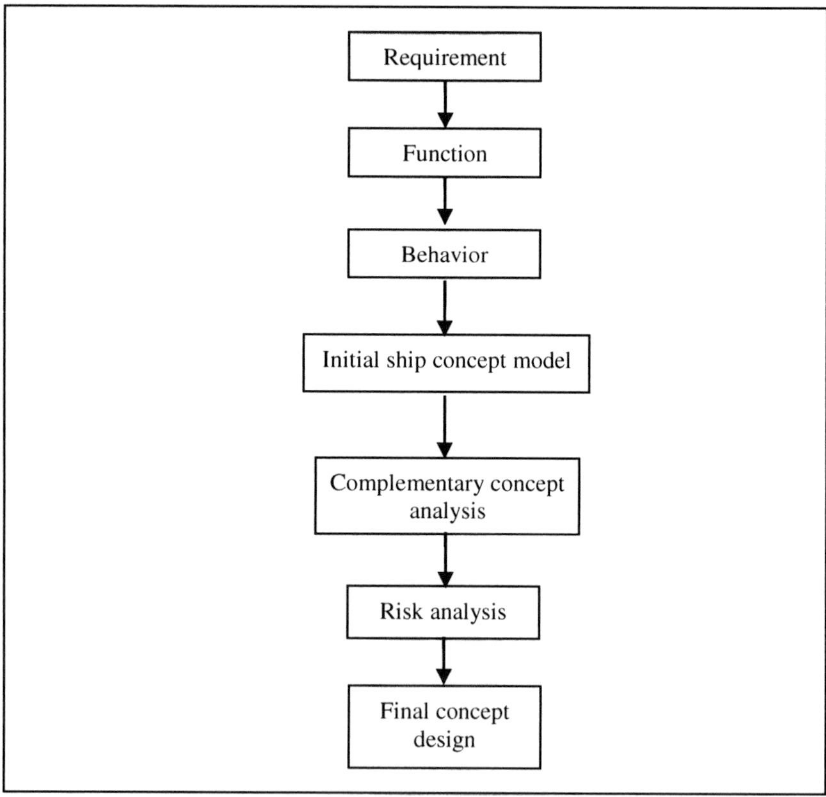

Fig. 1. Concept Design Process of Ship

One important designing skill is learning to place each project into the right perspective. When designers have decision demand in the right perspective, you can then determine how much time and effort to devote to each project[3].

Computer based Decision Support system provide current, timely information that is accurate, relevant and complete. A specific DSS for ship concept design presents information in an appropriate format that is easy to understand and manipulate. The information presented by a DSS may result from analysis of transaction data or it may be the result of a decision model or it may have been gathered from external sources. DSS can present internal and external facts, informed opinions and forecasts to Entrepreneurs. Entrepreneur wants the right information, at the right time, in the right format, and at the right cost.

3 Optimisation Model of Ship's Concept Design

The concept design work of ship includes a series of tasks that can define an object to meet the mission requirements and comply with a set of constraints. Objective attributes are not adequately synthesized or presented to support efficient and effective decisions. These attributes are usually qualitative, inconsistent, and not provided to design engineers in a format they can use. So the design space is very large, non-linear, discontinuous, and bounded by a variety of constraints and thresholds. Because ship design process involves a large range of technologies, the overall task of dividing and integration is very necessary. And the ship design task is very complex because of the design requirements and constraints that are virtually unique to the ship design.

Imagine a situation in which designers want to minimize the cost of producing the ship. Each ship j (j=1,…,n) includes per-unit production cost c_j associated with it, as well as an associated utilization rate a_{ij} of resources for each finished ship. In addition, the plant that produces the ship has a limited amount of each resource i (i=1,…,m), denoted by b_i. So, this paper had formulated a deterministic mathematical program for a single scenario s as follows:

$$\text{Min } z^s = \sum_{j=1}^{n} c_j^s x_j$$

Subject to

$$\sum_{j=1}^{n} a_{ij}^s x_j = b_i^s \qquad i=1,\ldots,m \tag{1}$$

$$x_j \geq 0 \qquad j=1,\ldots,n$$

Where c^s, a^s and b^s respectively represent the realization of the cost coefficient, the resource utilization and the resource availability data under scenario s. For example, ship designer who plan to design a kind of tanker, depends on the condition in the region whether the steel plate for the ships are obtained easily. The ship manufacture is also considering whether to design and produce this type of ship because every type of tanker is usually composed of a lot of parts. According to a ship concept design practice there are n projects. Each project is a assemble of d parts characterized by the cost level $C_i, i = 1, \cdots n$.

Supposing each of ships is set of four parts, A, B, C, D, so, a total of four parts would be considered. The four possible parts and associated parameters for ship are shown in Table 1. The first column corresponds to the particular parts; Column 2 denotes the different kind of every part; Column 3 shows the probability that each part is at current or purchased; Column 4 denotes the probability for each part whether it is at current and purchased; Column 5 shows the cost associated with each kind (L = low, M = medium, H = high); Column 6 denotes the utilization rate of each kind (L = low, H = high).

The optimization model needs to be solved once for each of the four parts. The design optimization approach can be summarized in two steps:

(1) Compute the optimal solution to each deterministic part.
(2) Solve a simulation model to find a single, feasible decision for all parts.

4 Genetic Algorithms for Ship Concept Design

Design optimization is accomplished using two genetic algorithms, GA1 and GA2. GA2 is a delta-coding GA operating on the chromosomes of GA1[4].

Ship manufacture cost is a control vectors and C is encoded as digital strings. The representation space I can be expressed as a ship parts' set:

$$I = S_1^1 \times S_1^2 \times \ldots \times S_1^d \times S_2^1 \times S_2^2 \times \ldots \times S_2^d \times \ldots \times S_n^1 \times S_n^2 \times \ldots \times S_n^d \tag{2}$$

GA1 uses a 4-bit scheme:

$$S_i^j = \{s_1, s_2, s_3, s_4 : s_k \in \{0,1\} \forall k = \overline{1,4}\} \tag{3}$$

Table 1. Possible Poject Choice for Ship Concept Design

Parts	Kinds	Station	P(S)	P(U)	Cost	Util
A	A1	Current	40%	30%	L	H
		Puchase	60%			
	A2	Current	50%	70%	M	M
		Puchase	50%			
B	B1	Current	70%	20%	H	M
		Puchase	30%			
	B2	Current	20%	40%	L	H
		Puchase	80%			
	B3	Current	50%	40%	L	H
		Puchase	50%			
C	C1	Current	30%	50%	M	L
		Puchase	70%			
	C2	Current	60%	50%	H	M
		Puchase	40%			
D	D1	Current	25%	10%	L	M
		Puchase	75%			
	D2	Current	35%	40%	H	H
		Puchase	65%			
	D3	Current	65%	50%	M	L
		Puchase	35%			

Suppose each cost level C_i takes an integer value in the range of 0 to 10 units. In general, with n ships demand and up to p cost levels for d parts there are up to npd design projects. For GA2, a sign scheme, $s_i^j = \{0,1,-1\}$ is used, representing either no change or an alteration of $\pm \Delta C$ to the drug levels C_i.

A GA1 choice set $x \in I_{\text{GA1}}$ can be expressed as:

$$x = \{s_1, s_2, s_3 \ldots s_{4nd} : s_k \in \{0,1\} \ \forall k = \overline{1,4nd}\} \tag{4}$$

A GA2 choice set $x \in I_{\text{GA2}}$ can be expressed as

$$x = \{s_1 s_2 s_3 \ldots s_{nd} : s_k \in \{0,1,-1\} \ \forall k = \overline{1,nd}\}) \tag{5}$$

Then the encoding functions on I_{GA1} and I_{GA2} will have the forms:

$$\text{GA1:} \quad C_{ij} = \Delta C_j \sum_{k=1}^{4} 2^{4-k} a_{4d(i-1)+4(j-1)+k}, \quad \forall i = \overline{1,n}, j = \overline{1,d} \tag{6}$$

$$\text{GA2:} \quad C_{ij}' = C_{ij} + a_{d(i-1)+j} \Delta C_j, \quad \forall i = \overline{1,n}, j = \overline{1,d} \tag{7}$$

This DSS uses a separate design simulation to evaluate each project. A project is deemed to be best if the cost is reduced to certain value or fewer for the set of four parts. The ship function also must satisfy the customer demand. For each project, the simulation returns the choice result of four parts at the end of each time. Fitness functions for GA1 and GA2 are now obtained by calculation of the optimization functions (1).

5 Conclusion

The concept design determines the final ship product and ship form, and the basic structure. Much of the ship's potential added value is set by concept design. The paper presented a based process conceptual design model of ship. The computer system for ship concept design is a three-tier decision support system running across the World Wide Web. The client is delivered as a Java Applet and is concerned with setting demand parameters and displaying results. The server contains a database of ship structure information along with intermediate objects for simulation and optimization of projects. Design optimization is carried out using genetic algorithms.

Acknowledgment. This work was supported by the Science & Technology Program of Shanghai Maritime University.

References

1. Coyne, R.D., Rosenman, M.A., Radford, A.D., Balachandran, M., Gero, J.S.: Knowledge-Based Design Systems, pp. 3–456. Addison-Wesley Publishing Company, Reading (1990)
2. Yuantao, J., Siqin, Y.: Study of Process based Conceptual Design Model for Ship. In: International Conference on Computer and Communication Technologies in Agricuture Engineering, pp. 31–34 (2010)
3. Committee IV.1: Design Principles and Criteria. In: Proceedings of the 16th International Ship and Offshore Structures Congress, vol. 1, pp. 20–25 (August 2006)
4. McCall, J., Petrovski, A.: A Decision Support System for Cancer Chemotherapy Using Genetic Algorithms. In: Proceedings of the International Conference on Computational Intelligence for Modelling, Control and Automation, Vienna, Austria, vol. 1, pp. 65–70. IOS Press, Amsterdam (1999)

Enterprise Performance Evaluation Based on BP Neural Networks

Lv Feng and Zhang Zhiwen

School of Mechatronics Engineering, Henan University of Science & Technology, Luoyang, China
sivajich2323@yahoo.cn

Abstract. The effective and practical performance evaluation method that can show the operational situation of the enterprises scientifically and objectively is in a great need. The paper puts forward a three-level enterprise integrated performance evaluation system combining theoretical study with empirical analysis in research because the traditional financial accounting- based performance measurement method is out of step and lagged. Then BP neural network model is applied to the performance evaluation of enterprises by building an evaluating model which avoids the uncertainty in estimating the weights subjectively on the basis of introducing the methods and steps of the model. Finally the empirical analysis result indicates the scientific nature and practicability of the proposed model.

Keywords: Enterprise performance, performance evaluation, index system, back propagation network.

1 Introduction

Enterprise performance management is very important to modern enterprise management. As the core of enterprise management system, enterprise performance evaluation must be studied. The study of enterprise performance evaluation started to rise in western industrial countries in 19th century[1], and traditional enterprise performance evaluation methods only consider financial index. At present, there are a lot of methods on enterprise performance evaluation. They can be broadly divided into qualitative and quantitative methodologies. Now the content of enterprise performance evaluation is more attention to the organic combination and interactive influence on strategic opportunity selection, core competence and sustainable development with enterprise governance structure, environmental adaptability and resource reasonable allocation.

In view of this, the paper builds the index system of enterprise performance evaluation based on analyzing influencing factors, and the paper uses BP neural network, whose characteristics is having strong self-learning, self-adaptive and fault tolerant property, to evaluate enterprise synthetic performance. It enables the evaluation to be more objective and reasonable, and provides a new approach to evaluate enterprise performance.

M. Dai (Ed.): ICCIC 2011, Part II, CCIS 232, pp. 101–108, 2011.

2 To Establish the Index System of Enterprise Performance Evaluation

The scientific characters of index system directly relates to the quality of enterprise performance evaluation, so the index system must be scientific, objective and reasonable in order to reflect all the influencing factors of enterprise business risk as comprehensively as possible. Many factors will influence enterprise performance, and it should be comprehensively considered with every factor's effect. Through analyzing [2-4], the index system of enterprise performance evaluation is built as Table 1 shows.

Table 1. The index system of enterprise performance evaluation

Objective layer	Index	
	First grade index	**Second index**
Enterprise performance evaluation	Financial performance (I_1)	Return on net assets (I_{11})
		Sales income growth rate (I_{12})
		Cost profit rate (I_{13})
		Net cash flow debt rate (I_{14})
		Earning per share (I_{15})
	Customer performance (I_2)	Customer satisfaction (I_{21})
		Market share (I_{22})
		Customer concentration ratio (I_{23})
		After service (I_{24})
	Internal operation performance (I_3)	Quality level (I_{31})
		Enterprise culture (I_{32})
		Enterprise informatization (I_{33})
		R&D coat ratio (I_{34})
		Intangible assets (I_{35})
	Human resources performance (I_4)	Employee satisfaction (I_{41})
		Productivity of staffs (I_{42})
		Technicians ratio (I_{43})
	Social responsibility performance (I_5)	Social contribution (I_{51})
		Social burden coefficient (I_{52})
		Social accumulation rate (I_{53})

3 Theoretical Basis

BP neural network which consists of some layers neurons is a multi layer perception structure[5]. The typical BP neural network is composed of three layers: input layer, hidden layer and output layer[6]. The structure diagram as Figure 1 shows.

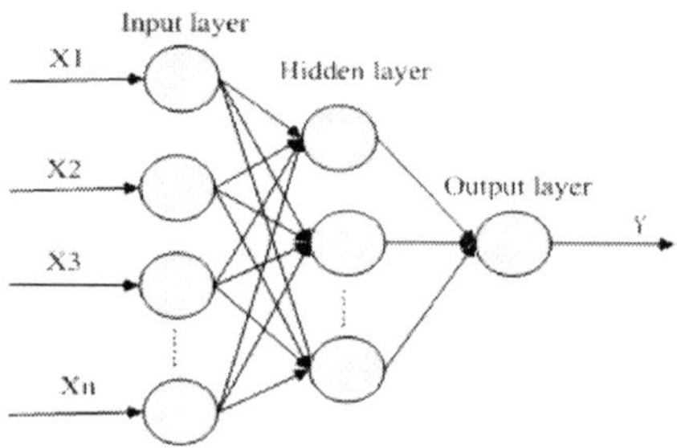

Fig. 1. The structure diagram of three layers BP neural network

The steps of the algorithm are as follows[7,8]:

3.1 *To initialize* w_{ji} *and* b_j

Where w_{ji} denotes the connection weight between the neuron i and neuron j, b_j denotes the threshold of neuron j.

3.2 The training sample set $\{x_{pl}\}$ and corresponding target output set $\{y_{pl}\}$ pretreatment

Where p, l denote respectively the number of sample and input vector.

3.3 To calculate the output of every layer neuron

To input layer:

$$p_{pi} = x_{pi} \tag{1}$$

Where x_{pi} denotes the ith value of p samples.
To hidden layer and output layer:

$$p_{pi} = f\left[\sum_i \omega_{ji} p_{pi} + b_j\right] \tag{2}$$

Where p denotes the input of the neuron i and the output of neuron j.

3.4 To calculate the error signal of every layer neuron

To hidden layer:

$$\delta_{pi} = \left(y_{pi} - p_{pj}\right) p_{pj}\left(1 - p_{pj}\right) \tag{3}$$

To output layer:

$$\delta_{pi} = p_{pi}\left(1 - p_{pi}\right)\sum \delta_{pj}\omega_{pj} \tag{4}$$

3.5 To calculate the error

$$E_r = \left[\sum_p \sum_k \right](bpk - ypk)^2 / 2 \tag{5}$$

When E_r is less than the given fitting error, the network training is finished

3.6 Back propagation and weight modification

Else return to (3), and continue to training.

$$w_{ij}\left(t+1\right) = w_{ij}(t) + \eta\delta_{pj}p_{pj} \tag{6}$$

Where η denotes learning rate.

4 The Enterprise Performance Evaluation Based on BP Neural Network

3.7 To construct quasi model based on GUI

1) To determine the number of hidden layer neurons

In general, the number of hidden layer neurons should be less than or equal to half of the dimensions of the input vector. The number of evaluation index set in this study is

20, the number of hidden layer neurons should be 7-10, and the number is 8 in quasi model.

2) To select training function

The learning algorithm should consider not only algorithm performance but also the complexity of the problem, the size of sample set, network scale, the goal error of the network and question type.

The generalization ability is one of the important symbols to measure the performance of neural network. There are two methods that can be used to improve the generalization ability in MATLAB neural network toolbox. They are regularization method and early stopping method.

In general, the mean square error function (mse) is adopted to evaluate the training performance function of the neural network.

$$mse = \frac{1}{N}\sum_{i=1}^{N}(e_i)^2 = \frac{1}{N}\sum_{i=1}^{N}(t_i - a_i)^2 \tag{7}$$

The performance function in regularization method shows as following:

$$msereg = \gamma . mse + (1-\gamma) msw \tag{8}$$

Where γ denotes proportional coefficient.

$$msw = \frac{1}{n}\sum_{j=1}^{N} w_j^2 \tag{9}$$

The network scale in this study is small, so trainbfg(), traingdx(), traind(), traindm() and trainscg() can be used to the training function of enterprise performance evaluation. In order to improve the generalization ability, the regularization method can be adopted. So the quasi model of enterprise performance evaluation based on BP neural network is constructed as Table 2 shows.

Table 2. The quasi model of enterprise performance evaluation

Item	Parameter
Network name	Mynet
Network type	Feed-forward backprop
Input dimension	20
Training function	TRAINSCG
Adaptive function	LEARNGDM
Network training performance function	MSEREG
Layer number of Network	3
The neurons of hidden layers	8
Output dimension	1
Transfer function	TANSIG

The structure of quasi model as Figure 2 shows.

The Quasi model based on GUI is built. It is a basic structure, so some training must be carried out in order to make the model be a steady state.

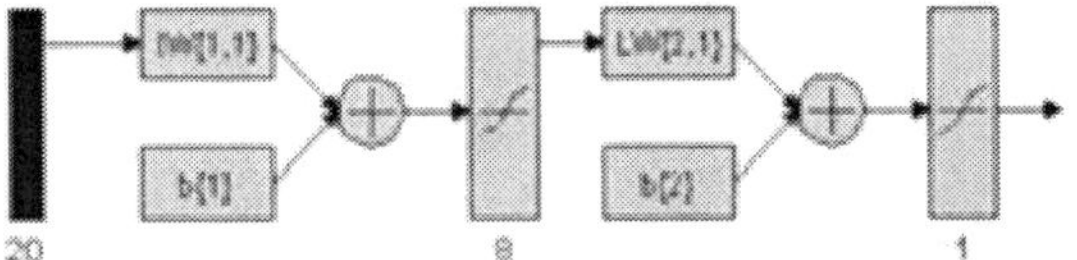

Fig. 2. The structure of quasi model

3.8 Data collection and processing

Taking 10 agriculture machinery enterprises as samples. It is necessary to normalize in order to eliminate the differences in index values and units.

To the-larger-the-better index[9]:

$$x_{ij} = \frac{I_{ij} - \min\{I_{i1}, I_{i2}, \cdots, I_{in}\}}{\max\{I_{i1}, I_{i2}, \cdots, I_{in}\} - \min\{I_{i1}, I_{i2}, \cdots, I_{in}\}} \quad (10)$$

To the-smaller-the-better index:

$$x_{ij} = \frac{\max\{I_{i1}, I_{i2}, \cdots, I_{in}\} - I_{ij}}{\max\{I_{i1}, I_{i2}, \cdots, I_{in}\} - \min\{I_{i1}, I_{i2}, \cdots, I_{in}\}} \quad (11)$$

To the moderate index:

$$x'_{ij} = \begin{cases} \dfrac{I_{ij} - \min\{I_{i1}, I_{i2}, \cdots, I_{in}\}}{I - \min\{I_{i1}, I_{i2}, \cdots, I_{in}\}}, I_{ij} < I \\ \dfrac{\max\{I_{i1}, I_{i2}, \cdots, I_{in}\} - I_{ij}}{\max\{I_{i1}, I_{i2}, \cdots, I_{in}\} - I}, I_{ij} > I \end{cases} \quad (12)$$

Where I_{ij} denotes the jth index value of the ith sample, I denotes the moderate index value.

The sample data standardization as table 3 shows.

Table 3. Sample data standardization

Index	Enterprise									
	A	B	C	D	E	F	G	H	I	J
I_{11}	0.558	0.547	0.673	0.563	0.759	0.787	0.916	0.865	0.996	0.655
I_{12}	0.523	0.073	0.944	0.769	0.097	0.450	0.188	0.282	0.608	0.029
I_{13}	0.542	0.539	0.618	0.561	0.685	0.612	1.000	0.676	0.679	0.601
I_{14}	0.800	0.641	0.746	0.689	0.851	0.875	0.717	1.000	0.794	0.000
I_{15}	0.349	0.588	0.325	0.340	0.508	0.905	0.823	0.690	1.000	0.473
I_{21}	0.143	0.000	0.571	0.429	0.857	0.714	0.286	0.571	0.714	1.000
I_{22}	0.012	0.271	0.048	0.000	0.303	0.182	0.381	0.284	1.000	0.502
I_{23}	0.877	0.000	0.853	0.787	0.497	0.520	0.284	0.928	0.000	0.963
I_{24}	0.000	0.333	1.000	0.333	0.667	0.667	1.000	0.167	0.833	1.000
I_{31}	0.125	0.000	0.250	0.500	0.750	0.750	0.250	0.625	0.750	1.000
I_{32}	0.000	0.167	0.333	0.333	1.000	0.667	0.667	0.667	0.667	0.667
I_{33}	0.286	0.000	0.571	0.286	1.000	0.429	0.857	0.571	0.571	0.857
I_{34}	0.037	0.055	0.067	0.040	0.185	0.084	0.833	0.228	0.111	1.000
I_{35}	0.821	0.790	0.331	0.895	0.322	1.000	0.198	0.846	0.300	0.214
I_{41}	0.500	0.500	0.750	0.250	0.625	0.750	1.000	0.500	0.750	0.625
I_{42}	0.352	0.340	0.428	0.159	0.416	0.567	0.765	0.342	1.000	0.561
I_{43}	0.231	0.424	0.739	0.649	1.000	0.107	0.519	0.401	0.539	0.095
I_{51}	0.292	0.508	0.508	0.326	0.545	0.664	0.804	0.731	0.698	0.565
I_{52}	0.932	1.000	0.770	1.000	0.851	1.000	0.000	0.352	0.511	1.000
I_{53}	0.199	1.000	0.251	0.347	0.408	0.270	0.108	0.268	0.396	0.805
Expected results	0.332	0.323	0.549	0.416	0.642	0.622	0.657	0.561	0.744	0.652

3.9 Model testing and modification

Taking the enterprises A, B, C, D, E and F as the learning samples. After numerous training, the results can be gotten as Table 4 shows.

Table 4. The results after the training

Item	Parameter
Training function	trainscg()
Network training performance function	msereg()
The neurons of hidden layers	10
Transfer function	tansig(),purelin()

The structure of modification model as Figure 3 shows.

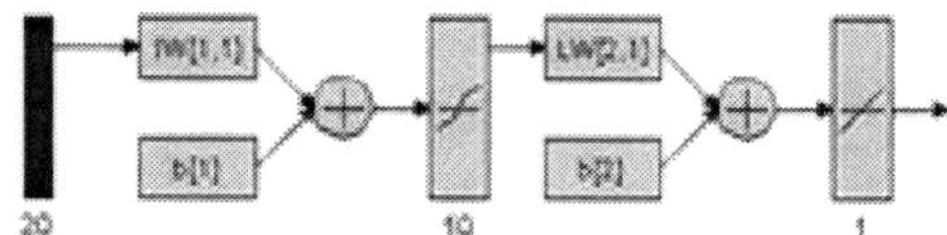

Fig. 3. The structure of modification model

The study of the model finishes after 582 epochs training.
The error curve of network training as Figure 4 shows.

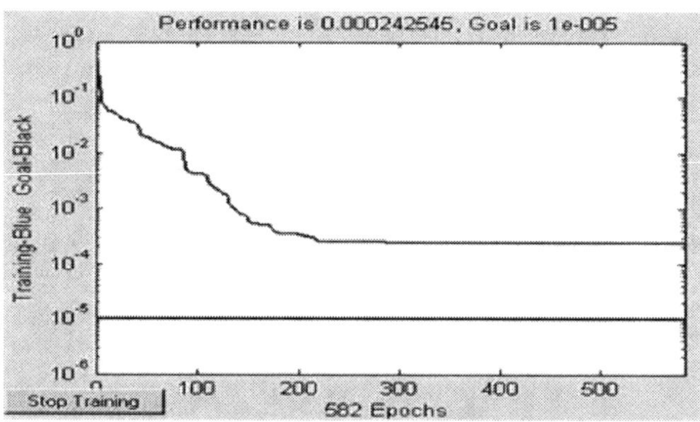

Fig. 4. The error curve of network training

3.10 Simulation calculation and result analysis

Taking the enterprises H, I and J as the simulation samples. The simulation calculation of the evaluation model of agriculture machinery enterprise performance based on BP neural network can be carried out.

The results are compared between simulation calculation and expected output, as Table 5 show.

Table 5. The comparison with test results and expected results

Result	H	I	J
Test results	0.562	0.738	0.624
Expected results	0.561	0.744	0.652
Relative Error	0.25%	0.86%	-4.34%

From Table 5, the relative error between test results and expected results is so small that BP neural network can be used to evaluate enterprise performance.

5 The Comprehensive Performance Evaluation

The comprehensive performance evaluation of 10 agriculture machinery enterprises can be carried out by the modification BP neural network. The results as Table 6 show.

Table 6. The comprehensive performance evaluation of 10 agriculture machinery enterprises

Enterprise	Test results	Expected results	Relative Error
A	0.331	0.322	0.30%
B	0.324	0.323	0.45%
C	0.549	0.594	-0.81%
D	0.414	0.416	0.28%
E	0.638	0.642	-0.59%
F	0.619	0.622	-0.33%
G	0.656	0.657	-0.04%
H	0.562	0.651	0.25%
I	0.737	0.744	0.86%
J	0.623	0.652	-4.34%

The performance level of 10 agriculture machinery enterprises can be gotten according to the discrimination criteria as Table 7 shows.

Table 7. The performance level of company

Discrimination criteria	Level	Enterprise
0.7-1.0	Excellent	I
0.5-0.7	Better	C, E, F, G, H, J
0.3-0.5	Common	A,B,D
0.1-0.3	Worse	None
Less than 0.1	Bad	None

6 Conclusion

The index system of enterprise performance evaluation is established in the paper, which includes 5 aspects that are financial performance, customer performance, internal operation performance, human resources performance and social responsibility performance.

The enterprise performance evaluation model based on BP neural network is built. The model avoids the impact of subjective factors, and it has strong self-learning, self-adaptive and fault tolerant property. Through test, the model has high accuracy, and the evaluation is more objective and reasonable. It not only enables to make the post-evaluation of current period management performance but also simulate and predict the management performance in the future. It will provide the scientific evidence for enterprise management decision.

Acknowledgment. The work is supported by Social Sciences Fund in Luoyang City (2009D037, 2009D074). The authors wish to thank anonymous reviewers for their constructive comments and the Editors for their editorial effort on the manuscript of this paper.

References

1. Zhen, L., Wang, J.: Enterprise Comprehensive Performance Evaluation System-Based on ANP, BSC and Performance Prism. Journal of Xidian University (Social Science Edition) 17, 1–7 (2007)
2. Liu, y.: On the stakeholders-orientated integrated performance assessment for natural monopoly enterprises. Management Review 12, 31–36 (2003)
3. Naughton, B.: Growing out of the plan: Chinese economic reform. Cambridge University Press, Cambridge (1995)
4. Wang, J., Wang, B., Zhao, Q.: Application of Balanced Scorecard and Analytic Network Process to Enterprise Performance Evaluation. Industrial Engineering Journal 9, 60–64 (2006)
5. Chi, L.C., Tang, T.C.: Artificial Neural Networks in Reorganization Outcome and Investment of Distressed Firms: the Taiwanese Case. Expert Systems with Applications 29, 641–652 (2005)
6. Hair, J., Anderson, R., Tatham, R., Black, W.: Multivariate Data Analysis. Prentice Hall, New Jersey (1998)
7. Hornik, K.: Approximation Capabilities of Multiplier Feed-forward Networks. Neural Networks 1, 68–72 (1993)
8. Sabuncuoglu, I., Gurgun, B.: A Neural Network Model for Scheduling Problems. European Journal of Operational Research 93, 288–299 (1996)
9. Tang, W.: The Study of the Optimal Structure of BP Neural Network. Systems Engineering–Theory and Practice 10, 95–100 (2005)

Design and Research of Traffic Accidents Simulation System

Yang Lei and Zhang Zhijun

The Department of Computer Science and Technology,
Shandong Jianzhu University, Jinan, China
dariuszk523@gmail.com

Abstract. Traffic accidents, one of the major hazards all over the world, are occurring increasingly frequently in China. Along with the expansion of cities and dramatic development of infrastructure, the capacity of motor vehicles and non-motor vehicles increased by 15%-20% each year. However, coupled with the amazing progress is the rise of traffic accidents, the annual incidence of which has reached staggering 100,000. As traffic accidents usually occurs in a flash, it is often impossible to get all the details. Consequently, the cause and responsibility of a traffic accident can not be judged arbitrarily. Thus the needs for thorough and just investigation of the truth of accidents, analysis of their causes and specification of responsibilities in them have become real and urgent. Based on information on the spot, this system is capable of simulating the whole process of an accident, which is of great help to the analysis of causes of it and specification of responsibilities.

Keywords: traffic accident, process simulation, simulation system.

1 The Interface Framework of the Traffic Accidents Simulation System

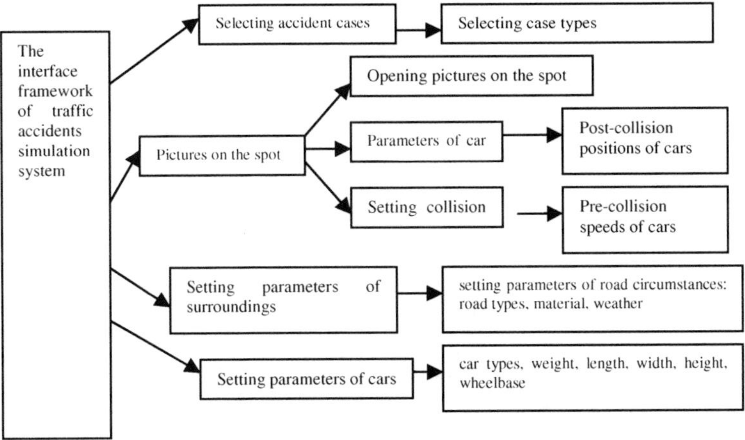

Fig. 1. The structure of the interface of traffic accidents simulation system

M. Dai (Ed.): ICCIC 2011, Part II, CCIS 232, pp. 109–115, 2011.

2 A Brief Introduction to Every Module of Traffic Accidents Simulation System

1) case selection: This module is responsible for selecting cases of traffic accidents, as is shown in figure 2.

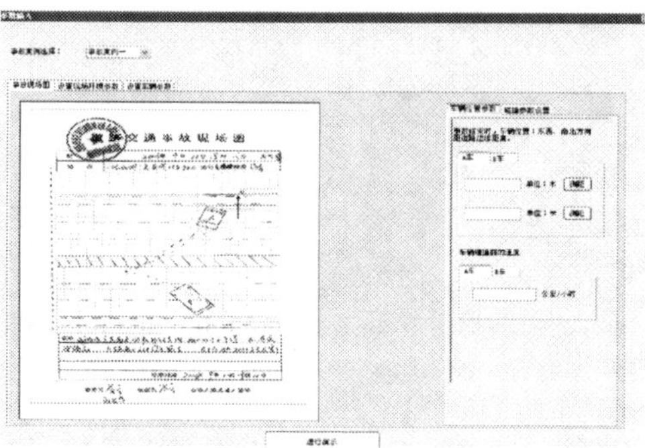

Fig. 2. The graph showing what happened on the spot (a)parameters of car positions

2) graphs showing what happened on the spot: opening this module, users can input both pre-accident and post-accident parameters about locations of cars. Moreover, collision parameters, including coordinates of two cars just before the collision and their respective sliding distance, can also be input, which is showed in figure 3.

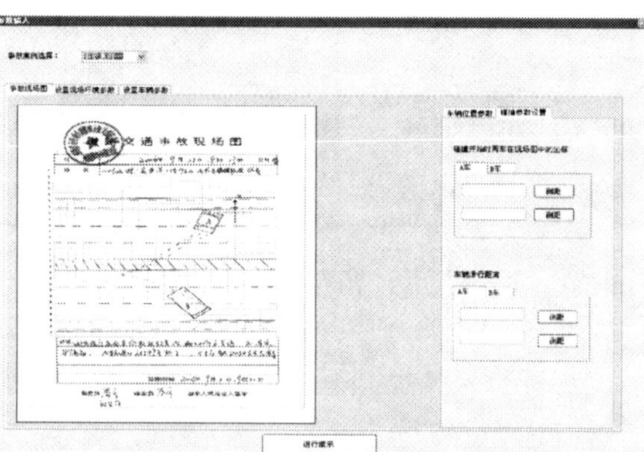

Fig. 3. Graphs showing what happened on the spot (b) setting parameters of collision

3) setting parameters of surroundings on the spot: this module allows users to set parameters of circumstances on the road, such as road types(four lanes, eight lanes or intersection), road materials(pitch, sand or stone), road conditions(dry or humid) and weather(sunny or rainy), which is showed in Figure 4.

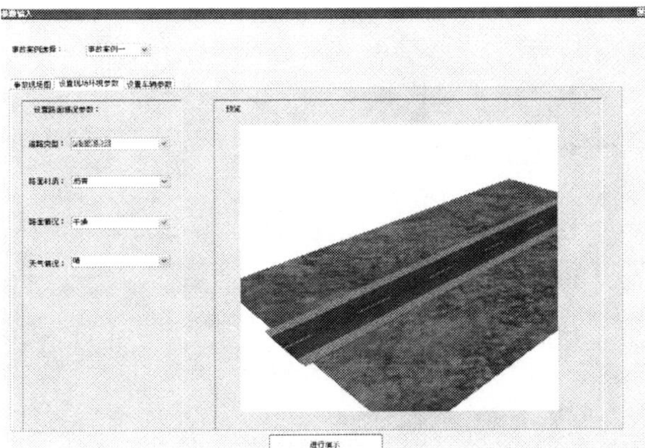

Fig. 4. Setting parameters of surroundings on the spot

4) setting parameters of cars: In this module, parameters of cars, say, car type, weight, length and width can be set, which is showed in Figure 5.

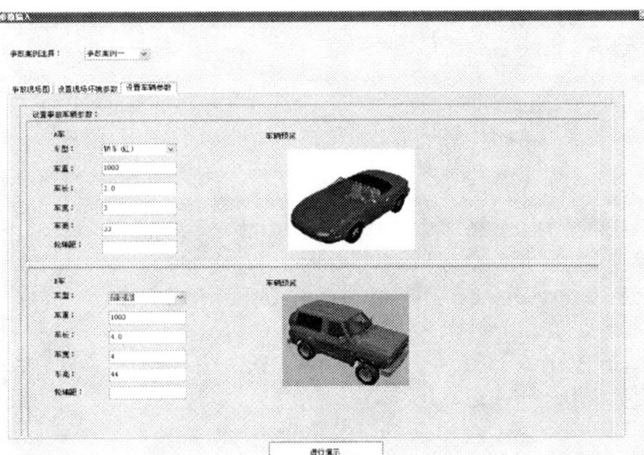

Fig. 5. Setting parameters of cars

3 The Development of Traffic Accidents Simulation System

3.1 Modules of System Development

This system mainly consists of three modules: modeling, simulating and displaying. Its framework is showed in the following figure 6.

3.2 An Introduction to Every Module

1) Modeling: In this module, geometric modeling is adopted and 3D models are established using 3DSMAX. Furthermore,

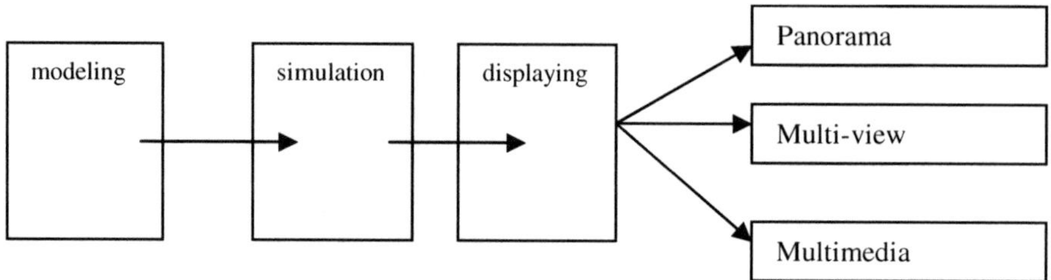

Fig. 6. The framework of system

2) Simulation: the whole process of an accident is divided into three steps: pre-accident, collision and post-accident. The pre-accident and post-accident movement of cars is specified according to kinetic model; the occurrence of collision is judged by employing the OBB surrounding box detection algorithm---if there is a collision, then the post-collision movement is simulated; otherwise the pre-accident movement is continued.

A collision detection class CollisionModel3D is established in this module to create an object for every model waiting to be examined. Its major structure is as follows:

```
Class Collision3D
{
Public
.......
addTriangle(float v1[3],float v2[3],float v3[3]);
//The coordinates of triangle's vertex are added.
void finalize();
//The OBB tree is established after all triangles are added
void setTransform(float m[16]);
//Transformation matrix is set to reestablish the OBB tree after transformation.
bool collision(CollisionModel3D * other);
//Whether the two models collide is judged
getCollidingTriangles(float t1[9],float t2[9]);
//The coordinates of triangles in which the colliding point of the two models are located are obtained.
}model1,model2;
```

The process of collision detection is as follows:

```
(1) for(int i=0;i<m_triangle.size();i++)
(2) //All slices of model1 are looped.
    {
     glBegin(GL_TRIANGLES);
     glVertex3fv(m_triangle[i].P[0]);
//The first vertex of slice[i] is displayed.
glVertex3fv(m_triangle[i].P[1]);
//The second vertex of slice[i] is displayed.
glVertex3fv(m_triangle[i].P[2]);
//The third vertex of slice[i] is displayed.
```

```
glEnd();
//Coordinates of vertexes in slices are added.
Model1->addTriangle(m_triangle[i].P[0], m_triangle[i].P[1], m_triangle[i].P[2]);
}
Model1->finalize();
//Adding is completed and OBB tree is established.
Float mat1[16];
glGetFloatv(GL_MODELVIEW_MATRIX,mat1);
model1->setTransform(mat1);
//The transformation matrix of model1.
```

(3) Object model2 is established in the same way that model1 is created.
(4) BOOL collision=model1->collision(model2); //Whether a collision has happened is judged.
(5) Corresponding measures are taken to deal with the collision.

This module utilizes VC++ and OpenGL to realize various operations of 3D models. It is capable of reading every parameters from the database established in module1, displaying 3D models on the monitor and placing them at appropriate positions. In addition, it takes advantage of various 3D algebraic transformations to realize diversified operations, including rotating and moving horizontally, vertically, obliquely and so on.

Models are created in 3DSMAX and texture maps are employed to achieve good displaying effects. In this way, detailed construction of models is reduced so that the number of vertexes and surfaces decreases greatly without distorting models. What is more, to enhance the performance of the system, other measures are also taken. All map files must be processed by Photoshop to minimize maps without making them ineffective; OpenGL requires that texture maps be bmp file, their size be the power of 2 without exceeding 1024bytes. Otherwise, reading them into OpenGL will be more time-consuming. After modeling cars and the road in 3DSMAX, files in 3ds format are output. Car models are stored as files in 3ds format, and then the files are output to 3d Exploration, a popular transformation software, and stored as files in cpp format. Afterwards, these cpp files are transferred to head files and added to the project. Then the class CModel2DExplore are used to call these files so that they can be displayed in lists and controlled. If it is found that the color or maps of a model cannot satisfy the need after the model is called by OpenGL, the model can be revised directly in head files mentioned above without returning to 3ds max. In head files, materials are represented by linear array, the data structure of which is showed as follows.

```
Struct MATERIAL{
GLfloat ambient[3];
GLfloat diffuse[3];
GLfloat specular[3];
GLfloat emission[3];
GLfloat alpha;
GLfloat phExp;
Int  texture;
};
```

Parameters can be changed to alter colors. Texture maps are represented by linear array, the data structure of which is as follows:

```
Struct TEXTURE
{
Char *name;
Glint id;
};
```

The first item is the name of graph used in texture maps. If maps are to be altered, only the first parameter needs to be modified, and the size of maps can also be changed here.

3) Displaying: This module uses animations to display the whole process of accidents, including panorama displaying, multi-views displaying and multimedia displaying. Panorama displaying provides users with panoramas which show all-round surroundings on the spot; multi-view displaying show the whole process of an accident from different perspectives by opening several windows simultaneously; multimedia displaying transforms the process of accidents into animations with high quality.

3.3 Effects of Traffic Accidents Simulation System

In this chapter, two cases of traffic accidents in real world are quoted to test the effectiveness of the simulation system. The consequence of collision, which is obtained using OBB surrounding box detection algorithm, is showed in figure 7. Applying other collision detection algorithms to the same cases, users can get the result showed in graph 3-7. As is shown in these two graphs, the OBB surrounding box detection algorithm can generate more immediate detection of collision than other algorithms. So such conclusion can be reached: using OBB collision detection algorithm and 3D algebraic modeling, this system enable users to detect collisions with great accuracy and efficiency. Moreover, it also provides us with more vivid models, animation pictures with high quality and speed.

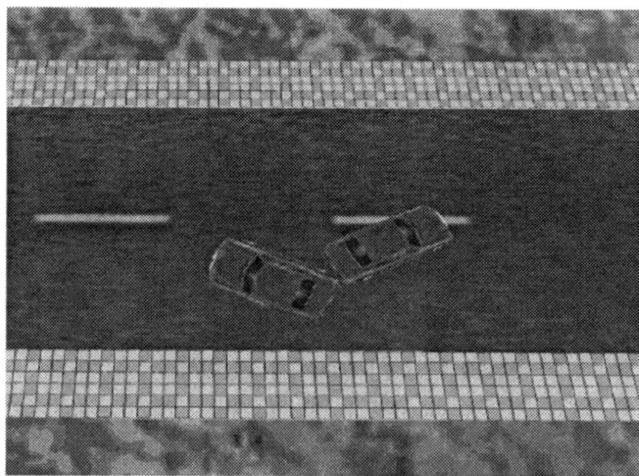

Fig. 7. Simulation graph of collision generated by adopting OBB algorithm

References

1. Li, S.: Course of Computer Graphics (OpenGlversion). China Machine Press, Beijing (2004)
2. Barrus, J.W., Waters, R.C.: QQTA: A Fast, Multi-Purpose Algorithm For Terrain Following in Virtual Environments, technical report 96-17. MERL Cambridge, MA (July 1996)
3. Du, Z., Liu, H., et al.: Study on Quick Production of 3D View in Digital City. Micro Computer Information 1-3, 249–251 (2005)
4. Chen, D., Luo, Y.: Virtual Designation. China Machine Press, Beijing (2006)

The Construction of Real-Time Integrated Surveillance System in Water Conservancy

Qing-Xun Ma

College of Geomatics
Xi`an University of Science and Technology
ShanXi Province, Xi`an City, China
tlelo.cuautle123@gmail.com

Abstract. The so-called 'integrated surveillance' means that such risks and disasters as flood, rainfall, drought, engineering, typhoon, etc can be synchronously and real-timely kept under surveillance. The designing style of the case system based on the 'integrated surveillance' concept is different from the systems which monitor the every sort of the risks and disasters separately. This system makes the user can quickly, duly, directly and thoroughly find out the information of current risks and disasters and also their spatial position. So it has practical significances for the water conservancy departments, and is much more adaptable to the requirements of combating flood, drought and typhoon disasters in time of the crucial flood season.

Keywords: Integrated Surveillance, Flood Conservancy, WebGIS, ArcIMS, ArcSDE.

1 Introduction

Along with the incessantly social economic increase and the advancement of substance civilization, the tasks of combating flood, drought and typhoon disasters are becoming heavier than ever. Higher requirement for the efficiency and response rate of handling accidental events are being made by society and government to the water conservancy department. Because of the differences in technical structure caused by development time and platform, the currently used risk-disaster surveillance systems and early-warning systems have some inconvenience in use. Thus, the simultaneous risks and disasters mostly cannot be monitored in one system, to say nothing of displaying all the information in the same interface of one system. Even if the relatively comprehensive function system being developed, it usually keeps the different risks and disasters under surveillance in individual subsystems, mostly because of the influence of traditional thinking and the separate founding of real-time database (such as the water-rain DB, the project DB, the typhoon DB). In flood season when some risks and disasters occur at the same time, for example, should the risks of typhoon, heavy rains, floods and engineering hazards come together; the system user can only get into individual subsystems to monitor the situation.

M. Dai (Ed.): ICCIC 2011, Part II, CCIS 232, pp. 116–121, 2011.

Here, a subsystem included in Guangdong Province (in southeast China) Water Conservancy Decision Support System (DSS) is given as an example to show how a typical kind of integrated-surveillance system is designed and constructed. Various sorts of risks and disasters such as flood, rainfall, drought, engineering, and typhoon can be synchronously and real-timely under surveillance in this subsystem. In this system, WebGIS thematic map fulfilled navigation the function, and the pre-defined water conservancy 'event' was taken as a core to realize the functions of surveillance, early warning, and information query and acquirement etc. Also because of using WebGIS as the main navigation means, the system interface is intuitional, practical and easy to be operated.

2 Construction of the Integrated Surveillance

2.1 Requirement Abstraction

The purpose of setting the functions of 'integrated surveillance' is to provide a convenient way for water conservancy departments to simultaneously and real-timely survey various risks and disasters in the target regions. The objects needed to be surveyed include flood, rainfall, drought, engineering hazards, typhoon as well as others (like hailstone, etc).

From the intentions mentioned above, the service logic of the 'integrated surveillance' can be abstracted into two levels: 'alert' and 'event'. 'Alert' objectively reflects the current risk information, using the real data show the risk status like strong rainfall in drainage area or district, the flood, and typhoon and so on. 'Event' is the synthesized current and predictive information, which extends the 'alert' information, stem from the existing alerts. For example, an 'event' was defined as 'twenty year-encountered flood' on a certain river; its information comes from the correlative 'alert' message. The function demand to the 'event' is that its evolution can be traced. To distinguish the integrated-surveillance logic into 'alert' and 'event' is favorable for the users to decide which is more important and what should be paid more attention to.

Bases of 'alert' are the real-time data like rainfall, water level, project accident status, which is most originally from sorts of hydrologic observation stations distributed in different region. That is to say, when the real-time data of certain survey object reach the level to give an alarm, the system should prompt the user 'alert' message. For instance, when the average rainfall of observation stations in one region gets to rainstorm level, this 'alert' should be generated. When water level of one river is higher than alertness level, this 'alert' also should be produced.

The root of 'Event' is 'alert'. The mode of generating 'Event' may be from two ways. One way is automatically made by the system according to the rules, for instance, the water level of River X exceeds the history tiptop, the system itself, without manual work, would create an 'Event': 'River X exceed the history tiptop'. The other way is to define the 'Event' artificially. When the man on duty (or specialist) ,after generally analyzing the information about the 'alert', thinks it is necessary to upgrade the 'alert' to an 'event' to attach importance to, the system should provide him event-defining function.

In time of 'event' is defined, the correlative data, such as the current the situation of a disaster, current investment, status of loss, upriver rainfall etc, can be organized by the system or user. The 'event' can be modified along with the evolution of the disaster. For instance the definition can be changed from 'a twenty-year-encountered flood'' to 'a fifty-year-encountered flood'. So when the 'event' needs to be conducted to an interlocution, all these correlative data can be submitted to the bargaining subsystem.

2.2 Interface Design

In this system, the function interface design adopted left-right framework. The left frame included the 'event' list area and the system menu area; the right frame was the WebGIS map area and message area (Fig1). This interface is the default logon interface of the whole DSS.

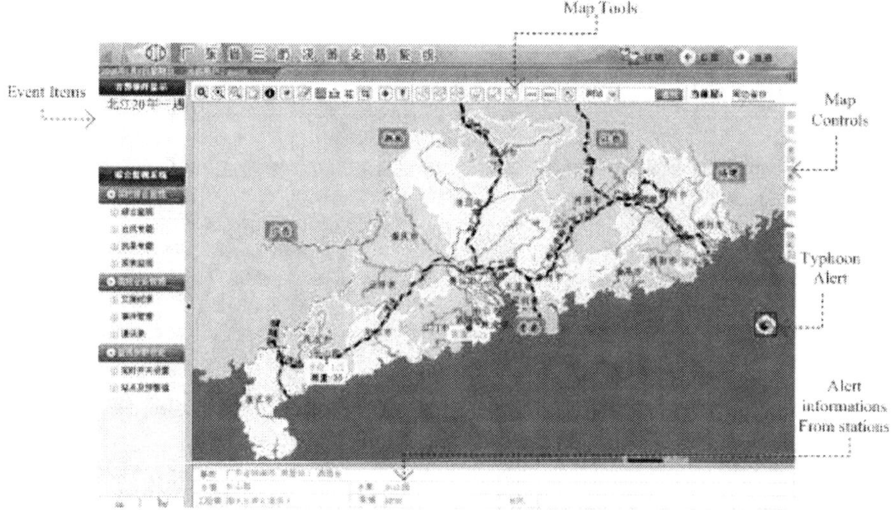

Fig. 1. Function Interface Design

In a default state of the DSS, the 'alert' info is expressed in two ways: by map and by list at the same time. The map uses spatial objects: points, lines, and polygons along with their labels to achieve giving alarms. The deeper query to the 'alerts' can be done through the GIS operation on these spatial objects. The way of list is that it shows all the 'alert' information in one list table.

The defined 'events' is shown on the left frame, the left-top of the whole interface and also the most notable position. The further-tracking function to every 'event' is performed by clicking the list item, and the right frameset will response to the event's mouse click showing the distinct area map and correlative information in the message area.

Apart from displaying the 'alert' information, the WebGIS map can also be used to show the district rainfall distribution, drought distribution, real-time water level and rainfall data of each observation station(after the map zoomed in) etc.

Abundant tools and control function are designed for WebGIS. Besides the accustomed tools, the fast layer switch, the quick query, the active layer remind functions were set. The query result list displays the different query at the same place and in the same style. It might be the result of Identify or Select by Rectangle and also might be result of Integrated Query, Quick query or Buffer Analysis. This interface design style greatly enhances the effective map extent on the computer screen, also ensuring the integrality of WebGIS function and simplifies the operations.

2.3 Realization of the Integrated Surveillance

This system was built on the J2EE MVC Strust structure, Oracleq10g as database, ESRI ArcIMS as WebGIS platform and ESRI ArcSDE as spatial database engine. The java API of ArcIMS java connector was used as programming technique to the development of map publishing.

The realization of the integrated surveillance can be summarized in two steps: the background data preparation and the forehead information display (include maps and lists).

1) Background Data Preparation

Relying on the database design criteria of the water conservancy, the DSS database system was logically composed of integrated DB, water-rain DB, engineering DB, typhoon DB, drought DB and so on. Its original real-time data came from observation stations (automatic or manual) distributed in different regions, as long as the associated department (for instance, meteorology department) database.

Thus, it was necessary to filter out the real-time data from these DB for alert and also to design new database tables to save and manage these data as well as the 'events' defined from these data. The data preparation course was as Fig 2:

A scheduled background timer process was contrived in the system, to perform the data preparative function. It timely accesses the real-time correlative data in the various DB, finding out if one new data record met the criteria of 'alert', picking out data according to the assumed algorithm. For example, the process timely accesses the water-rain DB to get the real-time rainfall data of all observation stations, it will firstly judge if the rainfall of every data record has reached the level of 'alert'(such as the daily rainfall exceeds 30mm), if true, the data will be extracted and stored in the 'alert table'.

2) Implementation of the Forehead Function

- Thematic map and 'alert'-listing function

The 'alert' thematic map involved in the 'alert' should be displayed in the map with a specific label. For rainfall, water, engineering and other types of the monitoring objects, the map directly marked up the positions corresponding the observation stations. Further query and analysis can be done on them. A specific alarm stations layer (an ArcIMS Acetate Layer) was dynamically created on the thematic map to show 'alert' to all kinds of stations and also to show typhoon position.

The organization of 'alert' listing information, such as rain and water is done according to the general rule of 'from big to small'. Firstly judge by the catchments, if the alarm criterion for the catchments area was suited to, the name of this area should be added to the 'alert' list; secondly judge by the administrative district, if the alarm condition was confirmed, the distinct name should be added to the list; and the last is that the each name of the exceeded criteria (no matter water level or rainfall) station.

A 'rainfall distribution' map layer (polygon layer) was set to display the district rainfall. The polygon feature of each district was filled with different color by the calculated average value of the stations rainfall of the whole district: colors from deep blue to shallow blue stand for the district rainfall from strong to weak.

- The conjunction of the 'alert' list to the map

The response of locating the 'alert' item on the map was achieved by transferring parameters to the WebGIS system. For the point object like observation station, the parameter should be its coordinate; for the line or polygon object like river, dike, reservoir, district, and drainage area the parameter should be its spatial Object ID (Feature ID).

- The implement of the WebGIS functions

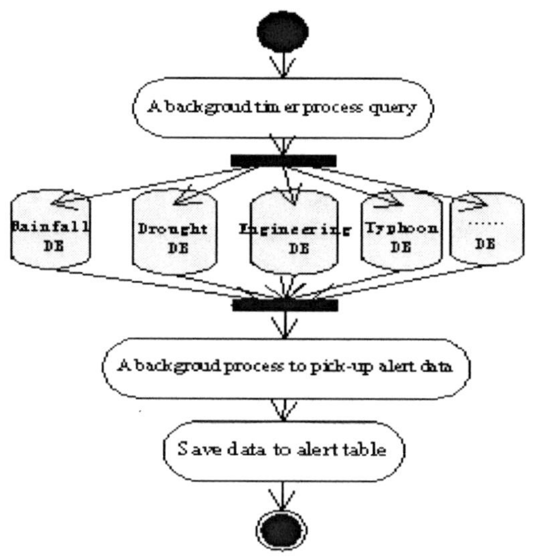

Fig. 2. The data preparation course

3 Conclusion

From the viewpoint of fulfilling the demand, since the business of water conservancy watching was abstracted in two-levels: 'alert' and 'event', not only the system keeps the objectivity of the alarm information, but also exerts subjectivity of the experts. The designing style of the case system found on the 'integrated surveillance' concept is different from the systems which monitor the every sort of the risks and disasters separately. So it has practical significances for the water conservancy departments, and is much more adaptable to the requirements of combating flood, drought and typhoon disasters in the crucial flood season.

References

1. Huang, K.-h., Qiu, C., Yu, K.-s., Ding, B.-l.: Design and Realization of Real-time Hydrological Information Issuing and Forewarning System Based on WebGIS. Journal of China Hydrology 4, 73–76 (2006)
2. Wang, X.-w., Zhang, G.-z., Wang-jun, et al.: Study on Development of Real-time Rainfall and Water Information System. Shandong Water Resources 1, 43–45 (2007)
3. Run, B., Wang, J.-x.: Discussion on Water Regime Information Transmission Channel Selection of Guangdong Provincial '3-Protection' Commanding Information System. Automation in Water Rescources and Hydrology 3, 4–7 (2007)
4. Cheng, Y.-s.: Discussion on Preventing and Decreasing Disaster System Framework Construction in Water Resources. Water Resources Development Research 6, 28–31 (2007)
5. Wang, Z.-y., Liang, Y.-m.: One stage design MIS of Water Conservancy. Guangdong Water Resources and Hydropower 2, 72–75 (2004)

Exploration on Oil Field Road Safety Quantificational Evaluation in the North of Shaanxi Zone

Qing-Xun Ma

College of Geomatics, Xi`an University of Science and Technology
ShanXi Province, Xi`an City, China
tlelo.cuautle123@gmail.com

Abstract. The security of the road is directly related with the oil production in oil field. The oil field roads in the North of Shaanxi have both characters of loess and mountainous areas. Segments of these roads usually pose serious threats to vehicles for its continuous zigzags, low-lying, steep slopes, cliffs etc. Upon the field road and risky point survey, this article synthetically exerts the advanced 3S spatial technology, computer information system and also the theory on road safety evaluation. A spatial technique which is called "Oil field road general evaluation method based on risk point grade value" was described in this article, which emphasized the importance of the risk sources along the road, and along with the technique, an exploration on the oil field road safety quantificational evaluation had been made.

Keywords: Road Safety Evaluation, Oil Field Road, Quantificational Evaluation, 3S Technology, Oil Production.

1 Introduction

Loess Plateau region in North of Shaanxi is the main oil-producing region of the Changqing oilfield and Yanchang oilfield. Because of its special features in the natural environment, various types of vehicles play an important role in the safe production. The production of crude oil needed for the production of subsistence material, the production of command, staff, emergency rescue, part of the transportation of crude oil and finished oil products all depend on the various types of general-purpose vehicles and special vehicles to complete [1]. The roads of the oil field have the characteristics of loess plateau and mountain and these roads usually have serious threats to the vehicle safety for its being continuous zigzag, low-lying, steep slope, cliff etc. So, oil road safety issue has always been attached to oil field production management departments and the oil road safety evaluation has great significance in improving the oil road conditions and enhancing the driving safety coefficient.

While developing the project –The Second Factory of Vehicles Management System of Changqing Oilfield– based on an idea called pre/post analytics in roads security evaluation, oilfield road general evaluation method based on risk point grade value is concluded in this article to preliminarily explore the quantitative method to safety evaluation of oilfield roads in North of Shaanxi, through surveying the field data of road and risk source, combining spatial-3S technology and computer information

M. Dai (Ed.): ICCIC 2011, Part II, CCIS 232, pp. 122–127, 2011.

management technology, and summarizing the road safety management experience of oilfield vehicles capacity security management department.

2 Data Acquirement

The data of Oilfield roads is the base for safety evaluation. The data in this article refers to that of the vector maps on the various types of roads in oilfield, as well as the so-called road "risk sources" of geospatial vector data on bends along the roads, steep slopes, low-lying, cliffs, narrow bridges, dense-populated areas and accident-prone sites. According to their different functions in oil industry, oilfield roads are classified into: the main trunk roads (grade highway-based), trunk roads (the main gravel road), and extension roads (mainly referring to pre-drilling dirt road). We combine the field measuring with indoor-map compilation to acquire these data. This map covers about 15000 km2 in seven counties and a region in the Longdong area in northern Shaanxi Province The roads are processed by the line layers and the risk sources are processed by the point layers.

2.1 Oilfield Road Map Compilation

The map of Oilfield roads is the 1:50000 scale digital map of Longdong oilfield, whose basic data comes from the original topographic map purchased and high-resolution satellite image maps. Due to the different scales, different mapping time and data incompleteness of the map offered by the surveying and mapping departments, we have to process the SPOT5 remote sensing image data which are 2.5m-resolution through local vector. The oilfield is very broad in area, so the work for map compilation is heavy and complicated. Its main work includes 12 layers of oil main trunk, trunk roads, extension roads, and contour lines, involving the workload of about 80 days per person.

2.2 Roads and Field Measurements of the Risk Sources

Because of its hysteresis, the data in the above-mentioned map can not fully reflect the current status of the roads, especially the road safety situation. Therefore we made field measurements on oilfield roads and risk sources. The job was done by 3 groups, and it lasted for two months. The group members took cars to measure the roads data from main roads to the station, well bases and well roads using hand-held GPS. At the same time, they measured various types of accident-prone risk sources such as curves, intersections, steep slopes etc. Road attribution collected some security-related attributes such as kilometers of road length, road width, road grade, road type, risk description etc. Risk sources' attribution covered names, category, respective sections, risk control tips, risk levels, risk scores and so on.

When the field survey was completed, through the combination of the inside data processing with the above-mentioned data, the compilation of risk-source map layers was completed which involved complete compilation of data compilation of oil main trunk roads, trunk and extension lines. Simultaneously, we accurately calibrated the topological relationship between the source of risk points and roads line layers using ArcGIS. We totally measured 4315 kilometers of roads and 2512 risk-source points (table 1). Eventually the measured data are saved at the space database.

Table 1. Statistics of risk points along the roads of oil field in north of Shaanxi zone

risk sources	steep slope (>25 degree)	steep slope (≤25 degree)	narrow bridge	zag curve	cross intersection	populous area	low-lying Section	cliff
Number	59	512	55	269	792	370	372	92

3 Quantitative Security Evaluation on the Oilfield Roads

3.1 The Composition of the Security Evaluation Factors

Experts from home and abroad have made a long-time and systematic research on the traffic security issues, and these studies are targeted at people, vehicles, roads and environment according to different research objectives. As for the studies on road conditions and environment, deep research is relatively late because of the shallow awareness of the environmental impact on the accidents. The researches mainly focus on the impact of road environment on road safety and the basis of the ideas fall into two main categories: 'post- research' and 'pre-research'. In addition, according to different perspectives on traffic safety, researches are divided into macro- and micro-traffic safety research. Security evaluation mainly aims at the objective condition of roads factors, which is in the scope of micro–traffic safety research.

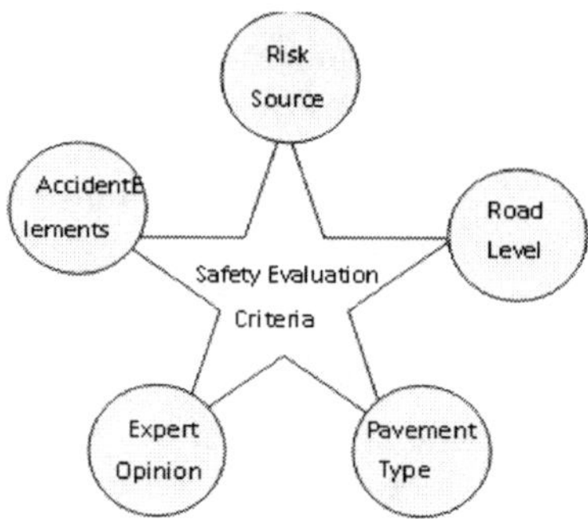

Fig. 1. Makeup factors of oil road safety evaluation

We consider that its own security evaluation factors mainly consist of five aspects: road levels, accident elements, pavement types, risk source and expert opinions, namely oilfield roads constituents of security evaluation criteria (Figure1). Of which:

Road level: the road level is divided into highway, grade 1 roads, grade 2 roads, grade 3 roads, grade 4 roads and grade 5 roads according to the "Highway Engineering Technical Standards" by Ministry of Communications Criteria, Oilfield roads are mostly non-hierarchical roads except part of the main road.

Risk Source: refers to the mentioned places of roads along the bend, crossroads, steep slopes, low-lying, narrow bridges, dense-populated areas which are the primary threat to roads traffic safety, which belongs to the category of "pre-accident" safety-evaluation factors. Accident-prone sites are not included.

Accident Elements: the road accident-prone locations, such location data are provided by oilfield road safety management departments, and they are in the scope of the "post-type" safety evaluation factors.

Types of road surfaces: refers to such types as asphalt, cement and sandstone, self-built gravel and dirt roads.

Expert opinions: opinions by experienced security experts and drivers who make their assessment to some roads.

Based on the above five factors composed of oilfield road safety evaluation criteria, objective factors (road level, pavement type, risk sources and accident elements) can be combined with the man-made subjective evaluation (expert opinion) ,and "pre-accident" factors can link with "post-accident" factors (accident elements), at the same time, risk sources of the road safety evaluation, this kind of 'pre-accident' objective factors stress on the importance of making the result more precise.

In order to facilitate level evaluation on the road security, the above-mentioned five security evaluations can be re-merged, that is to say, merging the road level (the main trunk, trunk, branch) and the road category (grade asphalt, non-grade asphalt, gravel, dirt road) into the road level; and road risk sources (steep slopes, sharp turns, etc.) and accident factors (accident-prone locations) into the road risk source; expert factors remain unchanged. Thus, risk level can be comprehensively and quantitatively assessed by road level, road risk source and expert opinions.

3.2 Quantitative Classification and Evaluation of Road Security Level

Based on the acquaintance of the above mentioned road safety assessment elements, we summarized the percentile comprehensive evaluation method that can make a quantitative classification and evaluation for safety level of road safety risk source. Method is as follows (Figure 2):

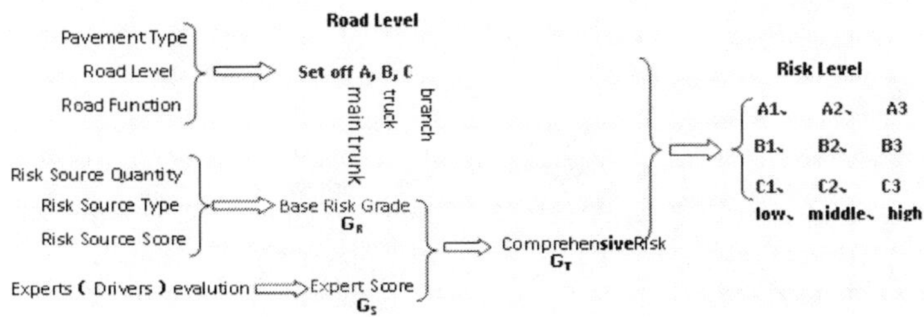

Fig. 2. Road safety evaluation flow chart

4 The Application of Evaluation Results

The evaluation method is achieved in the Second Factory of Vehicles Management System of ChangQing Oilfield, and applied to the "road file management," "risk source file management," "Vehicle Monitoring WebGIS system", "deploy the vehicles" and so on in this system [6] [7].

Figure 3 shows the results of road safety level displayed through visual map in the "Vehicle Monitor WebGIS system": the above of solid line "ZG45 (291m/20) A3" label, in which: ZG45 indicates that the road is the number 45 No. trunk; 291m shows the road length;20 shows the width of road is 20m;A3 indicates that this section is the main trunk road section (general grade asphalt) and its safety level is the high-risk section. "Fork in the road", "Bridge", "steep" with pointing arrows is the name and location of the risk sites. Thus the system plays an important warning role for vehicle schedule, safety management and drivers.

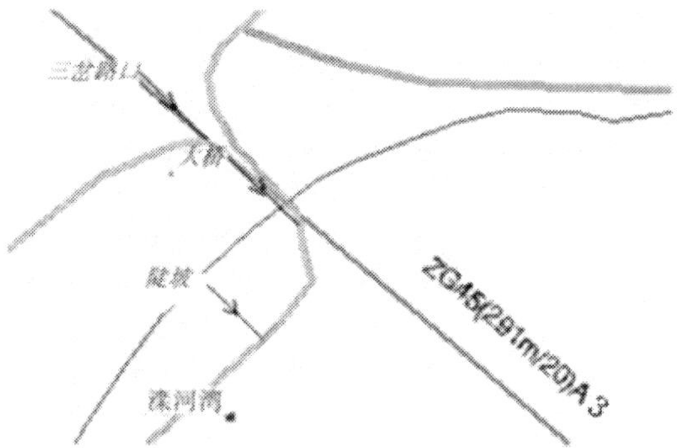

Fig. 3. The road,risk point and their annotation

In addition, the evaluation conclusion is applied to road safety assessment and road safety management decisions by vehicle capacity safety management. For example, based on the conclusions, the management department has taken such measures as designing pavement, engineering modifications and increasing the safety identity, which effectively reduce the happenings of serious accidents.

5 Conclusion

The "comprehensive evaluation method of oil road safety risk source score " has a broad and positive significance on quantitative safety evaluation of oilfield roads, roads management maintenance and traffic safety management. Although the method is not even very strict in the "risk source" technology classification, roads fragments and quantitative evaluation, it combines experts' judgment with objective risk factors. And based on the idea of pre/post analysis, it has incomparable advantages compared with conventional "post-type" evaluation. At the same time the method is simple and easy to understand and cost less, which is typically representative for safety assessment to the mountain roads and Loess Plateau area. I deem that it has some reference function at roads safety evaluation in such areas. At this point, I would like to sincerely thank those comrades from ChangQing Oil Field Plant, who involved in the project and also thank the project team for their hard work.

References

1. Martín, F.S., Ángeles, M.E.Q.: Prevention of traffic accidents: The assessment of perceptual-motor alterations before obtaining a driving license. A Longitudinal Study of the First Years of Driving 19(3), 189–196 (2005)
2. D'andrea, A., Cafiso, S., Condorell, A.: Methodological Considerations for the Evaluation of Seismic Risk on Road Network. Pure Appl. Geophys. (162), 767–782 (2005)
3. Ma, Q.-x.: Moden mine productive vehicle MIS combining 3S technology. Journal of Xi'an University of Science and Technology 27(1), 289–292 (2009)
4. Zhong, C.-y., Yue, L.: Geometrical Design and Safety for Highway. Communications Standardization 168(8), 93–95 (2007)
5. Zhang, T.-j., Tang, C.-c., Nan, S.: The Influence Analyses of the Vehicle Characters at a Downgrade followed with a blind bend Highway Section by HSEP. Journal of Highway and Transportation Research and Development 24(1), 130–132 (2004)
6. Wang, X.-w.: Research of Ji Lin Province Expressway Safety Appraisement. Ji Lin University (2007)
7. Huang, G.-y., Shen, Z.-f., Hao, S.: System design of vehicle information management platform and its key technology analysis. Science of Surveying and Mapping 32(1), 127–130 (2007)

Research of Ecological Landscape Assessment Systems of Road Based on GIS and ES

Fengling Wang and Yu Li

Department of Computer and Information Engineering
Harbin Deqiang Business College of Commerce
Harbin, China
J.J.Jung@hotmail.com

Abstract. With rapid development of China's road construction, road construction and its surrounding ecological landscape is not harmonious. The evaluation of the analysis, recovery and development is increasingly important issue. In view of this evaluation put forward in this paper, to apply GIS integrating with ES analyzes the applied status quo of the combined GIS with ES, applies two-way reasoning in the working process of fuzzy knowledge reasoning. Meanwhile the reliability transmits forward in the process of reasoning to realize the integration of GIS and ES. The realization of this system richens the ES theoretical knowledge, but also enlarges the Es applied fields.

Keywords: road landscape, fuzzy evaluation, fuzzy logic, expert system.

1 Introduction

Road construction plays a positive role in the national economic and social development, meanwhile, it also causes negative effect on the ecological landscape along the road such as, naked, vegetation and soil erosion, etc. It becomes a key point to make the surrounding landscape and its surrounding landscape harmonious. At present, the main resolution to solve the problem at home is to evaluate the road ecological landscape in order to reduce its negative effect on ecological landscape as far as possible. The existence of ecological depends on its properties and deep implication, but also on the subjective evaluation from watchers, in conclusion, evaluation on ecological landscape is a complicated process.

In this paper, the fuzzy logic is applied to evaluate ecological landscape, introduce some basic concepts about fuzzy logic and fuzzy reasoning, and describe the basic structure in its system. Because the evaluation on road ecological landscape is concerned about enormous fuzzy database and fuzzy rules. The paper interprets how to realize fuzzy reasoning and how to execute multidimensional reasoning process which is based on reliability.

2 The Applied Status Quo about the Combination of GIS and ES

A. The status quo about the combination of GIS and ES

We just apply the technology of combination between GIS and ES. To the database retrieval, the simple analysis on special database and the display of output. However, it

M. Dai (Ed.): ICCIC 2011, Part II, CCIS 232, pp. 128–135, 2011.

can not resolve some problems, it can not provide sufficient support for making decision on complicated, abstract, indefinite, fuzzy and dynamic special problems. Also, it is short of abilities to process and reason. So it is necessary to introduce reasoning system processing including artificial intelligence and expert system in order to provide a method to collect, organize and employ information by imitating human reasoning, and to provide a efficient tool for conducting a comprehensive analysis and reasoning special information [1].

B. GIS and ES combined form

At present, a combination of GIS and ES into the coupling: loosely coupled and tightly coupled two forms. The following table 1 to illustrate the two ways of:

Table 1. Gis and es combined form that

Binding pattern	**basic principle**	**Whether a unified interfaces**	**Gener alizability**
Loosely coupled	**ES outsourcing the GIS and GIS knowledge means and logic. don't change the structure of GIS**	yes	easily expanded
Tightly coupled	Use ES knowledge and mechanisms for that exercise of the internal structure of GIS be reformed. inefficient	yes	difficult to extend

C. GIS and ES the content

ES the core content is knowledge database and reasoning, and the integration of GIS knowledge database — — a mode of reasoning is the present study. Knowledge is of special knowledge database the geographical information content is extremely abundant, with time and space and the natural property of the multidimensional characteristics. Geography is essential to a factor which describe the geographical landscape basis, as technology, slope, rather thick, etc. The chief factor is the time and space, function, as can be said that slope p to P=f(x, y, z, t), meanwhile x, y, z is the space coordinate, coordinates t is time. Thus, the integration of knowledge database than purely an expert system. And the GIS and ES integration in the application logic and control strategies, employs mostly certainty, logic, such as three paragraphs, abduction, law, etc.

3 Fuzzy Logic and Fuzzy Reasoning

D. Geometry samples

In the collection of classical theory, domain is to discuss the question which refers to the object of a collection of the average. Vague collection is defined as domain U={x} the collection can be of A function μA(x), μA(x) in the x and [0, 1] in the value is called the x of vague set of A subject, if the closer one of the times, x of A degree of the more on the contrary, the less. That is a domain U={x} of vague set are the elements U x has a characteristic or quality of the domain of the elements and elements are distinct, but elements x of the program is a lack of A collection is A blur set.

If U domain are limited, namely $U=\{x_1, x_2, \ldots, x_n\}$, U of any collection can be expressed as a blur :

$$A=\mu_A(x_1)/x_1+\mu_A(x_2)/x_2+\ldots+\mu_A(x_n)/x_n=\sum_{i=1}^{n}\mu_A(xi)/xi$$

Meanwhile, $\mu_A(x_i)$ is x_i of the subject of A domain. If U is the domain, U as in any assembly can be expressed as A: $A=\int_{x\in U}\mu_A(x)/x$, $\int$ is not the point is infinite, domain of a vague set of symbols [2].

E. Fuzzy knowledge signify

1) Fuzzy proposition

People in our daily life use some vague and vague concepts of data, for example, Zhangsan is a young man, he stands at 1.76m. Here, "young" was a vague idea, "1.76" is a hazy data. In addition, people a judgment on what will happen, such as: this year's summer is not too hot. Here's a good chance, using fuzzy language value "great" describes the events will not be too vague "hot" or the possibility that extent.

Contain vague concepts, vague figures, or with a certain degree of statement is called a dim view. It is generally represent:

x is A

or x is A(CF)

Meanwhile, x is the domain of variables, represented by which the property of the object is blurry; A concept or vague, with the corresponding vague set of functions and depicted; CF is the dim view of certain degrees or consequential events, the possibility of, It can be a set of numbers, it can also be a fuzzy number or vague language. Language is vague values that size, length and speed, balance, how much of a modifier, etc. Specific application according to actual needs to determine their own vague language value set.

2) Fuzzy rule

Vague form of the rule of general: if E then H (CF, λ)

Meanwhile, E is a vague statement that the vague terms, it can be made by a single vague statement that the simple terms, can be more vague to constitute a combination of both requirements; H is using fuzzy view expressed in vague conclusion; CF is blurry rules of factors, it can be a set of numbers, it can also be a fuzzy number or vague language value; λ is the rule of the threshold, rules which can be used to indicate a restriction.

F. Fuzzy matching

The rules of vague terms as it is my view, the match to the evidence is also obscure view, therefore, should be a fuzzy matching calculate two dim view similar level that matches. For example, has blurred the rules and evidence:

if x is small then y is large (0.6)

x is lesser

Meanwhile, x is the domain of a U turn, the rules of the preconditions "x is small" can be expressed in vague set A threshold, the rules of evidence λ=0.6, as "x is smaller" can be expressed in vague set B:

U={1, 2, 3, 4, 5, 6, 7, 8, 9, 10}

A=1/1+0.76/2+0.6/3+0.3/4+0.2/5

B=1/1+0.89/2+0.75/3+0.62/4+0.42/5

To determine the rules of the term can match with the evidence as required on two obscure sets A and B to the match for the delta δ(A,B), if δ(A, B)≥λ is considered A and B match.

G. With the credibility of the multidimensional fuzzy logic

With the credibility of the multidimensional fuzzy logic a model for:
rule: if $(x_1 \text{ is } A_1) \wedge (x_2 \text{ is } A_2) \wedge \ldots \wedge (x_n \text{ is } A_n)$

then y is B CF_E

evidence: x_1 is $A^{'}$ CF_1

x_2 is CF_2

... ...

x_n is $A^{'}$ CF_N

conclusion: y is $B^{'}$ CF

Equations multidimension fuzzy logic conclusion acceptable CF steps are:

First choose a combination of terms and more evidence of the match, and combination methods of vague terms of more evidence of the match for the delta δ (E, $E^{'}$), matching the method is:

$$\delta(E, E^{'})=\min\{\delta(A_i, A_i^{'})/i=1, 2, \ldots n\}$$

If δ (E, $E^{'}$) ≥λ, the rules of the preconditions can match with the evidence ; otherwise, do not match.

4 Fuzzy Synthetic Evaluation Model

Vague comprehensive evaluation model is a geographic area planning scheme to evaluate important ways, it is appropriate to directly quantify the appraisal target and not directly to the evaluation of quantitative indicators, particularly for the latter [3]. This major steps are:

(1) Invited the relevant aspects of the expert review team.

(2) A set of appraisal target system F, F=(f_1, f_2, f_3, ..., f_n), the appraisal target system of n a target. The evaluation of each indicator evaluating the scale of the set E, E=(e_1, e_2, ..., e_m), Is to each of the indices are divided into different levels and to assign a header values. Indices of the assembly may also is a multi-level present rank collection.

(3) According to expert points, establish set of appraisal target system weight W, $W=(w_1, w_2, \ldots, w_n)$, weight assembly of elements that is more, and appraisal target number of the same.

(4) Has been formulated in accordance with the four of the evaluation criteria and indicators to evaluate review. Even with the same assessment of indicators and assessment of staff in different ways. Therefore, evaluate the results can only use of appraisal target f_i to the e_i evaluation criteria to the size of the extent to which degree. This may be called for, because there is m comment, so for the first appraisal target fi have an appropriate degree of dependence to R_i, $R_i=(r_{i1}, r_{i2}, \ldots, r_{ij}, \ldots, r_{im})$, $i=1, 2, \ldots n$. The replacement scheme R_i of appraisal target the subject, you can use of matrices R_i, the following:

$$R_k = \begin{bmatrix} r_{11}^k & r_{12}^k & \Lambda & r_{1j}^k & \Lambda & r_{1m}^k \\ r_{21}^k & r_{22}^k & \Lambda & r_{2j}^k & \Lambda & r_{2m}^k \\ \Lambda & \Lambda & \Lambda & \Lambda & \Lambda & \Lambda \\ r_{n1}^k & r_{n1}^k & \Lambda & r_{nj}^k & \Lambda & r_{nm}^k \end{bmatrix}$$

In the matrix R_i, elements $r_{ij}^k = \dfrac{d_{ij}^k}{d}$,Of experts expressed the opinion of spells, d_{ij}^k alternative solutions to the appraisal target fi make the evaluation criteria to evaluate the e_i experts. Therefore, the number of values that r_{ij} f_i e_j to make the possibilities.

(5) The replacement scheme A_k of appraisal target score. The calculation formula (1):

$$S_k = R_k E^T \tag{1}$$

E^T for evaluation criteria to measure of. $S_k=(S_{1k}, S_{2k}, \ldots, S_{nk})$ A_k scheme reflects the individual appraisal target score. It can be carried out a plan for each individual appraisal target comparison, can provide much useful information for decision-making.

(6) Comprehensive evaluation, the replacement scheme A_k general points, determine the priority. If the formula (2) shown :

$$N_k = WS^T \tag{2}$$

Use N_k size, can be carried out several alternative proposals priority for policy makers of the programmer provides direct basis for.

5 The Ecological Landscape Design and Implementation of Evaluation Systems

H. Basic Structure of system

The system, which employs the module programming technology is consist of 7 parts: the man-machine interface, comprehensive database, space database, knowledge databa-se, reasoning, knowledge and explanation procedure [4]. The structure of this system employs GIS improve the systematic functions of GIS, namely, to apply intelligent control and heuristic method reasoning, make use of expert knowledge to make a scientific decision and consultation [5].

The whole system runs controlled under the main list, and 7 modules run independently, this system program Delphi 7.0 as the system development SQL Server 2000 platform for the database by GIS SuperMap Objects to support.

(1) Synthesized database is used to store the fact and something in the estimate process, such as: the beginning data, solution state, middle estimate result, presumption, destination and the final estimate result.

(2) Knowledge database is used to construct and protect the relevant expertise and experience etc. in the process of estimatation and restoration.

(3) By knowledge to obtain program, expert will input the knowledge and experience or the changed knowledge and experience to computer system, this is the process of catalogue and arrangement.

(4) Inference machine, including the rules needed in the inferring process. We adopt the mixed obscure inference by considering the clear features of estimate samples. The reason is the system will give the restoring method based on the estimation, so we have to use the con and pro — —two mixed methods.

(5) Database in the space is the process of storing the graph of research area in the computer by electric map, by giving the estimation and restoration, according to the estimation and restoration plan, putting the changes in the space database, finally it will be shown on the electric map.

(6) Explanation process, i.e. showing the estimating process to the users by explaining program, which is useful to the expertise's in road ecological picturesque and beginning learners to learn directly by explaining the problem.

(7) The connection between human and machine, i.e. the process of translating the information inputting by expert and users to system acceptable forms, and changing the information from the system to expert and users. The adopted system is the friendly connection between human and machine.

I. Realization of obscure inference machine

Because of immense obscure rules in this system, such as "if the forestation is full of the two sides of the road , so we will have a good environment, and the estimation result will be 5" etc. and the result is composed of estimation on the seed of the trees both on the two sides and many estimated aspect to the inferior aspects. Each inferior status will have a different importance on the estimated result. So we need complete analyses to all inferior items and finally concluded the final estimation. This ES can be divided into the following parts"

1) The formation of inference machine

This inference is based on the knowledge, i.e. choosing information and using the information to solve the problem. Here information database and inference machine is the basic and core of knowledge inference [6]. The knowledge involved in the inferencing process can be divided into 6 parts. Natural data: data being entered into the natural database. Sample database: final data or instant data by analysing the math's sample by using the basic sample; exchanging data: data requiring in the operation of inference machine; dynamic data: the middle result in the matching of inference machine, they are put in dynamic buffer. It is used to inferencing or explaining the inference result; space data: showing various geographical elements by graph; multimedia data: it is useful for analysing the situation which users and experts are in vividly and objectively.

2) The process of inference

The working process is to match the fact from input of the screen and find the right rules from the knowledge database. Choosing all the rules of success and calculate the credible element. Finding the strategy to diminish the conflict to choose the rule and credibility amount which are not contained in the synthesized database, as the new fact and credibility of the fact to the synthesized database, and putting the estimated mark to the inference machine oppositely to get the relevant result, inspiring the machine will use the estimated result as the information for solving the problems for the decision-makers.

Inference process is a process of solving the problems, the quality of solving the problem and the efficiency of it rely on the strategies used on solving the problems, that is the control strategy of inference. We use two inference methods in the working process graph in this system, that is inference process positively and inference process oppositely. The positive process is to use the former rule to match the current content in the database. If we have many rules to choose from , we just choose one of them by using the conflict solving strategy. And adding the result to the synthesized database until the solution of the problem or no using of the rules. The inference process oppositely is to match the later part of the rule to the current content in the database, if we also have many rules to choose from, we choose one of them by using the conflict solving strategy. Adding the former part of it to the database, until we solve the problem or no available rules ,then the inference is finished.

3) Realization of the combination of GIS technique and ES technique

In the process of obscure estimation of system, expert will choose the numbers of the experts by totally knowing the multimedia information on the spot , relevant information in the space and natural element information. This choice will affect the numbers of experts in the marking process later, then choosing one or many of the choices. Protection degrees will change together with the choices. This system is decided by the fixed 5 types of roads and the outer styles of ecological picturesque.

6 Complimentary Close

The combination of GIS and ES will not only strengthen and perfect geographical information system, expert system and system function, but it will also provide scientific decision and consultation, giving perfect space information data for the application of expert system.

Acknowledgment. The author thanks to the support from the Project of Science and Technology Research Financed by the Education Department Heilongjiang Province under Grant No.11553040.

References

1. Huang, B., Wang, Y.: GIS and ES union and its applicationare. Environmental Remote (8), 11–13 (1996)
2. Huang, Q., Zhang, Y.: Hartificial intelligenceH the development of the present situation and outlook. Coal Mining Machinery (2002)
3. Wu, H.: The road of vague comprehensive evaluation. The Road 11, 31–34 (1998)
4. Xong, G., Luo, T.: Object-oriented the expert system system. Emulation Journal (1995)
5. Tian, M., Yang, B., et al.: Geographical information system. some study. Research and Design, Microcomputer Applications (2003)
6. Zhu, W., Zhu, M.: High-grade highways environmental appraisal method to study landscaping. Xi'an Road Traffic University Journal 19(supplement), 29–30 (1999)

The Measurement of Coordination Degree between Manufacturing and Logistics—Based on Gray Correlation System Model

Jian-Liang Peng and Kuai-Juan Zhang

College of Computer & Information Engineering
Zhejiang Gongshang University
Hangzhou, Zhejiang Province, China
caolb89@gmail.com

Abstract. Coordinated growth of manufacturing and logistics industry has become an important issue in the sustainable development of a city. The article firstly builds manufacturing and logistics system in index system, and then, with the application of gray model, makes a quantitative analysis of the degree of logistics coordination between manufacturing and logistics industry during 2000-2008 in Hangzhou. It finds that the coordinated development of manufacturing and logistics are in the critical state between coordination and lack of coordination. These conclusions are of practical significance.

Keywords: Coordination degree, Grey Relational Model, manufacturing industry, logistics industry.

1 Introduction

Manufacturing industry is the pillar industry of China's national economy, it is also the base needs of logistic socialization. Logistics is an important manufacturing service industry. It plays an important role for structural adjustment of manufacturing and industrial upgrading. Manufacturing and logistics industry has high degree of association and great space of coordinated development. In recent years, research on coordinated development of manufacturing and logistics industry has been proposed as a new hotspot. Many scholars at home and abroad put forward a number of related research methods and practical countermeasures.

Riddle[1] has proved manufacturing and production service relationships in his theory. Clifford F·Lynch[2] studies the logistics outsourcing from the aspects of logistics supply and logistics needs, then analyses the reason of logistics outsourcing. Joel D·Wisner, G·Keong, Leong, Keah-Choon[3]propose that using a third-party logistics provider can help enterprises to gain a competitive status in business. Companies do not need to make a special focus on supply chain management, but to put more resources into their core competence. Ye Mao -sheng[4]makes a comprehensive analysis on general mechanism of the role of modern logistics for upgrading manufacturing industry from enterprise and industry level, and points out that manufacturing and logistics should develop harmoniously to improve the logistic

M. Dai (Ed.): ICCIC 2011, Part II, CCIS 232, pp. 136–142, 2011.

level of manufacturing. Liu Juan[5]has pointed out that there is an ongoing two-way interactive relationship between manufacturing and logistics industry: manufacturing industry provides facilities and technical basis for the logistics industry, and logistics industry provides production services for the manufacturing industry. Zheng Ji-chang[6] takes Zhejiang Province as an example, discusses that the construction of advanced manufacturing base must be coordinated with service-supported industry to form an overall effort, so as to maintain competitive advantage.

At present, the weakest part of Hangzhou manufacturing competitiveness is not the manufacturing process itself, but the lack of international standard production service system, such as logistics services, etc. The coordinated development of manufacturing and logistics industry has become an important issue in the sustainable development in Hangzhou. Based on this condition, the article, with the application of grey correlation theory, makes quantitative analysis of the correlation between manufacturing and logistics in Hangzhou, and hope to reflect the coordinated state between the two through quantitative analysis, to provide quantitative basis in the way of looking for countermeasures of coordinated development.

2 Grey Relational Model of Manufacturing and Logistics Industry

2.1 Research Methods

Coordination degree is a measure of the degree of harmony with one another between systems or system elements within the development process, it reflects the trends of system from disorder to order, it is the quantitative indicators of how well the coordination situation[7].As we all know that manufacturing and logistics industries are systems containing multi elements. These two industries and its elements have already formed a complex, interrelated and interactive relationship. Through researches home and abroad, this paper uses a comprehensive multi-factor interaction analysis system which is called grey relational analysis, this method holds that: if the two factors change following the same trends in the system development process, then it can be called a high degree; On the contrary, it will be called a low degree[8].

2.2 Construction of Gray Correlation Model

Establish Master Sequence and Sub-Sequence:

$$x_i^{(t)} = \{x_i^{(1)}, x_i^{(2)}, x_i^{(3)} \cdots, x_i^{(k)}\} \tag{1}$$

$$y_j^{(t)} = \{y_j^{(1)}, y_j^{(2)} \cdots y_j^{(k)}\} \tag{2}$$

The original indicators of non-dimensional treatment:

In order to eliminate effects of magnitude and unit difference, we make initialization treatment to the original indicators, namely:

$$Z_{ij} = (X_{ij} - \overline{X}_{ij}) / \sigma_{ij} \tag{3}$$

Z_{ij} is the value of standardized indicators, x_{ij} is the original value of indicators, $\overline{X}_{ij}$ is the average value of indicators, σ_{ij} is the average value of standard deviation.

Calculate Difference Sequence:

$$\Delta_{ij}(t) = | Z_i^x(t) - Z_j^y(t) | \tag{4}$$

$$\Delta_{ij} = \{\Delta_{ij}(1), \Delta_{ij}(2) \ldots \Delta_{ij}(t)\} \tag{5}$$

$$\Delta_{\max} = \max_i \max_j | Z_i^x(t) - Z_j^y(t) | \tag{6}$$

$$\Delta_{\min} = \max_i \max_j | Z_i^x(t) - Z_i^y(t) | \tag{7}$$

$Z_i^x(t)$、 $Z_j^y(t)$ are the standardized indicators value of logistics and manufacturing indicators.

Calculate Association Coefficient:

$$\xi_{ij}(t) = \frac{\Delta_{\min} + \rho\Delta_{\max}}{\Delta_{ij}(t) + \rho\Delta_{\max}} \tag{8}$$

$\xi_{ij}(t)$ is the association coefficient, ρ is the identification coefficient, its value is between 0 ~ 1, we set ρ =0.5 in this article. We can find that, when $\Delta_{ij}(t)$ becomes larger, $\xi_{ij}(t)$ will be smaller. So the size of $\xi_{ij}(t)$ describes the degree of influence of $x_j^{(t)}$ on $x_i^{(t)}$.

Calculate Gray Correlation Degree:

We will seek correlation coefficient matrix by average number of correlation coefficient samples, which reflects the manufacturing and logistics relationships. Through comparing the correlation by the size of R_{ij}, we can analyze the factors in manufacturing and logistics industry the close relationship between the factors level.

$$R_{ij} = \frac{1}{n}\sum_{t=1}^{n}\xi_{ij}(t) \tag{9}$$

Calculate average value of rows and columns:

On the basis of the correlation matrix, we seek their average by rows or columns [9], then we can selecte the most important factor interaction between manufacturing and logistics industry according to the average size.

$$\begin{cases} R_i = \frac{1}{l}\sum_{j=1}^{l} R_{ij} \\ R_j = \frac{1}{m}\sum_{i=1}^{m} R_{ij} \end{cases} \tag{10}$$

Calculate the coordination degree(CD,) :

To judge from the whole manufacturing and logistics coordination degree between the two systems the size, we further constructed the coordination degree between the two models:

$$C(t) = \frac{1}{m \times l}\sum_{i=1}^{m}\sum_{j=1}^{l}\xi_{ij}(t) \tag{11}$$

2.3 Select Indicators

There are varieties of factors affecting the manufacturing and logistics correlation. To study these factors, based on the actual situation and combined with choice of target system with scientific principles, practical principles, quantified principle, we select 2000 -2008 years of relevant indicators of manufacturing and logistics in Hangzhou to make quantitative analysis. The index system shown in the following table:

Table 1. Manufacturing and logistics indicators system

System level	Indicators system1	Indicators system2
Indicators of Logistics Industry	Indicators of Logistics Infrastructure X_I	Freight of rail X1
		Freight of Road X2
		Freight of Sea X3
		Number of Logistics Employees X4
	Indicators of Logistics Industry Performance X_{II}	Logistics Outputs/GDP X5
		Freight Turnover X6
		Freight Volume X7
Indicators of Manufacturing Industry	Indicators of Manufacturing inputs Y_I	Number of Manufacturing Employees Y1
		Manufacturing Investment/Total Investment Y2
	Indicators of Manufacturing outputs Y_{II}	Manufacturing Outputs /GDP Y3
		Manufacturing Added Value Y4
		Value of profits taxY5
		Overall Labor ProductivityY6

Currently, as related statistics about manufacturing and logistics is quite little, alternative calculation is made for the data that cannot query. Related data explanations in the target system are as follows: As the manufacturing added value (MAV) takes the proportion of 80% in industry added value (IAV), we use MAV instead of IAV, the proportion of manufacturing output and GDP instead of the proportion of industrial added value and GDP; At same time, because the manufacturing sector accounts for a large share of secondary industry, the proportion of the secondary industry fixed assets investment in total investment is similar to the proportion of the manufacturing fixed assets investment in total investment.

3 Analysis of Manufacturing and Logistics Coordination Development — A Case Study of Hangzhou

3.1 Correlation Degree Matrix

Based on the above modeling steps, we get correlation degree matrix R of manufacturing and logistics industry, as shown in table 2:

Table 2. Manufacturing and logistics industry correlation matrix

		Y I (0.7081)		Y II (0.6824)				$\overline{X}$
		Y1	Y2	Y3	Y4	Y5	Y6	
X I (0. 7108)	X1	0.7715	0.7018	0.6803	0.7871	0.6163	0.7653	0.7204
	X2	0.9021	0.6615	0.6491	0.7699	0.4831	0.9186	0.7307
	X3	0.7183	0.6625	0.6649	0.6513	0.6342	0.6992	0.6717
	X4	0.7792	0.6784	0.6987	0.7605	0.5769	0.8293	0.7205
X II (0. 6644)	X5	0.4683	0.4888	0.4973	0.4815	0.7045	0.4871	0.5213
	X6	0.8497	0.6504	0.6421	0.8817	0.5279	0.8371	0.7315
	X7	0.8979	0.6827	0.6834	0.8258	0.4815	0.8719	0.7405
$\overline{Y}$		0.7696	0.6466	0.6451	0.7368	0.5749	0.7726	0.6909

If $0 < R_{ij} < 1$, we can say x_i and y_j are associated, the more R_{ij} is, the more associated they are. When $R_{ij}=1$, it shows a maximum of relevance between a certain indicator in logistics and certain indicator in manufacturing.

Integrated comprehensive studies home and abroad, the article sets:

①when $0< R_{ij} \leq 0.35$, correlation degree is weak, the coordinating role between the two systems target is weak.

②when $0.35 < R_{ij} \leq 0.65$, correlation degree is medium, the coordinating role between the two systems target is medium.

③when $0.65 < R_{ij} \leq 0.85$, correlation degree is strong, the coordinating role between the two systems target is strong.

④when $0.85 < R_{ij} \leq 1$, correlation degree is very strong, the coordinating role between the two systems target is very strong.

From Table (2), the relationships among individual indicators can be seen, minimum value of correlation degree is 0.4683, and the maximum is 0.9021. Majority of coordination degree is in the middle and strong range. On the basis of correlation matrix, if we calculate the average of the row, we can get the correlation degree between various indicators of logistics industry and manufacturing industry. If we calculate the average of the column, we can get correlation degree between various indicators of manufacturing industry and logistics industry. Therefore, from Table (2), we can get that the correlation degree between indicators within the logistics industry and manufacturing is 0.5213 ~ 0.7405, that is for medium or strong coordinating effect; while correlation degree between indicators within the manufacturing industry and logistics is 0.5749 ~ 0.7726, also for medium or strong coordinating effect.

3.2 Correlation Degree Curve

Coordination development of manufacturing and logistics not only manifests in the interaction and complexity of various elements, but also in the temporal phase of development. In order to reflect the evolution trend of coordinated development of manufacturing and logistics industry more clearly, we calculate coordinated development degree of logistics and manufacturing sector according to the formula (11) in Hangzhou from year 2000 to 2008, as shown in Table 3:

Table 3. 2000-2008 coordination degree of Hangzhou's manufacturing and logistics

Year	2000	2001	2002	2003	2004	2005	2006	2007	2008
CD.	0.74	0.70	0.71	0.67	0.63	0.73	0.70	0.71	0.62

Coordination degree curve is shown in Figure 1:

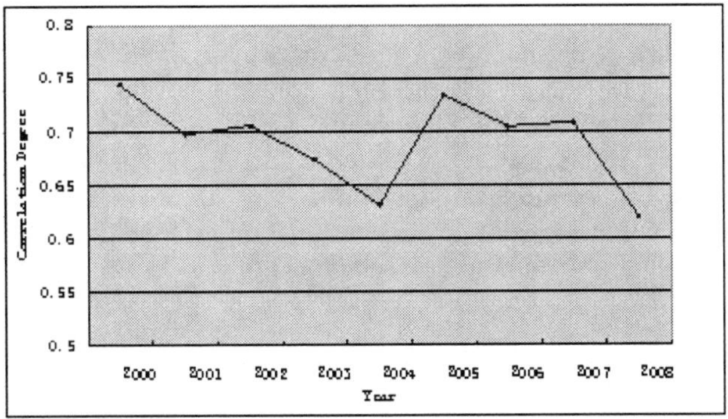

Fig. 1. Coordination degree curve of Hangzhou in 2000-2008

From figure1, we can see that coordination degree during 2000-2008 in Hangzhou between manufacturing and logistics shows significant fluctuations from 0.63 to 0.75. On the one hand, it shows the tightness and dynamic nature in coordination between manufacturing and logistics, on the other hand it illustrates that relevance degree and coordination intensity differences exist in different periods of historical development in Hangzhou. Coordinate curve can be divided into two phases according to fluctuation characteristics:

2000-2004 as the first stage, in this phase, the coordination degree of two systems has decreasing tendency, from 0.74 in 2000 to 0.63 in 2004. From the original data of Statistical Yearbook and Statistical Bulletin, it can be seen that the proportion of communication and transportation, storage and postal industry in GDP, the proportion of number of related employees, manufacturing fixed assets investment in total investment has declined during the few years. This leads to a downward trend for the coordinated degree of two systems.

2005-2008 as the second stage, it is the fluctuation period of the two systems. The development of manufacturing industry grows faster during 2004 in Hangzhou, the government increased its investment in logistics infrastructure, causing the coordination degree of two systems increased up to 0.73 in 2005. In subsequent years, because of the adjustment of national industrial policy, uncertainties of infrastructure invest and other factors, coordination degree of the two systems showed a slight change, but still remained at a level above 0.7. In 2008, as the global economic crisis spread, the manufacturing sector of Hangzhou had got great impact, the coordination degree of the two systems showed a significant of decline, down to 0.62.

4 Conclusion

Manufacturing is the main industrial activities of our national economy, is also an important source of logistics demand. With intensified market competition and national policy support, major manufacturing separates from its subsidiary business, logistics outsourcing pressure and momentum get further enhancement, manufacturing should further strengthens the cooperation with logistics industry to form a strategic partnership, coordinated development is increasing apparently. Combined with the actual situation of manufacturing and logistics industry in Hangzhou, and also with the application of gray correlation model, this paper analyzes the coordinated development of manufacturing and logistics in Hangzhou during 2000 to 2008. It finds that the coordinated development of manufacturing and logistics are in the critical state between coordination and lack of coordination. In order to promote the coordinated development of the two systems, we need to strengthen investment in logistics, grasp coordination mechanisms of the two systems correctly to promote sound and rapid development of regional economy.

References

1. Riddle: Service-led Growth, The Role of the Service Sector in World Development. Praeger, New York (1986)
2. Lynch, C.F.: Logistics outsourcing: A Management Guide. Oak Brook, IL (2000)
3. Wisner, J.D., Keong Leong, G., Tan, K.-C.: Principles of Supply Chain Management: A Balanced Approach. Thomson Learning (2005)
4. Ye, M.-s.: Modern logistics and manufacturing upgrades of interaction. Market Weekly · New Logistics (10), 62–63 (2007)
5. Liu, J.: Research on the coordinated development of the logistics service and manufacturing industries. China Logistics (2), 15–17 (2007)
6. Zheng, J.-c., Xia, q.: Based interactive service development and manufacturing competitiveness Relations - A Case Study of Advanced Manufacturing Industry in Zhejiang Province. Industrial Engineering and Management (4), 98–103 (2005)
7. Wu, Y., et al.: On the environment - economic system coordination degree. Pollution and Control (1), 25–29 (2001)
8. Deng, J.-l.: Gray theory, pp. 2–3. Huazhong University Press, Wuhan (2002)
9. Fu, L.: Grey system theory and its application, pp. 186–263. Science Press, Beijing (1982)

Studies on Prediction of Unsafe Events Caused by Human Factors in ERM

Yulong Zhan, Di Wu, Yitong Hao, and Yao Yu

Department of Marine Engineering, Shanghai Maritime University Shanghai, China
Dae-MKang11@hotmail.com

Abstract. This article makes use of a new management concept, Engine Resource Management (ERM). We researched the prediction of the unsafe events caused by human factors on the basis of the analysis of human factors in engine room. To reduce input samples the principal component analysis was led into computation before using BP artificial neural network to establish model. After the training and establishing model, insecurity events could be predicted at last.

Keywords: ERM, human factors, BP neural network, Principal Component Analysis, event prediction.

1 Introduction

Human factors cannot be ignored in shipwreck and damage accidents. Maritime accidents caused by human error account for 80% [1]. International Maritime Organization (IMO) developed a number of rules aiming for controlling human errors. To some extent, these rules reduced accidents above the sea, but the proportion of accident which caused by human errors had not changed. In shipping, the research of human factors focused on human error modeling, human factors classification, human behavior research, human reliability assessment etc. Especially human error modeling, which focuses on statistics and summary, considering few about the prediction of unsafe events carried out by human elements. Studies have shown that establishing model by using BP artificial neural network and principal component analysis can achieve a smaller error and provide data to help accident prevention [2].

2 Human Factors Analysis in ERM

2.1 Definition of Human Factors

The ways to define a human factor are various. In the theory of human safety engineering, human factors are human activities which impact goal of the system that has been set and the system structure, models. In a broad sense, human factors are all those factors that apart from all kinds of other natural factors. In this thesis, human factor in ERM is narrow, which is human factor about unsafe events in Engine Department [3].

M. Dai (Ed.): ICCIC 2011, Part II, CCIS 232, pp. 143–149, 2011.

2.2 The Inevitability of Human Errors

In Bernoulli trial, the proportion of A event is p (probability of not occur is 1-p):

$$P_k(n,p) = C_n^k p^k q^{n-k} \quad (k=0, 1, L, n).$$

The proportion of an error that will not occur:

$$P_0(n,p) = q_n,$$

Because $0 < q < 1$, this proportion is:

$$\lim_{n\to\infty} P_0(n,p) = \lim_{n\to\infty} q^n = 0;$$

On the other hand, in Bernoulli trial, the proportion of error, which might happens at least once:

$$\sum_{k=1}^{n} P_k(n,p) = 1 - P_0(n,p),$$

Taking the limit $n \to \infty$:

$$\lim_{n\to\infty} \sum_{k=1}^{n} P_k(n,p) = \lim_{n\to\infty} (1-q^n) = 1$$

It shows that the proportion of error, which happens at least once is 1. This fully explains the inevitability of human error [4].

2.3 The Law of Human Error in Engine Department

Human error "peak" often occurs in the two ends or boundary line in any work or certain activities. It showed as a "tub curve" distribution (as Figure 1)

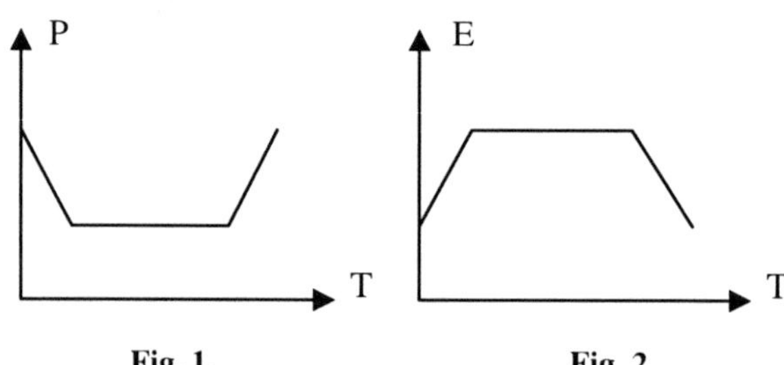

Fig. 1. **Fig. 2.**

If we regard the whole work which conducted by human labor as something consist of several parts of activity, human errors take place in the connection points of these activities. On the voyage, human errors are prone to happen on the "Tie Point". In the connection point, workers' psychological, physiological and energy concentration, or job preparation are at a relatively low. So E distribution is "inverted tub curve" (as Figure 2).

2.4 Human Factors Classification in Engine Department

From the system point of view, Human errors mainly due to the cause of psychological, physical, management decision-making and environment. Causes of human errors not only exist in the operator itself, but also in the entire system. In this paper, the factors of human errors are summarized as follows: Career adaptability factor, Knowledge and skills factors, Workload factor, Seafarer individual factors, Organizational management factor, Design factors, Factors operating and procedures, Educational training factors [4].

3 Prediction of Unsafe Incidents Based on Three-Layer BP Neural Network

3.1 Sample Data Processing

Statistical data collected from Engine Department of a shipping company show something about the factors which influenced the whole events. Because of more types of unsafe factors done by human, if apply BP neural network compute directly, network structure will be complicated and learning rate will decrease. So introduce principal component analysis could reduce the input data dimension. The data of main factors carried out by human and unsafe accidents are as Table 1and Table 2.

Table 1. Main factors carried out by human

Season / Human Factor	2007				2008				2009			
	1	2	3	4	1	2	3	4	1	2	3	4
Poor maintenance	1	3	1	0	0	0	0	1	2	1	1	0
Fatigue and stress	2	0	1	2	1	1	1	0	0	0	2	2
Violation of operating rules	2	0	1	1	0	1	1	2	2	0	1	3
Absence from duty	1	0	2	1	2	1	0	1	3	1	0	1
Lack of sense of responsibility	2	1	0	0	1	1	0	2	0	0	0	1

Table 2. Unsafe accidents

Season / Unsafe Event	2007				2008				2009			
	1	2	3	4	1	2	3	4	1	2	3	4
General Errors	9	3	6	3	6	5	3	4	7	5	4	
Serious errors	2	2	0	2	1	1	1	2	2	0	1	
Accident sign	1	2	1	0	1	1	0	0	0	1	0	
Accident	1	0	0	0	0	0	0	1	1	0	0	

As the data which has been collected not in the same order of magnitude, the data needs to be mapped to [1,-1].This will help us to improve the training speed.MATLAB provides a function of the normalized of data [6]:

[Pn,meanp,stdp,Tn,meant,stdt]=prestd(P,T) .

3.2 Determine the Parameters of the Network Structure

This paper adopted three-layer BP network with one hidden layer. Based on the results of foregoing analysis, we are able to determine the number of nodes of input layer which is 5. The number of neurons in the output layer could be determined by the number of prediction results, take 4.

3.3 BP Network Training Process

Step 1: Using a small random number to initialize the weights and threshold values of each layer, to ensure that the network is not saturate by large weighted input, meanwhile, initialize the following parameters;

- Set the minimum expected error: err_goal;
- Set the maximum number of cycles: max_epoch;
- Set learning rate of weight correction, lr=0.01-0.7;
- A cycle of training starting from 1;
- for epoch=1:max_epoch;

Step 2: Computing Network layers' output vector Al and A2 and network error E, the corresponding output sample is T;

A1=tansig (w1*p, b1); tansig is the S type activation function for the tangent;
A2=purelin (w2*A1, b2); purelin is linear activation function;
E=T-A;

Step 3: Computing the error variation D2 and Dl of back-propagation in each layer, and computing the modified value of each layer's weights and the new weights;

D2=deltalin (A2, E); deltalin is Purelin neuron's a (delta) function;
D1=deltatan (A1, D2, w2); deltatan is tansig neuron's a (delta) function;
[dw1, db1]=learnbp (p, D1, Ir); learnbp is the back-propagation learning rule;
[dw2, db2]=learnbp (Al, D2, Ir);
w1=w1+dw1; b1=b1+db1;
w2=w2+dw2; b2=b2+db2;

Step 4: Computing sum of squares of revised error again: SSE=sumsgr (T-purelin (w2*tansig (w1*p, b1), b2));

Step 5: Check that whether SSE is less than err-goal. If so, the training ended, otherwise, the training will be continued [7].

3.4 Realize by MATLAB

In MATLAB7.0, BP network's learning and training are mainly depend on inputting and calling the appropriate function. P is the input vector, T is the output vector. Take the front nine columns as the training sample data, take NO.10 and NO. 11 columns as test samples, lastly enter the last column of data to predict the probability of accident

1) Sample training. Train the input vector (9 columns) and output vectorH (5 columns):

$$P = \begin{bmatrix} 1 & 3 & 1 & 0 & 0 & 0 & 0 & 1 & 2 \\ 2 & 0 & 1 & 2 & 1 & 1 & 1 & 0 & 0 \\ 2 & 0 & 1 & 1 & 0 & 1 & 1 & 2 & 2 \\ 1 & 0 & 2 & 1 & 2 & 1 & 0 & 1 & 3 \\ 2 & 1 & 0 & 0 & 1 & 1 & 0 & 2 & 0 \end{bmatrix}$$

$$T = \begin{bmatrix} 9 & 3 & 6 & 3 & 6 & 5 & 3 & 4 & 7 \\ 2 & 2 & 0 & 2 & 1 & 1 & 1 & 2 & 2 \\ 1 & 2 & 1 & 0 & 1 & 1 & 0 & 0 & 0 \\ 1 & 0 & 0 & 0 & 0 & 0 & 0 & 1 & 1 \end{bmatrix}$$

After 1553 times computing, error reached to 0.0000000001:

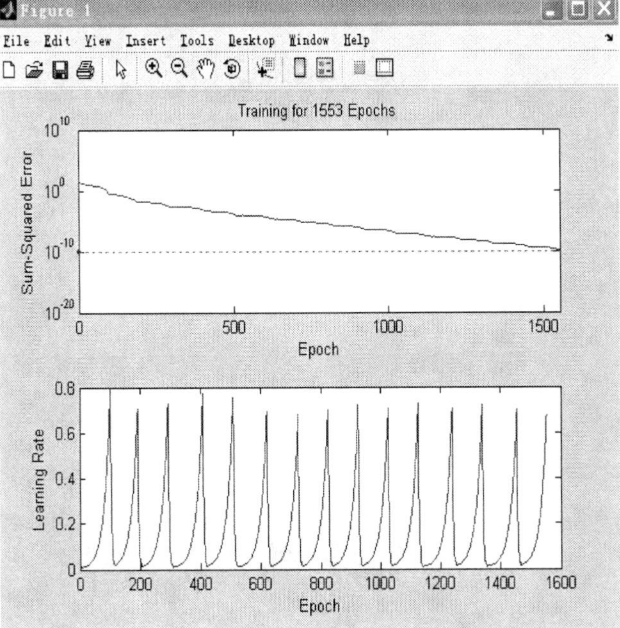

2) Test model. Test the model with10th and 11th column. Calculate the unsafe events' matrix a2:

$$a2=\begin{bmatrix} 4 & 3 \\ 0 & 1 \\ 1 & 0 \\ 0 & 0 \end{bmatrix}$$

Actual data:

$$\begin{bmatrix} 5 & 4 \\ 0 & 1 \\ 1 & 0 \\ 0 & 0 \end{bmatrix}$$

The above data suggest that the error between the data by model and actual data is very small. So we can use this model to predict.

3) Use the trained neural network to predict. Train the input vector (11 columns) and output vector (5 columns):

$$P = \begin{bmatrix} 1 & 3 & 1 & 0 & 0 & 0 & 0 & 1 & 2 & 1 & 1 \\ 2 & 0 & 1 & 2 & 1 & 1 & 1 & 0 & 0 & 0 & 2 \\ 2 & 0 & 1 & 1 & 0 & 1 & 1 & 2 & 2 & 0 & 1 \\ 1 & 0 & 2 & 1 & 2 & 1 & 0 & 1 & 3 & 1 & 0 \\ 2 & 1 & 0 & 0 & 1 & 1 & 0 & 2 & 0 & 0 & 0 \end{bmatrix}$$

$$T = \begin{bmatrix} 9 & 3 & 6 & 3 & 6 & 5 & 3 & 4 & 7 & 5 & 4 \\ 2 & 2 & 0 & 2 & 1 & 1 & 1 & 2 & 2 & 0 & 1 \\ 1 & 2 & 1 & 0 & 1 & 1 & 0 & 0 & 0 & 1 & 0 \\ 1 & 0 & 0 & 0 & 0 & 0 & 0 & 1 & 1 & 0 & 0 \end{bmatrix}$$

After 5773 times computing, error reached to 0.0000000001:

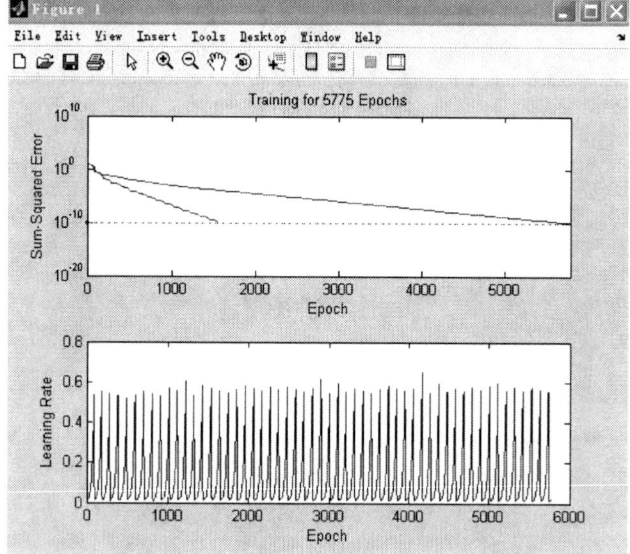

Enter the last column of data to predict the accident:

$$a2 = \begin{bmatrix} 11 \\ 1 \\ 0 \\ 1 \end{bmatrix}$$

4 Analysis the Predicted Results

The number of unsafe events in the fourth quarter of 2009 is [11, 0, 0, 1], it is more than the third season. Prediction indicates that general errors will increase significantly. So in security management, people should start from the detail and the factors of unsafe events, especially the five main factors, while improve on-site operators' vigilance and safety awareness.

5 Conclusion

Unsafe incidents' statistics show that the number of unsafe incidents is random and variable relatively with time-based within a certain range. Behind the seemingly chaotic data, possibilities of unsafe things are bound to hide some of the objective laws. Thus, from the perspective of the appropriate side, the overall level of development and trend of unsafe events can be analyzed and forecasted by appropriate mathematical methods. Effective prediction can help Ship managerial staff take appropriate measures, minimized the risk of accidents.

Acknowledgement. The authors wish to thank scientific research fund 09-22 of Shanghai Maritime University.

References

1. Fang, Q.: Bridge Resource Management. People's Transportation Press, Beijing (2006)
2. Lv, X.: Prediction of Unsafe Airlines Incident. China Civil Aviation University, Tianjin (2008)
3. Zhan, Y., Zhan, X.: Chief Engineer Business. People's Transportation Press, Beijing (2007)
4. Zou, J., Hu, Y.: Analysis of Human Errors in Shipping Damage Accidents. Academic Journal of Shanghai Maritime University (2003)
5. Yang, Z.: Studies on Human Errors and Accident Analysis and Countermeasures in ERM. Shanghai Maritime University, Shanghai (2009)
6. Pan, X., Liu, F., Wang, Y.: Venture Capital Project Evaluation Model Based on Principal Component Analysis. Technology Progress and Policy, 65–67 (2004)
7. Neural Network Toolbox User's Guide, The Mathworks (1994)

The Design and Implementation of Streaming Video Broadcast System Based on IPV6

Cai Wei, Wang Huixia, and Huang Kebin

Education Science and Technology Institute, Huanggang Normal University, Huanggang, China
luca.ml26@gmail.com

Abstract. From the campus network construction and application of teaching resources of today's streaming media to proceed, through the tunnel on the traditional IPV4 to IPV6 network of the transition network, enabling streaming video broadcast system based on IPV6 environment under the Windows Server2003 platform.

Keywords: Streaming media, IPV6, Video broadcast system.

1 Foreword

In recent years, many universities have established a strong network digital campus, full use of digital media technology on campus and campus bandwidth advantage, creating a campus video broadcast site. The campus classroom, professors lecture, students and cultural activities are extended to the campus network successfully, which greatly enriches teaching resources of the campus network of and students' entertainment.

The application of campus network multimedia has a very high demand on the stability of the transmission network, and IPV6, the next generation core Internet protocol standard, with its huge address space, optimized routing protocols, reliable QoS (Quality of Service QOS) and other advantages, ensures efficient and stable transmission. At present, the major campus network is based on the traditional IPV4 protocol, the campus network IPV4 transited to IPV6 network is a development trend and an inevitable choice of large campus network. Campus network upgrade is mainly based on dual stack and tunneling techniques, and upgraded campus network has a high degree of safety and quality of service, which provides the transmission of streaming media with a reliable protection.

2 The Concept and Application Demand Analysis of Streaming Video Broadcast System

2.1 The Related Concepts of Streaming Video Broadcast System

The concept of streaming media has broad and narrow senses, broadly sense, streaming media is the general of a series of techniques, methods and protocols which

M. Dai (Ed.): ICCIC 2011, Part II, CCIS 232, pp. 150–156, 2011.

makes audio and video media form a stable and continuous transport stream and playback stream. Narrowly sense, it is the streaming media , on Internet the client sends the streaming media requests for information requiring to wait for a few seconds to watch the video stream buffering.

2.2 The Application Mode of Live Streaming Video System

The application modes of live streaming video system in schools has mainly two kinds; one is the order flow (Progressive Streaming Transport), this transmission provides a high assurance for the quality of the video, such as video news on campus belonging to such transmission. The other is real-time streaming (Real-time Streaming Transport), it is more complex than the order flow, but it is a desirable video and audio transport protocol, because it can tolerate some packet loss. The streaming media broadcast system is used in this real-time streaming transmission. On the concrete realization of two ways as follows:

The order streaming transport, also called the web server method, uses application-level HTTP Hypertext Transfer Protocol and TCP transport layer reliable transmission protocol to respond and send program to the client. The process of concrete realization is that the original video and audio streaming is first compressed video file format, and is stored in web server, then a file that contains the URL of the web page is constructed in the web server. When a client is access to the web page, the client player will start to download the media file.

Real-time streaming transport, is also called streaming server method. It uses unreliable UDP transport layer protocol and network RTSP (Realtime Streaming Protocol) or MMS (Microsoft Media Server) and other agreements to complete the transmission of video and audio information, generally streaming media servers and web server are needed to work together to complete the flow of real-time transmission. Specific process is that collected video signal and audio signal will be transmitted to the streaming media server, the streaming media server is responsible for the analog audio signal encoded as streaming media format digital signal, generated by the video and audio streaming, or streaming media server (windows media server) the publication of the video streaming site or web server push given by the web server to publish the flow of information. The system uses a web server, a push to give way to complete the site posted video and audio information.

2.3 The Network Education Application Analysis of Live Streaming Video System

Online education refers to it that in the network environment, using one or multiple communication technology helps teachers and students of space-time separation complete a kind new personal teaching method of interactive teaching and learning of students. The most important in network teaching is that the teacher side of the multi-information (images, text, sound, pictures, etc.) is delivered to remote students sides, because of the amount of information and limited network bandwidth, so using live video streaming is no doubt a better option.

1) The use of streaming video live broadcast systems to achieve campus Internet classroom

Live in the campus classroom, the audio video equipment, firstly collects video and audio information in the classroom and transmits to the streaming media server, and then their streaming media server will release or send the encoded streaming information or push to web server release . A network client of campus Network can be live in the classroom so that students can be achieved teaching without leaving home. At the same time if the use of network technology will interconnect with campus network in the same provincial area, live online teaching between universities can be achieved.

2) The use of data synchronization to play electronic teaching plan

In the network teaching, flow of information delivered by teachers end not only has multi-media information, as well as real-time insertion of electronic teaching plan, based on windows of streaming media technology providing powerful data synchronization, that is in the video and audio time stamp information, command, URL are added, so that the computer which needs to play electronic lesson plan is established a link between the encoder, according to the time marking of video and audio electronic teaching plan spots in order to achieve electronic lesson plan and the logic of sync audio and video playback.

3 The Architecture Design of IPV6-Based Streaming Video Broadcast System

3.1 The Transition Strategy of the Campus Network from IPV4 to IPV6

As at present the number of the previous version IPV4 router used by the Internet and campus network is too large, it is impossible to change IPV4 network for the IPV6 network in a short period completely, because it needs to reconstruct large new IPV6 protocol routing equipment, increasing costs. In the current situation, combined with

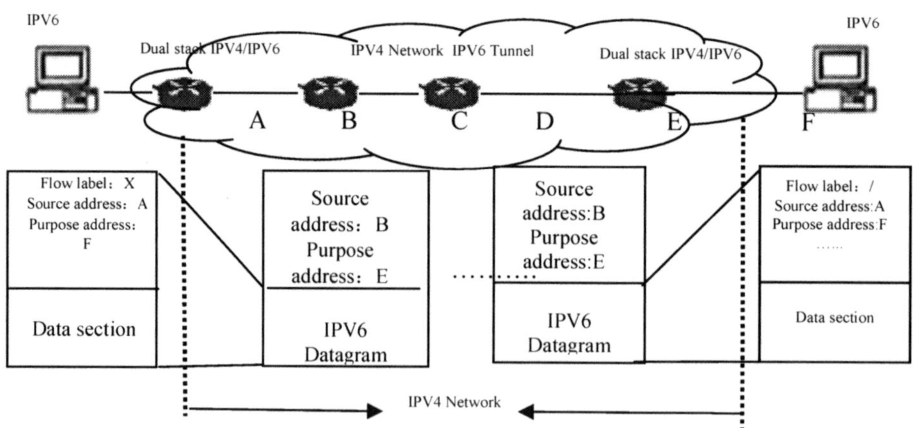

Fig. 1. Uses the tunnel technology from IPV4 to IPV6 transition

campus Network status we will take strategy of step- by- step lectures from IPV4 to IPV6 transition. Today the main campus network transition programs are dual stack and tunneling techniques. What the current campus IPV4 to IPV6 transition strategy of Normal Institutes takes is the ISATAP tunneling technology, the principle is shown in Figure 1.

When IPV6 data packet transmits in IPV4 network, the dual stack (IPV6/IPV4) router firstly encapsulates the IPV6 datagram in the IPV4 datagram, that is the IPV6 packets into IPV4 datagram data section, and then re-set the IPV4 Radical datagram protocol field value, change to 41 (41 means that the data portion of the data reported is the IPV6 data reported). When the packet transmitted to the other end of the dual-stack agreement routing, the route can identify and extract IPV6 packets of the data section of the IPV4. Then the data reported is forwarded to the appropriate IPV6 host.

3.2 Streaming Video Broadcast System

The system mainly consists of four modules, namely, acquisition module, code module, published module and receiving module. As shown in Figure 2. The system is achieved mainly based on Microsoft's Windows Media technology. Each module corresponds to a variety of videos and audio acquisition equipment, streaming media encoding server (Windows Media Encoder), streaming media distribution server (Windows Media server) and streaming media client (Window Media Player client).

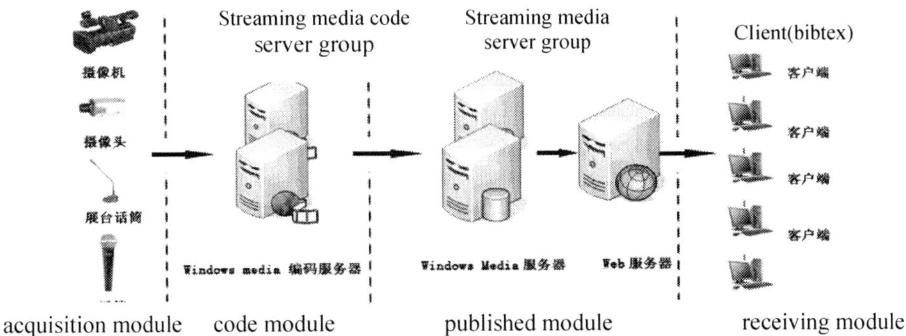

Fig. 2. Streaming media live system diagram

3) The video capture module design

Currently classroom teaching of many colleges mainly carried multimedia. Specific classroom information transmission is that the curriculum (electronic courseware) points of teachers' teaching through multi-media booth video signal to the video switcher, audio signals can be received through the microphone stand as an audio signal transmitted to the control of the way, and teachers' writings on the blackboard and video information of teacher activities can be received from the high definition camera or video camera installed in each classroom , then several ways' video and audio signal through the mixing of the video control is transmitted to streaming media encoding server as the original video and audio signals.

4) The video coding module design

The video and audio stream through the middle-control transmission is an analog signal, it needs to be converted to digital signals transmitting over the network, at this time streaming media encoding servers required streaming media encoding software and video capture card for video and audio encoding. In this system, streaming media encoding software is Microsoft's WMEncoder (Windows Media Encoder) encoder, while what video capture uses is a macro NV900_9.1 video capture card.

5) The video release module design

The streaming media encoding server will encode video and audio signal captured as video streaming signal of streaming media format and push to live video server, and video broadcast server through the Windows Media Services service sites in Windows Server2003 publishes the video and audio streaming, or the release sites are embedded into web page site to publish in web page sites' way.

6) The video receiver module design

For the client, as Microsoft operating system with Windows Media Player player, so there are two ways for access to the video broadcast site, the first is that in the address of the beginning of MMS protocol, the user enters in the client browser mms: / / IP address of server / release name, then tune out windows Media Player video player, start to be live; the other is that web-style browsing, but the premise is that video and audio stream publishes in the form of web site. Users simply enter the site in the web browser, so they are access to real-time high-definition video information.

4 The Realizition of Video Live System

4.1 The Configuration of IPV6 Network Environment

The experiment was conducted in Huang gang Normal Institute, the campus network ISATAP tunnel point IP address is 61.136.178.253. The end point router of the client setting ISATAP tunnel is 61.136.178.253. Configuration process can be divided into specific protocol configuration and network testing.

All host IPV6 protocol of video broadcast system is set as follows: Mouse Click "Start -> Programs -> Accessories -> Command Prompt", in a new opening command prompt window the following commands are executed netsh, int, ipv6, install, isatap, set router 61.136.178.253. Then close the window.

If the client is the Windows XP system, then at the command prompt, enter ping6:: 1, if the Windows 2003 system, enter ping:: 1, all cases show that packet loss is 0, installation is configured correctly.

After configuration, you can use the ipconfig / all to view IPV6 configuration information, in this streaming media, encoding server IPV6 address : 2001: da8: 300a: 1:6434:75 bb: 8b06: 7, video broadcast server IPV6 address : 2001: da8: 300a: 1:6434:75 bb: 8b06: 8, thus we complete the configuration of IPV6 network protocol.

4.2 The Implementation of Streaming Media Server

Web services can be used to publish HTML documents, and naturally video live broadcast services can be used to release streaming media files. Streaming media server, including encoding server and live server.

Windows Media Encoding Server, mainly change the file extension. avi, wav, mpg, mp3, bmp and jpg such as file transcoding into asf. wma and. wmv stream file that Windows Media Services uses.

Common streaming media broadcast live encodes the source of information, but also through the input of audio or video equipment, video or pictures and other sources of information codes operation, in order to convert them into the process of stream or stream files. Specific implementation process of encoding server is as follows: First, select the "broadcast live" incident to determine audio and video equipment, coding rate, etc., and then select the delivery method of pushing the streaming media, the live server by specified sends encoded broadcast content. After the coding, you can choose to save the news of live streaming video.

In order to put the encoded broadcast streaming media file out, it needs to publish with the Streaming Media Server. The implementation process of Streaming Media Server is as follows: Open Windows Media Services service with Windows Server, specify the server name in the list, select and enable the WMS HTTP Server Control Protocol, specify the port number issued streaming media file 8088 for the protocol, allow all IP addresses to use the protocol, you can realize stream media files live. When coding server WMEncoder start to encode, live video server under publishing point will automatically generate a live release point, this point shall be a live site.

4.3 The Implementation of Web Embedded Server

After the video broadcast site released, you can embed this broadcast live site into the web page in the web site server, what the code embedded in the main stream media uses is mainly object tags and param tags. The video object tag achieves the video embedding in web pages, param tag achieves the related properties of web page control of embedded video in the web. Param properties can be divided into the video playback controls properties such as AutoStart (Auto play), volume (default sound), Balance (channel balance), url (file address), rate (playback speed), etc., video interface control properties such as stretchToFit (ratio stretching), uiMode (display mode), windowlessVideo (full-screen mode) carrying video interface control, etc.. Main code as follows:

```
<Object id = "player" height = "223" width = "266"
classid = "CLSID: 6BF52A52-394A-11d3-B153-00C04F79FAA6">
<param NAME="url"  VALUE=
"mms://[2001:da8:300a:1:6434:75bb:8b06:8]/spzb">
<param name="rate" value="1">
<param name="volume" value="50">
......
</ Object>.
```

4.4 Receiver Implementation

Receiving terminal just follows the above method to configurate IPV6 protocol, within the campus network we can type: http:// server's IP address / publishing division in any a computer browser with IPV6 protocol to watch the video live on campus . In this study, the IPV6 address of video broadcast system access is: http:// [2001: da8: 300a: 1:6434:75 bb: 8b06: 8] / spzb. If you want to watch in any position of the public online, you needs to couple network IP address with the public server or from the firewall will map the server to the total network.

5 Summary

This paper, for the current situation and existing shortcomings of present live streaming video applications in the education system , through the tunnel from the traditional IPV4network to IPV6 network , designe and implement streaming video broadcast system based on IPV6 environment, Windows Server Platform. And in Huang gang Normal Institute campus information sources is broadcast live, experimental results show the effectiveness of the method. Following-up study can make further research for different sources (such as existing video files and Windows Desktop, etc.) live and different methods live of content distribution (such as multicast, anycast, etc.) and so on.

References

1. Khin, M.: Streaming media services in IPv6 Networks. Guangdong Polytechnic Normal University (6) (2006)
2. Lam: IPv6-based video-on-demand streaming media system design and implementation. Zhejiang Textile & Fashion Institute of Technology 8(3) (2009)
3. Wang, C., Zhao, C.-L., Qingtang, L.: Windows Media-based streaming media technology and its application in network education. Higher Correspondence Education (Natural Science) 17(6) (2004)

Government Audit and National Economic Security

Cheng Chen

Wuhan University of Technology
Wuhan, Hubei Province, China

Abstract. The fundamental function of government audit is supervision which can be described as monitoring, early warning, defense against harms and repairing in safeguarding nation's economic security.Government audit should employ scientific concept of development as guidance, strengthen the understanding on the importance of nation's economic security, and take national economic security as a permanent theme in government audit. Related institutions shouldmake good use of special audit investigation and audit notice to optimise policy audit, and explore to enhance the capacity of government audit to safeguard national economic security.

Keywords: government audit, national economic security, safeguard.

1 Introduction

National economic security is an important part of a nation's macroeconomic policy. Even though theory circle and practice circle interpret the connotation of national economic security differently (LeiJiasu2000[1] Zhang Youwen,2002[2]), the relatively consistent view is that national economic security refers to a country can use various kinds of effective measures to exempt from or decrease various threats from home and abroad and maintain the normal operation of the national economy and the capacity to achieve sustainable development. The main content include: national public finance security; national finance security; national industry and market security and national information security[3]

Facing the increasingly outstanding national economic security problem of our country, (Chen Songlin, 2003[4]; Chen Bo, 2005[5]; Zhao Xian, 2006[6]), The report of the 16th Party Congress of the Communist also mentions that In opening wider to the outside world, we must pay great attention to safeguarded our national economic security. In "The decision on issues regarding the improvement of the socialist market economic system" put forward at the 16th CPC Central Committee, comrade Hu Jintao mentioned that "we should establish and improve foreign trade operating monitoring system and balance of payments early warning mechanism system, safeguard our national economic security." In the 44th collective learning of Political Bureau of the Central Committee of the CPC on September 28, 2007, comrade Hu Jintao re-emphasized "we should effectively safeguarding our national economic security, improve the laws and regulations about national economic security, establish effective national economic security system and mechanism, enhance capacity of monitoring and early warning of national economic security as well as the capacity of crisis response and managing." Based on the social contract theory and commitement

M. Dai (Ed.): ICCIC 2011, Part II, CCIS 232, pp. 157–163, 2011.

responsibility, government audit ought to play an vital role in safeguarding the national economic security, it is an important part of our national economic security system (Tang Jianxin, 2008[7]). However, what function does government audit have in safeguarding the national economic security? How can it play its role in safeguarding the national economic security? The exist research is not deep and concrete, lacking operating instructiveness of audit practicing. Combining the practice of auditing work, this paper explored the problems such as what function does government audit have in safeguarding national economic security, how can it play its role in safeguarding the national economic security etc.

2 FontsFunction of Government Audit on Safeguard National Economic Security

The basic function of government audit is supervision, it covers the financialrevenue and expenditure of all departments of the State Council, local governments, national financial institutions and enterprises organization and their economic activities, embracing all aspects of national economic security. As the immune system of national economy and society, the supervise conduct of government audit appears in the monitoring, early warning, defense against harms and repairing in safeguarding nation's economic security. Relations as shown Table 1:

Table 1. Relations of govermet audit and national ecomic security

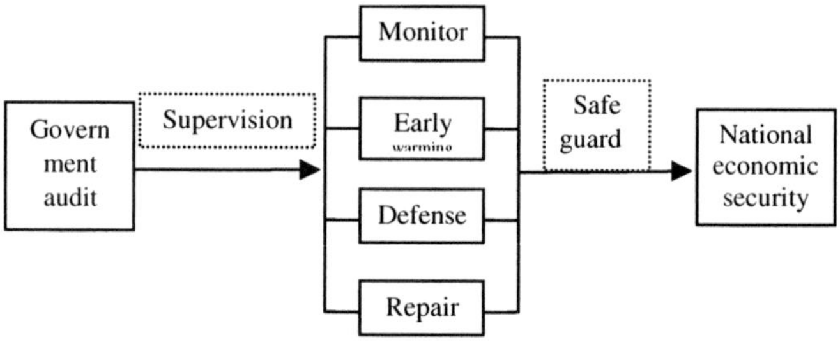

Government audit
Supervision
Monitor
Early warning
Defense
Repair
Safe guard
National economic security

2.1 Monitoring

Government audit body is both a country's economy supervisor and a huge information structure, it acquires macroscopical, medium and microcosmic economic information and other relevant information from all regions, departments, industries and units of the frontline of national economy, offering authenticity, authority and the possibility of development and utilization. Through professional, systematic and comprehensive analysis and evaluation of this information, we can discover some macro problems such as the inherent law of economy operation, common problems and economic development state, monitor all factors threatening national economic security. Through analyzing these different types of information and providing them to management and decision-making bodies, we can improve the accuracy of decision-making, discover and adjust the behaviors deviating targets and revise decision failure in good time. Therefore, government audit has strong information monitoring function in safeguarding national economic security.

2.2 Early Warning

Generally speaking, the process of continuous change in the state of economic security is often the process of slow deterioration of risk factors and acting upon the whole state of economic security. So discovering the change in the process of economic security turning to insecurity, prompting and warning this change in time and make decisive measures to turn safe is the best choice. Taking advantage of the information formed by monitoring economic activities, government auditing department can discover the factors threatening national economic security in time and exercise the power of reporting and releasing audit results according to law, build system dams of risk prevention by the authority of audit to prevent and warn national economic security.

2.3 Defensing

The risks of endangering national economic security are from various aspect,domestic, international, economic and social, we need to coordinate the various economic entities and regulatory bodies, achieve comprehensive, coordinated and sustainable economic development. Government audit can defense international market risk against spreading and transmitting to domestic to promote the healthy development of national economy by the implementation of national macroeconomic policies and the audit of effects; can regulate economic behavior by the audit of state budget execution, government fiscal and financial balance and state-owned enterprises; can prevent significant risks which may cause instability in the country and society by the audit of the industry and capital which are of vital importance to the nation's economy and the people's livelihood.

2.4 Repairing

Government audit perform their duties based on "Audit Law", supervise the operation security of the national economy, and can cross the interest's fetters between departments,industries and regions, objectively reflecting unprecedented change in the operation of national economy, prospectively reflecting various tendentious and incipient problems. With this comprehensive monitoring, on one side,we can find the defects in economic designing of relevant national economic system and economic policy-making, provide bases for government departments to repair the defects; on the other, government audit departments can also exert function of repairing by the exercising of the right of disposition and safeguarded national economic security.

3 The Rolr and Methods

3.1 Take National Economic Security as a Permanent Theme in Government Audit

General Auditor Liu Jiayi pointed out that scientific concept of audit is forming the consensus that devoting to the advancement of auditing work at a new ideology height at 2008 National Audit Conference. This requires us to employ scientific concept of development as guidance, emancipate minds, unify thoughts, forming the consensus of promoting stable and rapid economic and social development and safeguarding national economic security. First, we should form the consensus of serving for the Communist Party of China and the country's economic work. Secondly,we should form the consensus of executing of actions which break laws and regulations and economic cases clues firmly, highlight the points of audit work, and demonstrate government audit's monitoring functions. Thirdly, we should form the consensus of improving mechanism system firmly, use audit results to give full play to "immune system" functions of government audit in safeguarding national economic security.

3.2 Grasp the Focus of the Government Audit

The template is used to format your paper and style the text. All margins, column widths, line spaces, and text fonts are prescribed; please do not alter them. You may note peculiarities. For example, the head margin in this template measures proportionately more than is customary. This measurement and others are deliberate, using specifications that anticipate your paper as one part of the entire proceedings, and not as an independent document. Please do not revise any of the current designations.

*1) Around government investment security, we should to strengthen the audit supervision:*The key is to strengthen the audit tracking of project being fully funded and its management, prevent problems such as detention or retention and misappropriation or diversion, focus on investigating and dealing with developing items without considering national situations and actual conditions, illegally constructing of "two high" and the over-capacity projects and the problems like environmental pollution, resource destruction and unlawful appropriation of cultivated land caused in the construction; mainly focus on the efficiency of the use and management of construction funds, projects' quality and investment control, improving the benefits of investment. When facing huge, extraordinarily huge invest items, especially the new added central investment items to response to the global financial crisis, government should make measures of accrediting auditor and auditing regularly, implement the entire process of monitoring, prevent, disclose and defense various behaviors of breaking laws and regulations in investment construction field, effectively improve the level of investment audit.

2) Around financial security, we should to strengthen the implement of budget.: Therefore, in terms of audit objectives, we should change from the traditional "reality and legitimacy" to "efficiency", make efforts to explore ways of audit of financial benefit; in terms of audit links, we should change from "middle link" audit of budget execution to budgetary decision-making, the establishment of distribution and "two ends links" of final accounts, inspect the scientificity, rationality of the fixed expenditure and standard of budget and the authenticity of final accounts; in the terms of the contents of the audit, we should establish the "great finance" idea, change from general audit of revenue and expenditure of budget to the overall audit of extra-budgetary fund and government funds, We should expand the scope and object of audit which must to change general budget at the corresponding level from auditing departments to audit grassroots department; in terms of audit approaches, we should change from auditing to equal importance attached to auditing and audit investigation, strengthen special audit and audit investigation.

3) Around financial security, strengthen the financial audit.: Financial security is the first "firewall" of a country's economic security and social security, financial security audit is the content of the core functions in safeguarding national economic security. Firstly, focus on auditing of implementation situation of the financial institutions executing national monetary policy, carrying out the special audit investigations into major financial activities; secondly, attaches high attention to the quality and risk of financial assets, exposing financial institutions' problems at the aspects of "risk, management and benefit"; thirdly, attaches high attention to the economic crime cases in financial field , discover major cases clues in time, investigate and deal with the criminal acts in financial field, concerned about the creation of efficient, safe, steady financial operation mechanism, in order to creat a favorable financial environment for government macroscopic intervention. Fourthly, put forward some constructive comments in system and mechanism when facing problems of auditing, promote the construction of finance and legal system, and promote government financial supervisory authority to prevent from financial risks effectively, ensure the country's financial security.

*4) Around social security, we should strengthen audit supervision of people's livelihood funds.:*Government audit must establish the concept of people-oriented audit and increasing the audit supervision power of people's livelihood funds in order to play a greater role in safeguarding national economic security. Therefore, government audit should focus on the audit of people's livelihood funds and the major livelihood projects; focus on fiscal fund for assisting agriculture such as direct subsidies on farming, supporting housing invested by government, a minimum standard of living for urban and rural residents, the construction of county's and town's health care system, the investment and management situations of potable water security; focused on investigating and dealing with the problems like misappropriation, fraudulent applications and claims, loss and waste, corruption, destruction of resources and serious environmental pollution.; focus on revealing the outstanding problems like fulfilling national policies inadequately, not achieving the policy target and severely affecting and harming the interests of the masses, implement the policies benefiting people in real earnest, creating a good environment for the stable and rapid economic and social development.

5) Around the industrial safety and security of state assets, we should increase the intensity of audit supervision of state-owned enterprises.: Through the audit of the energy, equipment manufacturing and public infrastructure of state-owned enterprises which is related with the national economy and the people's livelihood, government audit departments should evaluate its effects on national political security and economic security, monitoring the security situation in important industries, ensure the security of the important national economic departments and the core industries. Based on the authenticity of audit of financial income and expenditure, we should focus on the audit supervision of management decision, asset acquisition, bulk purchase, new added investment project and big property transactions of state-owned enterprise, preventing the loss of state assets. Focus on auditing and supervising the hedge and increase of the assets in value of state enterprises, reducing the serious loss state-owned assets in property transactions. Focus on ascertaining the current operating status of state enterprises, the use efficiency of state-owned capital and the situation of maintaining and increasing the value of state assets.

3.3 Improving Capacity and Level

*6) The innovation of audit concep:*Concept is the forerunner of world outlook and behavior. Currently, we should establish three new concepts: the concept of employing scientific concept of development as guidance, coordinating the development of auditing work, give full play to "immune system" functions of government audit; the concept of taking nation's economic security as a permanent theme in government audit, always keeping authentic,lawful and effective in safeguarding national economic security; the concept of dialectical thinking, playing a role in safeguarding national economic security and improving capacity and level of safeguarding national economic security. In these three concepts, doing audit work by scientific concept of development is the core, which requires us to understand that the most important task is safeguarding national economic security, increasing the initiative, macroscopy, constructiveness, openness and scientificity of audit work; requires government audit be compatible with the whole development of national economy and society, be compatible with the course of construction of democracy and legal system, be compatible with audit management, constructions of audit institutions and audit business; requires us to use the scientific concept of development to realize the law of audit work and grasp the nature of audit, develop audit system with Chinese characteristics continuously, adhere to the line of audit with Chinese characteristics and play a role in safeguarding national economic security.

*7) The innovation of audit technology:*With the rapid development of modern information technology, government audit plays an important role in safeguarding national economic security, but has been profoundly affected by the development of informatization in audit range and audit method. Computerized auditing is the major method of modern audit, the important technology support of playing "immune system" function and serving national economic security. Currently, we should take the opportunity of phase II of "China's Golden Auditing Project", put emphasis on accelerate network construction, promote audit data center construction, achieving resource sharing. The innovations of computerized auditing, focus on implement the network audit system which is predominant by budget implementation audit while develop other audit cooperatively. Concentrate on this crucial point, on the principle of advancing step by step, focusing on key points, .emphasizing practical results, promote audit organization management of big audit project in the condition of informatization. At the same time, promote the operation of OA and AO system in audit engagement and management.

*8) The innovation of audit management:*The innovation of audit management is the important factor in promoting the scientific development of the audit work, and remains throughout the audit activity. Combining the need of safeguarding national economic security and the practice of audit institutions, the innovation of audit management should be developed from four aspects:Firstly, we must regard taking full advantage of audit resource as objective, innovate the audit organization management, resolve the problems of optimizing human resource. Secondly, we must take developing audit work scientifically as objective, innovate the management of audit projects. Thirdly, we must take developing the control of audit quality and prevention of audit risk as objective, innovate audit business management.Fourthly, we must taking applying audit results as objective, innovate audit information management.

9) *The innovation of audit theory:*According to the opinion that government audit is the "immune system" of the health of national economic security, how can government audit improve the level of quarantine, prevention and immunity? How can government audit keep a close watch on public finance, finance, people's livelihood, state-owned assets, energy, resources and environment and information from the independent, impartial and objective aspect? How can government audit play the inherent "immune" function in the inner part of government? In view of the problems like breaking laws and regulations, economic crimes, ruining resources, environment pollution, dangering national security and destroying democracy and legal system, how can government audit put forward constructive suggestions at the strategic height of safeguarding national economy security? How can government audit improve its "immune" function to prevent audit risk? Only by exploring and innovating in theory can government instruct audit practice better; only by innovating and deepening in theory can government audit function better in safeguarding national economic security.

References

1. Lei, J.X.: Theories and Methods of national economic security. Economic Science Press (2000)
2. Zhang, Y.W., Zhou, J.M.: Economic Security—The challenges of financial globalization. Shanghai Academy of Social Sciences Press (2000)
3. Patrick, J.D.: Economic Strategy and National Security: A Next Generation Approach. Westview press, Boulder (2000)
4. Chen, S.L.: Study on China's Financial Security Problems. China Financial Publishing House (2003)
5. Chen, B.: Comment on the Strategic Resources and National Security. China's Military Science 18 (2005)
6. Xian, Z.: Financial Security Problems and Security Measures in open economy. Modern Finance: Tianjin University of Finance 2 (2006)
7. Tang, J.X.: Government Auditing and national economic security, Theoretical basis and the role of path. Auditing 5 (2008)

A Metadata Management Model-Oriented Data Resource Planning and Application

Xiaojun Liu, Lianzhong Liu, and Qian Yang

School of Computer Science and Engineering, Key Laboratory of Beijing Network, Technology, Beihang University, Beijing, China
llsun1964@163.com

Abstract. To eliminate information silos, effective organization and management of metadata which describes the structure of data resources as well as tracking the changes of application data model are of great significance. This paper proposes a metadata management model, which tracks the entire life cycle of metadata, manages the existing information-coding standards, the data model of application software and the relationship, reach to make full use of achievement of data construction.

Keywords: Metadata management, resource planning, metadata application, version management.

1 Introduction

With the rapid development of information technology, most of corporations and institutions developed and applied various relational database-oriented application systems. But, the overall construction and application levels of systems are still not high, so are the levels of system integration and resource sharing. This issue deprived from that the database used by many databases didn't coincide with knowledge processing. it means that information systems resource structure is inconsistent with code standards. So it leads to kinds of information systems can not cooperate with each other. Data models of functional type systems and integration metadata of context knowledge environment play an important role of database management and information resource management. [1] The metadata which is used to describe data resource planning based on the information integration, sharing and exchange around organizations, meanwhile, it is the rules that functional system models should abide by. However, the application metadata which is used to describe functional system models is the foundation of evaluating, improving on and maintaining systems.

Metadata management has become a research hot spot in the field of software engineering, and one of the crucial technologies that realize information sharing and effective using of information. [2] This paper focuses on data resource planning and application metadata management model. The first part introduces related research. The second part introduces a kind of metadata management model that be proposed in this paper. The third part shows that metadata management model is applied to unified database security console (UDC). Finally, some concluding remarks and future works are mentioned in part 4.

M. Dai (Ed.): ICCIC 2011, Part II, CCIS 232, pp. 164–171, 2011.

2 Related Works

As metadata and metadata technology plays an important role in the data definition, description, using, sharing and document management, the formulation of a variety of metadata standards and the establishment of metadata system is very popular to international software engineering technology, particularly it becomes the core to establish large network information system. At present, several of industries and sectors at home and abroad have formulated metadata standards. More famous of all are the U.S. Federal Geographic Data Committee Spatial metadata content standards [3], NASA's Directory Interchange Format and the UK Dublin Core metadata standard Dublin Core [4].

Metadata are widely used in foreign countries, such as the United States Education Information Gateway (GEM), the European digital library and electronic resources, the Nordic Web Index (NWI), they are all successful example that metadata was applied in different fields. There are some famous generic metadata management tools like ASG's Rochade tools, Multistage tools developed by Ascential, Metacenter tool from DAG (Data Advantage Group) Company, their common defect is in short of safety control mechanisms and version tracking of features basically.

There are also a number of related metadata management systems or tools developed by domestic organization. Computer Network Center in Chinese Academy of Sciences developed the "Universal Data Management Tools" [5], "eco-metadata management tool", "Geographic Information Metadata System" researched and developed by Department of Computer Science and Technology in Peking University [7], Northeastern University Computer Architecture Research Institute developed "NEXT metadata management system" [8].But, most of which are industry-specific standards tools, so the function is simple and range of applications is limited, data resources can not be applied in the planning and management of unified data model. Moreover, Shengda Technology Co., Ltd. a professional computer in Shenzhen planning software tool data, "metadata management tool (MMT)" [9] is also a domestic generic metadata management tool, which provides business analysis, data analysis, and master data management. Kim Shin bridge TBSMDS metadata management system provides all kinds of metadata and object data editing, management, proofreading, but both of them lack change tracking based on metadata and version control of master data standards.

3 Metadata Management Object

3.1 Definition for Data Planning and Application Metadata

Metadata is "the data about data", it is the description information about data and information resource, and the key factor of managing information resource effectively [6]. Data planning and application metadata is one of subset of metadata, to serve as service information standard program and data model of functional application systems.

Data planning metadata is the description information about architecture framework for data planning information and mapping express the philosophical business entity world. Application metadata is the description about physical database structure, and abstract the database structure in functional application systems to heaven.

3.2 Component of Data Planning and Application Metadata

The data planning and application metadata are not only different, but also have relationship, which lead to the diversity and integrity of metadata. The data planning and application metadata divided into three levels, the metadata in data planning/application level, the metadata in information set/table level and the metadata in attribute/field level(shown in the figure 1).

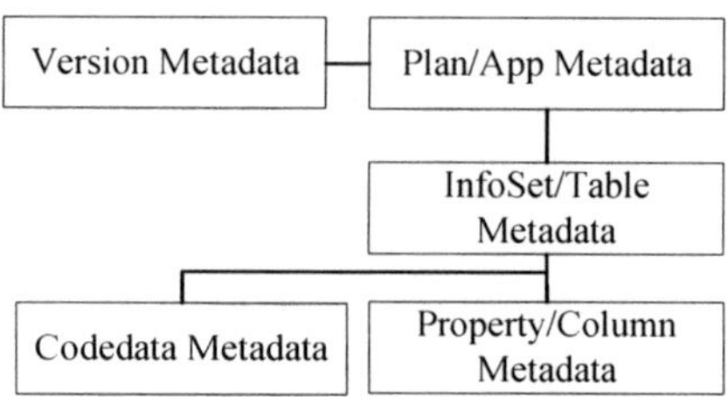

Fig. 1. Metadata level

- The metadata in data planning/application level, it means the integrity description about data planning and application data, which describes the general picture of data planning and application data. The version metadata describe the version information about data planning and application database, so version process is based on the general picture in data planning/application level.
- The metadata in information set/table level, describes the information about information set/code set in data planning ,meanwhile, it describes the data table and dictionary information in application database.
- The metadata in attribute/field level describes the characteristic of data planning and application data object, including the metadata about data planning information attribute and application database tables. The code set metadata describes code information, including the standard code set about data planning and user-defined code set about application database.

4 The Metadata Management Design

4.1 How to Choose the Manage Policy

There are two policies in metadata management [7] [8]. One is to build metadata repositories, which manage the metadata access and the whole metadata lifecycle, it is a platform for metadata access and aggregation, and attributed to centralized management model. The other is to establish a means of metadata exchange, metadata in different systems can exchange each other by this way, so as to bring the distributed and heterogeneous system integration with the implementation of metadata management. Resource planning and application of data-oriented metadata management model focus on the version management for standardization of existing data standards. For application of database modeling, creating the actual physical database, and providing the assessment and reference for application software standardized, the database version of the tracking applications change, which requires metadata management and application of the database in the same interconnected network environment, therefore, it uses centralized metadata management model, shown in Figure 2.

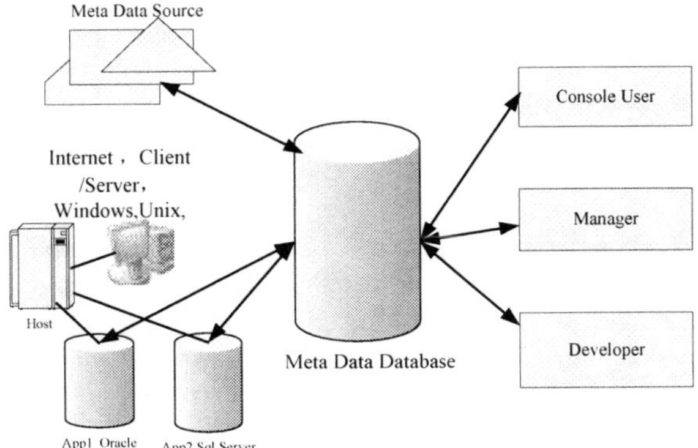

Fig. 2. Centralized management model

4.2 The Data Structure of Metadata

As the data planning metadata and application metadata have the size differences in describing information, and require to reflect the change about the version of data

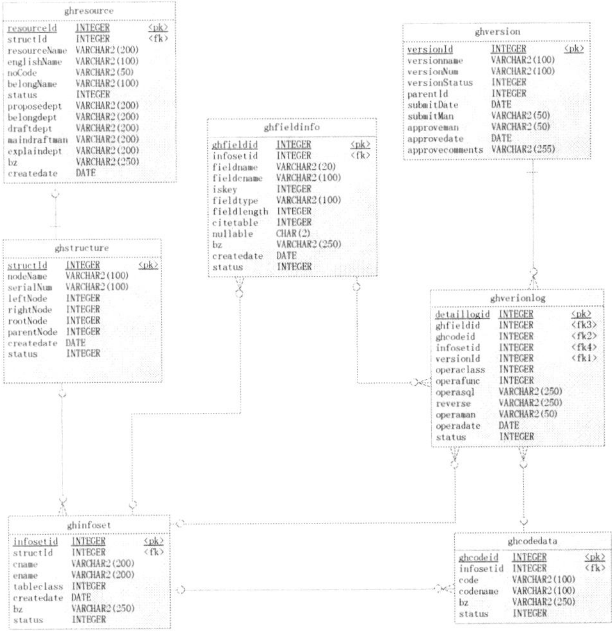

Fig. 3. Part of the datamodule

resources and the application version of the database structure,so the metadata version entity is introduced that based on hierarchical metadata version, shown in Figure 3. Metadata version information stored in the shared metabase directly, and build the appropriate view of version for data resources and database structure according to the record detail information ,so the shared metadata database only save the latest metadata information to achieve incremental version management.

4.3 The Overall Structure of Metadata Management

The data planning and application metadata management is based on that the data planning and application database structure organize, managet, publish metadata. In the process of managing data planning and applications for the metadata,which involves five components, namely, Meta Data Management Console, DataResource Register, AppDatabase Register, View Version Engine and Meta Data Import / Export, shown in Figure 4.

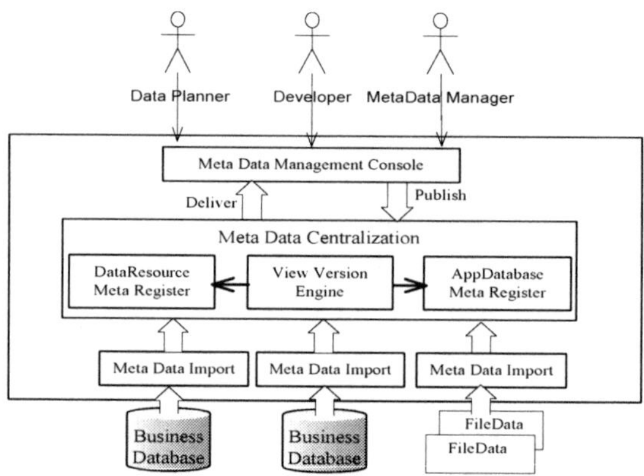

Fig. 4. Overall structure

The metadata distribution and query terminal is the main interface for resource manager, application database developers, metadata administrator, it manage the quote relationship between the application database structure and data resource standard system, access the application version of the database structure view, analyze application database meet the standard code system data resources or not. The data planning metadata registry module manage the existing built data resources and standards system, meanwhile ,it organize and maintain the investment of data, including data resources to establish, approve, publish, and then abandoned the whole process of revision and the standard code system for managing data resources. Applicationdatabase metadata registry module is key operation module for database developer, and make it adapt to the current standard system data resources, according to manage the physical model structure of application database and cite resource standards released by official data. The engine of version view is the core of data resources version and application database version of the management.Depending on the version details and the latest metadata to generate the view and the history of the state in accordance with historical versions, for users to track differences among versions.The import and export metadata modules do not only extract metadata element database into the database according to existing applications,but also make use of the formatted file data to import the metadata into the metadata database, and export data resource standard system during different periods,application database structure information and application database standardized report as needed.

5 Application of the Management Model

5.1 Introduction of Unified Database Security Enhancement System

The commercial databases used by domestic market only satisfy the national protection standard GB 17859-1999 and the second-level requirements of GB / T 20273-2006, but it can not satisfy the requirements to protect secret information classification [9]. Unified database security enhanced system passes the second-level requirement , it protect the database synthetically from account management, authentication, rights management and security auditing, to achieve "three separate"of competence, and cross-database management, in order to enhance the safety and reliability of database management , the overall structure as shown in Figure 5.

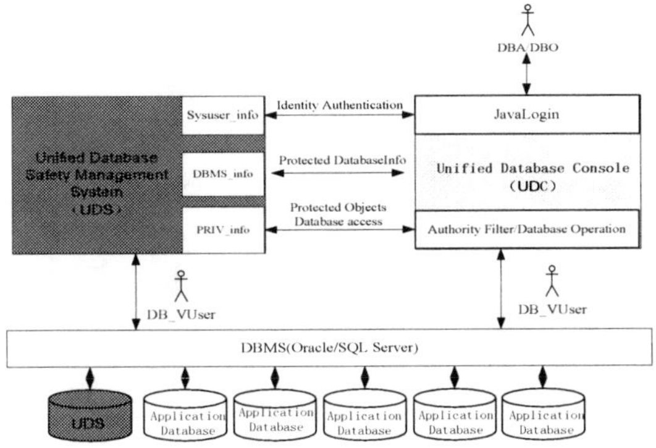

Fig. 5. Unified database security enhancement system structure

Unified database console(UDC) is a part of unified database security management system, it provide the user interface for the operator to authorize the application database, the specific function of which include: database management, database monitoring and metadata management. Database management include the maintenance of business data, scan and authority management business table structure .Database monitoring include the current running status and tuning the database status report management. Metadata management include the application database systems registration, application database version management, application database standardized assessment, data resources registration and version management.

5.2 Subsystem of Meta-data Management

Metadata management subsystem is the organic component of the database console (UDC), including data resources, database management and application metadata management, shown in Figure 6. Metadata management is consisting of three components: the Meta interface package lied in the layer responsible for interface control deployment, the data planning management package and the application Meta management. Meta-data management subsystem and the UDC's interface components shown in Figure 7. UDC provides data storage interfaces, log audit interface, and permissions granted to interfaces for metadata management system. Metadata management provides metadata import and export services, management services of data resources standards, application services, version view services and navigation services for application databases. Import / Export service mean that it initialize the application metadata and standard data resources and provide report for outputting.

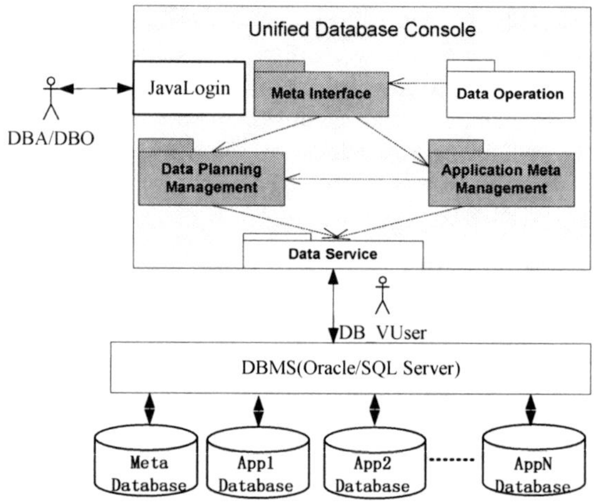

Fig. 6. Metadata management sub-system diagram with UDC

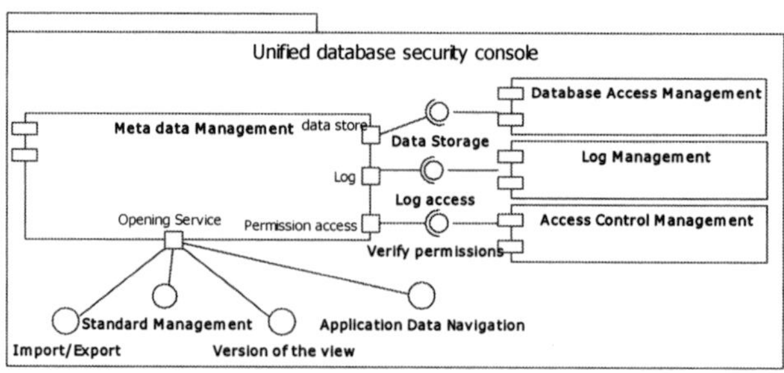

Fig. 7. Metadata management sub-system components

Meanwhile, it also track the version of evolution, standard management is in charge of standard code system management for data resources; version view tracking record the change about application database and data resources standard system to provide views of data during the different periods; application database navigation element can be used to generate the navigation tree catalog consistent with business organizations according to the stored database metadata, and to provide the other modules for database console.

6 Conclusion

The metadata management tools-oriented data resource planning and application provide the of version control during the whole process ,including the development of standards, audit and proof, the data resource standard release, it includes from the establishment of functional data model, modified to upgrade, to the application database assessment of the version management during the whole process .It provides the efficient programs for the data resource management and the management of functional data model , besides it improves the application value of construction of functional systems and makes use of the established value of data resources.

Acknowledgment. This work has been supported by Co-Funding Project of Beijing Municipal Education Commission under Grant No. JD100060630.

References

1. Poole, J., Chang, D., Tolbert, D., Mellor, D.: Common Warehouse Metamodel Developer's Guide, ISBN: 0-471-20243-6
2. Bouziane, M.: Metadata modeling and management, p. 18. Rensselaer Polytechnic Institute, Troy (1991)
3. Federal Geographic Data Committee. FGDC-STD-001-1998. Content standard for digital geospatial metadata. Federal Geographic Data Committee, Washington, D.C (June 1998) (revised)
4. Version 1.1, Dublin Core Metadata Element Set (January 14, 2008)
5. Electronic Publication: Digital Object Identifiers (DOIs): Article in a Journal
6. Chawathe, S., Gaarcia-Molina, H., Hammer, J.: The TSIMMIS Project:Integration of Heterroteneous Information Source. In: Proceeding of IPSJ Conference, Tokyo, Japan, pp. 7–18 (October 1994)
7. Object Management Group (OMG):Common Warehouse Metamodel (CWM) (2000), http://www.org/cgi-bin/doc?ad/2001-02-01
8. Harris, H.: What is CWM. IBM Corporation (2000)
9. Database Security—Concepts, Approaches, and Challenges Elisa Bertino. IEEE Transactions on Dependable and Secure Computing 2 (2005)

The Streaming Media Based Design of VOD System

Wang Huixia[1], Liu Zhibing[2,*], He Fang[3], and Cai Wei[4]

[1] College of Educational Science and Technology, Huang Gang Normal University, Huangzhou, China
[2] College of Mathematics and Information Science, Huang Gang Normal University, Huangzhou, China
Tel.: + 86-132-17256167; Fax:+86-713-8621649,
lzb8401552@hgnu.edu.cn
[3] College of Educational Science, Shan xi NormalUniversity, xi'an, China
[4] College of Educational science and Technology, Huanggang Normal University, Huanggang, China
380282773@QQ.COM

Abstract. This thesis took the streaming media technology as the starting point, stated the work principle of the streaming media based VOD system, put forward the design scheme of the whole structure, hardware structure and database structure of streaming media based VOD system .and realized the multimedia programmer watch on-demand and arbitrary broadcast, to provide users with an ordering service system which is a real-time, interactive and on-demand one.

Keywords: streaming media,VOD system, the database.

1 Introduction

With the gradual popularization of LAN, broadband Internet and the network, the network transmission no longer limits to data text and graphics, replaced by the multidirectional transmission of multimedia data gradually, the VOD system became an application hotspot. Along with the development of streaming media technology, more and more sites flow into the line of spreading multimedia audio information by this technology, providing users with more abundant contents, enriching the website, and will bring far-reaching influence to people's work and the life.

2 An Overview on Streaming Media Technology

Streaming media is using streaming transmission in Internet, such as video, audio or multimedia files. Streaming data flow can be transmitted and played at any time. Firstly, sending the first part of the multimedia documents in the network, other parts

* Corresponding author.

M. Dai (Ed.): ICCIC 2011, Part II, CCIS 232, pp. 172–180, 2011.

of the document will be sent out constantly as the first part broadcasted, and arrived timely for broadcasting [1].

The streaming media technology is a continuous real-time transmission technology bases on time, the key lies in the parallelism of network data transmission and client broadcast. The streaming media technology create a buffer in the client's computer firstly, download a small piece of data of files before broadcasting as a buffer, broadcasting program broadcasts data from this buffer and meanwhile the rest parts of the multimedia files download in the background to be filled to the buffer. So, when the network connections speed slower than actual data speed of broadcasting consumption, which can avoid the interruption, and maintained broadcast quality.

The continuous image and sound information are compressed into packages through a special way, transmitted to users continuously and real-timely by streaming service, let users watch and listen when download, do not need to download the whole compressed files to their computers. Using the streaming media technology can effectively break broadband bottleneck of low bit rate of Internet access way, overcome weakness of the download and transmission mode of files, realize the streaming transmission of multimedia information in the Internet [2].

2.1 The Making Process of Streaming Media

The making process of streaming media is a compression and code process, such as Microsoft's Media Encoder can make streaming files as WMV,ASF; And streaming Media coding tools Real Producer plus or HelixProducerPlus of RealNet company can transfer multimedia file format into Real streaming files. [3]

2.2 The Release of Streaming Media

Web page is stored in a Web server and information transmission between Web browser and server by HTTP protocol, so Web page using the address with the beginning of "http:// ", and the realization of information between Real Server and RealPlayer by using "RTSP, therefore, it takes rtsp / /" as opening address.

3 The Working Principle of the Streaming Media Based VOD System

The streaming media based VOD system consisted of streaming media server, Web server and database server three parts, as shown in figure 1 [4].

The structure of B/S (Browser/Server) is the structure of Server, under this structure; the achievement of users' interface is through the WWW Browser, and few business logic realized by browser, but the main business logic realized in Server. The streaming media based VOD system took the browser/server mode, namely the B/S model. The client can watch video online; the system is an open, flexible one.

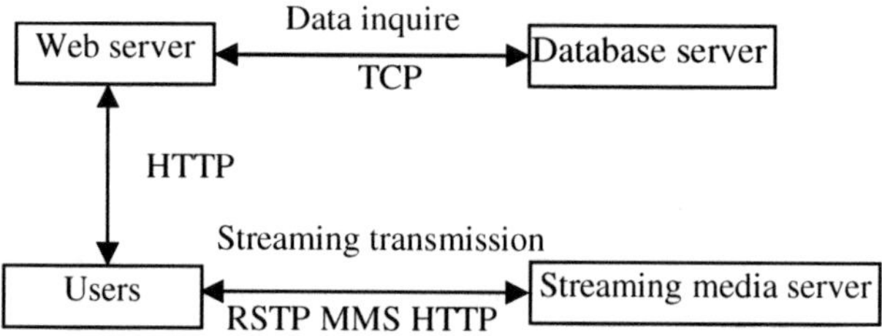

Fig. 1. The framework of VOD system

The working principle of the B/S based VOD system is to visit the Web server by browser and then returns to the URL from Web when the clients ordering; then the clients start streaming media player according to the URL programmer launched request, streaming media server accept the request, and send data, finally play on the clients' video player, finished the VOD process.

In the whole process, also need to complete necessary steps of identity authentication, access control, etc. Web server usually cooperates with database server, the database in charge for the information storage and data query etc, to reduce the pressure of Web server.

3.1 Streaming Media Server

Streaming media server is the core of the VOD system; its main functions are video storage: response to users' requests, provides stable video flow, respond to users' interaction during ordering, and undertake the control of contents access. Streaming media server requires a strong concurrent processing capability, and I/0 throughput capacities matching with the network and disk. The technological advancement and service of the whole system depends on the technology and performance of the Streaming media server.

3.2 Web Servers

The function of Web server is to provide a good interface through the website for users, easy to access video programs stored in the streaming media server.

Combining with the actual need, web design mainly realizes the following functions:

(1) Upload and management of the video program.
(2) Searching and streaming release of video program.
(3) User registration and rights management.
(4) Query and statistics of video program and users.

3.3 The Database Server

The function of the database server is complete database instructions come from the Web server, including query, adding and removing the program information and user information etc, separating the function of responding requests and data performance of Web server, reducing pressure and improving performance, which Request the database server possess a good performance, and can work stably and reliably.

4 The Structure Design of Streaming Media Based VOD System

4.1 The General Structure Design

Design of streaming media based VOD system contains four modules: user function modules, video player module, background management module, server management module. the structure is shown in figure 2. Here introduce background management module and user function module design in detail.

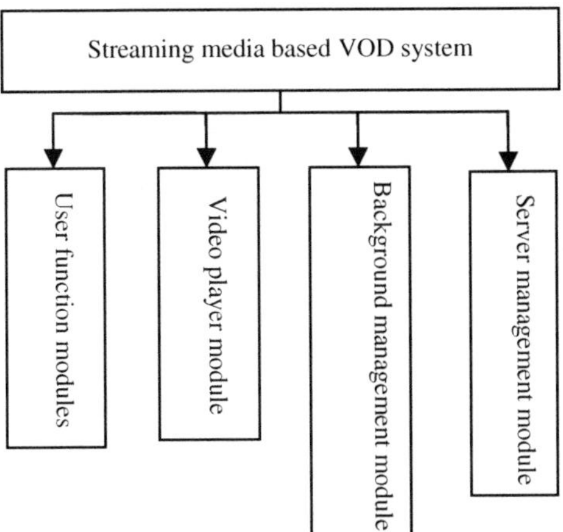

Fig. 2. Overall function figure

(1) The function design of background management module

The background function of System can be divided into four modules: video release and management sub-modules (used to manage video), registered users management sub-module (for manage and register users), administrator set sub-module (used to administrator management), system Settings sub-modules (system compound), as shown in figure 3 below.

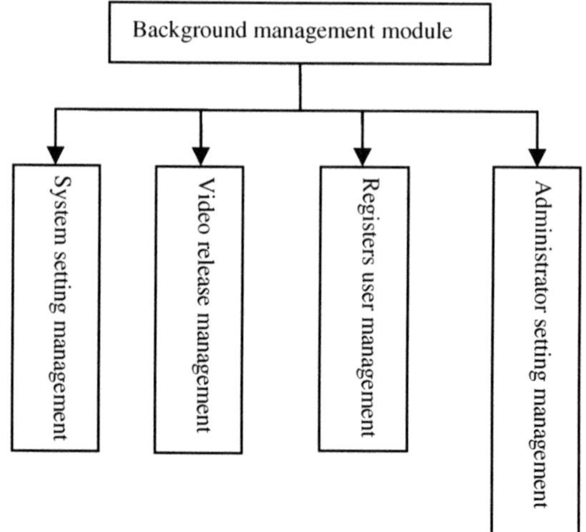

Fig. 3. Administrator function module

(2) Design of user function module

User function module consists of ordinary users and the registered user, as shown in figure 4. Ordinary users are tourists, who can register to be system users, can browse the video programs, order parts of the video programs. Registered users can log on the system for personal information changes, can upload and modify video; order and download video programs, also can comment, put forward error messages to the video programs, and finally exit system.

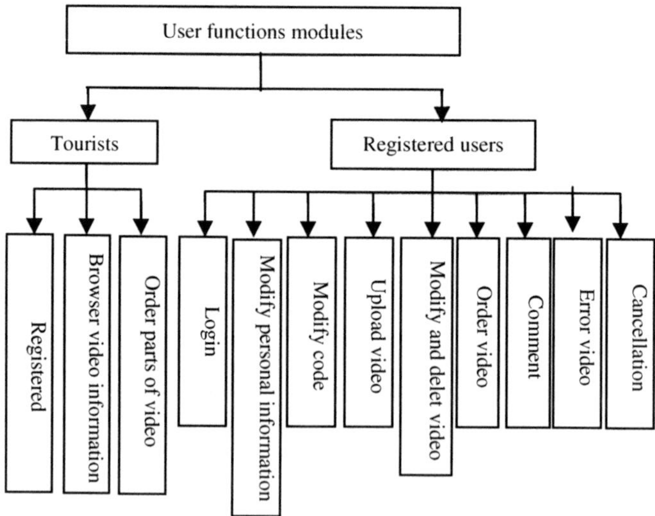

Fig. 4. User function module

4.2 The Structure Design of the Hardware System

The hardware structure Design of streaming media based VOD system consists of server, network equipment, librarian and user terminals, structure as shown in figure 5. Server composed by "streaming media server + Web server + database server", for cost saving, in general scale VOD system, these three video servers can compound as one usually, which means users can use a server to finish the work of three.

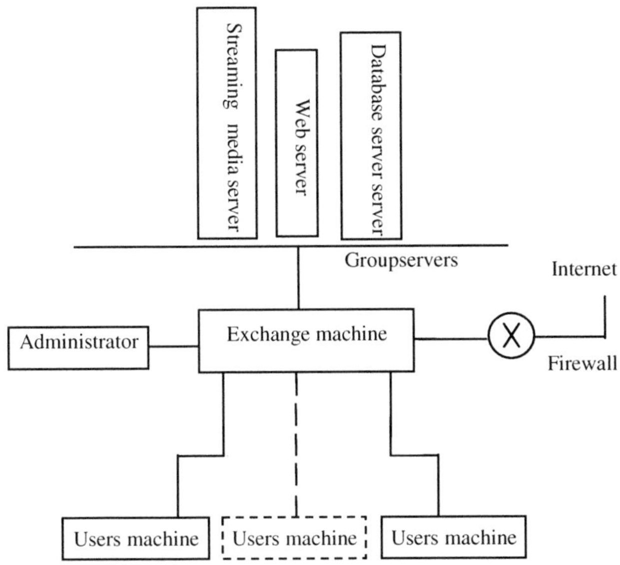

Fig. 5. Structure figure of hardware system

4.3 The Database Structure Design of System

A series of operations of users and administrator to this system are realized by Web page with database through a certain interface, therefore the database plays a very important role in system. The design of database directly affects the performance of the whole system.

In the practical application, the system takes Server2005 SQL database; this is the latest database of Microsoft.

(1) The administrator and the user e-r chart design

E-R chart is designed to abstract demands to information structure, which is the key of the entire database design.

Administrator has name and password is needed when login on, the distinction of number and rights are existed in storage, the e-r chart as shown in figure 6.

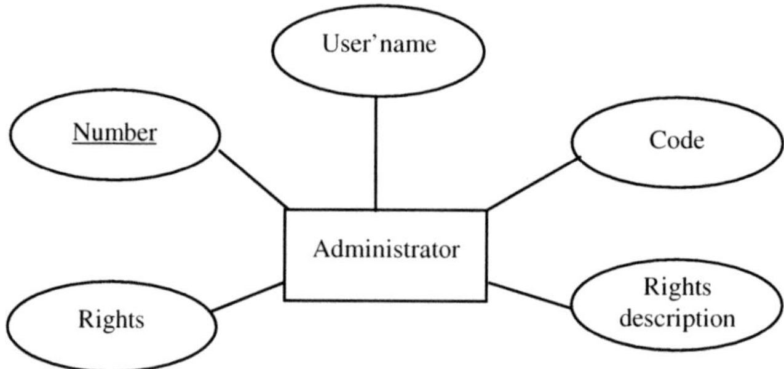

Fig. 6. Administrator E-R chart

Registration need user's name and password, user can continue to improve their information after login, such as gender, date of birth, nicknames, E-mail, QQ number, portraits, registration time, buddy list. in addition, login time will be reserved, there are other different privileges, such as users can write words what he or she likes. When user does things illegal his o rher account will be frozen, the user's e-r chart shown in figure 7.

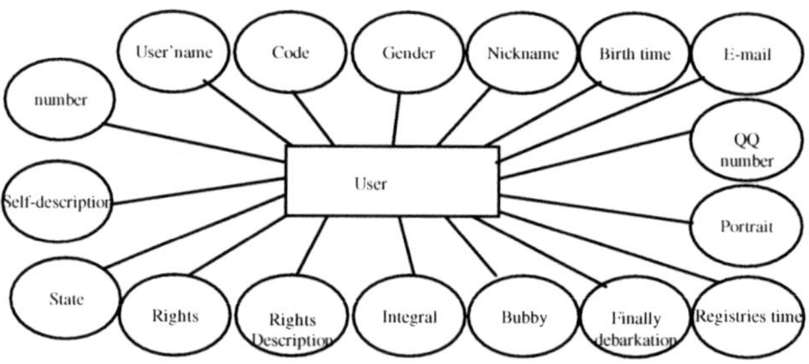

Fig. 7. User's E-R chart

(2) The data table design

Database structure design is converted all kinds of information into relevant items of data definition list on the basis of finishing the description of dependencies among kinds of data and classification of information. The function of a data definition list is to name for each table, the name of each field in table, the length of data type and allows the length, but in different database, the symbol and length of data type are different. The database tables of this system are shown in below, user data in table 1, administrator data in table 2, video data in table 3,. Comment data in table 4, Message data in table 5.

Table 1. User data Table

Field name	Data type	Field length	Allows null character	Description
ID	Auto number	5	no	Usernumber
UserName	Text	50	no	UserName
UserPassword	Text	50	no	UserPassword
UserName2	Text	50	yes	UserName

Table 2. Administrator data Table

Field name	Data type	Field length	Allows null character	Description
ID	Auto number	5	no	Adminnumber
AdminName	Text	50	no	AdminName
AdminPassword	Text	50	no	AdminPassword
AdminName2	Text	50	yes	AdminName

Table 3. Video data Table

Field name	Data type	Field length	Allows null character	Description
ID	Auto number	Long int	no	Video number
Big Class	Number	50	no	Broad heading
Small Class	Number	50	no	Minor heading
Title	Text	50	no	Video title
Content	Note	255	no	Video contents
Author	Text	255	no	author
Time	date/time	Long int	no	Add time
Read	Number	Long int	no	Browser times
Poster	Text	255	yes	Playbill address

Table 4. Comment data table

Field name	Data type	Field length	Allows null character	Description
ID	Auto number	Long int	no	Comment Numbers
BigClass	Number	50	no	Broad heading
SmallClass	Number	50	no	Minor heading
Title	Text	50	yes	Comment title
Content	Note	255	no	Comment contents
Author	Text	255	no	Comment author
Time	date/time	Long int	no	Add time

Table 5. Message data table

Field name	Data type	Field length	Allows null character	Description
ID	Auto number	5	no	Message Numbers
BBsName	Text	50	no	Name
BBsQuestion	Text	50	no	Question
BBsTime	date/time	Long int	no	Message time
Email	Text	50	no	E-mail
Answer	Text	50	no	Answer or not
Check	Note	50	no	Check

5 Conclusion

VOD system is the crystallization of many advanced technology, it can not only transmit video information smoothly and fluidly, but gives users the large space for chose by oneself, which meets the modern people's psychological eager of advocating freedom and participating. In China, this year, the number of Internet users has reached $4.04 billion people, who hope to get rich information resources. Therefore, the perfect combination of streaming media and VOD technology provide customers with broadcast servers as multimedia information, network movies, science and technology lectures, etc. and meanwhile create a new real-time, interactive network environment, improve the efficiency of information transmission, and meet the requirements of time, adapt to the development of informationization of society.

References

1. Liu, Q.T., Wang, F.: Multimedia technology foundation. Hubei science and technology press, wuhan (2006)
2. Wang, S.: The P2P-based streaming media distributed key technology. Journal of Henan University (February 2008)
3. Zhuo, J.L., Wang, P.: Personalized synchronous video flow courseware. Chinese Distance Education (August 2000)
4. Liu, Y.: The design of streaming media-based VOD system. Union Journal of Tianjin Vocational Colleges (March 2010)

Applications of Bioinformatics Based on Websites Services in Study of Environmental Microbiology

Yongliang Zheng [1], Lifang Long[1], Jun Xiang[1], Shiwang Liu[1], Deli Liu[2], and Yuling Zhong[1,*]

[1] Hubei Key Laboratory of Economic Forest Germplasm, Improvement and Resources Comprehensive Utilization, Huanggang Normal University, 146 Xingang II Road, Huangzhou, 438000, China
swzyl@hgnu.edu.cn
[2] College of Life Science, Central China, Normal University, Wuhan 430079, China
jianqiaoxu@gmail.com

Abstract. The quickly development of bioinformatics based on websites services promoted the study of microbial informatics. Microbial structural genomics and functional genomics try to illuminate the inner relation between the gene structure and function, and to construct gene regulatory networks. The application of Genechip based on bioinformatics became a stronger tool in environmental microbial ecological study and functional enzyme gene orientation. Bioinformatics of web-based services provide a new information platform and technology method for environmental microorganism study.

Keywords: Bioinformatics, Web-based service, Microbial bioinformatics, Environmental microbe.

1 Introduction

With the carrying out of Human Genome Project (HGP), bioinformatics was established and quickly developed. It has become one of the main domains in natural science in 21st century and impelled the establishment and development of microbial informatics [1-3], which was researched in microbes ecosystem, monitor and value the environment through the methods and theory in microbiology, and illustrated the interplay and relation among microbe, contamination and environment, and it is greatly important in protecting environment and benefiting mankind. Bioinformatics study quickly developed based on the web services [4]. Through bioinformatics study platform, we can index rich microorganism resources real-timely on websites, and share the environment microbe genome information[5]. Many specialized websites provide correlation information resources [6]. Therefore, Bioinformatics study has provided a brand-new information platform and research method for the environment microorganism research and development.

* Corresponding author.

M. Dai (Ed.): ICCIC 2011, Part II, CCIS 232, pp. 181–186, 2011.

2 Bioinformatics of Web-Based Services

2.1 Microorganism Resources Database

In recent years, highly developed Internet has brought the unprecedented opportunity to microbiology communication, resources sharing and international cooperation. Many large-scale websites and some microorganism specialized websites have provided rich and accurate real-time online microorganism resources and information for us. With the aid of the formidable search engine and huge electronic periodical database, we may timely and conveniently search information. Virtual library provided plenty of electronic documents, audio and video resource, any software as well as other kind of database about microorganism for us (Table 1). We can experiment such as electronic Northern, electronic PCR analysis in online virtual laboratory, microbe gene sequence can easily submit and blast through the global sharing specialized database (GenBank /EMBL /DDBJ).

Although microbiology was developed in recent 100 years, the new discovery species of microorganism were incessantly reported one after another. The concerned expert of international Union of Microbiology Societies (IUMS) estimated that there were 500,000- 600,000 kinds of microorganisms approximately in the whole nature. The rich microorganism resources bestowed by the nature are the inexhaustible precious wealth for humanity. At present, many countries have established respectively culture collection database on websites (Table 2.). User can index the need bacteria and obtain the biochemistry characteristic, classification evidence, culture condition and any other detailed information through microorganism partial characteristics.

Table 1. Some online microbe virtual libraries

Name	Website
ASM library	http://www.microbelibrary.org/
Mycology Image Library	http://www.medsch.wisc.edu/medmicro /myco/mycology.html
WWW Virtual Library	http://micxobiot.oxg/vlmicxo/vleduc.Ht ml
AIBS Library	http://www.aibs.org/virtual-library/
Virtual Library on Genetics	http://genome.gsc.riken.go.jp/hgmis/ge netics.html

2.2 Bioinfomatics Establishment and Development

With the Human Genome Project (HGP) was carried out, bioinformatics developed rapidly, and it impelled powerfully the research of environmental microbiology and theestablishment and development of Microbial Genomics, Microbial Functional Genomics and Microbial Structure Genomics. For completing the HGP, especially functional genomics, Model Organism Genome Project was launched followed. Some model microbes such as Escherichia coli, Haemophilus influenzae bacteria, Saccharomyces cevisiae have played an important role. The model microbial genome research not only is a major breakthrough and development in the field of microbial research but also supply and enrich the contents of bioinformatics.

Table 2. Websites of microbial strains and category resources

Name and abbreviation	Website
American Type Culture Collection (ATCC)	http://www.atcc.org/
China Center for Type Culture Collection (CCTCC)	http://www.cctcc.org/
China General Microbiological Culture Collection Central (CGMCC)	http://www1.im.ac.cn/typecc/junzhong/en.html
World Data Centre for Microorganisms (WFCC)	http://www.wfcc.info/
World Data Centre for Microorganisms (WDCM)	http://wdcm.nig.ac.jp/
Coding Microbiological Data for Computers (RKC)	http://micronet.im.ac.cn/RKC.html
Microbial Strain Data Network (MSDN)	http://micronet.im.ac.cn/msdn.shtml
Japan Collection of Microorganisms (JCM)	http://www.jcm.riken.go.jp/JCM/catalogue.html
Centre de Ressources Biologiques de l'Institut Pasteur (CIP)	http://cip.pasteur.fr/index.html.en
Belgian Coordinated collection of Microorganisms (BCCM)	http://www.belspo.be/bccm/
Australian Collection of Microorganisms (ACM)	http://www.micronet.cn/database/catalogsc.html

3 Application in Environmental Microorganism Research

3.1 Microbial Genomics Research

The sequencing of genome has caused the methods revolutionary improvement in microbe research. More bacterial genomes sequences were completed because of the smaller size of them. Since the length of 1.8 Mb Haemophilus influenzae bacteria genome sequence published in 1995, there were about 659 species of microbial genome sequencing partly or completely finished (http://www.ncbi.nlm.nih.gov/genomes/microbes/Complete.html).The Comprehensive Microbial Resource (CMR) (http://www.tigr.org/CMR) showed 150 new genomes have been added to the CMR till to 2010. Table 3 listed the microorganism genome database websites that have finished sequencing.

3.2 The Microbial Structure Genomic and Functional Genomic Study

In order to obtain a complete three-dimensional structure hologram of all proteins in atomic level and position in the cell and the various metabolic pathways, physiological way, signal transduction pathway,

Table 3. Database of microbial genomics and model microbial genome

Name	Website	Remark
EMGLIB	http://pbil.univ-lyon1.fr/ emglib/emglib.html	Bacteria and yeast genomics finished sequencing
NRsub	http://pbil.univ-lyuonl.fr/ nrsub/nrsub.html	Genomics of Bacillus subtilis
RsGDB	http://www-mmg.med.uth.tmc.edu/sphaero ids	Genomics of Rhodobacter sphaeroides
SGD	http://www.yeastgenome.org	Yeast genome
EcoCyc	http://ecocyc.pangeasystems.com/ecocyc	Genome, gene product and metabolize pathway of E.coli K12
CyanoBas e	http://www.kazasa.or.jp/cyano/	Genomic of Synechocystis sp.

Microbial Structural Genomics and Functional Genomics research were started from structure and function, by measuring all the details of complex three-dimensional structure of proteins and other biological molecules, comprehensively and systematically analyze all the genes function with high-throughput, large-scale experimental methods through the information provided by Structural Genomics, reveal the complicated and diversified mechanism of the origin and function of genes and their family in the evolutionary process by comparative genomics study. Some microbial structural and functional genomics data websites were showed in Table 4. Among them, gene regulation networks attempt to reveal the complex life phenomena by discovering the interaction law between genes from the system. Point of view, it is an important part of functional genomics research. The purpose of the study and its contents are as fellows: to identify and deduce gene network structure, properties and relation of regulation from gene expression map; understand regulatory process of complex molecular; know the basic principles of controlling gene expression and function; reveal information transmission laws in the process of gene expression; study genes function from the overall framework [7].

Table 4. Websites of model microbe structural genomics and functional genomics data

Name	Website	Remark
AresLab Intron Site	http://www.cse.ucsc.edu/research/ compbio/yeast_introns.html	yeast splicing and intron
DBTBS	http://elmo.ims.u-tokyo.ac.jp/ dbtbs	B.subtitls tran-acting factor and promoter
PromEC	http://bioinfo.md.huji.ac.il/ marg/promec	mRNA transcription initiation site in the E. coli promoter
RRNDB	http://rrndb.cme.msu.edu	changes of Prokaryotes ribosomal RNA operon
DPinteract	http://arep.med.harvard.edu/ dpinteract/	Binding site of E. coli DNA structure protein
YPD	http://www.proteome.com/ databases/index.html	Saccharomyces cerevisiae protein database
TRIPLES	http://ygac.med.yale.edu/triples/tr iples.html	Yeast interim transposon-inserted phenotype and expression of epitopes
GenProtEC	http://genprotec.mbl.edu/	Escherichia coli (K-12) genome, gene product and Homology.
SignalP	http://www.cbs.dtu.dk/servics/ signalp	Bacterial and eukaryotic proteins signal peptides and splice site

The main objective for functional genomics study were including that genome function annotation, high-throughput annotation of all biological functions of genomic coding production using bioinformatics method, and the main means of bioinformatics were that homology analysis, correlation analysis of bioinformatics, biotechnology functional annotation data exploring. The contents researched primarily involved three levels: identification of genome component, all ORF product functions notes, gene interaction and comparative genomic study [8]. Many online data or software platform supported corresponding gene annotation submitting or inquiries (Table 5). Worth mentioning is that there have also established genome annotation system platform in domestic, and provided web online services. The microbial genome sequence information platform established by Zhao Guijun provided gene sequence inquiries by gene access number, gene function and species or genus[9]. Automatic and manual classify according to the function codes in National Center for Biotechnology Information (NCBI), inquiring classification status, and establishing homologous gene mutual annotation function in several similar species with phylogenetic relationship. The Microbial genome annotation package (MGAP) established by Yu zhou was composed of two parts: genome annotation and Web-based user interface programe [10].Genome annotation system integrated numbers of gene identification, functional prediction and sequence analysis software, and protein sequence database, protein resources information system and orthologous proteins protein family databases, and used in Cyanobacteria gene annotation.

Table 5. Web of genome function annotation

Name	Website	Annotation
MGA	http://www.dkfz.de/mga/	Large-scale genome annotation website
COG	http://www.ncbi.nlm.nih.gov/cgi-bin/COG	orthologous Cluster analysis database
AAT	Http://genome.cs.mtu.edu/aat	Analysis and annotation genome tools
EcoCyc	Http://ecocyc.pangeasystems.com/ecocyc/ecocyc.html	E. coli genes and metabolism
CMR	http://www.tigr.org/tigr-scripts/CMR2/CMRGenomes.spl	microbial genome tools Annotation from TIGR Website
SAS	Http://www.biochem.ucl.ac.uk/cgi2bin/sas/query.cgi	Genome sequence analysis basis of structure
SGD	http://www.yeastgenome.org/	Yeast Genome Database
Indigo	http://195.221.65.10:1234/Indigo/	Complete genome-wide integrated information database of E. coli and B.subtilis
GIB	http://gib.genes.nig.ac.jp/	Microbial Genome Sequence Database
MBGD	http://mbgd.genome.ad.jp/htbin/Search.pl	Microbial genome integrated database
HAMAP	http://www.expasy.org/sprot/hamap/index.html	Automated coding and annotation system of microbial proteins
ARCHAIC	http://www.aist.go.jp/RIODB/archaic/	ancient bacteria nucleic acid sequence analysis database
ExPASy	http://www.expasy.ch/	Protein expert analysis system

Acknowledgment. This project was supported the National Key Project for Basic Research of China (2007CB116302), and the Key Grants of National Nature Science foundation of Hubei Province (2010CDA065),and supported by Educational Commission of Hubei Province of China (07BQ014), and National Natural Science Foundation of Hubei Province(2004ABA148, 2008cdz040), and Science & Research Program of Huanggang (07HG183).

References

1. Kong, W.D., Zhu, Y.G., Fu, B.J., Chen, B.D., Tong, Y.P.: A review on m icrobial gene and com m unity diversity in agricultural soil. Acta Ecologica Sinica 24(12), 2894–2898 (2004)
2. Kantachote, D., Naidu, R., Singleton, I.: Resistance of microbial populations in DDT-contaminated and uncontaminated soils. Applied Soil Ecology 16, 85–90 (2001)
3. Sergeev, N., Distler, M., Courthey, S., Al-Khaldi, S.F., Volokhov, D., Chizhikov, V., Rasooly, A.: Multipathogen oligonucleotide microarray for environmental and biodefense applications. Biosensors and Bioelectronics 20, 684–698 (2004)
4. Marsh, T.L., Saxman, P., Cole, J., Tiedje, J.: Terminal restriction fragment length polymorphism analysis program, a web-based research tool for microbial community analysis. Appl. Environ. Microbiol. 66, 3616–3620 (2000)
5. Zhang, Y.G., Li, D.Q., Xiao, Q.M., Liu, X.D.: Microarrays and Their application to environmental microorganisms. Acta Microbiologica Sinica 44(3), 406–410 (2004)
6. Lynda, B.M., Ellis Bo, K.H., Wen, J.K.: The University of Minnesota biocatalysis/ biodegradation database:post-genomic data mining. Nuclei. Acid Res. 31(1), 262–265 (2003)
7. Lei, Y.S., Shi, D.H., Wang, Y.F.: Reviewing the Study of Gene Regulatory Networks from Bioinformatics, vol. 26(1), pp. 6–12 (2003)
8. Xie, T., Liang, W.P., Dig, D.F.: Genome annotation in the postgenome era. Prog. Biochem. Biophys. 27(2), 166–170 (2000)
9. Zhao, G.J., He, Z.L., Lu, Y., Yie, L.T., Xu, A.L.: Establishment of a novel web-side bioformatics platform for the study of microbes genomes. Microbiology 2(4), 22–28 (2002)
10. Yu, Z., Li, T., Cai, T., Zhao, J.D., Luo, J.C.: MGAP-A microbe genome annotation platform. Acta Microbiologica Sinica 43(6), 805–808 (2003)

On the View of Criminal Legislation Model Driving Reform—A Perspective of Network Intellectual Property

Lu Zhen

School of Political Science and Law of Guangxi Teacher Education University
Nanning, China, 530001
ahn888168@gmail.com

Abstract. Network plays a crucial role in the community's political, economic, culture and life and so on. Internet technology has greatly promoted the development of social productive forces, but also changing the various social relations. Owing to the abuse of the present legislation model of intellectual property rights crime, the paper proposes the concept of network intellectual property by updating criminal law, which reforms current legislative model by full means of the accompanying model to achieve better protection of network intellectual property rights.

Keywords: network intellectual property rights, criminal law, legislative model, reform.

With the rapid economic development and network technology advances, the infringement of intellectual property rights has emerged increasingly in the network. It infringes upon the legitimate interests of intellectual property and violates the normal order of the network environment. The reason is because of limitation of legislation and poor punishment. Especially the criminal law can not effectively perform its function and fails to effectively curb infringement of intellectual property rights on the Internet. Therefore, it has focused on the study on the criminal jurisprudence in the intellectual property protection system, including how to deal with the challenges of knowledge economy and how to effectively protect the network intellectual property. Taken the limitation of the criminal law into consideration, it is urgent to improve the law protecting against network intellectual property crime.

1 The Concept and Characteristics of the Network Intellectual Property Rights Infringement

Network intellectual property rights infringement refers to behaviors seriously harm others intellectual property rights by means of internet. If the carrier of intellectual property rights only exists on a network, the network intellectual property rights infringement includes attacking its network itself. Broadly speaking, intellectual property crime is both a tool for network attack and to commit, but more important is the tool to commit in the network form of a traditional crime.

M. Dai (Ed.): ICCIC 2011, Part II, CCIS 232, pp. 187–193, 2011.

Different from the traditional infringement of intellectual property, network crime varies due to the scope of intellectual property crime [1]:

1.1 The Object

Infringement of network intellectual property characterizes complex objects, including the violation of the interests of intellectual property rights and of intellectual property management system and market economic order. In addition, the network intellectual property rights infringement also violates the normal order of network management. Network development requires the appropriate management system where standardizes network activity and protects the data. Under this circumstance, the normal information will be exchanged and normal economic order is guaranteed. Therefore, the network management laws and regulations are drawn up. The market economic order is obliged to be disrupted if the infringement of intellectual property rights has undermined the normal order of network management. The infringement abuses the IP-related science and technology protected by the national law enjoyed.

1.2 The Objective Aspect

The infringement is committed by abusing the rights of the obligee without permission. The relative law and regulation forbids anyone have the right to enjoy the intellectual property without the legal permission of the oblige. It may constitute a crime due to the severe harm.

Compared with the traditional intellectual property rights Infringement, the network infringement are not criminal acts committed, but the result of guilty or guilty of plot. The way of online infringement has so much change that the social harm appears much larger. In the judicial practice, however, standards of severity should refer to the judicial interpretation made by the state rights or justice organizations, combining with the specific trial.

1.3 The Subject

The subject of the infringement is a common person or the unit. The unit includes internet service provider, which makes one of difference between the network infringement and the traditional ones.

1.4 Subjective Aspect

The infringement is committed mostly on purpose while only acts of infringement of trade secrets can be constituted by the fault. On the intentional crime, though the network crime can't be excluded the profit purposes, network criminals have not direct commercial purposes compared with the traditional crimes. Thus, "for-profit" can't be a necessary element of the kind of crime.

2 Defects of the Legislative Protection against Network Intellectual Property Infringement

As the special form of intellectual property rights, the current network intellectual property has been recognized and protected in the world. The legislative model existing in China appears deficient which has impacted on judicial protection against network intellectual property infringement. Legislative protection is worthy to be recognized and improved to meet the current needs against the network crime.

Legislation on the intellectual property infringement is centralized model to maintain the law's lasting stability. However, an important feature of knowledge economy is the world of science and technology development and speeding up the process of economic globalization. With new problems increasingly emerging, as the relative rigidity of this legislative model fails to reflect new situations, the law protection against the intellectual property infringement lags behind changes in social life.

Technological progress is always a double-edged sword, namely facilitating the creation and spread of legal works as well as the pirate copy and spread. While the criminal law of intellectual property protection provides the main driving force and strong protection for technological development, it must constantly face the challenges of new technologies. In particular the rapid development of network technology, global liberalization for spreading brings out new situations and new problems for the criminal law of intellectual property, such as the domain of criminal law protection, the criminal law of copyright protection in the network environment, Jurisdiction of intellectual property infringement in electronic commerce and criminal evidence acquisition and so on. Therefore, the current situation of intellectual property legislation should be revised and perfected. Germany, France and other countries institute the combination-type pattern of criminal punishment on the base of the Penal Code and intellectual property laws. It can take into account not only the maintenance and stability of the Criminal Code, but the new situation and new problems IPR crimes. Thus the relevant provisions of the criminal law are timely amended and supplemented so that a reasonable organization react for violations of Intellectual Property Crime as the requirement of the network o Intellectual Property in the criminal law protection. [2]

In addition, for the legislative model of the intellectual property crime, the existing criminal law prescribes statutory findings exists in the intellectual property crimes. The findings are adjudicated on the base of two elements: the sales value or illegal gains; and the severity of cases or significant loss. The latter fails in the fight against crime owing to fuzzy meaning and lack of practical significance; the former, owing to the amount of illegal benefit as the standards, the legitimate interests of rights holders has been seriously damaged while legislation protect the competition order of market rather than the legitimate rights of intellectual property. Thus, it is difficult to pursue the criminal responsibility of infringer if the illegal gain or profit does not amount to prosecution under the standard,

3 Legislative Mode of Criminal Law on Intellectual Property Protection in the Network

The above suggested that it exposed many flaws for the existing criminal law of intellectual property protection system in the network. So it is urgent to establish a new system of criminal law protection making adjustments and norms. There are three ways to accomplishment as follows:

Updating the idea of the Criminal Code introducing into the network intellectual property

1) The equity between the personal interests and social interests and innovation encourage and technological progress

As the thought creating intellectual property, creators are obliged to enjoy the full benefits in order to create a sufficient stimulus. They are reasonable to be protected. However, the beneficiaries are unable to pay unreasonably high prices to obtain them. Thus, contrast to traditional unlimited protection for owners, the intellectual property rights protection takes the interests of both parties into consideration: the compensation for creators and artists as well as the public's real interests, which adjust and balance these two interests.

2) Criminal law as final sanction

Criminal law must be appropriately involved in the field of intellectual property on the premise of involving civil law, economic law, administrative regulations, which take the body and rights into full consideration as well as the corresponding obligations. That is the scope of the right behavior is restricted by the departments outside the criminal law. However, when other standards can't ensure the order of the legitimate presence, the criminal law should take effect as the final sanction. It is the time and logic reason why criminal law must be involved in the field of intellectual property.

In the field of intellectual property, the boundary between the crime and criminal is less clear than the traditional. laws and regulations of other departments will take on the task of determining boundary while the criminal law offer clear and certain negative evaluation on criminal act . Criminal law can't be introduced in the absence of other departments and regulations to define the case.

3) The extent of criminal law involvement

The effect-orientate idea holds two opposing views on criminal law involving into intellectual property rights, the week protection theory and strong protection one. The theory of the week protection, represented by the developing countries, as complete legal protection will contain the dissemination and application of knowledge, which affecting the country's economic and trade development. Therefore, it proposes the low level of intervention that criminal law shouldn't intervene the field of intellectual property rights. The theory of the strong protection, represented by the developed countries, holds that it protects at the expense of effective incentive mechanism for the development of intellectual property. Under the weak protection, it limits protection and deterrence of criminal law that serious violations can't be simply containment. It is necessary to strongly protect intellectual property [3].

The intellectual property should be strongly protected in the knowledge economy. In the present circumstances, however, this strong protection is mainly non criminal laws, such as civil law, administrative law and so on. That should be strong protection of intellectual property, which is an inevitable trend in rule of law and market economy today, but this should be relied upon the strong protection outside of criminal law rather than inside. A wide range of crime and severe punishment are not to implement the criminal law into strong protection of intellectual property violations.

Legislative model of criminal law protecting the network intellectual property

1)Accompanying legislative model

With the rapid development of the Internet, it appears out of date and inability of the provisions of existing criminal law on intellectual property infringement. So does the Criminal Code.

Taken the stability of the Criminal Code into consideration, the special model of the criminal should restrict the network intellectual property infringement to keep pace with social change. We can learn from Germany and France who combined criminal law code with to punish the intellectual property rights violations.

In the current legislative practice, law protection model of the network intellectual property rights should adhere to the basic principles of the criminal law. Besides the centralized provisions of blank crime and simple crime in the Criminal Code, it is practical to innovate and update the legal protection for the network intellectual property through the revision of the subsidiary legal regulation and the specific legal regulations such as patent law, trademark law, copyright law and so on [4].

With the function of hint, the accompanying legislation model establish on the premises of the provisions of criminal law. It, however, may be hardly applied due to its base on the provisions in the criminal law provided there is no relative provision in the criminal law [5].

Therefore, the accompanying legislation model should combine the Penal Code with the accompanying legislations. The Criminal Code prescribes the crime counts for violations of intellectual property rights and provides legal punishment while the subsidiary legal regulation prescribes the scope of criminal responsibility, which the crime committed shall be investigated for criminal responsibility. Its strengths is not only to take into account the provisions of the Criminal Code, but to avoid the lack of a single legislative model as the infringement of intellectual property characteristics a statutory offense. Of course, it is worth noting that there is no provision of crime counts and the punishment like the foreign law in our relevant administrative regulations and economic regulations. Although it isn't a criminal law norm in the strict sense, it still should be considered as a legislative form. Because the Criminal Code prescribes the crime of intellectual property rights must violate the patent law, trademark law, copyright law and other laws and regulation, which is decided by the principle of the statutory crime.

2) The possibility of special legislative model

Without breaking the concept of the existing criminal law, partial criminal acts could be punished. However, the criminal law deems to be revised with new forms of infringement of intellectual property, especially in the network. If not, they will not provide effective protection for intellectual property, and realize justice idea of the criminal law.

There is no specific criminal law on the network intellectual property crime in China. The existing legislative model fails in adequate protection for intellectual property owing not to consider the particularity of the network of intellectual property crime. The network intellectual property were mentioned on the judicatory interpretation cited from Some Legal Problems on Intellectual Property Criminal Cases Application by the Supreme People's Court, Supreme People's Procuratorate in 2004. But It is undoubtedly inadequate for a single article to contain the increasingly rampant violations of network intellectual property crime

Although the centralized legislative model is helpful to reveal the common features of intellectual property rights crimes, which facilitate comprehensive comparative analysis of different and relationship between various intellectual property crimes to achieve a systematic design adn increase deterrence of criminal law. But it may cause indulgence of network intellectual property crime as ignoring the individuality of network intellectual property rights. Within the existing system, It fails to handle the new cases and issues emerging in the new intellectual property practice areas such as network name, network copyright protection [6].

Expansion of the Criminal Code protection for network intellectual property

There is yet no specific criminal legislation on the network intellectual property crime. The existing criminal law on intellectual property crime only refers to the terms on the revised Penal Code in 1997. With the rapid development of the Internet, the terms of certain provisions appear gradually out of outdated and paralyzed. While article 287 in the criminal law hints the computer crime, the provision doesn't clarify the form of computer network crimes. On the rampant trend of network intellectual property crimes, it isn't conducive to evaluate a network criminal offense in the customary practice, but to protect intellectual property.

1) Protecting expansion of traditional intellectual property

According to article 217 and 218 in the State Criminal Law, it prescribes copyright focus on the partial use and payment as the criminal protection of copyright. It, however, excludes from the right and payment in other form of art works, such as performance, broadcasting, exhibition, film production, television, video and adaptation, translation, annotation, editing and so on. Besides, the rights of issue, modification and protection are not inclusive. So it is necessary to adjust the scope of criminal law protection through the adequate intervention of the criminal law under the more serious and frequent violations circumstances.

The existing criminal law excludes from the service marks as the protecting target. With the proportion of the tertiary industry growing in the national economy, service marks appear invaluable. It is easily indulge crimes without the protection of criminal law. Site provides network services platform rather than the transaction of goods. So the abuse of trademarks may also refer to the unauthorized use of the registered trademarks in the website.

In addition, our existing criminal law protection also does not extend into the phase of authorized sell, issue and rent. That is because the obligee is entitled lag the relative promised sale. The exclusive law doesn't prescribe the patentee is entitled to prohibit unauthorized offer to sell until the revision of the criminal law. However, there is still blank in criminal law protection, which is subject to modifiy the provision of the Criminal Code.

2) Specific protection for network intellectual property

In most countries, the criminal law expands the protecting scope of intellectual property. With the rapid development of the information technology, the international protection includes the copyright concerning the legal protection on the technical measures and authority management. Moreover, it is brought into the protecting system of the criminal law in some countries, such as the U.S. and Japan and so on. In our subsidiary law on the computer software, It should be added the corresponding provisions on technical measures and rights management. information corresponding to the protection of criminal law. Although the network intellectual property is inclusive in the relevant international conventions, civil administrative regulations, intellectual property like the domain name doesn't cover, which doesn't cohere with the above provisions. Therefore, it is necessary to reform the legal protecting form of the network intellectual property. Special criminal law on intellectual property infringement is ready to constitute in order to strengthen the network intellectual property protection.

References

1. Tao, Y.: On the Infringement of Network Intellectual Property. Liaoning Police Academy (6), 50 (2005)
2. Tian, H.: The Criminal Law on Intellectual Property Protection. China Law (2), 147 (2003)
3. Zhang, X.: Issues of Intellectual Property Protection. PhD thesis, Jilin University (12), 192 (2006)
4. Guan, R.: Study on Network Intellectual Property Crime. Politics and Law (4), 31 (2007)
5. Guan, R.: Issues of Network Intellectual Property Protection. Jiangsu Police Officer College (1), 63 (2008)
6. Li, F.: Legislative Comparison and Improvement on the Infringement of Intellectual Property Crime. Master thesis, China University of Political Science (4), 37 (2006)

The Research of the Meteorological Distance Education Based on Mobile Education

Yuan Feng[1], Xianzhi Zhang[1], Xiaoyan Gong[2], and Lejiang Guo[2]

[1] Department of Land-based Early Warning Surveillance Equipment
Air Force Radar Academy Wuhan, China
[2] Department of War Strategy Science and Engineering
The Second Artillery Command College Wuhan, China
Hakeemmo123@gmail.com

Abstract. With the constant development of meteorological technology, China has some new requirements for meteorological personnel training mode. Currently, the meteorological bureau leads meteorological distance training and has made some progress. However, there are still some problems. This paper attempts to apply 3G mobile technology in meteorological remote training, raises a new model to solve the problems. The result of this research shows the implementation of the meteorological mobile education services based on mobile mode and its performance analysis.

Keywords: distance education, mobile education, 3G, content provider.

1 Introduction

In August 2003, with the party and the country's development, the CPC Central Committee puts forward a large-scale training of cadres to improve the cadre's quality in large scale. With the end of the year, the CPC Central Committee, the State Council convened a national conference on human resources to complete the strategic mission. After the meeting, the decision on further strengthening the human resources work is made and published. It points out, on the basis of enhancing the universal ideological and moral qualities, scientific and cultural qualities and health qualities. China will focus on training people's learning ability, practical ability and strive to improve people's ability to establish a large education and training concept. It stresses to reform education and training mechanisms, content and methods [1].Immediately, the meteorological bureau proposes the national meteorology developmental strategy. In June 2005, Meteorology training center starts to conduct a large-scale meteorological distance training officially. A large number of people participated in training, the coverage is broad, the training approach is flexible, the management system is strict and the training effect is remarkable. In the certain extent, the training work has obtained success. However, there are also many problems. First, the union degree is not high between meteorological distance training and individual career development plan which causes the education training efficiency reduce. For personal career development plan, the training organization turn a blind eye, emphasizes the training

M. Dai (Ed.): ICCIC 2011, Part II, CCIS 232, pp. 194–201, 2011.

department's benefit constantly. It does not favor in the full utilization of training departments' human resources and does not tally "humanist" time management idea. Second, because of the lack of facilities, the majority of basic meteorological stations do not meet the distance training requirement, which affects the training effect. Third, the remote training system construction lags far behind. In the supporting online teaching resources, a long-range real-time interactivity and on-line testing areas, there are a large number of issues. Fourth, the training form and the time are highly fixed, which cannot satisfy the individualizing study request, lack of flexibility of the distance learning and the mobility.

Education is the cornerstone of economic development in any nation. Traditionally, formal education has been offered in a classroom setting where the teacher and students interact with each other face-to-face. This form of learning is group-based, and technology acts as a supplement to the teacher. For the student, this means that their physical presence and participation in group discussions forms an integral part of the institution's curriculum. The teacher has the challenge of meeting classroom schedules as well as the preparation and assessment of course materials. Despite these challenges, the traditional classroom offers a unique opportunity for teachers and students to interact with their peers. However, there is a problem that everyone has the opportunity to get to school. For instance, they may be living too far away, may be physically handicapped and the like. These limitations called for other forms of education that had the capability of reaching out to a larger audience. Distance learning (dLearning), electronic learning (eLearning) and mobile learning (mLearning) offer solutions that address the shortcomings of the traditional classroom.

The purpose of this paper is to apply 3G mobile technology in meteorological remote training, it may improve the distance learning condition, and the enough study time to meet the need of personalized the development.

2 Previous Researches

Famous scholar Figueiredo unifies the distance learning thought. Mobile learning is one kind of education methods, its formation and development is mainly due to the continuous development of distance education and electronic technology.

Initially, the distance learning is called the distance range education, the word appeared in1892. In 1947, the distance range education entered the adult evening schools of the Maryland University officially, then, this word has been widely used, It only took a hundred years time, this world has swept the world[2].

Distance education is education where teacher and pupils/students are separated by space and/or time. Technical media are used to impart knowledge and to make possible real to-way-communication, in support of the process of teaching. Distance learning offers students the opportunity to work or stay at home and study course materials when they find it convenient. Course material takes the form of printed material sent by post. This is called for improved road and rail transport especially to marginal areas. Advancements in information technology in the 1980s, it leads to the introduction of audio-visual aids, cable and satellite that further enhanced the learning experience. Through the application of these new technologies, it then also meant that it would be possible to link several geographically dispersed locations simultaneously, and create a virtual classroom. Technology thus extended the learning experience from one that was solely individual to one offering group-based, face-to-face teaching at a distance. Group-based learning is not limited to part-time students. It can be used for the simultaneous dissemination of didactical content to full-time students at several locations. By providing the teacher with an array of technological tools it became possible - among other things - to be joined by experts from a remote location who would further enlighten students on various subjects. Such educational moments provide students with a better understanding of a given area and aims at motivating the use of learning. Learning has also allowed teachers to have a more flexible time schedule as all teaching sessions could be stored on visual-audio aids and dispatched or broadcasted.

Currently, only in the United States, the total number of degree programs offered by educational background has achieved 49,000; moreover this number is also increasing. The distance learning has covered American College all disciplines and the specialty basically, include the meteorology specialty. The number of school performing distance education in the Internet has more than 60% in 1998. The long-distance learning's method presents the diversification the trend of development. Now there are following categories used in it, the individual pre-recorded TV (47%), asynchronous messaging technology (58%), bidirectional interactive television (54%), synchronization information transmission and processing system, such as chat systems, television and telephone system, conference system, etc [3]. Some University were Established like as the University of Phoenix City, the national technical university and so on. The United States National Technical University is a coalition of 45 well-known universities, which is committed to serving officers, remote master's degree education and short courses and distance continuing education by using satellite.

In order to do well the meteorological profession the continuing education system, the US had established the American country weather bureau. The bureau is composed of 4800 people, next governs training part, its duty is to manage the national weather bureau's training work, formulate training plan and so on. The training way mainly has two kinds of training include distance training and face-to-face training, the distance training mainly includes the web homepage education in Internet, the CD-ROM compact disc distribution education, pronunciation function interactive distance learning and the real-time video frequency alternately distance learning.

In US's meteorological department, distance learning training is widely applied. Regardless of socially oriented training, between profession cooperation training, Meteorological department selects the distance learning as internal training approach. It is the supplement mutually for the face-to-face training forms in classroom. Both of the training has formed the organic synthesis, which is a big characteristic in American meteorology training.

The Chinese first meteorological distance education appeared in 1950.It was held by Peking University, named as the meteorological correspondence course. In the late 70s, the central radio and TV University's establishment marks the second generation of distance education's formal launch in china, its course also involves knowledge of meteorology and related disciplines.

China's meteorological official starts modern distance education in 2000. Beijing institute of meteorology was converted into the China Meteorological Administration Training Center, it is authorized to establish the meteorological distance training systems and carry on the national meteorology system's distance education and aims at on-the-job training service in 2000. The center founded the meteorological distance learning training system, set up the meteorological bureau training centers, various provinces training centers and county meteorological bureau's third-level training stations[4].

The master station is the core of the whole system, which is responsible for training resources construction, distance learning platform and the entire weather system's education and training's planning include construction and maintenance.

The various provinces training centers are the second station which is responsible for learning counseling, teaching management and teaching information's feedback. This second station can be used to work up distance education platform for the province's distance education training. The county meteorological bureau's third-level training stations are the third station; this station is the main terminal of distance learning education and training point. Learners may learn the teaching materials broadcasted by meteorological satellite video or Internet. The transmission mode is one-way, the center is responsible for sending the materials and the stations are responsible for receiving. This stations is the distance learning spot, learners may study the master station and the second-level station teaching material.

The Chinese meteorological department has established an integrated application service system of meteorological satellite, its master station is located at Beijing, the two-way sites are located in the each provincial meteorological department, and the single-sites are located in the provincial meteorological departments and the meteorological stations. Now, there are more than 2000 stands, the overwhelming majority of stations are constructed at the county weather station, therefore, its coverage is very broad. The single-sites not only receive convention data information but also receive the video frequency programs from the master. In addition to receiving the master station's information, the two-way sites can also receive the master station's transmitter data, even the pronunciation information.

The experiment indicates that after ensuring the meteorological service carried on normally, the Chinese Meteorological Department may use part of satellite channel resources to carry on distance meteorological training by using the unidirectional video frequency broadcast and uses the exchange with the master station by applying the phonetic system. In the future, without increasing any equipments, each station still rely on integrated applications of meteorological satellite service system to carry out one-way broadcast video meteorological distance training.

At present, the meteorological distance training organization can provide four kinds of distance learning methods, the CD-ROM compact disc distribution education mode, the passive acceptance of one-way satellite video learning mode the two-way interactive TV learning method based on weather forecast television with simultaneous based on Internet network Web page learning method. The satellite video learning approach can be used in the third level stations, but the two-way interactive TV learning method can only be used in the provinces Bureau of Meteorology. Popularization is quite narrow, the number of personnel accepting training is so small, at the same time, the method based on Internet network Web page have been received sufficient attention.

3 Method

In recent years, depending on the mobile communication technology and the network technology, distance training has a new form, it is named mobile learning. Via mobile communication networks, computer networks, servers and mobile teaching devices, learners may achieve long-range training activities. In general, mobile devices mainly refer to mobile storage devices, such as notebook computers, mobile phones, learning machines and UMPC. Paul Harr said that mobile learning is an intersection of mobile computing technology and E-Learning, it can help learners study at any time and any where. At present, China also has a mobile learning model, which is mainly based on the traditional Client-Server system. The disadvantage of this system is that once the server is broken, all the customers can not use it. Subsequently, there is a dynamic networking environment, namely peer to peer network structure, which supports removable storage devices. Because of the JXTA structure, mobile devices have to use GSM and the P2P protocol. The communications technology is restricted to second-generation (2G), which severely limits the amount of data transmission, thus, mobile learning method was severely restricted. The International Telecommunication Union proposed the third generation mobile communication technology (the 3G technology) [5], which may provide kinds of wide band information services such as the high-speed data transmission, the television image transmission and so on, which cannot be provided by the first and two generation of technologies. There are a large promotion in the sound transmission and the data transmission; the transmission speed may get at least 2Mbps/second indoor, 384kbps/second outdoor. In 2005, South Korea, Japan applies this technology in the mainstream market; Western Europe also appears the tendency to use this technology. In 2007, 3G technology developed by Chinese information industrial department had obtained the license plate, the 3G is just round the corner. Using its quickly, multiplex service, the China Meteorological Administration Training Center can construct the meteorology distance training net, which will bring mobile education into reality in the near future[6].The advantages of using 3G technology are that a learner realizes the interactive behavior with the training organization any time and any where. Through the surfer terminals such as handset, wireless notebook, learner may watch the video frequency programs or select broadcast course content, even it may carry interactive exchange with the training mentors on the online. Through the equipment, learner may inquiry some quite urgent questions; it does not need the long-term waiting or is online. Learner may also browse multimedia meteorological data and teaching references. According to their interests, they may carry on tests and get answers after the end of exams. The training organization may carry on the online inspection to avoid cheating. At same time, according to learners' scores, the training organization may change the training material's difficulty and training key points in order to fit most of learners. There are the following several study methods based on the 3G distance meteorological migration Learning.

A. Making use of the multimedia services provided by 3G to carry on the multimedia study (MMS).

According to differences of the MMS terminal and the server, MMS may be divided into three categories. First, accept and transmit multimedia news mutually between the

MMS terminal, which is the meteorological multimedia news transmission between learners [7]. Some questions can be solved through the learners' exchange without access to the network. Second, it transmits and receives multimedia news mutually between MMS terminal and E-mail server's, which is the learner and the meteorological training organization, it can transmit or accept multimedia information each other through the Internet. Third, transmit and receive multimedia news mutually between MMS terminal and value-added service platform's in Internet. The ordinary text short news only include 170 byte length, but the MMS short news length may amount to 30~100 kilobytes. Besides text, it may also contain one kind or many kinds of combinations of the sound and the video. Learners may discuss any meteorological knowledge and the problems through the short news.

***B*. Using 3G WAP connected into Internet to browse.**

The WAP (wireless application protocol) is a open global standard protocol being used in the numeric move telephone, the Internet or other personal digital assistant machine (PDA) and computers' communication [8]. It is composed of a series of agreements and has been used for the standardized wireless communication equipment. The WAP is applied in the Internet visit, receiving or dispatching email, visiting page in WAP website and so on. At present many handset manufacturers have already developed the high-end hand-held mobile phone browsers, such as the WAP handset, the machine and the GPRS handset. The WAP browsing is similar to computer's browser. Compared with the traditional wireless communication system, the 3G system uses WAP2.0 to enhance the system content compatibility with the personal computing information, it support the utilizing content mark language W3C, taking HTML as foundation stipulation compatible, and apply CSS for enhancing the content expressive force. In addition, the WAP also supports the Internet standard the TCP/IP agreement, has a good compatibility with the Internet, and also may visit the www homepage directly. This study let learners get rid of time and place restrictions, so long as learners want to study the meteorological knowledge or to receive meteorological training, they may access the net through the hand-held equipment to get meteorological distance training or carry on downloading the training content. Learners might also study the content under the off-line state, reducing financial burden on the Internet. The mobile learning will have the unprecedented change in the conveniences. Meteorological distance training and individual learning will not receive the time, spatial and the region limit any more.

***C*. Using the 3G band increasing to carry on video-on-demand mobile leaning.**

Learners may share higher network transmission speeds, regardless of indoors, outdoors or process in moving. If the learners want to study video training courseware, they can carry out video-on-demand. Meteorological administration training center may take advantages of 3G mobile learning services to develop some packages for different training, assessment, practice, or course of curriculum. Compared with previous e-education and cable networks-based on-line education programs, this method has greater flexibility and is more suitable for learners working in remote stations.

***D.* Offline mobile learning methods.**
Taking into account the cost of access, learners may download e-books, multimedia courseware and other digital graphic content about meteorological training ahead of time, and then store them on portable mobile devices. Learners can carry on learning without connecting to the network anytime and anywhere.

4 Some Advice

The Chinese Meteorological bureau training center undertakes our country meteorology personnel's distance training work. The center has worked out the meteorological distance learning system's construction plan; it includes constructing four sub-systems, distance direct seeding teaching subsystem, based on Internet distance training subsystem, multimedia educational resources comprehensive development subsystem and real-time interactive mode distance training subsystem.

The four sub-system's constructions should integrate the mobile learning idea. For instance, the distance direct seeding teaching subsystem mainly bases on the system constructions. At present, single-sites has been spread in county stations, those sites can receive data from the satellite and undertake distance training. However, mobile learning idea may be introduced to transform the system. Broadcasting's video content should be issued on the Internet; learners may carry on the network direct seeding or the network data to study, instead of constructing the more satellite receiving stations again. Based on the Internet the distance training subsystem should take the meteorological distance teaching website system as the core, and provide distance learning in network. As long as holding a mobile termination equipment and access to the 3G communication network, learners can realize the distance training mission.

Providing the enough massive multimedia resources is very essential for training institutions. Thus, the developments of multimedia educational resources, construction of sub-systems are necessary. The training center must provide the basic hardware environment, it offer platform and element materials storehouse for multimedia resource development and develop software packages used in mobile termination equipment. The center must expand resources of storehouse such as test question, experiment and pseudo operation for learners to search in the network. At the same time, the training center may construct one learning service platform based on the 3G. This system should include the original meteorological network; meanwhile, this system should also include the module of supporting network service, turning on Internet, the 3G communication network and the enrollment platform. The training organization should let learners carry on the least operations, meet the needs of different level, specialty, disparity in age, learner's post demand. Learners may have custom-made in system's content, modify contents of the reception, carry on the online test, and inquire the individual performance and so on. After the debarkation, learners may register the materials, the help, and individual establishment.

References

1. Liu, Y.: National Meteorology Education Training Work Conference's Speech. Meteorological Soft Science (1), 123–128 (2006)
2. A bell Jiaozhuang. Foreign Distance Education. Information Technology Education (4), 324–329 (2004)

3. Gao, X., Wang, W.: American Meteorology Continuing Education And Training Development Situation and Characteristic. Chinese Meteorological Bureau Training Center, Learning From Others (2007)
4. Lv, Y.: Distance Education Help Meteorological Training. Distance Education in China (10), 114–118 (2006)
5. Keegan, D.: From Distance Learning To E-learning To Mobile Learning. Open Education Research (5), 211–217 (2000)
6. Liu, z.: Mobile Learning Is The Education of Modern New Direction of Technology Development. China Audio-Visual Education 9, 364–368 (2005)
7. Liu, Y.: Form Dynamic Learning - Summary of Current Situation of Overseas Research. Modern Education Technology (3), 286–290 (2004)
8. Liang, Z.: Based On 3G Technology. Mobile Learning, Information Science (2007)

An Empirical Research on Technological Innovation Capability of Enterprises Based on Logistic Regression Model

Na Li and Chuiyong Zheng

Business School
Hohai University Nanjing, P.R. China
877098408@qq.com

Abstract. Technological innovation is the power and source of enterprise development. According to the fundamental principle of logistic regression model, the paper did a principle component analysis of the selected indicators system to get the value of the dependent variable in the logistic regression model. Then, empirical studies were conducted with relevant data, getting the logistic regression formula to divide the enterprises into non-innovative enterprises and innovation enterprises with significantly high accuracy rate, and the analysis of the factors affecting technological innovation capability was carried out. We conclude that logistic regression model is an effective method for enterprise technological innovation capability research.

Keywords: technological innovation capability, technological innovative enterprises, logistic regression model.

1 Introduction

With the formation of economic globalization and the development of knowledge economy, the role of technological innovation has become increasingly prominent. Enterprise technological innovation capability determines the development and the competitive ability of the enterprise. Only with strong technological innovation capability could the enterprises create competition advantage in fierce market competitions and ultimately improve the competitive ability.

Technological innovation was first proposed by the famous American economist, Joseph Alois Schumpeter in 1912 [1]. The core competitive ability constructed by the technological innovation can bring sustainable competitive advantage to enterprises and have significant benefits to the development of enterprises. Government, enterprises and scholars focus more and more on the study of technological innovation capability. Seven Muller (1984) [2] proposed that the technological innovation capability of enterprises is the comprehensiveness of organization capability, development capacity, production capacity, adaptive capacity, analysis capability, improved capacity and obtaining ability of technology and information. Technological innovation was divided into product innovation and process innovation by Xu Qingrui(1986) [3]. He measured them respectively first and finally integrated

M. Dai (Ed.): ICCIC 2011, Part II, CCIS 232, pp. 202–210, 2011.

them into general technological innovation capability. Vangelis Souitaris (2002) [4] studied the technological innovation capability of Greek enterprises by means of cases. He believed that technological innovation was determined by enterprise consciousness, enterprise culture and other factors in European emerging industrialized countries. Han Huaying (2009) [5] was devoted to study the technological innovation of small and medium enterprises (SMEs) from resources, market, system and technology, and suggested to improve technological performance of SMEs from this four respects.

The problem of how to judge the technological innovation capability scientifically to help enterprises improve their independent innovation ability is urgent to be solved. There are several methods used in the evaluation of technological innovation capability. Fan Decheng, Zhou Hao (2006) [6] analyzed the technological innovation capability of Shanghai, Beijing and other 7 districts quantitatively using factor analysis. Based on DEA-Malmquist productivity indicator, Zhang Cheng, Zhu Shuying (2009) [7] measured variables such as the total factor productivity and technological progress. Xu Li, Zheng Ran, Zhou Shiwei (2010) [8] formed a new grey fuzzy evaluation method based on the combination of gray correlation and fuzzy evaluation method to help enterprises take effective measures to enhance technological innovation capability and core competitive ability. According to BP neural network theory, Chen Zhi, Zhang Dongliang, Shan Guyuan (2010) [9] designed the BP neural network model to assess the technological innovation capability of SMEs. Miao Chenglin, Wang Huating, Feng Junwen and Sun Liyan (2010) [10] studied the problem of technological capability integration based on ant colony algorithm. Currently, these evaluation methods are used to assess the area technological innovation capability, but there are fewer studies on the evaluation of enterprises. In this paper, regarding the technological innovation capability of enterprises as the focal point of study, a comparative analysis of innovative enterprises and non-innovative enterprises is carried out and a logistic regression model is established to find the indicator system which can identify the technological innovative enterprises, to analyze the technological innovation capability of enterprises.

2 The Construcion of Logistic Regression Model

A. The Principle of Logistic Regression Model

Logistic regression model is a nonlinear statistical method. There are two possibilities of the value of the dependent variable Y (usually denoted by 0 and 1). $Y=\begin{cases} 1 & event \quad will \quad occur \\ 0 & event \quad won't \quad occur \end{cases}$. It is assumed that the independent variables X_1, X_2, …, X_n can explain the probability of Y. $Y=\alpha_0+\alpha_1 x_1+\alpha_2 x_2+\cdots+\alpha_n x_n$. Considering that the reasonable value interval of the possibility is [0, 1], the value of the possibility p is logit transformed and the logistic regression equation is obtained as follows.

$$p = \frac{1}{1 + e^{-(\alpha_0 + \alpha_1 x_1 + \alpha_2 x_2 + \cdots + \alpha_n x_n)}} \quad (1)$$

where a_i is the regression coefficient corresponding to X_i, a_0 is the constant term independent of each factors.

In this paper, the dependent variable Y is introduced to represent the technological innovation capability of the enterprises. $p=p(Y=1)$ indicates the possibility of the enterprise with strong technological innovation capability, and $p=p(Y=0)$ indicates the possibility of the enterprise with weak technological innovation capability. The principal component analysis of the selected indicators system is needed to get the value of the dependent variable Y in the logistic regression model. Generally, it can be predicted that the event will not occur when $p< 0.5$, and the event will occur when $p> 0.5$.

B. The Selection of Research Samples

Since technological innovation project was carried out in 2006, the State of China has promulgated two groups of innovative enterprises. In order to make the results become more representative, considering the nature of these enterprises and the attainability of data, we remove the non-listed companies and select the remaining 24 technological innovative enterprises as enterprises with strong technological innovation capability. Meanwhile, with stratified random sampling, other 24 listed companies are chosen from enterprises outside innovative enterprises promulgated by the State of China. The data of these 48 listed companies in 2009 is used as the original sample set. All the financial data is from GuoTaiAn financial database and the industry data is from the “2009 Statistical Yearbook of high-tech industries”.

C. The Selection of Indicators

There are many factors affecting the technological innovation capability of enterprises, which include financial factors such as the total assets, current ratio, net assets per share and the industry environment, macro policy environment. However, the influence of the macro policies will be reflected in the indicators of the enterprises themselves and their industries. Therefore, according to the financial indicators and the industrial indicators of the enterprises, this paper selects 16 technological innovation capability indicators as follows, net assets value per share X_1, net assets income ratio X_2, equity ratio X_3, asset-liability ratio X_4, liquidity ratio X_5, quick ratio X_6, rate of return on assets X_7, ratio of cash flow to debt X_8, R&D personnel full-time equivalent X_9, R&D expenditure X_{10}, amount of new product items X_{11}, expenditure of the development of new products X_{12}, new product output value X_{13}, new product sales income X_{14}, amount of the application for patent X_{15}, and amount of invention patent number X_{16}.

D. Standardized Processing of Data

Regarding the 16 indicators of the 48 listed companies as variables, we can get the original data matrix. Because the nature and dimension of indicators are different, the data with different dimension can't be compared together. In order to reflect the actual situation, the impact caused by the different units of the indicators must be excluded. So standardized processing of the indicators' values must be taken to ensure that they are comparable.

E. Principal Component Analysis

By using SPSS 16.0, the eigenvalues and contribution rates of the principal components are obtained (see Table 1).

Table 1. Total Variance Explained

	Initial Eigenvalues		
Component	*Total*	*% of Variance*	*Cumulative %*
1	7.883	49.266	49.266
2	4.064	25.401	74.667
3	1.871	11.691	86.358
4	.765	4.784	91.142
5	.612	3.828	94.970
6	.375	2.344	97.314
7	.225	1.404	98.717
8	.069	.429	99.146
9	.046	.288	99.434
10	.033	.204	99.638
11	.024	.149	99.787
12	.017	.106	99.892
13	.009	.056	99.949
14	.007	.042	99.991
15	.001	.009	100.000
16	2.784E-05	.000	100.000

Extraction Method: Principal Component Analysis.

It is clear from table 1 that the cumulative contribution rate of the first 3 principal components reaches 86.358%. The first 3 principal components can reflect 86.358% of the original indicator system. So they are used to replace the original 16 variables for further analysis.

The eigenvectors of the first 3 principal components are obtained from the analysis results (see Table 2), and the linear expressions of these 3 principal components can be used to replace the original 19 indicators.

$$F_1=0.05X_1-0.008X_2+0.015X_3-0.017X_4+0.007X_5+0.010X_6 -0.007X_7+0.015X_8+0.131X_9+0.129X_{10}+0.125X_{11} +0.129X_{12}+0.127X_{13}+0.127X_{14}+0.126X_{15}+0.124X_{16} \quad (2)$$

$$F_2=-0.05X_1-0.133X_2+0.311X_3-0.301X_4+0.266X_5 +0.256X_6-0.019X_7-0.013X_8+0.001X_9-0.001X_{11}+ 0.008X_{13}+0.009X_{14}+0.006X_{15}+0.026X_{16} \quad (3)$$

$$F_3=0.292X_1+0.376X_2-0.102X_3+0.091X_4-0.022X_5- 0.007X_6+0.319X_7+0.282X_8+0.033X_9+0.014X_{10}+0.016X_{11} +0.009X_{12}-0.001X_{14}-0.001X_{15}+0.003X_{16} \quad (4)$$

Table 2. Component Score Coefficient Matrix

	Component		
	1	*2*	*3*
Zscore(X1)	.050	-.050	.292
Zscore(X2)	-.008	-.133	.376
Zscore(X3)	.015	.311	-.102
Zscore(X4)	-.017	-.301	.091
Zscore(X5)	.007	.266	-.022
Zscore(X6)	.010	.256	-.007
Zscore(X7)	-.007	-.019	.319
Zscore(X8)	.015	-.013	.282
Zscore(X9)	.131	.001	.033
Zscore(X10)	.129	.000	.014
Zscore(X11)	.125	-.001	.016
Zscore(X12)	.129	.000	.009
Zscore(X13)	.127	.008	.000
Zscore(X14)	.127	.009	-.001
Zscore(X15)	.126	.006	-.001
Zscore(X16)	.124	.026	.003

Extraction Method: Principal Component Analysis.
Rotation Method: Varimax with Kaiser Normalization.
Component Scores.

Taking the contribution rate of each principal component as weight, evaluation equation is educed as follows.

$$F=0.571F_1+0.294F_2+0.135F_3 \quad (5)$$

Equation (5) is the evaluation model of the technological innovation capability. By substitution of the data obtained from standardized processing into (2) (3) (4) (5), the comprehensive scores of the enterprises' technological innovation capability can be calculated. It is assumed that the listed firms with comprehensive scores greater than 0 have strong technological innovation capability, Y=1; and the ones with comprehensive scores lower than 0 have weak technological innovation capability, Y=0. Then logistic regression analysis can be taken by use of SPSS 16.0.

3 Logistic Regression Analysis

A. Significance Test of Logistic Regression Model

Table 3 shows the validation of the model. It can be seen that the value of -2 log likelihood is 0 after two steps and the value of Nagelkerke R Square is 1. It indicates that the equation fitting result is satisfactory and the model can fully demonstrate the difference between the innovation and non-innovative enterprises.

Table 3. Model Summary

Step	-2 Log likelihood	Cox & Snell R Square	Nagelkerke R Square
1	.000	.750	1.000
2	.000	.750	1.000

B. Logistic Regression Analysis Process

Table 4. Variables in the Equation

		B	S.E.	Wald	df	Sig.	Exp (B)
Step 2(a)	ZX1	51.386	8866.011	.000	1	.995	2.07E+22
	ZX2	101.854	23586.837	.000	1	.997	1.72E+44
	ZX4	-21.809	5478.689	.000	1	.997	0
	ZX5	-56.804	16657.407	.000	1	.997	0
	ZX6	42.642	16804.088	.000	1	.998	3.3E+18
	ZX7	-95.980	24629.099	.000	1	.997	0
	ZX8	-35.304	7593.155	.000	1	.996	0
	ZX9	-298.681	61287.571	.000	1	.996	0
	ZX10	343.416	107343.654	.000	1	.997	1.39+149
	ZX11	-94.986	31635.506	.000	1	.998	0
	ZX12	-127.354	86330.376	.000	1	.999	0
	ZX13	4427.301	1409057.723	.000	1	.997	.
	ZX14	-4482.017	1410908.087	.000	1	.997	0
	ZX15	140.650	46534.355	.000	1	.998	1.21E+61
	ZX16	108.590	27362.249	.000	1	.997	1.45E+47
	Constant	8.630	5121.651	.000	1	.999	5595.59

a Variable(s) entered on step 1: ZX1, ZX2, ZX3, ZX4, ZX5, ZX6, ZX7, ZX8, ZX9, ZX10, ZX11, ZX12, ZX13, ZX14, ZX15, ZX16.

After two steps selection, logistic regression model is obtained according to table 4.

$$Y = 8.630 + 51.386x_1 + 101.854x_2 - 21.809x_4$$
$$-56.804x_5 + 42.642x_6 - 95.980x_7 - 35.304x_8 - 298.681x_9$$
$$+343.416x_{10} - 94.986x_{11} - 127.354x_{12} + 4427.301x_{13}$$
$$-4482.017x_{14} + 140.650x_{15} + 108.590x_{16} \quad (6)$$

$$p = \frac{1}{1+e^{-Y}} \quad (7)$$

P is obtained by substitution of the data into (6) (7). If $p \leq 0.5$, it is said that the listed company has strong technological innovation capability. If $p \leq 0.5$, it means that the listed company has weak technological innovation capability.

According to the partial regression coefficients, it can be seen that there are 15 explanatory variables into the model as follows, X_1, X_2, X_4, X_5, X_6, X_7, X_8, X_9, X_{10}, X_{11}, X_{12}, X_{13}, X_{14}, X_{15}, and X_{16}. This indicates that with the implementation of technological innovation projects in China, the characteristics of technological innovative enterprises embodies their debt paying ability, profit ability, and industry status.

As is seen from the variables removed from the model, there is no significant difference in equity ratio X_3 between innovative enterprises and non-innovative enterprises.

In the 15 explanatory variables entered into the regression model, there are 7 indicators whose partial regression coefficient is positive. The partial regression coefficient of X_{13} is 4427.301, and it indicates that the output value of new products has absolute advantage in technological innovation. The partial regression coefficient of X_{10} is 343.416, X_{15} is 140.650, and X_{16} is 108.590. The three indicators show the fund investment and intellectual property are the key to technological innovation capability. So it needs enterprises to enhance their R&D investment and protect their intellectual property consciously. The partial regression coefficient of X_2 is 101.854, and X_1 is 51.386. This reflects the ability of return on enterprises' shareholders affects technological innovation. Also, the partial regression coefficient of X_6 is 42.642 and it means debt paying ability with funds on hand plays a role in technological innovation of enterprises.

According to the partial regression coefficient, asset-liability ratio X_4, liquidity ratio X_5, rate of return on assets X_7, ratio of cash flow to debt X_8, R&D personnel full-time equivalent X_9, amount of new product items X_{11}, expenditure of the development of new products X_{12}, and new product sales income X_{14} are the restraining factors of the development of innovative enterprises. These indicators don't have much promoting effect on the technological innovation capability of enterprises.

4 Discriminant Result of Logistic Regression Model

Table 5 shows that in the identification and classification of enterprises using 0.5 as the cut value, the total accuracy rate of the logistic regression model is 100% after 2 steps optimization. According to the distribution of predictive values, all samples are located in the vicinity of 0 and 1. It indicates the judgment result reliability is high and innovative and non-innovative enterprises can be fully identified. Overall, the logistic model describes the technological innovation capability of listed companies reasonably and objectively.

Table 5. Classification Table(a)

	Observed		Predicted		
			Y		
			.00	1.00	*Percentage Correct*
Step 1	Y	.00	24	0	100.0
		1.00	0	24	100.0
	Overall Percentage				100.0
Step 2	Y	.00	24	0	100.0
		1.00	0	24	100.0
	Overall Percentage				100.0

a The cut value is .500

5 Conclusion

It is important for the development of enterprises to identify whether the enterprises have strong technological innovation capability. It can help enterprises improve their independent innovation ability and maximize enterprises' whole value. Through regression analysis of the financial indicators and the industrial indicators, we can draw a conclusion that many indicators have an impact on the technological innovation capability. Technological innovation is a long process. The enterprises should improve their R&D investment, and protect intellectual property to create core competitive ability.

Because the attainability of data is difficult, empirical analysis of this paper is not carried out in different industries and different scales, and regional differences and other factors are not quantified into the model. These shortcomings should be amended in further studies.

References

1. Schumpeter, J.A.: Economic development theory, pp. 73–74. Commercial Press, Beijing (1990)
2. Westphal, L.E., Rhee, Y.W., Pursell, G.: Sources of Technological Capability in South Area. Technological Capability in the Third World, 163–279 (1984)
3. Xu, Q.: R&D Management. Higher Education Press, Beijing (1986)
4. Souitaris, V.: Firm-Specific Competencies Determining Technological Innovation: A Survey in Greece. R&D Management (12), 61–77 (2002)
5. Han, H.: SME Innovation System Model and Empirical Analysis. Economics and Management (8), 108–112 (2009)

6. Fan, D., Zhou, H.: Factor Analysis of Evaluation of Regional Innovation Capacity. Industrial Technology & Economy 25(3), 61–63 (2006)
7. Zhang, C., Zhu, S.: An analysis of enterprises technological innovation capability in China—empirical research based on Industry panel data and DEA. Economic Forum (23), 31–35 (2009)
8. Xu, L., Zheng, R., Zhou, S.: The Application of Grey Fuzzy Comprehensive Evaluation on the assessment of enterprise's technological innovation capability. Science and Technology Management Research (4), 149–159 (2010)
9. Chen, Z., Zhang, D., Shan, G.: The Evaluation about Technologic Innovation Capability of SMEs Based on BP Neural Network. Science and Technology Management Research (2), 56–58 (2010)
10. Miao, C., Wang, H., Feng, J., Sun, L.: Enterprise Technology Innovation Competence Aggregation Study Based on the Ant Colony Algorithm. Science of Science and Management of S.& T (2), 35–39 (2010)

Research on Channels Managerial Tactics Based on Product Life Cycle Theory

Rongsheng Lv and Jian Wang

Academy of Management
Tianjin University of Technology
Tianjin, China

Abstract. The study and application of product life cycle has great significance in promoting managers to establish channel strategy. According to the different characteristics of every stage of product life cycle, this article analyzed the ability requirement of different stages. In the end, according to these various requirement, the paper comes up with the channels managerial tactics should be taken to which are appropriate for each stage. And, the tactics should be practical and operability by the refinement of indicators and approaches.

Keywords: product life cycle, channel capacity, channels managerial tactics.

1 Introduction

Product life cycle started on research on the law of sales change after product entered markets. It was first put forward by Raymond Vernon who is a professor of Harvard University in the paper of "International Investment and International Trade in the Product Cycle" in 1966. It was accepted and used by many scholars up to now. The study and application of product life cycle has great significance in promoting managers to establish channel strategy. Many scholars have studied deeply on marketing strategy in product life cycle from different angles. To sum up, these studies can be divided into three categories: firstly, the study on pricing strategies in product life cycle; secondly, the study on sales promotion in product life cycle; thirdly, the study on channel strategy in product life cycle.

In general, at present, most of the work has been focus on pricing strategies and sales promotion, and has less addressed the issue of channels managerial tactics or less thorough study. This paper goes back to research on channel tactics based on product life cycle theory; propose concrete channels managerial tactics according to the concrete characteristics of every stage of product life cycle. The tactics should be practical and operability by the refinement of indicators and approaches.

2 The Stage of Product Life Cycle and Its Characteristics

Product life cycle (PLC) means the whole process from the market to be eliminated, also means market life or economic life, relative to product's material life or working life. Material life reflects the physical form of material goods consumption changes

M. Dai (Ed.): ICCIC 2011, Part II, CCIS 232, pp. 211–217, 2011.

process; the market life reflects the economic value of goods in the market process of change. Philip Kotler pointed out that product life cycle can divide into introduction stage, growth stage, maturity stage and decline stage in his book "Marketing Management", and made a graphic as shown in Figure 1.

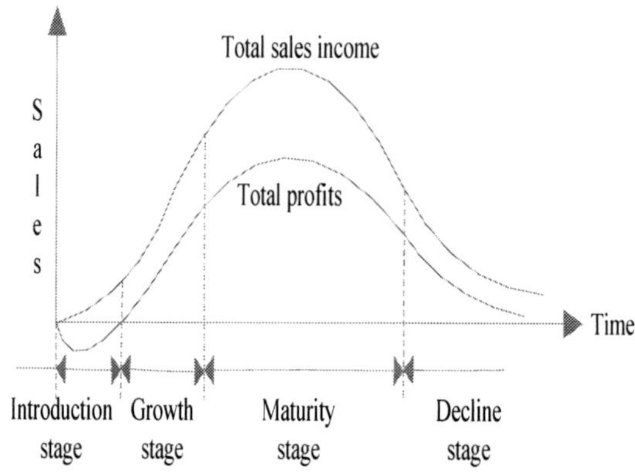

Fig. 1. Product life cycle curve

Every stage of product life cycle has different characteristics in market, sales, and corporate earnings as shown in Table 1. This means enterprises must have a concrete analysis of the actual characteristics of each stage, in order to formulate the appropriate channels managerial tactics.

Table 1. Characteristics of Each Stage of Product Life Cycle

		Introduction stage	**Growth stage**	**Maturity stage**	**Decline stage**
Characteristics	Market	little market, Few customers	To become greater or larger	Basic saturated, Few potential customers	Loss of customers, market to reduce
	Mode of Production	Can not be mass-produced	To begin mass production	Mass production	Quantity production
	cost	high	Higher (lower start)	Lower	Low
	Sales	Seldom	Begin to increase	Slow growth	Substantially reduced
	profit	Deficit	Increase	Start to decline	Substantially reduced
	competitor	few	Increase	Many	Substantially reduced
marketing objective		To enhance product awareness, strive for customers to try	To develop new markets, increase market share	To consolidate existing markets and to maximize profits	To cut spending, fight for the profits of as much as possible

A. Introduction Stage

When Products just listed, customers are few; enterprises need to have strong market development capability, developing the potential customer base. Products are sold less, but enterprises can have unit profitable, so warehousing capacity, cost control ability and financial support for capacity require low. Product is not very mature, customers contact with new products, and therefore the comprehensive service capabilities yet ask for not high.

B. Growth Stage

During the growth stage, many consumers are beginning to understand and accept the new products, buyers began to increase, and therefore there are more need for channel to develop new customers, helping manufacturers to continuously expand the market; sales began to increase, so the channel' warehousing capacity and financial support for capacity require more related to introduction stage, but the overall requirements are general; customers at this stage are beginning to pay more attention on product related services, which requires the channel should also strengthen its service capability, improve its service level.

C. Maturity Stage

At the mature stage, the market has basically saturated, there are very few potential customers, so market development capability's requirement is general; mature stage products have great sales, but lower unit profits, so warehousing capacity, financial support for capacity and cost control capacity require high; competition is fierce during the maturity stage, the product is very mature, so customers want to have high level of service, thus channel should supply good service for clients.

D. Decline Stage

At the decline stage, the market began to significantly decrease, consumers have turned to other types of products, the trend of this product out of the market is irreversible, it is no longer necessary that channel make great efforts to develop new markets; product sales dropped, the channel's warehousing capacity and financial support for capacity also requires general; but manufacturers want to make profit as much as possible, reduce all unnecessary input, and thus channel requires a high cost control capacity, in order to reduce costs to increase profit.

3 Channels Managerial Tactics for Different Stages of Product Life Cycle

A. Channels Managerial Tactics of Introduction Stage

At the introduction stage, the product has just listed, consumers also do not know the product, the market volume is small, thus marketing goal is to promote their products quickly, reduce the introduction stage, therefore, these determine that the overall import of channels managerial tactics should be short-channel based, early for product acceptance by consumers, specifically, companies can sell their own products or choose professional shops to test new products' market. But companies must understand that, as the market promotion, channel network is essential to full realization of market penetration. Therefore enterprises need to establish their own distribution network, the network is reasonable or not will directly determine the success or failure of market promotion, determine that the enterprise can quickly enter the growth stage or not.

The key of Channel network is the choice of brokers; the choice has a significant impact on distribution capability of enterprises. For consumers, distribution channels are often on behalf of manufacturers, so companies need a careful choice of the intermediary channel members. When selected middlemen, based on comprehensive collection of the information of middlemen's distribution capability, cooperative attitude, warehousing capacity, financial support for capacity, management capacity, comprehensive service capability and reputation, enterprises choose their suitable middlemen after making a careful and detailed analysis. Specifically, the indicators of selecting middlemen are as shown in Table 2.

Table 2. Evaluation Indexes for Middlemen

Index	**Ability Requirement**
Distribution capability	major Market coverage, large number of customers, good relationship with customers
Cooperative attitude	With the cooperation and business development initiative, cooperate actively with the enterprise sales work
Warehousing capacity	With long-range logistics and bulk storage capacity
Financial support for capacity	With strong financial support, the timely payment
Management capacity	Management practices, operational efficiency
Comprehensive service capability	Provide technical guidance, such as, delivery on this and other products needed to support services
Reputation	Focus on credit, bad credit history does not exist

B. Channels Managerial Tactics of Growth Stage

Products have been imported into the growth stage; consumers are beginning to understand and accept the new products, buyers began to increase. On the other hand, as corporate profits begin to increase, competitors are also stepping into this stage, so the marketing objective of an enterprise is to continue to develop new markets, increase market share. This requires the full expansion of the marketing channel network, and increasing market coverage as much as possible in order to achieve full market penetration as early as possible.

At growth stage, the expansion of distribution network mainly depends on strong support for middlemen to complete. The quantity and quality of middlemen in the channel network will directly determine the enterprise's distribution capability and market penetration. In order to enhance the enthusiasm of existing middlemen and attract new ones, middlemen can be supported by a variety of ways (as shown in Figure 2).

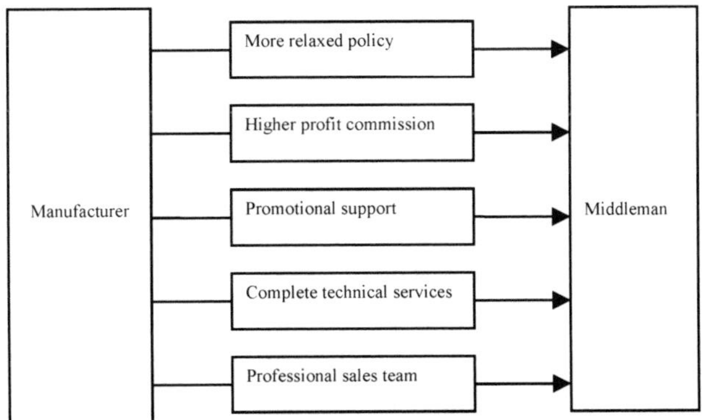

Fig. 2. The way of support middleman

C. Channels Managerial Tactics of Maturity Stage

When products enter into the mature stage, the market is basically saturated, there are few potential customers, and sales began to slow growth or even decline. At the same time, because there are many competitors, competition is stiff, the manufacturers' channel network has more maturity and fixed through a comprehensive channel network construction. At this time the enterprise marketing objective is to consolidate existing markets and maximize profits, which requires that business center of channel management strategy should be transferred from expanding channel network to network management. Only through the investigation and assessment on middlemen, eliminating unqualified middlemen, and to strengthen the management and control of the remaining brokers can better improve channel effectiveness, reduce costs and enable enterprises to maximize profits.

In order to improve channel effectiveness, enterprises must make comprehensive assessment of intermediaries (mainly including sales, delivery time to customers, the level of cooperation, etc.) and use it as the basis of reward and punishment to middlemen. Based on comparatively objective and comprehensive assessment, enterprise should give substance, honor and so on incentives reward to good brokers, and give punishment to low efficiency brokers, limits the period of time to improve, if he could not achieve goals, then enterprises may cancel its agent qualifications and instead to seek competent and qualified intermediaries.

According to the assessment, the inefficient middlemen have been phased out, then the rest of the brokers need to be strengthened management and control (as shown Figure 3), so as to reduce costs, increase efficiency of channels.

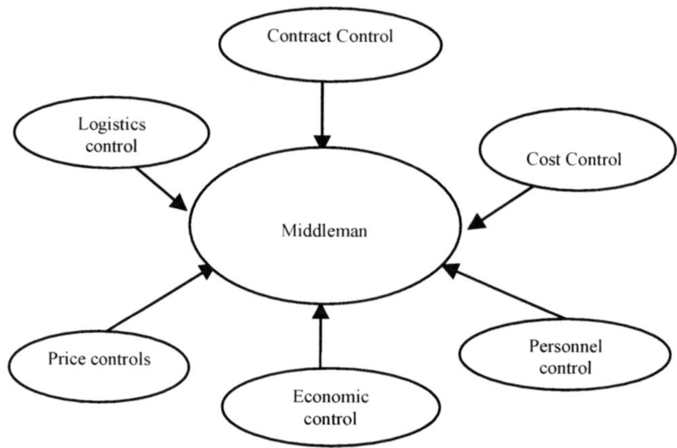

Fig. 3. Control of the middlemen

D. Channels Managerial Tactics of Decline Stage

When products enter into the decline stage, market has declined rapidly, profits have fallen sharply, and competitors have also withdrawn from the market. At this time the enterprise marketing goal is to cut spending as much as possible, get as much profit. Therefore, enterprises, at this stage, make substantial reduction in ad spending while beginning to reduce the number of middlemen; they keep only a small number of efficient intermediaries so as to reduce costs. At this stage, enterprise's channels managerial tactics is to safeguard the interests of brokers well when they gradually withdraw from the market, to keep brokers' loyalty to the enterprise so that enterprises can use the original channel network when they launch other new products.

Enterprises can safeguard the interests of middlemen from three aspects (as shown in Figure 4) in the process of withdrawing from the market so as to enhance the loyalty degree.

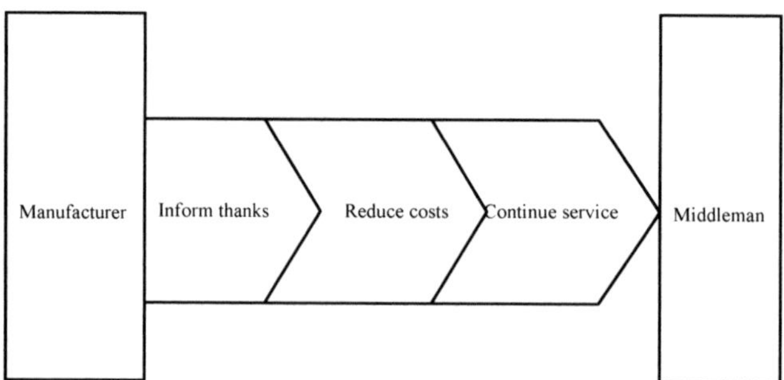

Fig. 4. The way of maintain interest of the middlemen

4 Conclusion

Different stages of product life cycle have different requirements to channel capacity. Enterprises should make matching channels managerial tactics at different stages according to channel capacity. At introduction stage, enterprises' channels managerial tactics should be committed to the establishment of distribution network, and make great effort on middlemen. At growth stage, enterprises should fully extend the marketing channel network as much as possible and increase market coverage. At maturity stage, channels managerial tactics' center should be transferred from expanding channel network to network management. At decline stage, enterprises' channels managerial tactics is to safeguard the interests of middlemen well when they gradually withdraw from the market, to keep brokers' loyalty so that enterprises can use the original channel network when they launch other new products.

References

1. Tang, B.: Application of product life cycle in Marketing Strategy. Commercial Economics Review 02, 64–66 (1999)
2. Huang, Y.: Discussion on different stages of product life cycle pricing strategy. Journal of Southwest Guizhou Teachers College for Nationalities 02, 79–82 (2000)
3. Li, C.: Different stages of product life cycle pricing strategy and consumer psychology. Market Modernization 14, 29–30 (2008)
4. Liu, Y.: Discussion on the product life cycle and advertising strategies. Science & Technology Information 26, 490 (2007)
5. Liang, Y.: Transformation of Advertising strategy from the t perspective of product life cycle. Journal of Guangxi University (Philosophy and Social Science) 29, 270–271 (2007)
6. Xu, B.: In The Product Life Cycle at Different Stages of Advertising Performance Demands and Application Strategy. Economic Research Guide 10, 106–107 (2009)
7. Huang, X.: The Study of Product Life Cycle. Commercial Research 17, 13–15 (2003)
8. Lin, C.: New products channel strategy choice based on Product life cycle theory. Popular Science & Technology 01, 120–121 (2006)
9. Kotler, P.: Marketing Management, vol. 10. The Peoples Press of Shanghai (2003)
10. He, Y.: Product Life Cycle And Choice of Channel Policy. Xiangtan University (2002)

Analysis of the Theory of Commercial Value in Chinese-Foreign Cooperation in Running Schools in Higher Education

Lihui Xie

[1] School of Political Science and Public Administration, Wuhan University, Wuhan, P.R. China, 430072
[2] School of Inter-cultural Studies, Jiangxi Normal University, Nanchang, P.R. China, 330022
tatsuokija@foxmail.com

Abstract. It is common practice that successful business organizations set up strategic objectives on explicit "value proposition". Chinese-foreign cooperation in running schools in higher education is also a sort of commercial presence, and its commercial value is embodied in the sum of value of education products or services in production, consumption and trade. This article is going to interpret the commercial value of Chinese-foreign cooperation in running schools from the perspectives of economics, management and sociology theory. As one of the means of education, Chinese-foreign cooperation in running schools is also likely to realize all value goals that can be realized by all education means.

Keywords: higher education, Chinese-foreign cooperation in running schools, commercial value.

1 Introduction

Attempt of Chinese-foreign cooperation in running schools started under the great background of the open-door to the outside world of China in the 80s of the Twentieth Century. In earlier 1990s, Chinese-foreign cooperation in running schools began to emerge in the field of education as a means of running schools. "Regulations of the People's Republic of China on Chinese-Foreign Cooperation in Running Schools" executed on September 1, 2003, provides definite legal foundation for development and supervision of Chinese-foreign cooperation in running schools. It is stipulated in "Regulations" that, "Chinese-foreign cooperation in running schools belongs to non-profit undertaking and is component of Chinese education. The country carries out the policy of expanding openness, standardizing school running, managing pursuant to the law and facilitating development for Chinese-foreign cooperation in running schools. China encourages bringing in Chinese-foreign cooperation in running schools with high-quality foreign educational resources. China encourages conducting Chinese-foreign cooperation in running schools in higher education and vocation education and encourages Chinese institutions of higher education to cooperate in running schools

M. Dai (Ed.): ICCIC 2011, Part II, CCIS 232, pp. 218–225, 2011.

with well-known foreign institutions of higher education. "Under direction of regulations and policies and push of social demand and economic development, Chinese-foreign cooperation in running schools in universities has gradually been developed.

2 Origin and Comprehension of Chinese-Foreign Cooperation in Running Schools in Higher Education

2.1 Development of Economic Globalization

Economic globalization has laid material foundation for ever-lasting higher education demand of people. Globalization has driven cross-border flow of manpower, capital, commodity, service, knowledge, technology and information, etc, and people are eager to learn knowledge of other countries and international conventions so as to find a position in the international labor force market that adapts to different working environment and can give full play to personal aptitude. Globalization has strengthened communication of all countries in educational resources and has enabled educational markets of all countries to be open the whole world and form a globalized educational market. Universities form university alliance and cooperate with foreign countries in running schools one after another to comply with the tide of social and economic development of economic globalization.

2.2 Advancement of Educational Popularization

After the Second World War, faced up with fierce competition of source of students and funds, quite a large number of universities chose to remould their image and transferred the elite education they had always been committed to into popular education. Higher education has been obviously expanded in terms of quantity, scale of world-wide higher education is rapidly enlarged and higher education begins to step into a popularization and even universalness stage. Investment in higher education lags behind development of its scale, educational resources lag behind the speed of expansion of enrollment scale, educational concept, curriculum system, personnel training method, teaching content and teaching method need urgently to be reformed and the teachership level needs to be improved. Universities can alleviate, to a certain degree, issues of insufficient high quality educational resources in the process of popularization of higher education by Chinese-foreign cooperation in running schools, rationally bringing in and making effective use of foreign high quality higher education resources.

2.3 Necessity of Educational Globalization

Service trade of international education and cross-border education opens broad space for exchange and cooperation of higher education in different countries and regions. Chinese-foreign cooperation in running schools is educational activity held by Chinese educational institutions with foreign educational institutions in which

Chinese citizens are the primary recruitment targets. As a kind of cross-border practice form of higher education, Chinese-foreign cooperation in running schools has set up a favorable platform for rational utilization of international excellent teaching resources and carrying on and promoting excellent cultural traditional of a nation. It has become a form of running schools to comply with internationalized demand and is also supplement for Chinese education (Qin Meiqiong, 2006).

2.4 Demand on Internationalized Talents

With more and more multi-national enterprises entering China, demand on talents is on the increase and talents with international education background are more and more favored by the society. It has become an important strategic choice for development of colleges and universities to cooperate with foreign higher education institutions, bring in high quality educational resources, set up disciplines, majors and personnel training mode that are urgently needed by the market but can not be provided by the schools contemporarily and realize internationalization of education.

2.5 Development of Colleges and Universities

With entry of China into WTO, as educational institutions and service industries, universities have to face up with a more open competition field. For any university to remain invincible in fierce competition, it has to continue to improve its own comprehensive level, which requires universities to further strengthen cooperation with foreign high-level universities at the time of reinforcing their own construction, to make up for each other's deficiencies and to absorb advanced foreign education experiences so as to motivate development of higher education in China.

In conclusion, Chinese-foreign cooperation in running schools is produced and developed under the great background of economic globalization and internationalization of higher education. With continuous expansion of Chinese openness to the outside world and unceasing advancement of educational reform, Chinese-foreign cooperation in running schools has become extremely rapid. By February 2007, institutions or projects of Chinese-foreign cooperation in running schools had expanded from the number of over 70 at the beginning of 1995 to more than 1400 (Meng Zhongyuan, 2008). It is common practice that successful business organizations set up strategic objectives on explicit "value proposition". Chinese-foreign cooperation in running schools in higher education is also a sort of commercial presence, and its commercial value is embodied in the sum of value of education products or services in production, consumption and trade.

3 Theory of Commercial Value of Chinese-Foreign Cooperation in Running Schools in Higher Education

And commodity or service has its value. Scholars summarize value as the function of income return to the price paid. As for common people, value means low price, interests they obtain from products or services and result of balance between "money paid" and "quality acquired" by customers. The value of Chinese-foreign cooperation in running schools comes from the commercial procedure of educational products or services offered by universities and is optimized in terms of its rationality and harmony to provide profits and assistance for consumption subjects in the aspects of products, services and technology. The connotation of its value is embodied as follows:

3.1 Political Value: Serving for Interests of the National State

"Internationalization of higher education is to foster first-class talents proficient in both eastern and western culture who can better serve for interests of their own country in the economic globalization" (Yang Fujia, 2001). Some developed countries have always been taking internationalization of higher education as an important component of strategy of global development and promote their thoughts and culture. As one of the means of globalization of higher education in China, Chinese-foreign cooperation in running schools borrows advanced foreign scientific culture, value concept and school running mode to cultivate academic elites, diminish its difference with the global level, improves school running level and educational quality of higher education and facilitates and improves higher education of the national state.

3.2 Social Value: Action of Motivation to Social Development

The most active value action of Chinese-foreign cooperation in running schools to development of higher education is also reflected in the fact that it intensifies its link with the society, makes the educational services and products it provides more in line with demand of the society on talents in the future, strengthens students' ability to adapt to multi-culture and the environment of globalization, improves competitive force of higher education and reinforces the action of motivation of higher education to social development. As for developed countries, internationalization of education can strengthen their cultural infiltration and influential capacity in developing countries, and can, in the mean time, absorb first-class talents from developing countries. As for developing countries and underdeveloped countries, internationalization of education can improve their educational development level and obtain some advanced technology and experience. At the same time, internationalization of education is favorable to expand the cultural vision of its social members, improve the degree of openness of the society and accelerate the progress of modernization of the society.

3.3 Economic Value: Economic Interest Is External Motive

Driven by economic interests, universities in many countries take a positive attitude in expanding outside communication and bring enormous economic profits for these countries through educational exportation. As the world economic power, America throw a lot of capital into higher education to attract international students to go to America for further study who contribute USD12 billion each year for American economy. Since 1980s, Australian Government has begun to export education by regarding it as an important service trade and its education service revenue in 2003 approximated to AUD4.9 billion (Gong Siyi, 2007). Britain is the first country that put forward the concept of "international student market". In 2002, the number of international overseas students in Britain broke through 0.16 million who contributed GBP1 billion for the country (Zhou Yan, 2002). More importantly, these international overseas students stay in these developed countries after they finished their school career and the economic value of talents these countries obtain is invisible wealth and can not be calculated with figures. Therefore, developed countries are optimistic about the enormous educational market of China one after another, establish cooperative partner relationship with China and lay foundation for Chinese overseas students to go to their countries.

3.4 Cultural Value: The Function of Cultural Exchange

1) To establish corporate cultural values through the strategy of alliance

Economic globalization, technological revolution and openness of markets of all countries throughout the world, more and more companies realize that it is unlikely for them to independently finish the strategic target of developing new markets merely relying on their own resources and technology, so companies from all works of life in the world choose to set up strategic alliance and cooperation. The value of entry into strategic alliance for an organization is that technical cooperation or cooperation in developing new products can supplement its technical or manufacturing deficiency, improve its efficiency in supply chain and obtain market or economy of scale (Thompson, 2006).

Strategic alliance can enable cooperative partners to learn and cooperate in the concept of interests and value, to adapt to changes of industrial environment and to come to know unfamiliar market and cultural knowledge. It is exactly on the basis of pursuing a common cooperation target, maintaining respective independence, and keeping respective strategic independence and particular interests that Chinese-foreign cooperation institutions implement together a project or activity by sharing resources and competence.

2) Cooperation with win-win results can bring cultural ideas with economic value for the two parties of cooperation.

Education products or services the alliance offers make it possible for consumers to frequently share network resources and obtain value of products or services supplemented and reduce the high amount of cost that customers have to pay in order to independently acquire international resources. A corporate organization can acquire value added by resorting to cooperation with organizations of alliance, making use of mutual resources, information and knowledge, collaborating with culture of different corporate organizations to create effect and strengthening competitive power of corporate organizations to obtain value added. Chinese education institutions (universities) can diminish gaps with advanced countries in organizational implementation and management of educational projects through Chinese-foreign cooperation in running schools, increase the diversity and selectivity of education supply and improve teaching conditions and environment. Foreign education institutions (universities) can directly or indirectly obtain the double profits of culture and talents through Chinese-foreign cooperation in running schools and can further get direct or indirect economic value for attracting more excellent talents to go their countries for further study and employment.

3.5 Value of the Subject of Running Schools: To Create Value for Stakeholders

Value of subjects is composed by three major parts: value brought by corporate organizations to consumers ("value obtained by consumers"), value that corporate organizations can obtain from consumers ("value obtained by corporate organizations") and life-time value of strategic cooperation partners that corporate organizations are mostly satisfied to be improved to the highest degree.

3) Value of consumption subjects

According to Philip Kotler, "Value is assessment on the competence of products to satisfy all varieties of demands by consumers." It is usually because consumers believe that a product or service can bring them incomparable value that they choose this product or service. Consumption subjects of Chinese-foreign cooperation in running schools are reflected in the talent labor market (namely, employing unit) and educational consumers. Selection and employment of personnel by employing units is usually based upon professional positions and industrial and corporate organization development changes and their demands on the type of talents and labor force, their quality, technology and skills are in accordance with development of the times. Economic globalization propels the labor force market of China to develop towards internationalization, which opens a steady flow of world-class and huge "assembly area" of labor force and which also accelerates the vigorous development of Chinese-foreign cooperation in running schools in colleges and universities of all levels. The consumption subjects of education refer to parents and teachers. Fostering of talents should be based on requirement of economic and social development and purpose and need of students in pursuing study and its value is usually restrained to economic development rule, social development rule and talent growth rule. Through cooperative means, teachers have more opportunities to go abroad for further study and academic exchange and have more chances to work and study together with foreign teachers and to be improved in teaching and scientific research. Thus, corporate organizations need to be familiar with the continuously changing needs of consumers and design and develop products or service projects that can furnish outstanding value for consumers.

4) Value of corporate organizations (universities)

Corporate organizations often make full use of resource competence of all parties on the premise of satisfying demands of consumers and taking the fundamental interest and long term objective of commercial value as the starting point, integrate resources, grow together with trading partners, cooperate with win-win results and create value. Through Chinese-foreign cooperation in running schools, higher education rationally brings in and makes effective use of excellent foreign higher education resources, which, to a certain degree, alleviates issues of deficient excellent education resources in the process of popularization of higher education. Higher education in China borrows foreign advanced higher education management experiences and school running modes, and multi-channel foreign education funds and cultivates talents full of international competitive power to facilitate reform of Chinese higher education, improve education level and international competitive force of Chinese higher education and promote cultural and economic cooperation.

5) To create value for cooperative partners

What the strategic partner of a corporate organization is knowledge-oriented competitive force, production technology and production and operation capacity or is to strengthen current production technology and competitive force of the corporate organization. With the means of cooperation, both of the cooperative parties can give full play to their production skill and production capacity up to the hilt and can create the most value through collaboration. Chinese-foreign cooperation in running schools is also a sort of commercial presence. Commercial presence means that suppliers of service of one member provide service within the border of the other member in the form of commercial institutions. For instance, educational institutions or citizens of one member party provide services within the border of the other member party by means of setting up subsidiary bodies or in the form of joint venture and cooperation. Foreign education institutions and universities acquire profits and value by exporting their education as products or services in the means of Chinese-foreign cooperation in running schools.

4 Conclusion

With the entire world propelled by the wave of globalization and informationization in recent years, more and more enterprises depend on innovation in order to continue to grow. In a survey initiated by the Economist Intelligence Unit, there were 54% CEO who thought that, business model innovation would become a more important strategy than innovation of product and service in the year 2010. Having established cooperative partner relationship through the strategic alliance --- Chinese-foreign cooperation in running schools in the field of higher education, Chinese and foreign universities develop and share resources together so as to reduce the cost risk in acquisition of resources and pursue development and, thus, realize the ultimate goal and final outcome of business model innovation in education field --- maximization of commercial value of business organizations. As a standard public product, the value target of Chinese-foreign cooperation in running schools is bound to be penetrated to all fields of politics, economy, culture and society through its subjects.

Acknowledgment. Research Project: one of achievements of social sciences planned projects [No: 08jy63] of the Eleventh Five-Year in Jiangxi Province.

References

1. Dai, X.X., Mo, J.H., Xie, A.B.: Marketisation of Higher Education. Peking University Press, Beijing (2004)
2. Christopher, M., Payne, A., Ballantyne, D.: Relationship Marketing, translated by Yi, W. China Financial & Economic Publishing House, Beijing (2005)
3. Hu, L.C.: Innovation of Models of International Cooperation in Running Schools. Hunan Normal University Press, Changsha (2008)
4. Brach of Chinese Association of Higher Education to Bring in Foreign Brainwork. Internationalization of Universities: Theory and Practice. Peking University Press, Beijing (2007)

5. Gong, S.Y.: Study on Models of Chinese-Foreign Cooperation in Running Schools in Universities. Shanghai University Press, Shanghai (2007)
6. Thompson, et al.: Strategy: Winning in the Marketplace, translated by Lan, H. L., et al. China Machine Press, Beijing (2006)
7. Zhou, Y.: On the Internationalized Education in Australia, England and USA. Journal of Chongqing Normal University (Edition of Social Sciences) 4 (2002)
8. Yang, F.J.: Internationalization — Necessary Trend for Development of Higher Education. China Higher Education 13 (2001)
9. Meng, Z.Y.: The Strategy for Development of International Cooperative Schools. Journal of Harbin University 29(7) (2008)
10. Qin, M.Q.: Development Strategy of Chinese-Foreign Cooperation in Running Schools. Sanjiang University Journal 2 (2006)

Empirical Study on Market Efficiency in Hubei-China Automotive Industry Based on SCP Paradigm

Xuetao Lee and Shuxiu Yu

Department of Economics and Management
Hubei Univercity of Automotive Technology
Shiyan, China
mfzhou123@foxmail.com

Abstract. Starting with the industry's market structure, resource allocation efficiency, level of technological progresst, market openness, this paper to construct the automobile industry market performance evaluation index system, and do an empirical analysis on the market performance of China's automobile industry by the fuzzy Borda number analytical method, giving a conclusion that market performance level of Hubei automotive industry has increased annually, but is still a big gap between Hubei province and other powerful provinces.

Keywords: Automobile Industry, SCP, Market Performance.

At present, China's auto industry has completed the first round of shuffling and formed six major automobile industry bases, including Beijing, Shanghai, Chongqing, Wuhan (Hubei Province), Guangzhou (Guangdong), Changchun (Jilin). With the establishment of strong position of the six provinces and municipalities above, the automotive industry distribution in China has basically shaped, but the more intense competition among them is following and the whole industry is bound to be difficult to avoid the re-shuffling. In response to competition, enterprises and the Government must formulate targeted and efficient development strategy, which requires the establishment of a scientific market efficiency evaluation system, to fully understand the rivals and clarity advantages and disadvantages in auto industry, to direct the development of automobile industry and find a rational path to improve the market efficiency.

In this paper, SCP paradigm is introduced into the study of market efficiency in automotive industry, to build evaluation index system on efficiency of industrial real market and potential market. Describe the Hubei automobile industry market efficiency profile through scale and efficiency of the industry, extent of technological advances and degree of market opening, and then render the weight of every evaluation index through the application of grid method and fuzzy Borda number analytical method. On this basis, a comprehensive evaluation will be given and scientific data and conclusions will be drawn.

M. Dai (Ed.): ICCIC 2011, Part II, CCIS 232, pp. 226–234, 2011.

1 Index System

In this paper, the automobile industry market performance evaluation indicators include industrial real market performance and potential market performance. Industrial real market performance refers to the level of industry growth characterized by industrial scale and efficiency, with characterization of industrial market concentration and profit margin. Industrial potential market performance refers to performance that is cumulative, potential and as a sign of industry sustainable development, with characterization of share of research funding in sales, engineering and technical personnel ratio, labor productivity, market share of imported cars.

A. B_1 industrial Scale and Efficiency

Industry scale and efficiency are the most intuitive measure of actual market performance. Scale structure and efficiency levels can be measured respectively by production concentration C_{11}, rate of return on sales $C_{12.}$

B. B2 Level of Technological Progress

Degree of technological progress is ultimately reflected through market performance of economic growth. It reflects the dynamic economic efficiency, an important aspect to measure market performance. The faster technology progress, the larger its effect on economic growth. The contribution of technological progress to economic growth can be represented by contribution rate of technological progress on economic growth, and described respectively by labor productivity C_{21}, proportion of research funding C_{22}, proportion of technical personnel C_{23}.

C. Market Opening Degree B3

Market opening degree reflects the performance of automotive industry in international competition. With the process of globalization in auto industry speeding up, the development of automobile industry must be oriented to domestic and overseas markets and two resources. Market opening degree of Chinese automotive industry can be measured by two indicators, that is, rate of import and export of equipment C_{31} and market share of imported cars C_{32}.

2 Market Efficiency Evaluation Model of the Automotive Industry

Automotive industry market performance has a bearing on the survival and development of automobile industry and it's an important symbol of the competitiveness of automotive industry, which needs to be evaluated with scientific methods. This method based on grid for the number of fuzzy Borda method. On the auto industry's assessment of market performance indicators of empowerment, and on this basis, a comprehensive evaluation. This paper renders the weight of every evaluation index through the application of grid method and fuzzy Borda number analytical method and gives a comprehensive evaluation on this basis.

A. Determine the Index Weight

Using this method, the basic steps of determining index weight are as follows:

1) **Hierarchical structure established**

It is the most important step in this method. The same as AHP, this method also decomposes complex issues down into various components called the index, and then continue to decompose until it is evaluable. The last form is a hierarchical structure with dominance relations from top to bottom.

2) **The establishment of grid**

Grid access method is a human judging and thinking model in personal construct theory put forward by Keller in 1955. A grid is composed of the element and attribute. In fact, with the establishment of index system, the elements have been determined. So this step is mainly to complete judgments of attribute, and then to get a complete grid through estimation accoding to degree of importance of the element under each attribute.

3) **Analysis on the grill, get the relative weight under the single criterion**

Set that scoring the first m attributes of indicators Dp for Bm (where m = 1, 2, ..., M; p = 1,2, ..., N). Steps using fuzzy Borda number analytical method to Analyse the grid are as follows:

a) **determine the membership degree**

Table 1 shows calculation of membership degree. M attributes in evaluation, membership Ump that each assessment index Dp is the "most important" was calculated. It is calculated as the following formula:

$$U_{mp} = B_m(D_p) / \max\left\{B_m(D_p)\right\} \tag{1}$$

b) **make fuzzy frequency tables**

Do fuzzy frequency statistics, the formula is as follows:

$$f_{hp} = \sum_{m=1}^{M} \delta_m^h(D_p)U_{mp} \tag{2}$$

$$R_p = \sum_h f_{hp} \tag{3}$$

In the formula, Dp came in the first h bits in priority order relations of m attributes, set $(D_p) = 1$; otherwise, $(D_P) = 0$. If Di, Dj m not in the same attributes in the Ump, and they should be ranked in h and h +1 bit, then σhm = σh +1 m = 1 / 2, and so do the rest.

c) **Calculate the fuzzy Borda FB (Dp)**

Render the weight for Qh if Dp is ranked h-bit in priority order, set Qh = (Nh) (N-h +1) / 2, then:

$$FB(D_p) = \sum_h \frac{f_{hp}}{R_p} \cdot Q_h = \sum_h W_{hp} Q_h \quad (4)$$

where,

$$W_{hp} = \frac{f_{hp}}{R_p}$$

d) normalized

Be normalized to obtain relative weight in a single criterion

$$W_p = FB(D_p) / \sum_{P=1}^{N} FB(D_p) \quad (5)$$

B. Determination of Consolidated Scores

Use linear weighted sum method to combine index score to a higher-grade index, until to get a composite score of the first- grade indicator. The formula is:

$$F = \sum_{P=1}^{N} (Y_p \cdot W_p) \quad (6)$$

3 Efficiency Analysis of Hubei Automotive Industry Market

According to the statistics of three-grade index value of Hubei and Shanghai Automotive Industry market Performance Evaluation from 2007 to 2009. At the same time, according to principles of evaluation criteria about automotive industry market performance evaluation proposed above, combining with consultation, to determine the assessment criteria and the evaluation index scores, and than use the index evaluation system established above to give evaluation to Hubei Automobile Industry market performance.

A. determination of weights in Evaluation system

On Design of Automotive industry market Performance Evaluation System, the establishment of a hierarchical structure and determination of elements of the grid have been completed. To get a complete grid, judgments to the grid attribute are to complete.

1) determine frequency of fuzzy of secondary indicators

According to the formula (1), (2), (3), calculate fuzzy frequency as shown in Table 1.

According to the formula (4), (5)calculate the fuzzy Borda FB (D_3) and the relative weight W_p of secondary indicators are:

FB (D_1)=1.57 FB(D_2)=1.92 FB (D_3)=0.92
W_1=0.36 W_2=0.43 W_3= 0.21

2) **determine frequency of fuzzy of the Third-grade indicators**

Analogy based on the above steps, obtain weights of the Third-grade indicators and calculate the index fuzzy frequency.

Table 1. Vague Frequencies Statistics Of the Second Estimation Index

p / f_{hp}	industrial scale and efficiencyB_1	level of technological progress B_2	*Market opening degree B_3*
1	1	1.5	*0.5*
2	0.4	0.5	*0.9*
3	1.4	0.6	*1.2*
Σ	*2.8*	*2.6*	*2.6*

Table 2. Statistical Chart of Fuzzy Frequency in Industrial Scale and Efficiency Indicator

f_{hp} / D_p	Production concentrationC_{11}	*Sales profitC_{12}*
1	2	*1*
2	0.6	*1.4*
Σ	*2.6*	*2.4*

FB (D_{11})=0.77 FB(D_{12})=0.42
W_{11}=0. 65 W_{12}=0. 35

Table 3. Statistical Chart of Fuzzy Frequency in Technical Advancement Degree Indicator

D_p / f_{hp}	Overall Labor ProductivityC_{21}	share of research funding in sales C_{22}	*engineering and technical personnel ratio C_{23}*
1	1.5	0.5	*1*
2	0.9	0.9	*0.8*
3	0.4	0.6	*0.6*
Σ	*2.8*	*2.0*	*2.5*

FB (D_{21})=1.93 FB(D_{22})=1.2 FB (D_{23})=1.58
W_{21}=0.41 W_{22}=0.25 W_{23}= 0.34

Table 4. Statistical Chart of Fuzzy Frequency in Market Opening Degree Indicator

D_p / f_{hp}	rate of import and export of equipment C_{31}	*market share of imported cars C_{32}*
1	2	*1*
2	0.8	*1.4*
Σ	*2.8*	*2.4*

FB (D_{31})=0.71 FB(D_{32})=0.42
W_{31}=0. 63 W_{32}=0. 37

Combine the results of the above secondary and third-grade evaluation indicators to get scores of the weights at all levels in the evaluation index system, as shown in Table 5.

Table 5. Index Right & Partly Value of Estimation Index System

Automotive industry market performance	**Secon-dary indicat-ors**	**Wei-ght**	**third-g-rade indicat-ors**	**relat-ive weig-ht**	**comprehensive weight**
	B1		C11	0.65	0.2307
		0.36	C12	0.35	0.125
	B2	0.43	C21	0.41	0.1782
			C22	0.25	0.1109
			C23	0.34	0.1463
	B3	0.21	C31	0.63	0.132
			C32	0.37	0.077

B. deteimine the consolidated scores

In accordance with the evaluation process of automotive industry market performance, this paper using the formula (6) to deal with the comprehensive evaluation results of market performance automotive industry in Hubei province and in Shanghai, in order to reach a general comments score of market performance. First of all, according to the formula (6), calculate scores of Industrial Scale and Efficiency Indicator B1, which is the secondary indicators in Hubei and Shanghai:

Similarly, in accordance with the above approach, scores of the secondary indicators like degree of technological progress B2, market opening degree B3 and general comments score of market performance can be calculated. The results are shown in Table 6.

Table 6. Table of Market Performance Evaluation of Automobile Industry

<table>
<tr><th colspan="3">Evaluation scores</th><th colspan="3">scores</th><th colspan="3">scores</th></tr>
<tr><td rowspan="9">Automotive industry market performance</td><td>Hubei</td><td>Shanghai</td><td>secondary indicators</td><td>Hubei</td><td>Shanghai</td><td>third-grade indicators</td><td>Hubei</td><td>Shanghai</td></tr>
<tr><td rowspan="8">0.523</td><td rowspan="8">0.832</td><td rowspan="2">B_1</td><td rowspan="2">0.47</td><td rowspan="2">0.79</td><td>C_{11}</td><td>0.0923</td><td>0.2307</td></tr>
<tr><td>C_{12}</td><td>0.075</td><td>0.05</td></tr>
<tr><td rowspan="3">B_2</td><td rowspan="3">0.52</td><td rowspan="3">0.83</td><td>C_{21}</td><td>0.0713</td><td>0.1782</td></tr>
<tr><td>C_{22}</td><td>0.0277</td><td>0.0943</td></tr>
<tr><td>C_{23}</td><td>0.1244</td><td>0.0878</td></tr>
<tr><td rowspan="3">B_3</td><td rowspan="3">0.62</td><td rowspan="3">0.91</td><td>C_{31}</td><td>0.099</td><td>0.1122</td></tr>
<tr><td>C_{32}</td><td>0.308</td><td>0.077</td></tr>
</table>

4 Analysis and Recommendations

From the above statistical results, there is a big gap between Hubei Automotive Industry market efficiency and market performance compared with Shanghai Automotive Industry.

A. Industrial scale and benefit analysis

1) Production concentration

Hubei Automotive Industrial production concentration showed a continuous upward trend in recent years, but growth is slow, indicating that the automotive industry in Hubei is still in the growth stage. The number of firms entering the industry is large and average scale is small.

2) Sales profit ratio

Sales profit ratio of the automotive industry in Hubei continuous growth in recent years. However, Automotive enterprises in Hubei is worse than those in Shanghai, indicating that in the same environment, in aspects of efficiency in resource allocation, automotive industry in Hubei will be much worse than Shanghai enterprises.

B. Analysis of degree of technological progress

1) Labor productivity

Personnel labor productivity of Hubei Automotive Industry increased year by year, but was far below the level of Shanghai. the main reason is that Hubei Automobile Industry has long been not performing well in digesting and absorpting the technology introducted, resulting in a relatively low level of production technology; Secondly, Hubei Automotive Industry is still in the extensive management and extensive management phase, and there is a significant gap in the implementation of lean production, resulting in low levels of labor productivity.

2) The proportion of research funding

Research funding ratio of Hubei Automotive Industry is well below that of Shanghai Automotive Industry. Mainly to the firm size of automotive industry in Hubei is generally too small to afford the cost of technology development; At the same time, the small enterprises size , low market share and small monopolistic power of products newly developed lead to the result that sometimes market benefit even lower than developing costs. Therefore, the developing desire of a large number of small-scale enterprise will be relatively low.

3) The proportion of technical personnel

In recent years the proportion of engineers and technicians in Hubei continuous growth, which is higher than that in Shanghai. But the proportion of scientists and engineers is far less than that in Shanghai, indicating that the technical staff engaged in product development are few. Compared with Shanghai enterprises, these staff are more likely distributed In research institutions, often out of touch with technological development.

C. Analysis of the market opening degree

Rate of equipment imported and exported

As the Chinese automobile industry is taking the road of technology import, Rate of equipment imported and exported of Hubei and Shanghai indicators line. However, the import car market share of Hubei Province has increased in recent years, but growth is slow, and has a relatively large disparity from Shanghai Automotive industry, reflecting the gaps in consumption ability and market opening degree of the two places, which limits the speed of absorption of new technologies for Hubei.

In short, market performance level of Hubei Automotive Industry has increased annually, but is still a big gap between Hubei province and other powerful provinces in aspects such as industry scale and efficiency, technological progress entent, market opening degree. With a new round of shuffling in auto industry began, Hubei Automotive industry will face new challenges. Therefore, effective measures must be taken in Hubei. To Enhance the competitiveness of the automotive industry through integrating resources, optimizing the industrial structure and industry organizations, in order to achieve success in the future competition in the automotive industry.

Acknowledgements. The paper has been supported by project "Empirical Study on Market Efficiency in Hubei China automotive industry based on SCP paradigm" (NO. 2010q077)of the Department of Education, Hubei Province China, hereby thanks!

References

1. Bergman, E.M., Feser, E.J.: Industrial and Regional Clusters: Concepts and Comparative Applications, Morgantown, p. 70. University of West Virginia, New York (1999)
2. Porter, M.E.: The Competitive Advantage of Nations. The Free Press, New York (1990)
3. Enright, M.: Regional clusters and economic development: a research agenda. Paper Presented to the Conference on Regional Clusters and Business Networks 1993, Fredericton, New Brunswick, Canada (1995) (revised version)
4. Humprey, J., Schmitz, H.: Principles Clusters & Networks of SMEs (1995)
5. Roelandt, T.J.A., Gilsing, V.A., Sinderen, J.: Cluster-based Innovation Policy: International Experiences. Research Memorandum. Erasmus University Rotterdam (2000)
6. Boekholt, P.: The Public sector at arms length or in charge? Towards a typology of cluster policies. Paper Presented at the OCED-Workshop on Cluster Analysis and Cluster Based Policy, Amsterdam, October 10-11

MapGIS-Based Research in "One Planning Map" Compilation of Township-Level Land Use
Take Nieshi Town of Linxiang City as an Example

Fengjuan Wei and Yanzhong Liu

School of Resources and Environment Engineering
Wuhan University of Science and Technology
Wuhan, China

Abstract. According to the disadvantages of less practicality, excessive workload, lower update speed caused by too much map-achievements during the process of compiling maps of the new township-level land-use overall planning, this paper used the MapGIS software platform to built a land-use planning database, in order to realize the idea of "one planning map" in land use, namely adding every planning content such as land use zoning, construction land controlling division and land remediation planning into one map. Meanwhile, it took the example of Nieshi Town of Linxiang City to verify the feasibility, rationality and practicality of the technical route of "one planning map".

Keywords: MapGIS, township-level land use planning database, map compilation, "one planning map".

1 Introduction

There were so many disadvantages in taking the traditional measure of hand-drawing during the last land-use overall planning, for instance, the planning maps were hard to be altered and renewed while compiling, the workload of statistics was huge and trivial, the colors and the filling patterns were much simple and less expressive. What's worse, it's difficult to manage and store the planning achievements. Hence, using the MapGIS software platform in the new round of planning to draw electronically and build database, the planning data can be updated timely and managed easily. The necessary maps of this township-level land-use overall planning are land-use status map, land-use overall planning map and two thematic maps, which one is construction land controlling and farmland protection map, the other is land remediation planning map. But these separate thematic maps are less practicality, difficult in updating and less associated with the land-use overall planning map. Furthermore, compiling them separately occupied too much manpower and material resources, increased the preparation cost, and got the compilation delayed. Therefore, it is practical to establish a land use planning database for town level, based on the concept of "one planning map".

Nowadays, there are two main thoughts of "one planning map" existing in Chinese scholars. One refers that integrate planning of each level such as urban overall planning, transport planning, tourism planning and land-use overall planning into one

M. Dai (Ed.): ICCIC 2011, Part II, CCIS 232, pp. 235–243, 2011.

picture so as to make each planning coordinate [1-2], and the other mentions that with the technology of GIS as an foundation, digging out and integrating the urban status electronic map with the planning related geographical and attribute data, such as planning approval and design, to construct "one planning map" database management system and exhibit it in form of one planning map to realize the information sharing and management of planning achievements[3-5]. Since there was no concept of "one planning map" in land use, this paper will apply the MapGIS software platform to construct a technical route of township land-use planning database based on land use "one planning map", aiming at realizing the information integration of all planning map-achievements. It'll also take the Nieshi town as an example to verify whether the technical route is feasible or not.

2 Main Contents of Township Land-Use Overall Planning

The core of the township lever land-use planning is to adjust the structure and layout of land use, namely implementing the superior planning's each controlling indicator of scale and the layout of various land use zones to realize the coordination of maps and figures [6]. The land use zoning aims at solving the problem of land use scale and structure, whereas this round planning emphasizes in settling land use layout, i.e. to define the boundaries of construction land controlling zones based on land use zoning further. So it is essential to reflect the four types of construction land controlling zones to the land-use overall planning map together with the land use zones to make them closely interrelated, coordinate the "rigidity" and "flexibility" of planning and prompt to form one intensive, efficient, coordinate and orderly land use pattern.

While the land consolidation, land reclamation and land development belong to land-use special planning and each has its unique planning system and standard, this planning just marks out the key areas of land remediation. However, compiling single land remediation planning map made the relation of interconnection and comparison with the land-use overall planning map more estranged and had less practical guidance. Therefore, combining with urban construction land increase/decrease linking projects, it's appropriate to exhibit the key areas of remediation in overall planning map to express the information of occupation of cultivated land for new construction and resupply of cultivated land by land remediation simultaneously, so as to reflect more directly the goal of identity between maps and figures.

3 Mapgis-Based Technical Route of Township Land-Use Planning Construction

The basic idea of MapGIS-based township land-use overall planning map is to use filling patterns of polygons to distinguish the planning land use from the present use, various colors to represent land use zoning types, single enclosed line files to identify each construction land controlling zone and the key areas of land remediation, numbers to express the scale of cultivated land resupplied by various types of land remediation. The technical route of land-use overall planning can be seen in fig. 1.

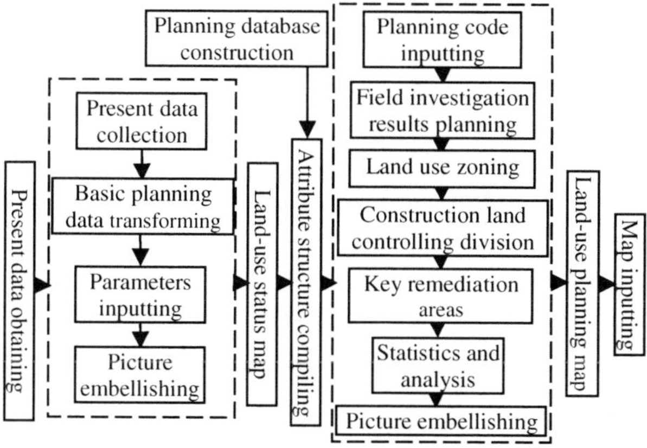

Fig. 1. MapGIS-based Technical Route of "One Planning Map"

A. Status Data Collection

Collect land use status database, as well as land use renovation and survey maps of the year of 2005, and then use the function of seamless jointing on MapGIS to get the MapGIS-projected township land-use status map merged by separate standard format maps. For last township-level planning period is 1997-2010, it adopted the land use classification of transition period .Meanwhile it is requested to get the planning basic data by using the MapGIS function of inputting parameters according to attributes. Modify the land use code abiding the corresponding relations between the above-mentioned classification and the new land use planning classification. Then input the information of colors and filling patterns to each file of polygon, line and point according to the latest drawing specification and standard of township land use planning map. After finishing the whole map, we can get a complete land-use status map.

B. Planning Database Construction

Establishing a unified standard and criterion of land use planning database can enhance scientificity, informatization, standardization and service-socialization of land use planning management [7]. The main route of constructing one land use planning database is to collect land use status database, the prophase specific research reports and maps and information of land use planning firstly, then analysis the needed polygon, line and point elements of planning to compile one standardized attribute structure and next input the data which needs tiered storage to obtain the land use planning database finally. So the key of building database is to construct attribute databases of each planning space factor, especially the planning polygon layer which can store current and planning information simultaneously.

C Attribute Structure Compilation

Based on the route of building planning database, in order to preserve the present land use information, using the MapGIS attribute database management subsystem to add other attribute fields to the attribute structure of the present polygon layer and then save it as planning polygon layer. The specific field variegated types can be seen in table 1 below.

Table 1. Added Attribute Fields Table

Field Name	Type	Length	Decimal	Note
XBHLB	string	8	---	Marking basic farmland
GHM	string	8	---	Land use type during planning period
YTM	string	8	---	Types of land use zones
QTQ	string	8	---	Marking settlements needed control
YLQ	string	8	---	Marking conditional construction land
JBNTZBQ	string	8	---	Marking basic farmland preparation zone
GZM	string	8	---	Construction controlling zone types
ZZM	string	8	---	Types of land remediation
SM	string	48	---	Instructions, e.g. project's name
JSNX	string	40	---	Marking the construction period

D. Maps Compilation

1) Field investigation results planning

The primary task of township land-use overall planning is to protect arable land and the basic farmland in particular, so firstly it needs to merge the town's basic farmland information extracted from the basic farmland verification database of the year of 2005 to the planning polygon layer by the operation of areas unionization in the MapGIS space analysis subsystem. The current round of planning is just a revision on the base of the last planning, so we can only modify the land use of part of the land on the land use present map according to the field investigation results and adjust the land use structure and layout. Then input GHM preliminary in accordance with the DLM (see table 2). Lastly, add the field investigation results, for instant, new rural resident, facilities, planning roads or trains, and tourist sites, to the planning polygon layer, using the function of cutting polygons and deleting arcs. Furthermore, modify GHM, SM, YSNX and other parameters.

2) Land-use zoning

According to the definition of various land use zones, we can get the corresponding relations between the land-use zoning and GHM. Combined with the actual situation of towns or villages and the above-mentioned land-use zoning system, YTM can be obtained through GHM (see table 2 and table 3). Then fill every polygon with corresponding colors to mark out various land-use zones. Since there are many small polygons which can not meet the smallest scale of land-use zones on the map after the work of cutting polygons during the above process, it's necessary to check the whole planning polygon layer and to merge the scattered small polygons to the neighbor land-use zones.

Table 2. Input GHM According To DLM

XBHLB	GHM	YTM
1 represents basic farmland	1	1
2 represents arable land except basic farmland	2	3
non-cultivated land code	Input GHM according to DLM(land type code)	
Non-arable land type code	---	---
Garden land(121~125)	12	3
Woodland(131~133）	13	13
Grassland(141~143)	14	4
Other cultivated land（151~155）	15	3
City(211)	211	211
Town(212)	212	212
Rural residential(213)	213	213
Mining use land(214)	214	215
Other independent construction land(215)	215	215
Other land use types	GHM equals the code of its three-level categories, e.g. if DLM=311, GHM=311	YTM equals the code of its two-level categories, e.g. if GHM=311,the YTM=31

3) Construction land controlling division

The work of construction land controlling division is conducted on the basis of land-use zoning and aims at balancing the urban and rural development, reserving land for construction projects whose locations are uncertain after making out the scale border of urban construction land, increasing flexibility of planning. According to the corresponding relations between the land-use zoning and construction land controlling division, input GZM and pick up various controlling linear files along the edge of polygons' arcs. The standards can be seen in table 3 and 4.

4) Land remediation planning

In order to put the information of land remediation into the land-use overall planning map similarly, it needs reference the superior planning, urban construction land increase/decrease linking projects together with the prophase specific research reports to input ZZM with Z, NZ, K and H to the polygons which are worthy of consolidation, development or reclamation, and then modify these polygons' other attributes. Mark out the land use remediation key areas with various lines and polygons files on the planning map, together with the remediation methods, serial numbers, scale of implementations and new arable land (see table 5).

B. Data Statistics

To test whether the land use planning structure meets the country land-use overall planning's given indicators, reaches the balance of demand and supply, realizes the consistent in maps and figures, or not, the task of data statistics on planning map is essential. MapGIS software could dynamically statistic and analysis the interaction conversion relations between different land uses to establish one comprehensive land use planning balance chart. Once it cannot meet those indicators, we should repeat the previous work and adjust the land use structure and layout again until it satisfies every aspect. Statistic data of scale and proportion of various types of land can be showed on the planning map in form of pie chart.

Table 3. Relations Between Land Use Zones and Construction Land Controlling Zones

Types of land use zone	YTM	Filling color	Types of controlling zone	GZM
Basic farmland protection zone	1	1021	Restricted construction land	2
Ordinary agriculture-use zone	3	1044	Restricted construction land	2
1)Basic farmland preparation land	8	1022	Restricted construction land	2
2)Conditional construction land	3	1015	Conditional construction zone	3
Woodland-use zone	13	1027	Restricted construction land	2
Grassland-use zone	4	1028	Restricted construction land	2
Town construction-use zone	211 or 212	1016	Permitted construction land	1
Settlements construction-use zone	213	1035	Permitted construction land	1
Settlements construction controlling zone	213	1045	Restricted construction land	2
Dependence construction-use zone	215	1036	Permitted construction land	1
Spots and tourist-use zone	5	1041	Restricted construction land	2
Ecological environment and security controlling zone	6	1042	Banned construction zone	4
Natural and cultural resources zone	7	1043	Banned construction zone	4
Planning code of non-zoning	---			
221~225	22	10	Restricted construction land	2
153、226、311~313、321、322	3 or 22 or 31 or 32	1031	Restricted construction land	2
227、331~335	22 or 33	Status colors	Restricted construction land	2

Table 4. Line Parameters of Controlling Zones

Types of controlling zones	Code	Parameters of line file (type, color, length, X, Y)
Permitted construction land	1	(1,1014,5,50,50)
Restricted construction land	2	None line files
1)Basic farmland preparation zone	2	(2,1020,5,50,50)
2)Settlements controlling zone	2	(1,20,5,50,50)
Conditional construction zone	3	(2,1014,5,50,50)
Banned construction zone	4	(2,1018,5,50,50)

Table 5. Polygon Parameters of Land Remediation Key Areas

Types of land remediation		Remediation code	Polygon files (filling color, filling pattern, length, pattern color)
Land consolidation	Settlements consolidation	Z	(9,197,50,5) Transparent
	Agriculture land consolidation	NZ	(9,130,50,5) Transparent
Land reclamation		F	(9,196,50,5) Transparent
Land development		K	(9,198,50,5) Transparent
Land comprehensive remediation		H	(9,131,50,5) Transparent

F. Graphics Output

After all geography elements and map elements are compiled into the township level land-use planning map, arrange the order of each single file to obtain one land-use overall planning map in which the planning layer is on the bottom and land category boundaries layer, linear features layers, lines of controlling zones and other elements are on the top orderly. We can get various format maps in different proportional scale through the function of project output.

4 The Application of Map-Gis on Nieshi Town Land-Use Overall Planning

Nieshi town is located in north-central of Linxiang city, Hunan province. It belongs to hilly terrain while the south is higher than the north. There are various types of land use reflected in different agriculture bases, rich forest resources and excellent tourist resources.

G. Compiling the Planning Polygon Layer

Obtain the Nieshi town land-use status map from the already compiled Linxiang city 1:10000 land-use status map which has realized the base figures conversion, then compile the attribute structure of Nieshi town planning polygon layer. Modify and renew the planning map orderly. In order to guarantee the arable land, basic farmland in particular, we should merge the information of basic farmland of the year of 2005 to the planning polygon layer. Firstly, it's guaranteed to protect important ecological security land and tourist facilities land, such as the Nieshi River, old stoned-street and Holy Water Temple. Then ensure the development of the market town and important construction projects. Mark out the rural and urban construction land scale borders of controlling and stretching appropriately depending on the actual situations of Nieshi. Next plan the new settlements, independent mining land, traffic and irrigation land, etc. Nieshi town is totally divided into 11 kinds of land use zones for its diverse land use types. Finally arrange the land remediation planning to fulfill the goal of dynamic balance on the whole arable land of Nieshi.

H. Compiling the Line Files of Each Zone

Following the task of reversing the attributes, compile the line files of each controlling zones according to the land use zones. Regarded Nieshi town is an important model town and has rapidly developing economic, the demand of construction land is also increasing and the conditional construction zone is 20% the size of the new urban land. There are three ways of land remediation in Nieshi town, namely the land consolidation, land development and land reclamation. Identify the land remediation key areas by using single line files and polygon files and referring the standard on the table 5.

I. Embellishing the Whole Map

Mark out the key construction projects on Nieshi town land-use overall planning map, for instance, the Linya road, Holy Water Temple, etc. Check out if villages' name, range and resident logos are right and then improve the legends to be more systematic and logical. Output the land-use overall planning map of Nieshi town whose proportional scale is 1:10000 and the format is TIFF, following the work of arranging other elements on the map.

5 Conclusion

Based on the idea of "one planning map", this paper built the township level land-use planning database, by the means of MapGIS software platform. It made it in integrating all land use information. This paper also verified that combined the land use status, "one planning map" can realize the unified management, modify and renew the planning contents conveniently by constructing one Nieshi town planning database. "One planning map" not only solves the problem of excess mapping workload and big cost stressed on the planning compiling unites, but also benefits the planning approval units to test and verify the consistent of maps and figures effectively. In one word, "one planning map" improves the instructions and operation of planning maps.

References

[1] Method of Country-level Land Use Overall Planning. Economic & Trade 6(6), 3–5 (2008) (in press)
[2] Sun, F.: Analysis of Planning Complication System and Performance Implementation in Building 'One Map' Arrangement-Oriented. North and South Bridges (8), 102–103 (2008) (in press)
[3] Huang, P., Huang, J.: Research on The Project of City 'One Planning Map' Overall Designing. Jiangsu Urban Planning (12), 4–8 (2009) (in press)
[4] Ye, Z., Zhou, N., Jiang, J.: Exploratory Construction of 'Living in Hangzhou' Planning Information Query Platform. Building Construction 25(1), 1–2, 12 (2008) (in press)
[5] He, M., Wu, Z., Xiong, W.: Research on the Date-Organizing System about Urban Planning Information Platform. Journal of Urban Planning (7), 236–238 (2009)
[6] Diao, C.: Discussion on the Mapping Methods of overall Land Use Planning at the Town and Township Level. Southwestern University, a master's degree thesis, pp. 27–30 (2008) (in press)
[7] Chen, Q., Wang, Q., Duo, H.: Building Qinghai Province Land Use Database of Country and Making an Inquire into Problem Based on GIS. Journal of Qinghai Normal University (1), 101–104 (2005) (in press)

Modeling and Analyzing of Farmer Specialty Co-operatives' Internal Movement Mechanism

Huifeng Zhao

Center for Post-Doctoral Studies,
China Agricultural University,
Beijing City, China
Ceciliasl@yahoo.cn

Abstract. The farmer Specialty Co-operative's movement mechanism may reflect its essential feature and the development request to a certain extent. In this article, the patronage amount which a member use the cooperative's service is acted as a variable amount. It is held together by members' profit target (i.e. benefit function) and services given by the cooperative to structural analysis model. Through the analysis of the model, you can effectively reveal the actual structure of the organization cohesive force.

Keywords: farmer specialty co-operatives, internal movement mechanism, modeling, Analyzing.

1 Introduction

Farmer Specialty Co-operative (Hereafter refers to as the cooperative) has many types. In this article, the cooperative organized spontaneously by farmers represent Farmer Specialty Co-operative. Principal cause is that its organization structure is simple and member's homogeneity is the best. Its movement mechanism may reflect the cooperative's essential feature and the development request to a certain extent. Its essential characteristics displays in two aspects: the profit and non-profit. To seek foreign profits are the sum total of the members to pursue the profit maximization behavior. Internal service level indicators is cooperative member uses its services. In this article, the patronage amount which a member use the cooperative's service is acted as a variable amount. It is held together by members' profit target (i.e. benefit function) and services given by the cooperative to structural analysis model. Through the analysis of the model, you can effectively reveal the actual structure of the organization cohesive force.

2 The Model Construction of the Cooperative'S Internal Movement Mechanism

A. The Model Construction

The basic hypothesis of the model is that economic party (i.e. members) in a cooperative is independent professional operators and their behavior is homogeneous.

M. Dai (Ed.): ICCIC 2011, Part II, CCIS 232, pp. 244–252, 2011.

Member's benefit function is that:

$$u_i = a_i^{\alpha_i} k_i^{\beta_i} g_i^{\gamma_i} l_i^{\eta_i} \qquad i=1, 2, \ldots, m \tag{1}$$

In the formula:

i—subscript, expresses the member I;
u—member's benefit function;
a—Member demand for technical services;
α—technical benefit function;
k—Physical capital elements;
β—Physical capital elements benefit elasticity;
l—Human capital factor;
η—Human capital benefit elasticity;
g—the patronage amount which member use the cooperative's service;
γ—benefit elasticity of he patronage amount.
Member need to pay for the cooperative. Suppose the total budget of member i is:

$$P_A a_i + P_K k_i + P_G g_i + P_L l_i = d_i \qquad i=1, 2, \ldots, m \tag{2}$$

In the formula:
d—total expenditure budget of member to the cooperative;
P_A—unit expenditures of technical service;
P_K—unit expenditures of material elements;
P_G—unit expenditures of the patronage amount to the cooperative;
P_L—unit expenditures of human capital.

P_A, P_K, P_G and P_L can be regarded as a cooperative internal price and have preferential to the cooperative 's members. We can educe that:

$$D = \sum_{i=1}^{m} d_i = P_A \sum_{i=1}^{m} a_i + P_K \sum_{i=1}^{m} k_i + p_G \sum_{i=1}^{m} g_i + P_L \sum_{i=1}^{m} l_i$$

$$D = P_A A + P_k K + P_G G + P_L L \tag{3}$$

In the formula:

D—total expenditures of all members to the cooperative's services;

$$D = \sum_{i=1}^{m} d_i$$

A—total mount of technical services provided by the cooperative;

$$A = \sum_{i=1}^{m} a_i$$

K—total mount of physical capital occupied by the cooperative;

$$K = \sum_{i=1}^{m} k_i$$

L—total mount of human capital occupied by the cooperative;

$$L = \sum_{i=1}^{m} l_i$$

G— the total patronage amount which member use the cooperative's service voluntarily;

$$G = \sum_{i=1}^{m} g_i$$

On the basis of formula (1) and formula (2), we can obtain external profit model:

Max $u_i = a_i^{\alpha_i} k_i^{\beta_i} g_i^{r_i} l_i^{\eta_i}$ (4)

S.t. $P_A a_i + P_K k_i + P_G g_i + P_L l_i = d_i$ (5)

i=1, 2, …, m

B. The Algorithm Results

First-order condition in model (4) - (5) is that:

$$\alpha_i a_i^{\alpha_i - 1} k_i^{\beta_i} g_i^{\gamma_i} l_i^{\eta_i} - \lambda_i P_A = 0 \tag{6}$$

$$\beta_i a_i^{\alpha_i} k_i^{\beta_i - 1} g_i^{\gamma_i} l_i^{\eta_i} - \lambda_i P_K = 0 \tag{7}$$

$$\gamma_i a_i^{\alpha_i} k_i^{\beta_i} g_i^{\gamma_i - 1} l_i^{\eta_i} - \lambda_i P_G = 0 \tag{8}$$

$$\eta_i a_i^{\alpha_i} k_i^{\beta_i} g_i^{\gamma_i} l_i^{\eta_i - 1} - \lambda_i P_L = 0 \tag{9}$$

$$d_i - P_A a_i - P_K k_i - P_G g_i - P_L l_i = 0 \tag{10}$$

In the formula:

λ_i—Lagrangeanmultiplier, ie shadow prices of di

We can educe from formula (10) that:

$$g_i = \frac{1}{P_G}(d_i - P_A a_i - P_K k_i - P_L l_i) \tag{11}$$

i=1, 2, …, *m*

We can educe from formula (6) and (8) that:

$$\alpha_i a_i^{\alpha_i - 1} k_i^{\beta_i} g_i^{\gamma_i} l_i^{\eta_i} = \lambda_i P_A$$

i=1, 2, …, *m*

$$\gamma_i a_i^{\alpha_i} k_i^{\beta_i} g_i^{\gamma_i - 1} l_i^{\eta_i} = \lambda_i P_G$$

i=1, 2, …, *m*

Therefore:

$$\frac{\lambda_i P_A}{\lambda_i P_G} = \frac{\alpha_i a_i^{\alpha_i - 1} k_i^{\beta_i} g_i^{\gamma_i} l_i^{\eta_i}}{\gamma_i a_i^{\alpha_i} k_i^{\beta_i} g_i^{\gamma_i - 1} l_i^{\eta_i}}$$

i=1, 2, …, m

$$P_A = P_G \frac{\alpha_i g_i}{\gamma_i a_i} \tag{12}$$

i=1, 2, …, m

We can educe from formula (7) and (8) that:

$$\beta_i a_i^{a_i} k_i^{\beta_i - 1} g_i^{\gamma_i} l_i^{\eta_i} = \lambda_i P_K$$

i=1, 2, …, m

$$\gamma_i a_i^{a_i} k_i^{\beta_i} g_i^{\gamma_i - 1} l_i^{\eta_i} = \lambda_i P_G$$

i=1, 2, …, m

Therefore:

$$\frac{\lambda_i P_K}{\lambda_i P_G} = \frac{\beta_i a_i^{\alpha_i} k_i^{\beta_i - 1} g_i^{\gamma_i} l_i^{\eta_i}}{\gamma_i a_i^{\alpha_i} k_i^{\beta_i} g_i^{\gamma_i - 1} l_i^{\eta_i}}$$

i=1, 2, …, m

$$P_K = P_G \frac{\beta_i g_i}{\gamma_i k_i} \tag{13}$$

i=1, 2, …, m

We can educe from formula (9) and (8) that:

$$\eta_i a_i^{a_i} k_i^{\beta_i} g_i^{\gamma_i} l_i^{\eta_i - 1} = \lambda_i P_L$$

i=1, 2, …, m

$$\gamma_i a_i^{a_i} k_i^{\beta_i} g_i^{\gamma_i - 1} l_i^{\eta_i} = \lambda_i P_G$$

i=1, 2, …, m

Therefore:

$$\frac{\lambda_i P_L}{\lambda_i P_G} = \frac{\eta_i a_i^{\alpha_i} k_i^{\beta_i} g_i^{\gamma_i} l_i^{\eta_i - 1}}{\gamma_i a_i^{\alpha_i} k_i^{\beta_i} g_i^{\gamma_i - 1} l_i^{\eta_i}}$$

i=1, 2, …, m

$$P_L = P_G \frac{\eta_i g_i}{\gamma_i l_i} \tag{14}$$

i=1, 2, …, m

Substituting formula (12), (13) and (14) to formula (11) reduce that:

$$g_i = \frac{1}{P_G}(d_i - P_G \cdot \frac{a_i g_i}{\gamma_i} - P_G \cdot \frac{\beta_i g_i}{\gamma_i} - P_G \cdot \frac{\eta_i g_i}{\gamma_i}) \tag{15}$$

i=1, 2, …, m

Formula (15)is die Aufloesung of model (4)-(5), that is the patronage amount which member i use the cooperative's service . From the standpoint of external profit, it is optimal demand of the patronage amount in the management process. This quantity decides level of dependency of member to the cooperative. Analysis its structure and the general trend can generally reveal agricultural cooperative's basic mechanism. [1]-[3]

3 The Model Analyses

C. The Analyzing of the General Movement Mechanism

Formula (15) can vary that:

$$g_i = \frac{1}{P_G}[d_i - P_G \cdot \frac{g_i}{\gamma_i}(\alpha_i + \beta_i + \eta_i)] \tag{16}$$

i=1, 2, …, m

For further derivation:

$$g_i P_G = d_i - P_G \cdot (\frac{\alpha_i + \beta_i + \eta_i}{\gamma_i}) g_i$$

$$g_i P_G (1 + \frac{\alpha_i + \beta_i + \eta_i}{\gamma_i}) = d_i$$

$$g_i = \frac{d_i \gamma_i}{P_G(\alpha_i + \beta_i + \gamma_i + \eta_i)} \tag{17}$$

i=1, 2, …, m

This shows that the g_i is a additional function of di and γ_i, is a decreasing function of $(\alpha_i + \beta_i + \gamma_i + \eta_i)$, i=1, 2, …, m. That means that, if other conditions unchanged, the higher of the total demand of member to the cooperative （i.e. di increase ）and the bigger function of the patronage amount provided by the cooperative（i.e. γ_i increase), the patronage amount which member use the cooperative's service voluntarily increases more and more (i.e. gi increases) .On the contrary, the bigger function of technology service , physical capital and human capital(ie the numerical value of $(\alpha_i + \beta_i + \gamma_i + \eta_i)$ increases), the smaller demand of the patronage amount which member use the cooperative's service voluntarily, that is gi will smaller and smaller. This shows that the stronger the member's capability, the smaller demand to the cooperative. Whether there are technical or capital, or other individuals, members will have this performance. This confirms in theory that cooperatives' essence is the weak's joint.

D. The Analyzing of the Economy Dealing

On the basis of Assignment only completely theory, we can obtain that:

$$\frac{\partial u_i}{\partial a_i} = \alpha_i \cdot a_i^{\alpha_i - 1} k_i^{\beta_i} g_i^{\gamma_i} l_i^{\eta_i}$$

$$\alpha_i = \frac{\partial u_i}{\partial a_i} / (\frac{u_i}{a_i})$$

i=1, 2, …, m

$$\beta_i = \frac{\partial u_i}{\partial k_i} / (\frac{u_i}{k_i})$$

i=1, 2, …, m

$$\gamma_i = \frac{\partial u_i}{\partial g_i} / (\frac{u_i}{g_i})$$

i=1, 2, …, m

$$\eta_i = \frac{\partial u_i}{\partial l_i} / (\frac{u_i}{l_i})$$

i=1, 2, …, m

(1) if it conforms to the assignment only completely theory,

$$\alpha_i + \beta_i + \gamma_i + \eta_i = 1$$

$$\frac{\partial u_i}{\partial a_i} = \alpha_i \cdot \frac{\partial a_i}{a_i} + \beta_i \frac{\partial k_i}{k_i} + \gamma_i \frac{\partial g_i}{g_i} + \eta_i \frac{\partial l_i}{l_i}$$

That is :

If in a fully competitive conditions, all of the elements vary in the same proportion, then:

$$\frac{\partial a_i}{a_i} = \frac{\partial k_i}{k_i} = \frac{\partial g_i}{g_i} = \frac{\partial l_i}{l_i} = \frac{d\lambda}{\lambda}$$

$$\frac{\partial u_i / u_i}{d\lambda / \lambda} = (\alpha_i + \beta_i + \gamma_i + \eta_i) = 1$$

So:

(2) $d_i = u_i$ (Distribution of the net balance)

$$\frac{\partial d_i}{\partial a_i} = P_{u_i A_i} = \frac{\partial u_i}{\partial a_i}$$

The same:

$$\frac{\partial u_i}{\partial k_i} = P_{u_i K_i}$$

$$\frac{\partial u_i}{\partial g_i} = P_{u_i G_i}$$

$$\frac{\partial u_i}{\partial l_i} = P_{u_i L_i}$$

In fully competitive conditions, we can define that:

$P_{u_i A_i}$ —Technical services to the market price,

i=1, 2, …, m

$P_{u_i K_i}$ —Substances on the market price of capital services,

i=1, 2, …, m

$P_{u_i G_i}$ —Cooperatives to the market price of the booking amount

i=1, 2, …, m

$P_{u_i L_i}$ —Human capital service market price,

i=1, 2, …, m

It is noteworthy that $P_{u_i A_i}$, $P_{u_i K_i}$, $P_{u_i G_i}$, $P_{u_i L_i}$ here is in terms of member individual and actual market efficiency which member individual has. According to these definitions, formula (15) can be changed to that:

$$g_i = \frac{1}{P_G}[d_i - P_G \frac{g_i}{P_{u_i G_i} / \frac{u_i}{g_i}} (P_{u_i A_i} / \frac{u_i}{a_i} + P_{u_i K_i} / \frac{u_i}{k_i} + P_{u_i L_i} / \frac{u_i}{l_i})]$$

$$= \frac{1}{P_G}[d_i - \frac{P_G}{P_{u_i G_i}} (P_{u_i A_i} a_i + P_{u_i K_i} k_i + P_{u_i L_i} l_i)]$$

i=1, 2, …, m (18)

Formula (18) indicates that the cooperative behavior has a close relationship with a variety of elements and services prices .It can therefore be considered that cooperative behavior is input-output process to price system for characterization of internal and external alignment. Inside and outside efficiency comparison decide the patronage amount which member use the cooperative's service voluntarily. The higher external efficiency is, the more willing to increase patronage amount members of cooperative. [4]-[6]

4 Conclusion

Based on the above analysis, it can be concluded that the following three main conclusions:

E. The Cohesive Force of the Cooperative Economy Organization to its Members is Decided by its Scale and the Benefit

The external benefit and internal non-profit characters of the cooperative may be abstract to external market receipts and expenditures of internal services accounting issues. The management behavior of each member can be described as the pursuit of maximizing external efficiency. Because Cooperative organization's internal structure has the non-profit the particularity, its cooperation cohesive force is different with the other Economic organization's important symbol. How many of the patronage amount which member use the cooperative's service voluntarily are one of the main reasons to decide cooperative organization change tendency. The larger the value, the greater the cohesion force of the cooperative organization to the Member. This shows that the larger the cooperatives, higher external efficiency. On the contrary, the smaller the cohesion force, lower external efficiency, there is the possibility of failure.

F. To Maintain the Energy Through Gradual Extending its Management Scope of the Farmer Specialized Cooperative Economy Organization

From the outcome of model (4) ~ (5), the development of the cooperatives directly affected by the number of d_i and indirectly gi quantity influence, ie the patronage amount which member use the cooperative's service voluntarily. This indicated that the farmer cooperative's development consistent with enhancement patronage amount internal as well as compatible the economical request essentially. Simultaneously also conforms to the agricultural technology regularity.

G. The Peasant Household of the Lower Production Level is Willing to Join the Cooperative Economy Organization

By formula (17) can be seen that g_i is increase function of d_i and γ_i, is decrease function of $(\alpha_i + \beta_i + \gamma_i + \eta_i)$. The patronage amount which member use the cooperative's service voluntarily will increase along with its function to the organization demand and decrease with the stronger force of factors of production and technology simultaneously. In the formula (18) is the benefit obtained by members' skill and other factors of production in the exterior market. The a_i, k_i and l_i are member-owned technology and material capital scale and levels of human capital. As can be seen from the type, if other conditions are invariable, the bigger these three variable's value is, the smaller the patronage amount g_i which member uses the cooperative's service voluntarily. Two formulas show that, the cooperative will display the strong development strength when members are willing to give their product to the cooperative or to use cooperative's other services .On the other hand, after members increase the income and sharpen ability or to master some production technology, they will decrease the demand to the cooperatives and have a tendency from cooperatives. Therefore may think that the first two factors are the decisive factors of internal characteristics and the latter three factors are the decisive factors of external characteristics. It can therefore be considered that the cooperative only strengthens foreign economical seeking to make a profit to be able to develop and their intrinsic cohesive force relay on enhancement of internal services to increase the amount of members of the patronage so as to maintain a certain scale.

In order to guarantee the stability of the cooperative development, the cooperative should concern the members' production strength differences in the early days. Those members who have similar economic strength are easier to reach agreement. Too much difference also leads too many difference demands to do business. Lack of cohesion force lead the organization loose and conflicts increase. Therefore, it is normal that the internal organizes cohesive force will change along with cooperative's development and members actually production level disparity enlarging. After the cooperative develops to a certain degree, it is possible that the cooperative presents the group to split up even restruct. Some cooperative evolve to enterprise. This is worth taking seriously in the cooperative practice. History of agriculture cooperative in the world wide indicated that many of cooperatives developed from pure specialty cooperatives to extensive multiple cooperation, from grass-roots cooperatives to National Trade Association, from single business to diversified management broad in scale.

References

1. Yao, J.: Study on Rural professional Technology Association. China Agricultural Science and Technology Publishing House, 11–21 (1996)
2. Tourte, L., Klonsky, K.: California's Organic Agriculture. Small Farm News 33(5), 52–55 (1995)
3. Yong, W.: Gambling analysis to enhance enterprise cohesive force. Management Science In China 9(supplement), 25–26 (2001)
4. Zhang, x., Yuan, p.: Cooperation in economic theory and practice. Chinese City Publishing house, Beijing (1991)
5. Zhang, x.: Go-to-market: Rural system change and organizational innovation. Management of economy publishing house, Beijing (1996)
6. Alfred, Haanel: The cooperative's vertical integration. China Supply and Marketing Cooperative (8), 19–20 (2001)

Security Analysis of WAPI Access Authentication Protocol WAI*

Zhang Ruihong and Yang Wei

Department of Computer Scinece and Technology,
Huanggang Normal University, Huanggang 438000, China
429657382@qq.com

Abstract. The authentication process of wireless local area network authentication and privacy infrastructure, namely, WAI protocol, is researched and analyzed, and the security analysis is made to its the security authentication and key-agreement process by using CK model. The analysis shows that: WAI can realize security attributes such as message integrity, mutual entity authentication, mutual key-control, key confirmation and so on, and it can also statisfy the secure goal of wireless local area network. Thus, it can be used to enhance the security of wireless local area network instead of WEP.

Keywords*:* Wireless Local Area Network, WAI, CK model, Unicast Key.

1 Introduction

Wireless communication service has been more and more widely used because of the character of convenience and flexibility, meanwhile, the security problem have become more and more prominent. In the paper CK model is used to analyze and verify the security of WAI protocol in the implementing scheme based on researching WAPI, the results indicate that the SK-secure of PFS will not be provided if elliptic curve encryption scheme adopted can resist choosing ciphertext (CCA2) attacks adaptively, and the key does not provide PFS's SK-secure when the protocol is negotiated by the key.

2 CK Model

CK model is a newly popular method for formal analysis of key-agreement protocol, it consists mainly of three parts: unauthenticated-links adversarial model, authenticated-links adversarial model and authenticator. It gives a definition of session key secure by indiscernible method.

* Foundation item: Supported by the Natural Science Foundation of Hubei Province (Q20102905).

M. Dai (Ed.): ICCIC 2011, Part II, CCIS 232, pp. 253–258, 2011.

2.1 Authenticated-Links Adversarial Model

AM model can be considered as an ideal environment. Under AM the attacker can only activate the subject through the message sent by another participant; the attacker can choose not to send message, but once the message is transferred, it can be transferred only once and to the final destination faithfully, in addition, the message can not be tampered.

2.2 Unauthenticated-Links Adversarial Model

UM model can be considered as a real environment. Except for having the ability in AM, the attacker under any UM can activate the session of another subject actively, and it can also tamper and replay the message arbitrarily.

2.3 Authenticator

Definition 1[2]: Let π and π' be two messages-driving n-party protocol, we call that π' emulates π under UM, only if there exists a attacker A under AM such that the protocol exports $AUTH_{\pi.A}$ and $UNAUTH_{\pi'.U}$ indiscriminating in calculation to the attacker U under any UM.

2.4 SK Security

Definition 2: A KE protocol π is SK(Session-Key) secure, only if the following two properties are stratified:

(1) The protocol π should make sure that any two honest entities can get the same private key when the protocol is finished;

(2) The attacker U under UM guesses the bite b(namely, $b' = b$) correctly is predicted to occur at a rate not in excess of $1/2$ and a negligible quantity.

3 The Security Analysis of WAI Protocol

3.1 The Introduction of WAI Protocol

The concrete contents of WAI protocol mainly as the following three aspects: the process of certificate identify, the process of unieast key negotiation and the process of multicast key negotiation. Among them the process of certificate identify includes 4 messages (message 1 to message 4): identify request, certificate identify request and certificate identify response. The process of unieast key negotiation comprises unieast key negotiation request and unieast key negotiation protocol response (message 5 and message 6). The process of multicast key negotiation contains multicast key negotiation request and multicast key negotiation protocol 1 (message 7 and message 8). The concrete contents can be found in reference [4].

3.2 The Security Analysis of WAI

3.2.1 Analysis of the Process of Certificate Identify of WAI

In fact, AP and STA do not know whether the opponent's certificate is valid, the previous 4 messages of WAI protocol will complete the mutual certification and gain the public key mainly. In the process, ASU will identify the certificate. Because AP and STA trust ASU completely and ASU sign to the result of certificate identify, the process can finish the corresponding mission.

3.2.2 Analysis of the Process of Unicast Key-Agreement Protocol of WAI

Let p denote unicast key agreement protocol in the WAPI implementation plan, the security of which is analyzed by CK model. It is proved that P does not provide SK-secure of PFS[7] in the following.

Assume that (G, ENC, DEC) are the key generation algorithm, encryption algorithm and decrypt algorithm respectively; let K be the security parameter, and STA and AP have transferred the algorithm G(K) and obtained their pair of private and public keys.

(1) To prove that P is a SK-secure key negotiation protocol, A and B are entities, and A can realize the function of decrypting Oracle, B is the attacker of protocol P and participates in implementation using the ability achieved from protocol attack, A has the pair of public key and private key of PK_{STA} and SK_{STA} (gained through the key generation algorithm G), and B knows PK_{STA} rather than SK_{STA}.

The implementation process is as following:

Stage 0: A provides challenged ciphertext $c* = ENC(PK_{STA}, r_1)$ to B, where $r_1 \xleftarrow{R} \{0,1\}^K$.

Stage 1: B sends a triple (x, r_i, t) to A, and $HMAC - SHA256_{k_a'}(t)$ is as the response, where $k_{a'} = last(KD - HMAC - SHA256(k'))$, $k' = r_i \oplus r'$, $r' = DES(SK_{STA}, c)$, ($last()$ denotes that the last 16 packet of 8-bit). B can repeat the process time after time, where it can choose every triple adaptively.

Stage 2: B sends a test string $t* = (SPI \parallel PK_{AP}(r_i))$ to A, and A chooses a bite $b \xleftarrow{R} \{0,1\}$, if b=0, then the response $HMAC - SHA256_{k_a''}(t*)$ will be sent to B, where $k_a'' = last(KD - HMAC - SHA256(k''))$, $k'' = r_1 \oplus ri$,where r_1 is a encrypted random number in stage 0, if b=1, then A will return a random string $s*$, whose length is the same as $HMAC - SHA256_{k_a''}(t*)$.

Stage 3: The stage is the same stage 1.

Stage4: B exports a bite b', which is a guess of b, $b = b'$ if and only if B attacks triumphantly.

(2) According to definition 2, to prove that p is SK-secure, we need to prove that it statisfies two conditions: (1) In the case that STA and AP have finished matching session, they will get the same secure session key, to be specific, the attack can not fabricate a key-agreement reply message sent to AP by STA, otherwise, they will get different secure session key. (2) The attacker can not distinguish between the private key k_s and a random number with non-negligible superiority. In the following we will prove that p can stratify the two conditions.

Lemma 1. If the adopted encryption schemes ECES is CCA2-secure, then the attacker can fabricate a key-agreement reply message in the execution process of P with non-negligible probability , and STA and AP can get the same secure session key when the protocol is terminated.

Proof. Assume that attacker B can fabricate a key-agreement reply message with non-negligible probability, namely, it can fabricate a message: SP, $PK_{AP}(r_2)$, $HMAC - SHA256_{k_a}(SPI, PK_{AP}(r_2))$. It can make use of the ability to participate in the execution, and choose r_2 as the random number r_i in the triple sent to A in the above execution process, however, c and t can be chosen by the attacker arbitrarily. Then in stage 2 it can calculate $HMAC - SHA256_{k_a''}(t*)$ with non-negligible probability (because the value is the same as the value of message authentication code in fabricated message).Then it can distinguish between $HMAC - SHA256_{k_a''}(t*)$ and $s*$ with non-negligible superiority, thus b can be guessed correctly with non-negligible superiority. Then the attacker can excute the above protocol successfully, and the encryption scheme is not CCA2-secure, which is contradicted with the hypothesis. Therefore, the attacker can not fabricate a key-agreement reply message with non-negligible probability. When STA and AP finish the , they will get the same secure session key.

Lemma 2. If the adopted encryption schemes ECES is CCA2-secure, then the attacker can not distinguish between the secure session key k_s and a random number in the execution process of protocol P with non-negligible probability.

Proof. Assume that the attacker B can not distinguish between the secure session key k_s and a random number in the execution process of protocol P with non-negligible probability. However, in the CK model, the attacker does not allow to attack test-session and its marching session (including entity capture, session state exposure, session key inquiry), so the attacker can not gain the secure session key k_s directly, where $k_s = first(KD - HMAC - SHA256(k))$, therefore, it can distinguish between k_s and a random number with non-negligible superiority only if it obtains k with non-negligible probability (because if the attacker can not calculate k, the attacker can not distinguish between k_s and the random number according to the property of Hash function), namely, in the case that the attacker knows $ENC(PK_{STA}, r1)$ and $ENC(PK_{AP}, r_2)$, then it can distinguish between $k = r_1 \oplus r_2$ and a random number with non-negligible superiority, because r_i in k'' is selected by the attacker, consequently the diffculty of distinguishing between k'' and a random number is less than the diffculty of distinguishing between k and a random number. Assume that the superiority of distinguishing between k and the random number by the attacker is λ_1 and the superiority of distinguishing between k'' and the random number is λ_2, then $\lambda_2 \geq \lambda_1$, however, $k_a'' = last(KD-HMAC-SHA256(k''))$, thus it can obtain k_a'' with non-negligible probability. Futhermore, it can calculate $HMAC-SHA256_{k_a''}(t*)$ with non-negligible probability, well then, the attacker can distinguish between $HMAC-SHA256_{k_a''}(t*)$ and $s*$ with non-negligible superiority. Then the attacker has participated in the above execution process, the encryption scheme is not CCA2-secure. However, this is contradicted with assumption, so the attacker can not distinguish between the session key and a random number with non-negligible superiority in the implementation process of protocol P.

Theorem 3. If the adopted encryption schemes ECES is CCA2-secure, then P does not possess SK-secure of PFS.

Proof. According to lemma 1 and lemma 2, we know that STA and AP obtain the same session key when the protocol is terminated, and the attacker can not distinguish between session-key and a random number with non-negligible superiority. Then from denifition 2, the protocol P is SK-secure. In addition, if the long-term private key of STA and AP is lost, then the attacker will gain the random number they exchanged, well then, all the negotiated session-keys before can be calculated, so the protocol can not provide PFS[7].

Meanwhile, because the protocol is the exact key authentication protocol, and from the above analysis it is known that the protocol is SK-secure, therefore, STA and AP can verify the opponent's identity when the protocol is terminated.

According to the above analysis, WAI protocol is secure.

4 Conclusions

This paper studies WAI protocol in detail, and proves that WAI can be proved secure by using CK model, the results show that the unicast key negotiation process can not provide SK-secure of PFS if the encryption schemes adopted ECES is CCA2-secure. WAI protocol can statify the secure goal of wireless local area network, which can be used in enforcing the security of wireless local area network. In addition, STA and AP have achieved the authentication of the opponent's identity respectively when the protocol is terminated.

References

1. Boyd, C., Mao, W., Paterson, K.: Key agreement using statically keyed authenticators. In: Jakobsson, M., Yung, M., Zhou, J. (eds.) ACNS 2004. LNCS, vol. 3089, pp. 248–262. Springer, Heidelberg (2004)
2. Canetti, R., Krawczyk, H.: Analysis of key-exchange protocols and their use for building secure channels. In: Pfitzmann, B. (ed.) EUROCRYPT 2001. LNCS, vol. 2045, pp. 453–474. Springer, Heidelberg (2001)
3. Bellare, M., Canetti, R., Krawczyk, H.: A Modular Approach to the Design and Analysis of Authentication and Key—exchange Protocols. In: Proc. of the 30th Annual ACM Symposium on Theory of Computing, pp. 419–428. ACM Press, New York (1998)
4. GB15629.11-2003/XGl-2006 information technology, remote communication and information exchange among systems. The Specific Requirements of LAN and MAN, the 11th Part: Wireless Local Area Network Specification. 1st Amendment (2006)
5. Canetti, R., Krawczyk, H.: Universally composable notions of key exchange and secure channels. In: Knudsen, L.R. (ed.) EUROCRYPT 2002. LNCS, vol. 2332, pp. 337–351. Springer, Heidelberg (2002); Bellare, M., Rogaway, P.: Entity authentication and key distribution. In: Stinson, D.R. (ed.) CRYPTO 1993. LNCS, vol. 773, pp. 232–249. Springer, Heidelberg (1994)
6. Günther, C.G.: An identity-based key-exchange protocol. In: Quisquater, J.-J., Vandewalle, J. (eds.) EUROCRYPT 1989. LNCS, vol. 434, pp. 29–37. Springer, Heidelberg (1990)
7. Mao, w.: Modern Cryptography: Theory and Practice. Publishing House of Electronics Industry, Beijing (2004)
8. Brown, D.R.L.: The exact security of ECDSA. Department of C&O. University of Waterloo, Waterloo: Technical Report CORR 2000-54 (2001)
9. Menezes, A., van Oorschot, P., Vanstone, S.: Handbook of Applied Cryptography. CRC Press, Boca Roton (1996)
10. Canetti, R., Krawczyk, H.: Universally composable notions of key exchange and secure channels. In: Knudsen, L.R. (ed.) EUROCRYPT 2002. LNCS, vol. 2332, pp. 337–351. Springer, Heidelberg (2002)
11. Li, H.-x., Cai, W.-d., Pang, L.-j.: Security Analysis and Verification of WAPI Access Authentication Protocol (WAI). Computer Engineering 34(3), 163–177 (2008)
12. Li, X.-H., Ma, J.-F.: On the Security of the Key-Agreement Protocol of Chinese WLAN Standard Implementation Plan. Chinese Journal of Computers 29(4), 577–579 (2006)

Research on Econometric Model for Domestic Tourism Income Based on Rough Set

He Xiaoya and Jie Zhiben

College of Science, Wuhan Textile University, Wuhan, China
sivajich2323@yahoo.cn

Abstract. This paper introduces a method for choosing the important factors from many influence factors on domestic tourism income by means of attribute reduction in rough set theory. Its advantage consists in reducing the number of explanatory variables for ensuring the degree of freedom as well as weakening the multiconlinearity. By using this method an econometric model for domestic tourism income about the selected explanatory variables based on their samples from 1994 to 2008 is established. According to the test result, it is a appropriate prediction model.

Keywords: econometric model, domestic tourism income, rough set, attribute reduction.

1 Introduction

With the improvement of material life, more and more people begin to enjoy their spiritual life in leisure time, and tourism has become one of the main pastimes. The rapid development of tourism industry attracts the great attentions of government at all levels and leads it to be a new economic growth point to promote the development of the regional economy. Tourism income directly reflect the economy of a country or a region and become an indispensable comprehensive index, which can measure the tourism economic activity and its effect, besides, it is an important symbol of a country or a region whether its tourism industry is developed. Many achievements have been made in academia on the prediction of the tourism demand. For example, Guo Lijun once studied the domestic tourism income with an econometric model. In this paper we try to propose a new idea of the research on the prediction by combining the rough set with the econometric methods. To begin with, analyzing the influence factors of the domestic tourism income, and then choosing the important influence factors using attribute reduction in rough set theory and finally establishing a prediction model for domestic tourism income by collecting data and using econometrics methods.

2 Analysis of Influence Factors

As tourism industry has strong relevance and dependency, many factors influence the development of tourism, such as socioeconomic status and economic relations. Tourism income is an important index which can measure the situation of the

M. Dai (Ed.): ICCIC 2011, Part II, CCIS 232, pp. 259–266, 2011.

development of tourism and it's a function of many factors. These factors include the following aspects: (1) residents, including the economic conditions, leisure time and physical qualities, (2) traffic, including the convenience and safety of routs, the condition of vehicles and the individual transportation, (3) reception, including the class, quality, quantity, security of hotel service, and (4) the close degree between people and the travel destinations in society, history and culture, etc. All factors above influence the development of tourist market from different aspects, as far as the degree of importance is concerned residents or social economic conditions is still the most important one in all factors leading people to have a trip. There are several reasons supporting this point. To begin with, any tourist activity is based on a certain economic condition. Only if people have enough money can they have a trip. So their economic status is first considered when they plan to have a trip. Secondly, the improvement of social economic condition inevitably brings the changes of traffic condition, information and consumer attitude, thus, it's beneficial for us to promote the development of tourism. In addition, the transportation, tourist conditions, and the leisure time and physical factors of residents affect the scale of tourism from different aspects.

3 Data Collection

Based on the analysis of influence factors on domestic tourism income and the availability of data, we consider the following explanatory variables:

- The variables which can measure the economic development and people's economic condition: gross domestic product, GDP for short, rural per capita annual net income, urban per capita disposable income.
- The variables which can measure the scale of domestic tourism market number of domestic tourists, tourism cost per capita.
- The variables which can measure traffic condition highway mileage, railway mileage, aviation mileage, inland river mileage, amount of domestic private car.

The domestic tourism income which serves as an explained variable and the explanatory variables above are symbolized by Y and X_i (i =1,2,..., 10) respectively. In China Statistical Yearbook 2010, we collected the data of the all variables above from 1994 to 2008.

4 Choosing Variables for Model

There are too many explanatory variables compared with the sample size to lead to multiconlinearity more probably and without enough degree of freedom, thus we must choose some important variables first in order to reduce the explanatory variables. We will use attribute reduction in rough set theory to reduce the explanatory variables. Let's give a brief introduction to related concept of rough set theory.

A. Information System and Equivalence Class

Rough set theory is a mathematical tool which can deal with vague and imprecise problems, and it is used in many fields, especially the attribute reduction method is an effective tool for data mining.

Assume $S=\{U, X, V, f\}$ is an information system, where $U=\{A_1, A_2,\ldots,A_n\}$ is a limited and non-empty set, namely, total samples set, and $X=\{X_1, X_2,\ldots,X_m\}$ is a limited non-empty attribute set, V_i signifies a attribute value range of attribute X_i, $V=\cup V_i$ is named the range of attribute set X, $f: U\times X\rightarrow V$ is named an information function, which is used to confirm attribute value of every object A_k in U, that is, for any $X_i\in X, f(A_k, X_i)\in V$. For any attribute subset R of X, U/R is named indiscernibility relation, i.e. the set of equivalence class.

B. Attribute Reduction and Kernel

Attribute reduction is one of key elements in the theory of rough set, which can relieve the work and improve the efficiency of evaluation through deserting redundant attribute in information system. According to this, we can find a smaller attribute set B which can take the place of X to describe the set of objects.

Define R as gens of equivalence relation, $r\in R$, if $U/R=U/R-\{r\}$, then we call r reducible or redundant; if not, we call r necessary. If every r is necessary, we call R independent, or else call R relevant. If the subset P of R is independent and $U/P=U/R$, we call P a reduction of R. R may have many reductions. If P is a reduction of R, then the set which is made up of all necessary relations in P are called the kernel of P.

In the following, we reduce the explanatory variables by using attribute reduction method. Considering each index include the explained variable has different dimensions of attributes, we compute the growth rate of each individual attributes, and then make them into discrete data by using cluster analysis. We get the initial decision table.

In Tab.1., Y, X_i and A_k represent decision attribute, conditional attributes and samples respectively. We can see

$$U/A=\{\{A_1\}, \{A_2\},\ldots,\{A_{14}\}\}.$$

For $U/A-\{X_i\}=U/A$, $i=1, 2,\ldots, 10$, every attribute is reducible individually but not simultaneously. To find out a smallest attribute set, namely, kernel set, to begin with, we compute the correlation coefficients between the decision attribute and each individual conditional attributes and correlation coefficients between two of all conditional attributes. We choose the attribute which has largest correlation coefficient with domestic tourism income as the element of the kernel set. If there is no contradictory decision rule in decision table which has the only attribute as conditional attribute, then the set made up of the only attribute is a kernel set. If there has at least one contradictory decision rule, then we must add a new attribute. For avoiding multicollinearity as much as possible, add the attribute which has relatively smaller correlation coefficients with the chosen attribute, and go on until finding out a kernel set.

Table 1. The Initial Decision Table

	X_1	X_2	X_3	X_4	X_5	X_6
A_1	3	3	2	1	2	2
A_2	2	1	2	1	3	2
A_3	1	1	3	1	3	3
A_4	1	1	2	1	1	2
A_5	1	1	2	1	2	2
A_6	1	1	2	1	2	1
A_7	1	1	2	2	2	2
A_8	1	2	2	1	2	2
A_9	1	1	1	1	2	2
A_{10}	2	3	2	1	2	3
A_{11}	2	2	2	3	2	1
A_{12}	2	2	2	1	2	2
A_{13}	3	2	2	1	2	2
A_{14}	2	1	2	1	2	2

(Continuation)

	X_7	X_8	X_9	X_{10}	Y
A_1	3	2	3	3	3
A_2	1	1	3	1	2
A_3	1	2	2	1	3
A_4	1	1	1	1	2
A_5	3	3	1	1	2
A_6	2	1	1	1	2
A_7	2	2	1	1	2
A_8	1	3	1	1	2
A_9	2	3	1	1	1
A_{10}	1	2	2	1	3
A_{11}	1	3	2	1	2
A_{12}	1	3	2	1	2
A_{13}	1	2	2	2	3
A_{14}	1	2	2	2	2

In Tab. 2, the correlation coefficient between Y and X_1 is largest, so we choose X_1 as the first element of the kernel set. According to the Tab. 1, if X_1 is regarded as the only conditional attribute, then the rule A_3 and A_4 are contradictory. So from the rest attributes, we add X_7, which has the smallest correlation coefficient with X_1, into the kernel set. If the conditional attribute set is only made up of X_1、 X_7, then the rule A_1 and A_{10} are contradictory. So we add X_3 again, which has smaller correlation coefficients with X_1、 X_7. Thus, if the conditional attribute set is only made up of X_1、 X_3、 X_7, then the rule A_2 and A_{10} are contradictory. We add X_5 again, which has smaller correlation coefficients with X_1、X_3、X_7. If the conditional attribute set is only made up of X_1、X_3、X_5、X_7, then the rule A_{10} and A_{11} are contradictory. So we add X_4 again, which has smaller correlation coefficients with X_1、X_3、X_5、X_7. Now it is not hard to see that there is no contradictory decision rule in the decision table based on the conditional attribute set made up of X_1、X_3、X_4、X_5、X_7. It's a consistent decision table and there is no reducible attribute, so$\{X_1、X_3、X_4、X_5、X_7\}$ is the kernel set and X_1、X_3、X_4、X_5、X_7 are important attributes influencing Y. We have done our best to avoid multicollinearity, but whether there exists should be tested.

Table 2. Correlation Coefficients Between Decision Attribute And Individual Attributes

	X_1	X_2	X_3	X_4	X_5
Y	0.993	0.988	0.842	0.944	0.917
	X_6	X_7	X_8	X_9	X_{10}
Y	0.972	0.768	0.985	0.990	0.992

Table 3. Correlation Coefficients Between Conditional Attributes

	X_1	X_2	X_3	X_4	X_5
X_1	1	0.994	0.789	0.954	0.904
X_2	0.994	1	0.761	0.964	0.886
X_3	0.789	0.761	1	0.715	0.913
X_4	0.954	0.964	0.715	1	0.852
X_5	0.904	0.886	0.913	0.852	1
X_6	0.967	0.960	0.869	0.906	0.957
X_7	0.738	0.721	0.901	0.690	0.868
X_8	0.997	0.993	0.753	0.959	0.880
X_9	0.992	0.982	0.828	0.936	0.930
X_{10}	0.998	0.991	0.810	0.951	0.921

(Continuation)

	X_6	X_7	X_8	X_9	X_{10}
X_1	0.967	0.738	0.997	0.992	0.998
X_2	0.960	0.721	0.993	0.982	0.991
X_3	0.869	0.901	0.753	0.828	0.810
X_4	0.906	0.690	0.959	0.936	0.951
X_5	0.957	0.868	0.880	0.930	0.921
X_6	1	0.816	0.952	0.973	0.974
X_7	0.816	1	0.710	0.756	0.772
X_8	0.952	0.710	1	0.981	0.994
X_9	0.973	0.756	0.981	1	0.991
X_{10}	0.974	0.772	0.994	0.991	1

5 Model Setting and Testing

After the above attribute reduction, we can use the multiple linear regression model as follows:

$$Y = \alpha + \beta_1 X_1 + \beta_3 X_3 + \beta_4 X_4 + \beta_5 X_5 + \beta_7 X_7 + u. \quad (1)$$

where Y represents domestic tourism income, and X_1, X_3, X_4, X_5, X_7 represent gross domestic product, tourism cost per capita, highway mileage, railway mileage and inland river mileage respectively.

Using OLS to estimate (1), we get the result as follows:

$$Y = 3245.358 + 0.026803X_1 + 6.846107X_3$$

$$+ 1.533316X_4 - 509.6332X_5 - 196.5797X_7. \quad (2)$$

C. Multicollinearity Test

We know that the signs of coefficient between X_5 and X_7 disaccord of the actual economic significance, this represents that there exists multicollinearity possibly. We use stepwise regression method to test and solve this problem. Finally, X_1 and X_3 are remained. The final model is as follows:

$$Y = \alpha + \beta_1 X_1 + \beta_3 X_3 + u. \quad (3)$$

Using ordinary least square method to estimate (3), we obtain the result as follows:

$$Y = -1137.75 + 0.026695X_1 + 3.738346X_3. \quad (4)$$

t=(- 4.812202) (24.34200) (4.359632)

r^2=0.994216 R^2=0.993252

F=1031.361 DW=2.156957

D. Heteroskedasticity Test

Using the white-test, we get the result in the follow table.

Table 4. White-test

White Heteroskedasticity Test:			
F-statistic	0.256734	Probability	0.925775
Obs*R-squared	1.872391	Probability	0.866505

P=0.866505 is large enough, so heteroscedasticity doesn't exist in the model.

E. Autocorrelation Test

Check the Durbin-Watson d statistic table, we have

$d_L = 0.946$, $d_U = 1.543$.

Here

$d_U < DW = 2.156957 < 4 - d_L$.

It is indicated that there is no autocorrelation in the model.

D. Statistics Test

According to the value of individual parameters' T-statistic in the model we know that all parameters of the sample regression are significant. F=1031.361 denotes that the regression function is also significant, and R^2=0.993252 means that the sample is better fitted by the regression function.

F. Economic Significance Test

We find that the domestic tourism income is positively correlated with GDP and travel cost per capita from the results of the model. It is consistent with the economic significance.

6 Conclusion

The tourism income has some common features of income. When GDP increases per 1 billion Yuan, the domestic tourism income will increase 0.027 billion Yuan. It indicates that the tourism income has little influence on GDP and the tourism income of China is still in a low level relatively, therefore, for majority, the travel cost of people is much a small part of the total amount of consumption. When the average expense spent on domestic tourism increases per one Yuan, the domestic tourism income will increase 0.374 billion Yuan. Comparing with the population of China, a large minority doesn't participate in the domestic tourism activity except a few wealthy residents who can travel abroad. It is still luxurious for majority. But on the other hand, the tourism market in China has a great room for development and it's still great potential.

In this paper we have chosen the influence factors on domestic tourism income by using attribute reduction in rough set theory before building a model, and its advantage consists in reducing the number of explanatory variables for ensuring the degree of freedom as well as weakening the multiconlinearity. The processing of data is based on the supposition that the data of growth rate can weaken multiconlinearity, in other words, if the data of growth rate has multiconlinearity, the original data must has. The discretization of continuous data will affect the real information of the original data. How to determine the value of an attribute advisably when it is discretized is worth researching further.

Acknowledgment. This work is supported by the Science Project of Hubei Provincial Bureau of Statistics #HB092-31(2009).

References

1. Junyi, L., Yaofeng, M., Min, Y.: A literature review on demand forecasting methods in China's Tourism. Commercial Research 3, 17–20 (2009)
2. Lijun, G.: Research on domestic tourism income based on econometric model. Cooperate Economy & Science 331, 16–17 (2007)
3. Yi, F., Zhiyong, Z., Guangshu, X., Peina, W.: The forecasting of logistics demand in china based on rough set theory. Logistic Technology 29, 60–62 (2010)
4. Qing, L.: Rough set and rough consequence. Science Press, Beijing (2001)
5. Hao, P.: Econometrics. Science Press, Beijing (2007)

Research on Exhibition Economy of Poyang Lake Ecological Economic Region*

Xiong Guojing

School of Economy and Management
Nanchang University
Nanchang, Jiangxi Province, China

Abstract. Building an integrated system from the urban agglomeration embrace Poyang Lake to start position to develop Exhibition Economy, to study and explore the economic development strategy of Poyang Lake Ecological Economic Region. It puts forward a plan of making full use of its regional advantages, both industry advantages and ecological advantages; stressing characteristics of the area, making every effort to innovate and build a base of exhibition in the central country, promote the sustainable development of the Poyang Lake Ecological Economic Region.

Keywords: Poyang Lake, Economy Ecological Region, Sustainable development, Exhibition Economy.

1 Introduction

Exhibition industry is a new industry which exhibits the trade of commodity, disseminates economic information, cooperates in the technology and business, integrates scientific and cultural exchange as a whole, and displays information consulting, trade and investment promotion, modern logistics, urban construction, marketing management, tourist services and many other features. After 20 years of the gradual growth of China's exhibition industry, during the "10th five years" period, the average increment of the industry has been over 14%, becoming one of the most dynamic industries in recent years.

In December 2006, Jiangxi Province put forward the plan to develop "the urban agglomeration embrace Poyang Lake ", taking China's largest freshwater lake, Poyang Lake as the core, which is surrounded by a total of five municipalities and districts include Nanchang, Jingdezhen, Jiujiang, Yingtan, Shangrao. The percentage of GDP and government receipts of this economic circle in the province arrived at 49.2% and 52.3% separately, and the economic circle is the region which has the best industrial base, the highest level of scientific and technological literacy, the top level of urbanization, and the most closely connected economy in Jiangxi province. As the collection and distribution centre of resources, traffic, and commerce in east China and the province, and as the central region adjacent to the Yangtze River Delta, Fujian Delta, the Pearl River Delta, it has unique urban location advantages which connects

* This work is supported by the Jiangxi Province Social Science Foundation Grant # 08SH37.

M. Dai (Ed.): ICCIC 2011, Part II, CCIS 232, pp. 267–273, 2011.

tightly with Guangdong, Fujian and Zhejiang and deep extends to Hong Kong, Macao and Taiwan, directly through the Yangtze and connects to Shanghai, which is the metropolis of China, and it plays the role to connect east and west region. Meanwhile, railways, highways, waterways, civil aviation and other transportation are very convenient, and it has formed the "5-hour Economic Circle" around Anhui, Hubei, Hunan, Zhejiang, and other nearby provincial capital.

2 The Integrated System of Exhibition Economy on Developmental Environment

The developmental environment for the Exhibition Economy is mainly composed of the natural environment, social environment and economic environment. It is propitious for the economic development to sponsor or undertake large-scale exhibition in virtue of the unique natural conditions and favorable social environment by combining local economic and cultural characteristics. The urban agglomeration embrace Poyang Lake has an excellent ecological environment, which also has provided favorable conditions to found Eco-Industrial Expo, Poyang Lake Economic Forum and Poyang Lake Economic Expo.

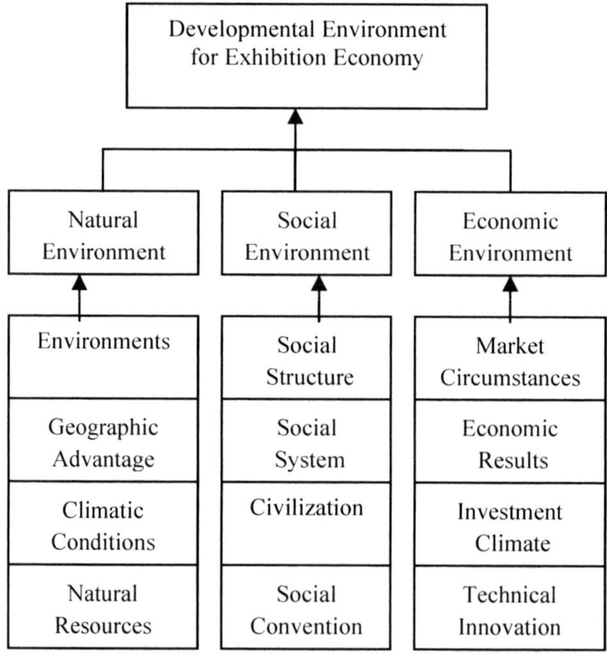

Fig. 1. The Integrated System of Exhibition Economy on developmental environment

The exhibition in the Poyang Lake Ecological Economic Region takes full advantage of its location advantages, industry advantages, and ecological advantages to set up a pageant to display its superiority on environments and resources, and to elevate the exhibition to be characteristic, brands, scale, cultural and effective event.

3 Using the Urban Agglomeration of Poyang Lake to Locate the Exhibition Economic System

A. Making Full Use of Existing Tourism Resources, Making Great Efforts to Cultivate Economic System of Exhibition on Tourism

We must put our advantages of tourism resources into practice, develop red tourism and green tourism industry, cultivate and develop the economic system of exhibition on tourism; We must speed up the development of tourism industry and the exhibition economy, integrate tourism resources and the resources of exhibition, create more tourist routes and tourist attractions, increase the investigation on hardware facilities and infrastructure of tourism. We must bring the function of tourism trade group into play, bring the guiding and coordinating function of government-led development of the industry into full play, to constantly enhance the tourism service standards and service quality.

B. The Exhibition Economy is a High-Efficiency, Non-Polluting Source of the Green Economy

Since the ancient days, the transportation of Poyang Lake Plain is very convenient both in the waterway and landway. It is a fortress close contacted with the eastern coastal, inland and western regions, It also has inherent advantages as a regional exhibition center. With the formation of economic integration, the exhibition has become an important platform for foreign investment.

C. Focus on Eco-environmental Protection, in Order to Win the Brand Features of Conference and Exhibition

1) Red tourism and historical and cultural folk exposition. Nanchang is the birthplace of the people's army and the "Hero City" of Chinese revolution. It is a famous city which has 2200 years of history and culture. The restoration of the temple fair of Shengjin Tower in Nanchang in 2002 has brought new feeling of "exciting, vibrant, dynamic, delicious, exotic" things for the tourists, has reappeared the historical accumulation and folk culture, and has promoted a rapid development on trade, tourism, catering and other related industry.

2) Jingdezhen international porcelain exposition. Jingdezhen, the city of porcelain, holds the international porcelain exposition taking the theme of "appreciate the world's rare porcelain products, carry forward Millennium Porcelain civilization", which has been listed in the activities disseminated by the Ministry of Commerce. In the year of 2008 in China, more than 600 well-known porcelain enterprises from all around the world and more than 2,000 people from abroad participated in Jingdezhen International porcelain exposition. Three major Exhibition Halls with 2810 exhibition booths attracted nearly 35 million people to visit and negotiate.

3) Lushan Trade Fair. Scenic Spots and Historic Sites of Lushan Mountain, which is a Natural and cultural heritage located in Jiujiang, are well known in the world. Taking use of the conference and exhibition in Lushan, the collaboration Annual Business of the Yangtze River basin and the high-level development forum of Trade circulation

has been extended to the whole country and even around the world. In the economic and trade cooperation seminar between Jiangxi and Taiwan, many Taiwan celebrities of business communities take part in, which makes it be a brand activity in the central and western regions of the country, and even sets off "Jiangxi hot" in Taiwan.

4) Zhangshu Herbs Fair. Zhangshu City is 80 kilometers away from Nanchang. As the old saying goes "Drugs are not complete until arriving at Zhangshu, drugs are ineffective until passing through Zhangshu ". So far, Zhangshu has successfully held 38th PHARMCHINA. In the year of 2008, the representatives of more than 6700 medicinal companies, pharmaceutical enterprise, health products manufacturer, processing and operating enterprise of traditional Chinese medicine, manufacturing companies of medical apparatus and instruments from all over the country and abroad took part in the PHARMCHINA in Zhangshu herbs, the number of participants reached six thousand, and the amount of contracts reached 3.495 billion Yuan.

4 The Sustainable Development Strategy of Poyang Lake Ecological Economic Region

A. Aim at the Needs of Exhibition Market and Exhibition Enterprise to Cultivate Professional Exhibition Economy Talents

We should combine academic education with the training of professional skills, beginning from various links of exhibition, to provide focused guiding for the students, strengthening the student's professionalism and using simulative experiments, to cultivate the student to be a man with the management capabilities about the project, themes, investment, exhibition, budget, management and resources of the exhibition.

B. Build Industrial Base, Attract the Headquarters of Multinational Companies to Station in

We should learn from foreign advanced management concept to build central business district, serving for attracting a number of multinational companies stationing in and introducing in investment and stay of the internationally renowned companies in the Poyang Lake Ecological Economic Region. Aiming at the regular and occasional national exhibitions and expositions, we should make full use of resource advantages to carefully nurture a conference and exhibition brands embrace Poyang Lake, and to vigorously promote the "exhibition economy".

C. Take Use of Logistics Parks and College Ground to Extend Exhibition Economy

In the recent years, Poyang Lake Ecological Economic Region was deluged with projects of conference and exhibition, involving trade, tourism, business, food, home design, building materials, agriculture, real estate, advertising, medicine, clothing, information industry and other aspects, and most of these were held in Jiangxi exhibition hall and Nanchang international exhibition center. East China International

Industry Fair use Qingyunpu industrial and logistics park in Nanchang to alleviate the shortage of exhibition space. Taking use of sports venues and other facilities in the College Park, it allows colleges and universities close to the community, and makes the resources of ground fully utilized.

D. Push the Exhibition to the Market to Enhance the Viability of Exhibition Enterprises

Nowadays, the number of enterprises dealing with exhibition in the Poyang Lake Ecological Economic Region is less than one hundred, so there is critical shortage of exhibition talents. The exhibition industry needs to be improved in the organization, management, service, planning level and operational level of the exhibition invitation, design, lay booth and exhibition period.

Taking the mode of market operation, guiding and providing chances for the exhibition, the government utilizes the operation of social capital to advance economic development of exhibition to promote the business of exhibition, raise the level of management and build brands of exhibition.

E. Protect Intellectual Property Rights of Exhibition to Attract More High-Tech Companies to Station in

We should pay attention to protect the intellectual property rights of exhibition, and *intellectual property rights of exhibition* should also be protected. We should require all exhibitors to sign a statement about the respect of the intellectual property rights, and also including that the government departments establish a rapid response mechanism to investigate and deal with infringement. We should strengthen the protection consciousness of intellectual property, cracking down on violations of exhibition on intellectual property rights to assure exhibitors. For overseas manufacturers, once weak intellectual property protection on the exhibition happens, it may lead to great negative impact.

F. Make Joint Effort to Build a Base of Exhibition in the Central Region to Bid for Hosting National and International Well-Known Exhibition

There are still some problems in the Poyang Lake Ecological Economic Region, such as the quality is not satisfied, most are small-and-medium-sized exhibitions, brand and large-scale exhibitions are few. We should strive to hold the international project of exhibition in virtue of the International brand of Conference and Exhibition Center. In this regard, we should take distinctive exhibition as the goal, relying on the industrial advantages and characterized location, and regarding various forms of meetings, exhibitions and large-scale competitions, concerts and festivals as support, further optimize the environment of development, standardize the running order, expand the overall economy, vigorously promote the branding, internationalization, specialization, market-oriented and standardized processes of exhibition, promote all-round economic and social progress, on the premise of ensuring that quality and efficiency are improved.

5 Conclusion

In this century, accompanied by the rapid economic development of Jiangxi Province, exhibition industry has entered an active period of market and the fast lane of development. However, compared with Exhibition Economy in the other province, exhibition industry in Jiangxi is on a small scale with poor quality. Many conferences and exhibitions are in the low level. Some have a title of "international conference and exhibition", but actually are nominal. At present, there are more than 30 companies of conference and exhibition in Nanchang, companies in the capacity of holding independent exhibition are not many, and the number of exhibition booth is less than 100 in most companies. We must cultivate and the introduce professionals especially versatile personnel, to upgrade the scale and the level of professional exhibition company to improve the overall level of conference and exhibition.

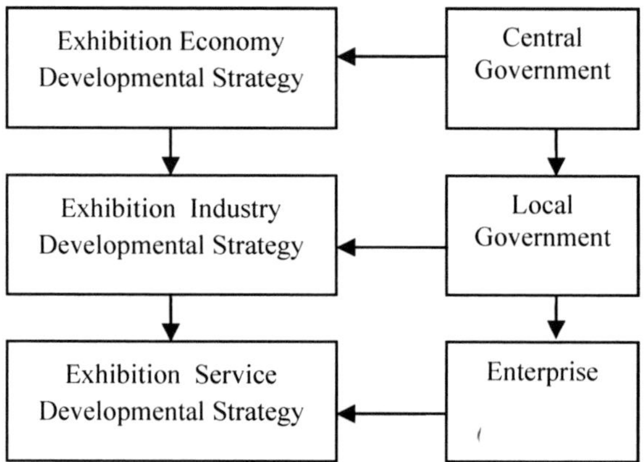

Fig. 2. The Strategic System of Exhibition Economy on development

Exhibition hall is the basis of economic development for conference and exhibition, if there is no considerable scale and supporting facilities of the exhibition hall, it would be very difficult to create influential exhibition brands. The location and layout of Exhibition hall would have great significance on exhibition efficiency, exhibition effect, bringing economic benefit into play after conference and exhibition, and coordinating development of Exhibition Economy. In the aspect of facilities in Poyang Lake Ecological Economic Region, there exists big gap not only in comparing with " The three magnates of Exhibition Economy " --Shanghai, Beijing, Guangzhou, but also in comparison with the neighboring provinces and cities,

Nanchang International Exhibition Center, which is the only modern, professional and international exhibition center, completed in Jiangxi Province in 2006. It has a total area of 180,000 square meters, including 77,000 square meters building area, 10 million square meters of outdoor exhibition space and 5 million square meters of indoor exhibition hall and conference area which are in use. But there is still no International Conference and Exhibition Center in the real sense, so it is very urgently to build a regional conference center. In Jiangxi Province, “Eleventh Five-Year Plan” proposed, following the accelerated trend of people, logistics, information flow, we should accelerate to develop Exhibition Economy, advertising display services, actively develop content services of information, technology services of information, network services of information, and other modern information service industry. Under the supervision of government departments, we should improve the trade law, avoid duplication of exhibition, waste of resources, and vicious competition, and strengthen the supervision of conference and exhibition, in order to provide a good environment for the development of Exhibition Economy in the Poyang Lake Ecological Economic Region.

References

1. Guo, x.: Research on Urban Development of the Modern Exhibition Industry. Theory Journal (9), 96–97 (2005)
2. Luo, W-z.: Research on Strategy of Development in Changsha Exhibition Economy. Systems Engineering (6), 56–59 (2005)
3. Qinengjie: Competitive Power Evaluation Model for Urban Competitiveness. Special Zone Economy Special Zone EC (1), 208–209 (2006)
4. Yangqun: Research on Sustainable Development of Tourism Economy in Shenzhen Conference and Exhibition. Special Zone Economy Special Zone EC (5), 192–193 (2006)
5. Zhangyuming: Research on Integrated Model and Innovative Approaches of Commercial Exhibition Marketing Promotion. Commercial Research (23), 133–135 (2006)

Land Use Change in the Coastal Area of the Pearl River Estuary Based on GIS and RS

Hengyao Tang and Yuan Fang

Department of Computer Science and Technology,
Huanggang Normal University,
Huanggang, Hubei, China
dariuszk523@gmail.com

Abstract. Land use conversion is the hottest issue in the research field of globe changing. The Coastal Area of the Pearl River Estuary where the zone has a typical feature of land use change and significant ecological effects is selected as a case. Applying the satellite images of Landsat-TM and the integrating techniques of RS and GIS, the present study analyzed the temporal and spatial processes and gravity center change in the Coastal Area of the Pearl River Estuary from 1988 to 2002. The classified results of multi-temporal TM remote sensing image data and transfer matrix of land use revealed that land use had been changed significantly from 1988 to 2002 in the Coastal Area of the Pearl River Estuary. Various types of land use convert frequently, which mainly reflect in the waters, the cultivated land loss and construction land increase and their different direction migration of the gravity center. After 1995 land use degree of the study area grows slower, which shows the Coastal Area of the Pearl River Estuary emphasized the overall development after the rapid expansion. On the east of the Coastal Area of the Pearl River Estuary the land use change which has experienced more rapid change represented the overall trend.

Keywords: component, LUCC, Spatial and temporal change, GIS, CAPRE.

1 Introduction

The Pearl River Delta is the forefront of our country' Reform and opening-up, driven by factors of various humanity and nature, the zone has converted rapidly from the traditional region of agricultural land into emerging highly urbanized areas, land use has taken place profound changes, which has the obvious impact on the regional ecological security. The Coastal Area of the Pearl River Estuary is the most typical region of the Pearl River Delta economic development, with social, economic and nature of various factors in the combined effect of different spatial and temporal scale, land use pattern in the Coastal Area of the Pearl River Estuary constantly tends to fragmentation, complexity and ecosystem stability and service functions are being constantly degraded. This paper applied the main techniques of RS and GIS, developing remote sensing mapping of classification of regional land use, promoting the ecological environment in the study region and socio-economic sustainable development.

This paper chose the Coastal Area of the Pearl River Estuary as the research area, and has been studied the conversion spatial pattern based on RS and GIS.

M. Dai (Ed.): ICCIC 2011, Part II, CCIS 232, pp. 274–280, 2011.

2 The Sutdy Area and Methods

A. The Overview of the Study Area

The Coastal Area of the Pearl River Estuary (CAPRE) is between longitude 113°09′~114°22′ and latitude 21°09′~22°27′, and adjacent to Hong Kong and Macao. The study area includes four administrative regions: Dongguan City and Shenzhen City in the east coast of the Pearl River Estuary, Zhongshan City and Panyu District of the west coast, the total area is about 6411 km2. Because of the restrictions on remote sensing image data, the study area is only related to part of region of the two administrative regions, Zhongshan and Shenzhen, respectively accounts for 71%,79% of the total area, but includes the major urban development and land use change region of the two administrative regions, Zhongshan and Shenzhen, it can reflect the two administrative regions of the land use pattern to a greater extent. It is mainly of the geomorphologic structure of the east coast of the Pearl River Estuary is relatively complex and diverse in the west coast, mesa hills and alluvial plains. Shenzhen and the eastern part of Dongguan are mountainous, and the mountains are huge, the altitude of them are between 200 m and 600 m, the terrain separates strongly, the most part of Zhongshan of the west coast and Panyu is flat open alluvial plain and the beach.

It is an important base for crop production in delta. Since reform and opening up, The Coastal Area of the Pearl River Estuary has made full use of the location advantage which is adjacent to Hong Kong and Macao and policy advantages of Shenzhen and Zhuhai Special Economic Zone, and has taken the transfer of industry and economic radiation of Hong Kong and Macao, rapidly developed the most active zone of economic development in Southeast coast of China.

B Data Analysis and Classification System

The study used the Landsat-5 TM (1988, 1995 and 1998) and Landsat-7 ETM (2002) remote sensing image as the basic data. The track number of the remote sensing image is 122/044. It extracted the classification data and cultivated land resources information of the different phase with remote sensing image processing based on ERDAS8.7, and ArcGIS9.0 [2]. All the spatial data are stored with 30*30 Arc GRID format. The method to process the grid data includes transfer matrix, spatial overlay, and GIS model[3].

This study is according to the factors such as China' Land Use Survey Technical Specification, the use of land, operating characteristics, the way of use, and the features of coverage and so on as the basis for classification of land use. From senior to junior level division, in the course of analysis, combined land use characteristics of the cross-strait zone of the Pearl River estuary and interpretation accuracy of remote sensing image, at the same time, considering the spatial variation of land use types and driving factors, the land use types is divided into arable land, garden plot, forest, grass land, settlements and construction land, waters and unutilized land, a total of seven types.

The results of remote sensing interpretation mainly referred to the type of map of land use from 1995 to 2002 in Guangdong Province, meanwhile, combined field survey data with the method of visual interpretation, conducting accuracy assessment of

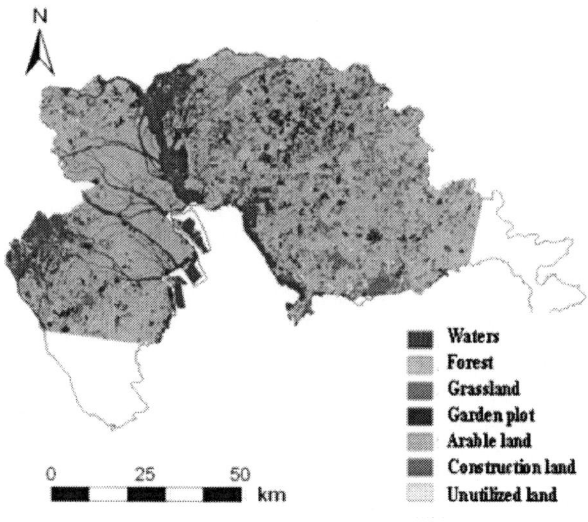

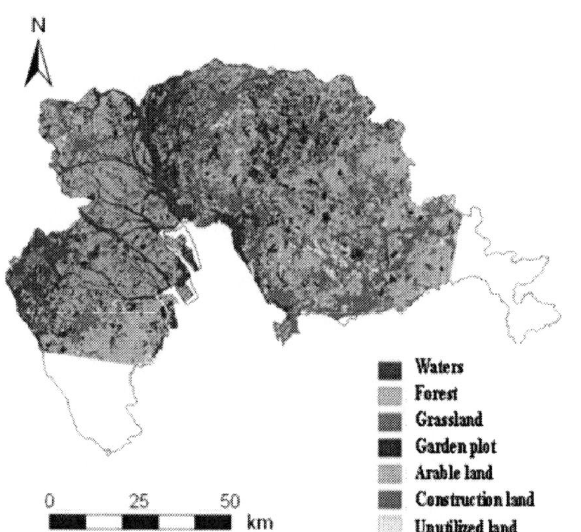

Fig. 1. The land use spatial pattern of CAPRE 1988 and 1995

classification results of the phase image. Accuracy Assessment mainly made use of accuracy assessment function of ERDAS classification module through randomly generating 256 samples and adopted the principle of the possibility of error matrix for the accuracy assessment of the explanation result of the phase of the remote sensing, got the assessment results of classification accuracy of four periods remote sensing images(Table 2).It can be seen from the table that the overall accuracy of the results of remote sensing classification of 1988,1995,1998,2002 are respectively as followings: 82.42%,82.03%,82.42%,81.64%, the kappa coefficient are respectively 0.774, 0.761, 0.792, 0.779, basically meeting the analysis requirements of land use change.

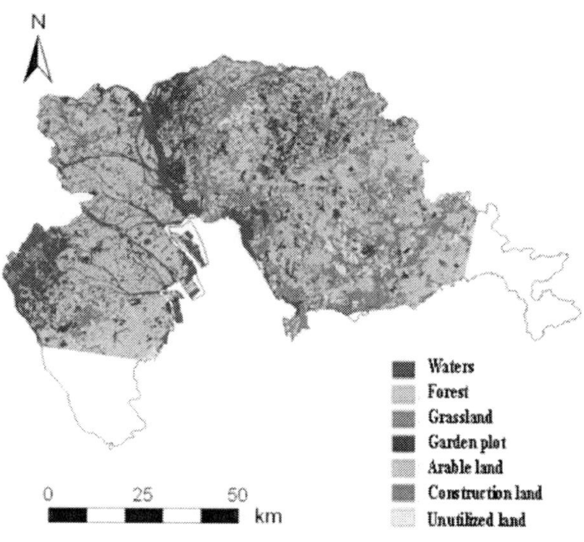

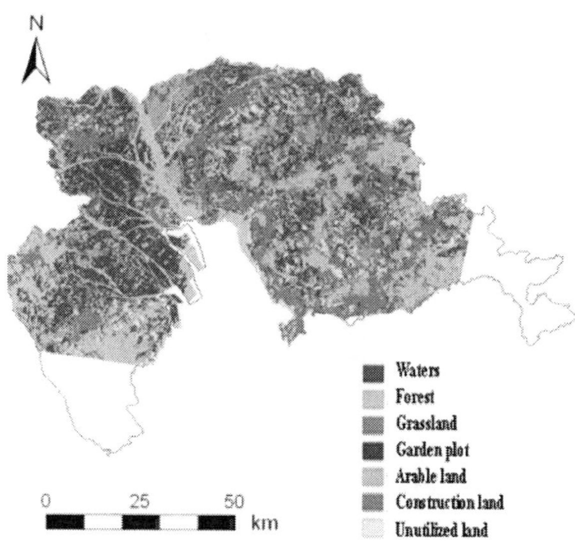

Fig. 2. The land use spatial pattern of CAPRE 1998 and 2002

3 Results

C. The Classification Results of Land Use

According to interpretation process as mentioned above, the classification results of remote sensing image was converted into Arc GRID data format, then used ArcGIS software drawing category mapping of different land use of four year for 1988,1995,1998 and 2002(figure1-2), and got out the type of land use of the Coastal Area of the Pearl River Estuary through making use of the administrative boundary map of the study area carrying out dynamic analysis of Land use patterns in different areas[4].

After interpreting the TM remote sensing image of different phase, added up respectively the classification results of land use of the study area and different administrative areas of the four different years from 1988 to 2002 with the support of ArcView, got the number of structural features of the corresponding land use types in the study area, then analyzed and compared the dynamic changes of land use of different years in the Coastal Area of the Pearl River Estuary. With the preliminary analysis it can be found that, land use patterns have taken place significant changes in the Coastal Area of the Pearl River Estuary from 1988 to 2002 with rapid development of the Coastal Area of the Pearl River Estuary of economy. The greatest feature of regional land use change was traditional agricultural land changing into construction land rapidly. Construction land and other areas have been continuing to increase, the areas of arable land and other types of agricultural land were continuing to decrease. Especially at the end of the last century 80's and at the early of 90's, The most dramatic change was the construction land and arable land among various land types in the Coastal Area of the Pearl River Estuary, the main feature of the loss of a large number of arable is the extension and expansion of construction land and the beaded and bulk distribution along the traffic. However, the main feature of the loss of agricultural land in the new period is that agricultural land was occupied in the developing zone.

D. Land Use Change

Combining with figure 1~2,it can be analyzed and found that the area of arable land continued to reduce, with the stimulation of the hot developing zone, hot urban construction and hot estate, urbanization and industrialization occupied a large number of land resources, which is the main cause of rapid reduction of arable land. In the past nearly 15 years, the number of the arable land sharply declined in the Coastal Area of the Pearl River Estuary, except that little arable land changed into grassland, forest and unutilized land, mainly into construction land and waters. It can c be seen that urbanization and industrialization developed rapidly, occupied a large number of arable land, arable land from 324959ha reduced to 185253ha. The area of arable land of reduction mainly flowed to construction land and waters from 1988 to 1995. Because of construction occupying land, about 100915.76ha arable land was occupied by construction land of towns, settlements and traffic mining, about 35055.45ha arable land was occupied by waters, other arable land about 1191.06ha changed into forest, 1561.44ha into grassland, and 3875.58haha into Garden. What's more, about 2053.09ha arable land was disserted. The reduction of arable land was less than pre -period in the years of 1995 to 1998, the arable land was mainly converted into waters and construction land. waters occupied about 10662.57ha arable land ,it was the land use types which occupied the largest number of arable land during this period, about 9846.68ha arable land was occupied by the land use of towns, settlements and traffic mining, other about 1191.06ha arable land was converted into forest, 302.67ha arable land into grassland, and 2153.2ha into Garden plot.

The phenomenon of abandoning arable land improved obviously than last period, the flow of the area of reduced arable land is similar to the flow of periods from 1995 to 1998. About 9846.98ha Among the construction land, about 9846.98ha arable land was occupied by the land use of towns, settlements and traffic mining, waters occupied about 12704.85ha arable land, the number that the arable land changed into other land-use types obviously reduced compared with last two periods, grassland was the least type which occupied the arable land among them.

In the Coastal Area of the Pearl River Estuary where the economy has been developing rapidly, the limited arable land resources is confronted with the demand pressures of the urban construction and food production and many other aspects. The contradiction between economic development and resources protection is prominent, in order to make up the loss of valuable arable land resources, and achieve the dynamic balance of the total arable land, people turned their view into "four disserted land" and so-called "four disserted land", which aggravated the vicious circle of ecological degradation and the vulnerability of natural ecosystems. With the analysis of 1~4,it can be found that while the arable land converted into other types of land use , and other types of land use can also convert into the arable land, Waters and forest are the main types of land use which has been converted into arable land, but the amount of them is obviously less than that of loss of arable land, from 1988 to 1995,there was 12186.5ha waters, 2855.34ha forest, 3456.27ha grassland , 4326.84ha Garden plot,599.44ha unutilized land changed into arable land ,however, the construction land was not changed into arable land. From 1995 to 1998,waters and Garden plot were the main types of land use which were converted into arable land, their areas were respectively 7416ha and 1049ha,the amount of unutilized land which was developed to arable land was 70.43ha,the amount that other types of land use were converted into arable land were relatively less ; from1998 to 2002,waters was type of land use which was converted into the largest number of arable land, with 8764.11ha,but it was far less than the amount of same period that the arable land was converted into the waters, the amount of forest, Garden plot, grassland and unutilized land that were developed to arable land was quite approximate, but all of them were larger than the amount of loss of arable land during the same period, construction land was still the only land type which was not converted into arable land.

4 Conclusion and Discussion

The study object of this paper is the Coastal Area of the Pearl River Estuary which is the typical area of the economic development in the Pearl River Delta, the main sources of information are TM Remote Sensing Image in four different stage and updating data through land use survey from 1996 to 2004, applying Remote Sensing Image processing and GIS technology deeply studied. The characteristics and laws of Spatial and temporal evolution about land use pattern and in the process of rapid urbanization and industrialization and the driving mechanism in the Coastal Area of the Pearl River Estuary.

The land use had taken place significant changes in the Coastal Area of the Pearl River Estuary during the 15 years from 1988 to 2002.The larger types of the range of land use change were waters, arable land and construction land, the land use change was relatively sharp in the east Coastal Area of the Pearl River Estuary among them, the degree of land use change and the rate of change were obviously higher than the average of the study and the west Coastal Area of the Pearl River Estuary, regional differences showed that Shenzhen>Dongguan>study area >Panyu>Zhongshan, it explained that human development activities tend to concentrate on the east coast, whose economy was more developed; It was the fastest time of the land use change from1988 to 1995,after that time the utilization extent of land use improved slowly in the study area, the change of land use pattern tended to relative ease and stability.

References

1. Zhou, J., Wu, Z., Li, D., Hu, Y.: A Quantitative Analysis on the Fragmentation of Cultivated Land on the Two Sides of the Zhujiang Estuary. In: Tropical Geography, vol. 25, pp. 107–110. Guangzhou Institute of Geography, Guangzhou (2005)
2. Lunetta, R.S., Balogh, M.E.: Application of Multi-temporal Landsat SRTM imagery for wetland identification. Photogrammetric Engineering & Remote Sensing, 1303–1310 (2003)
3. Pontius, R.G., Huffaker, D., et al.: Useful techniques of validation for spatially explicit land-change models. Ecological Modeling, 445–461 (2004)
4. Merten, B., Lambin, E.: Modeling land cover dynamics: integration of fine-scale land cover data with landscape attributes. International Journal of Applied Earth Observation and Geoinformation, 48–52 (1999)

Gravity Center Change in the Coastal Area of the Pearl River Estuary Based on GIS and RS

Chen Xiaolin and Zhou Fei

Department of Computer Science and Technology
Huanggang Normal University
Huanggang, Hubei, China
J.J.Jung@hotmail.com

Abstract. Land use change was the hottest topic in the research field of globe changing. The Coastal Area of the Pearl River Estuary where the zone has a typical feature of land use change and significant ecological effects was selected as a case. Applying the satellite images of Landsat-TM and the integrating techniques of GIS and RS, the present study analyzed the temporal and spatial processes and gravity center change in the Coastal Area of the Pearl River Estuary from 1988 to 2002. The classified results of multi-temporal TM remote sensing image data and transfer matrix of land use revealed that land use had been changed significantly from 1988 to 2002 in the Coastal Area of the Pearl River Estuary. Various types of land use convert frequently, which mainly reflect in the waters, the cultivated land loss and construction land increase and their different direction migration of the gravity center. After 1995 land use degree of the study area grows slower, which shows the Coastal Area of the Pearl River Estuary emphasized the overall development after the rapid expansion. On the east of the Coastal Area of the Pearl River Estuary the land use change which has experienced more rapid change represented the overall trend.

Keywords: component, LUCC, Spatial and temporal change, GIS, CAPRE.

1 Introduction

The Pearl River Delta is the forefront of our country' Reform and opening-up, driven by factors of various humanity and nature, the zone has converted rapidly from the traditional region of agricultural land into emerging highly urbanized areas, land use has taken place profound changes, which has the obvious impact on the regional ecological security. The Coastal Area of the Pearl River Estuary is the most typical region of the Pearl River Delta economic development, with social, economic and nature of various factors in the combined effect of different spatial and temporal scale, land use pattern in the Coastal Area of the Pearl River Estuary constantly tends to fragmentation, complexity and ecosystem stability and service functions are being constantly degraded. This paper applied the main techniques of GIS and RS, developing remote sensing mapping of classification of regional land use, promoting the ecological environment in the study region and socio-economic sustainable development.

M. Dai (Ed.): ICCIC 2011, Part II, CCIS 232, pp. 281–286, 2011.

2 The Study Area and Methods

A. The Overview of the Study Area

The Coastal Area of the Pearl River Estuary (CAPRE) is between longitude 113°09′~114°22′ and latitude 21°09′~22°27′, and adjacent to Hong Kong and Macao. The study area includes four administrative regions: Dongguan City and Shenzhen City in the east coast of the Pearl River Estuary, Zhongshan City and Panyu District of the west coast, the total area is about 6411 km2. Because of the restrictions on remote sensing image data, the study area is only related to part of region of the two administrative regions, Zhongshan and Shenzhen, respectively accounts for 71%,79% of the total area, but includes the major urban development and land use change region of the two administrative regions, Zhongshan and Shenzhen, it can reflect the two administrative regions of the land use pattern to a greater extent. It is mainly of the geomorphologic structure of the east coast of the Pearl River Estuary is relatively complex and diverse in the west coast, mesa hills and alluvial plains. Shenzhen and the eastern part of Dongguan are mountainous, and the mountains are huge, the altitude of them are between 200 m and 600 m, the terrain separates strongly, the most part of Zhongshan of the west coast and Panyu is flat open alluvial plain and the beach.

It is an important base for crop production in delta. Since reform and opening up, The Coastal Area of the Pearl River Estuary has made full use of the location advantage which is adjacent to Hong Kong and Macao and policy advantages of Shenzhen and Zhuhai Special Economic Zone, and has taken the transfer of industry and economic radiation of Hong Kong and Macao, rapidly developed the most active zone of economic development in Southeast coast of China.

B. Data Analysis and Classification System

The study used the Landsat-5 TM (1988, 1995 and 1998) and Landsat-7 ETM (2002) remote sensing image as the basic data. The track number of the remote sensing image is 122/044. It extracted the classification data and cultivated land resources information of the different phase with remote sensing image processing based on ERDAS8.7, and ArcGIS9.0 [2]. All the spatial data are stored with 30*30 Arc GRID format. The method to process the grid data includes transfer matrix, spatial overlay, and GIS model [3].

This study is according to the factors such as China' Land Use Survey Technical Specification, the use of land, operating characteristics, the way of use, and the features of coverage and so on as the basis for classification of land use. From senior to junior level division, in the course of analysis, combined land use characteristics of the cross-strait zone of the Pearl River estuary and interpretation accuracy of remote sensing image, at the same time, considering the spatial variation of land use types and driving factors, the land use types is divided into arable land, garden plot, forest, grass land, settlements and construction land, waters and unutilized land, a total of seven types.

The results of remote sensing interpretation mainly referred to the type of map of land use from 1995 to 2002 in Guangdong Province, meanwhile, combined field survey data with the method of visual interpretation, conducting accuracy assessment of

Table 1. The accuracy of classification result in study area

Phase	1988	1995	1998	2002
Sampling precision	82.42%	82.03%	82.42%	81.64%
Kappa coefficient	0.774	0.761	0.792	0.779

Table 2. The distance and direction of gravity center shift

	type	waters	forest	grassland	Garden Plot	arable land	construction land	unutilized land
The distance of gravity center shift(km)	1988~1995	3.370	1.435	2.531	2.084	8.359	6.399	5.079
	1995~1998	2.220	0.344	0.706	0.646	0.612	1.129	2.119
	1998~2002	1.849	0.629	0.382	1.294	0.946	0.540	4.076
	1988~2002	4.611	1.132	2.064	2.902	8.757	5.643	10.143
The direction of gravity center shift(^{0})	1988~1995	302.80	314.68	103.21	238.52	303.26	66.83	252.51
	1995~1998	264.00	328.81	210.48	132.25	3.48	268.20	262.64
	1998~2002	41.31	132.11	112.67	256.05	355.67	264.61	51.01
	1988~2002	307.61	318.80	135.01	235.37	293.01	15.62	85.66

Note: The direction of gravity center shift is with the angle of direction north.

classification results of the phase image. Accuracy Assessment mainly made use of accuracy assessment function of ERDAS classification module through randomly generating 256 samples and adopted the principle of the possibility of error matrix for the accuracy assessment of the explanation result of the phase of the remote sensing, got the assessment results of classification accuracy of four periods remote sensing images(Table 2).It can be seen from the table that the overall accuracy of the results of remote sensing classification of 1988,1995,1998,2002 are respectively as followings: 82.42%,82.03%,82.42%,81.64%, the kappa coefficient are respectively 0.774, 0.761, 0.792, 0.779, basically meeting the analysis requirements of land use change.

3 Results

C. The Classification Results of Land Use

According to interpretation process as mentioned above, the classification results of remote sensing image was converted into Arc GRID data format, then used ArcGIS software drawing category mapping of different land use of four year for 1988,1995,1998 and 2002(figure1-2), and got out the type of land use of the Coastal Area of the Pearl River Estuary through making use of the administrative boundary map of the study area carrying out dynamic analysis of Land use patterns in different areas[4].

After interpreting the TM remote sensing image of different phase, added up respectively the classification results of land use of the study area and different administrative areas of the four different years from 1988 to 2002 with the support of ArcView, got the number of structural features of the corresponding land use types in the study area, then analyzed and compared the dynamic changes of land use of different years in the Coastal Area of the Pearl River Estuary. With the preliminary analysis it can be found that, land use patterns have taken place significant changes in the Coastal Area of the Pearl River Estuary from 1988 to 2002 with rapid development of the Coastal Area of the Pearl River Estuary of economy. The greatest feature of regional land use change was traditional agricultural land changing into construction land rapidly. Construction land and other areas have been continuing to increase, the areas of arable land and other types of agricultural land were continuing to decrease. Especially at the end of the last century 80's and at the early of 90's, The most dramatic change was the construction land and arable land among various land types in the Coastal Area of the Pearl River Estuary, the main feature of the loss of a large number of arable is the extension and expansion of construction land and the beaded and bulk distribution along the traffic. However, the main feature of the loss of agricultural land in the new period is that agricultural land was occupied in the developing zone.

D. Land Use Gravity Center Migration

Land use is a kind of human activity with spatial location, scope and direction of change, dynamic change analysis of land use types as mentioned above was a kind of imitation analysis on the amount only based on the data of present spatial distribution but an overall feature of the land using spatial variation was using migration of type Gravity Center in this area, this feature can be reflected by gravity center coordinate.

Gravity center conversion is a vector problem with direction and distance, the direction of land using gravity center migration could reveal the distribution of dynamic change of land use in the space. If the area of land use change in all directions in space evenly grow and declined, its gravity center basically wouldn't change. If it showed rather obviously in one direction, its gravity center would shift significantly. The direction of gravity center also can reflect the direction of the land use change, and provide reference for the planning department of land use. Transferring distance can reflect the range of each kind of land use conversion to some extent, accordingly reflected the approximate level of the type of land increasing or declining in space and the original distribution, also can reflect spatial distribution and dynamic changes of Driving Factors which lead to land use change from the side.

With the urban development, the gravity center of all kinds of land use types also has taken place accordingly in space, its changes were different from each other, but they had close relationship and mutual constraints. Adopting the change model of gravity center of land use the gravity center shift of waters, Garden Plot, forest, arable land, construction land and unutilized land had calculated and researched to reveal the rules of spatial variation, the results of calculating had listed table2.

The direction information of the gravity center shift can be concluded from table 2, the turning point of gravity center of the land use types was mostly in 1995 among it. Therefore, the following analysis was divided into two periods. The gravity center of waters moved from 22.729N,113.642E in the direction of Northwest to

22.739N,113.620E from 1988 to 1995,the forest gravity center from 22.710N,113.853E towards the direction of north west moved to 22.710N,113.846E,the gravity center of arable land moved from 22.761N,113.707E towards the direction of Northwest to 22.764N,113.658E, the gravity center of construction land moved from 22.714N,113.832E towards the direction of Northeast 22.745N,113.845E, the grassland gravity center moved from 22.783N,113.890E towards the direction of east south to 22.782N,113.899E,the gravity center of Garden Plot moved from 22.837N,113.808E towards the direction of southwest to 22.830N,113.798E. The gravity center of waters towards North West again moved to 22.750N, 113.617E from 1995 to 2002.

During the 15 years from 1988 to 2002,the distance of gravity center shift of waters, arable land, construction land and unutilized land was quite large, the gravity center migration is between 1.132 and10.143km,these land use types were significantly affected by man-made, their gravity center shift may be influenced considerably by population migration and other factors, change intensity was quite considerably. The distance of the gravity center shift of forest, Garden Plot, grassland among the seven kinds of types of migration distance relatively smaller, which was the relatively stable land-use types in the study area, the migration distance of the Garden Plot was the smallest among them, because the Garden Plot in the study area lies in relatively large slope of the area, which is not good for development because of its strong stability, the gravity center can not easily shift. it was the time when the distance of the gravity center migration was the largest from1988 to 1995, arable land and construction land were the larger two types of land use of the gravity center migration which showed that arable land and construction land changed quite frequently during that time, and were affected considerably by human interference intensity; After 1995, the gravity center migration of all kinds of the land use was relatively small.

The migration direction of arable land, waters, forest and construction land is generally opposite, on the condition that the land area was fixed, the conversion of all the land use types in the area caused the change of the gravity center of land use type, they performed the direction of the movement of the gravity center in space, this is because the expansion of cities and towns would occupy lots of agricultural land, what' more, the movement range of the gravity center of arable land is larger than the gravity center of the construction land, because of the other factors which affected the change of the arable land . During the 15 years from 1988 to 2002, the angle of the gravity center of the construction land was relatively smallish showed that the change of forest and construction land in space was quite average, the direction of the gravity center shift of waters grassland and arable land was quite obviously, the conversion angle was also relatively large, it showed that the three kinds of land use types had obvious direction in the change of space.

4 Conclusion and Discussion

The study object of this paper was the Coastal Area of the Pearl River Estuary which is the typical area of the economic development in the Pearl River Delta.In the process of rapid urbanization and industrialization, various kinds of land use types converted frequently, which reflected in waters, arable land flowing and converting into construction land, whose conversion finally reflected the opposite of migration of gravity center direction of arable land, waters, forest and construction land in space[1]; The distance of gravity center shift was relatively large in the aspect of waters ,arable land, construction land and unutilized land in the Coastal Area of the Pearl River Estuary during the 15 years from 1988 to 2002, affected significant by the man-made, and the change intensity was relatively large, it was the largest time when the land use type converted most frequently and gravity center migration changed greatly from 1988 to 1995 ;the forest ,Garden Plot and grassland were the relatively stable land use type in the study area., the forest was distributed in the areas whose terrain conditions were relatively poor, it was not generally as the adjustments of other land use types and the source of expansion, type conversion was relatively little, and In space corresponding to the gravity center stability was strong.

References

[1] Zhou, J., Wu, Z., Li, D., Hu, Y.: A Quantitative Analysis on the Fragmentation of Cultivated Land on the Two Sides of the Zhujiang Estuary. In: Tropical Geography, vol. 25, pp. 107–110. Guangzhou Institute of Geography, Guangzhou (2005)

[2] Lunetta, R.S., Balogh, M.E.: Application of Multi-temporal Landsat SRTM imagery for wetland identification. Photogrammetric Engineering & Remote Sensing, 1303–1310 (2003)

[3] Pontius, R.G., Huffaker, D., et al.: Useful techniques of validation for spatially explicit land-change models. Ecological Modeling, 445–461 (2004)

[4] Merten, B., Lambin, E.: Modeling land cover dynamics: integration of fine-scale land cover data with landscape attributes. International Journal of Applied Earth Observation and Geoinformation, 48–52 (1999)

A Study on Conflict and Coordination between Industrial Policy and Competition Policy

Qiong Huang[1] and Renfa Yang[2]

[1] Nanchang Institute of Technology Nanchang, China
[2] School of Economics Nankai University Tianjin, China
caolb89@gmail.com

Abstract. Industrial policy and competition policy are the basic form of state intervention in the economy. They have differences in many aspects. But they are not irreconcilable. It is very important how to effectively coordinate between industrial policy and competition policy. In this paper, we analyze the conflict between industrial policy and competition policy based on the content and the relations of them, and then we propose the coordination path from coordination legal basis, coordination principle, coordination body, coordination methods.

Keywords: industrial policy, competition policy, conflict, coordination.

1 Introduction

Industrial policy was created in about 1950's in Japan. Ryutaro Komiya considered that industrial policy is to change the allocation of resources between industries and various private sector activities; Masu Uekusa argued that industrial policy is to foster the wide ranges of polices instruments in order to take the promising export industry for special protection; some other Scholars claim that industrial policy is that a government to improve their economic welfare policies implemented due to defects in a competitive market, when the result of competition of resource allocation and income distribution problems. Generally speaking, industrial policy is the sum of various interventions policy that a government in order to achieve a certain degree of economic and social objectives.

Competition policy has no strict definition although widely quoted. Competition policy is generally divided into two kinds of meaning. Broad competition policy is that all policies affecting competition in the market. Narrow competition policy is the enforcement of competition legislation and competition embodied in the practice, and sometimes is equated with anti-monopoly law Regardless of broad or narrow competition policy, Competition policy is the government formulated and implemented strategies to promote competition. The main purpose of competition policy is to protect and promote competition, prevent and sanction the behavior of various restrictions on competition, by maintaining free competition in a market economy order for the effective allocation of resources.

M. Dai (Ed.): ICCIC 2011, Part II, CCIS 232, pp. 287–293, 2011.

The relationship between industrial policy and competition policy gradually from "conflict" to "converge" with the development of national economy. In the early stages of economic development, the government implements powerful industrial policy. These will greatly compression competition policy implementation space, or even no competition policy. The relationship between the two policies is a "conflict."

And in the economy develops to a certain extent, governments and businesses have recognized the drawbacks of selective industrial policy, competition policy play the role in development of the national economy development. That the industrial policy and competition policy relationships or sometimes conflict, sometimes compatible. Then the relationship between the two policies called "nested type." When the national market economy system completely established, competition policy play the dominant role in the market, while industrial policy as support policies in the market, has only a market-oriented and remedy defects of market. This is the relationship between the two policies called "converge".

2 The Conflict Industrial Policy and Competition Policy

2.1 The Conflict of Specific Objectives Choosing and Data Processing

The aim of industrial policy is the development of specific industries, and competition policy will focus on the existence of the market competition mechanism and the market. Therefore, industrial policy emphasizes multi-elemental participation by formulating policies, the key enterprise vigorously support and encourage enterprises to increase investment and key through mergers and acquisitions, rapidly expand business scale, improve market share. In order to avoid the repetition of certain industry investment and excessive competition, the government often set up administrative barriers to entry to protect the interests of incumbent firms. Competition policy is to encourage competition among enterprises with the orientation of market. The government is alert to enterprises to expand the market share of market, concentration .Mergers and acquisitions among enterprises is even more rigorous scrutiny. Agreements such as fixed price among enterprises for the purpose of competition policy would have been strictly prohibited.

2.2 The Conflict of Specific Role of Object

With the individual nature of industrial policy, competition policy has universal application. Industrial policy only in terms of specific industries, such as resource-based industries and emerging industries; competition policy has universal application. Modern economics and legal theory show that monopoly has eroded not only the erosion of economic democracy, but political democracy. When the power is too concentrated related industries, economic democracy has been seriously eroded, competition policy will have a useless, at this time had formed to promote the industry to support the implementation of various industrial policies, you should give competition policy. Industrial policy should meet the requirements of competition policy; the relevant industries to implement industrial policies can only be a temporary use. Competitive market allocation of resources is the best way to compete when the market conditions change, the mission of the industrial policy will change accordingly.

2.3 The Conflict of Economic Adjustment

The implement industrial policy measures are mainly market access, price controls, financial subsidies and other support measures. For example, China telecom industry market competition is the market access control results. China's civil aviation market, the airline changed over by a new combination. While competition policy, mainly through defining the relevant product market and the company's market share, are judged by the impact of business-related acts. The main means of competition policy relief is the fine, prohibited in certain behaviors. In exceptional cases, enterprises engaged in some requirements in the concentration of circumstances require companies dispose shares or assets, or transfer business and so on.

2.4 The Conflict of Realizing Path

Market mechanism is not under any conditions at any time can play fully and effectively role, often occur “market failure” phenomenon. “Market failure” is caused by the market defects, such as the market for the provision of public products, the market for externalities, and information of non-symmetry. Only government through the industry policy to build public facilities, public utilities, can realize the public interests. For the blindness of the market, the lagging economic development plan, by formulating industrial development outline gives added. Industrial policy is to control the process of market mechanisms through the process of competition behavior control, offsetting market mechanism of failure. But competition policy is to make the rules by ex consequences. When the competition mechanism is suppressed, the positive function of competition can not play, then competition policy through the anti-monopoly law, unfair competition policy, sanction, maintain and give full play to the role of free market competition.

3 The Coordination Path of Industrial Policy and Competition Policy

3.1 The Legal Basis of Coordination

1) **The basic principles of macro-control**

Industrial policy and competition policy are two ways of modern macro. More industrial policy is to support and revitalize industries, to reduce excessive competition and the waste of resources. Competition policy is intended to promote market competition through removing the monopoly. This is like the two extremes state of market development, we do not need a disorderly market conditions, do not need no competition or competition in the market were too much on market conditions, we need a market in the middle of the state. Industrial policy and competition policy can be achieved the intermediate state of such a market. Therefore, industrial policy and competition policy can be a complementary relationship of the harmonization and cooperation, not opposition interests.

2) **Complying with the legal of competition policy law**

There are two characteristics of modern competition policy, from structuralism to behaviorism and the rule of reason principle of priority in itself illegal. That is characteristic of modern competition policy, much less rigid and more flexible components increased. For a monopoly is anti-monopoly regulation, industrial policy factors being taken into account. In a word, industrial policies and competition policy law that rigid, direct, pair of conflict in the modern society has become a history.

3) **Complying with the legal of industrial policy law**
There are many implementations of industrial policy means. As long as we greatly reduce direct intervention measures, using the indirect induction and information guiding measures, can reduce directly conflict of industrial policy and competition policy. At the same time, we can provide a legal reconcile space.

3.2 The Principle of Coordination

4) **The principle of competition policy priority**
To coordinate the relationship, the first problem to be solved is to conform which is the priority principle. On this issue, the establishment of competition policy priority has been widely accepted. First, competitive is the basis and premise of market mechanism. Maintenance of effective competition for the positive role of the market economy is self-evident. The industrial policy is various means including administrative measures taken by government, but the government is not omnipotent, in the case of government decision-making mistakes, government intervention will not match or even inconsistent on market demand. The economic impact of industrial policy is to be proved. Second, competition policy is to maintain competition in the normal state of the market economy. As long as there is a market economy, competition policy requires the protection of competition on the market. Industrial policy is the individual adjustment of the market with localized and stage. Finally, competition policy is the prerequisite and basis for industrial policy, industrial policy, only reflect the competitive factors can be effective.

5) **The principle of interests balance**
Any legal conflict is connect with the game of interest exists, but in order to avoid or reduce the cost game, they must be coordinated to balance various interests. In the coordination process of industrial policy and competition policy should adhere to the principle of balance. While the principles of competition policy priority of competition policy in many countries, Competition policy uncertainty for balance conditions of this. For example, in the process of implementing anti-monopoly law, administrative guidance or administrative departments of the issuance is a very good way to achieve coordination of antitrust and industrial policy. Administrative guidance is non-mandatory, guidance, soft flexible method of diversity, choose to accept other characters, which is different from a mandatory administrative enforcement actions, but the administrative guidance of the implementation process in the anti-monopoly law could play a complementary and alternative, counseling and promotion, coordination and clear, positive As the decline of Harvard School and the rise of the Chicago School, the development trend of modern competition policy principles to be judged by a reasonable variety of competitive behavior, and establish the system of exemption. All this has set aside some space for industrial policy. China "anti-monopoly law," Article 5, Article 15, Article 28 embodies the principle of balance coordination in line with world trends in anti-trust legislation.

6) **The principles** of **practical**

Competition policy as a "local" knowledge is required from national conditions. The basic system, the scope of application, and the principles of industrial policy is more dependent on their economic development stages and political factors. For example, the national competition policy of the United States has been the main priority is to uphold on market economy and respect for freedom and democracy. Japan after World War II, base on their goal of revitalizing and reshaping of the economic power political will, industrial policy is priority to competition policy.

3.3 The Measures of Coordination

7) **Specific areas of competition policy implementation**

The present stage should be emphasized in the overall competition policy, at the same time, we should full play the role of industrial policy In some areas. In order to apply the competition policy as wide as possible and consolidate its core position, industrial policy should be limited to the following industries: first, agriculture, forestry and fisheries. The purchasing of forestry and fishery products is not suitable for free competition, as well as marketing. Producers in many countries are allowed to enter into agreements restricting competition. Prices protection and subsides are often provided in these fields by the states, or the states participate in marketing activities directly. Second, the banking and insurance. Banking and insurance industry have their own special characters, and the stability of the entire national economy is closely related to them. Full and free competition Will seriously affect the economic stability and people's life. Therefore, some countries allow appropriate exemption to competition restriction in these sectors, for example, on loan interest rate, insurance policies, etc. Of course, exemption should be remained in moderate range. To prevent these enterprises to form a monopoly, abuse of dominant market, harm public interests, they should strictly supervised by the laws. Third, the high-tech industries. The degree of development of high-tech industries directly related to China's future position in the world economy. Therefore, Chinese government should encourage and help high-tech enterprises in collaborative research and market merger and acquisition activities for a long period in the future. Competition should be gradually introduced into this field. Fourth, the military enterprises. Military-industrial is an industry which is strict supervised and controlled by the state. It is related to the country's political stability and security. To some extent, military-industrial complex is not simply an economic issue but also involving the political field, comes as state monopoly. For the natural monopoly industries, they should be included within the scope of competition policy adjustment to conform the international trend of "generally applicable anti-trust law, exceptions exempt".

8) **Reasonable use of antimonopoly immunity**

Facing the intense economic competition, States are all use antimonopoly policy to protect their economies. Competition policy, regulatory process, "antimonopoly immunity" system for the use of direct expression of a country's specific industrial policy, antimonopoly immunity policy directly reflects a country's specific industrial policy, competition policy, but it fit with the inherent nature of competition policy. The reasonable and certain "antimonopoly immunity" system can not only protect except for the development of enterprises, promote the progress of technology, improve the competitiveness of enterprises, realize the maximization of social welfare, security market fair and orderly competition, so as to realize the economic and social benign operation, but also suitable for Chinese enterprise production period small scale, market competition is weak. Therefore, we must expand the business scale in order to achieve economies of scale. In this process, China must use indirect induction, direct control and administrative measures related to the implementation of specific industries tilt, focus on supporting some large enterprises, to accelerate industrial upgrading in China through industrial policy. The concept of "antimonopoly immunity" makes this possible. For example, Article 7 of China's anti-monopoly law: "For the undertaking in the state-owned economy controlled industries to which are related to national economic lifeline and state security, and in the industries to which the state grants special or exclusive rights, the state protect their lawful operation. The state also lawfully regulates and controls their operation and the price of their commodities and services, safeguards interests of consumers, promotes technical progresses."

9) **Perfect law enforcement agencie**

Another aspect of the relationship between competition policy and industrial policy is the issue of the implementing agencies set. Because the implementation of anti-monopoly law enforcement agencies must take into account the implementation of industrial policy, which involves the implementation of competition policy institutions and industrial policies. For example, when an industry is the list state-dominated industry, competition policy institutions should not excessive intervention on the industry of the merger and reorganization. Scholars have made extensive discussion on the anti-monopoly law enforcement agencies. When the scope of the competition policy and industrial policy of executing agency of actuators is overlap, the market economy is related to competition-related matters should be referred to the competition enforcement authorities, the implementation of industrial policy intervention in the market should not have to compete designated competitive landscape or affect the implementation of competition policy privileges. When the scope of implementation is industry supervision, the competition policy enforcement authorities should not intervene in industrial policy. That is, in the implementation of competition policy should protect the executive body of the high degree of independence and authority, highlighting the importance of competition enforcement agencies. At the same time, the implementing agency of the implementation of industrial policy privileges should be strictly defined.

10) **Enforcement the international cooperation of industrial policy and competition policy.**

Trends in international competition and competition policy will pay attention to the tendency of the international industrial policy and competition policy coordination. Transformations in the contemporary industrial policy, the changes of industrial policy objectives and content have taken place, which appeared to relax antitrust restrictions and enforce international cooperation. The former is reflected to promote mergers and acquisitions within the global scope, the latter shows memory in an international competition policy beyond the nation-state. The latter shows a competition policy beyond the nation-state, which formed a united anti-trust or anti-trust international cooperation in some international organizations or regional integration among the major developed countries. For example, the EU anti-trust law, and the cooperation agreements which signed the anti-monopoly law in 1995 between the United States and Canada.

References

1. Ye, W.: The impact of industrial policy on implementation of anti-monopoly law. Law and Business Research (Febraury 2007)
2. Song, X.: The coordination between competition policy and industrial policy in process of implementing anti-monopoly law. China Non-governmental Sciences Technology and Economy (June 2008)
3. Kai, Z.: The conflict and coordination between the industry policy and the competition law. Journal of Heze University (January 2010)
4. Shi, J.: A study on the coordination between competition policy and industrial policy after the implementation of anti-monopoly law in China. Social Sciences in Yunnan (January 2009)
5. Yang, S.: The conflict and coordination between competition policy and industrial policy. Exploring (January 2010)

The Key Update Algorithm Based on HIBE

Xiaocheng Lu and Fang Deng

School of Computer Science and Technology
Wuhan University of Technology
Wuhan, China
1083630901@qq.com

Abstract. In this paper, based on hierarchical identity-based encryption (HIBE) and combined with Key isolation mechanism (IKE), a new hierarchical key update algorithm is proposed. Above all, the security mechanism based on private key update on IKE is demonstrated; then a new encryption model (HIBE-IKE) is constructed, which combines hierarchical identity-based encryption and private Key isolation mechanism and provides a new Private key update method to solve the problems of private key update based on identity-based encryption system.

Keywords: HIBE, IKE, key update.

1 Introduction

Computer software is a difficult developed, costly, but easily copied goods. Piracy greatly do harm to the interests of software developers, undermine the order of software market, obstruct the development of the software industry. It is necessary to protect softwate property.

Among so many methods of software protection, software encryption becomes the mainstream method. Software encryption is also continually developed with the betterment of encryption algorithm. In 1984, Shamir [1] proposed identity-based password system concept. Identity-based encryption uses the user identity information, such as e-mail address, ID number, etc, as the user's public key. Key management is completed by private key generation center. With the development of Identity-based encryption scheme, Gentry[2] and some others designed the first hierarchical identity-based encryption (HIBE) program. The CA of PKG systems , do not like that of PKI, need to store large numbers of user's public key and certificate, but because the public key of identity-based encryption (IBE) exists social significance and the same as CA management to destroy public key and private key pairs in private key revocation list, can not thoroughly updated public key and private key pairs, can only be done by updating the private key to complete leaked key. This makes Key revocation becoming a problem that IBE needs to face. In 2001, BF-IBE algorithm first proposed by Boneh and Franklin, discussed the key revocation problem in IBE system. In the BF-IBE algorithm, the private key generation center (PKG) generates private key for the

M. Dai (Ed.): ICCIC 2011, Part II, CCIS 232, pp. 294–302, 2011.

user corresponding to the user's identity information together with the effective use period of the private key to operate private key. Dodi [3] and other scholars, first proposed in Eurocrypt'02 the the concept of key isolated to effective solve the problem of updating key.

This paper, the key isolate ideas used in identity-based password system, corresponding to the object hierarchy of the software distribution process in reality, uses the hierarchical structure of HIBE to manage key of the software distribution process. In key isolation mechanism, HIBE is used to organize key structure. Based on the above ideas, combinating HIBE and key isolation mechanism, the encryption system model of key update HIBE-IKE can be completed and proved to be secure.

2 Background Knowledge

A. Hierarchical Identity-based Encryption

HIBE program includes five algorithms [4-5]:

(1) root settings: root PKG selects safety parameters k, then the system parameters params and the root key s are generated, the system parameters including description of plaintext space M and ciphertext space C. System parameters is open to the public, root key is confidential and only public to the root PKG.

(2) low-level settings: In order to generate keys, each low-level PKG had best produce its own low-key, to generate private key for the next layer of user of its own.

(3) key generation: based on the identity tuple of users, public key is firstly created for users, and then the private key is calculated under the public key.

(4) encryption: the sender encrypt the message m, and send the ciphertext c to the receiver, by the identity tuple and params of receiver.

(5) The decryption process: using the private key and public parameters to decrypt ciphertext c to recover plaintext.

B. Identity-Based Key-Insulated Encryption

According to the characteristics of identity, public key is the same in the whole operation. Key isolation mechanism[6-8] divided system time into several time fragments, and the private key is updated at each time fragments, so different temporary private key is used at different time fragments, but public key always remains the same. Private key is divided into two parts: one part is the temporary private key for the control of user equipment, the other part is assist device key stored in the user key device (PD). All cryptographic operations are completed at user's terminal equipment, where PD interacts with the user equipment only at the beginning of each time fragment, to help users update the temporary private key, but PD do not participate in any other cryptographic operations. It is obvious that the safety of PD determines the security of the keys. In order to improve security of key, many PD could be used to update key, but the number and structure of PD can affect the updating efficiency of the key. In the literature[9], integrating number, structure and efficiency, two hierarchical structure of the key separation mechanism of PD are given. In the following, the definition of identity-based encryption algorithm key isolation of having two-tier PD is given.

A two-tier identity-based encryption and isolation key model consists of six stages and 8 algorithm:

Parameter generation: public parameter generation algorithm $PGen_{IKE}(1^k)$, where k is the security parameters, outputs a main key s and a public parameter p.

Key Generation: The user key generation algorithm for input, and the user's identity, the output capacity of the initial private key, among which d_0^0 is the initial decryption key of the identity U, and $d_0^i(i=1,2)$ is the initial i-tier key agreement stored in the i-tier PD of identity U. The above two generating algorithms are completed in PKG. PD update: This stage consists of two algorithm. In the first tier PD of the storage co-key ,algorithm $\Delta-Gen_{IKE}^1$ is used to update key updating information of the user decryption key. Similarly, In the second tier PD of the storage co-key, algorithm $\Delta-Gen_{IKE}^2$ is used to generate the updated information of first tier co-key. When $i=1,2$, algorithm $\Delta-Gen_{IKE}^i$ inputs $d_t^i, p, U, time$ and outputs the key update information $\delta_{T_{i-1}(time)}^{i-1}$ when $t=T_i(time)$, and $T_0(\square)$ and $T_1(\square)$ separately maps time to the time periods of decryption key and the first layer co-key.

Key Update: The stage consists of two algorithm. Algorithm Upd_{IKE}^1 using the decryption key and the key update information $\delta_{T_0(time)}^0$ of U to calculate decryption key when time is $time$, The algorithm Upd_{IKE}^2 is also using in the first tier co-key and update information $\delta_{T_1(time)}^1$ of U to update the first level of co-key when the time is $time$.

Encryption: encryption algorithm Enc_{IKE} ,as m U, p and time to be input, outputs ciphertext $<c, time>$

Decryption: decryption algorithm Dec_{IKE}, as $<c, time>, d_t^0, p$ to be input, outputs explicitly m or $\perp$, and $\perp$ means failed decryption. Decryption algorithm can correctly restore ciphertext only when $t=T_0(time)$.

The process of above algorithms can be presented by the following figure:

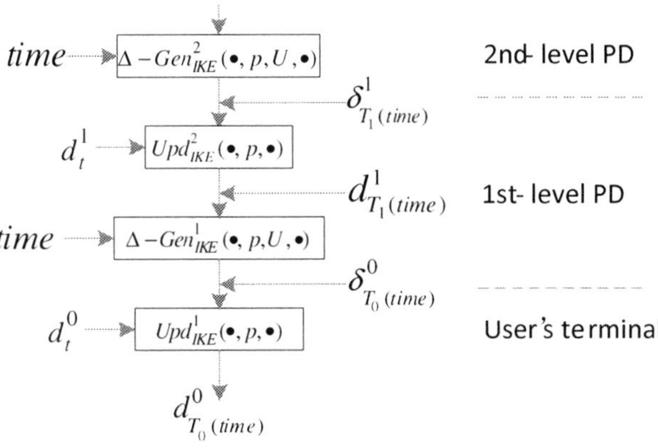

Fig. 1. Key update in IKE

3 The New Model

C. Model Description

(1) Setting of the root PKG Input: security parameter k,

1) produces two cyclic group, namely the additive group G_1 and the multiplicative group G_2, while producing a bilinear map $\hat{e}: G_1 \times G_1 \to G_2$.

2) Select any generator $P \in G_1$ in group G_1.

3) select $s_0 \in Z/qZ$ randomly and make $Q_0 = s_0 P$.

4) Select the anti-collision hash function

$$H_1: \{0,1\}^* \to G_1,\ H_2: G_2 \to \{0,1\}^n,\ H_3: \{0,1\}^n \times \{0,1\}^{k_1} \to Z/qZ,$$

where Clear space $M = \{0,1\}^n$, ciphertext space $G_1^t \times \{0,1\}^{n+k_1}$, the system parameters $param = (G_1, G_2, \hat{e}, P, Q_0, H_1, H_2, H_3)$, the root PKG's main key s_0.

(2) setting of the 1-tier in HIBE Randomly selecting integer $s_1^0, s_2^1, s_3^2 \in Z/qZ$, in case of $s_1 = s_1^0 + s_2^1 + s_3^2$, status being ID_1

1) calculating $P_1 = H_1(ID_1)$, $P_2 = H_1(ID_1, ID_2)$, where $U = (ID_1, ID_2)$ being used to express the identity of the user group.

2) calculating $S_1 = s_0 P_1$, $S_2 = S_1 + s_1 P_2$

3) Calculating $Q_1 = (s_1^0 + s_2^1 + s_3^2)P = s_1 P$

(3) The algorithm $Gen_{IKE}(s_1, p, U)$ generates the initial key,

1) Calculating $P_U = H_1(U) \in G_1 = H_1(ID_1, ID_2)$

2) calculating $S_1^0 = s_1^0 P_U$, $S_2^1 = s_2^1 P_U$, $S_3^2 = s_3^2 P_U$

3) generating the original key:

$$d_0^0 = (S_1^0, (*,*), (*,*,*))$$

$$d_0^1 = (S_2^1, (*,*))$$

$$d_0^2 = S_3^2$$

Return: (d_0^0, d_0^1, d_0^2)

(1) is completed in the root PKG in HIBE, and (2) and (3) are completed in the first-tier of PKG in HIBE. The following algorithms are completed by user except encryption algorithms, the organization of user's private key and the key using the same hierarchical organization. The 0-tier is the user's decryption key, 1,2 co-Key.

(4)encryption algorithm : $Enc_{IKE}(m, U, p, time)$

$$P_2 = P_U = H_1(U) = H_1(ID_1, ID_2)$$

$$P_{t_1} = H_1(U \square T_1(time))$$

$$P_{t_0} = H_1(U \square T_1(time) \square T_1(time))$$

$$g = \hat{e}(Q_0, P_1),\quad \sigma \in_R \{0,1\}^n,\quad r = H_3(\sigma, m)$$

Calculation: $c := < rP, rP_U, rP_{t_1}, rP_{t_0}, (m \| \sigma) \oplus H_2(g^r) >$

Return: $< c, time >$

(5) decryption algorithm

$$Dec_{IKE}(< c, time >, d_t^0, P)$$

$$c = (V, V_U, V_{t_1}, V_{t_0}, W)$$

$$m \| \sigma = W \oplus H_2\left(\frac{\hat{e}(V, S_2)\hat{e}(Q_2^0 + Q_3^0, V_{t_0})\hat{e}(Q_3^1, V_{t_1})}{\hat{e}(S_1^0 + S_2^0 + S_3^0, V)} \right)$$

In the above algorithm:

The algorithm $\Delta - Gen_{IKE}^2(d_t^2, P, U, time)$ is used to calculate the needed information updating the first-tier co-key. $d_t^2 = S_3^2$

Taking random integer $s_3^1 \in Z / qZ$

$$P_{t_1} = H_1(U \square T_1(time)) \begin{cases} \hat{S}_3^1 = S_3^2 + s_3^1 P_{t_1} \\ \hat{Q}_3^1 = s_3^1 P \end{cases}$$

Return: $\delta^1_{T_1(time)} = (\hat{S}_3^1, \hat{Q}_3^1)$

The algorithm $\Delta - Gen_{IKE}^2(d_t^2, P, U, time)$ is used to calculate the needed information of first-tier co-key.

$$d_t^2 = S_3^2$$

Taking random integer $s_3^1 \in Z / qZ$

$$P_{t_1} = H_1(U \square T_1(time))$$

$$\begin{cases} \hat{S}_3^1 = S_3^2 + s_3^1 P_{t_1} \\ \hat{Q}_3^1 = s_3^1 P \end{cases}$$

Return: $\delta^1_{T_1(time)} = (\hat{S}_3^1, \hat{Q}_3^1)$

The algorithm $Upd_{IKE}^1(d_t^0, p, \delta^0_{T_0(time)})$ is used to update the user terminal key through the updated information generated by the first tier co-key. $d_t^0 = (S_1^0, (S_2^0, Q_2^0), (S_3^0, Q_3^0, Q_3^1))$

$$\delta^0_{T_0(time)} = ((\hat{S}_2^0, \hat{Q}_2^0), (\hat{S}_3^0, \hat{Q}_3^0, \hat{Q}_3^1))$$

Return: $d_t^0 = (S_1^0, (\hat{S}_2^0, \hat{Q}_2^0), (\hat{S}_3^0, \hat{Q}_3^0, \hat{Q}_3^1))$

The algorithm $Upd_{IKE}^2(d_t^1, p, \delta^1_{T_1(time)})$ used to update the first-tier co-key through the information updated by the second co-key. $d_t^1 = (S_2^1, (S_3^1, Q_3^1))$

$$\delta^1_{T_1(time)} = (\hat{S}_3^1, \hat{Q}_3^1)$$

Return: $d^1_{T_1(time)} = (S_2^1, (\hat{S}_3^1, \hat{Q}_3^1))$

D. Security Analysis

The key separation mechanism of the proposed model is established which is based on HIBE, so to conceive of a challenger who could successfully challenge HIBE, this challenge can be completed by another challenger who could breach the proposed model. We conceived an algorithm B, public parameters of B are known, if the B in the IND-HID-CPA could breach HIBE, then in a sense, that is equivalent to breach the proposed model KE-CCA security with challenger A. If given that the advantage of B is ε_B, then the probability of successfully solving problem of CBDH is:

$$\varepsilon_{CBDH} \geq \frac{1}{3}\frac{2\varepsilon_B}{q_{H_2}}\left(\frac{3}{e(3+q_{KG})}\right)^3 \quad (1)$$

Where q_{KG} and q_{H_2}, respectively express the total number of query on the key generation oracle meachine KG and the random oracle meachine of HIBE.

For the public parameters:

$p=(G_1,G_2,\hat{e},P,Q,H_1,H_2)$ of HIBE, B selects $s_1,s_2 \in Z/qZ$,

and let parameters:

$p=(G_1,G_2,\hat{e},P,Q,H_1,H_2,H_3)$ to A as public parameters of IKE. Where $H_i(1\leq i\leq 3)$ is a random oracle meachine.

$$\varepsilon_B \geq \frac{1}{3}(\frac{1}{2}+\varepsilon_A - \Pr[H_{3^-}Ask])*\Pr[\neg D-Fail]+\frac{2}{3}\cdot\frac{1}{2}-\frac{1}{2}$$

Now, we come to estimate the probability of B being successful. LR, $H_h(1\leq h\leq 3)$ and KG is a perfect simulation, and KI will fail only if 2 is not the chosen special layer by A. Therefore, if we command the probability of A being successful is $1/2+\varepsilon_A$, then the probability of B being successful can be estimated to $1/2+\varepsilon_B$,where

$$\varepsilon_B \geq \frac{1}{3}(\frac{1}{2}+\varepsilon_A - \Pr[H_{3^-}Ask])*\Pr[\neg D-Fail]+\frac{2}{3}\cdot\frac{1}{2}-\frac{1}{2} \quad (2)$$

$H_{3^-}Ask$ denotes the event $(\mu_{\bar{b}},m_{\bar{b}})$ in quirying H_3, and $D-Fail$ denotes the rejected inquiry B to D which should not have rejected.

From information theory, $\mu_{\bar{b}}$ can not be found, then there is $\Pr[H_{3^-}Ask])\leq 1-(1-1/2^{k_1})^{q_{H3}}$, and q_{H_3} denotes the numbers of inquiry to H_3, and simulation of failure of D is only when the A present a ciphertext should not be rejected, and without advancing inquiry to correspond H_3, hence, $\Pr[\neg D-Fail]\geq(1-1/q)^{q_D}$,

that q_D denotes the inquiry numbers to D.

So, there are

$$\begin{aligned}\varepsilon_B &\geq \frac{1}{3}\left(\frac{1}{2}+\varepsilon_A-(1-(1-1/2^{k_1})^{q_{H_3}}))(1-1/q)^{q_D}+\frac{2}{3}\cdot\frac{1}{2}-\frac{1}{2}\right.\\ &\geq \frac{1}{3}\varepsilon_A-\frac{1}{3}\frac{q_{H_3}}{2^{k_1}}-\frac{q_D}{6q}\end{aligned} \quad (3)$$

Thus, let the probability of successfully solving problem of CBDH ε_{cbdh}, according to inequality (1), there are:

$$\begin{aligned}\varepsilon_{cbdh} &\geq \frac{1}{3}\cdot\frac{2}{q_{H_2}}\cdot\left(\frac{3}{e(3+q_{KG}+q_{KI})}\right)^3\cdot\left(\frac{1}{3}\varepsilon_A-\frac{1}{3}\frac{q_{H_3}}{2^{k_1}}-\frac{q_D}{6q}\right)\\ &\geq \frac{6}{e^3 q_{H_2}(3+q_{KG}+q_{KI})^3}\cdot\left(\varepsilon_A-\frac{q_{H_3}}{2^{k_1}}-\frac{q_D}{2q}\right)\end{aligned} \quad (4)$$

According to inequality (4), if ε_{cbdh}, $1/q$ and $1/2^{k_1}$ could be negligible, ε_A is also negligible, then, the key isolation mechanism in HIBE-IKE encryption system is KE-CCA secure. In summary, HIBE-IKE is the adaptive chosen ciphertext secure.

4 Summary

According to generating process of model of HIBE-IKE, the process will be applied to software releases and software in a hierarchical structure of the sector management, software developers can act as the root PKG, sellers can be the 1th layer of HIBE, software buyers act as the 2th layer of HIBE. The client's key update applies to the environment of a strict hierarchy, such as businesses, government agencies, and two-tier PD could be acted as higher-up to complete the key update, and the final executor has the final decryption key. In necessary conditions, the higher can recover the lower's key, monitor the actions of the lower ,because the whole encryption process is identity-based, the software all have identity records from development to release to use, which contribute to monitor and password protection, so HIBE-IKE in software protection has a good prospect.Through a combination of hierarchical identity-based encryption (HIBE) identity-based and key isolation mechanism HIBE-IKE encryption model is proposed and proved to be secure. HIBE in software protection has a good prospect.

References

[1] Shamir, A.: Identity-based cryptosystems and signature schemes. In: Blakely, G.R., Chaum, D. (eds.) CRYPTO 1984. LNCS, vol. 196, pp. 47–53. Springer, Heidelberg (1985)

[2] Gentry, C., Silverberg, A.: Hierarchical ID-based cryptography. In: Zheng, Y. (ed.) ASIACRYPT 2002. LNCS, vol. 2501, pp. 548–566. Springer, Heidelberg (2002)

[3] Dodis, Y., Katz, J., Xu, S.: Key-insulated public-key cryptosystems. In: Knudsen, L.R. (ed.) EUROCRYPT 2002. LNCS, vol. 2332, pp. 65–82. Springer, Heidelberg (2002)

[4] Lewko, A., Waters, B.: New techniques for dual system encryption and fully secure HIBE with short ciphertexts. In: Micciancio, D. (ed.) TCC 2010. LNCS, vol. 5978, pp. 455–479. Springer, Heidelberg (2010)
[5] Gentry, C., Halevi, S.: Hierarchical identity based encryption with polynomially many levels. In: Reingold, O. (ed.) TCC 2009. LNCS, vol. 5444, pp. 437–456. Springer, Heidelberg (2009)
[6] Ren, Y., Gu, D.: Key-insulated encryption without random oracles. Journal of Systems and Software 83(1), 153–162 (2010)
[7] Ohtake, G., Hanaoka, G., Ogawa, K.: An Efficient Strong Key-Insulated Signature Scheme and Its Application. In: Mjølsnes, S.F., Mauw, S., Katsikas, S.K. (eds.) EuroPKI 2008. LNCS, vol. 5057, pp. 150–165. Springer, Heidelberg (2008)
[8] Lu, H.-J., Su, Y.-X., Zhu, Y.-F.: Distribution of random session key based on key-insulated public-key cryptosystems. Wuhan University Journal of Natural Sciences 10(1), 251–254 (2005)
[9] Hanaoka, Y., Hanaoka, G., Shikata, J., Imai, H.: Identity-Based Hierarchical Strongly Key-Insulated Encryption and Its Application. In: Roy, B. (ed.) ASIACRYPT 2005. LNCS, vol. 3788, pp. 495–514. Springer, Heidelberg (2005)

Design and Implementation of Technology Data Sharing Platform with Web Services

Liu Dong-Ping[1], Chen Li[2], Chen Rui[2], and Jin Jie[2]

[1] Institute of computer GuangDong University of Technology
[2] Institute of computer GuangDong Communication Polytechnic
Guang-zhou, China
304858424@qq.com

Abstract. This paper use Web services in technology data-sharing platform to solve the data transmission problem in which the data is distributed and heterogeneous. Designed a data exchange model which apply to data sharing well, explained the principle of data transmission and the implementation methods of the core function's details. It achieved the data which is distributed and heterogeneous share effectively by using this design in technology program management system.

Keywords: Web Services, Data Sharing, Data Transmission.

1 Introduction

The technology projects is the important part of national economic plans and social development programs, the primary means for the government to organize scientific and technological research under the conditions of market economy, a very important technology management work which guide and support society to promote technology innovation. Technology information management has improved the office efficiency of the government and the level of management and decision, but it is easy to find one project be declared in several place, and one declarant declare several projects in one year, this makes the project be finished in time hard and can not manage the project well. That appears just because different technology management department are in different region, building their system independent, and the information in different database may Inconsistent. It is necessary to build a Distributed Heterogeneous Data Sharing service platform which is work for science and technology project and appropriate for Management departments at all levels of science and technology, for reduce duplication, save government funds and strengthen scientific and technological project supervision.

Distributed data sharing for manage Science and technology program is used to exchange data between different science and technology program database systems which are in different regions,or between the user and database systems. In a broader sense, it can data exchange between information publisher and technology project applicant, and achieve related protocols and services at the same time. Therefore, the data sharing are called to solve the following problem from the standards and

M. Dai (Ed.): ICCIC 2011, Part II, CCIS 232, pp. 303–311, 2011.

technology platform: (1) the elimination of heterogeneity. Data interaction can be achieved in different databases which run on different platforms; (2) standards-based. Reduce the hardware and software requirements which is needed when exchange data in heterogeneous environment; (3) loosely coupled. Asked not for a particular application program interface, the usage of system data can be controlled. [1] The technology of Web Services is just a good way to solve this problem.

2 Introduction of Web Services

A. Definition of Web Services

At present, different companies which support web services have different definitions. However, almost all definitions have these few things in common: First, web services provide useful functions to web users through standard web protocols. In most cases using the SOAP protocol. Second, web services can describe its interface in detail, which allows users to communicate with them by creating a client application. This description is usually included in XML document which is called web service description language (WSDL) document. Third, web services can be registered, so it can be easily find by potential users of these services, this thing completed by Universal Description, Discovery and Integration (UDDI) Protocol. [2]

B. Feature of Web Services

The applications and business services which use Web Services technology developed or deployed has the following characteristics: First, loosely coupled components. Application is composed of loosely coupled components, and is very easy to integrate with other platforms and other standard techniques. Second, self-description and self-adaptive. Describe the exchange information content with XML can guarantee the information self-descriptive and self-adaptive, eliminating the need of knowledge about application or interface. Third, distributed, and independence of position. Using ebXML and UDDI registration mechanism make business services unrelated with location and distributed. Fourth, dynamic and scalable. As the information for exchange packaged with XML, so that information can be dynamic convergence, dynamic conversion and real-time processing. Fifth, based on open standards. Web services architecture is based on open standards technology such as J2EE, XML, SOAP and UDDI and so on, not proprietary and vendor-defined technology. This makes the integration of components easier, makes the solutions have wider choice; at the same time, if adopt new technologies then, migration will be more convenient. [3]

C. Protocol stack of Web Services

Implement a complete Web service need a series of protocol and specification to support. Figure 1 shows a conceptual Web Services protocol stack. Layers above established on the functionality provided by the below layers, a vertical section means that each layer in the protocol stack must meet the needs shows in the vertical section, the text on the left said protocol stack layer should apply that standard technology.[4]

protocol	Service levels	Related issues of Web Services		
WSFL	Service Process	Security issue	Management	Quality of service issues
Static->UDDI	Service Discovery			
Direct->UDDI	Service Release			
WSDL	Service Description			
SOAP	XML-based messaging			
HTTP、FTP、Email、MQ、IIOP Etc.	Network			

Fig. 1. Protocol stack of Web Services

D. Architecture of web services

Web services architecture based on the interaction between three roles: service provider, service registry and service requestor. The Interactions involved in publishing, finding and binding operations. These roles and operations act on Web service component: Web services software module and its description. In typical cases, the service provider trustee can access software module(an implementation of Web services) through the network. Service provider defined the service description of Web services, and put it to the service requester or service registry. The requester search service description from the local or service registry by using find operation, then bind with the service provider by using the service description, and call the Web service implementation or interact with it. Service provider and service requestor is the logical structure, so can show two kinds of service features.[5] Figure 2 shows these operations, components which provide these operations and their interaction.

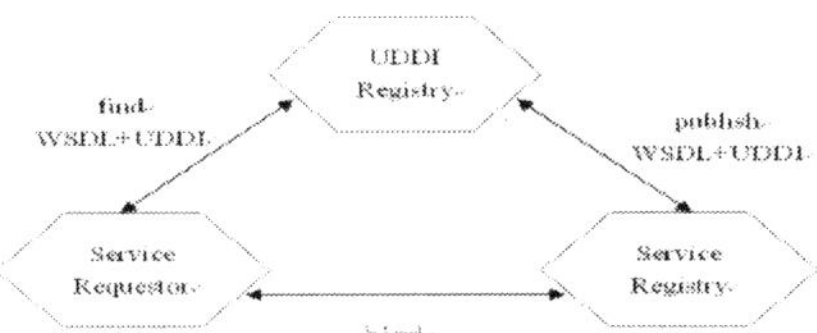

Fig. 2. Architecture of web services

Web Services components: Including three kinds of components.

Service provider: provide services to register in order to make services available.

Service Agent: switch servicer, the media between service providers and the service requestor.

Service requester: request services from the service agent, call these services to create applications.

The operations of Web Services: Including three kinds of operations.

Publish/Unpublish: the registration that the provider release to the agency (registered) service or not to release (remove) these services.

Find: implement the find operation from the service requester to the service agent, the service requester describe the service which should be found, service agents distribute matching results.

Bind: binding between the service requester and service provider, the requestor can access and invoke the service of provider through the two parts of consultations.

3 Project Platform and Tools

A. Project platform

This project used J2EE basic framework platform. J2EE is a set of technical architecture which is completely different from traditional application development, it contains many components, mainly to simplify and standardize development and deployment of application, thus enhancing portability, security and re-use value. J2EE core is a set of technical specifications and guidelines, which contains various components, services structure and technological level, they have common standards and specifications, so that the different platforms that all follow the J2EE architecture have a good compatibility. This solved the problem that the information products incompatible which used by the back-end user of the corporate, and internal or external hard interoperability. [6]

B. Related Tools of Project

Apache CXF = Celtix + XFire, Apache CXF's predecessor called the Apache CeltiXfire, and now, has been renamed as Apache CXF, and hereinafter referred to as CXF. CXF inherited the essence of Celtix and XFire which are open source project, provided comprehensive support for JAX-WS, and also provided a variety of Binding, DataBinding, Transport and various Format support, and can choose Code First or WSDL first easily to achieve the release and use of Web Services according to the needs of actual project. Apache CXF has been a formal top-level Apache project. [7]

4 Data Exchange

Data exchange is the core of research and implementation in data sharing platform. Data sharing platformt provide data exchange which is based on storage resources agent, the user use the data exchange component and middleware of storage resources agent to Make the data access request. Storage resource agent transform the user's logical request into a physical data requests by using the meta-data directory information, and sent the converted data access request to storage systems which in different regions or in different structures, then integrate the informations which are extracted from different storage systems, deliver to the user in the form customer expected. Data exchange chart which is based on storage resources Agent shown in Figure 3: [8]

The main part is composed by the components of exchange configuration management and the core components of data exchange. Messaging using JMS (Java Message Service) technology, the underlying communication protocol is SOAP.

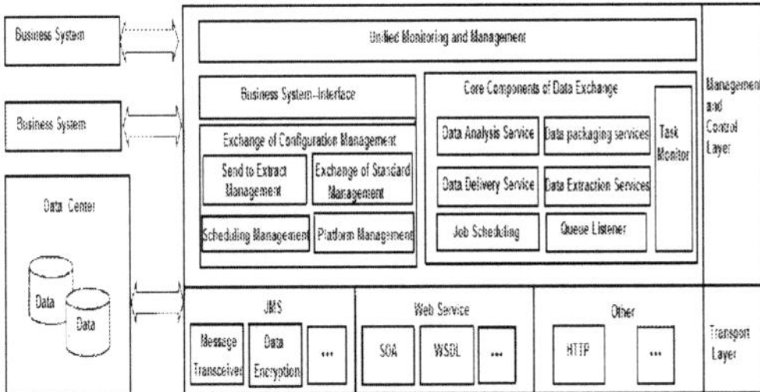

Fig. 3. Data exchange chart based on storage resources Agent

A. Configuration Management Components

Platform management work effectively for data exchange configuration information of each node, include data type management and security management for platform. The management of exchange standard, refers to the management of data exchange rules. It defines each type of data exchange format. Increase the flexibility of data exchange. Send/Extraction management, complete the flexible configuration of information which include extraction method, format and object units needed in data transmission/extraction process. Job scheduling management, used to set the job scheduling information.

B. Core Components for Data Exchange

Data assemble services complete the function which convert the data in the database to data format that the other side can recognize according to exchange standards, exchange standards defined by exchange configuration management component; Data analysis services, is the inverse process of data assembly services, analyze the received data according to data exchange standards, and write analyzed data into the node database. When write to the database, using the bulk submission. When writing is completed, sends arrival notification to the node system, the notification is sent using JMS, and the content of notification using XML format; Data transmission services, to receive requests for data exchange ,and package data in accordance with data packaging service, and then Send in accordance with a predetermined way or destination through transport layer; Data extraction services, sub-synchronous and asynchronous two ways, synchronous mode initiated by the data requirements, Call the data packaging service provided by the data provider to get data, then call the local data analysis services for data exchange; Asynchronous mode sent a selected task to the other side of the task queue by the data needer, send mission by the task monitor of other side; Job scheduling, is a key component of automatic exchange, defines the data exchange time, and system clock cycle, the tasks process generates the exchange tasks according to this, and put the exchange tasks in task queue , and exchanged by the task monitor; Task listener, listening for the task queue, call the send, implementation services to exchange operations when exchange task be send to task queue by job scheduling or extraction service; Queue listener, for monitoring the message queue which receive data, when data is sent to the message queue, the listener starts to get data from the message queue, call data analysis services to complete the asynchronous mode of data exchange. [8]

C. Structure of Data Exchange

The overall structure of data exchange center as shown in Figure 4, the entire structure is a joint topology ,at the center is the data exchange center, it is the centers for sharing and exchanging data, provide service for each data exchange node through a standardized Web Service interface. Each node only needs to interact with data exchange cente through Web Service, and use XML to exchange data, can obtain the needed data without having to visit each other which must be directly connected. The underlying implementation and memory mechanism of the whole data sharing and exchange is transparent to the application node. The structure has low coupling, and can be easily extended to snow level structure, built multi-level data exchange center structure to support a wider range of wide-area program. [8]

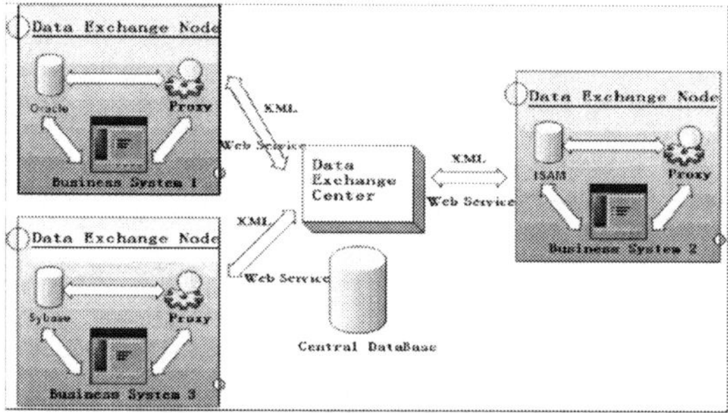

Fig. 7. The overall structure of data exchange center

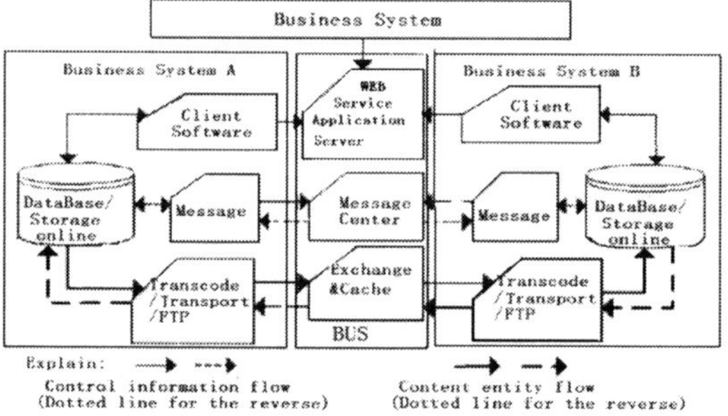

Fig. 5. Data exchange theory

D. Principle of Data Exchange

Figure 5 shows the data exchange principle. Supposing a business system B sends a data exchange request to the business system A through the platform If the exchange cache has the data which is B requested, then B analyze data directly and write to local database; if the cache have not. Then A need to package data following packaging services according to data exchange standard ; and then keep a data copy in exchange cache and then sent to B, B analyze target data using data analytic services ,and stored in the database. After this operation, send out a data arrival notification from the message center, notification is sent using JMS, the content using XML format. This completes the process of data exchange. [8]

5 Data Transmission

A. Mechanism of Data Transmission

Platform adopts the information transmission mechanism based on Web Service and message queue, shown in Figure 6. When exchanging the data, the task initiator (transmitter) organize the data first and put in the exchange buffer, then transfer the Web services components to initiate the content exchange's request, and then the bus will transmitte the exchange's request to the task receiver (receiver) with message; the receiver reads and verifies the legality of the contents from the exchange buffer, if lawful, then transfers the content to the system storage, and sends the feedback messages back with the message queue after the completion of migration and the transmitter receives messages for logging. [8]

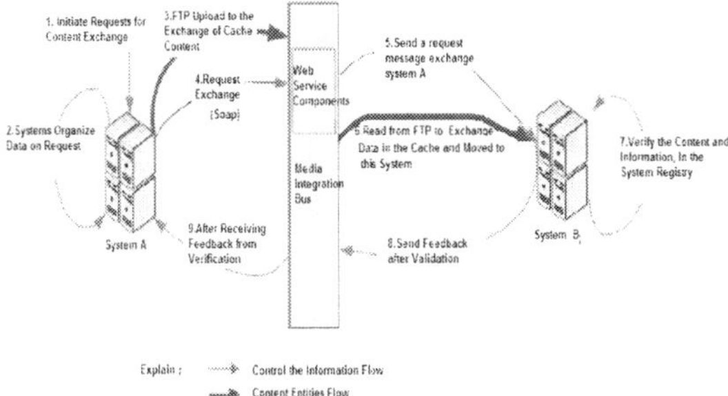

Fig. 6. Mechanism of Data transmission

B. Implement Details of Data Transmission

1) the simple process to achieve the service delivery with CXF

a) the preparation of interface and implementation class;

b) the preparation of the type converter Adapter

JAXB used in the CXF only supports the the List, string and other basic types, another types need adapters to convert;

c) configure the service information

Add in the applicationContext-serverbean.xml

```
<Jaxws: endpoint id = "dbconn"
implementor = "org.gd.deplatform.web.serverimpl.DBConnimpl"
address = "/ dbconn">
</ Jaxws: endpoint>
```

d) start the server;

2) simple processes to achieve service access with CXF

a) inquire about the related services address in the service center;

b) according to the service address automatically generate service interface and related classes;

c) in the configuration file ClientBean.xml create a instance anand a factory class;

d) according to the access interface supplied by the service program and then achieve the functions we need;

3)Details of data Transfer

Details of the data transmission shown in Figure 7. Data processing steps are as follows:

a) Use JDBC to access the database and the returned data type will be the ResultSet type.

b) Because the ResultSet type is not easy to deal with CXF, so I convert it into the List type which can be easy to deal with CXF. Transfer the public static List <HashMap> resultSetToList (ResultSet rs) throws java.sql.SQLException () method to convert it to List <HashMap> type.

c) And then use the adapter to convert List <HashMap> type to the type List <OtherValues[]>which can directly deal by CXF.

d) Data of List <OtherValues[]> types will be compiled into XML format used to transfer solution.

e) Data with XML format spread to the service petitioner, it will be formatted back into List <OtherValues[]> type.

f) Use the Adapter to convert the List <OtherValues[]> types of data back to the List <HashMap> type.

g) According to the needs of the service requester, it will processe the information which are got from the other service database.

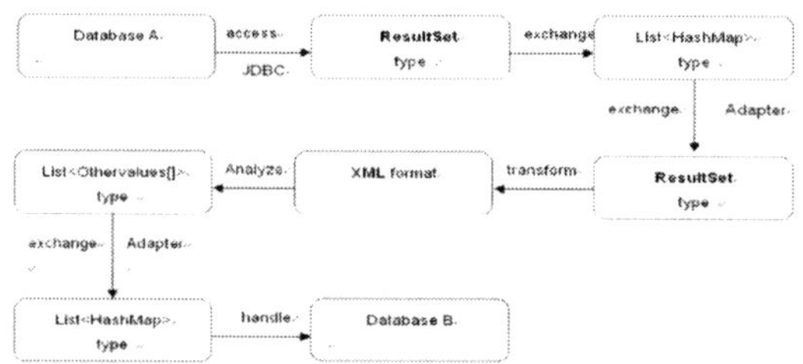

Fig. 7. The process of data transfer

Acknowledgment. First of all, I would like to show my deepest gratitude to my teachers, Professor Li Zhen-kun and Chen Ping-hua, they make many effort in this project which this paper based on. They have rich theoretical and practical experience, and teach me patience and careful.

Then I want to send my thanks to Mrs Chen, who provided me with valuable guidance in many stages of the writing of this thesis. At the same time, I want to say thanks to my classmate Chen Rui for all him kidness and help.

Last but not least, I' d like to thank my boyfriend Jin Jie for all his support and encouragement.

References

1. Zhang, L., Xian-Feng: Scientific data sharing based on Web Services. Computer and Applied Chemistry (May 2005)
2. Li, A.-y.: Web Services Technology and Implementation, p. 2. National defence industry press, Beijing (2003)
3. Ray, L.: J2EE Platform Web Services, p. 34. Publishing House of Electronics Industry, Beijing (2005)
4. Qiu, Z.-q., Chen, P.-h.: The data sharing standards and interface about Science and Technology Department of Guangdong Province, pp. 350–351. Jinke Information Network Center, Guang-Zhou (2007)
5. Qiu, Z.-q., Chen, P.-h.: The data sharing standards and interface about Science and Technology Department of Guangdong Province, pp. 351–352. Jinke Information Network Center, Guang-Zhou (2007)
6. http://baike.baidu.com/view/1507.htm?fr=ala0_1_1
7. http://baike.baidu.com/view/2742297.htm?fr=ala0_1
8. The materials of technology data sharing platform

A System Planning for a Coal Logistics Service Provider

Yang He

School of Computer Science and Technology
Huanggang Normal University
Huanggang, Hubei Province, China
luca.m126@gmail.com

Abstract. In China coal is the most important energy resource. Transformed by modern logistics, coal transportation and marketing will have a good profit. Many researches have been done in this field, but few companies have got a good solution. This article summarizes a program proposal for a traditional coal marketing and transportation company to transform into a coal logistics provider. The plan includes general solution, logistics planning and information system planning. At the end of this article, economic return and social benefic of the transformation are predicted.

Index Terms: coal transportation, railway transportation, logistics planning.

1 Introduction

Modern logistics is a new industry which combines transportation, warehousing, logistics information service and other logistics activities into a complete organism, and provides rapid, standardized, diversified service by means of information systems [1]. The market need of logistics service has impelled many companies in shipping, air transportation, land transportation, sales and international trade to adjust their strategy to occupy a position in modern logistics industry. In China, enterprises in railway transportation and coal industry have fallen behind in this trend.

Academics precede the market in many fields, in coal logistics in China, for example. Many researchers, officials and corporate executives have researched on coal logistics. Wang analyzed strategy on coal enterprises' business [2]. Rong analyzed the impact and challenge of coal logistics to railway transportation [3]. Han & Xia analyzed current informatization level of China coal logistics industry [4].

This article summarizes a project proposal for a railway multi-industry enterprise which operates coal selling and transportation in the traditional way, and wants to expand its business board to modern logistics industry, to search for a new profit growth, and to accomplish sustainable development. The following of this article includes the general logistics strategy, the logistics planning and the information system planning. Finally, a conclusion will be given.

M. Dai (Ed.): ICCIC 2011, Part II, CCIS 232, pp. 312–317, 2011.

2 General Strategy

2.1 Macro Situation of Coal Market

1) Supply-Demand Relationship: Chinese coal reserves rank the first in the world. In 2009, China produced 2.965 billion tons of raw coal (http://www.ndrc.gov.cn/jjxsfx/t20100129_327875.htm). Coal is the dominant fossil fuel in China which occupies about 70% of energy consumption. In 2009, coal-fired power occupies 68.5% of total installed capacity (http://www.cec.org.cn/news/showc1.asp?id=130657), and electric power generations consumed 1.399 billion tons of raw coal (http://www.serc.gov.cn/zwgk/jggg/201005/W020100514491452266286.pdf). With the rapid development of economy, China has an infinitely increasing need for coal-fired power supply. On the contrary, government has to close a lot of private small coal mines and control over the remaining ones rigorously for environment protection, resource conservation and production safety. Facing this contradiction, licensed coal mines are keeping a firm hold on pricing power and the power plants are in vulnerable situation. Government introduced a series of policies to mitigate this contradiction, but very little was achieved [3]. Experts say that the position of coal in Chinese basic energy supply will not change in recent 10~20 years. As a result, coal marketing and transportation will continue to experience a sustainable growth [5].

2) Coal Transportation by Railway: Most of coal mines are in north China, but coal consumption is mostly in the economically developed east and south [2], so a long-standing conflict exists between spatial distribution of production and that of consumption, which makes long-distance transportation a major concern of stakeholders. Coal is low attachment value product, so cheap, large capacity, low costs and long distance railway become the most suitable means of transportation. Coal is also the largest type of freight in railway transportation. Statistics show that in the first 7 month of 2010, China Railway has loaded 1.152 billion tons of coal, which occupies 54.66% of the overall goods send quantity (http://szb.peoplerail.com/shtml/rmtdb/20100805/20048.shtml). But the railway mileage experienced a very small increase from 1970s to early 2000s, which cannot meet the demand of economy development. Consequently, railway capacity becomes the bottleneck of coal supply. According to the plan for middle and long period railway net by Ministry of Railway (http://www.china-mor.gov.cn/tllwjs/tlwgh_6.html), more than 120 000 kilometers of railway will be available by 2020; high speed railway system and dedicated passenger lines are being constructed between large cities; quite a lot of existing railway have been or will be speed-raising, double-tracking and electrification; heavy haul trains, high-power locomotives and optimized train formation will enhance the carrying capacity. The plan demonstrates that in the next decade, passenger luggage division and existing line transformation will release the capacity of railway, and bring a broader space for coal transportation.

3) Environment Protection: Eliminating fossil fuel use and low carbon dioxide emission in human economy activity gains widespread attention. But making full use of coal is unable to avoid for coal resourceful China. Therefore, improving energy efficiency and reducing pollution in coal producing, processing and utilizing is necessary for China. Unfortunately, most coal contains a lot of impurities, such as gangue, ash and sulfur. Statistics show that every 10 tons of coal contains 1 ton of

gangue which affects the efficiency of combustion, generates pollution and adds cost to transportation. Coal washing will reduce these impurities, and have a significant influence on coal logistics. If all brown coal produced in China will experience washing, 42 billion ton kilometers of freight turnover and 340000 tons of carbon dioxide emission would be saved every year.

2.2 Internal Factors of the Company

The company we concerned locates in north China, which has long engaged in coal marketing and transportation, and has developed stable, equal and mutual-benefit long-term relations with suppliers, consumers. The company belongs to China Railway multi-industry system. Most of coal it keeps is produced in Shanxi, with high carbon content, low ash, high heat and other significant advantages; and is distributed to consumers located in east, middle and south China. But it has the same weaknesses like the other state-owned business, such as high cost and long cycle in transportation, poor human resource quality, low information integration, lack of enterprise culture, and weak awareness of logistics, which caused absence of core competitiveness and weak profit ability, and are obstacles for the company to transform to a logistics service provider.

2.3 General Solution

The goal of the transformation is to become a large logistics service provider, which integrates coal marketing, warehousing, transportation, washing and coal chemical industry. What's more, an integrated coal supply chain must be built. Share of local market and control over local coal resources must be enhanced at the same time. To accomplish this goal, the general solution is as follows:

1) Construct an Organization Form of Logistics Service Provider: A logistics service provider must be a modern company that provides consumers with uniformed logistics service. It must own or hire sufficient equipment, organize a certain network of freight distribution, and be equipped with sufficient organization, consumer service and staff. Finally, an information system to supervise the whole process of logistics activities is crucial.

2) Form Core Competitiveness through Logistics Business Restructuring: Suffering from market competition and increasingly strict need of consumers, only those with unique resources and competitiveness can achieve significant advance. A company with an organizational form of logistics service provider must conduct BPR (Business Process re-engineering) according to consumer need and logistics concept, making full use of modern logistics techniques and information technology, to enhance sense of service and ability to quickly respond to changing market needs, to make progress in management, and to form core competitiveness.

3) Supply Chain Integration: An integration of warehousing, transportation and information service, and effective supply chain management will set up a foundation for a higher level service network, which can provide large corporate consumers with full-line coal service. Supply chain integration means information sharing between upstream and downstream companies, and between supply chains.

3 Logistics Planning

Logistics planning of the company includes these major factors:

3.1 Logistics Node Scale and Layout

Key consumers of the company locate in Zhejiang, Jiangsu, Shanghai, Fujian, Guangdong, Annui, Hebei, Hunan, Hubei and Shandong. A logistics node is a circulation centre of logistics service, which usually posits at a transport hub, distributes resources, exchanges information, and controls over logistics process. The layout of logistics nodes must take into account many factors, including demand, land price, means of transportation, labor cost, economic and social environment, and the feature of coal business. Coal is piled, covered large area, large batch size and easy to pollute. Planning method and clustering method can be used to analyze spatial distribution and demand of the consumers, and plan the layout of logistics nodes.

A coal logistics node must be easy to access to coal and railway, to satisfy the demand of consumers in target area, to be able to store, transfer and distribute a certain amount of coal. The scale of logistics nodes must be planned according to expected transfer volume, and must reserve place for future development.

The company has 3 warehouses relying on the railway junctions, and has a link to the express way. The warehouses have a tight link with coal export regions by 2 railways. What's more, the company has another import points. These points are ranked into a T joint, which can take advantage of railway and road. Since the company wants a substantial increase in revenue, from 388 million Yuan to 1200 million Yuan in 3 years, the nodes must accommodate need of future 3 years, which asks the company to look for new providers and consumers, and site new nodes.

3.2 Transportation Planning

The aim of transportation planning is to eliminate vacancy rate of vehicles, convection, circuitry, meandering, repeating, backflow, and override, in order to cut costs, and compress transit time.

Most of coal turnover of the company is received from Shanxi and transported t o middle and south China by railway. Optimization of logistics path is the key for logistics enterprises to eliminate cost, control risk and improve economic performance.

In transportation planning, the algorithm of transportation problem, mini-cost flow algorithm can be used to make an optimized planning, to reduce cost, eliminate invalid transportation, and to accommodate more coal transportation.

3.3 Work Process Optimization

The transformation of company will of course impact current process. Four processes are important for work process optimization: marketing plan, human resource management, financial management and coal logistics management.

4 Information System Planning

Informatization must be carried out by the uniform information standard and integrative information platform. Information system project must be accompanied by staff information ability building. The information system of the company must include the following sub-systems:

4.1 Sales Management

Sales management provides support for consumer information management, coal pricing, contract management, and sales planning of the company. What's more, it will set a foundation of data for every sales-related department. This sub-system must provide a consumer interface, especially in contract management and consumer information management.

4.2 Distribution Management

Consumers are not spatial evenly distributed. Every node must arrange loading and vehicle number, optimize traffic flow, formulate appropriate transportation scheme, and select distribution path, according to volume of coal demand and the features of coal transportation.

4.3 Warehouse Management

Warehouse management provides support for the overall process of coal from inbound to outbound of coal, and reduces bill process and inventory check time, enhance accuracy and quality of delivering. This sub-system does not only provide inventory management, but also gives accurate and timely inventory information.

4.4 Coal Quality Control

Coal quality control provides support for coal sampling test, quality analysis, quality statistics and reports. Quality information of each batch must be saved and available for long time IOC (Incoming Quality Control).

4.5 Human Resource Management

Human resource management provides support for all activities referring to personnel and labor-capital relationship, including personnel files management, contracts, payroll processing, change management, checking-in, performance approval, training, leave management and business trip.

4.6 Financial Management

Financial Management provides tools for executive level. Executives can easily check various financial indicators. This part can analyze costs and return, which can be shown in pie chart, bar chart or trend chart. It must also accommodate examine and approve processes including reimbursement, borrowing, payment, purchasing. All the processes can be imported to financial system and integrated with accounting system.

4.7 Portal Platform

An E-commerce platform is very important for doing business in the information age. So a portal including company image display, product introduction, electronic order system, pre-sale and post-sale service center, information consultant must be built. This sub-system can produce economic return by raising its prestige, reducing transaction intermediate links, reducing costs and accommodating consumer interaction.

5 Conclusion

The above proposal can provide the company a lot of economic return. First, the company will be capable of guaranteeing high service level and timeliness to the customers. Second, logistics cost will be reduced greatly, and earning power will be enhanced. Third, logistics standardization will be achieved to meet ISO9000 and China Federation of Logistics and Purchasing specifications. Meanwhile, it will realize social benefits including energy supply insurance, pollution reduction, transporting efficiency improvement and logistics industry motivation.

Acknowledgment. This article is sponsored by Hubei Education Department. I will also thank my copartners in the project proposal, Hou Lixiang, Hao Weiming, Zhang Yong and Yuan Sheng. My wife Zuo Yanhong has revised my English expression.

References

1. Liu, Y., Zuo, Z.: A SWOT analysis of traditional transportation enterprises transforming to modern logistics service providers. Managers' Journal (14), 249–250 (2009)
2. Wang, H.: A strategy research on coal enterprises' business in logistics. Modern Economic Information (13), 144–145 (2009)
3. Rong, C.: The impact and challenge of coal logistics to China railway transportation. Chinese Railways (12), 31–35 (2007)
4. Han, G., Xia, Y.: An analysis about China coal industry informatization. China Coal 35(4), 29–30,120 (2009)
5. Ma, H.: A brief issue of the development of Shanxi coal logistcs industry. Journal of Shanxi Province CCP School 32(2) (April 2009)
6. Peng, C.: A logistics system plan and research on a large state-owned enterprise. Jiangsu University: Master Dissertation (2005)

On the Innovation of Finance Management under the E-Commerce Environment

Liu Jingzhong

Economic and Trade Department
Shang Qiu Polyltechnic
Shangqiu, Henan Province, China
llsun1964@163.com

Abstract. The internet-based information technology reform provides unprecedented impact for enterprise's management operating mode, ideological concept, etc., and it also proposes challenge for finance management. Compared with traditional finance management, the account management content, management mode, working mode and finance number has become under e-commerce environment. There are many disadvantages in traditional finance management, so it must timely create finance management to meet the new environmental change. This paper analyzes the innovation direction of finance management from the perspective of e-commerce environment: in idea, it should build the open "large finance" management concept; in finance management goal, it should change "shareholder wealth maximization" to multi-goals which takes intellectual property as its represent; the finance evolution system should increase non-finance information index, etc; in addition, the risk management and finance budget step under e-commerce environment should pay more attention and strengthen.

Keywords: E-commerce, Financial management, Reform, Innovation.

1 Introduction

With the wide application of modern information technology, especially the network technology, the e-commerce environment gradually forms, which makes the enterprise's production, operation and management deeply change. The e-commerce environment provides new development chance for traditional industries, while providing unprecedented impact for enterprise's management operating mode, ideological concept, etc.: such as international network strategy, e-commerce, virtual enterprise management, etc. these changes also provide challenge for finance management, so the traditional finance management can't follow the step of the information period, and the reform of the finance management can be inevitable. This paper analyzes the reform and innovation direction of finance management from the perspective of e-commerce environment.

M. Dai (Ed.): ICCIC 2011, Part II, CCIS 232, pp. 318–325, 2011.

2 The Reform of Finance Management under E-Commerce Environment

Under the e-commerce environment, as the digitalization and networking of the economic activity, there appears many new media space, such as virtual market and virtual bank. The e-payment, e-procurement and e-order will take place of many national business operating modes. The business activity is mainly in form of e-commerce in internet, which makes the enterprise's purchase and sale more convenient, the cost cheaper, and the quantification monitor of the storage productions more precise. This special business modes make the traditional finance management can't meet internet-based business operating mode. It mainly shows in the following aspects.

2.1 The Reform of Finance Management Content

Under e-commerce conditions, the proportion of intangible assets of network-based patent, trademark right, computer software, product innovation in enterprise capital structure will be largely improved. However, the theory and content of modern finance management are less involved intangible assets, because the traditional economic increasing mainly depends on the tangible assets of factory, machine, asset, etc., resulting in the incomplete and wrong evolution of the value of intangible assets in modern finance management activity, and it is not good at using intangible assets to operate capital.

2.2 The Reform of Finance Management Mode

It requires enterprise implements the centralized management of data processing and finance resources for its subordinate branch mechanism through network, including centralized entry, centralized accounting, entry account, report generation and collection; it can intensively process a lot of finance data and intensively allocate all the capitals in the group. However, as the limitation of the network technology, the traditional finance management has to apply the dispersed management mode, resulting in the feedback delay of supervision information, insufficient control for subordinate mechanism, low work efficiency, etc. so it can't meet the development requirement of the information period.

2.3 The Reform of the Working Mode

The enterprise's material purchase, production, demand and marketing, bank exchange, insurance, goods consignation and declaration all can be complete through computer network under e-commerce environment without human intervention. Therefore, it requires the finance management can implement business collaboration, remote processing and online management mode in management mode; can support online working and mobile office in working mode; and also can process the new medium of electronic bill, electronic money, Web page data, etc. However, the traditional finance management can only work in particular environment (because it is inner net- based system), so it can't meet the open requirement of information period. It requires the financial personnel can work when they leave the office under the e-commerce environment, namely mobile office. The real implementation of the online work only through implementing the changes from enterprise's inner net to internet.

2.4 The Reform of Finance Goal

The modern finance management goal takes "shareholder wealth maximization"," profit maximization" as its represent, it completely meets the industry period which the material capital takes up main position. However, as the implantation of finance goal is through client goal and business process to implement, with the coming of e-commerce period, the client goal and business process have a huge change, which requires the enterprises consider the following important elements, and relocate its finance management goal:

1. The benefit of relevant interest subject and its interest coordination. In the capital structure of e-commerce period, the position of virtual capital increases obviously, and this change gradually changes the position of owner of enterprises' elements. Different owner has different requirement for enterprise. However, as finance management goal, it should meet the benefit requirement of each relevant, thus to promote enterprise's finance management in benign cycle track.

2. The prospect economy and its value added. Prospect economy is enterprise' expected growth profit, and can predict the future profit degree. Under e-commerce economic condition, this goal shows that the enterprise completely implement the possible degree of technology industrialization, marketization, revenue maximization through product sales, venture capital, etc. In e-commerce period, the importance of enterprise's prospect economy, "growth power" and future value added will surpass the present profit.

3. Social responsibility. Under e-commerce condition, the knowledge capital takes the leading position. As the knowledge is enjoyable and transferable, it makes the connections of enterprise and society wider and deeper. The enterprise's success and failure depend on the contribution of the society for knowledge forming and developing, thus to require enterprise to pay more attention on its social responsibility. Meanwhile, the enterprise carries out social responsibility, such as: protect eco-balancing, maintain social public benefit, support social welfare and charity, etc. It not only can help to realize management goal, but also can build better image in social masses.

Above all, under e-commerce environment, the traditional finance management exists many disadvantages, it must timely create finance management, and structure the management mode that corresponding to information period, thus to meet the new environmental change and make enterprises' invincible position in the rapid international market competition.

3 The Innovation of Finance Management under E-Commerce Environment

3.1 The Innovation of Finance Management Concept

The bean counters' ideological concept and value judgment will change with the change of e-commerce development and finance management environment, and the innovation of the technology method, to gradually form and meet the financing concept in network period.

1. Cooperation and competition concept. With the appearance of global economic integration and e-commerce, the enterprise can rapidly pass and cope with various information, so it will bring two adverse effects: first, because the enterprise's capacity in capturing business information improves generally, which must promote the increasing intension of market competition; second, because the information is passed in larger scale, the enterprises can communicate and cooperate conveniently. It requires the enterprise can treat and coordinate the relationships between this company and other companies by using "double win" concept, thus to make the various economic benefits harmonious and unified.

2. Goal coordination concept. In e-commerce period, the international economy becomes a whole, the benefit of benefit body in each step of production and marketing is connected. A new mechanism of creating wealth appears, and the innovation of enterprise wealth completely depends on the timely passing and timely treating of the information in each step. The enterprise bean counters should surpass the organization boundary; it serves the relevant benefit for the whole chain of production and marketing form the perspective of strategic alliance.

3 Risk concept. The risk concept of e-commerce is different from the concept risk of traditional concept. Besides bearing traditional risk, as the increasing innovative and emergence of information technology and network technology, e-commerce also need to bear the risk of new innovations and the new financial risk it brings (Liu Jianqing, 2003). In the age of e-commerce, company's financial advisors must be able to scientifically predict the uncertainties caused by environment change, and take all precautionary approaches to minimize various risks it will face possibly.

4. Knowledge management concept. E-commerce period can effectively integrate the information (knowledge) and communications technology. The starting point of knowledge management is to consider the various types of knowledge attached to organizational internal as the most important resource, and take the control and use of knowledge as the key to improve enterprise competitiveness. Financial management personnel must establish knowledge management concept, digest all kinds of financial management knowledge, and creatively use and develop, in order to gain competitive advantage and implement companies' long-term survival and development.

3.2 The Innovation of Financial Management Mode

In the past, enterprises lack the technology tools to support centralized management, and the development of enterprise is restricted by the physical regions, so many large enterprises have to apply centralized management. As the feedback delay of supervision information, resulting in uncommon examples for the inadequate control of subordinate body and the emergence of enterprises crisis.

Under e-commerce economy condition, small businesses become into "big enterprises", and desktop management changes into the network way of non-desktop system. It makes centralized management possible; especially enterprises can comprehensively use various kinds of modern electronic information tools, to provide favorable condition for the integration of enterprise financial resources, the strengthening of the financial supervision of subordinate body, the reduction of the operation cost and the improvement of the efficiency.

Financial centralized management can be divided into three aspects:

1. The centralization of accounting. Timeliness of financial data process is a major feature of the network finance. Once confirming to deposit into the appropriate server and initiatively send financial information system to test all the times, business information real-timely converses automatically generates.

2. The centralization of financial control. The reduction of middle-level manager can make the accounting information directly send to high-level, maximum decision level can directly connect decision makers with the most grassroots staff, to control the financial expenditure and income. The company-owned units, departments, including the associated companies implement "major finance" management, thus can improve the use efficiency of idle fund, enhance the balance dispensing ability of internal capital, and put an end to corruption better.

3 The centralization of financial decisions. As the financial information is controlled by senior managers at all times, managers can according to the requirement to make virtual settlement, and it almost can instantly find the changes of market situations, thus to implement financial decisions timely.

3.3 The Innovation of Report Mode

Under e-commerce environment, financial accounting reports have greater change than traditional accounting reports, that is the goal of accounting report, it changes from providing and reflecting the management responsibility information for investors and creditors, to providing the relevant information helpful to decision-making for users to meet the diversification information demand of information users; report elements, it make a further refinement based on the traditional six elements, such as refine the rights as "material property proprietor rights" and "knowledge property proprietor rights", and assign the manpower property to handle as enterprise assets, then the accounting equation becomes: assets (the manpower property + material resources property) = debt + material property proprietor rights + knowledge property proprietor rights. Profit distribution, material capital appreciation should be supported by human capital, and the knowledge workers should participate in the distribution; report period, it changes from the regular reports to provide any place and any time information by using real-time accounting report system, and achieve on-line disclosure mechanism.

3.4 The Innovation of Financial Evaluation System

In future evolution system, if it doesn't reflect the customer satisfaction, employee fulfillment, enterprises long-term growth and other factors, only the financial indicators of accounting statements cannot meet the demand, the enterprise also need to provide comprehensive management examination table of a variety of non-financial information, such as: the development situation of new products, the impact of the industrial structure adjustment on enterprise and other background information, and even the enterprise should provide total employment, salary welfare, work conditions and staff training to reflect its social responsibility information. The establishment of comprehensive management examination table, on one hand, it can assess the enterprises development potential and social harmonious degree; on the other hand, it has the "lights" effect on directing the existing shortcomings of enterprises and the future development direction.

3.5 Risk Management and Risk Warning Be Taken Seriously

Professor E. Bell of U.S. Yililuosi University in his book "Future Trends of Accounting" analyzes the network economy risks, pointing out the great importance of risk management, and proposing the six major trends of future accounting development, one of which is the establishment of financial risk prediction and its model. The establishment of financial risk prediction model is an important part of risk management mode in network period to assess the enterprise risk. It is mainly composed of monitoring range and qualitative analysis, warning index selection, occurrence probability determination, etc. and reflects the sensitivity index in the process of enterprises economic operation, such as break-even point, income safety line, maximum debt limit, etc. In traditional financial management, enterprise risk management is often limited to a number of senior managers, and are mostly "mending" measurement with great random ("fire brigade operation"). However, in e-commerce economy period, as the improvement of technology, risk management will become active risk management, which requires predict and systematic to identify the possible risks.

There are four risks commonly encountered in traditional financial management: business risk, financial risk, disaster risk, and environmental and legal risk. With the wide applications of Internet in business, and as the nonlinear, mutagenicity and explosiveness of network economy, Enterprises will increase some risks, such as: information protection risks, internal and external intrusion risk, transaction integrity risks, and quick intangible assets investment, faster update of knowledge accumulation, increasing reduction of product life cycles, etc. As the uncertainty and complexity of risks, it is imperative to establish new risk management mode.

The comparisons of traditional financial management and risk management modes in Network period

traditional mode	new mode
Risk assessment is unspecified	Risk assessment is continuous
Looking for opportunities is impulsive	Assess opportunities according to risk and return
Finance department is responsible for most parts	Financial department takes the main responsibility
Operate independently of each sector	Emphasis on risk assessment and cooperation between departments
Focus on controlling financial risks and financial results	Focus on controlling various non-financial risks
Errors should be eliminated or corrected	Errors should be avoided
The main factor of risk is people	The main factor of risk is business process

3.6 Strengthen the Financial Budget Step

In e-commerce period, virtual enterprises exists widespread, each company and even competitors cooperate by using information technology to provide their own core advantages, namely, the best manufacturers product products, and the best market sellers sell products, thus to achieve their common goals; meanwhile, "debt management" and "risk management" are more prominent in enterprise, it needs enterprise appropriately to control debt and risk. In this environment, it requires enterprise integrates and coordinates to manage enterprises form the perspective of strategy for. It emphasizes on the integration of the enterprise plan, procurement and control, which makes the sub-targets of all the subsidiary companies and functional departments, which are almost the same as their overall targets, thus the cumulative cost can be minimum under the relationship of multilayer principal-agent. This requires financial management has a main line of "pre-plan --- control in the process of implementation --- post-analysis", and each department should develop around this main line. However, the prior analysis and financial budget are more important as a basic work. The financial budget will compile according to annual be based on objective business profits by "target profit --- selling budget --- cost budget --- purchase budget --- cash flow budget", Which changes the past production-centered compilation method. After the establishment of financial budget, due to the online operation of financial business, the network will supervise the implementation of enterprise financial budget like intangible hands; meanwhile, as the network has the ability of high speed transmission, it can rapidly pass the "exception management" and special exception business in financial budget management to senior person liable for approval exception. In this way, it ensures all the binding forces of financial budget in enterprise internal, and timely adjusts it according to market situations.

3.7 The Key of Financial Management Is the Enterprise Process Reorganization and Value Chain Analysis

The network economy in e-commerce period is a new trade service way, it takes place the traditional paper medium by using digital network and equipment, this approach breaks the one-way logistics operation pattern in traditional logistics enterprises, and implement the new operation which is based on logistics, takes information flow as its core, and the capital flow as the main body. In the new operation mode, the requirements of design and engineering services will be increased which is provided by customers for suppliers, so the companies will do much more non-core tasks; meanwhile, customers will requires their suppliers to provide more inventory management services the same time (such as database warehouse and order management). This requires the enterprises must restructure the existing business processes, to enhance the management level, and thus to adapt to the economic development needs.

If reorganizing the enterprise business process, it must analyze value chain. Value chain analysis is through the analysis of industry value chain from strategy (raw material suppliers - products - manufacturers - sellers), to understand the enterprise's position in industry value chain, thus to judge whether an enterprise is necessary or not to move forward or backward, and to implement enterprise management goal;

analysis from enterprise internal value chain (order - product research and design - manufacturing - sale - service) to determine how to reduce costs, and to make enterprise process optimization; analysis from competitors value chain, through comparing to the corresponding index with competitors to find the differences with competitors and their own cost situation, thus to enhance the overall competitiveness.

References

1. Jiang, S., et al.: Web-based Financial Management Innovation. Finance and Accounting Monthly (1), 89–90 (2008)
2. Fan, G.: Financial Management under Network Environment. Business Economics (4), 101–102 (2009)
3. Wang, F.: The Effect of Network Economy Development on Financial Management. Accounting & Control (9), 45–47 (2008)
4. Liang, T., et al.: Innovative Thinking on the Financial Management of Small and Medium Enterprises under Network Environment. Accounting Research (5), 56–57 (2003)
5. Tong, D.: Study on the Enterprise Marketing Strategy under E-commerce Environment. Shandong University of Technology (2007)
6. Zhang, R.: Real-time Control of Network Environment Accounting. Renmin University of China Press (August 2004)

Evaluative Conceptualization of Risk Prevention Mechanism upon Basic Principles of Environmental Law

Lin Youqu and Zhang Chunhong

Tianjin Polytechnic University, School of Humanities and Laws, Tianjin, China
luca.m126@gmail.com

Abstract. Environmental risk has become a direct result of high technology. The hazards of the environmental risk are latent and irreversible. These features of the environment risk make a lot of victims who are the contemporary people or the descendents, and the expenses of environmental modification are so high. All the above tell us that environmental risk precaution is so important and essential. In China, our environmental law has not a sound system focus on environmental risk precaution, so the definition of environmental risk is ambiguous and the relief channel of environmental risk is sole. Therefore, it has important theoretical and practical significances to establishing the legal system of environmental risk, to protect our environmental security, national security and the legal rights of the victims who be mired in environmental risk, meanwhile, it even becomes the require of the harmonious society.

Keywords: Environmental risk, environmental risk prevention.

1 Brief Introduction to the Theory of Environmental Risk Prevention Mechanism

1.1 Significance of Environmental Risk

Speaking from the perspective of law, environmental risk means the possibility of the environment being damaged, including the probability and frequency of the environment suffering from any risks and the severity of the damages caused by such risks. Viewing from the perspective of social significance, environmental risk refers to the public's recognition of the occurrence of environmental damages and the severity of the consequence of damages. It emerged after the disappearance of nature and tradition and is caused by human being's development, particularly the development of science and technology. Environmental risks bring people an unprecedented dangerous environment. Therefore, it is of great importance to adopt corresponding precautions[1].

1.2 Principles for Environmental Risk Prevention

Risk prevention principles are applicable when there is no certain recognition on the environmental damages and they are such rules using for preventions of environmental risks with scientific uncertainties. Today with the trend of globalization, our country also faces new challenges raised by environmental damages and risks caused by

M. Dai (Ed.): ICCIC 2011, Part II, CCIS 232, pp. 326–330, 2011.

economic construction, whereas the principles for environmental risk prevention are exactly the supplementation of the limitation that there is no specific scientific basis to prove the consequence between the behaviors and environment.

1.3 Features of Environmental Risks

Environmental risks cause great potential of the damages
The inherent properties of environmental risks result in long interval between the emergence of risks and the occurrence of consequent harms. Possibly it is the next generation who assume the evil consequence of the environment risks.

A variety and huge number of environmental risks
Due to the fact that human beings' activities have limited influences, one of the remarkable features of the traditional contamination is great declination in number. View from the standpoint of environmental risk, the rapid development and research of new technology brings a lot of new objects which do not exist in the nature before. These byproducts of high technologies have gone beyond the self cleaning capacity of the environment, causing great number of poisonous chemical products existing in the environment[2].

Expanding damaging range of the environmental risks
Traditional environment issues merely refer to the local or regional pollutions and damages which occur in developed countries mostly. However, environmental risk holds the background of rapid development of global scientific production forces. Thus, there problems are consequent expanding to developing countries. Own to the laggard steps, relative lagged industrial productive forces, simply focusing in economic development, weak concept in environmental protection, the environmental problems faced by developing countries are more difficult and tougher than that faced by developed countries.

2 Problems Existing in Environmental Risk Precautions in Our Country

2.1 No Systematic Law System of Environmental Risk Precautions in Established on Our Country

At present, the relevant system on environmental risk prevention still stays on the layer of political policies. Although there are norms like Agenda in the 21st Century in China—White Book of Chinese Population, Environment and Development in The 21st Century, Program of Long-Term Goals in 2010, National Ecologic Environmental Construction and Plan, etc., they are rules and creeds of political policies. Regarding the decision-making mechanism and measuring standard and countermeasures, there is no unified legislation.

2.2 The Law and Regulations for Environmental Risk Precautions in Our Country Is over Rigid

The law and regulations for environmental risk precautions are characterized in flexibility which is incomparable with that of other environmental infringing rules and regulations. In the existing law system in our country, environmental relief is mainly built based on certainty of environmental pollution and polluting object. Concerning the postponed environmental harm caused by environmental risk, the traditional environmental relief and compensation fail to satisfy the victims' needs. Sometimes we even can not find the department who should be responsible for suits about environmental risks due to the lack of scientific proofs to prove the consequence.

Wherever Times is specified, Times Roman or Times New Roman may be used. If neither is available on your word processor, please use the font closest in appearance to Times. Avoid using bit-mapped fonts if possible. True-Type 1 or Open Type fonts are preferred. Please embed symbol fonts, as well, for math, etc[3].

3 Establish Legislative Countermeasures for Environmental Risk Precaution in Our Country

3.1 Referring to Foreign Advanced Modes

German mode
In Germany, the principle of risk prevention is a part of "ecologic modernization" consciousness, which offers legal basis for the green development and growth of economy. The theory of ecologic modernization advocates that higher environmental standard is actually a chance for economic growth. High standards for environmental protection are of great potential as they can promote development of green technology and satisfy the public's higher requirement on the environment.

Australian mode
The features for risk prevention can be observed from the Austrian legislation: first of all, both the policies and legal documents have specific regulations on the principles of risk prevention, sometimes these documents are similar to international ones while sometimes they seem to be irrelevant to these international documents. Secondly, the principles of risk prevention can be regarded as one of the principles for ecologic sustainable development and contained in the legislations on ecologic sustainable development. Finally, the principles of risk prevention are required by the government department to be realized in legislative goals.

With reference to the Germany and Australian mode, there will be a more clear direction for the environmental risk prevention mechanism in our country. These two modes also offer valuable references to the establishment of environmental risk prevention mechanism in our country[4].

3.2 Establish Risk Prevention Mechanism with Chinese Characteristics

Build gross control system
Gross control system is a legal system which deices the discharging volume of pollutions in a region based on the regional environmental capacity and allocates the discharging volume of pollutions to each company according to the plan of discharging volume declination. The basic goal of this system is to restrict the resources reasonably within in the exploited region. In order to implement gross control of resources, it is necessary to work out regional resource plan to roughly specify the main contaminations and the allowed discharging pollutions for each company. Meanwhile,

such plans should coordinate and unify with the gross control plans for contaminations in each company.

Build environmental risk assessment system
Environmental risk assessment system means the regulatory system to indentify, measure, and assess the possible environmental consequence on human's health and ecologic safety caused on uncertain environmental risks by specific organization or organ. In order to reach the goal and requirement raised by sound environment risk assessment system, it is necessary to perform the following content: building advanced environmental monitoring and pre-warning system; establishing consummated monitoring system for execution of environmental laws; establishing environmental accident emergence system, enhancing comprehensive environmental assessment ability, offering environmental information wholly, accurately and in time; carrying out assessment of the environmental quality and ecologic changes as well as environmental economic calculation periodically.

Build clean production system under the background of environmental risk
Clean production under the background of environmental risk is actually the standardization and regularization of the clean production strategy and policy. It also an important tool and warrant for the implementation of clean production. Clean production fully conforms to the prevention principles, implements whole-process control, changes the management of waste and end to that of product and origin and represents fundamental changes of legislation principle, thus is a great historical advancement. It can alleviate the great pressure on the environment caused by over growth of economy, reduce the damages on the environment brought by production and service activities, realize double-win phase of economic development and environmental protection, and lay a good foundation for explore and develop "circulative economy"[5].

The rapid development of science and technology is the activator of the appearance of environmental risk prevention law and system. The economic globalization, and the good effect in implementing such systems in foreign countries have laterally reflected the historical inevitability of building environmental risk prevention legal system in our country. For an industrial developing country with rapid development of high-tech, our country's action of referring to the deeds in developed countries and building environmental risk prevention legal system under the background of environmental risk legal relief with the defect of no proof to prove the environmental harm is definitely a rational choice. The establishment of environmental risk prevention system not only reflects the orientation of social environmental policies in a country, nut also represents the depth and width of the realization of socialism, becoming an inevitable need for overall construction of socialism and harmonious society at present in our country.

References

1. Hu, B.: Tentative Discussion on Risk Precautionary Principle in International Environmental Law. Environmental Protection (6), 17–20 (2002)
2. Chen, Q.S.: Basic Theory of Environmental Law. China Environmental Science Press, Beijing (2004)

3. Cai, S.: Researches on Environmental Policy and Law. Wuhan University Press, Wuhan (1999)
4. Cai, S., et al.: Sustainable Development and Construction of Environmental & Resources Legal System. China Legal Press, p.296 (2003)
5. Tang, R.Z., Yu, Y.: Comparative Study of Circulation Economic Law - and Comments on the First Clean Production Promotion Law in Our Country. Journal of Hangzhou Commercial College, 26–28 (2002) (business)
6. Wei, S.: Environment Information Disclosure in Western Countries: Practice, Characteristics And Enlightens. Accounting Communication (7), 40–43 (2005)
7. Environmental Governance, Enterprises' Environmental Reports. Journal Of Environment and Sustainable Development (6) (2006)
8. Pan, J.: Tentative Discussion on Ancient Chinese Environmental Ethics. Journal of Ethics (9) (2007)
9. Chang, J.: Researches on Environmental Legal Liability Principles. Hunan Renming Publishing House (2001)
10. The ecological philosophy ZhengShaoHua. Harvard University press, Cambridge (2002)
11. Xiao, J.: Comparative Environmental Law. China Procuratorial Press (2002)
12. Xiao, J., Ouyang, G., et al.: Monograph of Comparative Environmental Law. China Environmental Science Press (2004)
13. Tang, S.: Researches on Environmental Risk Prevention Principle—A Dialogue Between Science and Law, pp. 144–149. Higher Education Press
14. Huang, X., Ceng, W.: New dissuasions on International environmental law, pp. 32–40. Chongqing University Press (2005)
15. Jin, R.: Environmental Law, pp. 55–61. Beijing University Press, Beijing (2002)
16. Chen, C.Y.: Overview of Environmental Law, p. 25. China University of Political Science and Law Press (2003)
17. Cai, S.: Textbook for Environmental Law, vol. 26. Science Publishing House (2003)
18. Wang, X.: An Introduction to American Environmental Law, pp. 45–49. Wuhan University Press, Wuhan (1992)
19. Wang, X.: Selection of International Environmental Law, pp. 55–62. Democracy and Construction Press (1999)
20. Lv, Z.: Environmental and Resource Law. China University of Political Science and Law Press (1999)
21. Lv, Z.: New Horizons of Environmental Law, p. 26. China University of Political Science and Law Press (2000)
22. Chen, Q.: Basic Principles of Environmental Law, pp. 23–27. China Environmental Science Press (2004)
23. Zhang, W.X: pp. 71–77. Law Press China, Beijing (2004)
24. Wang, X.: International Environmental Law, pp. 37–42. Law Press China, Beijing (2005)

A Comparative Study on SMEs External Environment

Liu Tanming

Business School, Central South University,
Changsha, Hunan, China
jianqiaoxu@gmail.com

Abstract. Based on a questionnaire survey of ten provinces and cities such as Guangdong and Zhejiang, this paper applies Structural Equation Model (SEM) to conduct quantitative researches into Chinese SMEs (Small and Medium Enterprise) external environment from the industry perspective. Research findings indicate that enterprise external environments of information transmission and computer service and software are the best, while that of Farming, Forestry, Animal Husbandry and Fishery is the worst; enterprise external environment of the eastern region as a whole, is superior to those of the central and western regions about which there exists little diversity. Causes of the distinction are also analyzed in this paper.

Keywords: External environment, SMEs, Industry.

1 Introduction

The growth rate of SMEs is connected with its external environment. Therefore, to accurately grasp and adapt to SMEs external environment turns out to be a crucial factor for accelerating the progress of SMEs.

2 Literature Review

There has been no agreed definition of external environment until now. In summary, most experts tend to hold that "enterprise external environment is a system which is mutually interacting and independent with enterprises and has significant impact on enterprise development".

As to studies on the content of enterprise external environment, related literatures focus mainly on two aspects: information uncertainty and resource liability. Tan(1994) first presented the idea to divide organization environment into three dimensions to carry out empirical researches[1]: dynamism, complexity and hostility. Domestic scholar Professor Xi Youmin (2001) categorized enterprise external environment as hard environment and soft environment in his monograph Analysis of Enterprise External Environment [2]. Professor Zhao Xibin (2004) divided enterprise external environment into three sub-systems[3]: social environment system, market environment system and natural environment system. Li Xiaoming (2006) held that it is a scientific and reasonable thinking to grasp external environment objectively and accurately by using the ecological theory for reference to study enterprise external

M. Dai (Ed.): ICCIC 2011, Part II, CCIS 232, pp. 331–341, 2011.

environment with systematic theory as the guidance and enterprise stakeholder theory as the basis [4].

Many management theories have come into being on account of studies on enterprise external environment centering on the extent of environment and strategy's influences on performance, and the controversy that between the selectivity of environment and the initiative adaptability of strategy which one should be dominant. These strategic management schools can be divided into three categories [5]: the first category lays emphasis on the decisive effect of environment on strategy; the second category highlights the effect of strategy on environment; the third category is not only an integration of the two views mentioned above but represents the latest research direction, namely, considering the relation of environment and strategy not as a one-way decision relation but as a two-way complicated collaborative evolution relation. However, we can see that most existing literatures focus on qualitative investigations at the level of studying contents and methods of external environment with only a few papers making quantitative research into the external environment of Chinese SMEs from the industry perspective.

The research framework of this paper is as follows: part two establishes the index system of enterprise external environment, and introduces the design method of questionnaires as well as research methods; part three deals with the sample data; part four makes a comparative study on SMEs external environment in different industries; part five conducts a comparative study on the comprehensive evaluation of SMEs external environment; part six is the conclusion part of this paper.

3 Enterprise External Environment Index System, Questionnaire Design and Research Method

Before creating the evaluation system for SMEs external environment, this paper classifies the contents of external environment (see Figure 1). According to Richard L. Daft's classification methods of partitions, elements and stakeholders [5], SMEs external environment mainly covers six partitions: economy, politics, technology, social culture, human resource and location resource (Figure 1).

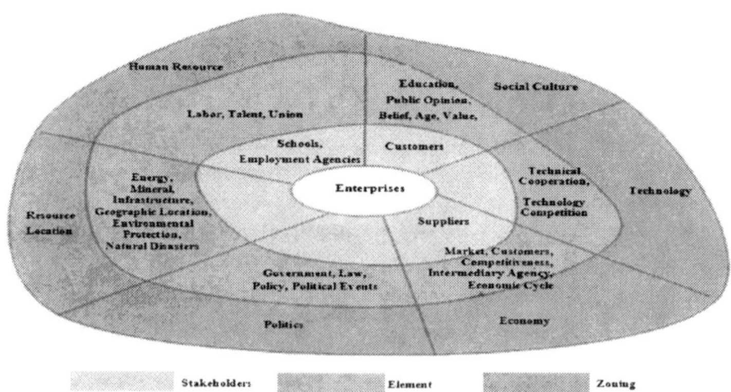

Fig. 1. Business division of the eternal environment

Base on content partitions, this paper establishes an evaluation index system of external environment from the perspective of external environment's influences on enterprises (organizations) (see Figure 2). The first level divides external environment into economy, politics, technology, social culture, human resource and location resource and makes comprehensive evaluation of external environment through the six partition indices. The second level evaluates the six partitions at the above level through 23 elements.

Based on the content of each element, the questionnaire evaluates each element (second-level index) subject to 54 indices. The questionnaire is designed in accordance with Richter's five-point scoring method. SMEs operators surveyed are required to rate the satisfaction with each specific index from 1 to 5, and the higher the score the more favorable this index is to enterprise external environment.

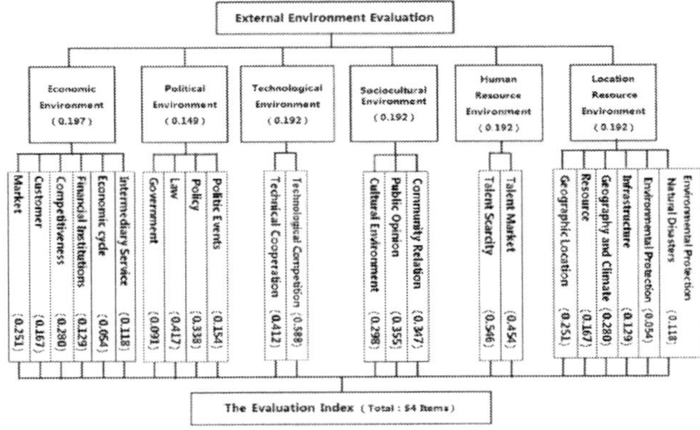

Fig. 2. Evaluation Index System of SMEs External Environment①

On the basis of obtaining research data, this paper plans to use structural equation to make confirmatory factor analysis of the evaluation model. Calculated by second order confirmatory factor analysis (after normalization), the factor loads of indices at different level (see the figures in brackets behind each index in Figure 2) all reach a noticeable level (t>2). The fit index of the model is shown in Table 1.

Table 1. Fit Indices of Confirmatory Factor Analysis②

Goodness of Fit Index	X^2 /df	GFI	AGFI	NFI	CFI	RM SEA
External Macro Environment	8.475	0.982	0.954	0.960	0.974	0.078

①Index weight is obtained through confirmatory factor analysis by using the structural equation model.

②Absolute fit measure x^2/df is a subjective goodness index of entire fit. x^2/df>3 indicates the index is general; x^2/df>5 shows the index is unsatisfactory; x^2/df>10 suggests the index is bad. In this model, the value of x^2/df is 8.475, unsatisfactory; the root mean square error of approximation (RMSEA) is 0.078, a little higher than the ideal level of 0.05; the rest of fit indices are all above 0.9. These fit goodness indices are all within the acceptable range, which means that the model structure is rational.

Based on the above factor loads of indices at different levels and the hierarchy structure diagram of external environment evaluation established in this paper, the scoring model of external environment is shown below:

$$HJ = \sum_{i=1}^{n} NW_i A_i, \quad A_i = \sum_{j=1}^{n} NW_{ij} B_j, \quad B_i = \sum_{k=1}^{n} NW_{ijk} C_k;$$

In the model, C_k is the score of each question in the questionnaire; B_j indicates the score of second-level indices (elements) in the hierarchy structure diagram; A_i means the score of first-level indices (partitions) in the diagram; *HJ* represents the final score of enterprise external environment; *NW* stands for the factor load (weight) of corresponding indices. At last, according to the industry classification of enterprises, this paper gets the SMEs external environment scores of different industries by means of arithmetic average.

4 Sample Data Processing

The data studied in this paper is the questionnaire survey data in the first half year of 2007 acquired by the SMEs Research Center of Central South University. Investigation methods include: telephone survey, mail questionnaire, and field research which contains five groups: western region, central region, Hunan region, Yangtze River Delta region and Pearl River Delta region. Of over 12000 questionnaires given out, 1933 valid questionnaires were received with reclaim rate 16.08%.

Synthesizing the features of survey data and Chinese national economic industry classification criteria, this paper categories the sample data into 12 industries for comparative study, namely, farming, forestry, animal husbandry and fishery (102), mining and quarrying (141), manufacturing (404), electric power, fuel gas (133), construction(173), transportation, warehousing (129), information transmission, computer service and software (243), wholesale and retail (141), lodging and catering (136), real estate (118), leasing and commercial service (106) and others (107).

In addition, because the questionnaire design is based on five-point scoring method, we have to multiply the scores of each index 20 times to make them scatter in the range of 0 to 100 during data processing, which is favorable to comparative studies on each index.

5 Comparative Study on SMEs External Environment in Different Industries

A. Economic Environment Evaluation of SMEs in Different Industries

Economic environment mainly includes many aspects that SMEs are faced with in the course of production and operation, such as market, customers, competition, intermediary service institutions, financial service institutions, and economic cycle that enterprise economic activities are at [6]. Based on this, factor loads determined by structural equation model (SEM) confirmatory factor analysis can get SMEs economic environment indices of different industries by using the scoring model of external environment (see Table 2).

Table 2. Economic Environment Indices of SMEs in Different Industries

Industry	Economic Environ ment Index	The Benchmark Index					
		Market	Custom er	Competitive ness	Financial Institutions	Economic Cycle	Intermediary Institutions
Electric Power & Fuel Gas	80.14	82.00	79.25	86.00	76.00	79.62	69.00
Information Transmission, Computer service & Software	76.79	72.73	78.35	78.48	80.26	72.87	77.86
Real Estate	75.45	78.00	74.60	72.00	78.00	79.60	75.40
Manufacturing	74.01	69.98	77.67	74.81	77.24	71.71	73.68
Leasing & Commercial	74.01	83.20	75.04	67.79	79.44	72.45	63.12
Construction	71.96	76 00	77. 68	70.48	66.70	71.51	65.31
Transportation & Warehousing	69.83	69.21	71.54	71.41	67.62	70.61	67.67
Mining	68.56	68.27	72.86	72.21	62.08	63.81	64.21
Lodging and Catering	66.54	72.60	76.07	65.35	58.40	66.57	52.40
Farming, Forestry, Animal Husbandry & Fishery	61.40	68.04	62.00	66.00	44.00	64.55	53.60
Wholesale & Retail	54.87	72.00	49.24	41.80	49.60	59.66	61.42

According to the evaluation indices of SMEs economic environment in different industries, industries with good economic environment index include electric power and fuel gas, information transmission, computer service, real estate, of which economic environment indices are above 75; farming, forestry, animal husbandry and fishery and wholesale and retail have worse economic environments with the indices being respectively 61.4 and 54.87.

B. Political Environment Evaluation of SMEs in Different Industries

Political environment where SMEs are involved in is mainly embodied in the government's administrative regulation, laws and regulations, policies, political events etc. See table 3 for the SMEs political environment index.

As is shown in table 3, SMEs political environment of different industries can be divided into three categories: the first category, the political environment index being above 70, includes farming, forestry, animal husbandry and fishery, information transmission, computer service and software, electric power and fuel gas while the second one, with the index between 65 and 70, covers real estate industry, manufacturing, transportation, warehousing. As for the third one whose index is below 65, it mainly includes wholesale and retail, lodging and catering, construction, mining, leasing and commercial service.

C. Technological Environment Evaluation of SMEs in Different Industries

The technological environment of SMEs in different industries is comprised of the technological cooperation environment as well as the technological competition environment. We can get a sound idea of the technological environment of those industries from those two dimensions (see table 4).

As is shown in table 4, the technological environment can be divided into two echelons. Echelon one with the index being over 70, while echelon two, the index being below 70. Meanwhile, it is found that technological environment indices of

SMEs in different industries are featured by the fact that the correlation coefficient of technological cooperation and technological competition reaches 0.82, which shows that better technological cooperation environment, ensures better technological competition capacity.

Table 3. Political environment indices of SMEs in Different Industries

Industry	Political Environment Index	Benchmark Index			
		Government	Law	Policy	Political Events
Farming, Forestry, Animal Husbandry & Fishery	78.53	76.00	78.00	79.20	80.00
Information Transmission, Computer Service & Software	70.62	74.48	76.00	66.24	63.41
Electric Power & Fuel Gas	70.33	81.70	72.00	68.84	62.34
Real Estate	67.87	78.86	73.66	60.28	62.34
Manufacturing	66.31	73.29	67.18	67.27	57.73
Transportation & Warehousing	65.01	76.06	63.98	64.67	62.01
Wholesale & Retail	64.51	70.92	66.48	61.98	60.95
Construction	64.20	65.24	65.98	63.83	59.58
Lodging & Catering	63.24	67.76	63.50	63.08	60.22
Mining	61.99	73.40	61.38	59.32	62.75
Leasing & Commercial Services	57.72	69.58	54.10	58.46	58.90

Table 4. Technological Environment Indices of SMEs in Different Industries

Industry	Technical Environment Index	Sub-index index	
		Technical Cooperation	Technology Competition
Manufacturing	77.88	78.00	77.80
Mining	72.89	77.44	69.70
Electric Power & Fuel Gas	71.44	73.22	70.18
Wholesale & Retail	71.37	69.98	72.34
Information Transmission, Computer Service & Software	70.81	69.25	71.90
Transportation & Warehousing	70.44	71.72	69.54
Real Estate	67.77	68.06	67.56
Construction	67.70	67.55	67.81
Farming, Forestry, Animal Husbandry & Fishery	66.75	64.40	68.40
Leasing & Commercial Service	65.97	65.06	66.61
Lodging & Catering	57.34	52.40	60.80

D. Sociocultural Environment Evaluation of SMEs in Different Industries

As a key component of enterprise external environment, sociocultural environment is composed of three parts, namely, cultural environment, social public opinion and community relations. These three factors boil down to sociocultural environment and refer to table 5 for sociocultural environment evaluation of SMEs in different industries.

Table 5. Sociocultural Environment Evaluation Indices of SMEs in Different Industries

Industry	Socio-cultural Environment index	The Benchmark Index		
		Cultural Environment	Public Opinion	Community Relations
Transportation & Warehousing	75.07	75.51	73.88	75.92
Electric Power & Fuel Gas	73.11	72.45	73.21	73.58
Information Transmission & Computer Service & Software	72.61	70.49	73.19	73.85
Manufacturing	72.50	70.62	72.72	73.89
Construction	72.16	71.71	71.23	73.49
Lodging & Catering Service	71.04	68.89	72.78	71.11
Wholesale & Retail	71.00	67.91	72.53	72.09
Leasing & Commercial Service	70.44	67.92	71.70	71.32
Mining	70.30	64.55	73.64	71.82
Real Estate	69.64	68.82	68.53	71.47
Farming, Forestry, Animal Husbandry & Fishery	53.61	59.68	53.26	48.76

Table 6. Human Resource Environment Evaluation Indices of SMEs in Different Industries

Industry	Human Resource Environment Index	Sub-index	
		Talent Scarcity	Talent Market
Leasing & Commercial Service	76.70	73.60	80.42
Information Transmission, Computer Service & Software	76.48	77.80	74.90
Wholesale & Retail	74.56	75.30	73.68
Manufacturing	70.00	68.00	72.40
Electric Power & Fuel Gas	67.86	59.60	77.80
Construction	63.34	56.70	71.32
Transportation & Warehousing	61.83	52.20	73.41
Real Estate	60.85	56.24	66.40
Lodging & Catering	57.85	55.72	60.42
Mining	57.22	52.17	63.30
Farming, Forestry, Animal Husbandry & Fishery	50.37	44.02	58.00

As is seen from table 5, the sociocultural environment index of farming, forestry, animal husbandry and fishery is obviously lower than those of other industries, except for which, indices of other industries are roughly equal. Generally higher than the other two indices, the social relations indices in different industries are almost equal.

E. Evaluation of Human Resource Environment of SMEs in Different Industries

The human resource is evaluated in terms of the talent shortage as well as the perfection degree of the talent market. Refer to table 6 for the evaluation of human resource environment index of SMEs in different industries.

It can be seen from the table 6 that there exist great differences in the human resource indices in different industries. Those industries enjoy obvious advantages like leasing and commercial service, information transmission, computer service, software, wholesale and retail. The human resource environment of manufacturing, electric power, fuel gas, construction, transportation, warehousing, and real estate industry is ordinary while that of farming, forestry, animal husbandry and fishery, lodging and catering, food industry and mining is the worst.

F. Evaluation of Location Resource Environment of SMEs in Different Industries

Location resource in this paper mainly consists of those six aspects, namely, geographic position, resource, climate, infrastructure, environmental protection and natural disasters. Refer to table 7 for location resource environment evaluation index of SMEs in different industries.

As is seen from table 7, those industries, like electric power, fuel gas, information transmission, computer service and software, transportation and warehousing, construction, enjoy obvious location resource advantages while real estate industry has worse location resources.

Table 7. Ocation Resource Environment Evaluation Indices of SMEs in Different Industries

Industry	Location Resource Index	Benchmark Index					
		Location	Resource	Geography and Climate	Infras-tructure	Enviro--nmental Protection	Natural Disasters
Electric Power & Fuel Gas	74.58	80.00	58.49	72.45	80.38	69.81	50.57
Information Transmission, Computer service & Software	72.99	78.16	53.33	73.25	75.69	68.53	53.45
Transportation Warehousing	71.97	80.00	61.84	71.22	75.51	63.67	51.43
Construction	71.90	77.26	56.71	71.23	77.88	63.84	49.59
Leasing & Commercial Service	69.65	68.30	57.45	69.43	72.45	72.45	50.57
Manufacturing	68.54	70.40	58.38	68.71	71.93	64.05	57.54
Wholesale & Retail	67.52	69.67	57.75	66.15	73.41	61.98	54.51
Lodging & Catering	66.76	73.33	55.83	64.44	72.22	58.89	52.22
Mining	65.24	63.81	64.76	65.71	67.62	64.76	52.38
Real Estate	64.11	67.94	55.59	64.12	67.06	58.24	52.35
Farming, Forestry, Animal Husbandry & Fishery	53.71	56.00	52.86	60.20	49.26	48.80	40.62

6 Comparative Study of Comprehensive Evaluation of the SMEs External Environment

G. Comprehensive Evaluation of SMEs External Environment in Different Industries

The external environment index is gained based on the six indices of SMEs in different industries (see table 8). Then according to the final external environment scores, it is divided into three echelons: the first one enjoys sound external environment, with the index over 70. The second one has an ordinary environment, with the index between 65 and 70.The third echelon refers to those industries with worse external environment index, which is below 65.

Table 8 offers a further reflex of the specific reasons for the differences of the enterprises' external environment. The external environment index of information transmission, computer service and software ranks first with the highest score near the top in every index, which shows the overall coordination in the development environment. The economic environment index of electric power and fuel gas industry ranks second by 0.38 due to the low human resource index.

Table 8. Comprehensive Evaluation of SMEs External Environment in Different Industries

Industry	External Environment		Benchmark Index					
	Index	Rank	Economic Environment	Political Environment	Technological Environment	Social Culture	Human Resource	Location Resource
Information Transmission, Computer service & Software	73.47	1	76.79	70.62	70.81	72.61	76.48	72.99
Electric Power& Fuel Gas	73.09	2	80.14★	70.33	71.44	73.11	67.86	74.58★
Manufacturing	72.01	3	74.01	66.31	77.88★	72.50	70.00	68.54
Leasing &Commercial Service	69.30	4	74.01	57.72?	65.97	70.44	76.70★	69.65
Transportation& Warehousing	69.12	5	69.83	65.01	70.44	75.07★	61.83	71.97
Construction	68.62	6	71.96	64.20	67.70	72.16	63.34	71.90
Real Estate	68.05	7	75.45	67.87	67.77	69.64	60.85	64.11
Wholesale& Retail	67.07	8	54.87?	64.51	71. 37	71.00	74.56	67.52
Mining	66.46	9	68.56	61.99	72 89	70.30	57.22	65.24
Lodging& Catering	63.69	10	66.54	63.24	57.34?	71.04	57.85	66.76
Farming, Forestry, Animal Husbandry & Fishery	60.87	11	61.40	78.53★	66.75	53.61?	50.37?	53.71?

NOTE: ? refers to the lowest score of the index; ★ refers to the highest score of the index.

H Comprehensive Evaluation of SMEs External Environment in Different Regions

As is shown from table 9, the SMEs external environment scores of all those industries in the east (mining excluded) are generally higher than those in the middle and the west, mirroring the better environment of the eastern region than those of the middle and the west. What's more, those eastern industries with best external environment include information transmission, software and computer service, and the western industry goes to mining, with the western industries with the best external environment being transportation and warehousing. Those industries with the worst external environment in the east, the middle and the west are in order mining, farming, forestry, animal husbandry and fishery and construction.

Table 9. Comparison of the External Environment Scores of SMES in Different Industries in the Three Regions of China

Region	East		Central		West	
Industry Name	Enterprise External Environment Score	Rank	Enterprise External Environment Score	Rank	Enterprise External Environment Score	Rank
Mining	64.48	11	70.05	1	69.68	3
Electric Power & Fuel Gas	69.34	7	69.78	2	65.08	8
Real Estate	73.80	2	64.32	9	66.60	6
Construction	69.79	6	66.86	4	61.82	10
Transportation & Warehousing	70.03	5	64.86	8	73.16	1
Farming, Forestry, Animal Husbandry & Fishery	65.85	10	63.34	11	-	-
Wholesale and Retail	68.69	8	63.80	10	66.21	7
Information Transmission, Computer service & Software	74.84	1	65.35	7	68.61	4
Manufacturing	73.52	4	65.49	6	66.90	5
Lodging & Catering	68.23	9	67.42	3	70.58	2
Leasing& Commercial Service	73.62	3	65.83	5	62.20	9

Note: the industry of farming, forestry, animal husbandry and fishery in the western region is deleted due to the little amount of samples

7 Conclusions and Enlightenment

(1) Information transmission, computer service and software, electric power and fuel gas industry belong to the first echelon. Though they enjoy general sound external environment, there exist potential dangers because of the lack of activation in human resource environment as well as the technological environment.

(2) In those industries of the second echelon, the key to the external environment improvement of wholesale and retail lies in improvement of economic environment. In addition, improvement of external environment also lies in improvement of the political environment, a common problem all SMEs are faced with.

(3) As for those industries in the third echelon, the external environment of farming, forestry, animal husbandry and fishery is better than before. However, the human resource index, economic index and location resource index are not competitive.

(4) Taking the external environment differences of the east, the middle and the west, authorities in the middle as well as the west are supposed to learn from the east in the improvement process of the SMEs external environment.

References

1. Tan, J., Litschert, R.J.: Environment—Strategy Relationship and its Performance Implication: An Empirical Study of the Chinese Electronic Industry. Strategic Management Journal 15(1), 1–20 (1994)
2. Xi, Y.: Business External Environment Analysis. Higher Education Press, Beijing (2001)
3. Zhao, X.: The External Environment Company of a Few Basic Questions. Wuhan University Journal (Social Sciences Edition) 1(57), 1 (2004)
4. Li, X.: Analysis on External Environment of Enterprises. Journal of Northwestern Polytechnical University (Social Sciences Edition) 26(3), 9 (2006)
5. He, Z., Tan, J., Lu, Y.: Organizational Environment and the Relationship Between Organizational Strategy and the Latest Research Literature Review. Management World (11), 144–150 (2006)
6. Daft, R.L.: Organization Theory and Design. Tsinghua University Press, Beijing (2003)

The Control Systems Design of Budgetary Slack in Chinese Enterprise

Shuang-Cai Zhang and Gui-Ying Liu

School of Management, Hebei University
Baoding, P.R. China, 071002

Abstract. This paper, with questionnaire survey conducted among 44 enterprises in China, got the conclusion that environment that fosters the production of budgetary slack exists in various links such as budgetary planning, budgetary control, final evaluation of performance, and choice of reward incentives. With the rising attention to budgeting enterprises, budgetary slack is becoming increasingly noticeable. This paper analyzed the basis of the current situation of budgetary slack in China in such aspects as budgetary target, budgetary participation, information asymmetry, and budgetary effect, and put forward the countermeasures that help solve issues of budgetary slack. These countermeasures include budgetary standardization, better supervisory communication, and redesign of reward and punishment system.

Keywords: Budget, Budgetary Management, Budgetary Slack, Information Asymmetry.

1 Introduction

As defined by Dunk & Nouri (1998), "budgetary slack" refers to the intentional underestimation of revenues or productive capabilities and /or overestimation costs or resources when completes budgeted task [1]. That is, along the budgeting process, due to information asymmetry at various levels existing within the enterprise, the individual manager makes the standard relaxation using the opportunity of participating in budgeting for satisfy personal motives.

Currently, the researches on budgetary slack focus on the following aspects:

A. Research on the Agent Behavior of Budgeting

Since 1980s, the effect of agent theory on budgeting management represents an important turning point of western budget management research. Although as early as the period of research of behavioral science oriented budget management, western scholars have begun to pay attention to the impact of incentive on budget. For example, H.O.Rockness (1977) set up the hypothesis based on expectancy theory [2], utilized the methods of experimental research, and tested the mechanism of effect of the forced budgetary rigidity and mechanism of frequency of bonus on performance and satisfactory. However, under the impact of research on agent theory, Western scholars began to pay attention to the use of principle of economics to explain the budget for the management of behavioral characteristics.

M. Dai (Ed.): ICCIC 2011, Part II, CCIS 232, pp. 342–349, 2011.

B. Budget Participation

Under the organizational background, subsidiaries own more accurate information about factors that affect performance than higher authorities, such as their working competence and efforts planned to pay. Meanwhile, the information of subsidiaries and higher authorities owns about uncertainty of working condition is not inconsistent. Therefore, the participation in budget making in order to provide the rule of information communication can play positive effect on eliminating of information asymmetric. However, some scholars think that the participation of budget provides the opportunity of budgetary slack (Baiman, 1982; Young, 1985)[3][4]. If subsidiaries think that the reward relies on the result of completion of budget, they will set up slack during the process of budget making(Lowe and Shaw, 1968[5], Waller, 1988[6]). Therefore, the participation of budget will lead to the production of budgetary slack[7] [8].

C. Budget Assessment

Because budgetary slack (Unrealistic prediction of performance capabilities from associates), more often than not, appears in the budget-based compensation contract environment, the design of incentive programs has aroused the concern of scholars. Desmond C.Y.Yuen(2004), through investigation and research, found that clear communication and incentive mechanism can specify the target and help solve budgetary issues when it is difficult to accomplish the target [9]. Moreover, the author thinks that these findings can be used in budget making system. The author also put forward some affective factors of communication and incentive mechanism: affective behavior of managers, necessary explanation of budget difference, budgetary feedback system, relationship between managers and associates, etc.

2 The Present Situation of Budgetary Slack in China

In order to have a profound and comprehensive understanding of the present budgetary slack in the enterprise, we specially designed a questionnaire and carry on the investigation in 44 enterprises. In order to make the coverage of target group to be broader, then reflect budgetary slack situation more comprehensively, we chose target enterprises including many kinds of nature, professions and different scales First the target enterprises basically covered each kind of nature in china, in which thirty-two enterprises belonged to "the national capital committee", the number of collective enterprise was one, the number of local state-owned holding enterprise was four, the number of universities and colleges or other institution holding enterprise was one, the private enterprise was one, the joint stock company was 1 and the number of other nature enterprise was four. Moreover, in order to make the investigation report more comprehensive, the industry of the enterprises are dispersed., including seven enterprises on excavation industry, eight enterprises on manufacturing industry , three enterprises on electric power and coal gas , four enterprises on architecture industry , one enterprises on transportation warehousing industry, two enterprises on information technology industry , one enterprises on financial insurance business, two enterprises on real estates, eight enterprises on social service industry , eight enterprises on comprehensive enterprise. Moreover, because participation budget which is easy to cause the budgetary slack, is mainly used in the major industry. Therefore, the choices of target enterprise's scale stresses on the major industry, the sales volume of 68%

target objects was above 300,000,000 Yuan. In conclusion, this research covers a broad target group. The nature and industry of the enterprises are dispersed. The size is large. As a result, the target group should comprehensively support this research.

A. Budgeting Goal

This part mainly investigates the six questions: the clarity of budgeting goal, the difficulty of budgeting goal, the reasons why budgeting goal is set in an attainable level, the emphasis of budgeting goal, the revision situation of budgeting goal, the detailed degree of budgeting goal and the tolerance degree regarding the deviation of the middle-term budgeting target.

Quastion 1----- Are their budgeting goals clear?
Quastion 2-----Are their budgeting goals easy to realize?
Quastion 3-----The budget can revise or not within the budget year?
Quastion 4-----Do the top management have very low tolerance regarding the deviation of middle-term budget?

we collect 83% of our target enterprises strongly state that their budgeting goals are clear, however, around 60% enterprises think that their budgeting goals are not easy to realize, but all enterprises agree that the budgeting goals may be realized if certain efforts are taken. All enterprises reach the same opinion that enterprises in china strongly emphasize budgeting goal; above 70% target enterprises cannot revise budgets within the budget year, only if certain significant situations happen; more than half of target enterprises think the top management has very low tolerance regarding the deviation of middle-term budget.

B. Budgetary Participation

Regarding budgetary participation study, we divide the topic into two kinds according to behaviour obligation: participation and communication. We design six questions including the willingness of divisional manager in participating in the budget planning process, the result of the participation etc., to study the participation situation of divisional manager in the budget planning process.

Quastion 1----- Are the divisional managers highly willing to participate in the budget establishment process?
Quastion 2-----Are leaders in the enterprises willing to discuss and construct budget together with the divisional manager and financial departments.?
Quastion 3-----Do the divisional managers communicate with the leaders usually?
Quastion 4-----The purpose of budgeting communication is to share information.
Quastion 5-----The purpose of budgeting communication is to control.

In over 70% target enterprises, the divisional managers are highly willing to participate in the budget establishment process. Subjectively, they are keen to discuss with higher level authorities in this process.

About the budgeting communication, we inspected in the degree of communicating the budget between top management and divisional manager, as well as the goal of such communication. The data displays that as high as 72% leaders in the enterprises are willing to discuss and construct budget together with the divisional manager and financial departments. On the contrary, unless there is disagreement in the communication which has negative impact on the budgeting plan, the divisional managers are not eager to keep daily communicate with the leaders. 60% target entities think that the purpose of budgeting communication is to share information; while 84% think the goal of budgeting communication is to control.

C. Budgetary Slack

About this part, we mainly investigate ten aspects.: the reasons of slack, the attitude of individual manager to the high-level management control system, the budgeting pressure on subordinate unit's, the right of subordinate unit's to budget independently, the condition of top management using budget, the attitude to the foundation of budget, the attitude to the relevance of budget to the performance evaluation, the general attitude to the budget, as well as the budgeting relevance.

There are some issues should be pointed out particularly: concerning to the reasons of budgetary slack, there are nearly 30% investigated enterprises indicate that guaranty and top management acceptance on reasonable budgetary slack from individual manager are the two major elements. Regarding to the attitude from top managers to individual manager, a more consistent attitude is delivered, which generally consider that obey and respect top management, clear instruction to the individual manager and fully dedicate employment are in favor of the development of enterprises, and help to reduce budgetary slack. According to the questionnaire, the investigated enterprises stressed the usage of budget, there are about 70% of the enterprises agreed on it, especially regarding to the prospects which the top management decision making based on the budget and cost control.

Enterprises demonstrate a more consolidated attitude towards the individual manager budget benchmark. More than half of individual manager are expecting to establish an easy target, nearly 90% of the enterprises prefer to over-fulfill the target instead of unable to complete it. There are about 60% of those surveyed management agree that the monetary incentives is mainly linked with budget completion. There are 57% surveyed subsidiaries believe that unfulfilled budgeting measure will lead to the top management discontent. There are 86% of enterprises consider that the "the ability of making individual manager to complete a task" is important to evaluate the management. On other issues, the investigated enterprises do not coincide in opinion, choice was relatively diverse.

D. Information Asymmetry

This part mainly investigates the five questions.

Quastion 1-----Who has higher amount of information of the activity in subordinate scope of official duty, the top management or the individual manager?

Question 2-----Who is more familiar with the information of the investment and return in subordinate scope, the top management or the individual manager?

Question 3-----Who has higher amount of information of the business activities process in subordinate scope, the top management or the individual manager?

Question 4-----Who is more familiar with the degree of technical part, the top management or the individual manager?

Question 5-----Who can know more clearly about the goal which subordinate can achieve, the top management or the individual manager?

More than half of the surveyed enterprises sense that about the five aspects below, the individual manager obtains higher amount of information than top management, and there is information asymmetry between the two phenomena. The five aspects are: the activity in subordinate scope of official duty, the investment and return in subordinate scope, the business activities process in subordinate scope, the familiar degree of technical part, the goal which subordinate can achieve.

E. Budgetary Effectiveness

On this issue, we conduct an investigation on three levels: budgeting effect on enterprises as a whole, the incentives of individual manager, as well as the budgeting effect on the top management.

Quastion 1-----Is budget critical for the enterprises?

Question 2-----The sense of non-material factors after budget completion is playing an important role to individual managers.

Question 3-----For the top management,the budget for improving the performance and ability has a positive effect .

Regarding to the budgetary effectiveness, almost all of the target top management reach the same opinion that, budget is critical for the enterprises; More than 80% of the surveyed individual manager believe that a sense of satisfaction, self-growth and development and other non-material factors after budget completion is playing an important role which promotes the subordinates' normative incentives; For the top management, more than 60% of respondents believe that the budget for improving the performance and ability has a positive effect, an effective budgeting mechanism can help them to become better managers.

3 Methods of Controlling Budgetary Slack

To control budgetary slack could not only limit to ex ante planning stage, but also need to control through the entire process ,including mid-term controlling, and ex post evaluation stages.

A. Making Measure Standardized

In the budget planning process, through analysis, and the unit cost decomposition, the top management should make budgetary measure establishment standardized, which provides a unified foundation of budget planning and verifying [10]. On this basis, the standard is determined beforehand, the proportion of artificial estimation contained in the data reduces. Thus, according to the predictive target of production next year, the top management can hold the precise data of cost and profit value, then reduce the lack of commutation between the top management and divisional manager. This probably can't eliminate the budgetary slack completely, but can make it slow down. The main methods of making measure standardized are standard costing and activity-based costing (ABC).

The standard costing produces in the 20th century 20's in US, under the influence of Taylor's production process standardization. This method mainly applied enterprise's scientific management to the cost measuring. Through formulation of standard cost, and making the costing plan, costing control, computation and analysis unified, standard costing is the method that takes the basis of controlling and inspecting cost disbursement.

ABC developed to provide more-accurate ways of assigning the costs of indirect and support resources to activities, business processes, products, services, and customer[1].The goal of ABC is not to allocate common costs to products. The goal is to measure and then price out all the resources used for activities that support the production and delivery of products and services to customers. Basis on this, activity-based cost system provides more accurate cost information. The procedures which calculate the cost produce good estimates of the quantities and the unit costs of the activities and resources deployed for individual products, services, and customers.

Otherwise, activity-based budget (ABB) produced on the foundation of mentality of activity-based management, it was a budget management, which took activity-based management as the foundation, took increasing value as the goal. According to the activity analysis and the service process improvement, it considers strategic target and the activity requirement forecasted, measures the cost which occurs in each activity-based department, and uses this information to stipulate the resources consumption quantity which each activity permits, implements control, evaluation and inspection effectively.

B. Enhance Information Communication

In this process, must have the smooth information communication system[11]. The good information communication may cause the actual production operating condition to issue smoothly, thus reduce information asymmetry, also may cause the difference between actual result and budget target to obtain prompt analysis and improvement. The methods which can strengthen the information communication are enhancement budgeting internal control, as well as establishment prompt information feedback system.

C. Redesigning Reward and Punishment System

Without a doubt, everybody is selfish. Regardless of what kind of reward and punishment system the enterprise implements, the staff members can discover the method which makes themselves benefit maximized, thus have the driving influence to create slack. But, the good reward and punishment system will consider the above factors. Through the reward and punishment system designing, the good system may make that the penalty is bigger than the earning when divisional manager creates a false budgeting, make the reward divisional manager obtained when he speaks truth is highest, thus reduce even eliminate divisional manager the power of "the irrigation", guide him to tell truth.

---

[1] Robert S.Kaplan, Anthony A.Atkinson. Advanced Management Accounting. Prentice Hall, Inc.1998(97-112).

The choice of performance measure is one of biggest challenges which the enterprise faces. The determination of measures is extremely important, and is able to decide the type of result. The measures which the enterprise chose can make the direction becoming to concrete application and mathematical quantification, turning to motion criterion of the staff in various departments and levels. After 1980's, the environment of business management has had tremendous changes, using the financial measure as the only standard to weigh the achievement of the enterprise, without a doubt, will urge the short-term behavior, also provide the power and possibility of twisting the information and creating a false budget too.

Therefore, adding the non-financial measure in the enterprise performance evaluation measure system appears extremely important. This is not only helpful to consider enterprise's logical relations between financial measure and other measures from the correct angle, but also helpful to reduce the spread of the false accounting information. Moreover, because the scope which individual manager establishes the false budgeting data is only limited to the financial measure, adding the non-financial measure in the system will decrease the important of budgeting goal to a certain extent, also will be helpful to reduce budgetary slack. Introducing the non-financial measure in performance evaluation measure system needs to utilize the management mentality of Balanced Scorecard. At this time, the budgeting target is no longer established only according to the anticipated data next year, but also needs to consider such factors, like the strategy, long-term target, and so on.

Without a doubt, one of the important reasons that divisional manager creates budgetary slack is that the level of completing budgeting measures is generally taken as the important standard of evaluating the performance of divisional manager. Based on this, this article proposes no longer taking the situation of completing the absolute data as the inspected standard, but introducing relative performance evaluation criteria. Under this kind of new evaluation criteria, not only considers the completion of budgeting measures, but also needs to consider the situation of achievement completing, compared with the other measures outside, such as the professional condition, national policy, and market condition on the budgeting year. At this time, whether budgeting measures complete will be no longer as the determining factor of the return of local manager. Thus, local manager also doesn't have the power to estimate slack. The utilization of relative performance evaluation criteria needs to consider the management mentality of Beyond Budget and Target Management.

Through the two methods, the impact of uncontrollable factors could be reduced by comparing the enterprise's performance with that of other firms in the same industry. On the basis of that, the individual managers of a enterprise whose earnings increased 20% while the industry average earnings increased 25% would not be rewarded for a good absolute but weak relative performance.

4 Conclusion

Through analyzing the questionnaire, the final conclusions can be drawn as follows: budgeting is taken more seriously, applied more extensively; in the Chinese enterprises. The individual managers are willing to participate in the management policy making process on the formulation of departmental budget, in addition, the information asymmetry is prevalent in enterprises, these two factors made the possibility of budgetary slack; The budgeting target of enterprises in china, normally keep unchanged, this factor will lead individual manager to create budgetary slack in order to reduce pressure.

To control budgetary slack could not only limit to ex ante planning stage, but also need to control through the entire process ,including mid-term controlling, and ex post evaluation stages.

References

1. Dunk, P.A.S.: Task uncertainty and its interaction with budgetary participation and budget emphasis: Some methodological issues and empirical investigation. Accounting, Organizations and Society 16(8), 693–703 (1991)
2. Rockness, H.O., Nikolai, L.A.: An Assessment of APB Voting Patterns. Journal of Accounting Research, 154–167 (Spring 1977)
3. Baiman, S.: Agency research in managerial accounting: A survey. Journal of Accounting Literature 1, 154–213 (1982)
4. Young, S.M.: Participative budgeting: The effects of risk aversion and asymmetric information on budgetary slack. Journal of Accounting Research 23(2), 829–842 (1985)
5. Lowe, E.A., Shaw, R.W.: An analysis of managerial biasing: Evidence from the company's budgeting process. Journal of Management Studies 5, 304–315 (1968)
6. Waller, W.S.: Slack in participative budgeting: The joint effect of a truth-inducing pay scheme and risk preferences. Accounting, Organizations and Society 13(1), 87–98 (1988)
7. Chenhall, R.H., Brownell, P.: The effect of participative budgeting on job satisfaction and performance: Role ambiguity as an intervening variable. Accounting, Organizations and Society 13(3), 225–233 (1988)
8. Cooper, J.C., Waller, W.S.: Participative budgeting: Effects of a truth-inducing pay scheme and information asymmetry on slack and performance. The Accounting Review 63(1), 111–122 (1988)
9. Yuen, D.C.Y.: Goal characteristics, communication and reward systems, and managerial propensity to create budgetary slack. Managerial Auditing Journal 19(4), 517–532 (2004)
10. Zhang, S., Yu, Z., Liu, Q.: The research on financial control system in enterprise group. Financial and Economical Press (2006) (in Chinese)
11. Dunk, A.S.: The effect of budget emphasis and information asymmetry on the relation between budgetary participation and slack. The Accounting Review 68(2), 400–410 (1993)

Treatment of Cr (VI) Contaminated Groundwater by PRB Simulation with Ash and Iron

Wei Zhang[1], Feng Ding[2], and Huasheng Wang[3]

[1] School of Energy and Environment Engineering, Hebei University of Technology, Tianjin, China
[2] Faculty of Architectural and Mapping Engineering, Jiangxi University of Science and Technology, Ganzhou, Jiangxi Province, China
[3] College Of Geoscience and Surveying Engineering, China University of Mining & Technology, Beijing, China
ahn888168@gmail.com

Abstract. The simulating PRB was filled with iron and fly ash, the ratio of two materials was 1:1. The groundwater contaminated by Cr (VI) was conducted by dynamic simulating test. The experiment showed that the pH was changing in the flowing water treated with simulating PRB and the water volume changes with the processing of experiment, also showed the removal ratio of Cr (VI). The testing results show when the pH of flowing water is 7-8,the effect of treated water is well. And, with the experiment is going on, the water volume is steady in a time, the removal ratio of Cr (VI) has close relationship with pH in flowing water treated by simulating PRB. As a result of Statistical data, there are great relationships between three factors which are pH in flowing water treated by simulating PRB, water volume treated by simulating PRB and the removal ratio of Cr (VI). The experiment show that PRB technology can be designed on site in right place to treat the Cr(VI) contaminated groundwater as soon as the media of PRB can be changed in time, and control the pH、 the ratio of the media.

Keywords: iron and ash, contamination of groundwater, Cr(VI), PRB.

1 Introduction

China is a country lack of groundwater.Especily in north area, overdraft of groundwater resulted from industry and agricultural water, the same time from domestic water. Groundwater contamination is one of concerns in field of environmental protection. Cr(VI) was a contaminant causing deformity、 cancer and mutation, which distributed in groundwater as forms of CrO42- and HCrO4-. And Cr(VI)has higher toxicity than Cr (III) about 100 times, at the same time , . Cr(VI) has greater migration and solubility. At present, there are two methods in controlling chromium- contaminated groundwater, which are pump-and-treat and in-situ remediation. The pump-and-treating method for the contaminated groundwater is pumping the contaminated water from the well situated at downstream of pollution plume body, and then treating and removing the contaminants dissolving in the pumping-groundwater by treatment

M. Dai (Ed.): ICCIC 2011, Part II, CCIS 232, pp. 350–356, 2011.

facilities. The pump-and-treat as a long term method for treating contaminated groundwater is not good for controlling the contaminated groundwater. Firstly, if pollution source is still existing, the method only control further spreading of the pollution, and can not remove the contaminant area.; secondly, the method need sustainable energy supply to pump the contaminated groundwater and operate the treatment facilities, which result in higher processing costs. Thirdly, long-time use of the method will result in groundwater funnel.

The permeable reactive barrier (PRB) is an in situ remediation technology where contaminated ground water is treated passively as it flows through a reactive medium. Referred as "reaction wall". PRB is filled with active materials to prevent the spreading of pollution plumes body. When the contaminated groundwater flow through the reaction zone filled with active medium, the pollutants can be degraded or fixed, which lead to groundwater quality of downstream from "reaction wall" reaching the appropriate environmental standards [1]. At present, PRB is becoming a major groundwater remediation technology, and gradually replacing the higher running costs pump–and-treat technology.

The type of PRB includes continuous treating system and funnel-channel systems, which have been widely used in practice [2]. The cheap and better active media filled in PRB is one of the key factors restricting the development of "reactive barrier", so primary research about PRB is the permeable media filled in PRB. Currently, in laboratory, usually active medias are activated carbon, zeolite, clay minerals, aluminum silicate, and phosphate, limestone, iron oxide, double-metal and microbial materials for the chemical adsorption, of which the most commonly used material is Fe(iron powder or iron filings) because of its effective absorption and degradation of heavy metals and organic pollutants.

However, the active media of PRB used in practical engineering has high demand in amount and the active media need regular replacing .economic and facilitation should be taken into account in choosing the active media of PRB.

Wei yang, Lidong Wang, etal [3] found that Cr (VI) removal rate increased with the increasing amount of Fe0 in the experimental research, at the same time, found that acidified dry fly ash has greater adsorption capacity for the Cr (VI) in static test.

Fly ash is the solid waste generated from power plant. In china, annual emissions of fly ash are more than 10,000 tons, which reach foremost in the world. Most of the fly ash pile up as waste, which not only occupy large land but also pollute atmosphere.

Using fly ash as filled media of PRB to control the pollution of groundwater is a worth exploring groundwater remediation technology.

In this paper, Iron and fly ash are filled as reactive media to control the Cr (III) contaminated groundwater, which discuss the function of the media in removing the heavy metal contaminants in groundwater.

2 Materials and Methods

A. Reactive Media Characterization and Contaminated Water Sample

As test water samples, the Cr (VI) contaminated water sample is deployed by distilled water and potassium dichromate.

The concentration of the Cr (VI) in sample water is 0.203mg/L.the Iron is the waste of mechanical factory and the fly ash is sampled from Douhe power plant. The components of filling iron and chemical composition of fly ash are as shown in table 1 and table 2, respectively. And, the effective diameter of sampled fly ash is 50um.

Table 1. The iron filling components

Component	C	Si	Mn	Other ingredients
Percentage(%)	3-3.3	1.2	0.8-1.0	1

Table 2. Chemical composition of fly ash sampled from DouHe power plant

Chemical composition	SiO_2	Al_2O_3	Fe_2O_3	CaO	MgO	SO_3	NaO	Loss of ignition
Percentage /%	55.4	27.5	8.67	2.23	1.02	1.02	0.25	2.3

B. Experimental Setup

Experiment simulates the principle of Infiltration grid, using in situ treatment of contaminated groundwater.. test water is flowing through the adsorption column made of glass tube (Φ15mm×40cm), water in container(1) flow through the tube, which has Controllable devices to control the speed of leaching water. The controllable devices of installed at the tube mainly keep the sample water in constant velocity to flow through the glass tube filled with iron and fly ash(together 5g,mass ratio is 1:1). The sample water flow through the glass tube filled with active materials , in the glass tube, the sample water react with active materials in Simulated PRB, and then, the water flow to Containers(5). The flowing speed in Simulated PRB (glass tube filled with active materials) is not contant, but the water pressure before flowing into the Simulated PRB is constant.

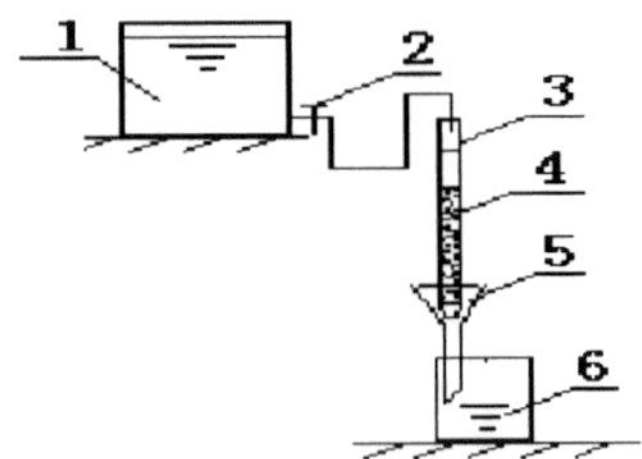

Fig. 1. The platform of dynamic simulation experiment

1.test sample 2.tube controllable water speed 3.glass tube4.reactive material 5. Funnel 6 water sample of outflow

C. Test Procedures

The simulating test conducting in platform is dynamic. The specific test is the sampled water flowing through the tube (simulating PRB) which is filled with 2.5g iron and 2.5g fly ash fixed uniformly.

The sampled water is remaining in the tube (simulating PRB) about 40 minutes. And then, when the sampled water flows out from the tube (simulating PRB), the treated water was collected every four hour to test the concentration of Cr (VI) until the concentration of Cr(VI) is below the 0.05mg/L. At the same time, the pH of every sampled water is tested, and meters the total treated water.

Using Spectrophotometry to determine the concentration of Cr (VI) in the flow water, and the removal ratio of Cr(VI) is metered.

3 Results and Discussion

A. The Change of PH in the Treatment

The change of pH can be obtained from figure2. With the experiments carried out, the pH of the water flowing out from the tube (simulating PRB) gradually changes smaller within 20 hours after the water flowing out. After 20 hours, the pH of the water flowing out from the tube (simulating PRB) is 8, the cause of which is the reacting of iron and fly ash. When iron and carbon in fly ash as an iron - carbon alloys, immersed in electrolyte solution, small iron-carbon primary batteries are formed. Iron is the anode, carbon is the cathode in iron-carbon primary batteries, and the electrode reaction occurs as follows:

In the anode:

$$Fe - 2e \rightarrow Fe^{2+};$$

$$Cr_2O_7^{2-} + 6Fe^{2+} + 14H^+ \rightarrow 2Cr^{3+} + 6Fe^{3+} + 7H_2O;$$

$$CrO_4^{2-} + 3Fe^{2+} + 8H^+ \rightarrow Cr^{3+} + 3Fe^{3+} + 4H_2O;$$

In the cathode:

$$2H^+ + 2e \rightarrow H_2;$$

$$Cr_2O_7^{2-} + 6e + 14H^+ \rightarrow 2Cr^{3+} + 7H_2O;$$

$$CrO_4^{2-} + 3e + 8H^+ \rightarrow Cr^{3+} + 4H_2O;$$

$$O_2 + 2H_2O + 4e \rightarrow 4OH^- \text{ (Alkaline, neutral)}$$

The electrochemical reaction formula shows that hydroxyl ions and trivalent chromium in cathode reaction will form hydrogen chromium. The reaction formula is as follow: $Cr^{3+} + 3OH^- \rightarrow 3Cr(OH)_3 \downarrow$. The reaction is the main causes to reduce the concentration of Cr6+ in the treated water. With occurrence of the reaction and consumption of iron, the function of the primary cell electrode reaction achieves the maximum. The weak deoxidization of fly ash and weak absorption can not promote the reaction to the concentration of Cr6+ in treated water. On the contrary, micro-cell electrode reaction (especially in the cathode) will be inhibited, which inhibits the formation of hydrogen chromium. In the reaction process of Cr^{6+}, the pH of the treated water is between 7 an 10, which is conducive to the precipitation of hydrogen chromium [7]. The fly ash has adsorption and catalysis in the process of removal of chromium contamination.

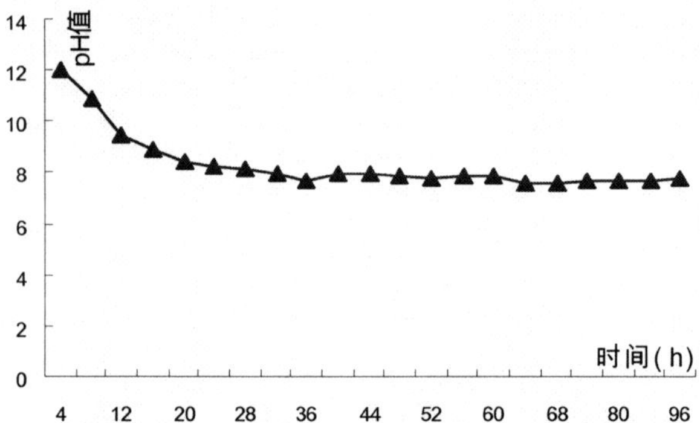

Fig. 2. The change of pH with flowing water

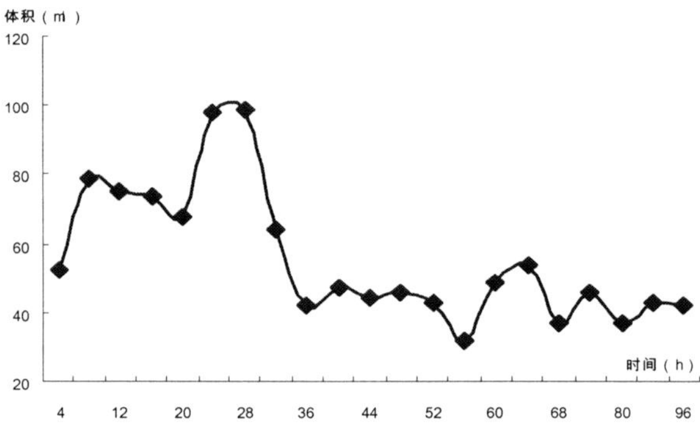

Fig. 3. The water volume changing with time

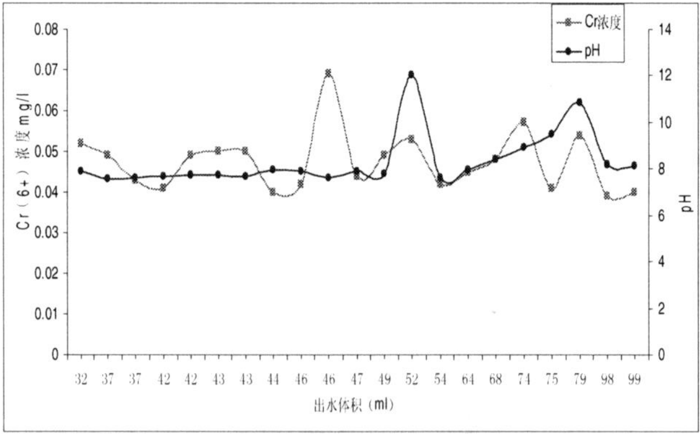

Fig. 4. The relationship between Cr6+、 pH and time of water effluent

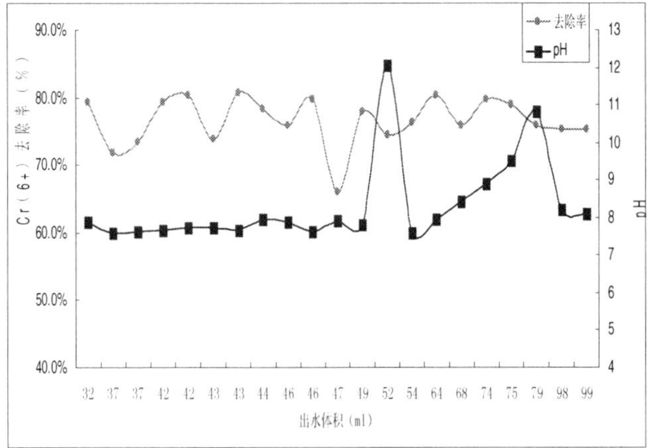

Fig. 5. Removal of Cr6 + concentration and pH with the water time

C. Water Volume Changes with Time in the Process

Seeing From figure 3, the whole processing treatment can be divided into three stages. The first stag is on the initial stage in treating the sample water. The second stag has an abrupt decline in the processing treatment. The third stage is that the water volume flowing out gradually becomes steady. On the first stage, the water volume of flowing out from the tube has an increasing tendency. And at the same time, the removal ratio of chrome has an increasing tendency, too. The figure 4 and figure 5 show the same phenomenon that the first stage is at the time 30 hours after the experiment. And as experiment is in progressing, iron in the tube (simulating PRB) is consumed, Cr (OH) 3 and Fe (OH) 3 produced in reactions are absorbed by slag-like and bead-like particles in fly ash, which resulted in lower porosity in simulating PRB. The results is that the water volume flowing out from the simulating PRB becomes stabilizing [8, 9].

The iron of reaction medium in simulating PRB has actively chemical properties and highly electronegativity with lower electrode potential and reducing power. Fe2+ has reducing power, when there is oxidants in the sampled water, Fe2 + can be further oxidized to Fe3 +., which forms the hydroxide iron with alkaline circumstance. Hydroxide iron can adsorb and flocculate the contaminants in solution.

The solution with lower pH has certain corrosion for iron. Seeing from figure 5, when the pH is 7-8, the removal ratio of Cr (VI) is 70%-80%.

4 Conclusion

A. The Following Results Concluded from the Experiment

(1) According to the redox, the pH is the main factor influencing the removal of Cr (VI).when pH is 7-8, the removal of Cr (VI) is good with 75% ratio of removing the Cr (VI).

(2) In the whole dynamic test, water flow is instability. With progressing of experiment, iron is oxidized hydroxide iron, and the medium is gradually losing the reactivity. The porosity is reduced with the forming of Cr (OH) 3 and Fe (OH) 3which result in lower flowing velocity. At this time, the media in simulating PRB should be cleared or updated.

B. Problems and Prospects

The aim of the dynamic test is simulating the effect in practical projects. The following issues need further considering.

1) Fly ash and iron have appropriate and economic proportion. And the influences of the changes of pH with composition of fly ash should be studied further. The removal mechanism of Cr (VI) resulted by the change of pH should be explored.

2) In practical application of PRB, How to install the PRB in the aquifer and how to determine processing time of the media filled in PRB are the main issues to allow water flow through the PRB under ensuring the treatment effect of groundwater.

References

1. USEPA. Pemeable reactive barrier technologies for contaminant remediation. EPA/600/R-98/125 (1998)
2. Powell, R.M., Blowes, D.W., Gillham, R.W., Schultz, D., Savages, T., Puls, R.W., Vogan, J.L., Powell, P.D., Landis, R.: Permeable Reactive Barrier Technologies for Contaminant Remediation. USEPA 1998 EPA/600/R-98/125 (September 1998)
3. Yang, W., Wang, L.-d., Xu, L., et al.: Experiment on Selection of PRB Media and Remediation of Chromium Contaminated Groundwater. Journal of Jilin University (Earth Science Edition) 38(5), 854–858 (2008)
4. Xia, C.b.: A study on the adsorption of toxic p-nitro phenol on impregnated fly ash. Environmental Science And Technology (3), 35 (2000)
5. Li, L., Zhu, Q., Xu, Y.-h., et al.: Advances in the Research on Wastewater Treatment Processes Using Fly ash. Fly Ash Comprehensive Utilization (4), 54–56 (2006)
6. Zhou, Q.-x., et al.: Application of Nanometer Zero-valent Iron in the Environmental Remediation. Journal of Anhui Agricultural Sciences 36(1), 283–284 (2008)
7. Ji, G.-j., Zhao, Y.-S.: Remediation of chromium contaminated groundwater by powered iron and fly ash. Ecology and Environment 15(3), 499–502 (2006)
8. Liu, F.-L.: Study on Removal of Cr(VI) with Zero-Valent Iron in Aqueous Solution. Lanzhou University (2010)
9. Guerin, T.F., Horner, S., McGovern, T., et al.: An application of permeable reactive barrier technology to petroleum hydrocarbon contaminated groundwater. Water Research 36(1), 15–24 (2002)

Study on Effective Elastic Thickness of Longmenshan Fault Zone after the Wenchuan Earthquake

Zedan Tao[1] and Xiwei Wu[2]

[1] College of Marine Geosciences, Ocean University of China, 238 Songling Road, Laoshan, Qingdao, Shandong, China
[2] Department of Agriculture and Plant Protection, Qingdao Agricultural University, 700 Changcheng Road, Chengyang, Qingdao, Shandong, China
Hakeemmo123@gmail.com

Abstract. After the Wenchuan Earthquake, the lithosphere structure of the Longmenshan fault zone was inevitable influenced by the earthquake. According to the interpretation of the topographic elevation and the gravity data of two line acrossing Longmenshan frault zone, we can research effective elastic thickness of the lithosphere and the flexure of the Moho. Finally we got that the effective elastic thickness of the northern Longmenshan fault is between 25 and 40km, and around the earthquake zone in the south, the effective elastic thickness was obviously thicker to between 35 and 70km.Bounded by the Longmenshan fault, the effective elastic thickness of the Tibetan Plateau in the west is smaller than the Sichuan Basin in the east.

Keywords: Terms- Wenchuan Earthquake, Longmenshan fault zone, effective elastic thickness.

1 Introduction

On May 12, 2008, in 31.0 degrees north latitude and 103.4 degrees occurred in Wenchuan of Sichuan province 8.0 magnitude earthquake[1].

The Main cause of the earthquake is the Indian plate subduct beneath Eurasian plate causing rapid uplift of the Tibetan Plateau and material continue to flow to the east. While the Longmenshan fault zone locates in the front of the of the material transporting and blocked by the South China block area, the compression was accumulated with strong and finally suddenly released in the Yingxiu area of the Longmenshan fault[2]. Since the earthquake had such a big structure change, so will inevitably lead to form the ground floor of the lithosphere changes. Furthermore ,the uneven compensation balance of the eastern Tibetan Plateau result in the Longmen Shan region continue to move. So the re-calculation of the effective elastic thickness in the Longmenshan fault after Wenchuan Earquake is Essentially important[3].

The elastic effective thickness of lithosphere is an emphasis of lithosphere dynamics, the ultimate key research is to solve geological problems. So it's the combination of geology and geophysics. Bouguer gravity anomalies contains a wealth of information within the earth[4]. Using Bouguer gravity anomalies and topographic

M. Dai (Ed.): ICCIC 2011, Part II, CCIS 232, pp. 357–363, 2011.

elevation data to calculate the effective elastic thickness of lithosphere based on the equilibrium model is the main computing means.

2 Tectonic History of the Longmenshan Fault Zone

The Longmenshan fault zone located in northeast of Tibet plateau is a famous overthrust fault zone and NE-SW distribution(Fig.1)[5]. It extends about 500km in length and 30km in width, the average elevation is about 3500m and has a big gradient in the fault terrain. It is one of the important activities of earthquake. The northwest is the Tibetan Plateau thin mantle zone while the southeast is the Sichuan Basin thin crust and mantle. There is a steep Moho for the west slopeof the change from the Longmenshan foreland basin to the west plateau. It shows that the Longmenshan fault zone slope to the west, lack of mountain root and it's a independent tectonic load system[6].

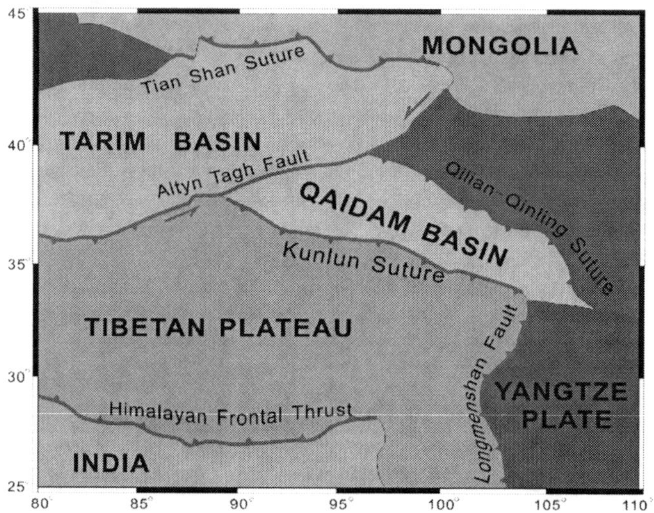

Fig. 1. The plate of the research zone. The red lines show the main fault zone in the study area and it is also the boundary of the plate.

3 The Data and Technology

Current calculation of lithosphere effective elastic thickness methods include Response Function, Correlation and Forward method The first two belong to spectral analysis method. Here to consider the use of Bouguer gravity data constrained inversion calculation of lithosphere effective elastic thickness.

In order to calculate the lithosphere effective elastic thickness of the Longmenshan fault zone after the Wenchuan Earthquake accurately, the data we used must have higher accuracy. For the sake of research the effective elastic thickness of the Longmenshan fault zone clearly, we selected the range of latitude 25 o -35 o N and

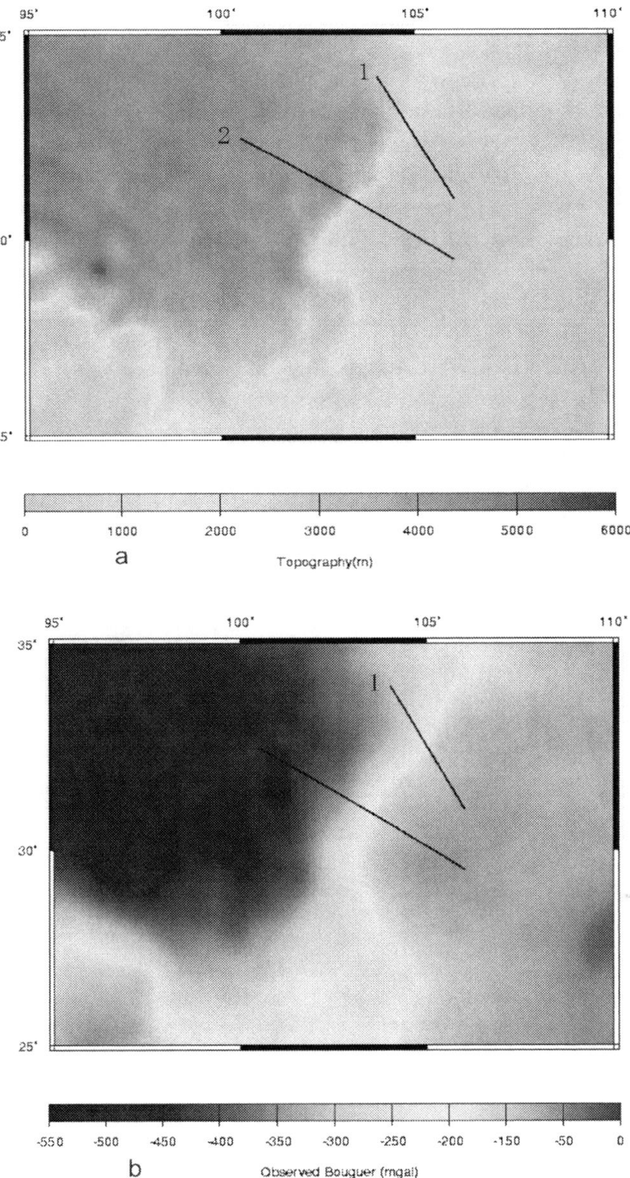

Fig. 2. is the actual measurement of the topography and the Bouguer gravity anomaly contour map. We can see from the chart(Fig.2_a) that the topography range of the research region is about 300m-5000m, decreasing from the northwest to the southeast. The corresponding gravity anomaly(Fig.2_b) changes from -100mgal to -400mgal, this is well reflected in the topography and Bouguer gravity anomalies corresponding relationship between the images.

longitude 95∘-110∘E, also chose the two survey lines across the Longmenshan fault zone as the profile of our study .They are line 1 and line 2 (Fig.2).

In the process of the effective elastic thickness calculation, we need to choose appropriate research model. But it is impossible to establish a fully same model to the actual condition. So we try to simplify the model with the premise of ensuring the accuracy. Moho is the first rank velocity interface of the lithosphere, and is also the biggest interface of density. we can use gravity data to calculate the depth of the Moho. The tectonic form can reflect on the deformation characteristics of upper mantle directly.

This paper used a 2d flexure model of spatial domain to calculate the lithosphere effective elastic thickness of the Longmenshan fault zone. Due to the flexure problem of the land lithosphere is more complex than the ocean crust, we set the rigidity is lateral variation[7].

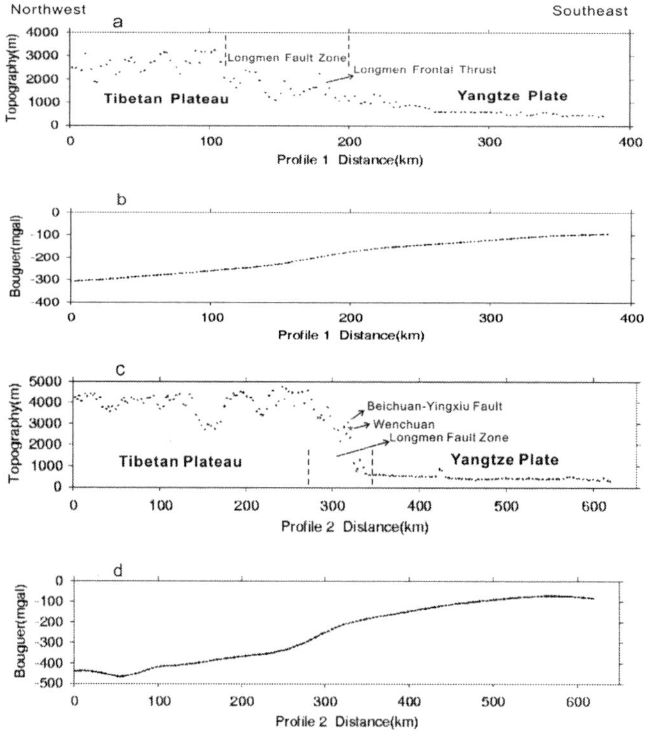

Fig. 3. is the topography and Bouguer gravity anomaly observation map of the two line. Line 1(Fig. 3a and 3b) the elevation is from 3500m gradually reduce to 400m from the northeast to southwest with an average height of 2500m. The survey lines within the relatively moderate and the Bouguer gravity anomaly curves are relatively moderate too. Line 2(Fig.3c and Fig 3d), from the northeast to southwest, the elevation gradually decrease from 5000m to 300m and the average height is 3500m. It has a steep terrain compared to line 1 and has larger degree steep terrain in the Longmenshan fault zone. Fig.3d show that the area that line across has dramatic changes in the Bouguer gravity anomaly and has image corresponds to the dramatic changes in the topography.

4 The Effective Elastic Thickness Calculation of the Two Line Some Common Mistakes

2d spatial domain flexure model fully consider the lateral non-uniformity rigidity of the continental lithosphere compared with the ocean lithosphere. We use the altitude data and the boundary conditions of Airy equilibrium model to calculate the flexure of the lithosphere and use the gravity calculated by Talwani formula to restrain the model parameters. Iteratively, until we get the effective elastic thickness of lithosphere to satisfy that the differences of the measured gravity anomaly and the theory of gravity anomalies reach the minimum[8].

Line 1 use Airy model and the single continuous variable elastic plate model using two-dimensional spatial domain model to calculate. Iteration to the end. From Fig.4c, we can see that the Bouguer gravity anomaly calculated by the Airy model has large difference with the observed Bouguer gravity anomaly. So Airy model can't interpretation the observed Bouguer gravity anomaly well. While the Bouguer gravity anomaly calculated by the single continuous variable elastic plate model meet to the observed Bouguer gravity anomaly. Obviously it can well reflect the lithosphere flexure of the Longmenshan fault zone.

From the Fig.4_c, we can see that the crust thickness decreases along line 1. But the change is not very big, this is just the vivid reflection that the topography of line 2 is more steep than line 1.There is a minimum point in about 150km distance, the depth is about 38km. Within the range of 200-400km, the curve is gentle, this is relational to the gentle topography and Bouguer gravity anomaly in the northwest of the Yangtze plate. Therefore, the Moho is lateral flat within the area.

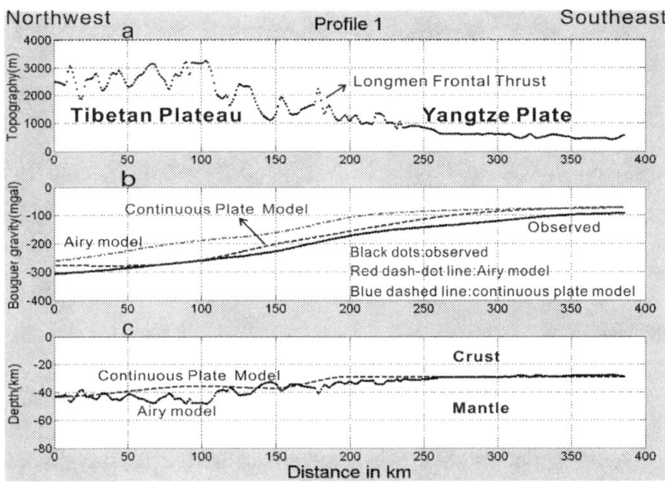

Fig. 4. Gravity modeling along the line 1.(a)Topography. (b) Observed Bouguer gravity anomalies (Black dots), predicted gravity from the Airy assumption (Red dash-dot line), a continuous elastic plate (Blue dashed line). (c) Depth model showing the deflection of the Moho from the Airy and continuous plate models.

In Fig.5 the theory gravity calculated by the single continuous elastic plate model can't meet the demand of precision. So we consider using broken plate model and Airy model to calculate the effective elastic thickness of line 2. From the Fig.5_b, we can see that the Bouguer gravity anomaly calculated by the Airy model has large difference with the observed Bouguer gravity anomaly, while the Bouguer gravity anomaly calculated by the broken plate model is exactly meet the observed Bouguer gravity anomaly. Therefore, the broken plate model can be used to calculate the effective elastic thickness accurately for line 2.

From the Fig.5_c, we can get that the lithosphere effective elastic thickness tends to decrease from northwest to southeast along line 2. The thickness decreases from 70km to 35km. The change range of Moho depth is much lager than line 1. This appearance is correlated with the larger topography steep than line 1. Similarly the topography gradually reach smooth after get into the stability of the Yangtze plate.

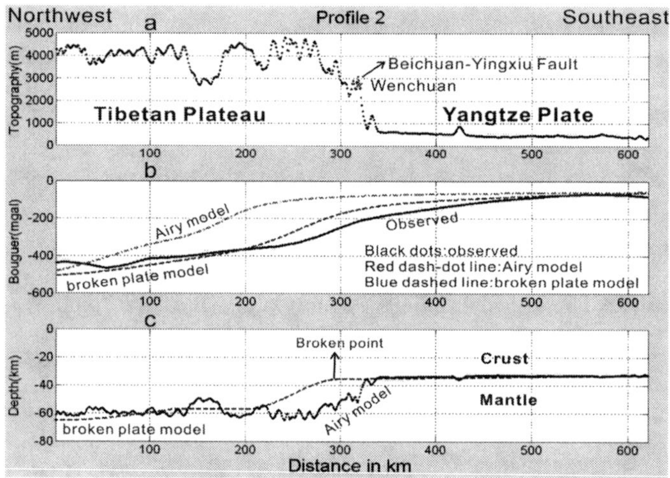

Fig. 5. Gravity modeling along the line 2.(a)Topography. (b) Observed Bouguer gravity anomalies (Black dots), predicted gravity from the Airy assumption (Red dash-dot line), a broken elastic plate (Blue dashed line). (c) Depth model showing the deflection of the Moho from the Airy and broken plate models[9].

5 Conclusion

With the calculation results by using 2d flexure equation of Longmenshan fault zone around the two line, we can get a conclusion: the topography in the north part of the Longmenshan fault is flat, with the lithosphere effective elastic thickness between 25km and 40km.The fault only occurred above the Moho, it didn't deep into the mantle. The area is mainly dominated by thin-skinned nappe structure. It is maybe due to the extrusion stress derived from the clockwise motion of the South China plate. The south part of the Longmenshan fault zone has steep topography and large gradient. The change range of Moho depth is large. The lithosphere effective elastic thickness is between 35km and 70km. The fault in the Wenchuan area doesn't only affect the thin-skinned crust of the Sichuan basin, but also affect the upper mantle. The effective elastic thickness of Longmenshan fault zone is bounded by the Longmenshan fault, decreasing from Tibetan Plateau to the Sichuan basin.

Acknowledgment. I would like to extend my sincere gratitude to my supervisor Xiaodian Jiang for her instructive advice and useful suggestions on my thesis.We thank her for providing us with laboratory equipment and technical guidance. All the persons involved in the research projects are thanked for their help.

References

1. Xue, Y., Liu, J., Mei, S., Song, Z.: Characteristics of seismic activity before 2008 Wenchuan M_S8.0 earthquake. Acta Seismologica Sinica 31(6) (November 2009)
2. Chen, Z.: Discussions on origin of Wenchuan earthquake and its continental quake dynamic source. Jiangsu Geology 32(2), 81–85 (2008)
3. Duan, H., Zhang, Y., Liu, F.: Study of the Gravity Variance in Chinese Mainland before and after Wenchuan Earthquake with GRACE Gravity Models. Journal of Seismological Research 32(3) (July 2009)
4. Du, X., Meng, L., Zhang, M.: Research on Fault Distribution and Tectonic Divisions in Northeast China in Terms of Gravity Field. Journal of Earth Sciences and Environment 31(2) (June 2009)
5. Li, C., Song, F., Ran, Y.: Late Quaternary Activity and Age Constraint of the Northern Longmenshan Fault Zone. Seismology and Geology 26(2) (June 2004)
6. Li, Y., Huang, R., Zhou, R.: Geological Background of Longmenshan Seismic Belt and Surface Ruptures in Wenchuan Earthquake. Journal of Engineering Geology 17(1) (2009)
7. Gao, H., Gai, Y.: Lithospheric Deformation Features in the Northeastern Edge of the Tibetan Plateau Obtained from Gravity Data. Periodical of Ocean University of China 36 (sup.) (December 2006)
8. Jiang, X., Jin, Y., McNutt, M.K.: Lithospheric deformation beneath the Altyn Tagh and West Kunlun faults from recent gravity surveys. Journal of Geophysical Research 109 (2004)
9. Jin, Y., Jiang, X.: Lithosphere Dynamics, pp. 59–96 (2002)

Optimization for Mix Design of High-Performance Concrete Using Orthogonal Test

Li Xiaoyong and Ma Wendi

College of Architecture, North China University of Technology, Beijing 100144, China
sivajich2323@yahoo.cn

Abstract. The paper presents a optimum approach to design concrete mixtures. It is based upon a set of tests relating composition and engineering properties of concrete use orthogonal method to identify the main influencing factors in mix ratio on compressive strength of concrete. Some of the raw materials of test are portland cement and fly ash. The effect factors are fly ash, water-cement ratio, water consumption, admixture. Every factor is at three levels. The array chosen was the L9(34) which has 9 rows corresponding to the number of tests. The results indicated that the effect of fly ash on concrete strength changes with time. The water cement ratio has important influence on both early and late CS. The optimal mix ratios for compressive strength of both 7 days and 28 days were achieved. This approach is illustrated through the design of a special high-performance concrete for road application.

Keywords: High-performance concrete, Orthogonal test, Mix design, Optimization.

1 Introduction

Nowadays, high-performance concretes (HPCs) are extensively applied in construction projects [1 and 2]. This new advanced concrete has been transferred from laboratory research to practical application; and it already occupies a noticeable share of the market. Based on the latest developments in concrete technology, HPC is characterized by a superior level of properties: workability, strength and durability. These advantages provided large-scale cost savings in many construction projects.

The parts of the world in which large-scale concrete construction takes place have extended enormously. Due to the recent trends in construction industries, construction of large and taller structures, and developments of construction techniques, the industries and companies in general strive to cast massive volume of concrete. When this large volume of concrete is used for construction, the safety and durability of cast concrete become fundamental issues. To ensure these issues, much effort has been focused on the developments of high-performance concrete [1, 2, 3, 4, 5, 6, 7, 8, 9 and 10].

High-performance concrete is designed to give optimized performance characterristics for a given set of materials, usage, and exposure conditions, consistent with strength, workability, service life, and durability. Engineers and constructors all over

M. Dai (Ed.): ICCIC 2011, Part II, CCIS 232, pp. 364–372, 2011.

the world are finding that using high-performance concrete allows them to build more serviceable structures at comparable cost. High-performance concrete is being used for structures in aggressive environments: marine structures, highway bridges and pavements, nuclear structures, tunnels, precast units, etc. [11 and 12].

The selection of mix proportions is the process of choosing suitable ingredients of concrete and determining their relative quantities with the object of producing as economically as possible concrete of certain minimum properties, notably strength, durability, and a required consistency [13]. Because the ingredients used are essentially variable and many of the material properties cannot be assessed truly quantitatively, selecting proportions for concrete can also be defined as the process of finding the optimum combination of these ingredients on the basis of some empirical data as stated in relevant standards, experience, and some rules of thumb [14].

The major difference between conventional concrete and high-performance concrete is essentially the use of chemical and mineral admixtures. The use of chemical admixtures reduces the water content, thereby at the same time reduces the porosity within the hydrated cement paste. The reduction in the water content to a very low value with high dosage of chemical admixtures is undesirable, and the effectiveness of chemical admixtures such as superplasticizer principally depends on the ambient temperature, cement chemistry, and fineness. Mineral admixtures, also called as cement replacement materials, act as pozzolanic materials as well as fine fillers; thereby, the microstructure of hardened cement matrix becomes denser and stronger. At ambient temperature, their chemical reaction with calcium hydroxide is generally slow. However, the finer and more vitreous the pozzolan is, the faster will be this reaction. If durability is of primary interest, then the slow rate of setting and hardening associated with the incorporation of fly ash or slag in concrete is advantageous. Also, the mineral admixtures are generally industrial by-products and their use can provide a major economic benefit. Thus, the combined use of superplasticizer and cement replacement materials can lead to economical high-performance concrete with enhanced strength, workability, and durability. It is also reported that the concrete containing cement replacement materials typically provides lower permeability[15], reduced heat of hydration, reduced alkali–aggregate reaction, higher strength at later ages, and increased resistance to attack from sulfates. However, the effect of cement replacement materials on the performance of concrete varies markedly with their properties.

Concrete mix design involves complicated issues, and the correct ways to perform this can be achieved with experts' advice and experience [16]. Mix design of High Performance Concrete (HPC) is more complicated because HPC includes more materials, like superplasticizer and supplementary cementitious materials. In addition, maintaining a low water-binder ratio with adequate workability makes the design process more complicated. Traditionally, experienced civil engineers, largely based on their experiential knowledge, do the job of mix design [17]. However, experts are not always available, nor do they always have time to consult all possible references, review available data, and so on. Some companies do not have personnel with the experience to make necessary decisions regarding concrete mix design. The conventional computer programs are useful only in manipulating the numerical data and providing mathematical reasoning for the final selection. They lack the intuitive reasoning based on heuristic knowledge such as experience and rules of thumb [18 and 19]. Many factors influence concrete mix design, and their mutual relationship is so complicated that it is impossible to formulate mathematical models to express their mutual actions and reactions [20, 21, 22, 23 and 24]. In addition, adjustments of trial mixes are always performed by taking into account the information from concrete quality tests, experts' advice and experience. It is believed that the problem of mix design and adjustment of HPC can be alleviated if the engineer's knowledge can be augmented with some ‘expert system’ for affirming his judgment.

This paper describes a optimization of mix design. The purposes were to improve the process of selecting and proportioning HPC constituents and to make the knowledge of HPC easily available to the concrete industry. It is also capable of diagnosing causes of mix performance failure and giving recommendations on corresponding performance adjustment.

2 Taguchi's Techniques

Taguchi's techniques have been used widely in engineering analysis. The techniques of Taguchi consist of a plan of experiments with the objective of acquiring data in a controlled way, executing these experiments, in order to obtain information about the behaviour of a given process. After the completion of the experiment the data from all the experiments in the set are analysed to determine the effect of the various design parameters. Conducting Taguchi experiments in terms of orthogonal arrays allows the effects of several parameters to be determined efficiently and is an important technique in robust design. The treatment of the experimental results is based on the analysis average and the analysis of variance (ANOVA) [12 and 13].

3 Experimental Procedure

A. Materials

Normal portland cement (NPC) and fly ash (FA) were used in the experimental program. The portland cement was characterized by the following Bogue's composition: C_3S—64%, C_2S—14%, C_3A—4%, and C_4AF—14%. The FA was composed of glassy microspherical particles with a diameter of 0.1–0.2 μm. The physical properties of the cement are shown in Table 1, the chemical analysis of the cement is shown in Table 2 and the technical indexes of fly ash is shown in Table 3. Crushed granite with a maximum size of 20 mm and specific gravity 2.69 was used as a coarse aggregate. Locally available natural sand with a fineness modulus of 1.96 and a specific gravity of 2.63 was used as a fine aggregate.

Table 1. Physical Properties of Cement

Content	Normal portland cement
Surface area (m^2/kg)	350
Specific gravity (kg/m^3)	3.15
Setting time (h:min)	
Initial	2:20
Final	3:50
Compressive strength (MPa)	
1 day	15.5
3 days	35.1
7 days	45.2
28 days	55.4

Table 2. Chemical Analysis of Cement

Content	Normal portland cement
SiO_2	4.87
Al_2O_3	4.91
CaO	66.9
MgO	0.42
Na_2O	0.15
K_2O	0.14
SO_3	4.05

Table 3. Technical Indexes of Fly Ash

Content	Technical indexes
Degree of fineness	7.6
Water demand	92
loss on ignition.	0.93
water content	0.16
sulfur trioxide	0.65
chloride ion	0.013
alkali content	1.07

B. Plan of Experiments

For the elaboration of experiments plan we used the method of Taguchi for four factors at three levels. By levels we mean the values taken by the factors. Table 4 indicates the factors to be studied and the assignment of the corresponding levels.

The array chosen was the $L_9(3^4)$ which has 9 rows corresponding to the number of tests, as shown in Table 5. The factors and the interactions are assigned to the columns.

Table 4. Assignment of Levels to Factors

Level	Factor			
	A	B	C	D
	Fly ashto mixe quantity (%)	Water-cement ratio	Water consumption (kg/m^3)	Admixture to mix quantity (%)
1	15	0.3	135	1.0
2	20	0.32	150	1.5
3	30	0.35	162	2.0

Table 5. Orthogonal Array $L_9(3^4)$

Test	A	B	C	D
1	1	1	1	1
2	1	2	2	2
3	1	3	3	3
4	2	1	2	3
5	2	2	3	1
6	2	3	1	2
7	3	1	3	2
8	3	2	1	3
9	3	3	2	1

C. Results of Experiments

The responses to be studied are the compressive strength (CS). The tests were replicated, resulting in a total of 9 tests, to allow the analysis of the variance of the results. The orthogonal arrays to obtain CS may be observed in Table 6 and Figure 1.

Table 6. Orthogonal Test Results $L_9(3^4)$

Test number	Compressive strength for 7day (MPa)	Compressive strength for 28day (MPa)	Slump (mm)
1	52.4	61.5	161
2	50.8	63.7	184
3	37.6	58.9	195
4	46.8	65.4	176
5	43.9	67.8	186
6	35.1	54.8	174
7	38.9	59.4	182
8	32.8	56.8	195
9	33.6	52.7	164

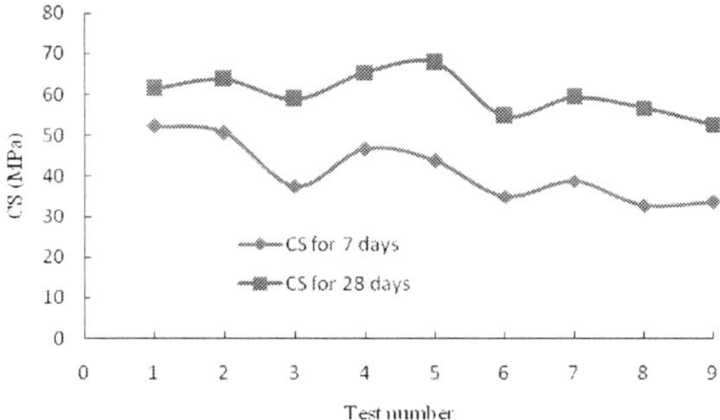

Fig. 1. Compressive strength

4 Analysis of Experimental Results

A. Range Analysis

The sum of compressive strength of 7 days and 28 days for same level is seen in Table 7 and Table 8 respectively. The mean and extreme difference of compressive strength of 7 days and 28 days for same level is seen in Table 9 and Table 10 respectively. Extreme difference of compressive strength of 7 days and 28 days for same level is seen in figure 2 and figure 3 respectively.

Table 7. Compressive strength statistics for 7 days

Factor	Sum for level 1	Sum for level 2	Sum for level 3
A	140.8	125.8	105.3
B	138.1	127.5	106.3
C	120.3	131.2	120.4
D	129.9	124.8	117.2

Table 8. Compressive Strength Statistics for 28 Days

Factor	Sum for level 1	Sum for level 2	Sum for level 3
A	184.1	188	168.9
B	186.3	188.3	166.4
C	173.1	181.8	186.1
D	182	177.9	181.1

Table 9. Mean of compressive strength statistics for 7 days

Factor	Mean for level 1	Mean for level 2	Mean for level 3	Extreme difference
A	46.9	41.9	35.1	11.8
B	46.0	42.5	35.4	10.6
C	40.1	43.7	40.1	3.6
D	43.3	41.6	39.1	4.2

Table 10. Mean of Compressive Strength Statistics for 28 Days

Factor	Mean for level 1	Mean for level 2	Mean for level 3	Extreme difference
A	61.4	62.7	56.3	6.4
B	62.1	62.8	55.5	7.3
C	57.7	60.6	62.0	4.3
D	60.7	59.3	60.4	1.4

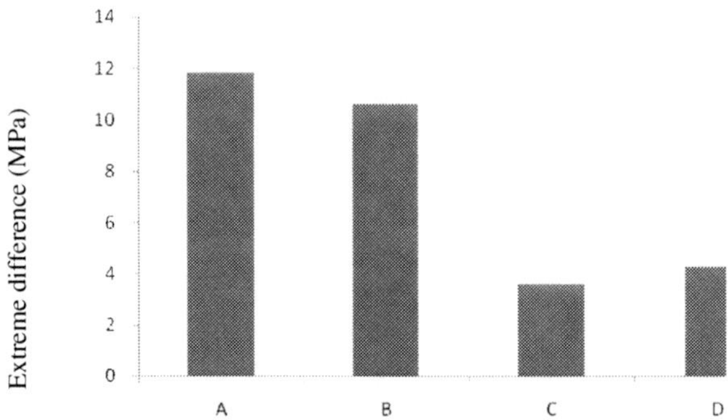

Fig. 2. Extreme difference for 7 days

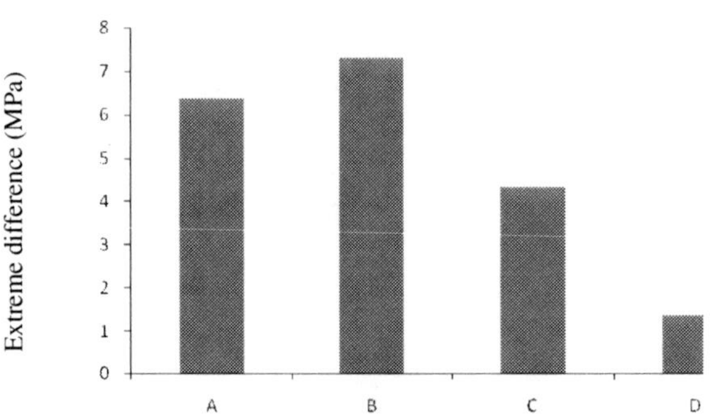

Fig. 3. Extreme difference for 28 days

Table 11. Variance Analysis for CS of 7 Days

Variance originates	Sum of squares	Freedom degree	Variance	F ratio	Remarkable
A	231.5	2	115.8	11.6	*
B	163.1	2	81.6	8.2	
C	19.9	2	9.9		
D	29.5	2	14.6	1.5	

Table 12. Variance Analysis for CS of 28 Days

Variance originates	Sum of squares	Freedom degree	Variance	F ratio	Remarkable
A	61.5	2	30.8	10.7	*
B	158.6	2	79.1	27.5	**
C	12.7	2	6.5	2.2	
D	5.8	2	2.9		

B. Variance Analysis

Variance analysis for CS of 7 days and 28 days is seen in Table XI and Table XII respectively. The critical value, $F_{0.1}(2,2)=9.0$, $F_{0.05}(2,2)=19.0$, $F_{0.01}(2,2)=99.0$.

5 Conclusions

The effect of fly ash on concrete strength changes with time. The activity of fly ash is little for the CS in 7 days, so its strength is provided by the cement. The activity of fly ash has some for the CS in 28 days, the compressive strength first increases and then decreases with fly ash content increasing.

The water cement ratio has important influence on both early and late CS. The object strength can be achieved by controlling water cement ratio. The low water cement ratio tries to be used to achieve the early strength.

Based on range and variance analysis, the optimal mix ratio for compressive strength of 7 days is $A_1B_1D_1C_2$, ie fly ash 16.3%, water cement ratio 0.3, water 149kg/m^3, additive content 1.2%; the optimal mix ratio for compressive strength of 28 days is $B_2A_2C_2D_1$, ie fly ash 20%, wate cement ratio 0.33, water 149kg/m^3, additive content 1.2%.

Acknowledgment. The works was provided financial aid by Youth Focus on Fund in North China University of Technology and Funding Project for Academic Human Resources Development in Institutions of Higher Learning under the Jurisdiction of Beijing Municipality (PHR 20110868).

References

1. de Larrard, F.: A method for proportioning high-strength concrete mixtures. Cement Concr. Aggr. 12(2), 47–52 (1990); View Record in Scopus | Cited By in Scopus (18)
2. Gutierrez, P.A., Canovas, M.F.: High-performance concrete: requirements for constituent materials and mix proportioning method. ACI Mater. J. 3, 233–241 (1996); View Record in Scopus | Cited By in Scopus (19)
3. Sobolev, K.G., Soboleva, S.V.: High strength concrete mix design and properties optimization, concrete technology in developing countries. In: Proceedings of the 4th International Conference, Famagusta, TRNC, pp. 189–202 (1996)
4. Kasperkiewicz, J.: Optimization of concrete mix using a spreadsheet package. ACI Mater. J. 6, 551–559 (1994)
5. Dewar, J.D.: A concrete laboratory in a computer-case-studies of simulation of laboratory trial mixes. In: ERMCO-1995, Proceedings of the XIth European Ready Mixed Concrete Congress, Istanbul, pp. 185–193 (1995)

6. Islam, M.N., Al-Mattarneh, H.M.A., Zain, M.F.M., Basri, H.B.: Towards an expert system for HPC mix design. In: Proceedings of the World Conference on Concrete Materials and Structures, Shah Alam, Malaysia (May 2002)
7. Malasri, S., Maldonado, S.: Concrete mix designer. Comp. Appl. Conc. Tech., ACI SP113-3, 33–41 (1988)
8. Islam, M.N., Al-Mattarneh, H.M.A., Zain, M.F.M., Basri, H.B.: Expert systems and concrete mix design: a review. In: Proceedings of the Sixth International Conference on Concrete Technology For Developing Countries, Amman, Jordan (October 2002)
9. Malier, Y. (ed.): High performance concrete: from material to structure. E and FN Spon, London (1992)
10. Shah, S.P., Ahmad, S.H. (eds.): High performance concrete and applications. Edward Arnold, London (1994)
11. Nawy, E.G.: Fundamentals of high strength high performance concrete. Longman Group Limited, London (1996)
12. Aitcin, P.C.: High-performance concrete. E and FN Spon, London (1998)
13. Safiuddin, M.: Influence of different curing methods on the mechanical properties and durability of HPC exposed to medium temperature. MSc Thesis, Universiti Kebangsaan Malaysia (1998)
14. Day, K.W.: Concrete mix design, quality control and specification, 2nd edn. E and FN SPON, London (1999)
15. ACI Committee 211. Standard practice for selecting proportions for normal, heavyweight, and mass concrete (ACI 211.1-91). American Concrete Institute, Detroit (1991)
16. ACI Committee 363. State-of-the-art report on high-strength concrete (ACI 363R-92). American Concrete Institute, Detroit (1992)
17. ACI Committee 211. Guide for selecting proportions for high strength concrete with Portland cement and fly ash (ACI 211.4R-93). American Concrete Institute, Detroit (1993)
18. ACI Committee 201. Guide to durable concrete. ACI Manual of Concrete Practice: Part 1 (ACI 201.2R-92). American Concrete Institute, Detroit (1995)
19. de Larrard, F.: A method for proportioning high-strength concrete mixtures. Cem. Conc. Agg. 12(2), 47–52 (1990); Mehta, P.K., Aitcin, P.C.: Principles underlying production of high-performance concrete. Cem. Conc. Agg. 12(2), 70–78 (1990)
20. Rougeron, P., Aitcin, P.C.: Optimisation of the composition of high-performance concrete. Cem. Conc. Agg. 16(2), 115–124 (1994)
21. Mehta, P.K., Aitcin, P.C.: Microstructural basis of selection of materials and mix proportions for high-strength concrete. In: Proceedings Of The One-Day Short Course On Concrete Technology/HPC: Properties and Durability. University Malaya, Kuala Lumpur (1997)
22. Taya, M., Arsenault, R.: Metal Matrix Composites, pp. 1–9. Pergamon Press, Oxford (1989)
23. Clyne, T., Withers, P.: An Introduction to Metal Matrix Composites. Cambridge Solid State Science Series, pp. 1–10 (1995)
24. Chadwick, G.A., Heat, P.: Machining metal matrix composites. Met. Mater. 6, 73–76 (1990)

First Order Dynamic Sliding Mode Control for Wheeled Mobile Robots

Da Lingrong[1] and Tian Zhixiang[2]

[1] 723 Institute, China Shipbuilding Industry Corporation, Yangzhou, Jiangsu Province, China
[2] College of Mechanical Engineering, Nanjing University of Aeronautics and Astronautics, Nanjing, Jiangsu Province, China

Abstract. Based on the sliding mode variable structure control theory, a first order dynamic sliding mode control algorithm is proposed for a nonholonomic wheeled mobile robot system. In this paper, a new switching function which related to the derivative of the control input is designed by modified conventional sliding mode control switching function using differential block, and the dynamic sliding mode control algorithm transfers the discontinuous input terms into the derivative terms that can reduce the chattering of the system. The Lyapunov function and the exponential approximation law using saturation function instead of sign function which also can reduce the chattering are used and combined with the first order dynamic sliding mode control algorithm the control law of the wheeled mobile robot is derived. Finally, the control law is designed and simulated by the proposed algorithm for the wheeled mobile robot, and the simulation results show that the first order dynamic sliding mode control algorithm can make the system convergence fast and also can reduce the chattering of the system that caused by the characteristic of the sliding mode control.

Keywords: sliding mode variable structure control, dynamic sliding mode control, nonholonomic, wheeled mobile robot.

1 Introduction

In recent years, the development direction of the wheeled mobile robot is miniaturization, intelligence, high speed and so on, and its stabilization of control and trajectory tracking problem become more and more concerned and a hot research area. As the velocity constraints between the wheel of the wheeled mobile robot and the ground are non-integrable that is nonholonomic constraints, the wheeled mobile robot system does not exist smooth or continuous time invariant static state feedback and satisfy Brockett[1] necessary condition for smooth feedback stabilization, that makes the trajectory tracking of the wheeled mobile robot is much more difficult than general nonlinear control systems. Appeared in the 1950s, the sliding mode variable structure control become a new design method for linear and nonlinear systems,

M. Dai (Ed.): ICCIC 2011, Part II, CCIS 232, pp. 373–381, 2011.

continuous and discrete systems and certain and uncertain systems. The difference between the sliding mode control and other control methods is that the structure of the sliding mode control is not fixed but changing with the current state of the system in the dynamic process and forcing the system move according to the predetermined trajectory. The design of the sliding surface has nothing to do with the disturbance and object parameters that make the sliding mode control method have fast response, insensitivity to parameter changes and disturbances, no parameter identification and simple physical realization[2]. But the disadvantage of the sliding mode control is that when the phase trajectory of the control system reaches the sliding surface, due to the inertia and other factors, the phase trajectory is difficult to move along the sliding surface stably, but sliding back and forth on both sides of the sliding surface which produces chattering problem. For such shortcomings, it is easy to activate the unmodeled characteristics of the system, thus affecting the performance of the entire control system. In this paper, the trajectory tracking of the wheeled mobile robot is studied, and established the kinematic model of the nonholonomic wheeled mobile robot and proposed a first order dynamic sliding mode control[3] method to implement the trajectory tracking for the wheeled mobile robot.

2 Kinematic Model of Wheeled Mobile Robot

In this paper, the three wheeled mobile robot with two wheeled differential drive is studied. The front wheel is a universal wheel, and the two rear wheels each have a motor independently which through the differential of the rear wheels to achieve steering. The front wheel only plays a supportive role, neither steering nor driving the robot, so it can be ignored in the kinematic model. The structure is shown in Fig.1

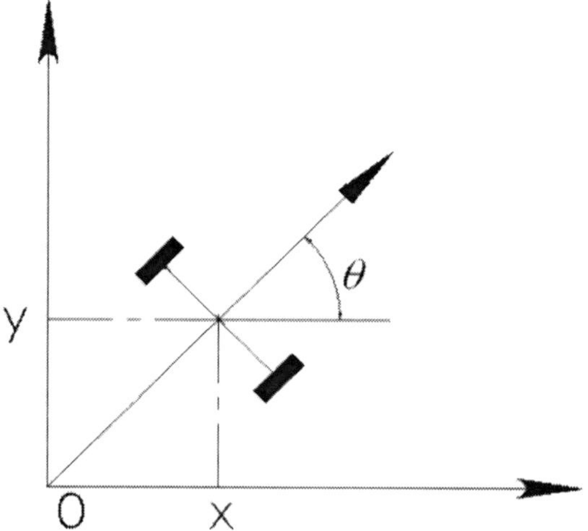

Fig. 1. Wheeled mobile robot

θ denotes the angle between the move direction of the wheeled mobile robot and the axis X, expressed as a course. The coordinate (x,y) is the midpoint of the two driving wheel axis. The kinamatic equations of mobile robot are as follows:

$$\boldsymbol{p} = \begin{pmatrix} \dot{x} \\ \dot{y} \\ \dot{\theta} \end{pmatrix} = \begin{pmatrix} \cos(\theta) & 0 \\ \sin(\theta) & 0 \\ 0 & 1 \end{pmatrix} \cdot \boldsymbol{q} . \tag{1}$$

where $\boldsymbol{p} = (x \quad y \quad \theta)^{\mathrm{T}}$ and $\boldsymbol{q} = (v \quad \omega)^{\mathrm{T}}$. v and ω denote linear velocity and angular velocity of the wheeled mobile robot respectively, and in the control system they are control input.

3 The Design of Switching Function

The operation of the wheeled mobile robot trajectory tracking is to find the control input $\boldsymbol{q} = (v \quad \omega)^{\mathrm{T}}$ that makes the any initial position error, posture error and velocity error converge to zero and the system state $\boldsymbol{p}$ bounded. The kinematic model of the wheeled mobile robot is a multi-input nonlinear system, and the design of its switching function is a difficult problem. In this paper, the Backstepping[4] algorithm is used to design the switching function. Consider the position, posture and velocity tracking control for the wheeled mobile robot, the desired position, posture and velocity are defined as follows:

$$\begin{aligned} \boldsymbol{p}_d &= (x_d, y_d, \theta_d)^{\mathrm{T}}, \\ \boldsymbol{q}_d &= (v_d, \omega_d)^{\mathrm{T}}. \end{aligned} \tag{2}$$

And the position and posture error are defined as:

$$\boldsymbol{p}_e = (x_e, y_e, \theta_e)^{\mathrm{T}} . \tag{3}$$

Where $\theta_e = \theta_d - \theta$. According to the coordinate transformation formula, the position and posture error equations[5-6] of the wheeled mobile robot are

$$\boldsymbol{p}_e = \begin{pmatrix} x_e \\ y_e \\ \theta_e \end{pmatrix} = \begin{pmatrix} \cos(\theta) & \sin(\theta) & 0 \\ -\sin(\theta) & \cos(\theta) & 0 \\ 0 & 0 & 1 \end{pmatrix} \cdot \begin{pmatrix} x_d - x \\ y_d - y \\ \theta_d - \theta \end{pmatrix} . \tag{4}$$

Then the differential equation of the position and posture error equations are obtained:

$$\dot{\boldsymbol{p}}_e = \begin{pmatrix} \dot{x}_e \\ \dot{y}_e \\ \dot{\theta}_e \end{pmatrix} = \begin{pmatrix} y_e\omega - v + v_d \cos(\theta_e) \\ -x_e\omega + v_d \sin(\theta_e) \\ \omega_d - \omega \end{pmatrix}. \tag{5}$$

The linear velocity and angular velocity error equations are as follows

$$\boldsymbol{q} = \begin{pmatrix} v \\ \omega \end{pmatrix} = \begin{pmatrix} v_d \cos(\theta_e) + k_1 x_e + y_e v_d \sin(\theta_e) / x_e \\ \omega_d - \eta \cdot sat(s) - k \cdot s \end{pmatrix}. \tag{6}$$

Define the Lyapunov function of the wheeled mobile robot as

$$V = y_e^2 / 2. \tag{7}$$

Supposed that $\theta_e = -\arctan(v_d y_e)$ and combing with (6), derivate (7), then we could obtain that

$$\begin{aligned} \dot{V} &= \dot{y}_e y_e \\ &= (-x_e\omega + v_d \sin(\theta_e)) y_e \\ &= -x_e\omega y_e + v_d y_e \sin(-\arctan(v_d y_e)) \end{aligned} \tag{8}$$

When $v_d y_e = 0$, then we get

$$v_d y_e \sin(-\arctan(v_d y_e)) = 0.$$

When $v_d y_e > 0$, $-\arctan(v_d y_e) \in [-\pi/2, 0]$, we get

$$v_d y_e \sin(-\arctan(v_d y_e)) < 0.$$

When $v_d y_e < 0$, $-\arctan(v_d y_e) \in [0, \pi/2]$, we get

$$v_d y_e \sin(-\arctan(v_d y_e)) < 0.$$

So we could obtained the conclusion

$$\dot{V} \le 0. \tag{9}$$

If and only if $v_d y_e$=0, $\dot{V} = 0$. When $x_e = 0$, and θ_e converge to $-\arctan(v_d y_e)$, the system state y_e also could converge to zero. So the entire control system meets the requirement of accessible condition. According to the conclusion, the switching surface is designed as:

$$\boldsymbol{s} = \begin{pmatrix} s_1 \\ s_2 \end{pmatrix} = \begin{pmatrix} x_e \\ \theta_e + \arctan(v_d y_e) \end{pmatrix} \tag{10}$$

By the design of the sliding mode controller, make $s_1 \to 0$ and $s_2 \to 0$, we could achieve x_e converge to zero and θ_e converge to $-\arctan(v_d y_e)$, and finally achieve $y_e \to 0$ and $\theta_e \to 0$.

4 Design of Dynamic Sliding Mode Controller

The switching function of (10) is about the position and posture of the wheeled mobile robot, but the control inputs of the system are $\boldsymbol{q} = (v \quad \omega)^{\mathrm{T}}$, so (10) needs to be derivative to make the switching function is about the control inputs. Combing (5) and (10), obtained that

$$\begin{aligned} \dot{s} &= \begin{pmatrix} \dot{s}_1 \\ \dot{s}_2 \end{pmatrix} = \begin{pmatrix} \dot{x}_e \\ \dot{\theta}_e + \arctan(v_d y_e)' \end{pmatrix} \\ &= \begin{pmatrix} y_e\omega - v + v_d \cos(\theta_e) \\ \omega_d - \omega + \partial\alpha / \partial v_d \dot{v}_d + \partial\alpha / \partial y_e \dot{y}_e \end{pmatrix} \\ &= \begin{pmatrix} y_e\omega - v + v_d \cos(\theta_e) \\ \omega_d - \omega + \partial\alpha / \partial v_d \dot{v}_d + \partial\alpha / \partial y_e(-x_e\omega + v_d \sin(\theta_e)) \end{pmatrix} \end{aligned} . \tag{11}$$

Where

$$\partial\alpha / \partial v_d = y_e / (1 + (v_d y_e)^2), \; \partial\alpha / \partial y_e = v_d / (1 + (v_d y_e)^2).$$

In this paper, we are going to design the dynamic sliding mode controller, and the switching function must be related to the first order derivative of the control inputs, only by this method we could obtain the continuous sliding mode control law in the time domain which can reduce the chattering of the control input. In order to design the first order derivative of the control input, that is the linear acceleration and angular acceleration control input, derivate (11), we obtained that:

$$\begin{aligned} \ddot{s} &= \begin{pmatrix} \dot{y}_e\omega - v + v_d \cos(\theta_e) \\ \omega_d - \omega + \partial\alpha / \partial v_d \dot{v}_d + \partial\alpha / \partial y_e \dot{y}_e \end{pmatrix}' \\ &= \begin{pmatrix} \dot{y}_e\omega + y_e\dot{\omega} - \dot{v} + \dot{v}_d \cos(\theta_e) - v_d \sin(\theta_e)\omega \\ \dot{\omega}_d - \dot{\omega} + \partial\alpha / \partial v_d \ddot{v}_d + (\partial\alpha / \partial v_d)' \dot{v}_d + (\partial\alpha / \partial y_e)' \dot{y}_e + \\ \quad \partial\alpha / \partial y_e(-\dot{x}_e\omega - x_e\dot{\omega} + \dot{v}_d \sin(\theta_e) + v_d \cos(\theta_e)\omega) \end{pmatrix} \end{aligned} . \tag{12}$$

Take the exponential approximation law

$$\ddot{s} = -\boldsymbol{k}\,\mathrm{sgn}\,\boldsymbol{s} \tag{13}$$

where $\boldsymbol{k} = (k_1, k_2)^{\mathrm{T}} > 0$. In order to reduce the chattering caused by using sliding mode control method, use the saturation function instead of sign function

$$\ddot{s} = -\boldsymbol{k}sat(\boldsymbol{s}) \tag{14}$$

Where

$$sat(\boldsymbol{s}) = \begin{cases} 1 \;\;, s_i > \Delta \\ m \cdot s, |s_i| \le \Delta \\ -1 \;\;, s_i < -\Delta \end{cases} \quad m = \frac{1}{\Delta}, i = 1, 2$$

Δ denotes the boundary layer. In the control progress, the essence of the saturation function is that when phase locus outside the boundary layer the switching control is used, when inside the boundary layer the linear feedback is used. Combing (12) with (14), the dynamic control law is as follows:

$$\dot{q} = \begin{pmatrix} \dot{v} \\ \dot{\omega} \end{pmatrix} = \begin{pmatrix} k_1 sat(s_1) + \dot{y}_e\omega + y_e\dot{\omega} + \dot{v}_d\cos(\theta_e) - v_d\sin(\theta_e)\omega \\ (k_2 sat(s_2) + \dot{\omega}_d + \partial\alpha/\partial v_d \ddot{v}_d + (\partial\alpha/\partial v_d)'\dot{v}_d + \\ (\partial\alpha/\partial y_e)'\dot{y}_e + \partial\alpha/\partial y_e(-\dot{x}_e\omega + \dot{v}_d\sin(\theta_e) + \\ v_d\cos(\theta_e)\omega))/(1 + x_e\partial\alpha/\partial y_e) \end{pmatrix}. \tag{15}$$

$(\partial\alpha/\partial v_d)'$ and $(\partial\alpha/\partial y_e)'$ are not including $\dot{\omega}$.

5 Simulations

The circular trajectory is tracked by wheeled mobile robot in the Matlab environment. Supposed that the tracking linear velocity and angular velocity are uniform circular motion, taking

$$v_d = 1, \omega_d = 1.$$

And the desired position and posture are as follows

$$\boldsymbol{p}_d = \begin{pmatrix} \cos(t) \\ \sin(t) \\ t \end{pmatrix}.$$

The initial system state is (-3, 0, 0). Simulated in Matlab from time 0 to 20 seconds, the simulation results are as shown below. Fig. 2 is the dynamic sliding mode control input of linear velocity which is namely the linear acceleration of wheeled mobile robot. Fig. 3 is the dynamic control input of angular velocity that is namely angular acceleration of the wheeled mobile robot. Fig.4 is the linear velocity control input for the wheeled mobile robot. Fig. 5 is the angular velocity control input. Fig. 6 is the simulation result of circular trajectory tracking.

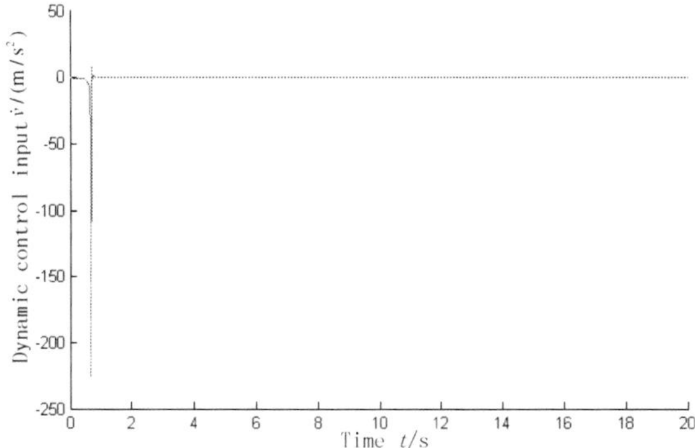

Fig. 2. Dynamic control input of linear velocity

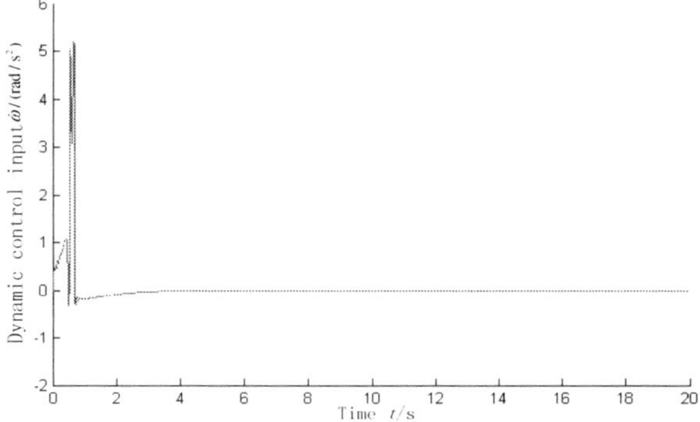

Fig. 3. Dynamic control input of angular velocity

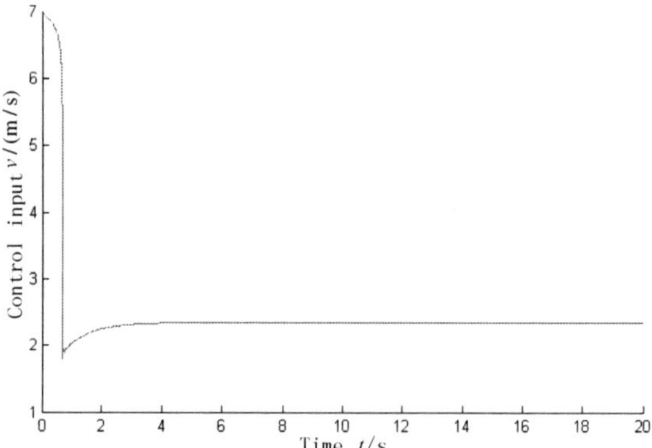

Fig. 4. Control input of linear velocity

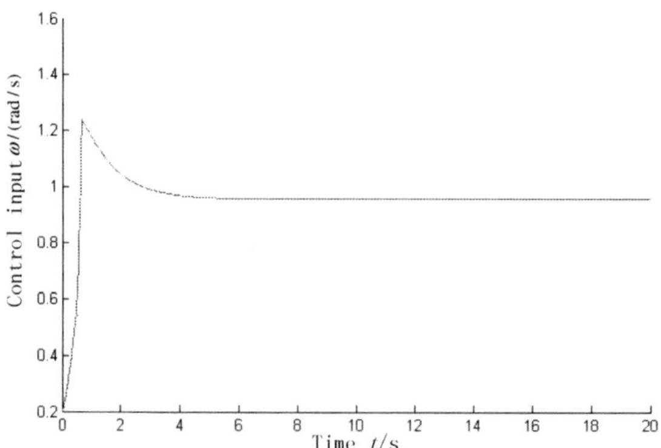

Fig. 5. Control input of angular velocity

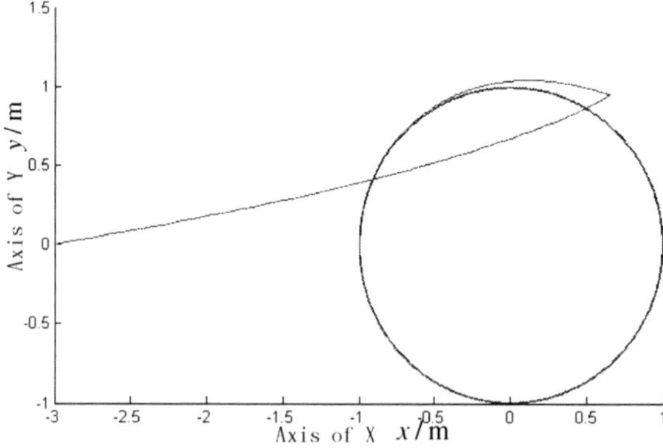

Fig. 6. Circular trajectory tracking

6 Conclusions

In this paper, the trajectory tracking of the wheeled mobile robot nonholonomic system is studied, and proposed the first order dynamic sliding mode control method for the wheeled mobile robot which implements the trajectory tracking. The simulation results show that the first order dynamic sliding mode control method is efficient, and this method not only can complete the tracking trajectory quickly but also can inhibit the chattering of the control input.

References

1. Brockett, R.: Asymptotic stability and feedback stabilization. Differential Geometric Control Theory. Birkhauser, Boston (1983)
2. Liu, J.: MATLAB Simulation for Sliding Mode Control. Tsinghua University Press, Beijing (2005)
3. Pioper, J.: First order dynamic sliding mode control. In: Proceedings of the 37th IEEE Conference on Decision & Control, Tampa, Florida USA, pp. 2415–2420 (1998)
4. Weiguo, W., Huitang, C., Yuejuan, W.: Global trajectory tracking control of mobile robot. Acta Automatica Sinica 27(3), 326–331 (2001)
5. Kanayama, Y., Kimura, Y., Miyazaki, F.: A stable tracking control method for autonomous mobile robot. In: IEEE International Conference on Robotics and Automation, pp. 384–389 (1990)
6. Shim, H., Kim, J., Koh, K.: Variable structure control of nonholonomic wheeled mobile robot. In: IEEE International Conference on Robotics and Automation, pp. 1649–1699 (1995)

Residual Strength for Concrete after Exposure to High Temperatures

Li Xiaoyong and Bu Fanjie

College of Architecture, North China University of Technology,
Beijing 100144, China
azgad11@yahoo.cn

Abstract. An experimental research is performed on such strength as compressive strength and tensile strength for concrete after heating to temperatures of 100–600°C. Some concrete specimens are standard concrete cylinders of 150 mm diameter×300 mm height, the others are cubes of 150×150×150mm, made with siliceous aggregate. The heated specimens are tested at heating rate of 5°C/min after they are cooled to room temperature. From the results of 63 specimens with two original unheated strengths, a formula for the strength of heated concrete varying with temperature is proposed. Through the regression analysis, the relationships of the mechanical properties with temperature are proposed to fit the test results, including the residual compressive strength and elastic modulus. In addition, the split-cylinder tests of 42 specimens are also carried out to study the relationship of splitting tensile strength with temperature. The experimental results show that the compressive strength of concrete after 200℃~300℃is increased with the increase of temperature and its critical temperature is around 400℃.

Keywords: Temperature, Compressive strength, Elastic modulus. Concrete, Tensile strength.

1 Introduction

Although the probability of occurrence of a fire may be small, its impact on a structure is high. Several cases in the recent past show the effect of such an accident on civil structures [1]. Concrete structures in most cases behave very well during a fire and although they suffer from a certain degree of strength loss, it could be interesting to repair these structures. Repair shows some economic benefits, since costs of demolition and rebuilding can be avoided, and the building can be reused in a shorter time period [2].

Fire remains one of the serious potential risks to most buildings and structures [3]. Since concrete is widely used in construction, research on fire resistance of concrete becomes more and more important.

Concrete has been well known as a low cost building material with high strength and versatility. Though high in compressive strength, concrete is quite brittle with a tensile strength of only 10% of its compressive strength [4].

M. Dai (Ed.): ICCIC 2011, Part II, CCIS 232, pp. 382–390, 2011.

Concrete is a nonhomogenous material consisting of hardened cement paste and aggregates. With an increase in temperature, cracking is initiated due to thermal incompatibilities between the aggregates [5]. Generally, at elevated temperatures, the cement paste would shrink due to the dehydration/decomposition of the hydrates while the aggregates usually expand before disintegration. Thermal stresses and cracks develop under conditions of high temperature exposure [6-8].

When concrete is heated at a rapid rate, a steep thermal gradient may develop between the outer and inner layers of concrete because concrete is a poor conductor, this gradient can also cause cracking [9]. The thermal gradient largely depends on the heating regime and the concrete thermal properties, such as specific heat, thermal conductivity and thermal diffusivity.

Concrete structures generally behave well in fires. Most fire-damaged concrete buildings can be repaired and put back to use even after severe fires [10-12]. Certainly, the damaged structural members must be repaired to reach again the minimum strength, stiffness and ductility they ought to have had before the fires. When concrete is exposed to heat, chemical and physical reactions occur at elevated temperatures, such as loss of moisture, dehydration of cement paste and decomposition of aggregate. These changes will bring a breakdown in the structure of concrete, affecting its mechanical properties. Therefore, concrete members without visible damage may have reduced strength due to elevated temperatures [13-18]. To evaluate and repair the fire-damaged concrete members, it is essential to understand the effect of temperature on the mechanical properties of concrete.

Exposure to fire or any extreme heat source can have adverse effects on concretes' mechanical properties; for plain concrete, changes can occur in the pore structures, cracking and spalling, the destruction of the bond between cement paste and aggregates and the deterioration of the hardened cement paste [19-24].

Many studies have been made on the residual mechanical properties of concrete after exposure to elevated temperatures such as compressive strength, splitting tensile strength and elastic modulus [25], [26] and [27]. The results obtained by different works in different countries are not easy to compare quantitatively with each other.

The purposes of this paper are to establish a database of the mechanical properties of concrete after heating to temperatures up to 600°C. The compression and split-cylinder tests are carried out to examine the validity of the relationships of temperature with the residual compressive strength, elastic modulus and splitting tensile strength.

2 Experimental Procedure

A. Materials

Concretes used in this study consisted of plain concrete. Properties of cements, coarse and fine aggregate, are given in Table 1. The chemical properties of cement is as shown in Table 2. And the properties of aggregate are shown in Table 3. The concrete mix proportions were calculated according to strength using the Graf formula and the full details of these mixes are given in Table 4.

Table 1. Property of Raw Materials

Materials	Properties
Cement	Portland type I with specific gravity of 3.16
Fine aggregate	River sand with fineness modulus of 2.71, absorption of 1.4%, and specific gravity of 2.72
Coarse aggregate	Natural rock with maximum size of 19 mm, FM of 6.34, absorption of 1.0% and specific gravity of 2.71
Water	Tap water

Table 2. The chemical properties of cement

Bulk oxide	(%) by mass for Portland Cement
SiO2	21.12
Al2O3	5.62
Fe2O3	3.24
CaO	62.94
MgO	2.73
LOI	1.42
Specific surface area (cm^2/g)	3430
Specific gravity (g/cm^3)	3.10

Table 3. Properties of Aggregate

Aggregate type	Aggregate size	Specific gravity	Water absorption (%)
Natural river sand and gravel (Siliceous agg.)	0–2	2.26	6.48
	2–4	2.41	3.69
	4–8	2.59	2.92
	8–16	2.61	2.24

Table 4. Mix Proportions of Groups

Mix group	I (C20)		II (C35)	
	Volume (dm^3)	Weight (kg)	Volume (dm^3)	Weight (kg)
Cement	103.00	307.97	131.75	393.93
Water	194.00	194.00	194.00	194.00
Air	10	–	10	–
Agg. 0–2	138.60	334.03	132.85	320.17
Agg. 2–4	138.60	360.36	132.85	345.41
Agg. 4–8	138.60	358.97	132.85	344.08
Agg. 8–16	277.20	723.49	265.70	693.48

B. Specimens and Test Temperatures

Some concrete specimens are standard concrete cylinders of 150 mm diameter×300 mm height and the others are cubes of 150×150×150mm, made with siliceous aggregate, which is more representative of the quality of normal concrete at room temperature.

The specimens are made with the Portland cement of Type I and the siliceous aggregate commonly used in Beijing. For compression tests, two kinds of compressive strengths are tested. Six specimens of 35MPa and three of 25MPa are carried out for each of seven temperatures: room temperature, 100, 200, 300, 400, 500, 600°C. A total of 63 specimens are tested to obtain the complete stress–strain curves for different temperatures. For split-cylinder tests, two kinds of compressive strength are also tested. Three specimens of 30MPa and three of 20MPa are tested for each of the same seven temperatures. A total of 42 specimens are tested to provide the splitting tensile strength for different temperatures.

C. Heating Regime

The specimens were heated at a rate of 5 °C/min and then kept for 1 h at the peak exposure temperature to establish a stable temperature profile in the samples (as shown in Fig. 1). An electrical furnace with 600×450mm cross section×500mm height is used. The temperatures of the specimens are monitored by thermocouples. The rising rates of average surface temperatures are followed as closely as the assigned heating rates by adjusting the heat output of the electrical furnace.

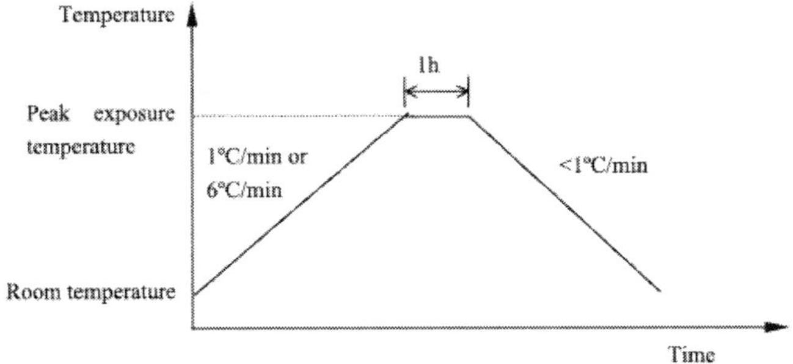

Fig. 1. Temperature versus time

D. Test Procedure

The tests are performed with a universal testing machine capable of 100kN. In the uniaxial compression test, a compressometer is attached to the specimen surface to measure the average strains over a central 20cm length. The tensile strength of heated concrete for different temperatures is obtained by the split-cylinder tests.

Three specimens are heated in the furnace at the same time. When the average surface temperature of the specimens reaches 20°C more than the specified test temperature, the surface temperature is kept constant for about 2h by adjusting the heat output of the furnace until the centre temperature reaches the same specified temperature. This is followed by natural cooling down to room temperature in the furnace.

3 Experimental Results and Analysis

A. Experimental Results

Fig. 2 and Fig. 3 show the effect of temperature on the residual compressive strength f_c , elastic modulus E and splitting tensile strength. The relation between compressive strength and elastic modulus are shown in Fig. 4. The compressive stress–strain curves for different temperatures are shown in Fig. 5

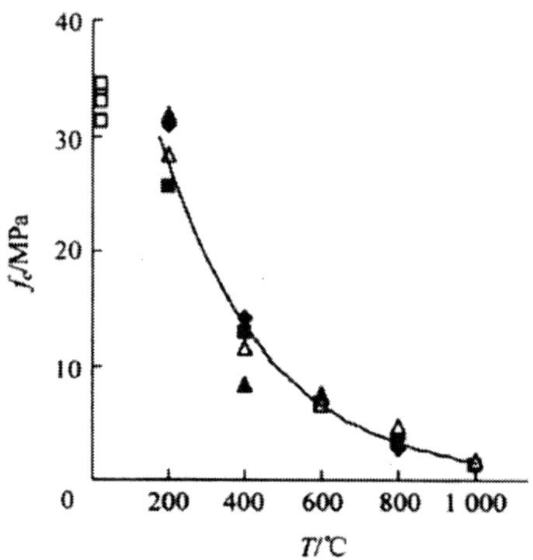

Fig. 2. Compressive strength versus temperature

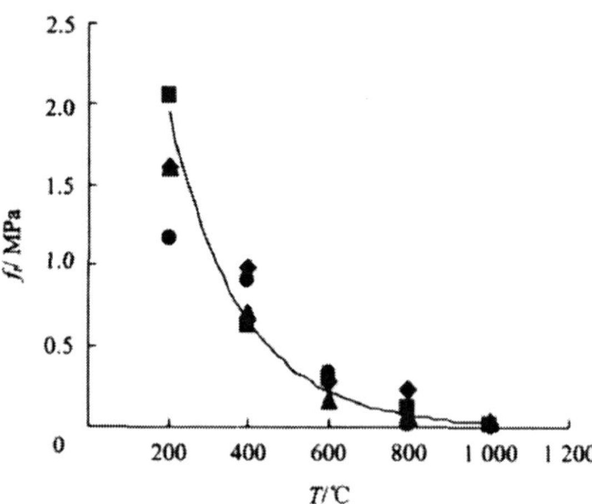

Fig. 3. Tensile strength versus temperature

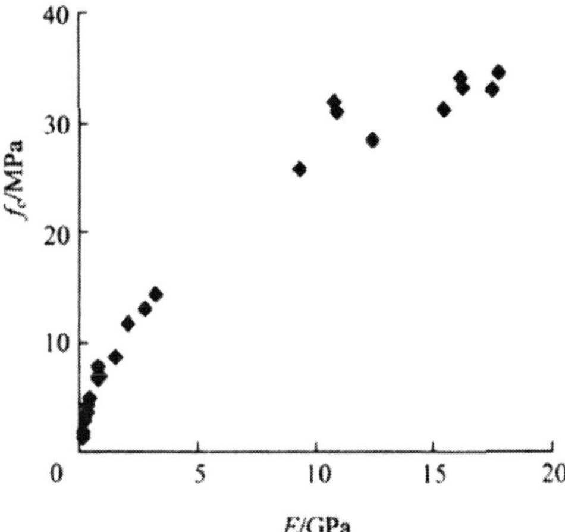

Fig. 4. Compressive strength versus elastic modulus

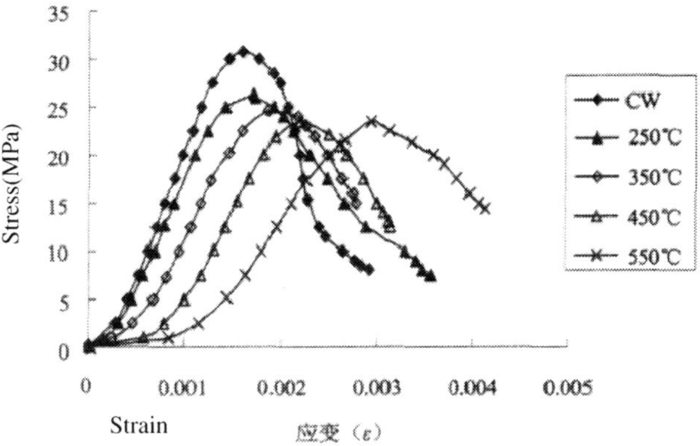

Fig. 5. Stress–strain curves

B. Regression Analysis

Through the regression analysis, the relationship of the normalized compressive strength f_c^T/f_c with temperature T can be expressed as Eq. (1).and (2).

When 20℃≤T≤400℃, R^2=0·942:

$$\frac{f_c^T}{f_c} = -3.11(\frac{T}{1000})^2 + 0.96(\frac{T}{1000}) + 0.97 \tag{1}$$

When 400℃≤T≤600℃, R^2=0·962:

$$\frac{f_c^T}{f_c} = -2.4(\frac{T}{1000}) + 1.77 \tag{2}$$

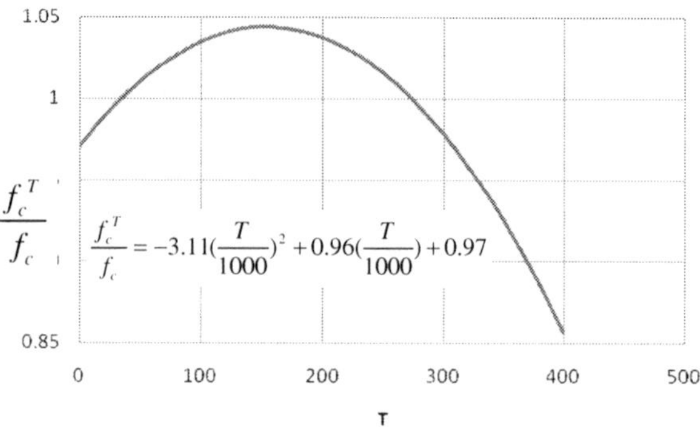

Fig. 6. Relationship of the normalized compressive strength f_c^T/f_c with temperature T for 20℃ ≤T≤400℃

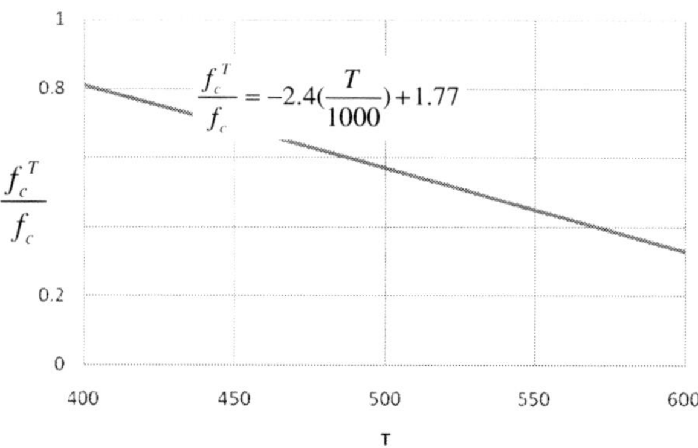

Fig. 7. Relationship of the normalized compressive strength f_c^T/f_c with temperature T for 400℃ ≤T≤600℃

C. Experimental Analysis

The mechanical properties of the tested concretes (compressive strength, tensile strength and elastic modulus) generally decreased with the temperature.

Between 20 and 150°C, a small loss of strength was observed. It was associated to an evaporation of free water as well as to an increase in porosity of the tested concretes. This porosity increase is an expansion of the pores diameters and therefore leads to an increase in permeability.

Between 150°C and 300°C, an increase in compressive strength was observed. Nevertheless, the other mechanical properties (tensile strength and elastic modulus) continued to decrease in a similar way to the observed evolutions between 20 and 150°C, due to the departure of bound water, corresponding to a large mass loss. The increase in strength could be attributed to a modification of the bonding properties of the cement paste hydrates.

Beyond 300°C, the mechanical and physical properties of the tested concretes decreased quickly. The specimens subjected to a heating up to 600°C showed very weak mechanical properties. The decrease of the mechanical properties was associated to that of physical properties.

4 Conclusions

The following conclusions can be drawn from the experimental results on the concrete specimens after heating to temperatures up to 600°C:

The test data indicate that the original compressive strength of concrete fc′ has no significant effect on residual compressive strength.

The reductions after exposure to temperatures decrease one by one in this order: elastic modulus, tensile strength and compressive strength.

The compressive strength of concrete after 200℃~300℃ is increased with the increase of temperature and its critical temperature is around 400℃.

Acknowledgment. The works was provided financial aid by Youth Focus on Fund in North China University of Technology and Funding Project for Academic Human Resources Development in Institutions of Higher Learning under the Jurisdiction of Beijing Municipality (PHR20110868).

References

1. Papayianni, J., Valiasis, T.: Residual mechanical properties of heated concrete incorporating different pozzolanic materials. Mater. Struct. 24, 115–121 (1991)
2. Nassif, A.Y., Burley, E., Rigden, S.: A new quantitative method of assessing fire damage to concrete structures. Mag. Concr. Res. 47(172), 271–278 (1995)
3. Wu, B., Ma, Z.C., Ou, J.P.: Experimental research on deformation and constitutive relationship of concrete under axial loading and high temperature. J. Build. Struct. 20(5), 42–49 (1999) (in Chinese)
4. Tsai, W.T.: Uniaxial compressional stress–strain relation of concrete. J. Struct. Eng. 114(9), 2133–2136 (1988)
5. Mander, J.B., Priestley, M.J.N., Park, R.: Theoretical stress–strain model for confined concrete. J. Struct. Eng. 114(8), 1804–1826 (1988)
6. Georgali, B., Tsakiridis, P.E.: Microstructure of fire-damaged concrete. A Case Study. Cement Concrete Compos. 27, 255–259 (2005)
7. Handoo, S.K., Agarwal, S., Agarwal, S.K.: Physicochemical, mineralogical, and morphological characteristics of concrete exposed to elevated temperatures. Cement Concrete Res. 32, 1009–1018 (2002)
8. Powers-Couche, L.: Fire damaged concrete-up close. Concrete Repair Digest, 241–248 (1992)
9. Gustafero, A.H.: Experiences from evaluating fire-damaged concrete structures – fire safety of concrete structures. American Concrete Institute SP-80 (1983)
10. Annerel, E., Taerwe, L.: Revealing the temperature history in concrete after fire exposure by microscopic analysis. Cement Concrete Res. 39(12), 1239–1249 (2009)

11. Lau, A., Anson, M.: Effect of high temperatures on high performance steel fibre reinforced concrete. Cement Concrete Res. 36, 1698–1707 (2006)
12. Poon, C.S., Shui, Z., Lam, L.: Compressive behavior of fiber reinforced high-performance concrete subjected to elevated temperatures. Cement Concrete Res. 34, 2215–2222 (2004)
13. Chen, B., Liub, J.: Residual strength of hybrid-fiber-reinforced high-strength concrete after exposure to high temperatures. Cement Concrete Res. 34, 1065–1069 (2004)
14. Peng, G.F., Yang, W.W., Zhao, J., Liu, Y.F., Bian, S.H., Zhao, L.H.: Explosive spalling and residual mechanical properties of fiber-toughened high-performance concrete subjected to high temperatures. Cement and Concrete Research 36(4), 723–727 (2006)
15. Kupfer, H.: Behavior of concrete under biaxial stresses. ACI Journal 66(8), 656–666 (1969)
16. Husem, M., Gozutok, S.: The effects of low temperature curing on the compressive strength of ordinary and high performance concrete. Construction and Building Materials 19(1), 49–53 (2005)
17. Lu, X.B., Hsu, C.T.T.: Behavior of high strength concrete with and without steel fiber reinforcement in triaxial compression. Cement and Concrete Research 36(9), 1679–1685 (2006)
18. Luo, X., Sun, W., Chan, Y.N.: Residual compressive strength and microstructure of high performance concrete after exposure to high temperature. Materials and Structures/ Materiaux et Constructions 33(6), 294–298 (2000)
19. Chan, S.Y.N., Peng, G.F., Chan, J.K.W.: Comparison between high strength concrete and normal strength concrete subjected to high temperature. Materials and Structures/ Matdriaux et Constructions 29(12), 616–619 (1996)
20. Elsen, J., Lens, N., Aarre, T., Quenard, D., Smolej, V.: Determination of the w/c ratio of hardened cement paste and concrete samples on thin sections using automated image analysis techniques. Cement and Concrete Research 25, 827–834 (1995)
21. Jakobsen, U.H., Brown, D.R.: Reproducibility of w/c ratio determination from fluorescent impregnated thin sections. Cement and Concrete Research 36, 1567–1573 (2006)
22. Alarcon-Ruiz, L., Platret, G., Massieu, E., Ehrlacher, A.: The use of thermal analysis in assessing the effect of temperature on a cement paste. Cement and Concrete Research 35, 609–613 (2005)
23. Poon, C.S., Azhar, S., Anson, M., Wong, Y.L.: Performance of metakaolin concrete at high temperatures. Cem. Concr. Compos. 25, 83–89 (2003)
24. Kalifa, P., Menneteau, F.-.D., Quenard, D.: Spalling and pore pressure in HPC at high temperatures. Cem. Concr. Res. 30, 1915–1927 (2000)
25. Nishida, A., Yamazaki, N.: Study on the properties of high strength concrete with short polypropylene fiber for spalling resistance. In: Proceedings of the International Conference on Concrete under Severe Conditions, CONSEC 1995, Sapporo, Japan, pp. 1141–1150. E&FN Spon, London (1995)
26. Kalifa, P., Chene, G., Galle: High-temperature behaviour of HPC with polypropylene fibers from spalling to microstructure. Cem. Concr. Res. 31, 1487–1499 (2001)
27. Chan, Y.N., Luo, X., Sun, W.: Compressive strength and pore structure of high-performance concrete after exposure to high temperature up to 800 °C. Cem. Concr. Res. 30, 247–251 (2000)

Control Strategy for Wind and Solar Hybrid Generation System

Xin Gao

College of Electrical Information and Engineering,
Southwest Nationalities for University,
Chengdu, Sichuan Province, China, 610041
2218322269@QQ.COM

Abstract. Solar energy and wind energy are the two most viable renewable energy resources in the world. This paper presents a control strategy for wind & solar hybrid power generating systems. If the power generation sources produce more energy than the one required by the loads, the surplus energy can be used either to charge the battery or to provide a dump load (electric heater or electrolysis-hydrogen). If the amount of energy demanded by the loads is higher than the one produced by the power generation sources, the control strategy determines the battery will release energy to cover the load requirements until the battery is fully discharged. This paper explains the strategy developed and shows the control flowchart of hybrid power generation system.

Keywords: Control strategy, Hybrid system, MPPT, Charge-Discharge control.

1 Introduction

Tibet Plateau at high altitude has a strong solar radiation. Annual average hours of sunlight is 3000-3300 hours, Ultraviolet radiation is 6700-8400 MJ/m^2. Tibet Plateau also has plenty of wind energy. The density of effective wind power is 150-200 W/m^2. There are, in annual average, about 4000-5000 hours when the wind speed is higher than 3m/s. Also, about 3000-4000 hours when the wind speed is higher than 6m/s.

Even though Tibetan Plateau has plenty of solar and wind energy, at present, most of this natural energy has not been used for generating, heat and electricity. To make the better use these kinds of energy to satisfy the big potential market requirements, to consider better environment protection and to improve herdsmen living conditions, there is an urgent necessity in developing portable wind & solar hybrid power generating systems. The power generation hybrid systems are usually more reliable and lest costly than the systems that use a single source of energy [1, 2]. Particularly, central government has determined and made a long term policy to support the social, economic and environmental developments in Tibet area and inject big funding to sponsor projects for these development. This will further guarantee the future market requirements on these kinds of systems. The system proposed in this paper will greatly help to ease the shortage of electricity supply to herdsmen living in the wide grassland.

M. Dai (Ed.): ICCIC 2011, Part II, CCIS 232, pp. 391–395, 2011.

2 Control strategy of hybrid power generation system

A hybrid solar/wind power generation system consists of the PV module, wind turbine, battery, inverter, controller and load. A schematic diagram of a basic hybrid system is shown in Fig. 1.

Figure 1 shows a schematic block diagram of a "Wind & Solar PV Hybrid Power Generation". In this system, both PV array and wind turbine supply electricity to load. PV array can also directly provide DC supply to the application equipments connects. Wind turbine produces AC electricity, which will be converted into DC electricity in PV & turbine control. Then the DC electricity is supplied to loads. In a normal operation the PV array and wind turbine work together to satisfy the load demand.

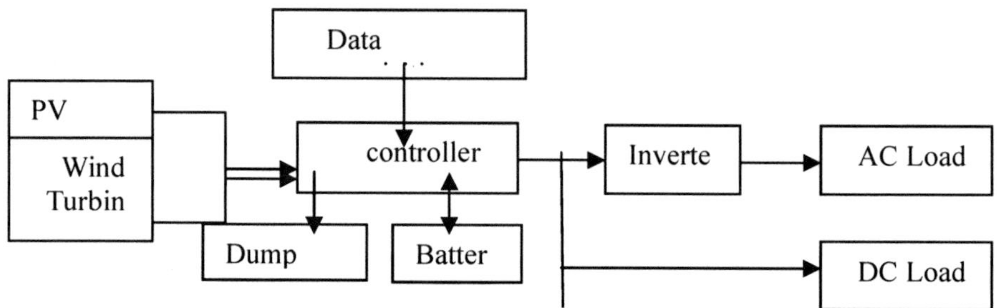

Fig. 1. Schematic diagram of a basic hybrid system

When the energy sources (solar and wind energy) are abundant, the surplus power will be used to charge the battery until it's fully charged. When the battery is fully charged, the extra energy will be abandoned by disconnecting the PV array to cut off the solar energy generation. After PV array is cut off, if there is still surplus power, i.e. the power generated by the wind turbine is higher than the load demand and the battery is fully charged at the same time, then, a dump load (electric heater or electrolysis-hydrogen) will be turned on to discard the spare energy from the wind turbine. In some other conditions, when the energy sources are poor, the battery will release energy to assist the PV array and wind turbine to cover the load requirements until the battery is fully discharged. The main task of the controller is to continuously adjust and switch the battery working conditions based on the insolation, wind speed and load demand. This will also extend the life span of a battery and greatly reduce maintenance costs.

A. PV charging-discharging control with MPPT

Solar energy has become a promising alternative source due to its advantages: abundance, pollution free and renewability. The main drawbacks are that the initial installation cost is considerably high, and the energy conversion efficiency is relatively low. To overcome these problems, the following two essential ways can be used: (1) increase the efficiency of conversion for the solar array, and (2) maximize the output power from the solar array. Many MPPT control techniques have been conceived for this purpose in the last decades [3,4], such as Voltage feedback based methods, Current feedback based methods, P&O and IncCond methods. There are less known but sometimes very appropriate methods such as fuzzy logic control, neural network, sliding mode control, genetic algorithm. As we stated above, there are many methods to realize MPPT to PV array. However, we would like to use a combination of the artificial intelligence methods and perturbation and observation (P&O) methods. Because of artificial intelligence controllers have been introduced in the tracking of the MPPT in PV systems. For example, the fuzzy logic controllers have the advantage to be robust and relatively simple to design since they do not require the knowledge of the exact model. The study shows that the fuzzy controller is faster than the P&O controller in the transitional state, and presents also a much smoother signal with less fluctuation in steady state. Meantime, to improve the design and further improve the performances of the fuzzy logic and P&O controller, genetic algorithms are used to find the optimal membership functions. Ongoing research will involve an implementation of the proposed artificial intelligence controller.

B. Battery charge-discharge control strategies

The battery control strategy determines the effectiveness of battery charging and energy source utilization, and ultimately, the ability of the system to meet load demands [5]. It should have the ability to prevent overcharge and over-discharge of battery regardless of the system design and seasonal changes in the power generation and load profile. When the energy sources are abundant, the battery will work in charging mode. After the battery voltage rises up to the overcharge protection voltage, the PV array is disconnected and the dump load is turned on to maintain the battery voltage below the threshold. Three stages charging control mode is used in the charging control of battery, that is, Floating charging, constant voltage charging and constant current Charging. For the discharging mode, the control strategy prevents aggressive discharging of the battery by disconnecting the load when the battery voltage goes below the over-discharge protection voltage. And only when the battery voltage rises up to the load reconnection voltage, can the load be reconnected. Different kind of loads has different control strategies according to their priorities. So we need consider the deep-discharge-protection (disconnection voltage) and the discharge-reconnect voltage (reconnection voltage) to every different load.

3 Control Flowchart of Hybrid Power Generation System

The system overall software configuration is shown in appendix. It involve five function modules, that is, A/D convert module, MPPT control module, Charge control module, discharge control module. The charge control module include constant current charging module, constant voltage charging module and floating charging module. This software design can increase the complementarity of PV & wind turbine and improve the life span of a battery which will reduce maintenance costs.

4 Conclusion

This paper presents a control strategy for wind & solar hybrid power generating systems and shows the systemic control flowchart. Researches show that the control strategy may be well applied to the charge and discharge control for the wind & solar hybrid power generating systems. Further research and experiment will be carried out in the Tibetan Plateau.

Acknowledgment. Project supported by the Base of the Tibetan Plateau High-tech Research and Development of SWUN.

References

1. Muselli, M., Notton, G., Louche, A.: Design of hybrid-photovoltaic power generator with optimization of energy management. Solar Energy 65(3), 143–157 (1999)
2. Diaf, S., Notton, G., Belhamel, M., Haddadi, M., Louche, A.: Design and techno-economical optimization for hybrid PV/wind system under various meteorological conditions. Applied Energy 85, 968–987 (2008)
3. Salas, V., Barrado, A., Lazaro, A.: Review of the Maximum Power Point Tracking Algorithms for Stand-alone Photovoltaic Systems. Solar Energy Materials & Solar Cells 90, 1555–1578 (2006)
4. Tarik, H.: Maximum power tracking algorithm based on Impp = f(Pmax) function for matching passive and active loads to a photovoltaic generator. Solar Energy 80, 812–822 (2006)
5. Zhou, W., Yang, H., Fang, Z.: Battery behavior prediction and battery working states analysis of a hybrid solar–wind power generation system. Renewable Energy 33, 1413–1423 (2008)

Appendix

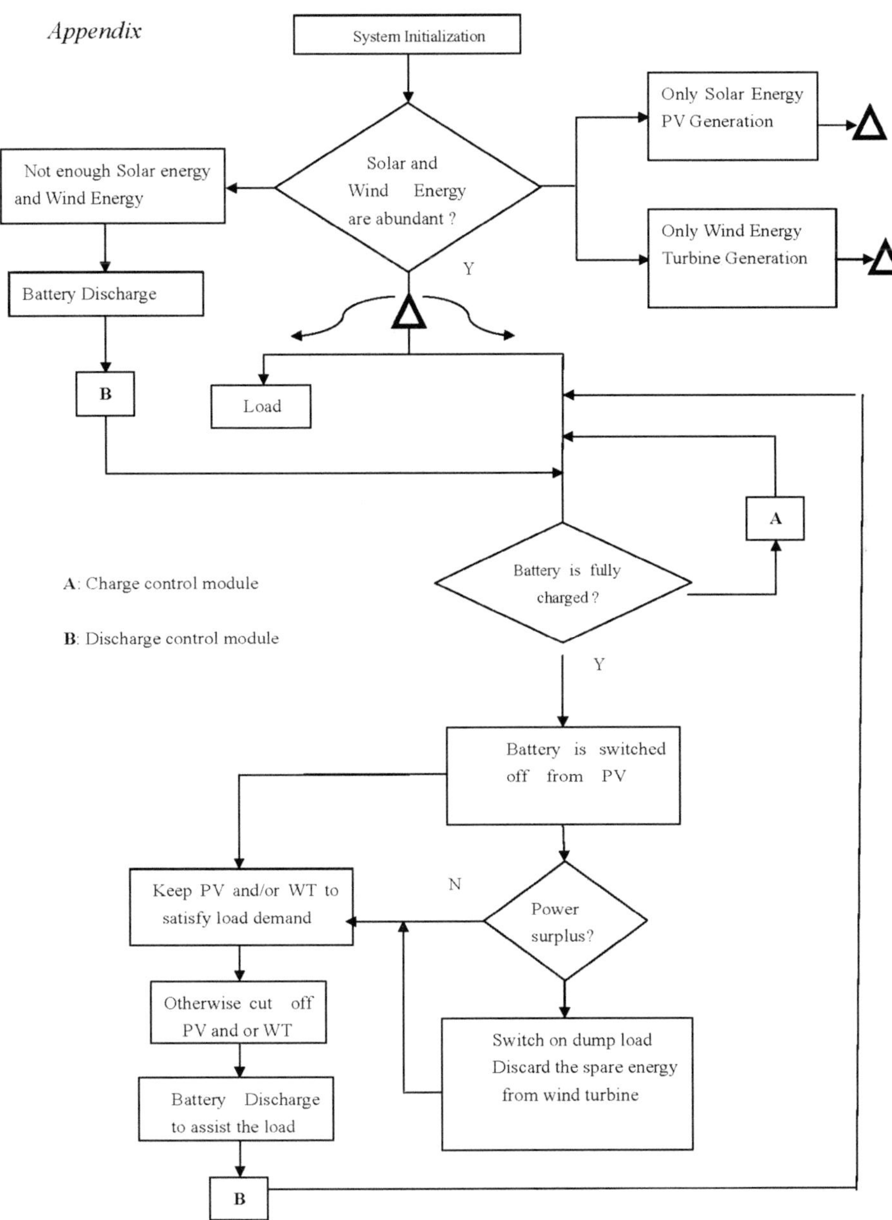
System Initialization
Solar and Wind Energy are abundant ?
Not enough Solar energy and Wind Energy
Only Solar Energy PV Generation
Only Wind Energy Turbine Generation
Y
Battery Discharge
B
Load
A
A: Charge control module
B: Discharge control module
Battery is fully charged ?
Y
Battery is switched off from PV
Keep PV and/or WT to satisfy load demand
N
Power surplus?
Otherwise cut off PV and or WT
Switch on dump load Discard the spare energy from wind turbine
Battery Discharge to assist the load
B

Deep Heat Transfer Performance and Ratio of Length to Diameter in Shell and Tube Heat Exchangers

Fuhua Jiang and Xianhe Deng

School of Chemistry and Chemical Engineering,
South China University of Technology,
Guangdong Province, 510641, P.R. China
mfzhou123@foxmail.com

Abstract. The relationship between ratio of length to diameter (L/D) of shell and tube heat exchangers (STHXs) and deep heat transfer was studied experimentally. The comparison of heat transfer and pressure drop performance of five STHXs with tube number of 10, 20, 30, 40, 50 are presented in this paper. The experiment is carried out in STHXs with cold air in shell side and hot air in tube side. Overall heat transfer coefficients are calculated and heat transfer coefficients of shell side are determined by Wilson plots technique. It shows that heat transfer performance decrease and pressure drop increase with the decrease of L/D, and critical point of deep heat transfer state (hot air outlet temperature equals to that of cold one) is achieved when L/D at some point between 3.08 and 4.62. When a certain heat transfer task is given, reasonable L/D can be chosen based on the experimental results.

Keywords: pressure drop, friction factor, flow distribution, ratio of length to diameter, deep heat transfer.

1 Introduction

When hot and cold fluid go through shell and tube heat exchangers(STHXs), the ratio of outlet temperature of hot fluid to that of cold one(α) indicates heat exchange depth. When outlet temperature of hot fluid is equal to that of cold one, α = 1. When outlet temperature of hot fluid is lower than that of cold fluid, α <1, which we calls STHXs run into deep heat transfer state. Generally, deep heat transfer state exists in industry such as sulfuric acid transformation system[1], the petrochemical ethylene and oil refining system.

In recent years, STHXs in chemical, power and petroleum refining industries have an enlargement trend which the traditional configuration of STHXs can't meet. In order to enhance heat transfer, various types of baffles such as segmental baffles[2-3], hollow ring[4-6], helical baffles[7-10] and twisted leaves[11-12] have been used in STHXs. By inserting baffles, shell side fluid was forced to flow across the tubes to ensure high heat transfer rates, but pressure drop also increased and flow patterns became comprehensive. Pressure drop increasing lead to more pumping power needed which is uneconomic. And flow pattern comprehensive lead to flow pattern be far away from counter flow which lead to heat transfer performance reducing greatly. So this article did research on STHXs without baffles.

M. Dai (Ed.): ICCIC 2011, Part II, CCIS 232, pp. 396–404, 2011.

The reason why deep heat transfer state can't be achieved when STHXs become larger is the traditional configuration of shell side is unreasonable. Baffles can improve heat transfer in a certain extent, but the basic way of solving the problem is changing the traditional configuration of shell side. To solve the problem of deep heat transfer state limited as ratio of length to diameter (L/D) of STHXs decrease, DENG[13] proposed multi parallel channel (MPC) structure (see Figure 1)which split the whole tube bundles into some districts with small tube numbers in shell side of STHXs. This is equivalent to set some sub-heat-exchangers with small diameter (D_P, the diameter of parallel sub-heat-exchangers) in heat exchangers with large diameter(D_W, the diameter of the whole heat exchangers). Hence D_P can be artificially adjusted, L/D_P can be much larger than L/D_W. Therefore, ratio of cross flow area to the whole heat transfer area can be limited under a reasonable value and deep heat transfer limiting problem can be well solved.

This paper studied the heat transfer performance and pressure drop of five STHXs with L/D_P range from 1.85-9.23. And at which range of L/D_P, deep heat transfer state can't be achieved has been given.

2 Experimental Study

Tubes were made in Φ10*2000mm which decreased five times of industry model Φ51*6000mm according to geometrically similar principle. Five heat exchangers were made with different tube numbers of 10, 20, 30, 40, 50. Though the model is contracted, but L/D_P of experiment size and industry size is the same. Take 10tube STHXs as example, industry size L=6000mm, D_P=650mm, tube pitch is 65mm, L/D_P=6000/650=9.23, experimental size L=1200mm, D_P=130mm, tube pitch is 13mm, L/D_P=1200/130=9.23.

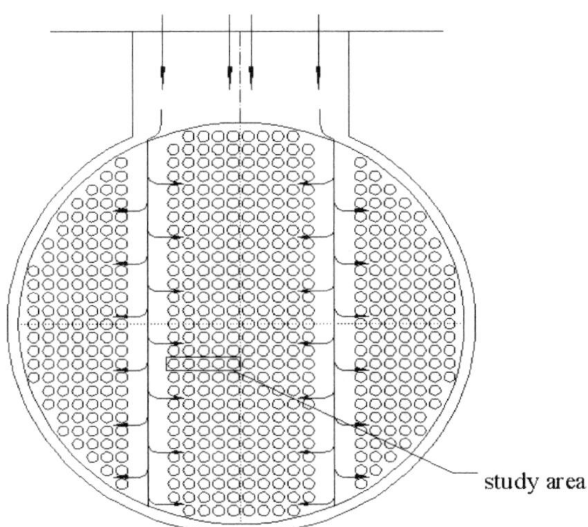

Fig. 1. Schematic of shell-side fluid flow in STHXs with MPC

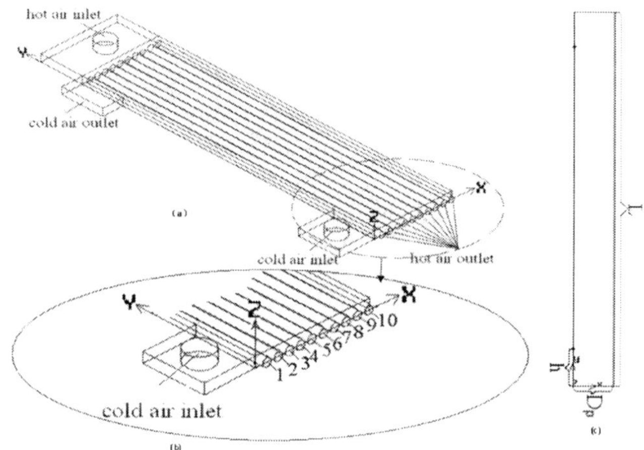

Fig. 2. (a) schematic of 10tube STHX, (b) tube order of hot air outlet, (c) Detail view of 10 tube STHX

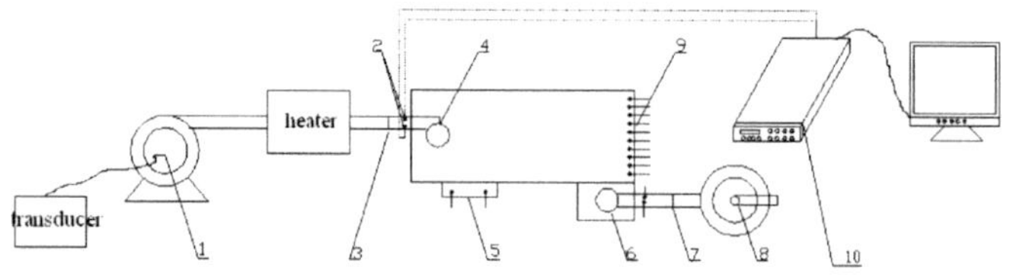

1.air pump 2.thermalcouple in tube side 3.bourdon's tube in tube side 4.inlet of hot air 5.outlet of cold air

6.inlet of cold air 7.bourdon's tube in shell side 8.air pump 9.outlet of hot air 10.Data Acquisition System

Fig. 3. The schematic diagram of experiment setup

Fig.2(a) is the schematic of 10tube STHX of width 130mm, depth 13mm and length 1200mm. Fig2(b) illustrates the tube order of hot air outlet. Detail view of 10tube STHX is shown in Fig.2(c) which indicates h is proportional to D_P.

The experiment setup of the study is shown in Fig.3. The system includes two independent loops: a cooling air loop and a heating air loop. The heating air loop consists of an air pump, a volumetric flow meter, a heater, and a heat exchanger. The air is heated up by a heater to reach a predetermined inlet temperature value before inlet the tube side of the heat exchanger. Then it is pumped to the tube side, where it is cooled down. Finally, the cooled air was pumped in to the air. The cooling air loop consists of an air pump, a volumetric flow meter and a heat exchanger. The cooling air is pumped to the shell side of the heat exchanger for heat-up. Then it is pumped into the air. A dedicated valve is used to control the cooling air's volumetric flow rate. To minimize heat loss of the facility, refractory aluminium silicate fiber insulation at 40mm thickness is covered on the outer surface of the heat exchanger.

Measurements of inlet and outlet fluid temperature are carried out using T-type thermal couple. The volumetric flow is measured with a compensation micro-pressure meter. The pressure drop between inlet and outlet of shell side is measured with a U-type differential draft gauge.

The experiment was being conducted under steady state conditions with air as the working fluid. The procedure was repeated a few times for different flow rates of the shell side ranging from 22.81 to 48.87 m3/h, while the flow rate of the tube was maintained constant. And the procedure was repeated a few times for different flow rate of the tube side ranging from 19.78 to 42.39 m3/h, while the flow rate of the shell side was maintained constant. Prior to each experiment, an energy balance test was conducted. Usually it took approximately 120min to reach a steady state which was judged by the temperature reading fluctuation of with ±0.1℃. After reaching the stable condition, the temperature measured by T-type thermalcouple was recorded by a Data Acquisition System for 10min maintaining a span of 5s between two successive readings. At the same time, the volumetric flow rate and the pressure data were recorded.

3 Results and Disscussuions

A. Model Validation

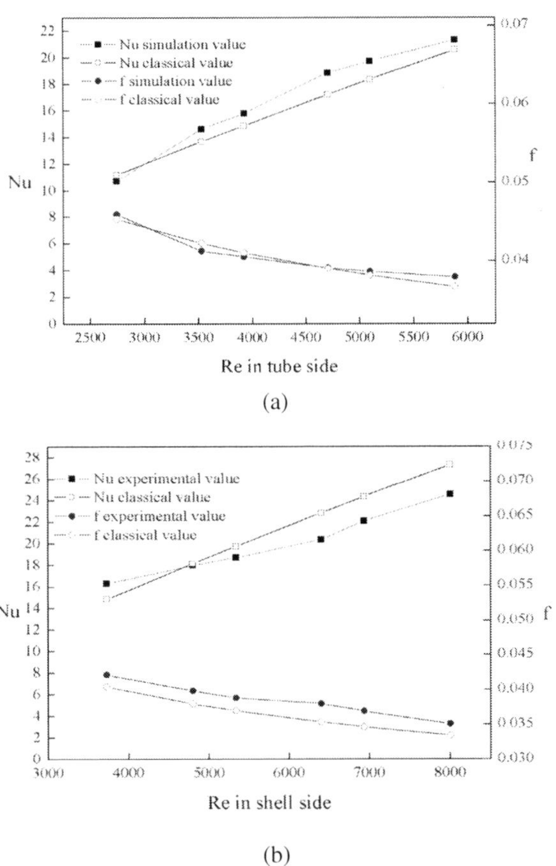

Fig. 4. Comparison of experiment results of Nusselt number with the data from Dittus-Boelter method for10tube STHX (a) tube side (b) shell-side

In order to verify the experimental set-up, a heat exchanger with ten tubes is used to investigate heat transfer and pressure drop at the early stage of the experiment. The heat transfer measurements of the present work are compared with the data from Dittus-Boelter[ ]. Fig.4 and Fig.5 show the comparison of experimental results of Nusselt numbers with the data from Dittus-Boelter method in tube side and shell side, respectively. The difference between the present experimental data and the results from the Dittus-Boelter method is approximately 6%. The comparison of experimental results of pressure drop with the data from Dittus-Boelter method in tube side and shell side is also presented in Fig.4 and Fig5. It can be seen that the deviation between the present experimental measurements and the results from the literature is about 5%. The present experimental results are in agreement with the data from Dittus-Boelter method. It shows that the experiment setup is reliable for the experimental research of shell-and-tube heat exchangers.

B. Experimental results

Table 1. Experimental Parameter Setting

Number of tubes	Tube side Re_i	Shell side Re_o	Volume flux of tube side $m^3 \cdot h^{-1}$	Volume flux of shell side $m^3 \cdot h^{-1}$	Average velocity in tube side $m \cdot s^{-1}$	Average velocity in shell side $m \cdot s^{-1}$
10tubes	5866.71	4325.29	33.88	39.55	11.99	12.14
20tubes	5357.14	3820.48	54.98	68.35	9.73	10.49
30tubes	6142.88	4195.83	95.22	111.77	11.23	11.44
40tubes	5295.92	3398.83	117.29	120.27	10.37	9.23
50tubes	4846.94	3278.31	123.39	144.79	8.73	8.88

Table 2. Experimental Results

Tube number	L/D	$t_{s,in}$	$t_{s,out}$	Δt_s	$T_{t,in}$	$T_{t,out}$	ΔT_t
10	9.23	43.6	68.9	25.3	96	58.4	37.6
20	4.62	41.1	60.9	19.8	83.4	55.5	27.9
30	3.08	46.6	60.8	14.2	82.4	62.1	20.3
40	2.5	51.8	64.4	12.6	83.4	66	17.4
50	1.85	47.7	57.4	9.7	82.3	69.7	12.6

(1) Table1 shows the experimental parameters. Table2 shows the experimental results. From table2 we can see that, cold air goes through heat exchangers with different length to diameter, temperature rise of cold air is smaller and smaller, temperature drop of hot air is smaller and smaller. Heat transfer reduced as tube numbers increases.

(2) It can be observed that cold air outlet temperatures of 10 tube STHX with length to diameter 9.23 and 20 tube STHX with length to diameter 4.62 are higher than hot air outlet temperature, respectively. That is to say, in 10tube STHX and 20tube STHX, deep heat transfer state can be achieved. If L/D≥4.62, deep heat transfer state can be achieved, and if L/D≤3.08, deep heat transfer state can't be achieved any more. Cold air temperature equals to hot air temperature when L/D at the range of 3.08-4.62. In order to achieve deep heat transfer, L/D should be designed larger than 3.08.

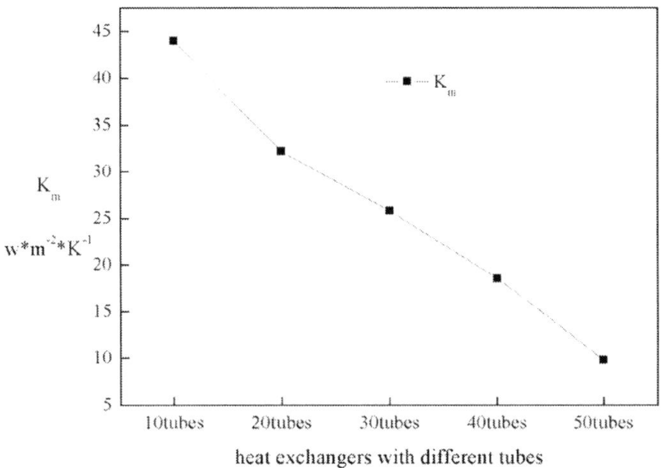

Fig. 5. Heat transfer coefficient of different STHXs

Fig.5 illustrates the heat transfer coefficient of STHXs with different tube numbers. It can be clearly observed that the heat transfer coefficient decreases with the increase of tube numbers. In other words, the heat transfer coefficient decreases with the decrease of L/D. The reason for this phenomenon appears to be as follows, cold air impinge on the shell side in normal direction first then along with the tube and hot air impinge in the tube always along the tube, in other words, cold air and hot air first exchange heat with cross flow first, then counter flow, and cross flow finally. As known, heat transfer efficient is higher when hot air and cold air change heat in counter flow than in cross flow. If cross flow proportion is larger, the heat transfer efficient is smaller, that is heat transfer coefficient will be smaller. For STHXs with 10tubes, the ratio of cross flow to the whole flow type is 19.5%, and for STHXs with 50tubes, the ratio of cross flow to whole flow type is 97.5%. Flow maldistribution is another reason. Flow maldistribution can be seen from the temperature of hot air outlet.

Fig.6 shows outlet temperatures of hot air in every tube. Tube order is shown in Fig.2(b). From the figures, it is found that temperatures of hot air outlet increase as the tube order increase. In other words, the further the tube away from cold air inlet, the higher the temperate of hot air outlet is. The reason for this phenomenon appears to be as follows, there are dead zone in shell side. Fig.6 also clearly shows that the deviation between outlet temperature of the first tube and that of the last tube is 5.9%

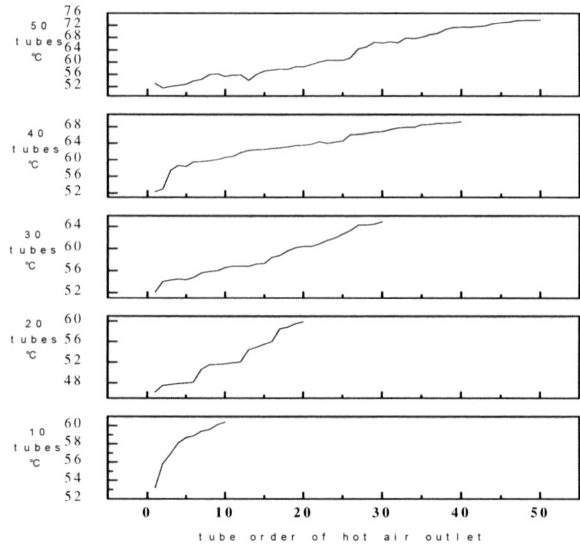

Fig. 6. Outlet temperature of hot air in STHXs with different tubes

for STHXs with 10tubes whereas that is 27.5% for STHXs with 50tubes. And the deviation between outlet temperature of the first tube and the last tube for STHXs with tube number of 20,30,40 are between 5.9%-27.5%. This phenomenon indicates the flow distribution is more and more uneven.

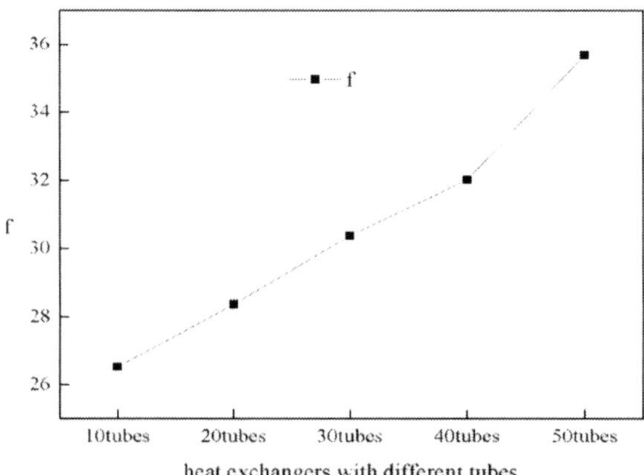

Fig. 7. Resistance coefficient of shell side in different heat exchangers

Fig.7 shows the resistance coefficient in shell side of different STHXs with different tubes. It can be seen that resistance coefficient in shell side increase with the increase of tube numbers in different STHXs. In other words, the resistance coefficient in shell side increase with the decrease of L/D. The reason for this phenomenon appears to be as follows, flow separation at the edge of tubes causes abrupt momentum change and severe pressure loss.

4 Conclusions

Experimental investigations of five STHXs with different tubes are performed in the present work. Hot air flow is in the tubes while cold air acts as a coolant flowing in the shell side. The heat transfer coefficients and pressure drop on the shell side of five STHXs based on the experimental study are reported.

It shows that

(1)the heat transfer coefficient decreases with decreasing L/D on the shell side for a constant volume flow rate in tube side. And the resistance coefficient increases with decreasing L/D.

(2)the critical point of deep heat transfer state will happen when L/D ranges from 3.08 to 4.62. When L/D of STHXs is bigger than 4.62, hot air and cold air can act deep heat transfer. When L/D of STHXs is smaller than 3.08, hot air and cold air can't act deep heat transfer.

(3)To avoid the decrease L/D or design a shell side structure which has a relatively uniform flow distribution is required. The present study provides a powerful reference for design of STHXs.

References

1. Liu, S.-w., Qi, Y.: Sulfuric Acid Production Technology. South East University Press, Nanjing (1993)
2. Zhang, J.F., Li, B., Huang, W.J.: Experimental performance comparison of shell-side heat transfer for shell-and-tube heat exchangers with middle-overlapped helical baffles and segmental baffles. Chemical Engineering Science 64(8), 1643–1653 (2009)
3. Li, H., Kottke, V.: Analysis of local shellside heat and mass transfer in the shell-and-tube heat exchanger with disc-and-doughnut baffles. International Journal of Heat and Mass Transfer 42(18), 3509–3521 (1999)
4. Wang, C., Zhu, J.G., Sang, Z.F.: Experimental Studies on Thermal Performance and Flow Resistance of Heat Exchangers with Helical Baffles. Heat Transfer Engineering 30(5), 353–358 (2009)
5. Peng, B., Wang, Q.W., Zhang, C.: An experimental study of shell-and-tube heat exchangers with continuous helical baffles. Journal of Heat Transfer-Transactions of the Asme 129(10), 1425–1431 (2007)
6. Wang, Q.W., Chen, Q.Y., Chen, G.D.: Numerical investigation on combined multiple shell-pass shell-and-tube heat exchanger with continuous helical baffles. International Journal of Heat and Mass Transfer 52(5-6), 1214–1222 (2009)
7. Deng, X., Huang, W.: Construction and application of gas heat exchanger with sharp expansion and accelerated flow converging-diverging tubes. Sulphuric Acid Industry (5), 22–24 (2005)
8. Wang, C., Zhu, J.G., Sang, Z.F.: Experimental Studies on Thermal Performance and Flow Resistance of Heat Exchangers with Helical Baffles, vol. 30, pp. 353–358. Taylor & Francis, Abington (2009)

9. Wang, Q., Chen, Q., Chen, G., Zeng, M.: Numerical investigation on combined multiple shell-pass shell-and-tube heat exchanger with continuous helical baffles, vol. 52, pp. 1214–1222. Elsevier, Amsterdam (2009)
10. Peng, B., Wang, Q.W., Zhang, C., Xie, G.N., Luo, L.Q., Chen, Q.Y., Zeng, M.: An experimental study of shell-and-tube heat exchangers with continuous helical baffles, vol. 129, p. 1425 (2007)
11. Wang, Y.-j., Deng, X.-h., Li, Z.-w.: Compound heat transfer enhancement of converged-diverged tube supported by twisted-leaves. Journal of Chemical Industry and Engineering 58, 2190–2193 (2007)
12. Wang, Y.-j., Deng, X.-h., Li, Z.-w., Hong, M.-n.: Heat transfer and flow resistance characteristics of tube bundle supported by twisted leaves, vol. 58, pp. 21–26 (2007)
13. Deng, X.-h., Zhang, Y.-j.: Shell and tube heat exchangers with multi-parallel-channel inlet and outlet structure, CN1719176 (2006)

Study of the Free Surface Fluctuations in a GMAW Weld Pool with Globular Transfer Mode*

Zhao Pengcheng and Li Dasen

College of Electromechanical Engineering,
Qingdao University of Science and Technology,
Qingdao, Shandong, China 266061
dariuszk523@gmail.com

Abstract. The transient free surface fluctuations during one droplet impingement period in a gas metal arc welding (GMAW) weld pool with globular transfer mode are studied to investigate the formation of cripples on weld bead surfaces by both experimental and numerical methods. Capillary waves and gravity waves are observed on the free surface of weld pools by using high-speed photography. Theoretical analyses indicate that the capillary waves contribute to the formation of cripples. The wave equation is established to simulate the dynamics of 3D free surface fluctuations. The predicted wave parameters show good agreement with the experimental results in current study.

Keywords: free surface fluctuation, weld pool dynamics, capillary wave, GMAW.

1 Introduction

In nuclear industry, the gas metal arc welding (GMAW) is widely used in the fabrication of reactor pressure vessels. At the surface of a GMAW bead, ripples are inevitably observed. Generally, even distributed fine ripples are acceptable and contribute to reduce the weld stress. But few studies involve in reasons why ripples form and in measure how to eliminate coarse ones. Hu[1] studied the transient weld pool dynamics and he considered that the phenomena of "open and close-up" for a crater in the weld pool was caused by the periodical impingement of filler droplets. Besides, he predicted ripples at the surface of a solidified weld bead by his model for the first time and discussed mechanisms leading to the formation of ripples. But details about ripple formation still remain unclear.

Theoretically when the free surface fluctuation caused by the impingement of transferred droplet in GMAW spread out to the back edge of a weld pool and solidify immediately, a ripple takes place at the surface of welding bead. Many reports investigated the impingement of filler droplets, the surface deformation of a weld pool, and the heat and fluid flow in GMAW weld pool by using numerical methods. Hu and Tsai[2,3] developed a model to predict the resulting crater in the weld pool

* This work is supported by the Scientific Research Foundation of QUST.

M. Dai (Ed.): ICCIC 2011, Part II, CCIS 232, pp. 405–413, 2011.

and the weld-pool oscillation due to periodical droplet impingement in GMAW. They chiefly focused on the transient distributions of current density, temperature and pressure in an arc, as well as the transient melt-flow velocity and temperature distributions in the droplet and in the weld pool. Guo[4] calculated the transient weld pool shape and the distributions of temperature and velocity by a three-dimensional numerical model, and predicted the formation of the crater formed in a GMAW of aluminum alloy 6005-T4. Wu[5] developed a numerical model for fluid flow and heat transfer in metal inert gas (MIG) weld pools. He analyzed how the droplet impact affects the MIG weld pool geometry and gave a set of algorithm to calculate weld reinforcement and weld pool geometry. Sun[6] established a model to study the influence of weld pool surface shape on the distribution of current density. The predicted results showed that the distribution of current density is bimodal distribution near the arc centerline. The distribution mode of current density was markedly modified by the shape of weld pool surface. But all the studies above didn't refer to the transient fluctuation on the free surface of a GMAW weld pool, which play a key role in the formation of both ripples and craters.

This article devotes to investigate the transient formation of fluctuation on the free surface of a GMAW weld pool by means of high-speed photographing and numerical simulation, which could discover the formation of ripples even humps on the surface of welding bead and could provide basic data for the droplet transfer strategy.

2 Model

A. Experiments

Different experiments are conduced on the observation of free surface fluctuation formed in a GMAW weld pool by high-speed photography to acquire a globular transfer mode. Table 1 gives the used welding parameters.

Table 1. Welding Parameters

Welding parameters	Value
Arc Voltage, V	14V
Welding current, I	160A
Welding speed, vw	2.5mm/s
Droplet transfer frequency, f	50Hz

Results show that during one droplet transfer period, when the filler droplets impact on the free surface of molten liquid, the surface is quickly depressed and part of the droplet blend into the weld pool immediately. Then the surface and the residual part of droplet restore and continue to rise till a liquid peak forms. It's worth noting that a small droplet takes shape just on the top of liquid peak. After that, the droplet and liquid peak fall again to restart a new sequence. At the same time, a train of waves or fluctuation form and spread out from the impingement point at a great speed. Those waves are characterized by high speed, short wavelength and low amplitude, which are mainly caused by surface tension of liquid metal. In hydraulics, they are known as capillary waves. Finally after capillary waves on the free surface pass off in a short time, irregular oscillations on the free surface emerge under an interaction of surface tension and liquid gravity, they are gravity waves. Because there are no specific spreading directions, the oscillations would have no influence over the formation of ripples.

The results indicate that after a droplet contacts the free surface of a weld pool, about seven waves with equivalent frequency will come into being in about 0.0014s. Compared with droplet transfer period of 0.02s, the effect of capillary wave on free surface deformation of weld pool is minimal. Some experimental parameters used and observed are indicated in table 2.

Table 2. Experiment Parameters

Parameters	Value and unit
Droplet velocity, v_d	0.5m/s
Wire feeding speed, v_s	0.05m/s
Wire diameter, D	1.2mm
Wave peak amplitude, A	0.1mm, max
Wave period, T	About 2×10^{-4}s
Wave velocity, c	About 2.0m/s

B. Wave equation

In GMAW weld pools, a droplet gains momentum under the interaction of arc pressure and its gravity as it falls down from the tip of a welding wire, which will result in the fluctuation on free surface of weld pools. Then the fluctuation will spread out in the form of waves. According to wave theory[7], we denote those waves with their wavelength longer than critical wavelength the gravity waves, because the gravity effect is dominant, while waves with their wavelength shorter than critical wavelength the capillary waves, since the effect of surface tension is dominant. The critical wavelength can be written as in (1).

$$\lambda_c = 2\pi\sqrt{\frac{\sigma}{\rho g}} \quad (1)$$

Where λ_c is the critical wavelength, σ is surface tension, ρ is density of liquid metal and g is acceleration of gravity.

Here in GMAW, we take σ = 1.5N/m[8], ρ = 7860kg/m3, g =9.8m/s2, hence λ_c = 27.7mm. In experiments, as the weld pool length is about 10mm and 7 waves are observed in weld pool, so the wavelengths in current study are much shorter than the critical wavelength. It is concluded that they are capillary waves.

Some assumptions are made to simplify the model as follows:

(1) The liquid metal is incompressible.

(2) Surface depression of weld pool caused by arc pressure is neglected.

(3) The capillary waves are considered as deep water waves and reflection of waves on weld pool boundaries is omitted.

(4)Every wave in the wave train has same frequency and same wavelength.

As shown in Fig.1, a train of capillary waves is given by

$$y = A\sin(\omega t - kx) \quad (2)$$

Where A is amplitude, ω is angular frequency, and k is wave number.

In (2), parameters A, ω and k must be determined to describe the train of waves.

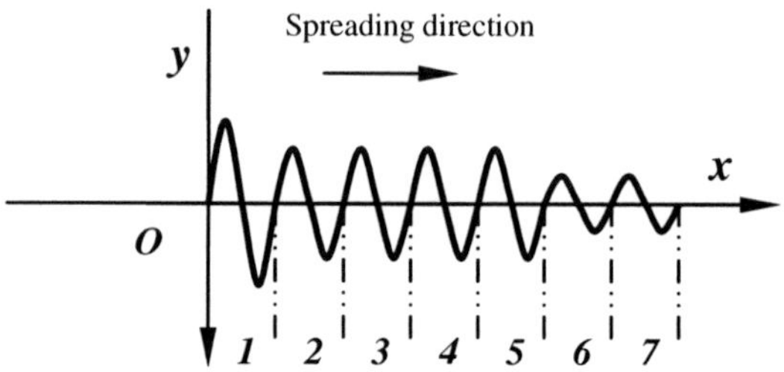

Fig. 1. Schematic of fluctuation on weld pool surface

Suppose the kinetic energy carried by droplets leads to the fluid flow inside the weld pool and an addition in surface area. So we have

$$7E = \eta E_d \quad (3)$$

Where E is surface energy of very wave, η is rate of potential energy converted from droplet kinetic energy, and E_d is the kinetic energy carried by one droplet.

The E_d is defined as[9]

$$E_d = \frac{\pi D^2 v_s \rho}{8f} v_d^{\ 2} \quad (4)$$

Where D is diameter of welding wire, v_s is wire feeding speed, ρ is wire density (same as metal liquid), v_d is droplet velocity at the moment it enters weld pool, and f is droplet transfer frequency.

As indicated in Fig.1, the train of wave is composed of 7 single waves with same amplitude. Therefore the surface energy has another expression

$$E = \sigma \Delta S \quad (5)$$

Where ΔS is the incremental surface area of single wave, and σ is surface tension.

Fig.2 shows an increase of surface area in half wave, thus for one wave we have

$$\Delta S = 4 \times \left[\pi \frac{\lambda}{4} l - \pi (\frac{\lambda}{4})^2 \right] \quad (6)$$

Where, l is the arc length in x direction, and λ is wave length.

Since l is close to line segment L in value when amplitude A is small, l could be replaced by L in equation (6). Based on the geometry relationship in Fig.2, we get

$$l \approx L = \sqrt{A^2 + (\frac{\lambda}{4})^2} \quad (7)$$

From equation (3)-(6), we obtain

$$A \approx \sqrt{(\frac{\eta D^2 v_s \rho v_d^2}{56 f \sigma \lambda})^2 + \frac{\eta D^2 v_s \rho v_d^2}{112 f \sigma}} \quad (8)$$

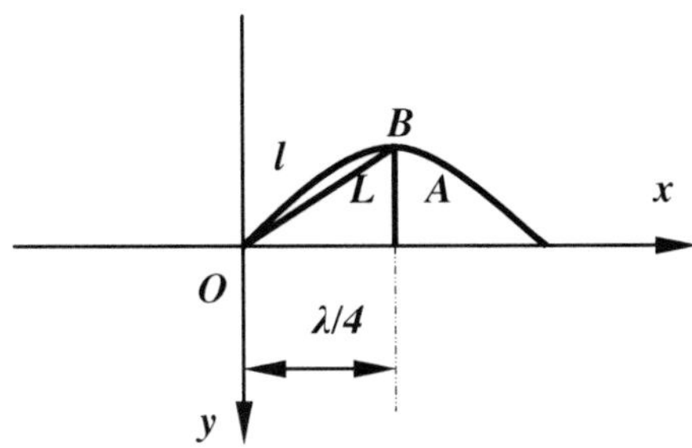

Fig. 2. Schematic diagram of a half wave

By using parameters shown in Table 2, we have an approximate expression of A

$$A = \sqrt{\frac{7.9 \times 10^{-8}}{2\pi\sigma}} \quad (9)$$

Angular frequency ω can be expressed as[7]

$$\omega = \frac{2\pi}{T} \quad (10)$$

In current study, we get ω = 31416s-1.
The wave speed in capillary wave is expressible in the form[10]

$$c = \sqrt{\frac{2\pi\sigma}{\rho\lambda}} = \frac{\lambda}{T} \quad (11)$$

Where, c is the wave speed. So from equation (10) and (11) we get

$$\lambda = 2\pi\sqrt[3]{\frac{\sigma}{\rho\omega^2}} \quad (12)$$

And wave number is

$$k = \frac{2\pi}{\lambda}. \tag{13}$$

Thus all the required parameters in equation (2) can be determined.

3 Numerical Results and Discussion

A. Numerical method

Numerical simulations on 3D transient free surface fluctuation in GMAW weld pools are performed by using the same welding parameters in case of experiments. First the heat field of workpiece is calculated, and then weld pool shape is obtained. After that, the free surface fluctuation subroutine is called to predict the generated wave train.

In current study, the weld pool will keep stable relative to the torch 3 seconds after welding starts. So the calculation of wave begins from the 3rd second. Besides, the surface tension of liquid metal is temperature dependent[11]. Fig.3 shows the schematic of GMAW operation system.

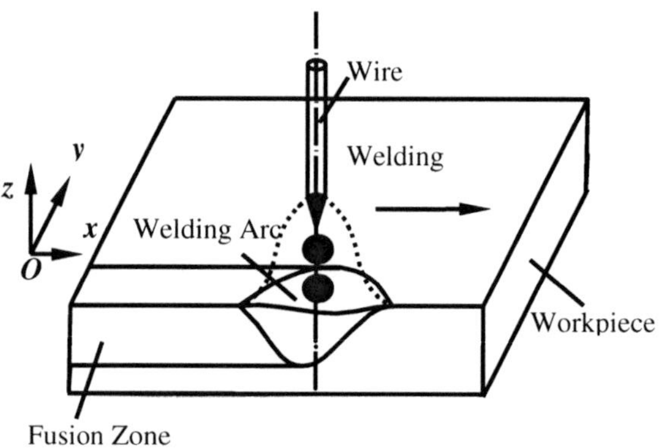

Fig. 3. Schematic of GMAW operation system

B. Predicted 3D waves on free surface

The predicted transient 3D waves are shown in Fig.4, which demonstrate the dynamics of free surface fluctuation in an impingement period. It can be seen that five waves generate at 3.001s, with average amplitude about 0.09mm and wave length about 0.5mm. The wave train first reaches at the front edge of weld pool, then both the side boundaries, finally the rear trailing of weld pools. The calculated wave speed is around 2m/s. At 3.003s, wave train only exists at the back of weld pool. At the same time other part of free surface restore to original equilibrium position.

The amplitude and wave length in very single wave and in different position are not the same because the surface tension is temperature dependent. Projections of the wave train on bottom surface clearly reveal the size and number of waves on free surface of the weld pool. At 3.001s, five waves form and spread out. At 3.002s, all the seven waves have taken their shapes and the center area restore to horizontal position under the action of surface tension. At 3.003s, only four waves left. The predicted parameters of the wave train have a good agreement with experimental ones.

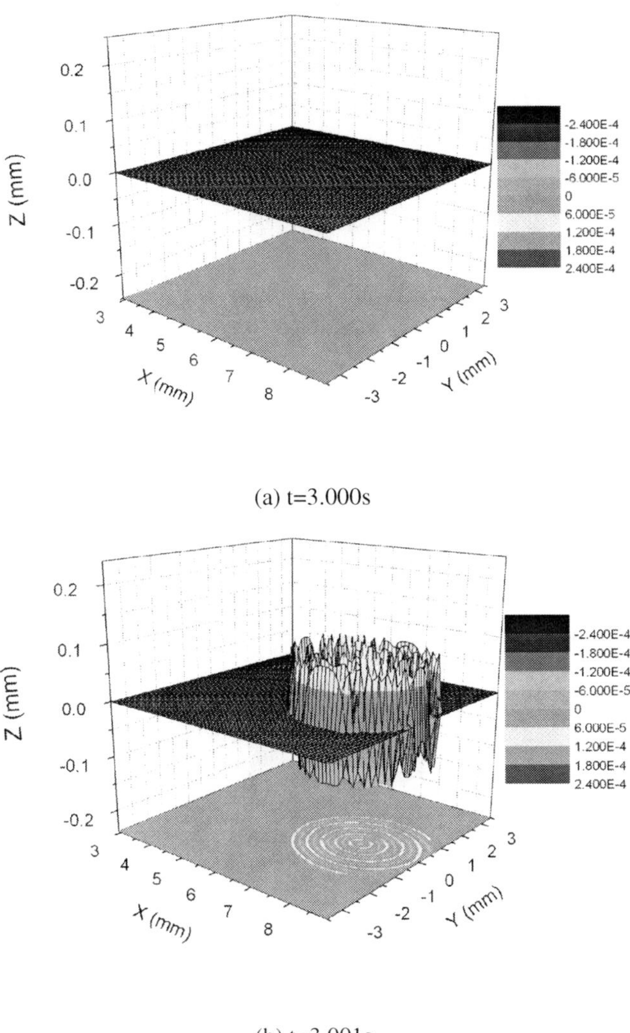

(a) t=3.000s

(b) t=3.001s

Fig. 4. The predicted free surface waves in 3D view (enlarged in Z axis) The impact point is at point (7.5, 0, 0)

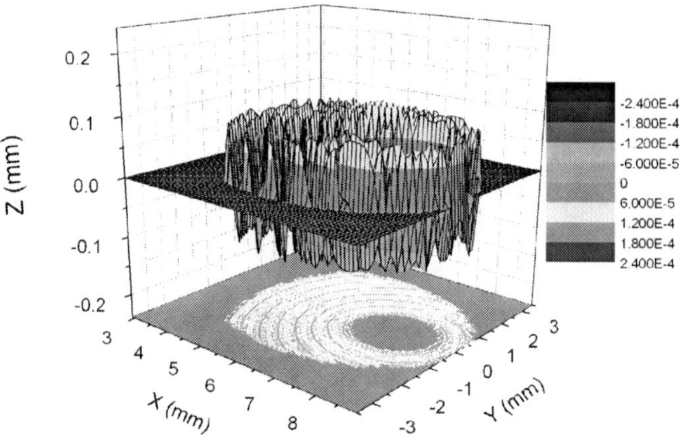

(c) t=3.002s

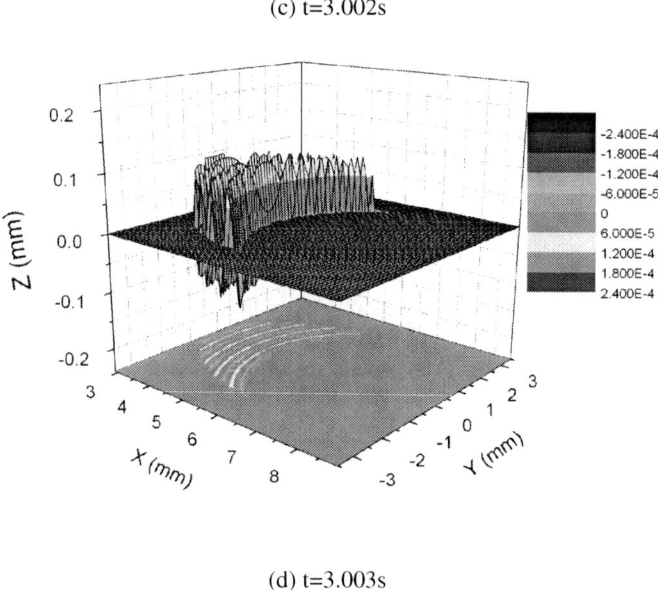

(d) t=3.003s

Fig. 4. *(continued)*

4 Conclusion

The transient free surface fluctuations in a GMAW weld pool with globular transfer mode is investigated experimentally and numerically. The wave model is established and the dynamics of wave train in one droplet impingement period are predicted.

(1) Both capillary waves and gravity waves are observed on free surfaces of a GMAW weld pool. Capillary waves contribute to the formation of cripples on weld bead surface.

(2) As the existing time of capillary waves is very short, they have small effect on the arc shape and heat input distribution mode of a GMAW arc in comparison with gravity waves.

(3) Seven waves in one wave train with average amplitude 0.1mm, period 0.0002s, and wave speed 2.0m/s, respectively, are obtained by using numerical analysis in current study. The predicted results have a good agreement with measured ones

References

1. Hu, J., Guo, H., Tsai, H.L.: Weld pool dynamics and the formation of ripples in 3D gas metal arc welding. International Journal of Heat and Mass Transfer 51(9-10), 2537–2552 (2008)
2. Hu, J., Tsai, H.L.: Heat and mass transfer in gas metal arc welding. Part I: The arc. International Journal of Heat and Mass Transfer 50(5-6), 833–846 (2007)
3. Hu, J., Tsai, H.L.: Heat and mass transfer in gas metal arc welding. Part II: The metal. International Journal of Heat and Mass Transfer 50(5-6), 808–820 (2007)
4. Guo, H., Hu, J., Tsai, H.L.: Formation of weld crater in GMAW of aluminum alloys. International Journal of Heat and Mass Transfer 52(23-24), 5533–5546 (2009)
5. Wu, C.S., Dorn, L.: The influence of droplet impact on metal inert gas weld pool geometry. Acta Metallurgica Sincia 33(7), 774–779 (1997)
6. Sun, J.S., Wu, C.S.: The influence if weldpool surface shape on the distribution of arc current density. Acta Physica Sinica 49(12), 2427–2430 (2000)
7. Hsieh, D.-Y., Ho, S.P.: Wave and stability in fluids. World scientific publishing Co. Pte. Ltd., Singapore (1994)
8. Iida, T., Guthrie, R.I.L.: The physical properties of liquid metals. Oxford University Press, New York (1988)
9. Sun, J.S., Wu, C.S., Gao, J.Q.: Effects of distribution model of droplets heat content on fluid flow in weldpool. Acta Metallurgica Sinica 35(9), 964–970 (1999)
10. Probstein, R.F.: Physicochemical hydrodynamics: an introduction, 2nd edn. John Wiley & Sons, Inc., New York (1994)
11. Zhao, P.C., Wu, C.S., Zhang, Y.M.: Numerical simulation of the dynamic characteristics of weld pool geometry with step-changes of welding parameters. Modeling and Simulation in Materials Science and Engineering 12, 765–780 (2004)

Development of Visual Analysis System Based on Visual Basic

Haibo Lin[1], Yingqian Zhang[1], Yumei Luo[1], and Yan Shi[2]

[1] School of Mechanical Engineering,
Sichuan University of Science and Engineering, Zigong 643000, China
[2] Process Equipment and Control Engineering of Key Laboratory,
Sichuan Province, Zigong 643000, China
WZX00722@YAHOO.CN

Abstract. Based on finite element theory, ANSYS software was encapsulated by VB software. The visual analysis system for structure field and flow field of high-parameter gate-valve was developed through their seamless integration. Conducted with APDL, simulations for gate-valve's structure field and flow field promoted the efficiency of serial design and optimize design. Making full use of prominent advantage in its graphical user interface, VB was efficiently linked with ANSYS. Friendly human-computer interactive interface reduced requirements to technicians' level of English and ANSYS. This system reserved user defined function interfaces to improve its generality and expansibility.

Keywords: high-parameter gate-valve, visual analysis system, structure field, flow field.

1 Introduction

Ultra - supercritical units is the inevitable development trend of thermal power generating unit for its advantages such as low coal consumptions and few pollution emissions[1]. High-parameter is one effective way to increase operation efficiency and decrease production cost. But it is shows that increasing pressure, temperature and flow of medium that result in higher requirement for strength and life of power station valve[2].

Structure of high-parameter Gate-valve is complex. Valve body cavity shape is serious mutation irregular. Traditional vale design relied mainly on empirical formula and experience to production. Distribution laws of structure and flow are difficult to be mathematical characterized, which can not reflect overall force condition of valve so as to limit the design of new style and large scale valve. With the development of computer technology, finite element analysis (FEA) method is frequently used to solve practical engineering problems. Large numbers of excellent software are as an important calculation and simulation tool provide us an excellent platform.

M. Dai (Ed.): ICCIC 2011, Part II, CCIS 232, pp. 414–419, 2011.

2 Technical Scheme

ANSYS program is large finite element software (FTEA) to solute questions on structure, flow, power, electromagnetic field and collision, et al.. User should be better related mechanical knowledge and rich experience for its generality that means there are different analysis methods to professional module in different industry. Meanwhile, the complicated interface is a serious obstacle to technicians engaged in FTEA

Visual Basic (VB) is a structured high-level programming language that is engineered for productively building type-safe and object-oriented applications. Visual Basic was one of the first systems that made it practical to write programs for the Windows operating system, which included software tools to automatically create the detailed programming required by Windows. These software tools not only create Windows programs, they also take full advantage of the graphical way that Windows works by letting programmers "draw" their systems with a mouse on the computer. Visual Basic also provides unique and complete software architecture such as Windows and VB programs, work together [1].

ANSYS software was integrated with Visual Basic to develop a simple user interface. When VB was used to encapsulate ANSYS software, visual analysis system was developed through the seamless integration of them, which is easy to use. Users can use it only by entering the corresponding structural parameters and analysis parameters. The analysis of design work on the valve can be completed by simply clicking on the button [2].

The specific steps were designed as follows:

A. The solid model was constructed by ANSYS to analyse the structural field and the flow of the gate-vale.

B. After these ANSYS steps had been completed, the next procedure in VB was as follows:

a. Visual parameter input interface for user were established in VB, and the number of interface was determined by user's demands.

b. The script was written to use the commercial finite element code ANSYS to form the APDL.file, and VB program execute the file to reach the purpose of parameter design.

c. the program was developed to automatically obtain and preserve these analytical results.

d. Contents of command were saved as *.Mac format by Visual Basic protocol.

e. VB was used to encapsulate ANSYS software, which means that the protocol for automatically calling macro command of VB was inputted. The system can automatically call ANSYS to generate model, simulate operating mode, and get analysis results meeting design requirements [3].

f. Calculating results can be outputted and analysed.

3 Implementation of System Technology Scheme

A. Implementation of ANSYS Analysis

In GUI-graphical user interface of ANSYS, solid model of gate valve was built and dissected to analysis. After the mesh generation of the model, restraint and loading was exerted, different contours will be obtained including displacement contour stress contour strain contour among the series of structures and loads. And the stress which happened of the gate valve dangerous position will be performed linearization operation; at last the linearization results will be received [4].

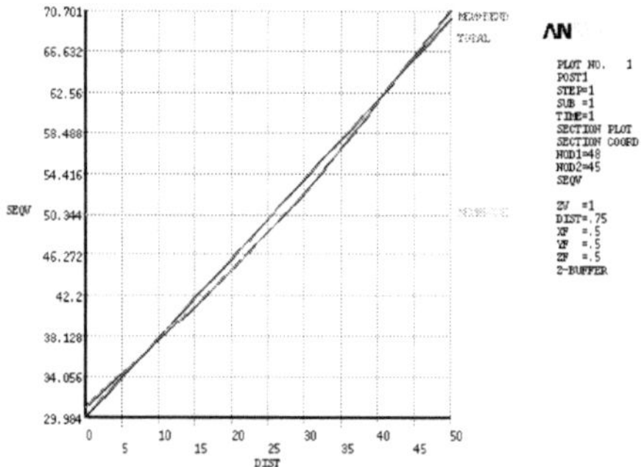

Fig. 1. Linear analysis graph

The precondition of fluid analysis are the fluid's form and the force of the fluid, and these can be got through the contours, including the fluid's pressure contour and velocity contour etc.. The contour in Fig. 2 was pictured for turbulence.

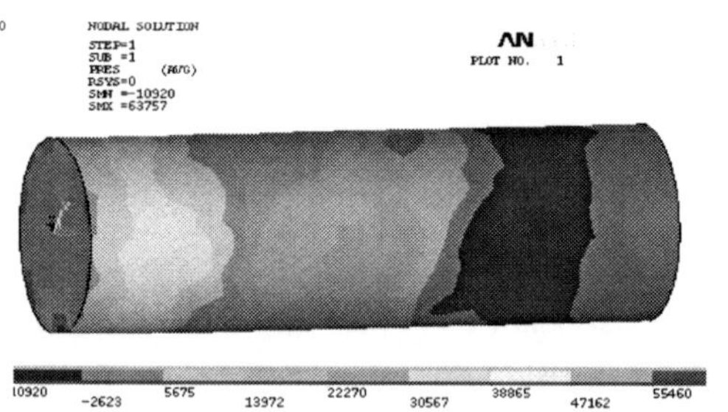

Fig. 2. Fluid pressure contour

B. Visual Basic Implementation

a. Define global variable

Forms will be created when VB program launched, due to the variable's exchange, the template modules has been created to define global variable. When the global variable been defined, different forms can share the public data.

b. Create the structure parameter interface

The purpose of parameter design is to realize the product's series modelling, which is to say server user. Base on this purpose, the software's interface as fig.3 shown, the function is providing with parameter's input, which is the model's geometric properties.

c. Create the analysis parameter interface

When the input of structure parameter is done, a dialog will be needed to finish inputting analysis parameter, the interface as fig.4 shown:

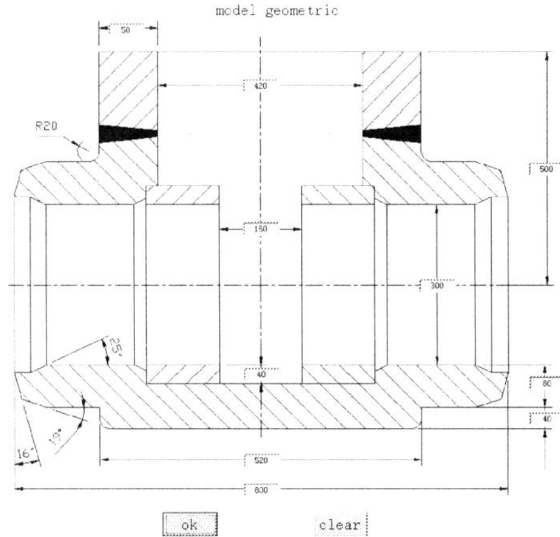

Fig. 3. Structural parameters input interface

analysis parameter

pressure (Mpa)	30	dens(Kg/m^3)	998
temp (℃)	20	velocity(m/s)	5
possion	0.3	c (KJ/Kg. ℃)	4.183
speed of sound (m/s)	340	gravitity (m/s^2)	9.81
Time (s)	10	D(m^2/s)	345
v(MPa. s)	1.005	E (MPa)	200000
u(m^2/s)	0.000001006	cc (1/MPa)	0.0005
k(W/(m. ℃))	0.599	btc(N/m)	0.0728

create flow parameter

Fig. 4. Analysis parameters input interface

Series of flow parameters will be inputted in the dialog, when the input is done, the software can calculate the flow parameters automatically.[5] When the software has been launched, user can adapt the default data or input data freely, click the "create flow parameter" button and finish the input.

d. Create flow parameter interface

The flow parameter which calculated previous step can be displayed in this dialog, user can check and verify the flow parameter, the "create macro" button as fig.5 shown has functions as follow: create macro with *.mac extension, gather and save the result.

e. Create the macro

Generally, an APDL file always contains several words which functions are setting parameters. According this character, the scripts of APDL and assign code are mixed in VB program. VB program print this codes line by line, at last form a file which extension is *.Mac.

f. ANSYS calling interface

The user only need to click the "execute" button, and the software will call ANSYS code in batch, execute mesh apply load and solve problem automatically. After the analysis is done, the software will pump a dialog, notice user the complete of the analysis. User can do post-processing due to the result, which including contours and data etc...

Fig. 5. Call interface of ANSYS

3 Conclusions

The gate valve's structure and flow feature can be obtained through the developed software, so the designer can understand the structure's stress field and displacement field intuitively. Base on the result, the designer can master inner flow mechanism easily, and even many problems in the traditional design can be solved. The developed software employs the idea of ASME stress rules, so the purpose of optimizing the valve can be reached, and it also can reduce the cost.

The developed software based on Visual Basic program, so the software has many traits including friendly convenient works easy and so on. The software seal the scripts of ANSYS background, user only need to input the geometric data the property of material and load data, when the software running, it can capture pictures and form files automatically. When the analysis is completed, a report will be formed immediately.

In a word, the developed software has a friendly interface, and it also has a working easy trait. So under the help of this software, the designer can master the design of the gate valve with high parameter rapidly, even the designer has no concept of ANSYS or poor in English.

Acknowledgment. The authors would like to acknowledge the financial support of the Process Equipment and Control Engineering of Key Laboratory of Sichuan Province (No. GK200807) and the Key Program of Sichuan Provincial Education Department (No. 07zz019).

References

1. Information on, `http://visualbasic.about.com/od/applications/a/whatisvb.htm`
2. Ma, C., Meng, X.: Parametric design method based on a directed acyclic hyper graph and object oriented technology. IEEE 4, 2383–2387 (2000)
3. Hardee, E.: CAD-based design parameterization for shape optimization of elastiesolid. Advances in Engineering Software (30), 185–199 (1999)
4. Hajela, R.: Neurobiological Computational Models in Structural Analysis and Design. Computers & Structures 41, 657–667 (1991)
5. Apion, E.R.: Finite element analysis in manufacturing engineering, pp. 1–18. ChMcGraw-Hill, inc., New York (1992)

Research on Entropy-TOPSIS in External Environment Evaluation of Power Grid Corporation

Qingyou Yan, Xiaoya Wang, Siqi He, and Lili Zhu

School of Economics and Management, North China Electric Power University,
2th Bei Nong Road, Hui Long Guan Town, Chang Ping District, Beijing, China
leeislee@hotmail.com

Abstract. This paper developed external environment impact assessment index system based on the asset management process of power grid Corporation. It established an entropy-TOPSIS environment impact assessment evaluation model and adopted the general procedure by Matlab language with this above comprehensive evaluation model to sort the external environment factors according to the impact degree so as to choose the important factors, and provided decision support to develop asset management strategies. This model introduced information-entropy to calculate every scoring expert weight in order to avoid determining subjectively the weight.

Keywords: External environment, Evaluation, Information Entropy, TOPSIS, Matlab Toolbar.

1 Introduction

Power Grid Corporation as a typical asset-intensive business has a huge asset scale. With the rapid economic and social development and the growing of electricity load, the corresponding power grid also should be accelerated, thus the operation, maintenance, update, and transform task of power grid assets would be even more arduous. Therefore, the traditional management methods have not been met requires of the development of Grid Corporate in new situation. Only to implement the Life Cycle Asset Management, could ensure the security of power grid, improve the efficient of assets, reduce life cycle costs and achieve a whole-process and comprehensive management. In the process to implement the Life Cycle Asset Management, it is basic to understand and grasp correctly the external environment of assets and its variation for developing scientific decision-making. At present, there was no separate literature in academic field, while plenty much research about the corporation external environment had been done.

International study on the external environment mainly about the relationship between environment and organizational strategy, forming three major theoretical schools: (1) Emphasized the environment's effect on the chosen organizational strategy, representatives as *School of Population Ecology and Contingency Theory*. (2) Emphasized organizational strategy's environment impact, representatives as the *Strategic choice theory and the Resource-Based Theory* thought: focusing on the

M. Dai (Ed.): ICCIC 2011, Part II, CCIS 232, pp. 420–427, 2011.

management and conduct their own choice from the point view of the enterprise, the common feature was that organizations do not always passively respond but subjectively against the external change by the strategic behavior at a considerable extent, meanwhile affected the environment to change its situation to achieve a more favorable position in the process of choosing to adapt to environment or strategic. (3) Emphasized the collaborative relationship between evolution of organizational environment and organizational strategy, representatives as *Organizational Learning Theory and Complexity theory* thought: it was wrong to simply take the relationship between environment and organizational strategy as one decided another, but make specific analysis according to time condition, and the collaborative evolutionary relationship[1] should be existed between these two. Foreign scholars' researches on the corporation external environment were all focused on the relationship between environment and organizational strategy, and generated a lot of research results, proposing the most classical mode *Environment - Strategy – Performance* in Strategic management.

Domestic scholars' studies were mainly concentrated on how to divide the corporation external environment and how to evaluate it. Li Lin divided the external environment of cooperate into political environment, economic environment, social environment, technological environment, industry structure and market environment[2]. Zhou Guohong divided that into legal and policy environment, institutional and socio-cultural environment, financing, environment, market environment, technical environment, human resources environment, social services environment and industrial environment[3]. Xi Youmin divided that into the economic environment, the political environment, the technological environment, social and cultural environment, population and natural resources environment[4]. Cheng Xiaohong divided that into the economic environment, the political environment, technological environment, social and cultural environment, human environment and natural resources environment[5]. Besides, almost all these literatures focused on business or strategy to study advantages and disadvantages of the external environment conditions, few started from the perspective of a management activity to look into the impact of external environment's importance, also few took corporation internal environment into effect index system from the perspective of environment division.

The structure of the paper was as follows: Section 2 developed the external environmental impact evaluation index system of Power Grid Corporation; Section 3 developed environmental impact assessment of improved information entropy TOPSIS model; Section 4 dealt with data processing, including questionnaire reliability test and relative similarity; Section 5 dealt with conclusions which determined the fatal external environmental factors and proposed corresponding strategy.

2 The External Environmental Impact Evaluation Index System about the Asset Life Cycle Management of Power Grid Corporation

The corporate external environment asset management is a multi-agent, multi-level, multi-dimensional structure of system with development and changes. In this paper, we took the asset management process of Power Grid Corporate and comments related with network asset management personnel into consideration to build strategic asset model of Power Grid Corporate, as shown in fig.1.

On this basis, we constructed the environmental impact assessment of improved TOPSIS model based on information entropy, according to the severity of impact to sort external environmental factors, finding factors which should be paid attention, and proposing appropriate strategies. Moreover, this paper developed the Matlab toolbar of Entropy-TOPSIS. The relative similarity of each external environmental factor can be obtained only entering the initial experts rating matrix.

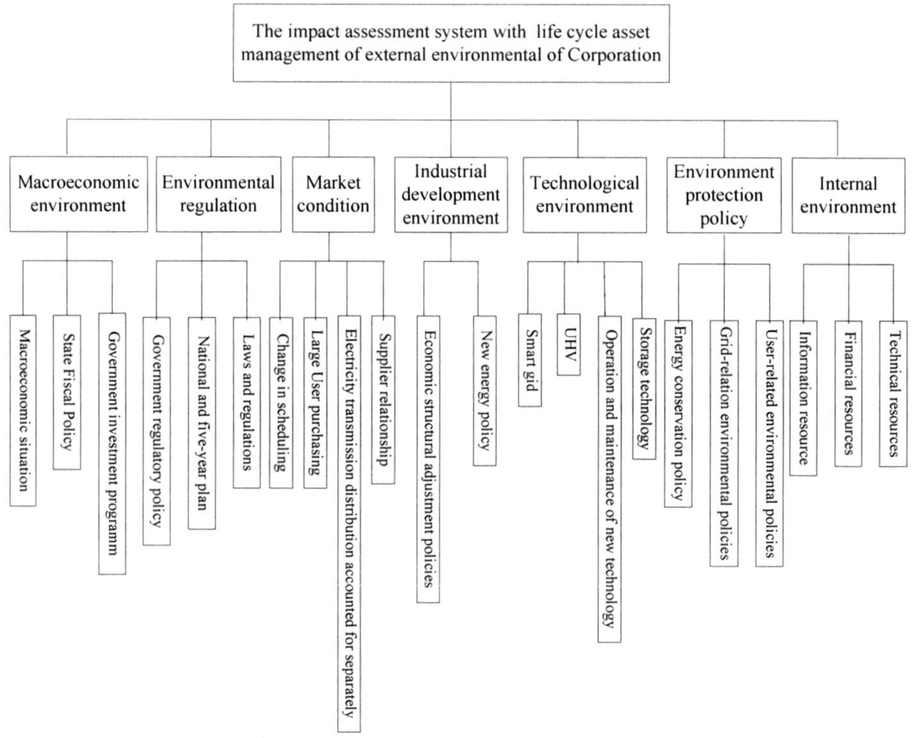

Fig. 1. The external environmental impact evaluation index system about the life cycle asset management of Power Grid Corporation

3 TOPSIS Method Based on Information Entropy

Technique for Order Preference by Similarity to Ideal Solution (as TOPSIS) was proposed by Hwang and Yoon in 1981. The basic idea[6,7] was to define a Ideal solution and negative ideal solution, finding a scenario which was nearest from ideal solution and farthest from negative ideal solution. The ideal solution was assumed scenario taking the best value, commonly not feasible. The negative ideal solution was assumed scenario taking the worst value, not feasible either. Any scenario from the ideal solution and the negative ideal solution had a weighted Euclidean distance measurement (Euclidean norm). But a certain solution which was nearest from ideal solution often happened not farthest from negative ideal solution, or not the nearest distance from another ideal solution but the farthest from negative ideal solution, and opposite happened if otherwise. TOPSIS method based on information entropy[8,9] considered the distance through the relative proximity, and avoided subjectivity on determining the weight of each index by introducing information entropy .

m denoted evaluation objects (external environmental factors), and n was represented as the number of the experts. X denoted the scoring matrix of external environmental factors, where x_{ij} was represented as expert j 's score about external environmental factor i .

$$X = \begin{matrix} \\ A_1 \\ A_2 \\ \vdots \\ A_m \end{matrix} \begin{matrix} X_1 & X_2 & \cdots & X_n \\ \left[\begin{matrix} x_{11} & x_{12} & \cdots & x_{1n} \\ x_{21} & x_{22} & \cdots & x_{2n} \\ \vdots & \vdots & \cdots & \vdots \\ x_{m1} & x_{m2} & \cdots & x_{mn} \end{matrix}\right] \end{matrix}$$

Formula of regularization (the proportion treatment) treatment for indicators gave as:

$$p_{ij} = \frac{x_{ij}}{\sum_{i=1}^{m} x_{ij}} \tag{1}$$

The information entropy of expert j was given from the definition of information entropy:

$$E_j = -k\sum_{i=1}^{m} p_{ij} \ln p_{ij} \qquad (j = 1, 2, \cdots n) \tag{2}$$

Where $0 \le E_j \le 1$ can be ensured with the coefficient k , through $k = 1/\ln m$.

Generally, index with smaller information entropy E_j had a greater variation, also provided greater information and gained greater weight; Otherwise, The weight should be smaller. Calculated weight through deviation d_j :

$$d_j = 1 - E_j \qquad (j = 1, 2, \cdots n) \tag{3}$$

The weight of scores of experts gave as:

$$w_j = \frac{d_j}{\sum_{j=1}^{n} d_j} \qquad (j = 1, 2, \cdots n) \tag{4}$$

The basic steps of TOPSIS method [10]

(1)According to formula (1)-(4), we could determine the weight of each expert's sore $w = (w_1, w_2, \cdots, w_n)$

(2) By constructing weighted normalized matrix Z , its element z_{ij} gave as,

$$Z = (z_{ij})_{m\times n}$$

$$z_{ij} = w_j z'_{ij} \qquad (i = 1,2,\cdots,n; i = 1,2,\cdots,m)$$

Where w_j was the weight of goal j ;

(3) A^* denoted the ideal solution and A^- denoted the negative ideal solution; J denoted the effective subset of goals, while J' was represented as the subset of cost targets:

$$A^* = \left\{ (\max_i z_{ij} \mid j \in J), (\min_i z_{ij} \mid j \in J') \mid i = 1,2,\cdots,m \right\} = \left(z_1^*, z_2^*, \cdots, z_n^*\right)$$

$$A^- = \left\{ (\min_i z_{ij} \mid j \in J), (\max_i z_{ij} \mid j \in J') \mid i = 1,2,\cdots,m \right\} = \left(z_1^-, z_2^-, \cdots, z_n^-\right)$$

(4) Calculating the external environmental factor's distance from ideal point S_i^* and distance from negative ideal solution S_i^- :

$$S_i^* = \sqrt{\sum_{j=1}^{m}\left(z_{ij} - z_j^*\right)^2} \qquad (i = 1,2,\cdots,m) \quad S_i^- = \sqrt{\sum_{j=1}^{m}\left(z_{ij} - z_j^-\right)^2} \qquad (i = 1,2,\cdots,m)$$

(5) Calculating each external environmental factor's relative proximity of ideal point C_i^* ;

$$C_i^* = S_i^- / \left(S_i^- + S_i^*\right) \qquad i = 1,2,\cdots,m$$

(6) Sorting scenario according to relative proximity.

$$A = \left\{ A_i \mid \max_{1\le i\le m}\left(C_i^*\right) \right\}$$

Sorting the impact of external environmental factor by relative similarity, a greater relative similarity meat a nearer distance from ideal solution and a farther distance from negative ideal solution hence reflected more importance.

4 Numerical Example

This paper obtained data through questionnaires, and the respondents were close-related professionals of network asset management. The main contents were two parts: (1) Profiles under investigation—the unit and work experience. (2)20 problems of the external environmental factors on the severity of asset management of Power

Grid Corporation. The propose was to conduct respondents to give comments about external environmental factors which were applied to the strategic assets, and determined the strategic impact and further the external environmental factors impact on power grid.

Respondents only choose from 5 ranks against every question, 5 for the extremely important factor, 4 for important factor, 3 for ordinary factor, 2 for unimportant factor, and 1for very unimportant one.

A. Test the reliability of the questionnaire

This study based on a questionnaire, so it was necessary to test the reliability. Reliability meat the possibility of getting the same result when used the same techniques repeatedly[11]. This paper judged the credibility through Cronbach-Alpha method by SPSS[12]. The Cronbach-Alpha coefficient was 0.784, and *Statistics* generally believed that the value fit test if α achieved 0.7[13], hence this survey was reliable.

B. Data Processing

By the reliability of the questionnaire and coming back to calculation steps in section 2, we implemented processs[14] through Matlab. After running, we obtained tool bar shown as fig.3.Sorting the decision matrix (ie, the questionnaire results) into.txt files as required, we clicked the button *Browse* to open decision matrix files, fill k value as demarcation point between efficiency indicators and cost-based indicators(the questionnaire have shown the scoring rules, saw all involved targets as efficiency index, let $k = 15$),then clicked the button *Relative proximity*, the text box *Result Output* would show the relative similarity of external environmental factor(shown as fig2) for us to assess further the extent of its importance.

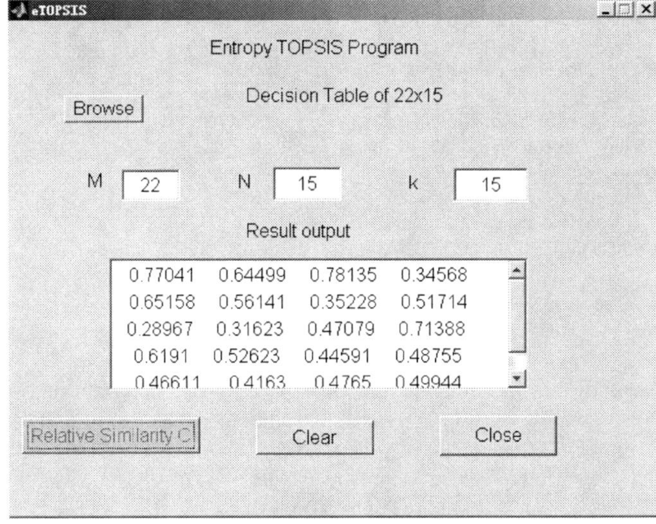

Fig. 2. Operational Results

5 Conclusions and Recommendations

A greater relative proximity indicated that the evaluated external environmental factors should be closer to the ideal solution, meanwhile farther away from the negative ideal solution, representing the more important impact on external environment. Shown as table 1, government investment plan had the greatest impact for power grid company asset life cycle management, followed by the macroeconomic situation, the new energy policy, national and regional five-year plan, the state fiscal policies and other external environmental factors. Therefore, when power grid company develop asset management strategy, firstly it should consider the impact on government investment plan, macroeconomic situation, the new energy policy, national and regional five-year plan, the state fiscal policies. Precisely, the third column in table 1 was the considering order of the impact.

Table 1. The relative similarity of each external environmental factors and order of importance

External Environmental Factors	Relative Similarity	Order of Importance
Government investment program	0.78135	1
Macroeconomic situation	0.77041	2
New Energy Policy	0.71388	3
National and regional five-year plan	0.65158	4
State Fiscal Policy	0.64499	5
Smart Grid	0.6191	6
Financial resources	0.60283	7
Technical Resources	0.5752	8
Laws and regulations	0.56141	9
UHV	0.52623	10
Large Users Purchasing	0.51714	11
information resource	0.49944	12
Operation and maintenance of new technologies	0.48755	13
User-related environmental policies	0.4765	14
Economic structural adjustment policies	0.47079	15
Energy conservation policy	0.46611	16
Storage Technology	0.44591	17
Grid-related environmental policies	0.4163	18
Change operation mode	0.35228	19
Government regulatory policy	0.34568	20
Relationships with suppliers	0.31623	21
Electricity transmission and distribution accounted for separately	0.28967	22

References

1. He, Z., Tang, J., Lu, Y.: Strategic relationship between organizational environment and organizational review of the literature and the latest research trends. Management World (11), 144–150 (2006)
2. Li, I., Wang, H.: Enterprise environment evaluation and diagnosis of the fuzzy AHP. Shanghai University of Technology 23(1), 91–94 (2001)

3. Zhou, G., Lu, L.: Tech SMEs environmental evaluation index system. Quantitative Technical Economics Research (2), 32–35 (2002)
4. Xi, Y.: Analysis of external environment for enterprises. Higher Education Press, Beijing (2001)
5. Cheng, X., Wang, F.: SMEs in China based on SEM evaluation system of the external environment. Business Economics and Management 204(10), 42–47 (2008)
6. Dong, Y.: Evaluation Theory, Methods and Applications. Science Press, Beijing (2007)
7. Yang, Y., Zhang, Q., Wu, L.: Entropy-based supplier selection TOPSIS method. Beijing University of Technology 26(1), 31–35 (2006)
8. Cheng, Q., Yang, X.: TOPSIS method based on entropy weight in water environment quality assessment. Environmental Engineering 25(4), 75–77 (2007)
9. Zhang, X., Liang, C., Liu, H.: Entropy-based TOPSIS method to improve water quality evaluation. Harbin Institute of Technology University 39(10), 1670–1672 (2007)
10. Liu, R., Wang, X.: TOPSIS method based on information entropy evaluation projects in the power grid in the application. In: Decision Sciences Systems Engineering Society of China Committee of the Eighth Annual Conference, vol. (10), pp. 136–141 (October 2009)
11. Earl, B.: The Practice of Social Research, 8th edn. Wadsworth Publishing Company, Belmont (1998)
12. Zhang, W.: SPSS 11 statistical analysis (Advanced section). Hope Electronic Press, Beijing (2002)
13. Nunnally, J.C.: Psychometric Theory, 2nd edn. McGraw-Hill, New York (1978)
14. Zhang, Z.: Proficient in Matlab 6.5 version. Beijing Aerospace University Press, Beijing (2003)

A New Mixed Variable Step Size ELMS Algorithm and Its Application in ANC

Sun Li Jun, Zhang Shou_Yong, and Wang Xiang_Li

School of Electrical Engineering
Henan University of Technology
Zhengzhou 450001, China
Sun5454@yeah.net

Abstract. In this paper, we proposed a new mixed variable step size ELMS algorithm (MVSS-ELMS) which combined the mean square error and the correlation of the error to modify the step size. The approach is general in the sense that it not only retains the benefits of ELMS algorithm lower steady-state error, but also improves the system convergence speed. In comparison, the new approach performance is much better than VSS-ELMS algorithm and VFSS-ELMS algorithm in the convergence speed and anti-noise capacity. Effectiveness of the proposed algorithm is demonstrated through computer simulations.

Keywords: adaptive filtering, noise canceller, LMS algorithm, ELMS algorithm.

1 Introduction

Noise pollution is a common phenomenon in signal transmission process, such as long-distance telephone communication system. Filtering technology can be used to pick up the using signal from the noise filed where the signal is very weak or the conventional method is invalid, but one limitations of this design is that it must be based on a priori knowledge of signal and noise. One modification of the best filtering technology is Adaptive Noise Cancellation (ANC) which uses the technology of adaptive filters with input from two micro-phones. One is for a reference noise input and the other is for a voice signal where the noise overlaps [1]. So it can extract the useful signal and suppress the effects of interference and noise signal by automatically adjust the adaptive filter weights to more effectively use the original signal, without knowing or requiring very little prior knowledge of the signal noise. The widely used least-mean-square (LMS) algorithm has been successfully applied to many filtering applications, including signal modeling, equalization, control, echo cancellation, or beam-forming, for its simplicity, low computational complexity, and ease of implementation, however, the main drawback of the LMS algorithm is that it will produce a big steady-state error and low convergence speed. Many ANC algorithms have been proposed in the past years using modified LMS algorithm in order to simultaneously improve the speed of convergence and tracking ability

M. Dai (Ed.): ICCIC 2011, Part II, CCIS 232, pp. 428–435, 2011.

including normalized LMS (NLMS),extended LMS (ELMS) algorithms [2]. The NLMS algorithm has advantages in convergence time and steady-state, however, the ELMS performance is much better than the NLMS algorithm in steady-state. The fixed step-size ELMS algorithm is contradictive in the request of step-size μ for diminish μ can improve the convergence precision and reduce the steady-state error, but the decrease of μ in turn lead to the reduction of convergence speed and tracking rate. Increase factor μ can speed up the convergence rate, but it will lead to steady-state error increases, even lead to the divergence of the algorithm. Therefore, there are scholars used the method of variable step-size to solve the above contradiction. In [2], [3], faster converging algorithms called variable step-size NLMS algorithm (VSS-NLMS algorithm) and VFSS-NLMS, respectively, are proposed. The VSS-NLMS algorithm use the mean square error to control the step-size, and it is easily to be disturbed by the independent noise. The VFSS-NLMS algorithm which use the correlation of error signal to adjust the step size, however, analysis point out that adaptive error is non-correlated in the process of closing to the best value of weight, but its relevance possibly is also very small in the convergence procedure when the filter order is large, so use the correlation of the error signal to control the step size may cause the step size reduced very quickly in the adaptive process, and then slow down convergence rate, result with bad performance of the algorithm in the limited time.

In order to achieve a good performance of ANC, therefore, the above two variable step-size methods are introduced into the ELMS algorithm and get VSS-ELMS, VFSS-ELMS algorithms to compare with the new mixed variable step-size ELMS algorithm (MVSS-ELMS) proposed in this paper which combined the mean square error and the correlation of the error signal to modify the step- size. We will show that our proposed method greatly improve the effectiveness and reliability of ANC

2 ELMS Algorithm

The ELMS algorithm used a revisionary instantaneous gradient estimate as (1), so it guarantee a stable steady-state performance than the LMS algorithm due to the error vector $-2s(n)X(n)$ which is produced for using transient error gradient $\hat{\nabla}(n)$ in the LMS algorithm to represent the mean error gradient $\nabla(n)$ [4].

$$\begin{aligned}\hat{\nabla}(n)elms &= -2[e(n)-\hat{s}(n)]X(n) = -2[s(n)\\ &-\hat{s}(n)]X(n) - 2[n_0(n) - X^T(n)W(n)]X(n)\end{aligned} \tag{1}$$

Where $\hat{s}(n)$ is the forecast estimate of the using signal $s(n)$, and then the ELMS algorithm can be described by the following equations:

$$
\begin{aligned}
&e(n) = d(n) - X^T(n)W(n) \\
&\hat{s}(n) = E^T(n)W_1(n) \\
&W_1(n+1) = W_1(n) + 2\mu[e(n) - \hat{s}(n)]E(n) \\
&W(n+1) = W(n) + 2\mu[e(n) - \hat{s}(n)]X(n)
\end{aligned}
\tag{2}
$$

Where $E(n) = [e(n), e(n-1), \cdots, e(n-L+1)]^T$, L is the order of the wiener forecast estimator. A conventional method, the wiener forecast estimator, was used to estimate the signal $\hat{s}(n)$. Adopt this kind of estimator can guarantee the superiority of the ELMS algorithm for $\hat{s}(n)$ can tracking the using signal $s(n)$ effective and simultaneous, and the more approximate of the forecast estimated signal $\hat{s}(n)$ to the $s(n)$, the better of the ELMS algorithm's steady state performance is [5].

3 Variable Step Size ELMS Algorithm

The convergence rate of the ELMS algorithm should be slower than LMS for it needs to estimate the wanted signal, in order to improve the ELMS algorithm convergence rate, many improved algorithms have been proposed of which the variable step size ELMS, use variable step size $\mu(n)$ to replace fixed step size μ, was the most commonly used. In [3] a method was used to control the step size which using the mean square error. Substituting the step-size into the ELMS algorithm, we can obtain a variable step-size ELMS(VSS-ELMS) algorithm and rewrite (2) in (3) as

$$
\begin{aligned}
&\mu(n+1) = \alpha\mu(n) + \gamma[e(n) - \hat{s}(n)]^2 \\
&\mu(n+1) = \begin{cases} \mu_{\max} & \mu(n+1) > \mu_{\max} \\ \mu_{\min} & \mu(n+1) < \mu_{\min} \\ \mu(n+1) & else \end{cases}
\end{aligned}
\tag{3}
$$

Where $0 < \alpha < 1$, $\mu_{\max}$ is a step size which is closing to the unstable spot of the standard ELMS, the parameter α always take the value close to 1 to obtain the maximum possible convergence rate. The prominent advantage of this algorithm compared to the conventional ELMS is: the value of $e(n) - \hat{s}(n)$ is very big and then the value of $\mu(n)$ is large too, so the VSS-ELMS algorithm has fast convergence rate in the preliminary stage of adaptive process; Along with the algorithm converge to the stable state, the value of $e(n) - \hat{s}(n)$ will reduces to a minimum and the same to $\mu(n)$.So the misadjustment will be very small when the weight tends to the optimal weight. It is worth pointing out that compared to the conventional ELMS algorithm the performance of the VSS-ELMS algorithm has promoted greatly, however, it is sensitive to independent noise and easy is disturbed, and it would cause quite large steady-state error when it was used in a low signal-to-noise ratio environment.

Therefore, an improved method to control the step-size was proposed in [2], and we apply it into the ELMS algorithm to get a new kind of variable step-size ELMS algorithm (VFSS-ELMS) which is using the correlation of error signal to adjust the step size. We recognize that (3) can be rewritten as :

$$p(n) = \beta p(n-1) + (1-\beta)\{[e(n) - \hat{s}(n)][e(n-1) - \hat{s}(n-1)]\}$$
$$\mu(n+1) = \alpha\mu(n) + \gamma p^2(n) \tag{4}$$

$\beta(0 < \beta < 1)$ is a weight coefficient constant, used to control the convergence time, and $\mu(0) = \mu_{\max}$, $p(0) = \mu(0)$, to guarantee quick convergence speed in the adaptive preliminary stage. In contrast to the VSS-ELMS algorithm, its sensitivity to independent noise has decreased greatly, however, it is sensitive to initial step-size and not track to jumping system simultaneously.

4 New Mixed Variable Step Size Elms Algorithm (Mvss-Elms)

In this section, we present a novel mixed variable step size ELMS algorithm ELMS (MVSS-ELMS) which using associated value of the mean square error and correlation of the error to adjust its step-size showed in (5). This new algorithm has many advantage in steady state, convergence rate, and anti-noise capacity; meanwhile, it brings remarkably improvement of the VFSS-ELMS algorithm drawback that step-size decrease too fast [5][6][7]

$$p(n) = \beta p(n-1) + (1-\beta)[(e(n) - \hat{s}(n))(e(n-1) - \hat{s}(n-1)) + (e(n) - \hat{s}(n))^2]$$
$$= \beta p(n-1) + (1-\beta)\{[e(n) - \hat{s}(n)][(e(n-1) - \hat{s}(n-1)) + (e(n) - \hat{s}(n))]\}$$

$$\mu(n+1) = \alpha\mu(n) + U_{\max}((1-\alpha)(1 - \frac{1}{1 + bp^2(n)})) \quad \mu(n+1) = \begin{cases} \mu_{\min} & \mu(n+1) < \mu_{\min} \\ \mu(n+1) & else \end{cases} \tag{5}$$

Following we will give the analyses of the new algorithm's performance: supposing that $\hat{s}(n)$ would be the better evaluate of $s(n)$ along with the adaptive process i.e.

$$\hat{s}(n) = s(n)$$

$$e(n) = s(n) + X^T(n)W_{opt} + v(n) - X^T(n)W$$

$v(n)$ is independence noise with zero mean value uncorrelated to $X(n)$, the error signal can be as follow in ANC [3], [9]

$$e(n)-\hat{s}(n)=s(n)-\hat{s}(n)+v(n)+X^T(n)W_{opt}$$
$$-X(n)W^T(n)=v(n)-X^T(n)\Delta W$$
$$\Delta W=W(n)-W_{opt}(n),$$

define $e(n)-\hat{s}(n)=m(n)$, and then

$$m(n)[m(n)+m(n-1)]=v^2(n)+v(n)v(n-1)-$$
$$2v(n)X^T(n)\Delta W-v(n)X^T(n-1)\Delta W-v(n-1)X^T(n)\Delta W$$
$$+\Delta W^T X(n)X^T(n-1)\Delta W+\Delta W^T X(n)X^T(n-1)\Delta W$$

The feature of error signal correlation can be obtained by expected mean. For $v(n)$ is mean-zero, independent to $X(n)$, and to itself

$$E\{m(n)[m(n)+m(n-1)]\}=E[\Delta W^T(n)X(n)$$
$$X^T(n-1)\Delta W]+E[\Delta W^T X(n)X^T(n)\Delta W] \tag{6}$$

From (6), we know that the associated value of the error of the error signal correlation and the mean square error is not influenced by the noise $v(n)$, so the new algorithm using

$$[e(n)-\hat{s}(n)]\{[e(n)-\hat{s}(n)]+[e(n-1)-\hat{s}(n-1)]\}$$

to modify the step size and then it guarantee faster convergence rate and lower steady state error for the step size is only correlated to the input signal and not correlated to the noise. Especially when it is used in the low signal-to-noise ratio environment can maintain the good performance. At the same time it overcome the VFSS-ELMS algorithm drawback that step-size decrease too fast by introduce the least step size μ_{min} to control the scope of step size.

5 The Computer Simulation Result and Analyzes

In this section, the performance of the proposed method is assessed via computer simulations. For comparison purposes, the parameter settings chosen for the following simulations are as follows: 1) adaptive filter order L=4; 2) we use sine signal for the input signal $s(n)$; 3) a white Gaussian noise was added as the reference input signal $X(n)$ and the resulting signal-to-noise ratio(SNR) is 10db, and takes this white noise as jamming signal $N(n)$ of the useful input signal. 4) Independence noise $v(n)$ is white noise and the SNR is 5db. In this paper, 5) U_{max} =0.25, μ_{min} =0.002 and the initial step size is U_{max} .

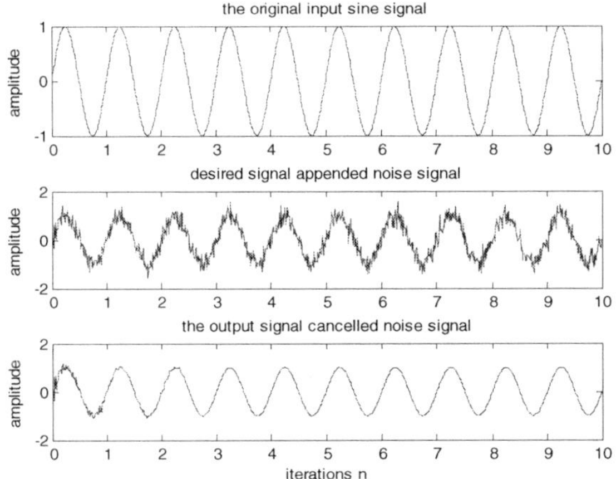

Fig. 1. The output of MVSS-ELMS algorithm

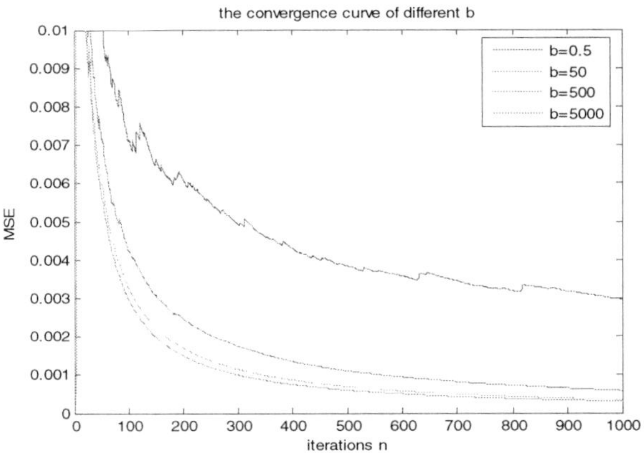

Fig. 2. The convergence curve of different b

The noise cancellation effects of MVSS-ELMS algorithm are shown in Fig.1. We can see that the new algorithm remarkably improved the noise cancellation and convergence performance.

In Fig.2, we show the convergence curve obtained with the MVSS-ELMS algorithm where b take 0.5, 50, 500, 5000 separately; the step size of the wiener predictor μ is 0.5, a =0.05, b =0.1. We notice that the convergence rate is faster when b takes bigger value on the condition that other parameters are the same.

Fig.3 shows the anti-noise capacity of the VSS-ELMS, VFSS-ELMS, MVSS-ELMS algorithm where b =0.5, μ =0.5, a =0.05, b =200. We can see that initial anti-noise performance of the VFSS-ELMS is superior to that of VSS-ELMS and MVSS-ELMS; however, the MVSS-ELMS algorithm can achieve the same anti-noise capacity with VSS-ELMS as iteration goes on.

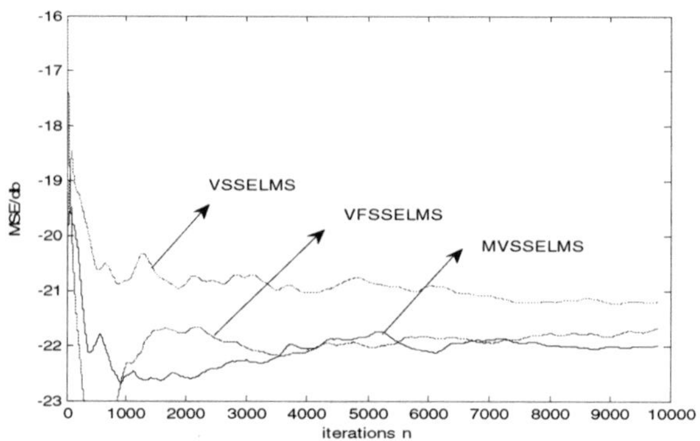

Fig. 3. The anti-noise capacity of different step size algorithms

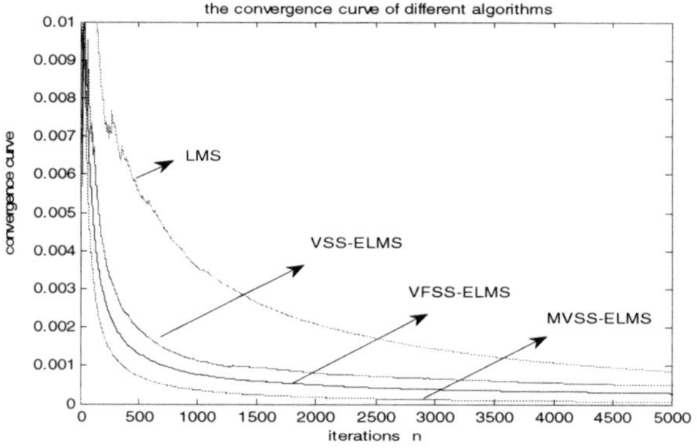

Fig. 4. The convergence curve of different algorithms

The convergence curves of different approaches are shown in Fig.4. We can see that the MVSS-ELMS algorithm remarkably improved the convergence curve performance compared to LMS, VSS-ELMS, VFSS-MLMS algorithm (sampling points is 5000, the mean value of 200 independent simulation), and the steady-state error of the new algorithm is lower than those algorithms.

6 Conclusion

In this paper, we proposed a novel method to control the step-size of the ELMS. The theoretical analysis show that it has the good properties of fast convergence speed and a small steady state error, the algorithm is not affected by presence of uncorrected noise. Under certain conditions, the proposed ANC based on the MVSS-ELMS algorithm offers a minor improvement in computational complexity. However, as the simulations show, it may improve the noise cancellation performance compared to other algorithms.

Acknowledgment. This work is supported by Zhengzhou Science and Technology Project (No. 2-41).

References

[1] Wu, L.C., Sheng, L.C.: Discussion on Variable Step LMS Algorithms. Ship Electronic Engineering 5(28), 175–176 (2008)
[2] Qian, F.C., Shun, Z.Y.: Research on ELMS Algorithm and Variable Step Size Algorithm. Journal of Air Force Engineering University 5(2), 77–80 (2004)
[3] Xiao, Y., Rui, H.G.: ELMS and Variable step size Algorithm in ANC. Journal of Shanghai Jiaotong University 32(4), 92–96 (1998)
[4] Xiao, Y., Qicai, W.: An extended LMS algorithm in ANC. In: ICNN SP 1995, Nanjing, China, vol. (12), pp. 737–740 (1995)
[5] Yu, L., Zhong, W.: New variable step size LMS-Type algorithm and simulation based on Decorrelation method. Electronic Measurement Technology 30(1), 52–55 (2007)
[6] Gorriz, J.M., Ramirez, J.: A Novel LMS Algorithm Applied to Adaptive Noise Cancellation. IEEE Signal Processing Letters 16(1), 34–37 (2009)
[7] Yao, S.C., Bo, L.H.: Variable step size LMS adaptive filtering algorithm and analysis. Journal of Information Engineering University 7(2), 190–192 (2006)
[8] Tingchan, W., Sangaroon, O.: Performance comparison of adaptive algorithms for multiple echo cancellation in telephone network. In: ICCAS 2007, pp. 789–792 (2007)
[9] Qian, F.C.: A new variable step size LMS algorithm and its simulations. Radio Engineering 34(4), 31–32 (2004)
[10] Tobias, O.J., Seara, R.: On the LMS algorithm with constant and variable leakage factor in a nonlinear environment. IEEE Signal Processing 54(9), 3448–3458 (2006)
[11] Tandon, A., Ahmad, M.O.: An efficient, low-complexity, normalized LMS algorithm for echo cancellation. In: Circuits and Systems, NEWCAS 2004, pp. 161–164 (2004)

A New Variable Step-Size Constant Modulus Blind Equalization Algorithm

Sun Li Jun[1], Zhang Shou-Yong[2], and Dai Bin[2]

[1] School of Electrical Engineering,
Henan University of Technology,
Zhengzhou 450001, China
[2] School of Information Science and Engineering,
Henan University of Technology,
Zhengzhou 450001, China
Sun5454@yeah.net

Abstract. In order to overcome the shortcoming of fixed step- size constant module(CM) blind equalization algorithm, this paper proposes an new adaptive variable step- size constant module blind equalization algorithm, in which we use mean square error (MSE) to improved function as step- size control factor. Computer simulations and theory analyses show that the proposed algorithm has advantages of low complexity, fast convergence, and low computational load.

Keywords: Blind Equalization CMA, Variable Step-Size, MSE.

1 Introduction

In modern communication systems, high-speed data communication over a band-limited channel is subject to inter-symbol interference as a result of transmitter receiver filtering and multipath propagation. Mitigation of such kind of distortion calls for equalization. The conventional equalization algorithms need some training sequences. And transferring the training sequences would occupy some frequency resource which is valuable and in short. Blind equalization doesn't need referring to a training sequence to maintain normal work and only utilizes the prior information of transmitted signals to equalize the channel character. So it can raise the channel's efficiency and may get better equalization ability at the same time. In the last two or three decades, the blind equalization techniques have gained an increasing intrest. In a variety of blind equalization algorithm, the most popular is constant modulus algorithm (CMA), which was firstly introduced by Godard and Treichler. The CMA has calculated the amount of small, easy real-time algorithm to achieve better robustness and the advantages of widely used. However, the traditional CMA using a fixed step size, the algorithm convergence speed and steady-state residual error as a contradiction.

M. Dai (Ed.): ICCIC 2011, Part II, CCIS 232, pp. 436–442, 2011.

2 Cma

CMA is one kind of Bussgang-type blind equalization algorithms, (also a special case). The nature of the Bussgang algorithm for blind equalization model is shown in Fig. 1.

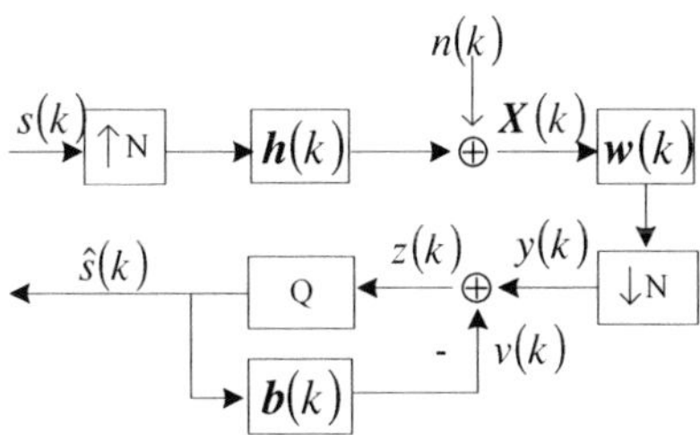

Fig. 1. The nature of the Bussgang algorithm for blind equalization model

where x(n) is the transmitted symbols, h(n)is the channel impulse response, n(n) is the complex white noise, y(n) is the equalizer input, $\tilde{x}(n)$ is the equalizer output, $\hat{x}(n)$ is the output of the decision device , $g(\cdot)$ is non-linear function of memoryless estimate, $e(n)$ is error signal.

According to the theory of signal transmission, the equalizer input is given as follow:

$$y(n) = h(n) * x(n) + n(n) = \sum_i h_i(n)x(n-i) + n(n) \tag{1}$$

the output of equalizer:

$$\tilde{x}(n) = w(n) * y(n) = \sum_i w_i(n)y(n-i) = W^T Y(n) \tag{2}$$

CMA cost function as follows:

$$J(w_n) = \frac{1}{4} E[(|\tilde{x}(n)|^2 - R_2)^2] \tag{3}$$

Where R_2 is the mode of the algorithm:

$$R_2 = \frac{E[|x(n)|^4]}{E[|x(n)|^2]} \tag{4}$$

In constant modulus algorithm e(n) is given by

$$e(n) = \tilde{x}(n)[R_2 - |\tilde{x}(n)|^2] \tag{5}$$

The equalization tap coefficients are updated according to the following algorithm:

$$W(n+1) = W(n) - \frac{\mu \partial J[W(n)]}{\partial W(n)} = W(n) + \mu \tilde{x}(n)[R_2 - |\tilde{x}(n)|^2]Y^*(n) \tag{6}$$

Where * denotes conjugate complex conjugate transposition, μ is the iteration step-size factor, usually taken the small normal number. By the type (6) can be known, Step-size parameter is a key factor to decide convergence speed and excess MSE. A fast convergence speed needs large step-size, but a small excess MSE requires small one. It means that these two criterions can not be optimized concurrently when using fixed step-size. For solving this problem, the variable step-size technology[1] is introduced in equalization. Variable step-size equalization algorithm has both the fast convergence speed and small excess MSE. Early in the algorithm convergence, increased step length and speed up the convergence rate; near convergence, the step-size reduced to improve the convergence precision.

3 New Adaptive Step-Size CM Blind Equalization Algorithm

Jingfan Tan and Jingzheng Ouyang [3] combined step-size μ with the error signal's non-linear function and obtained a new variable step adaptive filter algorithm (SVSLMS), which could overcome the tradeoff in convergence rate, track rate and convergence precision. During this algorithm , Variable step size was the excess error of Sigmoid function, $\mu(n)$ was given by:

$$\mu(n) = \mu\{1/[1 + \exp(-a|e(n)|)] - 0.5\} \tag{7}$$

Where a is a constant which controls the shape of the Sigmoid functions and decided to increase the speed curve, μ is a constant which controls the scope of Sigmoid function and needs to experiment to determine.

Sigmoid function is too complicated in here, and the excess function error is not steady when closes to zero Department, because the direct use of the residual error to control the step size, there are some deficiencies, so as to improve the algorithm as follow:

$$\mu(n) = u\{1 - \exp[-a|MSE(n)|]\} \tag{8}$$

Where μ is the scale factor control which Control the range of $\mu(n)$. a is determined parameters which is used to control the pace of step size. Where the mean square error expressed by the following formula:

$$MSE(n) = E\{e^2(n)\} = E\{[\hat{x}(n) - \tilde{x}(n)]^2\} \tag{9}$$

Style (5), (6), (8) and (9) constitutes a self-adaptive time-varying step-size constant modulus algorithm.

4 The Improved Algorithm Convergence Analysis

As a result of

$$0 \le 1 - \exp(-a|MSE(n)|) \le 1 \tag{10}$$

Reference type (9), we can see:

$$0 \le \mu(n) \le \mu \tag{11}$$

Therefore, we can see that in the case of channel interference, the step change has always been in $[0, \mu]$, and could have been avoided as a result of unforeseen circumstances resulting from misuse of transfer or divergence algorithm, in order to ensure good tracking performance. At the same time, by selecting the parameters a, you can change the pace of different curve-step, easy to select suitable for the control of step-size curve.

At the same time in order to ensure convergence, step-size factor that must be met [4]:

$$0 \le \mu(n) \le 2/3tr(R) \tag{12}$$

Where R is the equalizer input signal's auto-correlation matrix, $tr(R)$ is the track of R. Also by the type (11), we can see:

$$u \le 2/3tr(R) \tag{13}$$

Therefore, in type (13) conditions, the algorithm convergence in certain, But does not satisfy the conditions of u and a, all can enable the algorithm in the initial phase of a larger step, and after convergence in the algorithm step size smaller.

5 Simulation Results

In this section, we illustrated the performance of the improved CMA proposed in this paper. We have simulated a QPSK source signal. The signal to noise ratio (SNR) was fixed to 20db/symbol in simulation. The length of the equalizer was taken as 11. The middle tap of the equalizer was initialized to the nonzero value 1, and the rest of the equalizer weights were initialized to 0. The impulse response of the channel is h= [1, 0.3,-0.3, 0.1,-0.1]. The parameter μ in CMA was set to 0.003, while improved the variable step-size algorithm was chosen as 0.07 and $a = 5$.

Fig.2 shows that comparison of convergence curve of two algorithms on 4PSK in Common channel. Fig.3 shows that QPSK signal through the common channel the improved algorithm step curve. As can be seen from the figure that the improved algorithm has higher convergence speed and steady-state error of smaller, with the algorithm convergence, steady step length adjustment value down gradually.

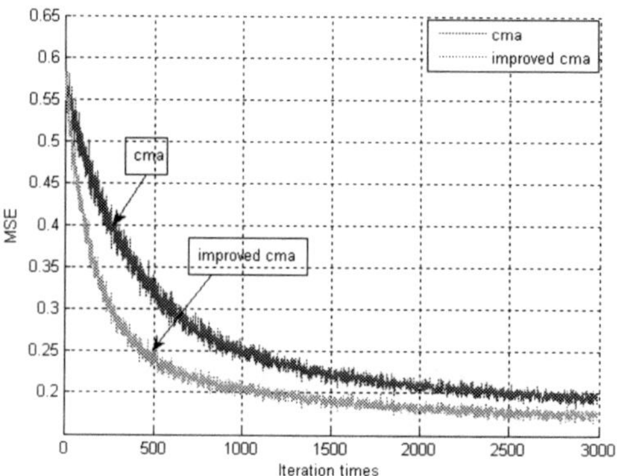

Fig. 2. Comparison of convergence curve of two algorithms on 4PSKin Common channel

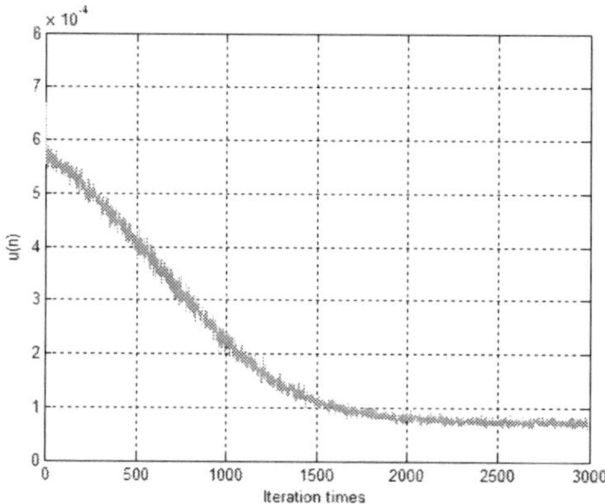

Fig. 3. The improved algorithm step curve

Fig.4-a is QPSK signal convergence Constellation of CMA in common channel. Fig.4-b is 4PSK signal convergence constellation of improved CMA in common channel. From the figure can be clearly seen, after algorithm convergence, the constellation concentrate of the improved algorithm is more clear and centralized, so the improved algorithm has smaller residual error and BER.

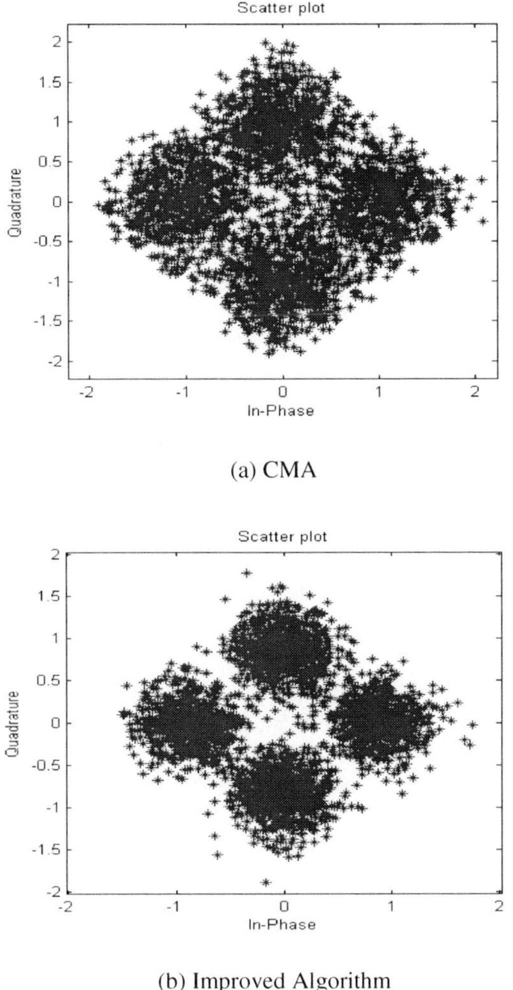

(a) CMA

(b) Improved Algorithm

Fig. 4. After the convergence of two algorithms compared constellation diagram

6 Conclusion

In this paper, by applying mean square error (MSE) to improved Sigmoid function to control step-size, we proposed a new variable step-size constant modulus blind equalization algorithm. The theoretical analysis and computer simulation show that the improved algorithm has higher performance for blind adaptive channel equalization than the fixed CMA algorithm.

Acknowledgements. This work is supported by Zhengzhou Science and Technology Project (No. 2-41).

References

[1] Sun, L. Q., Ge, L. D.: A new dual-mode blind equalization based on estimated error variance. In: Proc. Computer-Aided Industrial Design and Conceptual Design (CAIDCD 2006). IEEE Press, Los Alamitos (2006)

[2] pp. 1–4, doi:10.1109/CAIDCD.2006.329486

[3] Raymond, H.: A Variable Step Size LMS Algorithm. IEEE Trans. On Signal Processing 40, 1633–1642 (1992)

[4] Kilfoyle, D.B., Baggeroer, A.B.: The state of the art in underwater acoustictelemetry. IEEE J. Oceanic Eng. 25(1), 4–27 (2000)

[5] Labat, J., Macchi, O., Laot, C.: Adaptive Decision Feedback Equalization: Can You Skip the Training Period. IEEE Transactions on Communications 46(7), 921–930 (1998)

[6] Liyi, Z., Lei, C.: Variable Step-size CMA Blind Equalization based on Non-linear Function of Error Signal. In: Proc. Communications and Mobile Computing (CMC 2009), pp. 396–399. IEEE Press, Los Alamitos (2009), doi:10.1109/CMC.2009.77

[7] Proakis, J.G.: Digital communications, 4th edn. McGraw-Hill, Boston (2001)

[8] Meng, C., Tuqan, J., Ding, Z.: A Quadratic Programming Approach to Blind Equalization and Signal Separation. Signal Processing 57, 2232–2244 (2009)

A New Algorithm of Echo Cancellation in Mobile Applications

Sun Li Jun[1], Dai Bin[2], and Zhang Shou-Yong[2]

[1] School of Electrical Engineering
Henan University of Technology
Zhengzhou 450001, China
[2] School of Information Science and Engineering
Henan University of Technology
Zhengzhou 450001, China
Sun5454@yeah.net

Abstract. Mobile communication network echo is mainly caused by two factors: mobile terminals and wireless network delay. Several adaptive algorithms are found to offset the echo of wireless network delay, such as the LMS-type algorithm (including the NLMS, BLMS), and RLS algorithms. By analysis and comparison of their performances, a new algorithm (NLMS-BRLS) is obtained for echo cancellation in mobile communication systems, and the simulation results demonstrate the efficiency of the proposed method.

Keywords: Least Mean Squared, Recursive Least Squared, Echo Cancellation, Adaptive Filter.

1 Introduction

In communication systems, echo exists in many situations, like the video-conferencing system, the mobile hands-free phone, the videophone terminal, the mobile communication and other personal applies, satellite communication and so on. The echo seriously influences pronunciation clarity, and what more fatal is when the feed back is serious the system will be unable to work, so it is essential to eliminate echo. In motion network, similarly with the fixed-line telephone it will receive this kind of echo's influence; therefore to design an effective echo canceller will be an important content to guarantee the connection quality of the mobile communication system. Because the echo in mobile communication is real-time changeable, generally the adaptive filtering technology is used to realize the echo cancellation, and the adaptive algorithm is the core of this technology.

2 Echo Canceller's Principle

A. The model of an acoustic echo counter-balance system

The characteristic of the echo way is first estimated by the echo canceller, and then an echo transcription is produced, the echo again is subtracted from the received signal,

M. Dai (Ed.): ICCIC 2011, Part II, CCIS 232, pp. 443–449, 2011.

then the expectation receive signal estimate value is obtained. This is the echo canceller's principle. Because the echo way is unknown and it is time-variable, it is difficult to achieve echo cancellation. One of the methods which are accepted by everybody is generally: the echo is simulated via the adaptive filter; the goal of echo cancellation is achieved after this echo again is subtracted from the received signal. Figure 1 is the model of an acoustic echo canceller:

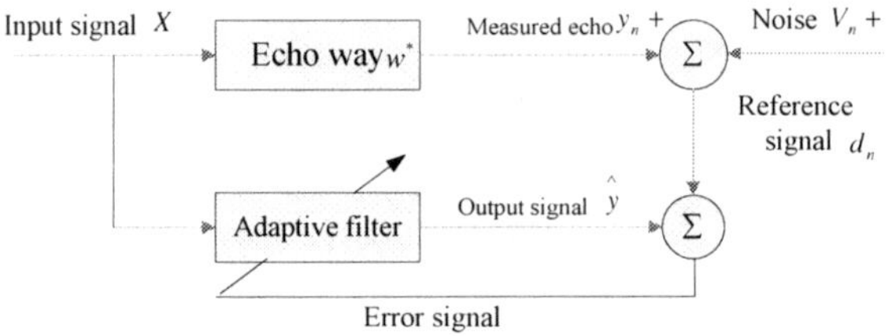

Fig. 1. The model of an acoustic echo canceller

On one hand, the far-end talker signal x_n through the echo channel w^* turns the measured echo y_n,then y_n adds the near-end noise v_n to form the expectation signal d_n; On the other hand, x_n through the adaptive filter H_n produces the synthesis echo $\hat{y}_n$ which is similar with the expectation signal, the error signal $e_n = d_n - \hat{y}_n$, $\hat{y}_n = X_n^t H_n$, where $X_n = (x_n, x_{n-1}, \cdots x_{n-L+1})$ is the input signal, H_n is a vector of the filter in time n. When the adaptive filter's unit pulse response can simulate the echo channel's transfer function well, after undergoing echo cancellation processing, the stable state echo error $e_n = d_n - \hat{y}_n$ will approach to 0, thus echo cancellation is realized. The entire acoustic echo canceller not only contains the adaptive filtering functional module, but also includes the near-end signal measuring ability module, far-end signal detection additional modules and residual echo suppression module. In this paper we mainly discuss the adaptive echo cancellation algorithm which holds an important role in the echo canceller.

B. Acoustic echo canceller in mobile communication system

ITU-T stipulated echo suppression measure must be adopted, when the echo delay achieves above 100ms. The reasons for the echo delay in the wireless way mainly include: (1) the time delay of wireless link transmission information; (2) the time delay of BTS (Base station) or MS (Mobile Station) using balanced technology to overcome multi-diameter detention; (3) the time delay of TC to realize the voice arranges the decoding .All time delay total quantity surpasses 100ms, therefore the echo cancellation must be used in the mobile communication system.

The echo channel is simulated by impulse response w(k) and the local noise signal n(k),in this paper the simulation's expectation signal obtains by input signal x(k) convolution impulse response c(k).

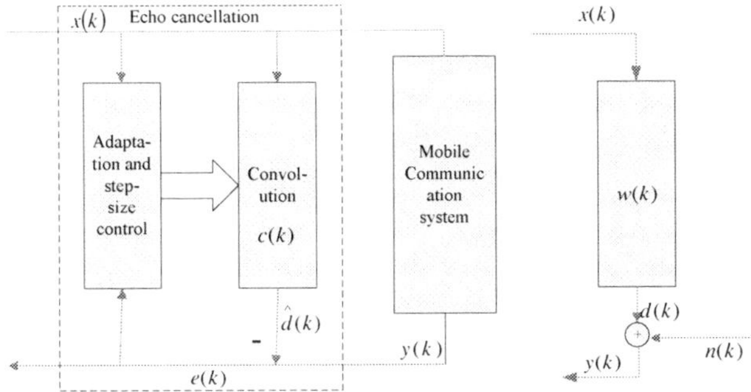

Fig. 2. Echo canceller in mobile communication system

3 Adaptive Algorithms

The research of the adaptive algorithm is now one of the most active topics. There are two main adaptive algorithms in echo cancellation: One kind is the smallest mean square error method and the other is the recursive least square.

$x_n = [x_n, x_{n-1}, \cdots x_{n-L+1}]^T$ represents input signal vector of the time n, and it constitutes by the final L signal sampling values. $w_n = [w_{0n}, w_{1n}, w_{2n} ... w_{(L-1)n}]^T$ is frequently the adaptive filter's order coefficient. L is the length of filter. d_n is the excepted output signal, e_n is the error signal, μ is a parameter to controls stable and the convergence rate, and it is called the length of stride factor or the gain also.

A. LMS algorithm

In steepest descent method, the precise gradient is replaced by gradient vector's estimate each iteration, and then form the common LMS algorithm.

The LMS algorithm's fundamental equation is:

$$y_n = x_n^t + w_n \tag{1}$$

$$e_n = d_n - y_n \tag{2}$$

$$w_{n+1} = w_n + 2\mu e_n x_n \tag{3}$$

The convergence condition of LMS algorithm is: $0 < \mu < \lambda_{\max}$, $\lambda_{\max}$ is the input signal autocorrelation matrix R maximum characteristic value, also is the biggest diagonal element of the diagonally characteristic value matrix.

Regarding crosswise filter, the condition convergence of weight vector [1] is:

$$0 < \mu < 1/10\, NP_{in} \tag{4}$$

This formula is the stricter limit formula, N is the length of the adaptive FIR filter, p_{in} is the input Signal power.

From the former equation, it is clear that The LMS algorithm is simple, but an adjust parameter is needed, namely the stride factor μ .It is used to control the speed of convergence and the selection of μ is limited by the system's Stability; therefore, the algorithm convergence rate is limited.

B. RLS algorithm

Besides the LMS algorithm which is introduced above, another kind of algorithm is commonly used by the FIR adaptive filter, namely the recursion least squares method (Recursive Least Squares, RLS).This algorithm is one kind of the Weina filter's time recursive algorithm, and it is strictly to take the smallest two involution criterion as the basis algorithm[2]. Its principal advantage is character of the quickly convergence rate, and its major drawback is that each time iterates the computation amount is very big (the length of the filter is M , and then the computation is M^2).

The RLS algorithm is to take the least error sum of squares as the optimized goal, according to smallest two rides the criterion to define the cost function. Namely

$$J(w)=\sum_{n=0}^{t}\lambda^{t-n}\left|y_n - w^T x_n\right|^2 \tag{7}$$

Where $0<\lambda<1$ is Forgetting factor.

The RLS algorithm may be realized by the following steps:

1) Initialization: $H_0 = 0, P_0 = I/\delta, n = 0$ .And δ is the small positive number.

2) Renew $n = n+1$, the RLS algorithm's essential method is:

Where $P = E[d_n x_n]$, k_n is the Kalman gain vector. Formula (8) has composed the RLS algorithm.

$$\begin{aligned} &y_n = X^T w \qquad e_n = d_n - y_n \\ &k_n = {(p_{n-1}x_n^3)}\big/{(\lambda + x_n^T p_{n-1}x_n^3)} \\ &p_n = \lambda^{-1} p_n - \lambda^{-1} k_n x_n^T p_{n-1} \\ &w_n = w_{n-1} + k_n e_n \end{aligned} \tag{8}$$

C. NLMS-BRLS algorithm

For the BRLS algorithm's iterative formula is as follows:

$$w_{n+1} = w_{n-N+1} + (x_n x_n^t)^{-1} x_n^t E_n$$

Introduces the LMS algorithm's the normalized length of stride formula, the improved NLMS-BRLS algorithm's iterative formula is obtained to be as follows:

$$w_{n+1} = w_{n-N+1} + \alpha (x_n x_n^t)^{-1} x_n^t E_n^f \tag{9}$$

Where $\alpha = \gamma /(\beta + x^T x)$, $\gamma = \exp(|e_n|^2)$ and $\beta = \log_{0.5}^{|e_n|}$. The length of stride value is selected following by the improved NLMS algorithm proposed in this paper.

4 Simulation Result and Analysis

To simulate the echo cancellation algorithm, first, an echo way impulse response model is needed. The simulation and the comparison are made separately of the Return loss gain, the mean error and the residual echo's result. The PCM code's sampling rate is 8KHz in the common telephone channel, so the adaptive filter length's choice criteria is: 1 millisecond to choose 8, 32 milliseconds are 256,and so on[3]. The curves demonstrate the changes of the mean error or the return loss gain along with the iterations. 400 error samples' average value is taken in this paper to smooth the curve.

1) The input signal, we use the tape recorder in Windows to record a section of wav pronunciation document, and preserves for the telephone voice data (the 8 KHz sampling rate, which is the standard frequency of PCM voice). The time delay is 300ms, and the number of sampling points is 2400[4]. Then the voice data file is read to a vector in namely the voice data with the MATLAB wavread function.

2) The expectation output signal is obtained by convolution of the echo way and the input signal. When a noise signal is needed to add, we consider a Gauss whose average value is zero, and signal-to-noise ratio is 20dB.

3) The impulse response function is the envelope exponential decay function, whose impulse response function is expressed: $w(i) = R(i)\exp(-(i+1)/64)\delta(n-i), i = 0,1,\ldots L-1$, and $R(i)$ is uniform distribution random number between[-0.6 0.6] .

4) The impulse response and adaptive filter's length L is selected 1024.

The adaptive NLMS algorithm and the BRLS algorithm belong to the extreme case of the new algorithm. The performance of the NLMS-BRLS algorithm is more superior than the traditional NLMS algorithm or the pure BRLS algorithm, because the new algorithm has a very low complexity of computation (to be lower than other adaptive algorithms). The research analysis indicated that the block size is smaller (big block length waste massive memories, and brings big input output delay), the algorithm performance is more superior. However, in the peculiar circumstance, the algorithm will be out of balance, such as the noise is added to reference signal or input signal is non-steady. The question of imbalance will be improved greatly through the introduction of invariable length of stride. This algorithm is potential, which had been proved: the new algorithm's restraining performance and track capacity is not as good as NLMS algorithm, but it has Lower complexity of computation [5]. Thus it suits to apply to the acoustic echo cancellation system. Its adaptive characteristic may be close to the RLS algorithm, and the complexity of computation is actually smaller than the RLS algorithm.

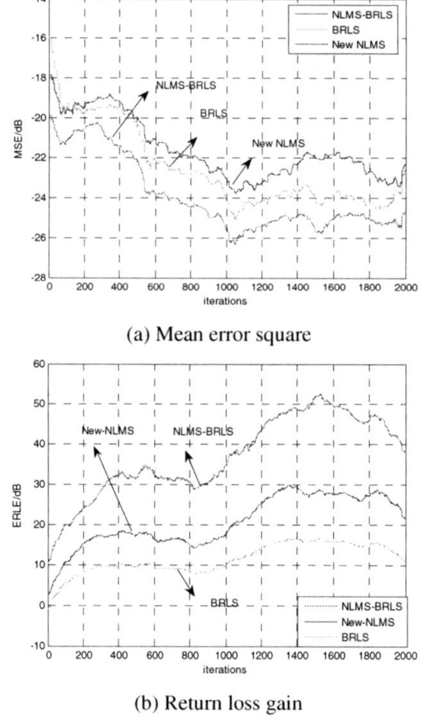

(a) Mean error square

(b) Return loss gain

Fig. 3. This paper improved NLMS algorithm, BRLS algorithm and improved NLMS-BRLS algorithm comparison

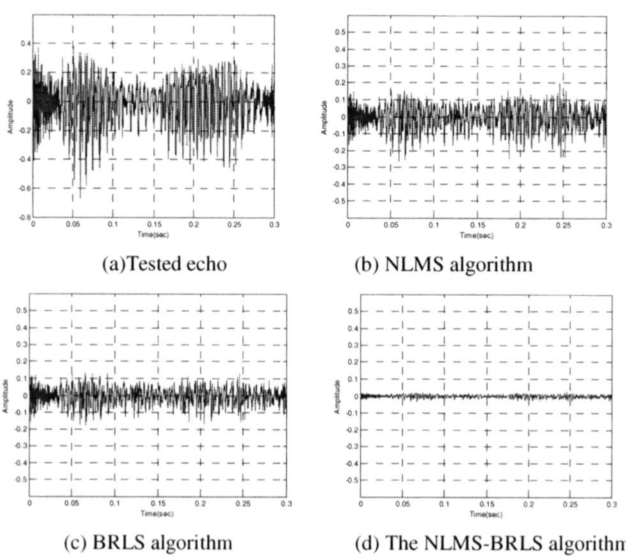

(a)Tested echo (b) NLMS algorithm

(c) BRLS algorithm (d) The NLMS-BRLS algorithm

Fig. 4. Simulation of three algorithm cancellation residual echo and test echo comparison

5 Conclusions

By the analysis and comparison for the principles and performances of those algorithms, their advantages and disadvantages may be obtained: the LMS algorithm is most simple, and is easily realized on the general digital signal processor. However, the LMS algorithm's convergence rate relies on seriously the distributed characteristic of input signal, therefore, it is necessary to study other adaptive algorithm which has nothing to do with input signal's distributed characteristic and to enhance the serviceability of adaptive algorithm in the acoustic echo cancellation system.

The recursion least squares (RLS) algorithm in fact is one kind of the Weina filter's time recursive algorithms, which is strictly to take the smallest two involution criterion as the basis algorithm. This algorithm's merit is the quick convergence rate, and its major drawback is that the computation is too big (Regarding the M order filter, then the computation is M^2).

In this paper, we improved the traditional NLMS algorithm on the base of the full research of existing classical algorithm, and combined it with the BRLS algorithm to apply them to the acoustic echo cancellation system of mobile communication domain. Finally, computer simulation results show that the performance of the NLMS-BRLS algorithm has surpassed the tradition adaptive algorithm obviously.

Acknowledgment. This work is supported by Zhengzhou Science and Technology Project (No. 2-41).

References

[1] Gao, Y.: Cumulant-based adaptive filter theory and its applications (Doctorate paper), pp. 13–45. South China University of Technology, Guangzhou (2002)
[2] Amand Benesty, F., Gilloire, A., Grenier, Y., et al.: Adaptive filtering algorithms for stereophonic acoustic echo cancellation. In: Proc. ICASS P, pp. 3099–3102 (1995)
[3] Lin, Y.-R.: Adaptive filtering theory and in echo cancellation applied research (Doctorate paper), GuangZhou, pp. 12–46 (1999)
[4] Zhou, Y.-J., Xie, S.-L.: One kind of new adaptive filtering fast algorithm and in multi-channel echo cancellation application, vol. 2, pp. 352–359 (2003)
[5] Song, W.-Q.: Adaptive echo cancellation engineering research in mobile communications (Master's degree paper). Henan University of Technology, Zhengzhou (2009)
[6] He, Z.-Y.: Adaptive signal processing. Scientific Publishing house, BeiJing (2002)
[7] Clark, G.A., Mitra, S.K., Parker, S.R.: Block implementation of adaptive digital filters. IEEE Trans. Acoust. Speech, Signal Processing ASSP-29(3), 744–752 (1981)

A System Integration Approach for E-Government System Development

Wen-Qian Liang[1], Hui-Jin Wang[2], and Shun Long[2]

[1] Municipal Construction Committee of Guangzhou
Guangzhou, P.R. China
[2] Dept. of Computer Science, JiNan University
Guangzhou, P.R. China
Wen_33@yeah.net

Abstract. This paper discusses in depth the key design and implementation issues of e-government system integration. These key issues include core management services, Internet-based integrated administrative service, cross-bureau collaboration, as well as system architecture. The discussion is based on an integrated e-government system for GuangZhou municipal Construction Committee which has been successfully developed and deployed.

Keywords: e-government, system integration, government management, administrative service, workflow.

1 Introduction

E-government[1][2] promises a comfortable, transparent, and low-cost interaction between government and the public, government and business/industry sectors as well as those between different government bureaus.

In the past two decades, the Chinese government has actively encouraged and invested in the growth of the Internet to capture the technology's vast commercial potential and social benefic for the people. Rapid progress has been made since, with vast number of information systems successfully deployed and more going underway. Most of these systems focus on improving internal administrative efficiency and intra-bureau information sharing, whilst few fulfills its promise to the public in providing both sufficient information and fast, convenient and integrated administrative services. This is mainly caused by the following reasons[4]:

1) A mismatch between the current administrative services and the requirements of e-government: Due to lack of experience, decades of poor practice has turned the government infrastructure into a clumsy, gigantic one characterized by its high cohesion and low coupling nature. The key to e-government is to establish a long-term, organization-wide strategy to constantly improve administration efficiency. In order to achieve this, reformation on staffing, technology, processes and work flow management is a must. However, the current administrative hierarchy makes it very difficult to coordinate the efforts of all parties involved in order to fulfill the public demands on e-government.

M. Dai (Ed.): ICCIC 2011, Part II, CCIS 232, pp. 450–457, 2011.

2) Although most government departments have been equipped with modern computer hardwares, in many cases, they provide little more than a traditional portal which is rarely updated. Even for those equipped with dedicated software systems, most target work efficiency within the office, whilst contribute little to the general public and to fellow-government bureaus. It is believed that our efforts of informationization should be better integrated with that of a restructuring of governmental functionalities, so that local efforts could contribute more to the overall administration efficiency.

3) A lack of industrial-level e-government development standards: this inevitably led to arbitrary system development approaches. The resulting systems vary in architecture, data storage, and software platform, etc, It is therefore even more difficult to share information among these ad hoc systems.

4) Severe information silo: this seriously hinders information sharing across different bureaus and for the public. It is difficult to coordinate efforts in order to provide integrated service and decision support via modern techniques such as data mining.

5) Security is a major concern with the fact that that the Internet is constantly under threats. Sufficient measures must be taken to protect the information involved when a e-government system is provided to the public.

This paper discusses in depth our first-hand experiences in e-government integration. Our discussion is based on an integrated e-government system for GuangZhou municipal Construction Committee (GZCC)[5][6] which has been successfully developed and deployed. It focuses on key design and implementation issues such as core management services, Internet-based integrated administrative service, cross-bureau collaboration, as well as system architecture. The paper is organized as follows. Section 2 will briefly outline the system requirements. Key factors in system design are discussed in section 3, and key implementation decisions are explained in section 4, followed by some concluding remarks.

2 Requirements of GZCCS

Driven by the enormous demands from both within and from the public, GZCC has put on a lot of efforts in various areas such as urban construction, management, and metropolitan layout, etc., particularly in the past decade or so. These efforts have significant improve its work efficiency, management, and quality of service to the public. For instance, GZCC has developed its OA system which covers all of its 8 authorization and 25 management missions. A smart-card system has been deployed for construction site management, with 600,000+ cards issued and 1,000,000+ data records kept about employment, insurance, and salaries, etc. On-spot construction project management has been achieved via a management system which coordinates the efforts of 53 related government bureaus on quality and safety of construction projects. 5 databases have been set up in GZCC, which are databases of Key Projects, Construction Sector Intendance, Office Automation and Internet Websites respectively. Software systems have been set up for information sharing among subsidiary departments and with fellow bureaus. They cover sharing and/or exchange of data about 90+ administrative operations across 18 different departments. This helps to ensure timeliness, integrity and accuracy of data for authorization operations, and significantly improve the work efficiencies of departments involved.

To raise the administration efficiency and service quality to the next level, GZCC aims to develop an integrated e-government system (*GZCCS* as it is called) which can unify both of its internal administrative operations and its external services to the public. This GZCCS is expected to 1) integrate all the administrative operations and public services of all of GZCC departments, 2) seamlessly connect all the existing OA systems in order to avoid major changes at work, 3) provide a unified interface for all the information needed, particularly for those to be provided on various websites. It aims to provide an e-government solution that integrates applications, managements, services as well as intendance of GZCC.

The duties of GZCC include: 1) routine administrative operations, such as document transfer and processing, complaint processing, etc.; 2) examination and approval of construction projects, which shall follow standard processing routines; 3) construction sector intendance, which aims to monitor all the construction-related sectors (such as design industry, building trade and real estate industry, etc.) via the analysis of operational data collected; and 4) public service, which is to provide a unified and interactive online platform for the public to access all construction-related information, and do their business whenever necessary.

GZCCS is expected to be a unified platform for all these four duties. More specifically saying, it aims to provide a common ground for effective information sharing and efficient coordination among all bureaus involved, in order to support decision-making, help reduce the staff's workloads, improve work efficiency and lower the operational costs.

3 System Design

A. Principles of Design

In order to achieve the above targets, we believe that the design of GZCS shall abide the following principles: 1) strictly follow all the existing industrial standards and specifications imposed by the corresponding authorities, 2) make full use of not only the current hardware resources but also the data and workflows[3] of the existing systems, 3) a forward-looking design to help ensure the resulting system remain effective for long after deployment; 4) rationality and practicality are two primary concerns, so that the final system can be of a rational architecture easy to use and to maintain; 5) adopt a component-based development approach and use mainstream software products available in the market; and finally 6) easy maintenance and enhancement, security and reliability shall be considered.

B. Approach

We believe that the right approach to GZCCS is to build on top of the existing network infrastructure. Its core is a data center which is responsible for integrating all the data available from the existing GZCC systems listed above. A set of interfaces and services shall therefore be developed on basis of this data center, in order to achieve an integrated system for both internal administrative operations and public services.

More specifically, for internal administrative operations, all the operation logics of GZCCS shall be centered around a workflow engine which unifies all the administrative workflows within GZCC. This workflow engine is the core of the new application system which supports all the internal administrative operations. A new interface shall then be developed to provide a single unified information exchange interface between GZCC and fellow bureaus.

Different application systems shall be developed for different sectors of potential users such as the public, fellow bureaus as well as different subsidiary departments within GZCC. For instance, public services shall be set up for the general public to access information in a user-friendly and web-based manner, portal services shall be provided for construction sector companies to carry out their works with GZCC. Joint examination and approval services shall be set up so that different departments can cooperate efficiently in their corresponding operations.

In order to achieve this, we classify the GZCCS functions into four sections: 1) *Administration*, which covers routine workflows, document management, examination and approval services, etc; 2) *Construction sector management*, which include managements for construction companies, projects, employees and various construction sector surveys; 3) *Public service*, which provides online business applications, announcement of examination and approval results, general announcement, etc.; 4) *Coordination*, which is responsible for maintaining connections with the GuangZhou municipal administration center, as well as those with fellow bureaus, in order to carry out exchange, archive and surveillance of large volumes of administrative documents. This is achieved via a unified information exchange interface.

C. System Infrastructure

The GZCCS has a layered infrastructure as illustrated in Fig.1, which is followed by more detailed explanations.

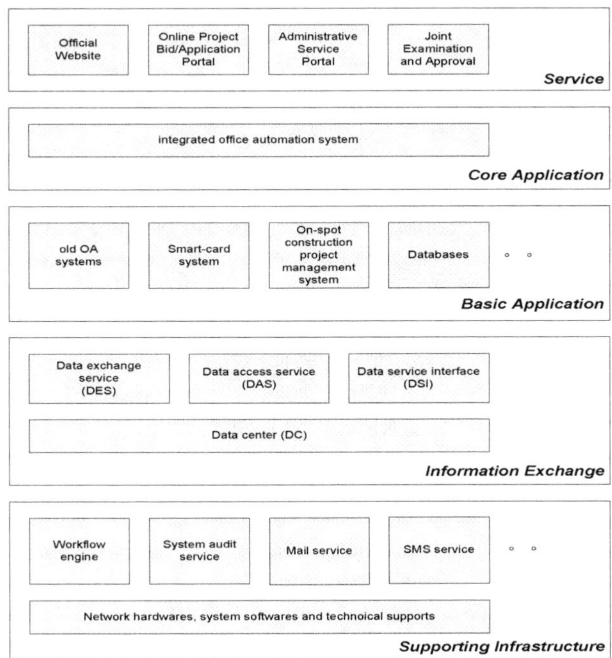

Fig. 1. The infrastructure of GZCCS

The bottom layer is the *Supporting Infrastructure (SI)* layer which includes 1) networking hardware, 2) system software and 3) technical support for operation administration. The first two parts make the runtime environment, which is a 100M local network connected to all desktops within GZCC. It provides interfaces to not only the GZCC intranet but also the Internet. Twenty servers have been deployed and they are equipped with Microsoft software packages and ArcGIS software products. The technical support for operation administration support includes workflow engine, system audit, and mail service, etc. This supporting infrastructure layer is the foundation to build GZCCS. However, we do not intend to rebuild it from scratch, since most of them have already been in service.

The *Information Exchange (IE)* layer includes the data center and data exchange services. Data are collected from the operational data from both the current GZCC application systems and fellow bureaus. A renovated data center (DC) is to be set up based on the current one. On top of this new data center, we have 1) a *Data Exchange Service (DES)*, which is responsible for data exchange with all the GZCC internal systems, 2) a *Data Access Service (DAS)*, which provides data storage and retrieval service to applications of the higher layers, and 3) a *Data Service Interface (DSI)*, which provides remote data access for fellow governmental bureaus of GZCC. GZCCS must provide a comprehensive DSI for users from outside.

On top of the Information Exchange layer we have a *Basic Application (BA)* layer which contains all the existing basic application systems within GZCC, for examples those systems mentioned in section 2. They implement all the basic operation procedures and generate large amount of data on a daily basis.

The fourth layer is *Core Application (CA)*, which contains an integrated office automation system. This system covers all the GZCC administrative duties, including document management, administrative workflow management, internal processing of examinations and approvals, complaint and proposal processing for the regional people's congress, as well as other sector-related administrative works.

On the top of GZCCS we have a *Service* layer which provides various tailor-made operation/business services to the public. Examples of these services include online project bid/application and administrative service portals (for construction sectors), joint examination and approval workflows (for internal use across multiple GZCC departments), and official website (for the public), etc.

4 Key Implementation Issues of GZCCS

The GZCCS adopts the popular *.Net*-based multi-layered Service Oriented Architecture (SOA)[8]. Data transfer is achieved in XML format whilst data package encapsulation and routing are implemented via Simple Object Access Protocol (SOAP). The core JKCFLOW platform supports graphic-based visual workflow control, time bound control, and role authority control, etc. This significantly eases the burden of administrative workflow management and workflow control.

The listed functionalities of GZCCS can be divided into three major groups, as illustrated in in Fig.2.

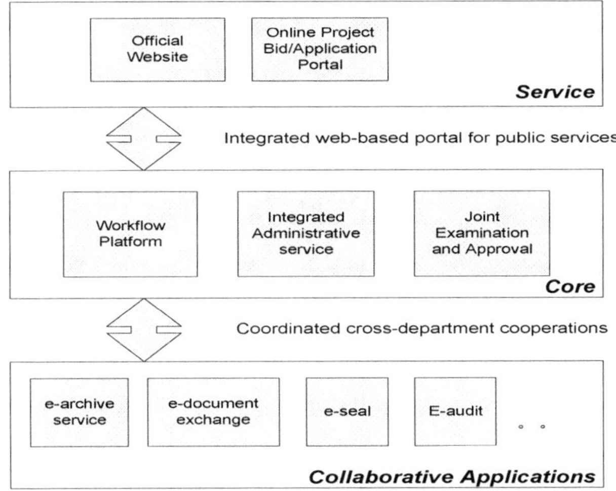

Fig. 2. The GZCCS service architecture

The key to the success of GZCCS is obviously to provide 1) the integrated administrative service, 2) an integrated web-based portal for public services, and 3) a unified approach to coordinate cross-department cooperation. We will explain in depth how our GZCCS provides the 1), before giving a brief introduction of how 2) and 3) are achieved.

D. Unified administrative services

GZCCS uses the workflow control provided by JKCFLOW platform[7] to achieve the standardization of all administrative works and workflow management. Currently, there are 70+ standard workflows within GZCCS. JKCFLOW platform provides the necessary tools to design these workflows, before implementation. This helps to ensure that all the operational data needed are available throughout the corresponding workflows.

The first step to achieve this unified administrative service is to build a workflow meta model. Based on our requirement analysis, we extend the WFMC meta model in order to provide effective support to complex administration logics. The extension can be grouped into five categories. 1) *activity*, 2) *workflow-related data*, 3) *workflow-related application*, 4) *executor* and 5) *resources*. Activity is the smallest unit of a workflow, i.e. the atomic operation within the administrative process. GZCCS unifies all executable applications, operations and functions as functions call, in order to implement all the necessary steps within a workflow as a series of function calls. The executor contains basic information about the staff and departments/offices related to the corresponding workflow. The resource refers to all the spreadsheets and databases needed during the process.

For convenience, we defined six different basic execution models for GZCCS. The first is a *sequential model*, which all actions are taking in sequential order. The second is a *selection model*, where a series of actions are executed based on the user's request or a predefined condition. The third is a *parallel model* which presents the fact that once a certain action is completed within a workflow, a predefined action will be launched in parallel to the next action within the workflow. But this parallel action will have no impact on the main workflow. This model is used when documents must be cc to fellow departments for references at work. The fourth is a *collaboration model* which is a variant of the selection model but differ in that the main workflow does not have to wait for the results from its sub-workflows. The fifth is a *pipeline model* where the completion of a workflow will automatically launch the execution of the next one. Finally, the sixth model is a suspend model which is a variant of the selection model but embedded with sub-workflows that can be executed independently. These sub-workflows will be launched when the execution of the workflow reaches a specific step (i.e. an action). The execution of the workflow will be suspended until these sub-workflows are completed.

All the GZCC workflows can be represented by the following six execution models, or the composition of them. By doing this, we re-shuffled all the current systems currently in service and unified all the administrative services in GZCCS.

E. Portals and cross-deparment collaborations

GZCCS portal aims to bridge the gap between its core internal administrative workflows and external services to the public. This means to provide not only a seamless connection between the online application systems and the internal administration workflows, but also a unified interface to provide the progress of user applications.

GZCCS provides a web-based online application system for users to launch an application. Once the forms are completed and the required supporting documents are provided, the corresponding examination process is launched. There are two types of data associations within this process. One refers to the associations within the corresponding examination workflow. It is supported by a unique reference number generated by the workflow engine, which is used to represents this specific workflow in all tables within the database. The other type of associations refers to those between the data within the database and those to be presented in the web-based forms. A dedicated tool has been developed for the GZCC staff use to explicitly specify this type of associations.

The portal provides an interface for users to make enquiry about the progress of their applications, and for GZCC to publicize the results of its examinations and approvals. This generates a demand for synchronizaction between the portal and the GZCCS' internal systems. A *WebService* interface is used to implement real-timed synchronizations, whilst less demanding synchronizations are supported by the exchange center within the JKCFLOW workflow platform. Once the examination/ approval data becomes available, a procedure is triggered to send this data to the portal automatically. In addition, the JKCFLOW workflow platform provides timer for the administrators to set in order to provide automatic data release to various destinations.

5 Conclusion

GZCCS has been successfully implemented and deployed in 2008. It provides a platform for all departments within GZCC to integrate their internal administrative works as well as public services. It is an comprehensive office automation system that covers all 55 administrative operations of GZCC, which can now be carried out in an online manner. In 2008, GZCC has received 8525 examination/approval applications, with 4991 documents received and 2434 delivered. Feedbacks (from both the staff and the public) show that the administrative efficiency has been significantly improved with a much lower cost. GZCCS has become an e-government hub by sharing information not only within GZCC but also with fellow municipal service sectors. A seamless information connection with the GZCC official website has also been achieved so that all examination and approval progresses and results are available for the public in a timely manner.

References

[1] Andersen, K.: E-government and public sector process rebuilding: dilettantes,wheel barrows, and diamonds. Kluwer Academic, Dordrecht (2004)

[2] Abramson, M.: E-Government, 2003 (IBM Endowment Series on the Business of Government). Rowman & Littlefield (2002)

[3] Fischer, L.: The workflow handbook 2005. Future Strategies Inc. (2005)

[4] Guangzhou Informationization Office, Report of Guangzhou Informationization Development (2001-2005) (2006) (in Chinese)

[5] Guangzhou Construction Committee, Technical report of the Integrated e-government system for Guangzhou Municipal Construction Committee (2008) (in Chinese)

[6] Information Center of Guanzhou Construction Committee, Blueprint of Informationization for Guangzhou Construction Industry (2007) (in Chinese)

[7] Sichuan, J.K.C.: Geographical Information Technologies Co., Ltd., http://www.jkcchina.com

[8] Papazoglou, M., Heuvel, W.: Service oriented architectures: approaches, technologies and research issues. The VLDB Journal 7(16) (2007)

The Effects of Goods Sorting Mechanisms on Consumer Behavior and Seller Strategy in Online Marketplaces

Zhuzhu He[1], Shanshan Wang[1,2], Yuewen Liu[2], and Kaiquan Xu[2]

[1] College of Computer Science, Inner Mongolia University
Hohhot, P.R. China
[2] Department of Information Systems, City University of Hong Kong
Hong Kong, P.R. China
zhuzhu2325@sina.cn

Abstract. This paper studies the effects of sorting mechanisms in online marketplaces. Two sorting mechanisms, including sorting mechanism by price and sorting mechanism by seller reputation, are studied. Using a simulated experiment, this paper examines consumers' search behavior and sellers' strategy when sorting mechanisms are presented. The implications of the research findings are discussed.

Keywords: sorting mechanism, online marketplace, seller reputation, homogeneous goods, heterogeneous goods.

1 Introduction

The electronic marketplace develops rapidly in recent years, and generates overloaded goods offering in the market. For example, if consumers search "Nokia N73" in "Cell Phone > Nokia > N73" category on *Taobao*, a dominant Chinese online marketplace, they still can get more than 6,000 offerings. A lot of methods and tools are developed in helping consumers make judgments, for example, sorting mechanisms, recommending agents and filter systems. This paper will focus on the sorting mechanism, which is one of most direct method in help consumers narrow down their choices. Sorting mechanisms also have been used in most online marketplaces. For example, *Amazon* and *eBay* allows their consumers sort the goods listings by goods price.

It seems that consumers may choose the cheapest goods when there is a price sorting mechanism. However, firstly, there are different types of goods, homogeneous goods and heterogeneous goods [2, 3]. For heterogeneous goods, sorting by price may not be a good solution, since the goods quality varies from one good to another. Secondly, online marketplace is of high uncertainty and risks [1, 4]. In such a context, seller reputation is an important factor [1]. Sorting by seller reputation may also be a good way to help consumers choosing goods from the overloaded goods offerings. Then a question is, when both of the two sorting mechanisms exist, what the consumers' search strategies will be, and how should sellers react? Obviously, sorting mechanisms will enhance the competition in the online marketplace. Should an online marketplace adopt the sorting mechanisms?

M. Dai (Ed.): ICCIC 2011, Part II, CCIS 232, pp. 458–465, 2011.

This study tries to examine the effects of sorting mechanisms, including a price sorting mechanism and a seller reputation sorting mechanism. To the best of our knowledge, this is the first piece of study which focuses on the sorting mechanism. Because sorting mechanisms are not practically available in conventional marketplace, it has not been studied explicitly in the literature. However, there are three streams of studies which are related. The first stream of literature is the studies which discuss search cost in economics [8, 9, 12]. This stream of literature offers a framework to examine the consumer behavior when there is a sorting mechanism. This study compares the search behavior with and without sorting mechanisms, thus will extend the traditional search models and benefit the understandings of search behavior. The second stream of studies is related to online marketplace. The topics include the effects of seller reputation [5, 15] and consumers' search and purchase behavior [4, 13]. However, these kinds of studies have not considered the effects of sorting mechanisms. Given that sorting mechanisms can change consumers' search and browse sequence, it should have important effects on consumers' search and purchase behavior. The third stream of literature focuses on the price dispersion and transparency of online marketplace [6, 11, 14]. However, when there are sorting mechanisms in online marketplaces, the price transparency may be sharply increased, and price dispersion may be sharply decreased. Therefore, examining the effect of sorting mechanism will also benefit to this stream of research.

This paper firstly uses a search model (which is extended from [9]) to illustrate consumer's search behavior. Then we conduct a simulation to compare consumers' search behaviors both with and without sorting mechanisms. We examine consumers' cost and surplus. In the end of this paper, we discuss consumers' search strategy and sellers' strategy based on the findings.

2 Research Model

A. Online Marketplace

As mentioned in the introduction section, online marketplaces are of overloaded goods listings as well as insufficient goods quality information. Assume there is an online marketplace where N sellers are retailing the same product. A single seller is denoted by seller i. We study two types of goods, homogeneous goods and heterogeneous goods. Homogeneous goods are identical, and have the same quality, q; while heterogeneous goods have the same functions, but their quality are drawn from a normal distribution $F_q(q_i)$.

Seller reputation is a reputation score, r, which follows a distribution $F_r(r_i)$, and indicates a seller's experience in conducting transactions. For example, the reputation score in eBay, Amzon and Taobao indicate the number of consumers the seller has deal or the number of transactions the seller has conducted. For the sake of simplicity, we transform the reputation sore to $0 < r < 1$, and interpret the seller reputation as the relationship between goods quality and goods price. Suppose the goods price of seller i follows a distribution $F_p(p_i)$, then r is the correlation coefficient between q_i and

p_i. This assumption is reasonable compared with the reality. An experienced seller may charge goods price relate to the quality. If the goods quality is significantly lower than the goods quality, then consumers will complain and damage the seller's reputation. If the goods quality is significantly higher than the goods quality, then the seller's profits will be harmed without other benefits (since the seller has already set up his/her reputation, he/she does not have to invent on the reputation). Therefore, the goods price of experienced sellers will be closed to the goods quality. On the contrast, inexperienced sellers may charge goods price less related to goods quality. They may charge low price for a quick increase of seller reputation [10]; or charge normal price; or charge high price to target inexperienced consumers or even fraud those consumers [7].

We use the search model in [9] to as a start. In the following inequity, $E(B_n)$ indicates the expectation of the highest utility in all the n times search. s denotes the search cost. The following inequity shows that, other if the marginal benefit of one additional search is higher than the search cost, consumer will stop searching [9].

$$E(B_{n+1}) - E(B_n) > s \tag{1}$$

For the sake of simplicity, we assume that consumers' surplus equals to the goods quality minus the goods price.

B. Search Models without Sorting Mechanism

1) Homogeneous goods:

For homogeneous goods, since the quality is constant, the inequity is equivalent to:

$$E(\min\{p_1,\ldots,p_n\}) - E(\min\{p_1,\ldots,p_{n+1}\}) > s \tag{2}$$

2) Heterogeneous goods:

Heterogeneous goods have different quality, thus the condition of keep searching is:

$$\begin{aligned} &E(\max\{q_1 - p_1,\ldots,q_{n+1} - p_{n+1}\}) - \\ &E(\max\{q_1 - p_1,\ldots,q_n - p_n\}) > s \end{aligned} \tag{3}$$

C. Search Models with Sorting Mechanism

We consider two searching strategies: searching following the price sequence (from low to high) and searching following the seller reputation sequence (from high to low).

1) Homogeneous goods:

a) Sorting by price: Consumers can directly find the cheapest goods in the first place of the list. Because all the goods have identical quality, thus the consumer can directly purchase the cheapest goods.

b) Sorting by seller reputation: Reorder the list of price and quality according to seller reputation, and denote the as list with new sequence as

$$\{(q_{(1)}, p_{(1)}),\ldots,(q_{(1)}, p_{(1)}),\ldots,(q_{(n)}, p_{(n)})\}$$

The condition of keep searching is:

$$E\left(\max\left\{q_{(1)}-p_{(1)},\ldots,q_{(n+1)}-p_{(n+1)}\right\}\right)- \\ E\left(\max\left\{q_{(1)}-p_{(1)},\ldots,q_{(n)}-p_{(n)}\right\}\right)>s \tag{4}$$

2) *Heterogeneous goods:*

For heterogeneous goods, the goods quality is different between different goods from different sellers.

a) Sorting by price: Reorder the list of price and quality according to seller reputation, and denote the as list with new sequence as

$$\left\{\left(q_{[1]},p_{[1]}\right),\ldots,\left(q_{[i]},p_{[i]}\right),\ldots,\left(q_{[n]},p_{[n]}\right)\right\}$$

The condition of keep searching is:

$$E\left(\max\left\{q_{[1]}-p_{[1]},\ldots,q_{[n+1]}-p_{[n+1]}\right\}\right)- \\ E\left(\max\left\{q_{[1]}-p_{[1]},\ldots,q_{[n]}-p_{[n]}\right\}\right)>s \tag{5}$$

b) Sorting by seller reputation: The condition of keep searching is the same with (4).

3 Methodology

We simulated a marketplace where 1,000 sellers are selling the same goods (homogeneous goods) or the goods with the same functions (heterogeneous goods).

To conduct the simulation, we have to coin the distributions mentioned in the model. We assume the distribution of seller reputation is a uniform distribution between 0 and 1. The distribution of heterogeneous goods quality is a normal distribution, $N\left(q,\sigma_q\right)$.

Notice that the correlation coefficient between price and quality is r_i. We assume the distribution of the price of homogeneous goods is $N\left(q,\sigma_p\sqrt{1-r_{i2}}\right)$; and the distribution of the price of heterogeneous goods is $N\left(q_i,\sigma_p\right)$. The conditional distribution of seller i 's goods quality given the goods price q_i is

$$N\left(q+\frac{\sigma_p}{\sigma_q}r_i\left(p_i-q_i\right),\sigma_p\sqrt{1-r_i^2}\right)$$

The values in the experiment: $q=10$, $\sigma_p=\sigma_q=1$, and the search cost is 0.05.

We conduct the simulation in the following steps:

(1) Generate 1000 sellers, each one has two goods: homogeneous goods and heterogeneous goods. We generate a random number as the price of the homogeneous goods, and two random numbers as the price and the quality of the heterogeneous goods, from their distributions separately.

(2) We randomly draw one goods from these 1000 homogenous goods and 1000 heterogeneous goods, and record the best consumer surplus. This process will repeat 1000 times until no goods are left.

(3) We sorted the sellers by their reputation score (from high to low). Then we draw one goods each time following the seller reputation sequence, and record the best consumer surplus. This process will also repeat 1000 times until no goods are left.

(4) We sorted the sellers by their goods price (from low to high). Then we draw one goods each time following the price sequence, and record the best consumer surplus. This process will also repeat 1000 times until no goods are left.

These four steps will be repeated 10,000 times. Average and standard deviations of several values are calculated. The experiment results will be discussed in the following section.

4 Data Analysis

The results of the experiment are illustrated in Table 1. The left panel of table shows the experiment results in the case of homogeneous goods, and the right panel of table shows the experiment results in the case of heterogeneous goods. As shown in the second row, we examined three searching strategies (i.e. search by random, search following seller reputation sequence and search following price sequence) in each of the two cases.

The third row of the table shows the optimal times a consumer should search to maximum his/her surplus. We found that when no sorting mechanism is offered in the marketplace, consumers have to search 9 times for homogeneous goods, and 7 times for heterogeneous goods. However, when sorting mechanisms are offered, the optimal search times are 0. In other words, consumers can directly purchase the goods in the top of the list. In general, sorting mechanisms reduce the cost and time consumers should spend in purchasing goods in online marketplaces.

Table 1. Best Search Times and Payoffs

	Homogeneous Goods			**Heterogeneous Goods**		
Sorting	***No*** [a]	***Rep.*** [b]	***Price*** [c]	***No*** [a]	***Rep.*** [b]	***Price*** [c]
Optimal Search Times	9	0	0	7	0	0
Price	8.781	10.000	7.057	8.409	10.006	5.713
Quality	10	10	10	9.114	10.007	7.659
Consumer Surplus	0.769	0	2.943	0.355	0	1.895
S.D.	0.553	0.046	—	0.770	0.045	0.780
Seller Profit	3.781	5	2.057	3.852	5.003	1.884
Seller Reputation	0.401	0.999	0.233	0.339	0.999	0.321

a. "No." stands for search by random;

b. "Rep." stands for search following price sequence;

c. "Price" stands for search following seller reputation sequence.

We also compared the standard deviation of consumer surplus and seller profit in the different cases. The 7th row of Table 1 shows that, the standard deviation of consumer surplus is much less when searching following seller reputation sequence than both when searching following price sequence and searching randomly. The 8th row shows that seller profits when consumers search following seller reputation sequence.

To examine sellers' reputation score when transaction is conducted, we also compared the expected seller reputation in each case, which is illustrated in the 9th row. Searching following seller reputation sequence generates the highest seller reputation. The seller reputation when consumers search randomly is also higher than the seller reputation when consumers search following price sequence. We also illustrated the research results in Figure 1.

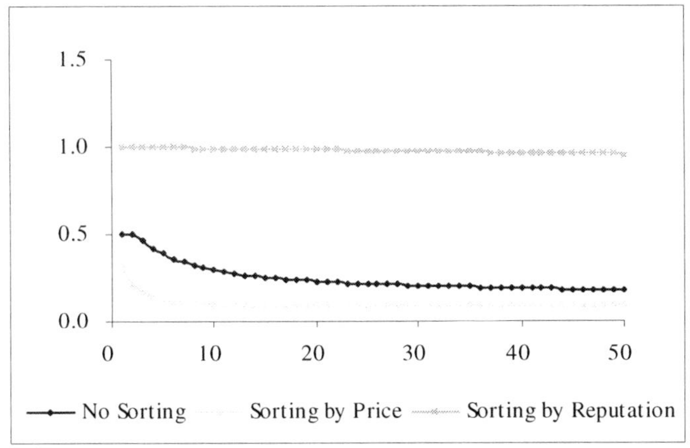

Fig. 1. Seller Reputation of Heterogeneous goods

5 Discussions

This study has several key findings: first, the presence of sorting mechanisms can reduce consumers' optimal search times, as well as the search costs; second, in the perspective of consumer surplus, search following price sequence is more efficient than search by random, while search by random is more efficient than search following reputation sequence; third, the standard deviation of consumer surplus when search following reputation sequence is lower than both search following price sequence and search by random. These findings have several implications.

D. Consumers' Search Strategy

When consumers are searching for homogeneous goods, search following price sequence is the dominant strategy. Because the quality of homogeneous goods is identical, consumers can directly purchase the goods with the lowest price to achieve the highest consumer surplus. This may induce a highly competitive marketplace.

When consumers are searching for heterogeneous goods, search following price sequence can generate a high expected consumer surplus; however, the variance of the consumer surplus is also large, which indicates a high uncertainty and risk. On the contrary, search following seller reputation sequence can generate a low expected consumer surplus, but it can assure a low quality variance. Therefore, a consumer may sort the goods listings by price when looking for high surplus, and he/she may sort the goods by seller reputation when looking for stable goods quality [10].

Both the sorting mechanism by price and by seller reputation can reduce optimal search times and search costs, especially when the goods listings are overloaded. Therefore, consumers are benefited by the sorting mechanisms in online marketplaces.

E. Sellers' Strategy

The sorting mechanisms also can improve sellers' payoffs. First, it increases sellers' profits when consumers search following the seller reputation sequence. Second, the sorting mechanism by price offers new sellers (whose reputation has not been established) the chance of growing quickly. By charging low prices, new sellers can appear in top positions of the list of goods, and transact more goods to build up "seller reputation". They may choose homogeneous goods to assure consumers of the goods quality. Third, the sorting mechanism by seller reputation can offer high reputation sellers the opportunity of charging price premium. Without the seller reputation sorting mechanism, their goods may be hided in the overloaded listings and seldom be browsed and purchased. The seller reputation sorting mechanism brings the goods listings from high reputation sellers to the surface, and thus enhanced their payoffs.

F. Marketplace Strategy

Sorting mechanisms can increase the market transparency, and reduce consumers' search costs [11]. *eBay* and *Amazon* have already adopted price sorting mechanisms in their online marketplace platform. However, our findings suggest that only a price sorting mechanism may be not enough. To help consumers to search stable goods quality, and to help high reputation sellers to fetch price premiums, a sorting mechanism by seller reputation is also necessary.

G. Future Research

This study is a preliminary study on the effects of sorting mechanisms. It can be strengthened in the following perspectives in the future.

First, this paper has simply treated consumers' utility as the difference between goods quality and goods price. However, the utility function may be much more complex. Future research may consider a more sophisticated utility function, and especially considered the utility functions of risk-alike and risk-aversive consumers. Second, the experiment assumed the distribution of seller reputation as a uniform distribution. However, it may be a long tail in the reality. Future study may test the research results when the distribution of seller reputation is different. Third, this paper used simulated data to draw conclusions. Field data from online marketplace may be collected to verify the model and the results.

In a conclusion, this paper studies the effects of sorting mechanisms in online marketplaces. The model in this paper can be used in designing and testing new sorting mechanisms as well as recommending agents. The results in this study can shed some lights on the practices in online marketplaces.

References

[1] Ba, S.L., Pavlou, P.A.: Evidence of the effect of trust building technology in electronic markets: Price premiums and buyer behavior. MIS Quarterly 26(3), 243–268

[2] Bailey, J.P., Faraj, S., Yao, Y.: The Road More Travelled: Web Traffic and Price Competition in Internet Retailing. Electronic Markets 17(1), 56–67

[3] Brynjolfsson, E., Smith, M.D.: Frictionless commerce? A comparison of Internet and conventional retailers. Management Science 46(4), 563–585

[4] Ghose, A.: Internet Exchanges for Used Goods: An Empirical Analysis of Trade Patterns and Adverse Selection. Mis Quarterly 33(2), 263–291

[5] Ghose, A., Ipeirotis, P.G., Sundararajan, A.: The Dimensions of Reputation in Electronic Markets. Working Paper

[6] Jin, G.Z., Kato, A.: Dividing online and offline: A case study. Review of Economic Studies 74(3), 981–1004

[7] Jin, G.Z., Kato, A.: Price, quality, and reputation: evidence from an online field experiment. Rand Journal of Economics 37(4), 983–1004

[8] Nelson, P.: Advertising as Information. Journal of Political Economy 82(4), 729–754

[9] Nelson, P.: Information and Consumer Behavior. Journal of Political Economy 78(2), 311–329

[10] Snijders, C., Zijdeman, R.: Reputation and Internet Auctions: eBay and Beyond. Analyse & Kritik 26(1), 158–184

[11] Soh, C., Markus, M.L., Goh, K.H.: Electronic Marketplaces and Price Transparency: Strategy, Information Technology, and Success. MIS Quarterly 30(3), 705–723

[12] Stigler, G.J.: The Economics of Information. The Journal of Political Economy 69(3), 213–225

[13] Yen, C.H., Lu, H.P.: Factors influencing online auction repurchase intention. Internet Research 18(1), 7–25

[14] Zhang, J., Fang, X., Sheng, O.R.L.: Online consumer search depth: Theories and new findings. Journal of Management Information Systems 23(3), 71–95

[15] Zhou, M., Dresner, M., Windle, R.J.: Online reputation systems: Design and strategic practices. Decision Support Systems 44(4), 785–797

A Study on R-TOPSIS Method and Its Application to Web Site Building Alternatives Selection

Ling Zhang and De-Qun Zhou

College of Economics and Management
Nanjing University of Aeronautics and Astronautics
Nanjing 210016, China
lingzhang2556@sina.cn

Abstract. In the multi-attribute decision-making problems, interaction can exist among the decision-making attributes and experts' preference, the weights of the attributes (or experts) are not additive. The new decision making method named R-TOPSIS is proposed based on TOPSIS method and fuzzy measures to solve the decision-making problem with interaction. The fact that the R-TOPSIS method is the general form of the original TOPSIS method is pointed out. And then the new group decision-making method is established according to R-TOPSIS method. Finally, R-TOPSIS method and its corresponding group decision-making method are validated through selecting e-business's web site building solution for enterprise.

Keywords: Fuzzy measures, R- TOPSIS, Group decision making, E-business's web site building solution.

1 Introduction

TOPSIS (Technique for Order Preference by Similarity to Ideal Solution) is one of the attributes decision making methods[1], which evaluate the alternatives based on two rules: one is close to the idea solution, the other is far away from negative idea solution[1, 2]. TOPSIS has already been applied to many fields (such as risk evaluation[3], performance evaluation[4, 5], and suppliers selection[6]) since it was proposed by Hwang and Yoon in 1981. Similar to other traditional decision-making methods, TOPSIS method can only be applied to those decision-making problems which attributes are independence because in which probability is used to weighet the decision-making attributes. However, interavtive exists in most real decision-making problems[7]. References [8, 9] show some instances in which decision-making attributes are not independence. At the same time, group decision-making method often be used in the real lifes to avoid human deflection[10-12]. But experts' preference is effected by their social class, power, knowledge and expectation, which can bring interaction into expert's preference. For example, experts' preference is similar when their social class, power, knowledge and expectation are close to each other.

M. Dai (Ed.): ICCIC 2011, Part II, CCIS 232, pp. 466–474, 2011.

In multi-attribute decision-making problems, the weights of the attributes cannot be modeled through probabilities because the attributes' interaction ruins its additive. To weight the attributes for the decision-making problems with interaction, the concept of fuzzy measure was proposed by Japanese scholar Sugeno[13]. Marichal summarized that fuzzy measure can model all kinds of interaction among things, for example correlation, relationship of preference, and complementary/redundancy[8]. Based on fuzzy measure, Sugeno integral and Choquet integral are often used to synthesize attributes' value for the decision-making alternatives [7-9, 13]. Sugeno integral is suitable for aggregating ordinal information, while Choquet integral is suitable for aggregating cardinal information[8]. Both Sugeno integral and Choquet integral evaluate alternatives according to maximum rule. In order to value alternatives based on two criteria when decision-making attributes are interactive, the new decision-making method named TOPSIS with interaction (R-TOPSIS) is proposed based on traditional TOPSIS and fuzzy measure. According to which, new group decision-making method is proposed, and then the R-TOPSIS method and its corresponding group decision-making method are verified by an instance.

2 Fuzzy Measure

Before we define R-TOPSIS method, we introduce the concept of fuzzy measures [13]: a (discrete) fuzzy measure on A is a set function $\mu : P(A) \to [0,1]$ which satisfies the following axioms:

(1) Boundary conditions: $\mu(\phi) = 0$ and $\mu(A) = 1$;

(2)Monotonic conditions: $\forall T \subseteq R \subseteq A$, $\mu(T) \leq \mu(R) \leq \mu(A)$.

For any M, $N \in P(A)$, $M \cap N = \phi$, $\mu(M)+\mu(N)<\mu(M \cup N)$ when M, N are redundancy; $\mu(M)+\mu(N) >\mu(M \cup N)$ when M, N are complementary; $\mu(M)+\mu(N) =\mu(M \cup N)$ when M, N are independence. Where $P(A)$ is the power set of A.

3 R-Topsis Method

R-TOPSIS is defined according to traditional TOPSIS method and fuzzy measure which is used to weight the set of attributes. For a decision-making problem with attribute set $A= (a_1,\ldots,a_n)$ and alternative set $U=(u_1,\ldots, u_m)$. The steps of R-TOPSIS are listed as follows:

Step 1: Decision-making matrix T ($T =[t_{ij}]_{m\times n}$) is built after that each attribute value of alternatives is obtained.

$$T = \begin{bmatrix} t_{11} & t_{12} & \cdots & t_{1n} \\ t_{21} & t_{22} & \cdots & t_{2n} \\ \vdots & \vdots & \vdots & \vdots \\ t_{m1} & t_{m2} & \cdots & t_{mn} \end{bmatrix}$$

Where t_{ij} is the value of attribute $a_j (a_j \in A)$ of alternative u_i ($u_i \in U$).

Step 2: Normalized decision-making matrix Y ($Y=[y_{ij}]_{m\times n}$) is obtained after formulation (1) is applied to decision-making matrix T.

$$y_{ij}=t_{ij}/\sqrt{\sum_{i=1}^{m}t_{ij}^{2}},(i=1,\ldots,m;\ j=1,\ldots,n) \tag{1}$$

Step 3: Idea-solution and negtive idea-solution are determined according to decision-making matrix Y.

Idea solution is

$$z^{*}=(z_{1}^{*},\ldots,z_{n}^{*})=(y_{1}^{*},\ldots,y_{n}^{*})$$

where

$$y_{j}^{*}=\{<\max_{1\le i\le m}y_{ij}\Big|\,j\in J^{+}>,<\min_{1\le i\le m}y_{ij}\Big|\,j\in J^{-}>\},1\le j\le n,$$

J^{+} is the set of benefit attributes and J^{-} is the set of cost attributes.

Negtive idea solution is

$$z^{0}=(z_{1}^{0},\ldots,z_{n}^{0})=(y_{1}^{0},\ldots,y_{n}^{0}),$$

where

$$y_{j}^{0}=\{<\min_{1\le i\le m}y_{ij}\Big|\,j\in J^{+}>,<\max_{1\le i\le m}y_{ij}\Big|\,j\in J^{-}>\},1\le j\le n.$$

Step 4: The distance of a alternative $u_i(u_i\in U)$ far from idea-solution and negtive idea-solution are calculated.

Matrixes P ($P=[p_{ij}]_{m\times n}$) and Q ($Q=[q_{ij}]_{m\times n}$) are built according to $p_{ij}=|y_{ij}-z_j^0|$, $q_{ij}=|z_j^{*}-y_{ij}|$, $(1\le i\le m,\ 1\le j\le n)$, where z_j^0 and z_j^{*} are jth unit of vector z^0 and z^{*} respectly.

The distance of alternative $u_i(u_i\in U)$ to idea-solution and negative idea-solution are calculated according to formula (2) and (3) respectly.

$$d_i^{-}=\sqrt{\sum_{j=1}^{n}[p_{(ij)}(\mu(A_{(j)})-\mu(A_{(j+1)}))]^{2}}\ ; \tag{2}$$

$$d_i^{+}=\sqrt{\sum_{j=1}^{n}[q_{(ij)}(\mu(A_{(j)})-\mu(A_{(j+1)}))]^{2}}\ . \tag{3}$$

Where $_{(ij)}$ is the transformation of vector $(p_{i1},\ldots,p_{in})$ and $(q_{i1},\ldots,q_{in})$, $(1\le i\le m,\ 1\le j\le n)$, so that $0\le p_{(i1)}\le,\ldots,\le p_{(in)}$ and $0\le q_{(i1)}\le,\ldots,\le q_{(in)}$; $A_{(j)}=(a_{(j)},\ldots,a_{(n)})$; μ is the fuzzy measure defined on $P(A)$ and $\mu(A_{(n+1)})=0$.

Step 5: The alternatives are ranked according to their relatively close degree which can be calculated with formulate (4).

$$c_i=d_i^{-}/(d_i^{+}+d_i^{-}),\ 1\le i\le m. \tag{4}$$

Where c_i is the relatively close indexes of alternative u_i ($u_i\in U$).

And then the alternatives can be ranked according to their relatively close degree. The larger close degree is, the better alternative is because the alternative with large close degree means it close to the idea solution and far away from negative idea-solution.

The following theorem discovers the relationship between R-TOPSIS and traditional TOPSIS method.

Theorem 1: R-TOPSIS is equal to traditional TOPSIS when decision-making attributes are independence.

Prove

Since decision-making attributes are independence, the weights of the attributes are additive. So that the following equations can be obtained:

$$\mu(A_{(i)})\text{-}\mu(A_{(i+1)})=\mu(a_{(i)}),$$

$$\mu(a_1,\ldots,a_n)=\sum_{k=1}^{n}\mu(a_k)=1\cdot$$

The relatively close indexes of alternative ui(ui∈ U) can be calculated according to R-TOPSIS method:

$$c_i=\frac{d_i^-}{d_i^-+d_i^+}$$

$$=\frac{\sqrt{\sum_{j=1}^{n}[p_{(ij)}\mu(a_{(j)})]^2}}{\sqrt{\sum_{j=1}^{n}[p_{(ij)}\mu(a_{(j)})]^2}+\sqrt{\sum_{j=1}^{n}[q_{(ij)}\mu(a_{(j)})]^2}}$$

$$=\frac{\sqrt{\sum_{j=1}^{n}[p_{ij}\mu(a_j)]^2}}{\sqrt{\sum_{j=1}^{n}[p_{ij}\mu(a_j)]^2}+\sqrt{\sum_{j=1}^{n}[q_{ij}\mu(a_j)]^2}}$$

$$=\frac{\sqrt{\sum_{j=1}^{n}[\left|y_{ij}-z_j^0\right|\mu(a_j)]^2}}{\sqrt{\sum_{j=1}^{n}[\left|y_{ij}-z_j^0\right|\mu(a_j)]^2}+\sqrt{\sum_{j=1}^{n}[\left|z_j^*-y_{ij}\right|\mu(a_j)]^2}}$$

$$=\frac{\sqrt{\sum_{j=1}^{n}[(y_{ij}-z_j^0)\mu(a_j)]^2}}{\sqrt{\sum_{j=1}^{n}[(y_{ij}-z_j^0)\mu(a_j)]^2}+\sqrt{\sum_{j=1}^{n}[(z_j^*-y_{ij})\mu(a_j)]^2}}$$

Set $\mu(a_{(i)})=w_j$ ($1 \leq j \leq n$), and then:

$$\frac{\sqrt{\sum_{j=1}^{n}[(y_{ij}-z_j^0)w_j]^2}}{\sqrt{\sum_{j=1}^{n}[(y_{ij}-z_j^0)w_j]^2}+\sqrt{\sum_{j=1}^{n}[(y_{ij}-z_j^*)w_j]^2}}.$$

The formula listed above is same to which is used to calculate relatively close degree for alternatives in traditional TOPSIS method (ref [1]). And then R-TOPSIS method is equal to traditional TOPSIS method when decision-making attributes are independence.

According to Theorem 1, it is clear that traditional TOPSIS is R-TOPSIS method's especial instance. And the R-TOPSIS method is more general than the traditional one.

4 Group Decision-Making with R-TOPSIS

R-TOPSIS method can also be used to solve the group decision-making problems when interaction exist among both experts' preference and decision-making attributes.

The detail steps of group decision-making according to R-TOPSIS method are listed as follows:

Step 1: For a group decision-making problem with alternative set $U=(u_1,\ldots,u_m)$, attribute set $A=(a_1,\ldots,a_n)$ and expert set $D=(d_1,\ldots,d_h)$, decision-making matrix T^k ($T^k=[t_{ij}^k]_{m\times n}$) is built after that each attribute of alternatives is valued by expert $d_k\in D$.

$$T^k=\begin{bmatrix} t_{11}^k & t_{12}^k & \cdots & t_{1n}^k \\ t_{21}^k & t_{22}^k & \cdots & t_{2n}^k \\ \vdots & \vdots & \vdots & \vdots \\ t_{m1}^k & t_{m2}^k & \cdots & t_{mn}^k \end{bmatrix};$$

Step 2: Normalized decision-making matrix Y^k ($Y^k=[y_{ij}^k]_{m\times n}$) is obtained after decision-making matrix T^k ($k=1,\ldots,h$) is normalized;

Step 3: Determining the weights of the attributes and its subsets;

Step 4: Determining the weights of the experts and its subsets;

Step 5: The relatively close degree c_i^k ($i=1,\ldots,m$; $k=1,\ldots,h$) of alternative $u_i\in U$ is calculated according to matrix Y^k and R-TOPSIS method;

Step 6: Matrix C ($C=[c_i^k]_{m\times h}$) can be obtained after each element c_i^k ($i=1,\ldots,m$; $k=1,\ldots,h$) is calculated;

Step 7: The relatively close degree c_i ($i=1,\ldots,m$) of alternative $u_i\in U$ is calculated based on matrix C according to R-TOPSIS method;

Step 8: Ranking the alternatives according to their relatively close degree c_i ($i=1,\ldots,m$).

In the following part, R-TOPSIS method and its corresponding group decision-making method will be verified through selecting e-business web building solution for enterprise.

5 E-Business Web-Site Building Solution Selection for Enterprise

Many enterprises plan to build their e-business web site, but how to select a suitable building solution is very important. Here, four attributes are considered when enterprises select their building solution of e-business web site, which is building risk (a_1), economic benefit (a_2), social benefit (a_3), and cost (a_4). Among which, a_1 and a_4 are cost attributes; while a_2 and a_3 are benefit ones. All attributes' value of each alternatives are obtained through expert surveying. The weights of attribute and attributes are also given by expert, which are listed as follows: $\mu(a_1)$=0.25, $\mu(a_2)$=0.30, $\mu(a_3)$=0.20, $\mu(a_4)$=0.30, $\mu(a_1, a_2)$ =0.60, $\mu(a_1, a_3)$=0.50, $\mu(a_1, a_4)$=0.52, $\mu(a_2, a_3)$=0.45, $\mu(a_2, a_4)$=0.65, $\mu(a_3, a_4)$ =0.48, $\mu(a_1, a_2, a_3)$=0.85, $\mu(a_1, a_2, a_4)$=0.90, $\mu(a_1, a_3, a_4)$=0.85, $\mu(a_2, a_3, a_4)$=0.95, $\mu(a_1,a_2,a_3,a_4)$=1.00. Three alternatives are considered by an enterprise when its e-business web site start to build, that is, building by itself (u_1), building by both software company and itself (u_2) and buy existing software (u_3). Three experts are considered in this instance (d_1~d_3), whose weightes are $\mu(d_1)$=0.40, $\mu(d_2)$=0.40, $\mu(d_3)$=0.40, $\mu(d_1, d_2)$ =0.75, $\mu(d_1, d_3)$=0.75, $\mu(d_2, d_3)$=0.75, $\mu(d_1, d_2, d_3)$=1.00. Tab 1~3 show attributes value of alternatives (u_1~u_3) given by expert. According to which, the best building solution of e-business web site can be selected.

Table 1. Decision-making matrix given by expert d1

	a_1	a_2(mil.RMB)	a_3	a_4(mil.RMB)
U_1	0.90	2.00	0.70	1.00
U_2	0.70	1.75	0.90	1.50
U_3	0.80	1.87	0.75	1.35

Table 2. Decision-making matrix given by expert d2

	a_1	a_2(mil.RMB)	a_3	a_4(mil.RMB)
U_1	0.80	2.08	0.70	1.20
U_2	0.70	1.62	0.75	1.50
U_3	0.73	1.78	0.72	1.30

Table 3. Decision-making matrix given by expert d3

	a_1	a_2(mil.RMB)	a_3	a_4(mil.RMB)
U_1	0.90	1.75	0.80	0.80
U_2	0.80	1.80	0.90	1.00
U	0.88	1.75	0.82	0.85

3

Normalized decision-making matrixes 4~6 are obtained after formulation (1) is applied to Decision-making matrix Tab 1~3 respectly.

Table 4. Normalized Decision-Making Matrix R^1 According To Tab 1

	a_1	a_2	a_3	a_4
U_1	0.65	0.61	0.51	0.44
U_2	0.50	0.54	0.66	0.67
U_3	0.57	0.58	0.55	0.60

Table 5. Normalized Decision-Making Matrix R^2 According To Tab 2

	a_1	a_2	a_3	a_4
U_1	0.62	0.65	0.56	0.52
U_2	0.54	0.51	0.60	0.65
U_3	0.57	0.56	0.57	0.56

Table 6. Normalized Decision-Making Matrix R^3 According To Tab 3

	a_1	a_2	a_3	a_4
U_1	0.60	0.57	0.55	0.52
U_2	0.54	0.59	0.62	0.65
U_3	0.59	0.57	0.56	0.55

Firstly, R-TOPSIS method is used to solute decision-making matrix R^1, and its corresponding idea-solution, negative idea-solution, P matrix and Q matrix are listed as follows:

$$Z^*=(0.50\ 0.61\ 0.66\ 0.67);$$
$$Z^0=(0.65\ 0.54\ 0.51\ 0.67);$$
$$P=\begin{bmatrix} 0.00 & 0.08 & 0.00 & 0.23 \\ 0.15 & 0.00 & 0.15 & 0.00 \\ 0.08 & 0.04 & 0.04 & 0.07 \end{bmatrix},$$
$$Q=\begin{bmatrix} 0.15 & 0.00 & 0.15 & 0.00 \\ 0.00 & 0.08 & 0.00 & 0.23 \\ 0.07 & 0.04 & 0.11 & 0.16 \end{bmatrix}.$$

The distance of alternative u_1 to idea-solution and negative idea-solution is 0.07 and 0.05 respectly after formula (2) and (3) are applied to matrix R^1.

The relatively close degree of alternative u_1 is calculated through formula (4):

$$c_1^1=0.07/(0.05+0.07)=0.58.$$

Based on the analysis mentioned above, the relatively close degree of alternative u_2 and u_3 are c_1^2=0.42, c_1^3=0.34 according to decision-making matrix R^1. And the relatively close degree of alternative u_1~u_3 are c_2^1=0.74, c_2^2=0.26, c_2^3=0.52 according to decision-making matrix R^2. The relatively close degree of alternative u_1~u_3 are c_3^1=0.62, c_3^2=0.38, c_3^3=0.58 according to decision-making matrix R^3.

Step 2:As a result, matrix C can be obtained:

$$C=\begin{bmatrix} 0.58 & 0.74 & 0.62 \\ 0.42 & 0.26 & 0.38 \\ 0.34 & 0.52 & 0.58 \end{bmatrix}\cdot$$

The synthetical relatively close degree of alternative u_1~u_3 are 1.00, 0.11, 0.44 respectly according to matrix C and R-TOPSIS method. And then, the rank of u_1~u_3 is $u_1 \succ u_3 \succ u_2$. That is, this enterprise should build its e-business by itself.

And the synthesis value of alternatives u_1~u_3 are 0.95, 0.91 and 0.92 and their rank is $u_1 \succ u_3 \succ u_2$ if the instance mentioned above is resolved through Choquet integral (ref [8]).

Obviously, the rank of u_1~u_3 obtained through R-TOPSIS method and Choquet integral are same. But, R-TOPSIS method can evaluate the decision-making alternatives based on two criteria.

6 Conclusions

Interaction exists in most real decision-making problems, the new decision-making method named R-TOPSIS is proposed and applied to group decision-making with interaction. The steps of how to apply R-TOPSIS is discussed. Several conclusions can be drawn from this study:

(1) In R-TOPSIS method, fuzzy measure is used to weight the attribute and attributes instead of probability measure. So that it can deal with the decision-making problems with interaction;

(2) R-TOPSIS method is a general version of traditional TOPSIS method. R-TOPSIS method is equal to traditional TOPSIS method when decision-making attributes are independence;

(3) Since interaction exist in most real group decision-making problems, R-TOPSIS method can get scientific and reasonable result. And R-TOPSIS method is more general than traditional TOPSIS method;

(4) Similar to Choquet integral, R-TOPSIS is suitable for aggregate cardinal information when it is used to deal with decision-making problem with interaction;

(5) Group decision-making method based on R-TOPSIS deals with group decision with interaction, which provides new way to deal with group decision problems.

References

[1] Wei, S.X., Zhou, X.Z.: Multi-attribute decision making and its application in the C3I. National defence industry press, Beijing (1998)

[2] Yu, Y., Liang, L.: Extensions of the TOPSIS for Multiple Criteria Decision Making. Systems Engineering (2), 98–101 (2003)

[3] Wang, Y.-M., Elhag, T.M.S.: Fuzzy TOPSIS method based on alpha level sets with an application to bridge risk assessment. Expert Systems with Applications 31(2), 309–319 (2006)

[4] Yu, J.X., Tan, Z.D.: Research on Quantificational Performance Evaluation Based on Combination Weighting and TOPSIS. Systems Engineering-theory & Practice 11, 46–50 (2005)

[5] He, Q.C., Wang, X.N., Han, D.Y., et al.: Application and comparison of comprehensive evaluating the achievements of scientific and technological professionals of health science by peer review and TOPSIS method. Science Research Management 4, 16–22 (2004)

[6] Lv, Q.: Application of TOPSIS Comprehensive Evaluation in Suppliers Selection. Value Engineering 1, 66–68 (2004)

[7] Bi, K.X., Sun, J.H.X., ZHANG, T.Z., et al.: Measurement and Evaluation of Regional Technological Innovation in Small and Medium Enterprises Based on Fuzzy Integral. Systems Engineering-theory & Practice (2), 40–46, 61 (2005)

[8] Marichal, J.L.: An axiomatic approach of the discrete Choquet integral as a tool to aggregate interacting criteria. IEEE Transactions on Fuzzy Systems 8(6), 800–807 (2000)

[9] Wang, Z., Leung, K.S., Wang, J.: Determining nonnegative monotone set functions based on Sugeno's integral: an application of genetic algorithms. Fuzzy Sets and Systems 112(1), 155–164 (2000)

[10] Chen, C.-T.: Extensions of the TOPSIS for group decision-making under fuzzy environment. Fuzzy Sets and Systems 114(1), 1–9 (2000)

[11] Leyva-Lopez, J.C., Fernandez-Gonzalez, E.: A new method for group decision support based on ELECTRE III methodology. European Journal of Operational Research 148(1), 14–27 (2003)

[12] Beynon, M.J.: A method of aggregation in DS/AHP for group decision-making with the non-equivalent importance of individuals in the group. Computers & Operations Research 32(7), 1881–1896 (2005)

[13] Angilella, S., Greco, S., Lamantia, F., et al.: Assessing non-additive utility for multicriteria decision aid. European Journal of Operational Research 158(3), 734–744 (2004)

Research on Strategic Human Resource Management Innovation-Oriented

Sun Bo

School of Economics and Management
Jiaying College
Meizhou, Guangdong Province, P.R. China
sunli8896@sina.cn

Abstract. System of human resource management innovation-oriented is precisely the important way supporting enterprise's innovation. This research reviewed innovation theories from aspects of economy, management and sociology, summarized domestic & foreign scholars' studies on human resource management and enterprise performance, and outlined related domestic & foreign researches on human resource management innovation-oriented. On the basis of all those, this paper constructed system of strategic human resource management innovation-oriented via method of normal research.

Keywords: Innovation-oriented, Human resource management, Enterprise performance, Strategy.

1 Introduction

In present era, economic globalization and knowledge economization dominate. Enterprise cannot just rely upon rich material capital, inexpensive labor force and plenary monetary fund of its own to make it larger & stronger. Instead, enterprise should concentrate its attention on its innovative ability. Regardless of from product, service, flow, or management, innovation will win unique competitive advantage for enterprise. This is also the sure choice of organizations for the present and the future.

A. Birth of the problem

At present, change and innovation are the theme of the time. The only unchangeable subject is 'change'. Under such situation, how should organization deal with competitions and challenges from various aspects? How to maintain its agility to the changing external environment? These all request organization to establish innovation mechanism facing to the environment and avoid homogeneous competition. Through continuous innovation, to win by innovation in change, enterprise could set up competitive advantage of its own. However, human is the carrier of organization's activities and the most active factor of productive forces. Enterprise's every innovation should be done by worker or team. Since scale of enterprise's innovation ability is decided by staff's consciousness and motion to a great extent, enterprise should fully arouse staff's enthusiasm, initiative and creativity to shape its overall innovation power through stipulating human resource management system and policy

M. Dai (Ed.): ICCIC 2011, Part II, CCIS 232, pp. 475–483, 2011.

suitable to innovation. This is a direction of human resource management research - human resource management innovation-oriented.

To construct system of human resource management innovation-oriented is precisely the important way supporting enterprise's innovation. But there're still questions need to be clarified such as what the difference between human resource management innovation-oriented and traditional human resource management system is, what the common features are, how to construct and so on. Enterprise's every innovation will finally be manifested by promotion of enterprise performances. Human resource management innovation-oriented will also be similarly helpful to enterprise performances' promotion.

Therefore, the following research should pay attention to the intrinsic mechanism of how human resource management innovation-oriented influence enterprise performances. On the one hand, qualitative research will discuss how to link parts of human resource management with innovation-orientation to highlight innovation's conduction. On the other hand, quantitive research will study the intrinsic relations between human resource management innovation-oriented and enterprise performances. This paper dialyses the impacts of strategic human resource management innovation-oriented on enterprise performances, and it could be regarded as a sub-research of the above topic.

B. The research background

The report of the party's 17th session in October, 2007 explicitly declared to construct innovative country through promotion of independent innovating competence! Our country's scientific innovation level still lags behind world level and there remains big disparity. Lu Yongxiang, the vice chief of Standing Committee of the National People's Congress committee, chief of Chinese Academy of Science and a dual academician wrote <To Improve Independent Innovating Competence Is A Significant Strategic Mission to Construct Innovative Country> which proposed that promotion of independent innovating competence must be guided by scientific development concept, scientific innovation must be guided by scientific development concept, and request of scientific development concept must be implemented to scientific innovation's every aspect.

To insist Chinese characteristic independent innovation path should take promotion of independent innovating competence as the important task of the current microscopic subject - enterprise organizations. Therefore, constructing system of human resource management innovation-oriented helps to promote enterprise's independent innovating competence and accelerates implementing strategy of to construct innovative country.

C. The research method

This research will construct strategic human resource management innovation-oriented through normal research. Because human resource management innovation-oriented is a new concept, the academic circle still lacks research on this domain. Therefore, on foundation of combing related literatures and building theoretical platform, this research will adopt method & mode of normal analysis to discuss strategic human resource management innovation-oriented.

2 Literature Review

As a new viewpoint and a new thought, strategic human resource management innovation-oriented receives little systematic research. The research results are also quite limited. Related theories are mainly in innovation theories, human resource management theories and enterprise performances theories. This paper will review the literatures from aspects of theoretical foundation and related research to build up the theoretical platform of normal analysis and theoretical foundation of empirical research.

A. Innovation theories

Although innovation has already become a popular vocabulary, experts from different domains hold varied understandings of it.

1) Innovation theories in economic domain

Innovation was first brought forward by J. A. Schumpter, a famous Austrian economist. He elaborated innovation from angle of production elements' substitution: 'to introduce new factors or combination of old & new factors in Industrial organizations' [1]. The new factors here include innovative discovery, introduction and combination on product or product quality, production method, market, supply source, form of Industrial organization and so on. What worth pointing out is that Schumpeter equated management innovation and technological innovation in discussion, as effectively expanded innovation's range of study and established broad research cornerstone for enterprise to obtain and maintain competitive power.

2) Innovation theories in management domain

Knowledge management theories founded by Peter F. Drucker, the grand Master of management science, more involves how to utilize knowledge to realize innovation. In Drucker's opinion, systematic innovation refers to seven origins to trace innovation opportunity. The first four origins exist inside enterprise; the latter three involve exterior changes of enterprise or industry. Each origin has its own unique attributes. So these seven origins need to be analyzed respectively. However, each origin is not inherently more important or more productive than others. Patterns of innovation are by no means fixed. It possibly comes from thought's miraculous glow or just opportunity or coincidence. Drucker's viewpoint seems like disorder. But deep taste of it might actually provide technical guide for research of stimulating and inducing innovation. Successful entrepreneurs won't just wait for innovation opportunity to grant them a 'good idea', they diligently resort to practice. This is not only of extraordinarily meaningful to this article, but also of guiding significance to rewrite innovation concept for enterprise, school and other organizations.

As knowledge management research dominates from recent years, scholars attempt to solidify innovation and creation from technical aspects. Wiig, a Norwegian scholar thought that innovation might expand previous knowledge through individual intellect and analysis, and it might also test by experiment or exploration while study was the best way to obtain and create new knowledge [2]. Japanese scholars Ikujiro Nonaka and Hirotaka Takeuchi thought that knowledge transition should go through the following four modes: socialization, externalization, combination and internalization [3]. Through these four modes, knowledge of different levels like individual, team and organization proliferate gradually, as forms so-called 'knowledge screw'. Knowledge unceasingly innovates as it circulates unceasingly in conversion process. Viewpoints of Wiig, Nonaka and Takeuchi provided new thoughts on aspect of mechanism construction for enterprise to pursue vision of innovation. They're especially worth referring to enterprise training.

3) Innovation theories in sociological domain

According to Durkheim's sociology theory, innovation starts on the micro aspect. Microcosmic innovations will constitute national innovation system with stronger cohesiveness. Nation then can influence innovation process from aspect of policy. And innovation process inside enterprise can also be influenced by social structure. This is the relationship between macro- and micro- innovation processes [4]. This paper leaves away from macro viewpoint, only discusses how to induce, stimulate and cooperate with innovation in terms of micro management. Durkheim theories' revelation to enterprise is: while under the rule's control, enterprise could apply it in its internal subsystem to theoretically support adjustment of innovation on enterprise level and individual level. This is also what this research should concern while discussing human resource management's support, initiation and induction to innovation.

B. Review of related research on human resource management and enterprise performances

Both domestic and foreign scholars have made effective research on discipline of human resource management, thus classical theories of human resource management also get continuous enrichment and development. And there doesn't lack unique & new HRM theories and viewpoints profoundly influencing to the field. Anyway there's a point for sure that pertinent HRM is indeed helpful to enterprise performances' promotion.

1) Foreign related research review

Foreign scholars started to pay attention to problem of HRM practices and enterprise performances in early 1980s. The related research could be summed up as the following aspects.

The person called 'change technician' by Kanter is an important role in company to support innovation [5]. Function of successful change technician could be comprehended as interaction in & between different levels of enterprise, as magnifies enterprise's possibility to succeed compared with its competitors. Recruitment & selection, training & development, feedback, compensation and cognition of ones staff are the most important factors organization input. Factors like cohesion, motive, etc. are correlated with organization performances [6]. Innovation on enterprise aspect needs interaction to coordinate [7]. All these HRM practices are related with enterprise interior. Empirical study demonstrates that HRM practices and company performances are mediated by top managers' social network [8]. To adapt to environment, organizations pursuing reliability should keep open & flexible to expanding information to acquire reliability of innovation. Hiring adept casual laborers could produce better financial performances [9]. Group structure influences team validity and further affects organization performances. Effective HRM system helps staff to effectively establish network relations while top managing team's internal & external social network is the very adjustment variable of company performances.

Strategy of innovation brings unavoidable pressure of change to traditional HRM. Since interaction in & between enterprise's different interior levels could foster innovation, such interaction should be focus of attention. Organization intervention and organizational structure influence performances, so they should be concerned. Vogus & Welbourne's point that dynamic environment is more likely to produce innovation the viewpoint is quite inspiring to the author: If dynamic environment could produce innovation more easily, could environment's state of dynamic & static be the dividing line to study HRM and enterprise performances? Guzzo's point of organization intervention suggests the author to consider performance promotion on organizational aspect. Collins & Clark's point about staff's network relations coincide with the author's. Effective staff's network relations are nothing but: network structure taking staff as its node helps to improve enterprise performances! Dr. Kanter's point about change technician encourages scholars to propose hypothesis on 'interaction'. Axtell's related point on 'interaction' further strengthens the determination to propose such hypothesis.

2) Domestic related research review

Chinese domestic scholars started to study problem of HRM practices and enterprise performances later than foreign scholars. And their most research results are close with foreigners'. As a whole, their related research could mainly be narrated by the following.

Innovation is closely correlated with culture, thus enhancing enterprise's core competitiveness should begin from constructing culture innovation-oriented [10]. We should emphasize not only technical experts' role in enterprise innovation, but also all staff's station and function in enterprise's strategy of innovation [11]. Lack of innovation strategy and planning are the main organizational influencing factors, and 'innovating tendency' is one of creativity's foundations. 'Performance management basing on gradual innovation strategy' could advance continuous innovation. Constructive recruitment is a direction of HRM development. Irrational technical human resources' disposition influences their output, and the re-disposition to correct & compensate would inevitably exhibit flowing of human resource.

Wang Zhongming's point is a little bit advancing, but still a valuable anticipation of HRM's development direction. Sun Jianmin's point fore-mentioned requires enterprise to hike innovation to strategic degree and clarify its procedures - or 'esoterica'. Zhao Shuming from Nanjing University provides a benchmark for related study by his empirical research on relations between innovation strategy, HRM and performance. According to the above, this research puts forward the concept of strategic human resource management innovation-oriented.

C. Review of related research on human resource management innovation-oriented

1) Foreign related research review

Early in 1994 at promulgation ritual of America Human Resource Excellence Award, Smith noted 'Winning innovations in human resource', namely to win innovation through human resource. This could be regarded primitive thought of 'human resource management innovation-oriented'. Atuahene-Gima, an innovation management professor in Sino-Europe International Business School, put forward HRM's innovation-orientation's influence in new product development, as clarified that HRM could really do something in innovation-orientation. His viewpoint consolidates confidence of both enterprise and researchers including the author: practice and research of 'HRM innovation-oriented' could be potential. Searle & Ball further proposed that HRM policy could be used to support innovation, and he did empirical study on data from Britain [12]. In 2003, professor Edvardsson, an Icelandic scholar, put forward 'knowledge management and creative HRM' in his work paper, and he interpreted on aspects of recruitment, selection, training, development, performance management, compensation, professional career, learning environment and so on, as brought forward a more comprehensive model and drew innovation even closer with HRM. Vassalou, the first prize winner of 2005 European HRM Doctoral Dissertation proposed HRM's innovative nature, and chose variables in internal environment, external environment and individual characteristics. However, Vassalou didn't effectively differentiate HRM innovation and HRM innovation-oriented.

2) Domestic related research review

Domestic research on HRM innovation-oriented started a little bit late. The first person putting forward concept of 'management innovation-oriented' is not from academic circle. He is from Huaneng International Electric Power Development Company Nanjing Subsidiary, and his name is Liu Guosheng. Basing on enterprise practices, he proposed 'management innovation-oriented' and introduced ways of his enterprise in 2000. Liu Guosheng's point was obviously practical. Li Baoshan et al. from People's University opined on management innovation-oriented's illumination to reform of state-owned enterprise in 2001. What needs to point out is that Li Baoshan and his partners' point were also from practices of Huaneng Nanjing Power Plant. Meng Qingwei et al. from Harbin Industry University studied enterprise culture's technological innovation-orientation in 2002, as also symbolized trend of enterprise innovation's infusion to HRM research. But hereafter, research on enterprise management's innovation- orientation once stagnated, until in 2007 Wan Houfen et al. from Zhongnan University of Economics and Law proposed merging of innovation-orientation and market-orientation. But the merging they mentioned was on aspect of marketing but not domain of HRM. Yang Jingzhao et al. from Nanjing University released an article 'Performance management strategy innovation-oriented', which led theme of innovation into aspect of performance management, as symbolized that innovation officially entered domain of HRM.

In an article 'High-tech Enterprise's HRM Practices Innovation-oriented' printed in <China Human resource development>, a Chinese domestic periodical in May, 2007, 'human resource management innovation-oriented' appeared for the first time in China. This article thought that High-tech enterprise's knowledge creation competence is the source of its retainable competitive advantage. It systematically analyzed factors influencing enterprise knowledge creation competence, and brought forward an interactive model of four factor deciding high-tech enterprise's knowledge creation output. It also indicated concrete HRM measures to promote enterprise knowledge innovation and advance its retainable competitive advantage, namely HRM practices primarily basing on stimulation including appraisal, compensation and so on. But it's a pity that this article's author didn't make further study after proposing 'human resource management innovation-oriented' [13]. Just at the same time of that article's publication, this paper's author's research paper 'Innovation's Support: Outsourcing, Culture and Vocational Career' got released in Proceedings of the first International Conference on Enterprise Growth and Management Innovation (May, 2007, Wuhan University). 'HRM innovation-oriented' was also brought forward.

This paper's author started research on HRM innovation-oriented from 2006. Some English papers have been released and indexed by EI and ISTP. These research attempt to establish a systematic model of HRM innovation-oriented constituted by internal & external, dynamic and static, organizational structure, etc., which has induced scholars' attention in international conferences. After conference exchanging and professors' remarking, this model has been revised and perfected.

3 Constructing System of Strategic HRM Innovation-Oriented

To enterprise, innovation means to seek not only new product, but also new materials, new market, new control system and new methods, etc.. Managers need to purposedly search source of innovation and grasp every chance to successfully realize innovation. The so-called 'innovative innovation' is just to implement innovation-orientation in HRM practices to stimulate and induct enterprise innovation. In other words, that is innovation theories and practices' application in HRM domain. In HRM innovation-oriented, HRM is the method while to direct enterprise innovation is the goal. The so-called 'HRM innovation-oriented' is not to create opening new space of HRM, but to reorganize in existing space whose principle is to insist enterprise's demand of to innovate.

The 'strategy' here is actually 'strategic human resource management'. It's designed HR utilizing mode and varied HRM practices aiming to realize enterprise's goal. Strategic HRM requests enterprise to break through traditional localization as 'personnel affairs'. Instead, it should consider enterprise's human resource deployment at a more macroscopic angle for and from all staff. Therefore, 'strategic development direction' becomes our first index to investigate strategy. Strategy should be formed by top managers rightly to enterprise's specifics and must be fully exchanged with intermediate & foundational level. The second index to investigate strategy is defined as 'different levels' discussion on strategy'. Enterprise pursues innovation, thus it has to rely on knowledge workers. Therefore, the degree of enterprise's emphasizing on knowledge workers reflects its strategic angle of view. Then the third index is 'to focus on knowledge workers'. 'Human resource investment' is a representative one among numerous details of strategic HRM since it could reflect enterprise's human resource value concept and is also the strategic viewpoint when human, capital and material are weighed to choose. Thus it becomes the final index to investigate strategy.

In enterprise's numerous innovations, the first one need to solve should be macroscopic innovation which is just strategic innovation. Compared with other innovations, strategic innovation is one kind is most radical and the most deciding innovation content. Facing to tide of knowledge economy and complicated international competition, enterprises are generally challenged by strategic innovation. Successful managers mostly take more care of strategy. That is, successful enterprise policy-makers must speed up strategic innovation by brand-new idea, brand-new vision, brand-new method, globalized judgment and strategist's courage.

Outstanding enterprise policy-makers mostly have sober or even advancing understanding of strategic innovation. Choate, the president Ford Company's board of directors had a profound sentence: 'leading enterprise is always working for tomorrow's requests', as actually means strategic innovation. There's diversity in human's ability. If we can design a kind of mechanism that could automatically adjust work load and difficulty and allocate interest according to this to fully expose talents, it will be a goal HRM satisfies and pursues. To let the most 'weighted' person automatically 'leak' out could be called HR's 'funnel' theory. Haier Group's way of 'to horse race but not choose' is of similar thought. And design of this kind of multi-channel competition system could be fostered and developed on aspect of strategy.

From practice of enterprise development, strategic innovation is a kind of comprehensive, long-term and foundational arrangement & planning of enterprise. For demonstration and design of future strategic development direction to instruct direction of enterprise innovation, enterprise needs to answer the following questions: Do enterprise's top leaders emphasize innovation and endeavor to push it? Has enterprise drawn up its innovation vision? Do departments like production, research & development, marketing and so on arrange periodic innovation scanning? Are enterprise's new development direction & strategy the regular topics of top managers' conference? Do top managers hold different opinions on its best strategic development direction? Has enterprise officially empowered top managers to improve executive procedures to support innovation? Do top managers regularly discuss strategic development direction together with staff? Do employees often challenge top managers' understanding of enterprise's present situation? Does enterprise's HR strategy suit with its innovation strategy? ......

Strategic innovation is not so mystical & remote as in imagination. Enterprise should try to learn after different professions and different enterprises. A little change of thought in practice might be the starting point of strategic innovation. For example, to change production line from 'push' to 'pull', as seems only a change of direction, but actually a series of innovations on production line started, and the famous lean manufacture pattern comes into being. To research & develop via staff is considered perfectly justified, but if customers are introduced to participate in research & development and opine on critical parameters or even break through product's traditional model design, surely it is innovation.

4 Conclusions

Enterprise's strategic innovation is one kind of 'soul' innovation, should be the first to solve in enterprise's numerous innovations. Human resource is just like enterprise's mineral resource. Whether it is gold, silver or copper mine is decided by different HR strategy. Strategic innovation fosters, instructs and supports enterprise innovation, as has already aroused attention of far-seeing leaders. Enterprise should intend to guide, because it's no so remote and out of touch. Besides comprehensive strategy of manpower exceeding, selection, utilization, training and so on constitute other items of HR strategy innovation-oriented.

Individual innovation doesn't definitely lead to improvement of organizational performance. So the following concerns should be how to lift individual innovation to organizational level. The author advocates theorists and practitioners to seriously regard HRM innovation-oriented, further study its branches, and ultimately implemented it to practitioners' HRM practices.

Acknowledgment. The author appreciates the precious opportunity given by sponsors & organizers of EEEE 2010. The organizers are especially thanked for their timely & efficient instructions.

References

[1] Schumpeter, J.A., He, W., Yi, J., et al.: Economic development theory. Commercial Press, Beijing (1991)
[2] Wiig, K.M.: Knowledge management: The central management focus for intelligent-acting organizations. Schema Press, Arlington (1994)
[3] Nonaka, I., Takeuchi, H.: The Knowledge Creating Company. Oxford University Press, New York (1995)
[4] Durkheim, E., Dong, Q.: Social division of labor. SDX Joint Publishing Company, Beijing (2000)
[5] Kanter, R.M.: The Change Masters: Innovation for Productivity in the American Corporation. Simon & Schuster, New York (1983)
[6] Guzzo, R.A., Shea: Group Performance And Intergroup Relations In Organizations. In: Dunnette, M.D., Hough, L.M. (eds.) Handbook Of Industrial And Organizational Psychology, pp. 269–313. Consulting Press, Palo (1992)
[7] Axtell, C.M., Holman, D.J., Unsworth, K.L., Walt, T.D., Waterson, P.E., Harrington, E.: Shopfloor innovation Facilitating the suggestion and implementation of ideas. Journal of Occupational and Organizational Psychology 73, 265–285 (2000)
[8] Collins, C.J., Clark, K.I.: Strategic human resources practices and top management team social networks: An examination of the role of HR practices in creating organizational competitive advantage. Academy of Management Journal 46, 740–751 (2003)
[9] Vogus, T.J., Welbourne, T.M.: Structuring for high reliability: HR practices and mindful processes in reliability-seeking organizations. Journal of Organizational Behavior 24, 877–903 (2003)
[10] Wang, Y., De Zhang: Empirical study on relations between innovative culture and enterprise performance. Metascience Research 12, 475–479 (2007)
[11] Li, G., Zhao, S.: Research on relations between enterprise innovation strategy, human resource management and performance. Foreign Economy and Management 4, 17–24 (2008)
[12] Searle, R.H., Ball, K.S.: Supporting Innovation through HR Policy: Evidence from the UK. Creativity and Innovation Management 3, 50–62 (2003)
[13] Sui, X.: Practices of human resource management innovation-oriented in high-tech enterprises. China Human Resource Development 5, 4–9 (2007)

A Database Integration Method for Small and Medium Information System

Bing Wang

Zhejiang GongShang University, 310018,
Hangzhou, Zhejiang, China
Wangbb33@126.com

Abstract. The paper presents a database integration method named MysqlInside which mainly for small and medium information system, describes its composition and structure, introduces some key attributes and functions of its components, and gives the core code in Java language for example. With the performance advantages of Mysql itself, MysqlInside is easy to use and has fully competent for small and medium information system's database application requirements.

Keywords: database integration, small and medium information system, Mysql, Java.

1 Introduction

The application of relational database has becoming an essential part of information system, how to choose an appropriate database product must be considered at the beginning of design. This article discusses the database integration is mainly aimed at small and medium information system which have two characteristic: one is the end-users of these systems are almost SMEs or individuals, and the other is the scale of one-table-data within a number of years will not exceed one million. In this case, a database product only with the following features can be competent for[1]: First, low cost, customers and dealers are unwilling to bear the additional cost of database; Second, easy maintenance, due to the lack of professionals to maintain the database's daily operation, the best way is making the database "transparency"; Third, data security, here is considered more about the flexible data backup&restore mechanism; Fourth, fast and efficient, most end-users have strict speed demanding, slow or lag will affect their spending choices; Fifth, easy migration, there often do not have a fixed server to run the system, program various from one PC to another at any time; Sixth, small disk occupation, the size of program code itself only a few dozen MB, so a huge size DBMS is not acceptable.

At present, there are many popular database products which have lot of difference on scale, performance and price. Orcal, DB2, SQLServer, Sybase ASE are becoming the representatives of large and medium database[2][6], while Mysql, Access, Firebird, Sqlite are of small and medium database[8]. Considering this situation, Mysql stands out. First, according to the developer, said Mysql may be one of the

M. Dai (Ed.): ICCIC 2011, Part II, CCIS 232, pp. 484–492, 2011.

fastest database, in addition to technical reasons, Mysql streamlines a number of unnecessary and non-common features, comparing to some other large database product, which do not affect the using within system; Second, Mysql is relative easy, and supports network application; Third, Mysql has obvious advantages on price, it is all free if without the technical support from the developer; Fourth, Mysql has very small disk occupation and can be fully integrated into the system software; Fifth, Mysql has huge data capacity, after version 3.23 it uses MyISAM as table type, with which the data capacity is no longer limited by database itself but the Operating System[4][7].

According to above, this paper presents a database integration method named MysqlInside which implements in Java. MysqlInside provides some interfaces and functions for other programs to invoke, which do the jobs of database install, start, stop, uninstall, backup, restore and transmit effectively[5], it truly integrates the database into the grogram, and completely frees the end-users from the database maintenance.

2 Structure of MysqlInside

Mysql product itself provides some management tools for different OS, and its core data file is cross-platform, here uses Windows for example. See figure 1:

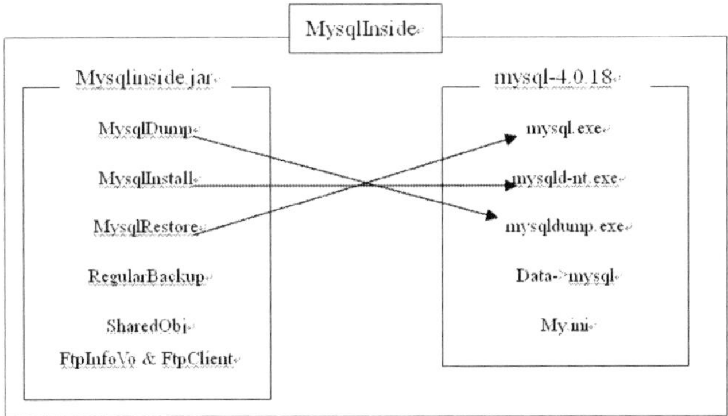

Fig. 1. The Structure OF MysqlInside

MysqlInside consists of two main parts, one is the "MysqlInside.jar" which contains components of MysqlDump, MysqlInstall, MysqlRestore, RegularBackup, SharedObj, FtpInfoVo&FtpClient; the other is "mysql-4.0.18" which is the DBMS, it only reserves some necessary parts of the whole version, on Windows platform, they are mysql.exe, mysqld-nt.exe, mysqldump.exe, My.ini and data Folder. After streamlining by the author, size of "mysql-4.0.18" is only 4.66MB.

The main job of the components in "MysqlInside.jar" is invoking the specific tools for specific requirement, sometimes put them together.

3 Function and Implementation

A. Class SharedObj

Class SharedObj defines a set of shared properties and methods which for other components to invoke. These methods seal some underlying operating as one module. See figure 2:

```
public static List<String> actCMD(String cmd);
public static int isPortInUse(int port);
public static int getWinServiceState(String serName);
public static String getDBName(File file);
public static Date getDumpDate(File file);
public static String getOSType();
```

Fig. 2. The shared method of class ShareObj

1) Method actCMD

Implements functions that using Java to run Windows Command Line. It is the bridge between Java program and the Mysql management tools. Core code is:

```
Process p1 = Runtime.getRuntime().exec("cmd /c "+cmd);
```

Fig. 3. Core code of method actCMD

P1 is an independent thread, it receives a string type command line as input, and puts the process information into List<String> as return.

2) Method isPortInUse

Implements functions that determining whether a particular port number is taken up by other program. Core code is:

```
List<String> list = actCMD("netstat -an");
```

Fig. 4. Core code of method isPortInUse

3) Method getWinServiceState

Implements functions that judging the current state of Mysql service, there are three types of state: Uninstalled, Running and Stopped. The last two indicates Mysql service has been installed. Core code is:

```
List<String> list = actCMD("sc query "+serName);
```

Fig. 5. Core code of method getWinServiceState

Param “serName” is the service name of Mysql on Windows platform.

4) Method getOSType

Implements functions that getting the current type of operating system.

5) Method getDBName and getDumpDate

They are mainly for data restoring, their functions are getting the database name and backup date from the dump file.

B. Class MysqlInstall

Class MysqlInstall implements functions that installing, uninstalling, starting and stopping the Mysql service. See figure 6:

```
private String mysqlDirPath;          private boolean isParamValid();
private String mysqlServiceName       private boolean reWriteMyIni(File file);
private int mysqlPort;                public void install();
                                      public void unInstall();
                                      public void start();
                                      public void stop();
```

Fig. 6. Key properties and methods of class MysqlInstall

1) Property mysqlDirPath

Specifies the path of "mysql-4.0.18" directory.

2) Property msqlServiceName

Specifies the name of Mysql service on Windows platform.

3) Property msyqlPort

Specifies the port number of Mysql service when running. Setting the msqlServiceName and msyqlPort properly can construct multi-instance of Mysql at the same time, and avoids conflicts with existing services

4) Method isParamValid

Implements functions that judging whether the tool "mysqld-nt.exe" is existed or not. This tool is necessary for Install and Uninstall.

5) Method reWriteMyIni

Implements functions that re-generating file "My.ini" properly, it is the very file for Mysql configuration, which contains basic information of data path, port number, etc.

6) Method install

Implements functions that installing the Mysql service, main steps as following:

Step 1: execute method isParamValid to sure the correctness of parameters.

Step 2: execute method reWriteMyIni to re-generate file "My.ini" according to the context.

Step 3: execute method SharedObj.getWinServiceState to get the service state, if the service is already installed then do not need to re-install.

Step 4: execute method SharedObj. isPortInUse to determine whether current port number is in use, if is, then change it.

Step 5: execute the command line to install, core code is:

```
String newpath = this.mysqlDirPath.replace('/', '\\');
String cmd = newpath+"\\bin\\mysqld-nt.exe -install "+
this.mysqlServiceName+" --defaults-file=\""+newpath+"\\my.ini\"";
SharedObj.actCMD(cmd);
```

Fig. 7. Core code of install Mysql service

Step 6: re-execute SharedObj.getWinServiceState to check whether the service is installed successfully.

7) Method unInstall

Implements functions that uninstalling the Mysql service, main steps as following:

Step 1: execute method isParamValid to sure the correctness of parameters.

Step 2: execute method SharedObj.getWinServiceState to get the service state, if the service is not installed yet then do not need to uninstall.

Step 3: execute the command line to uninstall, core code is:

```
String newpath = this.mysqlDirPath.replace('/', '\\');
String cmd = newpath+"\\bin\\mysqld-nt.exe -remove "+this.mysqlServiceName;
SharedObj.actCMD(cmd);
```

Fig. 8. Core code of uninstall Mysql service

Step 4: re-execute SharedObj.getWinServiceState to check whether the service is uninstalled successfully.

8) Method start and stop

Implements functions that starting and stopping the Mysql service after it be installed, on Windows, using "net start" and "net stop" command line respectively.

C. Class MysqlDump

Class MysqlDump implements functions of backup database. See figure 9:

```
private String dumpToolsDir;      private String paramPassword;
private String paramServerIp;     private String lastDumpFilePath;
private int paramServerPort;      private boolean isParamValid();
private String paramUsername;     public boolean dump(String dbName,
                                  String outPutDir);
```

Fig. 9. Key properties and methods of class MysqlDump

1) Property dumpToolsDir

Specifies the path of tool "mysqldump.exe".

2) Property paramServerIp and paramServerPort

Specifies the IP address and port number of the Mysql service for which to backup.

3) Property paramUsername and paramPassword

Specifies the Authentication information for the Mysql service with which to login[3].

4) Property lastDumpFilePath

Records the latest dump file path, it can be used for other processing.

5) Method isParamValid

Implements functions that judging whether the tool "mysqldump.exe" is existed or not. This tool is necessary for backup.

6) Method dump

Execute the backup operation. It receives two parameters: parameter dbName specifies which database need to backup; parameter outPutDir specifies where to output the dump file. Core code is:

```
File toolDir = new File(this.dumpToolsDir);
String cmd = toolDir.getPath()+"\\mysqldump.exe -u"+paramUsername+
      " -p"+paramPassword+" -h"+paramServerIp+" -P"+paramServerPort+
      " --complete-insert --opt --extended-insert=false "+
      dbName+" > "+dir.getPath()+"\\"+dumpfilename;
List<String> list = SharedObj.actCMD(cmd);
```

Fig. 10. Core code of method dump

D. Class MysqlRestore

Class MysqlRestore implements functions that restoring database. See figure 11:

```
private String dumpToolsDir;     private String paramPassword;
private String paramServerIp;    private boolean isParamValid();
private int paramServerPort;     public boolean restore(String dbName,
private String paramUsername;      String inputFile);
```

Fig. 11. Key properties and methods of class MysqlRestore

Some properties and methods are as same as MysqlDump.

1) Method restore

Execute the restore operation. It receives two parameters: parameter dbName specifies which database need to restore; parameter inputFile specifies which dump file will be used to restore. Core code is:

```
File toolDir = new File(this.dumpToolsDir);
String cmd = toolDir.getPath()+"\\mysql.exe -u"+paramUsername+
      " -p"+paramPassword+" -h"+paramServerIp+" -P"+paramServerPort+
      " "+dbName+" < "+inFile.getPath();
List<String> list = SharedObj.actCMD(cmd);
```

Fig. 12. Core code of method restore

E. Class RegularBackup

Class RegularBackup implements functions that backing up database automatically. See figure 13:

```
private Timer timer0;              private long intervalSecs;
private String dbName;             private boolean isStarted;
private String outPutDir;          private List<MyFtpInfoVo> ftpList;
private MysqlDump dumpObj;         private boolean isParamValid();
private Date lastDoDate;           public void start();
private Date nextStartDate;        public void stop();
private int hour;                  public Date getNextStartDate();
private int minute;                private class DumpTask extends TimerTask;
```

Fig. 13. Key properties and methods of class RegularBackup

1) Property time0

It is the instance of class java.util.Timer for executing regular tasks.

2) Property dumpObj

It is the instance of class MysqlDump, and it is the true executor of backup operation.

3) Property lastDoDate and nextStartDate

Specifies the latest dump time and next will-be dump time respectively.

4) Property hour and minute

Specifies the hour and minute numbers that the first backup operation will be executed.

5) Property intervalSecs

Specifies the backup cycle time, in seconds, it is used to calculate the next backup time.

6) Property ftpList

It is a list for FTP sites, RegularBackup will put the latest dump file to the specific FTP sites automatically if they in this list.

7) Method start and stop

Implements functions that starting or stopping the RegularBackup task.

8) Inside class DumpTask

It is an inside class that extends java.util.TimerTask. After each backup process, a new instance of DumpTask will insert into the task schedule.

F. Class FtpInfoVo & FtpClient

Class FtpInfoVo defines the formation of one FTP site including IP address, port number, login code and file path, while FtpClient defines one method sendFile, see figure 14:

```
public static boolean sendFile(MyFtpInfoVo ftp,String sourcefile,String destName);
```

Fig. 14. Definition of method sendFile

This method receives three parameters: parameter ftp specifies one FTP site; parameter sourcefile specifies the file which will be put onto the FTP; parameter destName specifies the new name of the file.

4 System Integration

With MysqlInside it is very convenient to integrate components into specific parts of information system. See figure 15:

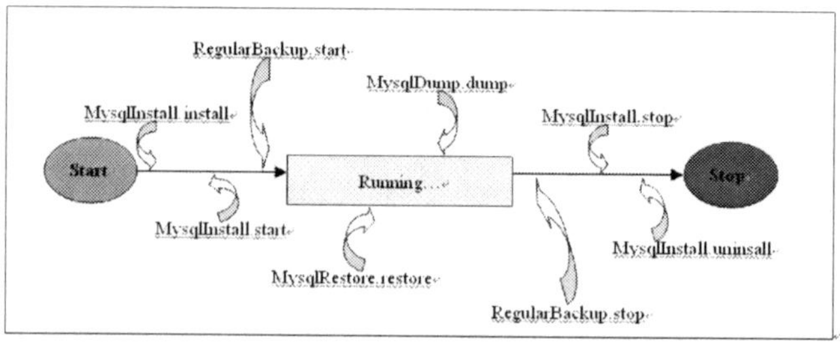

Fig. 15. Integrate MysqlInside into information system

1) After system starting and before running

First, execute method MysqlInstall.install to install the Mysql service; Then, execute method MysqlInstall.start to run the Mysql service; At last, execute method RegularBackup.start to start the automatic backup program.

2) In sytem running process

Can execute method MysqlDump.dump or MysqlRestore.restore to operate specific functions.

3) Before system stopping

First, execute method RegularBackup.stop to stop the automatic backup grogram; Then, execute method MysqlInstall.stop to stop the Mysql service; At last, execute method MysqlInstall.uninsall to uninstall the Myql service.

Through such a process, Mysql will be started when system start and stopped when system stop, that is the "transparency".

Using Java for example, here is the core code of MysqlInside integration:

```
MysqlInstall obj = new MysqlInstall();
obj.setMysqlDirPath("C:/mysql-4.0.18");
obj.setMysqlPort(3318);
obj.setMysqlServiceName("MysqlInsideDB");
obj.install();
obj.start();
```

```
MysqlInstall obj = new MysqlInstall();
obj.setMysqlDirPath("C:/mysql-4.0.18");
obj.setMysqlPort(3318);
obj.setMysqlServiceName("MysqlInsideDB");
obj.stop();
obj.unInstall();
```

```
RegularBackup rbc = new RegularBackup();
rbc.setDumpObj(obj);
rbc.setDbName("testDB");
rbc.setOutPutDir("C:/DbBackup");
rbc.setIntervalSecs(86400);
rbc.start();
......
rbc.stop();
```

```
MysqlRestore obj = new MysqlRestore();
obj.setDumpToolsDir("C:/mysql-4.0.18/bin");
obj.setParamServerIp("127.0.0.1");
obj.setParamServerPort(3318);
obj.setParamUsername("root");
obj.setParamPassword("");
obj.restore("testDB",
    "C:/DbBackup/testDB_1270962533296.sql");
```

Fig. 16. Core code of MysqlInside integration

5 Conclusions

MysqlInside seals and optimizes some local tools of Mysql database provided, reduces the complexity of operation and maintenance of Mysql database for developers and end-users, makes the work of database integration easier. With the performance advantages of Mysql itself, MysqlInside is easy to use and has fully competent for small and medium information system's database application requirements.

References

[1] Li, J., Si, Q.: The application of Mysql with open source in SMEs. Modernization of Mark (January 2009)

[2] Wu, D.: SQL Relational Database and Itegration of JAVA Development Language. China New Technologies and Products (15) (2009)

[3] Zhu, H.: Security Vulnerabilities and Prevent Method of Mysql Database. Information Technology, Information Science

[4] Ma, X., Fen, W.: MSSQL and MySQL database Comparing the Merits and Prospects. Science and Technology Innovation Herald (11) (2009)

[5] Zhao, Z.: Database Backup & Recovery of Mysql. Computer Learning (December 2009)

[6] Comparison of the four major databases, http://tech.ccidnet.com/art/1105/20050610/265929_1.html
[7] Mysql Data Capacity, http://hi.baidu.com/xiyouwang/blog/item/73180a2d7f68473e349bf7ea.html
[8] Comparison of several small database, http://www.cppblog.com/woaidongmao/archive/2008/10/26/65138.html

E-Government: An Approach to Modern Public-Service Oriented Government

Yong Wu[1], Fang Zhou[2], and Jun-Min Liu[3]

[1] Department of Automobile Management, Automobile Management Institute, Bengbu Anhui 233011, China
[2] Basic Department, Bengbu Navy Petty Officer Academy, Bengbu Anhui 233012, China
[3] Department of Automobile Management, Automobile Management Institute, Bengbu Anhui 233011, China
yongwu2526@sina.cn

Abstract. E-government could make room for the development of modem public-service oriented government. The establishment of e-government will play a important role in facilitating the development of the public- service oriented government. This article defined the meaning and function of the e-government firstly, discussed the e-governments' stimulative function to establish the public-service oriented government, so as to draw the conclusion that construct a structure- rational' economic and effective e-government service system based on the public- service oriented and learning-oriented government. In order to finish the purpose, it is necessary to change the government's function and construct the service oriented government, perfect the system of laws, expand the service targets and cultivate supportive culture of, improve operational mechanisms.

Keywords: E-government, Public- service oriented government, Innovation of the rule.

1 The Meaning and Function of the E-Government

The e-government is also called as the electronic government, it's meaning to use the info and communications technology to break the framework limit of the administration, construct the e-department, in order to realize the network of information which government agency obtain and supply, and come true the electronic-interaction between the government and the public. It also means that the information-management system and administrative management system based on network that faces to the government agency inner, others agencies, corporation and public. But, the e-government is unequal to traditional government-electronic. It is a sort of system innovation, that is re-constructing and changing the traditional government based on the information and network technology. It acts the citizenship as the client of government, and focus on the citizenship' requirements, improve radically the relations between government and government, government and corporation, government and individual, Urge to the

M. Dai (Ed.): ICCIC 2011, Part II, CCIS 232, pp. 493–498, 2011.

governments make more service for the masses with the new govern model. Concrete to say, the e-government could bring out those functions:

Firstly, it is contribute to change the government' function and enhance the ability of service

The basic character of the e-government lies in focusing on citizenship' requirements, making full use of the information-technology to enrich the content and form of government' service, to build up the ability of service, to urge its service results to the maximize. So, we can say the emergence of the e-governments push the changing for the government service functions. Through comparing with the traditional government, the services of the e-government supply the rationalization and reality of social requirements with an eye to more areas and higher layers, it also provides more chances with the masses that obtain government public services. So, the construction of the e-government means the changing deeply of government's function.

Secondly, it is contribute to increment the governmental clarity and realize the governmental affairs openly

Constructing the e-government contributes to increment the governmental clarity, for it's framework and behavior tend to"can be seen", it can be as low as lowest degree to inequity, unfair and corruption phenomena. Making the rational system circulated on the machine with more steady, credibility, availability. So as to restrict with government's power, lowered the indetermination of the government public service with maximum limit ， reduce the unreasonable government' behaviors because of the information dissymmetry and imperfection.

Thirdly, it is contribute to building up the government's competition ability and providing with more superior quality service for the society

At present, it is more obvious that the competition among governments. The e-governments contribute to building up the government's competition ability for its' more public service ability, Higher administration management efficiency, larger governmental affairs clarity. So, if a government owns e-government, It would own better market environment, higher in line with level with nations, greater investment attraction. And that will build up the government' competition ability further.

2 E-Governments Accelerate to Establishment the Public-Service Oriented Government

The public-service oriented government is a new type of the government manage mode. It's service corpus is an all levels governments and others public organizations, it's service object is citizenships, society organization and society, the direction of service is public benefits, the service of the contents is public service, the service of the way is a public transparent way. The e-government has an inherent and natural contact with the public-service oriented government. From a certain angle to see, the character of e-government lies in it's the public-service oriented government, namely innovation government' service in virtue of electronics means. As the professor Wang-Yu Kai pointed out "information-based government and work via network are an important measure for the public-service oriented government." Seen from the essence, the e-government embodies fully the basic principle on constructing the public-service oriented government, provide the importance path to construct he public-service oriented government. Seen from the essential meaning, the relation between the e-government and the public-service oriented government embody as: the public-service oriented government is a purpose and the e-government is a means.

Firstly, it contributes to changing the working-means for the public-service oriented government

E-governments make full use of modern information and correspondence technology, break off the organization boundary to tradition government, and construct a new type of information dissemination mode via network, according to form a kind of open and matrix organization structure. The information can flow and pass quickly through a network, come into being the information-flowing which maneuver interleave, lead to everywhere, even surpass the national boundary, time and space boundary. E-governments make the centralization management system transited to the mutual, networked and flat management system, carry out the outline that the information delivering to all-directions, multilayer, multiformity types, many paths and surpass time and space boundary. The outlet that the information is delivered except perpendicular outlet arrive bottom by top, and has also a horizontal outlet. E-governments own the dissipation of type path to networked dissemination. It can make central governments' order reach to the basic level without obstruction. Whereas, the feedback of the basic level also deliver quickly and upward, the layer class' information deliver function which tradition perpendicular of organization is instead of network'.

Secondly, it contributes to enhancing the scientific decision for the public-service oriented government and the quality of the public policy

The decision of the government is a certain policy or the choice of the activity which governments deal with some important social problems. The scientific decision call for democratization, if it has no full democracy, it couldn't widen to open speech road, benefit by canvassing various opinions, couldn't exertive creative power with maximum limit. within the administrative area of e-government, the objective which "small government, big society" will be established gradually, the function is divided explicitly between government and brainpower organization, make full use of the assistance decision of function which policy-research institution and society expert system, many performanced works become more and more systemize, at end come true numeral. Make the decision become professional, specialize more. Scientific and right decision-making can bring out a excellent performance, it can contribute to social and economic development and the masses' benefits. So, the governments act as the spokesman of public interest, Property and behavior aim of itself ask for decision exactitude and valid in work. In order to come true the aim, it is vital important that democratization of benefit by canvassing various opinions and make full use of various science result of scientific during the decision-making. So, we can say e-government contributes to enhancing the scientific decision for the public-service oriented government and the quality of the public policy.

Thirdly, it contributes to strength the supervise-strength of policy-carrying, lowering the transform opportunity of policy-carrying

The implement of the e-government contributes to carrying out and consolidating on the avail of public supervise-mechanism. First of all, e-government simplify the deliver outlet which supervise-information feedback via network technology. The trivial supervise-information deliver process is simplified, the inspector and decision-maker will be eliminated, drive off artificial separate phenomenon will be cancelled that the decision-layer connects with masses' network terminal directly through its web page or website. In this way, simplify the center-link which information-delivering, avoiding to the information's losing true which the information of feedback in the process of delivering. Secondly, e-government can insure the supervisor especially masses presume to supervise via "by secret ballot" or "anonymous direct". Through the network's surveillance, it can safeguard effectively the interests of supervisors, get rid of the worry, This contributes to providing with a guarantee for supervision activity.

Fourthly, it contributes to strengthen the clarity of government operation and induce to the clean-government's construction

Opening-information is the foundation of democracy, is the ultimate requirement of the open-government. Using to the network, government can make the handling affairs procedure opened to public, exaltation government work' efficiency, promote clean-government's construction. E-government can publish the name of government departments, function, organization structure, handling affairs rules etc. government provide open information of index to public depend on its property toward the society, organization, business enterprise. So as to the public can understand quickly, increment handling affairs of clarity. At the same time, government can accept the opinions of every trade public, accept public supervision, attain the governmental affairs to open. So, e-government contributes to strengthen the clarity of government operation and inducing to the clean-government's construction. Therefore, after the e-government's foundation, with the continuously strengthen of the degree of integration of the social resource, it will consumedly promote government operation of public, decrease corrupt, promote clean-government's construction.

3 The Research on the Path to Establish Our E-Government

The construction of e-government is a complicated systemic engineer, there exists many problems, difficulties and challenges among them. Therefore, it needs to judge the hour and size up the situation, make full using of the most important chance which overall construct middle-class family society and push forward modernization quickly. It takes the e-government consideration into carrying on systemic integration on all kinds of resources and values. It contributes to pushing up the e-government's development on the whole. Seeing from the angle of non-technique, the path to construct the e-government includes the following faces:

First of all, changing the government function: change the government from the supervised government to public-service oriented government

Government' function is a duty which administrational system takes on in the society and economy, changing and renovating government's function is a basic way that administrational system according to environment's change. Facing up to the globalization' impaction that taking information technique as the carrying body, the motive that is changed by market. And the knowledge economy's challenge that takes knowledge innovation as core, takes the industry information as important character.

The establishment and impelling of e-government brings up the important material equipments and technique-support that government function' conversion from the supervised government to public-service oriented government. It makes conversion become necessity that from the supervised government to public-service oriented government. The character of e-government lies in it's a public-service oriented government, namely innovating the government's management and service via e-medium. E-government wish for forming a kind of ideal service form: citizenship can obtain the abundant information without walking in to government office. Citizenship can deal with anything in any office. The service of future develops toward to "single unit" "overpass department" "twenty-four hours" "self-service". In other words, e-government requires the government innovate the service way, make the government's service faster, more convenience, more unimpeded, more direct, more fair, have higher additional value.

Secondly, establishing the perfect laws system, providing with institutional guarantee for establishing e-government

E-government could get away from the perfect framework of law and system, if it hasn't a healthy development. In overseas, many states constitute and promulgate special laws, rules and executive orders in order to guarantee to government information-based development. Those laws and rules have a method to depend on, have a chapter to follow, have a according to depend on for constructing the e-government. Therefore, we should draw lessons from advanced experience which abroad governments construct the e-government on legislation and system. According to our concrete state of the nation, the actual condition of the e-government's construction, speeding up the establishment on the related laws and system, in order to provide with powerful law support and guarantee for e-government's smooth development and administrative service of valid operation.

Thirdly, stepping up the speed of learning-government's construction, cultivating the support culture of e-government

In the knowledge-based economical and informational society, if a government attains only last advantage for long time, it must have more ability of study. It contributes to government's development as a system which has continuously and innovative ability that base on knowledge, through molding the learning-government. Therefore, the construction of e-government that from changing the government's function, reengineering-process to remould the organization's culture. Namely cultivate the inside support-culture which contribute to the e-government's development. Making the e-government's construction attained a new cultural-strength. So, we should inspire the desire for study to government organization and members, cultivate the ability of their study, Make it liked to accept a challenge with supportive and o reformational mindset, realize the ego-surmount, devote to e-government's construction creatively, at last finishing the taking customers' requirements as center of value system, At the same time, as possible as adopt to the circulate mode of e-government. So as to improve intelligence mode, establish common vision, strengthen government inner work's cooperation. exalting to e-government's construction level; Strengthen a government organization and its members' forward-looking consciousness and innovation consciousness in order to push group's study, and heighten the ability of systemic thinking, enhance the ability of initiative, forward-looking, foresee which include decision and plan, organization and leadership, control and innovation of active, more availably reach a construction strategy target to e-government. At last, it promotes the support culture of the e-government.

Fourthly, Drawing lessons from the management style for enterprise, perfect the circulate mechanism to e-government

During the construction of e-government, we should establish the quality management standard and information management system according to the requirements of service object, so as to heighten the service validity. Among them, we can draw lessons from ISO9000, we can use the ISO9000 that used widely in enterprise to the service system of the e-government; establishing the scientific, procedure management way of e-government and realizing the standardize and norm of administrational service process, Making the e-government circulate on a new higher quality terrace more efficiently, heightening the satisfaction for e-government's service, In order to accomplish the e-government service quality which the masses require with more economic way.

References

[1] Cai, L.-H.: E-affairs: the remold of government In Information era. Chinese Social Science Publisher, 314–315 (2006)

[2] Tan, Z.: Change the process of the e-affairs. Science Publisher, 102 (2006)

[3] Li, C.-J.: E-government and service oriented government. Modern Education Publisher, 225 (2008)

[4] Zhang, R.-T.: General outline of e-government. Chinese People's Publisher, 125 (2004)

[5] Li, C.-J.: The end of managerialism-the historyand logic of service oriented government's development. Chinese People's Publisher, 255 (2007)

[6] Wang, Y.-K.: The e-affairs should emphasize service oriented. The People's Tribute, 50–54 (June 2006)

[7] Li, C.-J.: Construction of e-government and service oriented government. The Study Tribute, 45–48 (June 2009)

[8] He, Z., Wei, Q.: The analysis on the government administrative process in the e-affairs view. E-affairs, 48–52 (August 2005)

An Empirical Analysis on Effecting Factor of Urban-Rural Income Disparity in Heilongjiang Province

Guangji Tong and Cungui Li

College of Economics and Management
Northeast Forestry University
Harbin, Heilongjiang Province, China
guangji4545@sina.cn

Abstract. The imbalanced urban-rural development and continuously enlarging urban-rural income disparity have already become the important bottleneck of social economic sustainable development in Heilongjiang. First, this paper analysed the actual situation and historical evolvement trend of income disparity between urban and rural residents in Heilongjiang. Then, according to the statistical data from 1978 to 2008, this paper built a multiple linear regression model to empirically analyzes the effecting factors of the income gap between urban and rural residents. The empirical results show that there is a positive correlation between the urban-rural income disparity and the urban-rural dual economic structure, industrial structure; there is a negative correlation between the urban-rural income disparity and urbanization level, the level of rural financial development. In the end, some countermeasures and suggestions on how to narrow the income disparity between urban and rural residents are proposed.

Keywords: urban-rural income disparity, effecting factor, multi-linear regression model.

1 Introduction

Since the reform and opening up, Heilongjiang's economic strength increased substantially, the people's living standards improved significantly, both urban and rural incomes increased considerably, and most families had more property than before. However, like other domestic regions, after the task of industrial system was basically accomplished, the urban biased policies and institutions have not been adjusted completely and timely, which are characterized by strong path dependence. Thus, the rural residents have not fully shared the fruits of economic development, and the income disparity between urban and rural residents shows a trend of continuous expansion.

The enlarging income gap between urban and rural residents would certainly affect economic sustainable development and social harmony and stability in Heilongjiang province. In 2008, the third plenary session of the seventh central committee clearly put forward that China has entered the development stage of industry promoting agriculture and urban areas helping rural areas as a whole, and entered a new period of

M. Dai (Ed.): ICCIC 2011, Part II, CCIS 232, pp. 499–509, 2011.

eradicating the urban-rural dual structure and form a new pattern that integrates economic and social development in urban and rural areas. Speeding up to build a new socialist countryside and effort to balance urban and rural development are of decisive significance for building a moderately prosperous society in all respects. The No. 1 central documents for 2010 again confirm that we must regard balancing urban and rural development as the fundamental requirement for building a moderately prosperous society in all respects and regard improving people's lives as the important part of adjustment of distribution pattern of national income.

In recent years, there are very much literature on effecting factor of income disparity between urban and rural residents. Domestic and foreign scholars analyzed the effecting factors from the follow respects: heavy industrialization strategy, urbanization, household registration system, labor transfer, urban-rural dual structure, rural financial development and so on. LIN Yi-fu (1996) holds that the urban-rural income disparity stems from differential social policies for the surpassing development strategy of heavy industries [1]. By empirical analysis on the income distribution effect of rural labor mobility, LI Shi (1999) draw a conclusion that rural labor outflows play an active role in reducing the income gap between urban and rural areas. On the one hand, rural labor mobility can increase the income of rural migrant workers directly or indirectly; on the other hand, working out of home can improve rural labor productivity by reducing rural surplus labor [2]. Joshua Levin (2001) thinks that like many other developing nations, China's urban-rural income disparity is the result of long-term urban-biased policies [3]. Thomas Hertel (2006) draws a conclusion that household registration system, rural land contract system, non-agricultural labor flow restrictions have significant effects on urban-rural income disparity [4].

To sum up, although the above literatures are important to our study, most of them study the urban-rural income gap from single aspect. The existence of the income disparity between urban and rural residents is a series of events. So, on the base of these studies, according to the statistical data from 1978 to 2008, this paper will make theoretical explanation to the relationship between urban-rural income disparity and urban-rural dual economic structure, urbanization level, growth rate of per capita GDP, and rural financial development level, industrial structure and employment structure. Then a multi-linear regression model will be built to empirically analysis on these factors. The hope is to find out the key factors of reducing the urban-rural income disparity and provide references for eradicating the urban-rural dual structure and forming a new pattern that integrates economic and social development in urban and rural areas.

2 The Status and Historical Evolvement Trend of Urban-Rural Income Disparity in Heilongjiang Province

As shown in Fig. 1, since the reform and opening up, both the per-capita disposable income of urban households and the per capita net income of rural households increased considerably, but the income gap between the urban and rural residents is widening, too. From 1978 to 2009, the per capita disposable income of urban households and the per capita net income of rural households have increased from 455 Yuan and 172 Yuan to 12 566 Yuan and 5 206.8 Yuan. Because the income of urban residents grows faster and urban base period level is higher than rural, the absolute gab of urban-rural income is becoming wider. In 2009, the relative income disparity between rural and urban residents once again reach to 2.41, which is lower than China's average level 3.33:1, but is much higher than the safety standard 1.6:1 asserted by international labor organization. In addition, all kinds of subsidy in kind are not included in the per capita annual disposable income of Chinese urban households, such as medicate, insurance, education, old-age pension, unemployment insurance and subsistence allowances. If took them into account, the income disparity between rural and urban residents would be much greater [5].

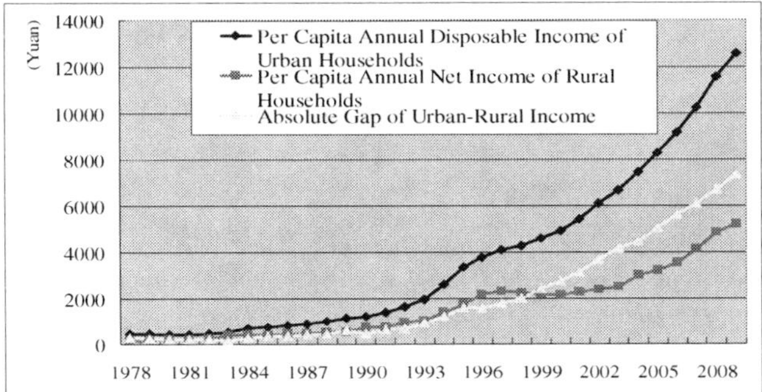

Fig. 1. The changing trend of urban-rural residents' income and disparity from 1978 to 2009 in Heilongjiang province

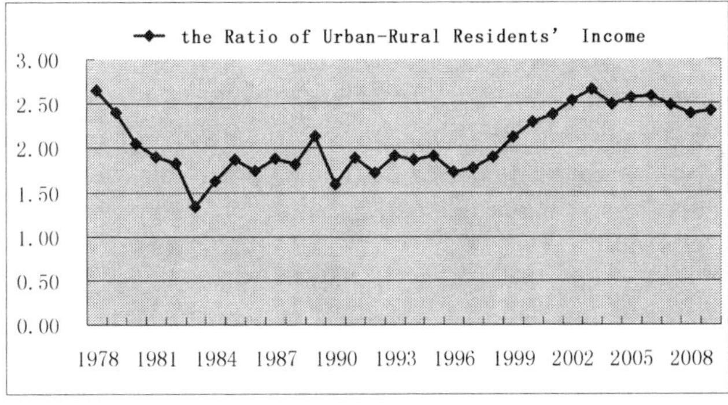

Fig. 2. The changing trend of the ratio of urban-rural residents' income ratio from 1978 to 2009 in Heilongjiang province

It can be seen from the Fig. 2 that the income disparity of urban and rural residents presents shows distinguishing stage characteristics since the reform and opening up in Heilongjiang province. (1) The first stage (from 1978 to 1983), the income disparity between urban and rural residents shows a fast diminishing trend. (2) The second stage (from 1984 to 1989), the income disparity between urban and rural residents shows the trend of rapid expansion as a whole. (3) The third stage (from 1990 to 1997), the income disparity between urban and rural residents shows a steady fluctuation state. (4)

The forth stage (from 1998 to 2003), the income disparity between urban and rural residents shows the trend of expansion once again. (5) The fifth stage (from 2004 to present), the income disparity between urban and rural residents shows tendency a gentle reduction.

3 Empirical Analysis

A. Variable Selection and Theoretical Basis

1) Dependent variable

This paper takes the urban-rural income disparity (Y) as the dependent variable, represented by the ratio of the incomes of urban and rural residents. Urban-rural income disparity = disposable income of urban residents / per capita net income of rural residents. The larger of the ratio, expressed greater of the urban-rural income disparity.

2) Independent variables

It is unrealistic and unnecessary to take account of all variables that affect the urban-rural income disparity. According to the theoretical analysis, experiential judgement and availability of data, we mainly consider the following key factors.

a) Urban-rural dual structure coefficient(X_1). W. A. Lewis (1954) proposed economic development model with unlimited supplies of labor, facing the dual structure in developing countries. This model thought that traditional agricultural sector has unlimited supplies of labor, whose marginal labor productivity is equal to zero or negative, lower than urban labor productivity generally. The gap between labor productivity has led to the differences between urban and rural areas. Along with the transfer of rural surplus labor force, the dual economic structure will gradually reduce [6]. The world economics social development's practice indicated that along with the economical development, the dual structure coefficient will decrease, and the urban-rural dual structure will inevitably change to the urban-rural integration. Urban-rural dual structure coefficient=(Secondary and tertiary industries output / Secondary and tertiary industries labor force)/(Primary industry output / Primary industrial labor force).

b) The level of urbanization(X_2). Urbanization is the transformation from rural traditional natural economy to urban socialization large-scale production. In general, along with the increase in the level of urbanization, the urban-rural income should show the trend of decreasing. On the one hand, the aggregation effect of town can absorb a number of rural surplus labor, then raises the agricultural productivity, increases farmers' income; Meanwhile, the increase in urban labor supply will increase competition in urban labor markets, reduce the wages of the urban labor force [7]. On the other hand, the town, as center of production, finance, trade, transportation, information and service, has a strong radiation and leading role to the countryside. The town can promote economic development in rural areas through technology transfer, industrial transfer, capital output, information dissemination and other means [8]. But, Heilongjiang's current urbanization is a urbanization of incomplete, which would cause land waste, scale management of agriculture can not be achieved, rural remaining problems, the role transformation of rural migrant workers in cities is blocked, and other social issues [9]. At the same time, among rural residents, only those who have higher human capital or have certain physical capital have the opportunity to live in the city; those who left in rural areas are mostly low educational level, no professional skills, old and sick and poor groups. The negative impact of loss of human capital in rural areas has the trend of widening income gap between urban and rural residents. Therefore, whether the urbanization can reduce the urban-rural income gap or not, depending on the role of these positive and negative results.

c) Growth rate of per capita GDP (X_3). Simon Kuznets (1995), a famous economist in the United States, put forward the "inverted U" shaped model to explain the changes of income distribution gap in industrial countries. Kuznets Reversed U Curve suggests that when the economy is at a stage of low development, along with per capita GDP growth, the income gap among residents will expand; when the economy develops to a certain stage, with further increases in per capita GDP, the income gap will gradually reduce [10]. As can be seen from Fig. 3, at present, the urban-rural income disparity in Heilongjiang begin to decline with the growth of per capita GDP.

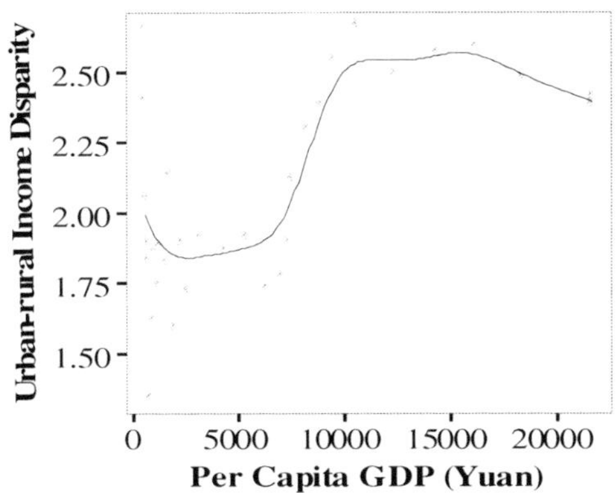

Fig. 3. The scatter plot between urban-rural income disparity and per capita GDP

d) The ratio of fiscal expenditure for agriculture(X_4). Changes in the structure of government expenditure are the most direct reflection of government policy preferences. The growth of agricultural expenditure rate reflects the government's emphasis on agriculture. The growth of fiscal expenditure for agriculture is helpful to improve agricultural production conditions, raise the level of agricultural technology, and promote agricultural development. If the prices of agricultural products remained stable or rose, the increase in the number of agricultural products arising from the improvement of agricultural production will inevitably result in the growth of farmers' income, thus the urban-rural income disparity will decrease too.

e) Rural financial development level (X_5). Production theory in economics suggests that the increase of capital will lead to output growth, given other conditions unchanged. The development of rural financial will increase the capital stock in rural

Table 1. The data of urban-rural income disparity and its effecting factors in Heilongjiang province

Year	Urban-rural Income Disparity	Urban-rural Dual Structure Coefficient	Urbanization Level	Growth Rate of Per Capita GDP	Ratio of Fiscal Expenditure for Agriculture	Rural Financial Development Level	Industrial Structure	Employment Structure
Unit		(%)	(%)	(%)	(%)	(%)	(%)	(%)
Code	Y	X_1	X_2	X_3	X_4	X_5	X_6	X_7
1978	2.65	3.63	35.9	10.37	14.51	19.83	76.5	47.36
1979	2.40	3.08	37.3	5.32	17.28	20.72	76.3	51.12
1980	2.05	2.64	38.5	16.84	17.60	20.13	75.0	53.22
1981	1.89	2.44	39.4	2.16	17.99	29.03	74.7	54.70
1982	1.83	2.30	39.9	7.48	17.61	33.28	74.4	55.74
1983	1.34	1.97	41.0	10.37	17.39	29.14	71.5	56.01
1984	1.62	2.03	42.0	14.03	15.54	33.43	73.0	57.03
1985	1.86	2.53	42.9	10.74	13.03	39.87	78.3	58.79
1986	1.74	2.30	43.9	11.96	10.49	35.52	76.9	59.10
1987	1.88	2.65	44.9	12.28	11.65	40.82	80.0	60.26
1988	1.82	3.04	45.9	20.00	10.12	42.65	82.9	61.51
1989	2.13	3.73	46.9	12.86	10.66	45.34	85.1	60.54
1990	1.59	2.27	48.0	12.17	10.78	28.92	77.6	60.40
1991	1.89	2.81	49.0	13.91	8.46	36.51	82.0	61.82
1992	1.72	2.76	50.1	15.67	8.84	26.59	82.6	63.23
1993	1.91	3.11	51.3	23.73	8.53	17.49	83.4	61.83
1994	1.86	2.48	52.4	32.79	8.22	16.02	81.0	63.21
1995	1.91	2.54	53.7	23.05	8.00	15.17	81.4	63.22
1996	1.73	2.43	53.8	18.14	8.31	14.66	81.3	64.10
1997	1.77	2.62	53.9	11.77	8.18	15.75	82.7	64.68
1998	1.89	5.17	54.0	3.39	10.34	19.39	84.5	51.38
1999	2.12	6.30	54.2	2.75	8.60	29.03	86.8	51.16
2000	2.29	7.28	51.9	9.45	9.48	23.46	87.8	49.79
2001	2.38	6.93	52.4	7.31	8.91	22.97	87.2	49.48
2002	2.54	6.77	52.6	7.20	9.10	23.70	87.0	49.62
2003	2.66	7.41	52.6	11.50	7.34	25.35	87.6	48.72
2004	2.49	6.55	52.8	17.02	7.84	27.46	87.5	51.69
2005	2.57	6.00	53.1	15.95	7.10	32.38	87.6	54.01
2006	2.59	5.99	53.5	12.43	7.59	34.61	87.9	54.82
2007	2.48	5.22	53.9	13.86	8.00	34.95	87.0	56.30
2008	2.38	5.08	55.4	17.58	8.62	32.59	86.9	56.61

areas, and then result in growth of agricultural output and raise of farmers' income. The rural financial development level is measured by the ratio of agricultural loans to the out of primary industry.

f) Industrial structure (X_6). The adjustment and upgrading of industrial structure are the most important factors affecting the distribution of income. Along with the change of industrial structure, the production factors will shift from Agriculture sector with low marginal productivity to non-Agriculture department with high marginal productivity, until the marginal productivity and return of the two sectors are equal. Therefore, a region where the ratio of the modern sectors (non-agriculture industries) in the industrial structure is higher means that the urban-rural income gap may be smaller. This paper regards the ratio of the secondary and tertiary industrial output to the primary industrial output as the indicator to measure the industrial structure.

g) Employment structure (X_7). In general, with the labor force shifting from the primary industry to secondary and tertiary industries, the income disparity between urban and rural residents will show a trend of decreasing. The main reason is that the transfer of the primary industrial labor force is favorable to achieve the appropriate large-scale operations of land, and promote the agricultural labor productivity. Moreover, the rural labor employing in the secondary and tertiary industries is helpful to improve their wage income, which would narrow the income disparity between urban and rural residents. However, under the influence of China's special national condition and relevant policies, the change of employment structure will not necessarily narrow the income disparity between urban and rural residents. Since the reform and opening up, although the restrictions on rural labor mobility were relaxed gradually, a series of urban biased welfare systems that take household registration system as the core still exist. When the rural migrant peasants look for work or work in town, they will encounter discriminatory treatment of industry access, post acquisition, wages, rights and interests maintenance, and so on. Therefore, if change of employment structure will lead to urban-rural income gap narrowed, it needs to make further empirical analysis. The employment structure is represented by the ratio of non-agricultural industries employed persons to total employed persons.

Data resources: Heilongjiang statistical yearbook and China compendium of statistics 1949-2004.

Table 2. Regression Analysis Result Using the Method of Enter—Coefficients

Model		Unstandardized Coefficients		Standardized Coefficients	t	Sig.	Collinearity Statistics	
		B	Std. Error	Beta			Tolerance	VIF
1	(Constant)	0.364	2.003		0.182	.857		
	Urban-rural dual structure coefficient X_1	-0.137	0.132	-0.696	-1.036	0.311	0.015	65.547
	Urbanization level X_2	-0.037	0.018	-0.624	-2.049	0.052	0.074	13.471
	Growth Rate of Per Capita GDP X_3	0.012	0.007	0.223	1.861	0.076	0.480	2.084
	Ratio of Fiscal Expenditure for Agriculture X_4	-0.018	0.028	-0.182	-0.668	0.511	0.092	10.823
	Rural Financial Development Level X_5	-0.002	0.005	-0.056	-0.486	0.632	0.516	1.937
	Industrial Structure X_6	0.097	0.030	1.375	3.254	0.003	0.039	25.922
	Employment Structure X_7	-0.067	0.032	-0.972	-2.079	0.049	0.031	31.757

B. Model building and empirical results

Multiple linear regression model is often used as empirical model or approximating function when more than one independent variable is involved, which can approximate the true unknown functional relationship between the dependent variable and independent variables [11].

Using the time series data from 1978 to 2008 in Heilongjiang province, as shown in Table 1, according to the above theoretical analysis, the multiple regression model was built to test the relationship between urban-rural income gap and its effecting factors. Taking the urban-rural Income disparity Y as the independent variable, X_1, X_2, X_3, X_4, X_5, X_6, X_7 as the dependent variables, the following multiple linear regression model is proposed.

$$Y = \beta_0 + \sum_{j=1}^{7} \beta_j \cdot X_j + \varepsilon \tag{1}$$

Where ε is random error term of the predictive model, β_0 is a constant term, $\beta_j (j = 1,2,\cdots,7)$ are called the regression coefficients and represent the variation of the predicted score when the corresponding independent variable Xi varies 1 unit, which are estimated by $\hat{\beta}_j (j = 1, 2, \cdots, 7)$ respectively.

Table 3. Regression Analysis Result Using the Method of Stepwise—Coefficients

Model		Unstandardized Coefficients		Standardized Coefficients	t	Sig.	Collinearity Statistics	
		B	Std. Error	Beta			Tolerance	VIF
1	(Constant)	-1.532	1.098		-1.395	0.175		
	Urban-rural dual structure coefficient X_1	0.083	0.036	0.424	2.311	0.029	0.236	4.234
	Urbanization level X_2	-0.057	0.013	-0.957	-4.570	0.000	0.181	5.526
	Industrial Structure X_6	0.077	0.021	1.088	3.639	0.001	0.089	11.267
	Rural Financial Development Level X_5	-0.009	0.004	-0.218	-2.157	0.040	0.779	1.283

1) Multicollinearity diagnosis

Variance inflation factor (VIF) is estimated for each independent variable to identify causes of multicollinearity. VIFj>20 implies that the jth independent variable is highly correlated with other independent variables of the model.

SPSS (18.0) statistical packet programs was used in the present statistical analysis, using the enter method in regression analysis, the results shown in Table 2. The result of equation fitting showed that the sample multiple correlation coefficient R=0.842, its value gives the proportion of the variance of the dependent variable that can be predicted from the independent variables. The determination coefficient R^2=0.917, F-statistics =17.456, significant P≈0.000, reflecting that the strength of the straight-line relationship is high. But, as is seen from Tab.2, the regression coefficients of X_1, X_2, X_3, X_4, X_5 and X_7 can not pass the t-Test of significance. At the same time, the variance inflation factors (VIF) of X_1, X_6, and X7 are much larger than 20, showing that the model has multicollinearity.

2) Result of stepwise regression analysis

In econometrics, there are many methods of eliminating multicollinearity, such as to expand the sample size, stepwise regression, ridge regression, principal component regression, partial least square regression and so on. In our study, the stepwise regression is adopted to solve multicollinearity problem. According to Table 3, the following multiple-linear regression model was obtained for the relationship between the urban-rural income disparity and the above-mentioned affecting factors using the data sets of the Table 1.

$$\hat{Y} = -1.532 + 0.083X_1 - 0.057X_2 - 0.009X_5 + 0.077X_6 \tag{2}$$

The result of equation fitting showed that the sample multiple correlation coefficient R $=0.891$, the determination coefficient $R^2=0.794$, F-statistics =25.004, significant $P\approx0.000$, less than 0.05, passing the F-test, showing that there were significant correlations between dependent variable and independent variables. It can be seen in Table 3 that, all the regression coefficients pass the t-Test of significance and the estimated VIF coefficients of all variables are less than 20, showing that the multicollinearity have been eliminated and the regression models are effective, which can be used to approximate the true functional relationship between the dependent variable and independent variables.

4 Conclusion

1) There is a positive correlation between urban-rural dual structure coefficient and urban-rural income disparity. From the regression results of the model, we know that the regression coefficients of X_1 is positive and maximum, showing that urban-rural dual structure is the most primary factors that result in the expansion of urban-rural income gap in Heilongjiang. Therefore, changing the dual economic structure should be the first choice to reduce the income gap between urban and rural residents.

2) There is a negative correlation between urbanization level and urban-rural income disparity. According to the model, the regression coefficient of X_2 is -0.057, showing that the urban-rural income disparity will decrease by 0.057 unit when the urbanization level increases by 1 unit. Therefore, to promote urbanization is an important way to narrow the urban-rural income disparity.

3) There is a negative correlation between the level of rural financial development and urban-rural income disparity. According to the mode, the regression coefficient of X_5 is -0.009 showing that the urban-rural income disparity will decrease by 0.009 unit when the level of rural financial development increases by 1 unit. The development of rural financial plays a significant role to narrow the income gap between urban and rural residents.

4) There is a positive correlation between industrial structure and urban-rural income disparity. According to the model, the regression coefficient of X_6 is 0.077, showing that the urban-rural income disparity will increase by 0.077 unit when the ratio of secondary and tertiary industrial output to the primary industrial output increases by 1 unit. This may be related to the upgrading of the industrial structure did not bring about a fundamental change in the employment structure in Heilongjiang province.

5 Suggestions

A. Balance urban and rural development and change the urban-rural dual economic structure

Balancing urban and rural development, is to take the urban development and the rural development a whole, combine the expansion of rural employment with the transfer of surplus rural labor, combine tapping the potential of agriculture itself with industry nurturing agriculture in return, and combine building a new socialist countryside with steadily promoting urbanization. First, we should vigorously develop rural education, efforts to enhance rural human capital, increase the capacity of scientific farming; should intensify pre-employment training for surplus labor transferred from rural areas, enhance the market competitive ability of rural migrant workers in cities. Next, to balance urban and rural industry development, through rational division of labor and cooperation of industries between urban and rural areas, to guide a rational flow of capital, technology, human resources, management and other production factors from urban to rural area. Guide the agglomeration of rural enterprises in county region and concentrate development area, support labor-intensive industries shift from cities to countryside, and make greater efforts to form a new pattern that Industrial layout is scientific, division is rational and draw on each other's strengths.

B. Steadily promote urbanization and implement the policies conducive to transfer rural labor out of farming

According to the requirements of the No. 1 central documents for 2010, urbanization should focus on strengthening the development of medium-sized and small cities and small towns. First, we should better integrate small town construction, develop rural enterprises and the industrialized operation of agriculture. We should vigorously develop and cultivate agricultural products processing enterprises in the construction of small towns, improve and perfect the whole service system of before, during or after agricultural production. Develop the small towns into agricultural processing and marketing center, and information and technology service center of agricultural industrialization. Secondly, we should put gradually promoting the qualified rural migrant workers to work and settle down in town as the important task of promoting urbanization. Relax the restrictions on household registration in small cities and towns, to realize the transformation of farmers into townspeople. Finally, gradually establish a system of population free migration. Eliminate a series of urban-biased welfare system attached to household registration system and give equal treatment to rural migrant workers in the aspects of Employment, housing, wages, health care, children education and so on. To create a good institutional environment for surplus labor transferred from rural areas.

C. Promote innovation in the rural banking system to meet the demand of rural credit

Firstly, encourage rural credit cooperatives, agricultural bank of China, postal savings bank of China and other financial institutions to further increase credit loans to peasants and organizations of agricultural production. Moderately relax the market access conditions, guide and regulate the development of rural informal financial institutions. Secondly, actively promote small credit loans in rural areas, expand the scope of small credit loan and encourage private capital come into the rural small credit market to enhance the supply of financial markets. Increase loans to rural township enterprises and solve the funds bottleneck of township enterprises. Finally, actively perfect the agricultural insurance system and expand the scope of agricultural insurance premium subsidy.

References

[1] Lin, Y.-f., Cai, F., Li, Z.: The China miracle: development strategy and economic reform. The Chinese University Press, Hong Kong (1996)

[2] Li, S.: Rural labor mobility, income growth and income distribution in China. Social Sciences in China (2), 16–33 (1999)

[3] Levin, J.: China's divisive development. Harvard International Review 23(3), 40–42 (2001)

[4] Hertela, T., Zhai, F.: Labor market distortions, rural–urban inequality and the opening of China's economy. Economic Modeling 23(1), 76–109 (2006)

[5] Zhu, X.-j.: The reason analysis and policy choice of China's urban-rural income gap continued to widen. Technology and Market (7), 41–42 (2008)

[6] Lewis, W.A.: Economic development with unlimited supplies of labor. The Manchester School of Economics and Social Studies 22(2), 139–191 (1954)

[7] Lu, M., Chen, Z.: Urbanization, urban-biased economic policies and urban-rural inequality. Economic Research Journal (6), 50–58 (2004)

[8] Tong, G.-j.: Consideration about the promotion of county's economic competition in Northeast China, pp. 108–109. Heilongjiang People's Publishing House, Harbin (2006)

[9] Ma, X.-s.: The negative effect and countermeasures of incomplete urbanization. Jiangxi Social Sciences (1), 176–185 (2008)

[10] Kuznets, S.: Economic growth and income inequality. The American Economic Review 45(1), 1–28 (1995)

[11] Zhu, L., O'Dwyer, J.P., Chang, V.S., Granda, C.B., Holtzapple, M.T.: Multiple linear regression model for predicting biomass digestibility from structural features. Bioresource Technology 101(13), 4971–4979 (2010)

The Economic Disparities of Shenyang Economic Region with Cluster Analysis

Guangji Tong[1] and Tiankuo Wang[2,3]

[1] College of Economics and Management, Northeast Forestry University
Harbin, Heilongjiang Province, China
[2] College of management and economic Northeast forestry University Harbin
Harbin, Heilongjiang Province, China
[3] Shenyang Aerospace University
Shenyang, Liaoning Province, China
guangji4545@sina.cn

Abstract. According to the emerging non-equilibrium conditions of the cities in Shenyang Economic region along with economic development, in this paper analyze the same set of indicators of the eight cities in the economic region by the different methods that cluster analysis and SPSS software, investigate the economic disparities among those cities in Shenyang Economic Region, The result of classification is that eight cities are divided into four classifications, which expresses the economic progress and economic condition of each city, in order to find out the causes of economic disparities among those cities ,at the same time put forward proposals for future development in this region.

Keywords: Clustering Analysis, Economic Disparities, Shenyang Economic Region.

1 Introduction

Shenyang Economic Region became a national comprehensive reform experimental area of new-type industrialization in April 2010. After a decade's rapid development, it has grown into an influential industrial urban agglomeration area, the largest industrial base with its key equipment manufacturing industry and raw materials. Its leading industry leads a competitive advantage in china. At present, integration of the dominant industries in the region has made significant progress, and the connection is increasingly closed between these cities. As the core area and typical representative of the old industrial bases in Northeast China, its economic development facilitates not only the resolution of its own institutional and structural problems, but also the optimization and upgrading of industrial structure in Northeast China. Its success poses a positive demonstration to industrial bases both in the Northeast old industrial base and the whole country, lighting up a road to new-type industrialization. However, due to traditional distribution of productive forces and differences between cities in geography, resources, technology and policy, regional economic development differs from city to city, resulting in inter-regional imbalance. This paper, through clustering

M. Dai (Ed.): ICCIC 2011, Part II, CCIS 232, pp. 510–517, 2011.

analysis, presents a classification, comparison and analysis of economic development in the eight cities in Shenyang Economic Region. It aims to figure out the reasons for differences in economic development, thus formulate a targeted strategy to reduce the difference and promote integration of the economic regional.

2 Clustering Analysis

Clustering analysis is a multianalysis way to study "Like attracts like"[1]. In other words, it classifies the objects according to their characteristics, depending on degrees of kinship among sample data (or variables) without prior knowledge. The guiding principle is that the same class possesses a high degree of homogeneity while different classes are highly heterogeneous[2,3]. It has been widely used for people to understand social, economic and technical systems.[4] As a branch of mathematics from the numerical classification, based on data analysis, it gives the same classification process consistent quantitative methods to avoid the subjective and arbitrary manner in the general classification. It is a more accurate, more detailed scientific classification tool.

3 Construction of the Indicator System for Clustering Analysis in Shenyang Economic Region

A. Shenyang Economic Region

The economic region centers around Shenyang with a radius of 100 kilometers, covering Shenyang, Anshan, Fushun, Benxi, Yingkou, Fuxin, Liaoyang, Tieling. With a total population of 23.59 million and an area of 75,000 square kilometers whose urbanization rate is 65%, it possess one of the highest level of urbanization and most integrated transportation system, towering as the first and the largest industrial base with its key equipment manufacturing industry and raw materials. In 2009, GDP in Shenyang Economic Region is 998.47 billion Yuan, accounting for 66.3% of that in Liaoning Province and 32.7% of that in the three northeastern provinces. In order to have a clear understanding of the economic development in eight cities, this paper chooses 12 national key indicators of the eight cities in 2007, and explores nearest neighbor for a clustering analysis of economic developments in eight cities coupled with an interpretation of its economic significance and the individual city's position in the region's economic development.

B. selecting key indicators for clustering analysis

Between the cities in Shenyang Economic region there are distinct regional differences. In order to better evaluate the differences and make a comprehensive evaluation of economic developments in these different cities, first of all, it is desirable to select a series of key indicators. These indicators, first, need to demonstrate the coordinated regional economic development strategy, reflecting not only the present but also the potential economic development. [5] Second, they should be representative of not only clear social and economic significance but also an aspect of socio-economic development. Third, with the existing differences between cities in

Table 1. Main index of national economy of 8 cities in Shenyang Economic Region

City	GDP per capita (yuan)	GDP growth rate (%)	Urbanization rate	The proportion of tertiary industry	Public library collection per hundred people (che)	Hospital and the number of beds per million people in (zhang)	Gross of industrial output (wanyuan)
Shenyang	45582	22.75	0.64	46.54	125.98	47.37	47860210
Anshan	38387	16.30	0.51	39.65	54.05	42.52	13252681
Fushun	24451	16.10	0.66	37.37	43.36	46.12	9792161
Benxi	31066	14.50	0.67	32.19	60.85	57.13	6727940
Yingkou	24597	21.30	0.46	34.76	38.20	34.82	9868844
Fuxin	10025	16.20	0.45	39.56	20.41	31.72	1938323
Liaoyang	25564	16.70	0.44	29.80	49.95	47.44	8917693
Tieling	13249	19.90	0.32	29.77	18.70	26.41	5493748

City	Green area per people (square meter)	Total retail sales of social goods (wanyuan)	Foreign investment (ten million dollars)	Total investment for fixed assets	Cargo volume (wandu)
Shenyang	44.66	12318501	504451	23618726	19092.30
Anshan	34.59	2988137	25817	4771198	8734.00
Fushun	30.13	2356183	6850	2814872	6171.00
Benxi	46.27	1159832	8530	1653014	7716.00
Yingkou	35.65	1441016	13016	4178208	8084.00
Fuxin	25.51	875925	2521	1040931	2587.00
Liaoyang	38.90	1217199	6178	1804943	5108.00
Tieling	33.37	1316567	8656	3092144	6377.00

Source of data: *China City Statistical Yearbook* 1990～2008.

size and the population, total index is not comparable. Therefore, the selected indicators are comparable average indicators. Finally, full consideration is required of the availability of these statistical data, practicality of the indicators and the operability of the approach. According to Delphi and expert evaluation method, the following 12 indicators are selected for evaluation of regional economic development[6]. They were shown in Table 1.

Indicators reflecting the economic development of these cities: GDP per capita, which is an effective tool to reflect the region's macroeconomic performance and to measure living standards. Indicator reflecting the city's economic development rate: GDP growth rate, for economic growth means enhancement of goods, services and productivity; it is the basic content and performance of economic development. Indicators reflecting the level of economic development: urbanization rate, which is closely linked with industrialization. Gross industrial output, which is the most basic and most important indicator, reflecting the city's economic development at large. Indicator reflecting local industrial structure: the proportion of tertiary industry, for economic development should be matched with optimization and adjustment of industrial structure for mutual promotion of all the three industries. Indicator reflecting the region's economic vitality: total retail sales of social goods, mainly reflecting transmission of goods through various channels to residents and social groups to meet their needs. It is an important indicator to study living condition, purchasing power of consumer goods, currency and other issues. Indicator reflecting living standard public library collection per hundred people, hospital and the number of beds per million people, green area per person, which generally reflect the city's living environment, living standard and the stage of socio-economic development and so on. Indicators reflecting development sustainability: foreign investment utilization, which is an important symbol of international economic cooperation and competition. Total investment for fixed assets, which is a further adjustment of economic structure and regional distribution of productivity to enhance the economic strength and improve people's material life and cultural life. Cargo volume, which can reflect a city's transportation network in the modern system of logistics.

4 Cluster Analysis of the Economic Differences between Cities

A. Data Processing

As the dimensions of each index and index under the same dimension vary, there will be discrimination of certain indicators when considering the distance among classes. Therefore, it is necessary to process the data. As people are more concerned about ranking of each unit's different indicators in the clustering analysis of the economic development, we chose the ranking of each index as the basis for data processing.

B. clustering analysis

In order to have a clear understanding of the status of the cities in Shenyang Economic region during the process of economic development, we use clustering analysis method to process these data. As there are 12 ranked results of each city, each city corresponds to a 12-Dimension index ($x_1, x_2, \ldots, x_{12}$), which is the basis for the classification of the samples. If we mark Shenyang as G1, Anshan as G2,

Table 2. Position of 13 cities in Shenyang Economic Region in the order of their main index of national economy

City	GDP per capita (yuan)	GDP growth rate (%)	Urbanization rate	The proportion of tertiary industry	Public library collection per hundred people (che)	Hospital and the number of beds per million people in (zhang)
Shenyang	1	1	3	1	1	3
Anshan	2	5	4	2	3	5
Fushun	6	7	2	4	5	4
Benxi	3	8	1	6	2	1
Yingkou	5	2	5	5	6	6
Fuxin	8	6	6	3	7	7
Liaoyang	4	4	7	7	4	2
Tieling	7	3	8	8	8	8

City	Gross of industrial output (wanyuan)	Green area per people (square meter)	Total retail sales of social goods (wanyuan)	Foreign investment (ten million dollars)	Total investment for fixed assets	Cargo volume (wandu)
Shenyang	1	2	1	1	1	1
Anshan	2	5	2	2	2	2
Fushun	4	7	3	6	5	6
Benxi	6	1	7	5	7	4
Yingkou	3	4	4	3	3	3
Fuxin	8	8	8	8	8	8
Liaoyang	5	3	6	7	6	7
Tieling	7	6	5	4	4	5

Table 3. D(0)

	G1	G2	G3	G4	G5	G6	G7	G8
G1	0							
G2	4	0						
G3	6	4	0					
G4	7	5	6	0				
G5	5	3	5	6	0			
G6	7	6	5	7	6	0		
G7	6	5	5	6	4	5	0	
G8	7	6	6	7	4	5	6	0

Fushun as G3, Benxi as G4, Yingkou as G5 , Fuxin as G6, Liaoyang as G7 , Tieling as G8 , and the distance between the two different samples x and y as Cheby-shev Distance: $d\infty(x, y) = \max_{1\le i\le 12} \left|x_i - y_i\right|$, the distance of the symmetric matrix D(0) between samples is shown in Table 3.

The smallest element in D (0) is 4, so G1, G2 and G3 can be combined into one group, denoted by G9. By calculating the distance matrices between new class G9 (Shenyang, Anshan and Fushun) and other types, the smallest element is 5, so G9, G4, G7 can be combined into one group, denoted by G10. Repeat the above approach, G5, G6, G8 can be combined as one class, denoted by G11. Finally, G10 and G11 as one group is denoted by G12 as the process is terminated. Results from the clustering process are as follows.

Category 1	Shenyang、anshan、fushun
Category 2	Benxi、liaoyang
Category 3	Yingkou、fuxin、tieling

In order to get the more scientific and rational results, use the software SPSS to analysis the 12 indicators are shown in table 1 simultaneously. As the selected indicators differ in their dimensions, the variables should be standardized[7] before clustering analysis from 2 to 6 classes is carried out with statistical software SSPS16.0.[8] The results are as follows.

Cluster membership					
Case	6 clusters	5 clusters	4 clusters	3 clusters	2 clusters
Shenyang	1	1	1	1	1
Anshan	2	2	2	2	2
Fushun	2	2	2	2	2
Benxi	3	3	3	2	2
Yingkou	4	4	4	3	2
Fuxin	5	5	4	3	2
Liaoyang	6	3	3	2	2
Tieling	4	4	4	3	2

As in shown in the above table, when clustered into four categories, the first category is Shenyang, the second category Anshan and Fushun, the third category Benxi and Liaoyang, the fourth category Yingkou, Fuxin and Tieling. This results from the above clustering analysis is basically similar to realistic level of economic development in the eight cities. It should be noted that only the ranking is employed when the clustering analysis is conducted. Reference to real economic development and the actualization of the selected indicators confirms that Shenyang possessed a much higher absolute value than other cities, establishing itself as the core among eight cities. Therefore, it is reasonable for Shenyang to be classified as a separate class. So it is the classification of the eight cities within Shenyang Economic Region.

5 Conclusion

It can be seen from the clustering results that on the overall scale, Shenyang is an absolutely leading core among eight cities. 1) The overall economy can be divided into three major sections: The first category is the head plate consisting of Shenyang, Anshan, Fushun, the second category the body plate of Benxi and Liaoyang, the third category the tail plate of Yingkou, Fuxin and Tieling. 2) The leading section can be divided into two subsections: the first is Shenyang as the core, the second being Anshan and Fushun.

Located in the center of the economic region, Shenyang is the transportation hinge between north and south. As the core in Northeast old industrial base and the heart of Shenyang Economic Region, the city of Shenyang boasts 8 out of the 12 first-level evaluating indicators. In the future, Shenyang will connect Fushun and Anshan through traffic, industrial zones and other connections to strengthen integration. A one-hour traffic circle is to be built to further enhance the attractiveness and radiation to other neighboring cities. Eventually Shenyang should to be the world's equipment manufacturing base, the National Center City and an important economic hub in Northeast Asia. Anshan and Fushun have an advantage with regard to their GDP per capita, urbanization rate, proportion of tertiary industry, industrial output, total retail sales of social goods, foreign investment, total investment for fixed assets and freight volume, etc. They are comprehensively high-level economic development areas, second only to Shenyang. As the only way to sea for Shenyang economic region, Anshan is a most important industrial base of Shenyang Economic region and the window to the outside. Fushun, due to its spacial edge possess an inborn advantage to its integration with Shenyang. Also as the only pilot transition cities of resource depletion in Northeast, Fushun is faced with new development opportunities. The railway connecting these three cities has become a driving force for rapid interaction. Benxi and Liaoyang possess a certain high level of overall economic development in the area, with Benxi enjoying a higher urbanization rate and a better development than Liaoyang. Benxi should focus on its integration with Shenyang so as to make full use of Shenyang's advantages in information, technology and business. Liaoyang in the future will give priority to the development of chemical fiber industry, pharmaceutical machinery and papermaking machinery and as key industries. As Liaoyang is an developed regions of agricultural and rural economy in this region, it is more important to develop a "high-yield, high-quality, efficient" agriculture in the future. The city is to be expanded through the building of Hedong new city to foster population concentration. Since Yingkou, Fuxin, Tieling enjoy rich natural resources and convenient traffic, these cities should speed up their introduction of technology, capital and talent to take full advantage of their resources to develop their industry. Yingkou is the only port city in Shenyang Economic region, so it must play its coastal edge to facilitate the passage. Fuxin will become a new energy area in the economic region, with its sufficient supply of coal and natural gas. At the same time it will become the shield to protect Shenyang Economic region for a good ecological environment. Tieling will focus on the building "one area, two zones". "One area" refers to the construction of Tieling new city, while "two zones" to that of industrial zone between Tieling and Shenyang, so as to promote urbanization and enhance comprehensive economic strength.

The observations in this analysis highly recommend that the government in Shenyang Economic Region should take full account of the region's actual economic performance when they conduct their city planning, to make it appropriate and targeted.

References

[1] Zhang, r., Fang, k.: Introduction to Multivariate Statistical Analysis. Science Press, Beijing (1982)
[2] Xue, w.: Statistical Methods and Applications with SPSS. China Renmin University Press, Beijing (2001)
[3] Yao, Z.-q.: Cluster Analysis of Social Strata with Different Views on the Social Problem. Operations Research and Management Science (2), 111–116 (2002)
[4] Shenyang and others 6 Cities around it to fight for Northeast Center City. First Financial Daily (February 23, 2005)
[5] Tong, G.: Consideration about the promotion of county's economic competition in Northeast. Heilongjiang People's publishing House (2006)
[6] City Statistical Yearbook 2008. China Statistics Press, Beijing (2008)
[7] Lu, X.-h., Zhu, S.-f.: Discussion on Comprehensive Economic Strenghth of Chongqing. Journal of Chongqing Institute of Commerce (5), 1–4 (2002)

An Empirical Study on Effecting Factor of Migration of Rural Labor in China

Guangji Tong and Jingli Lan

College of Economics and Management
Northeast Forestry University
Harbin, Heilongjiang Province, China
guangji4545@sina.cn

Abstract. The migration of rural labor has become the breakthrough of solving the problem of agriculture, countryside and farmers. This paper constructed an analytical framework of effecting factors of rural labor migration from aspects of push, pull, the system influence and personal influence, and made empirical analysis on the effecting factors of rural labor migration by establishing multiple linear regression model using the data from 1983 to 2008. The empirical results show that per capita net income of rural households, the number of rural employment, the proportion of secondary industry output value, the ratio of non-state sector employment, the development level of rural non-agricultural industries, culture conditions of rural labor force are the significant factors of affecting the migration of rural labor force. Finally, specific countermeasures based on above conclusions are proposed.

Keywords: China, Rural Labor, Migration of Labor, Effecting Factor, Multiple Regression Analysis.

1 Introduction

The migration of rural surplus labor force not only is the inevitable result of industrialization and urbanization, but also is an important factor of promoting the development of industrialization and urbanization. Surplus rural labor causes the increasing pressure to the rural economy with the continuous improvement of agricultural productivity, per capita arable land increasingly scarce resources and seasonal factors of agricultural production, etc. Development experience around the world shows that, a reasonable migration of surplus rural labor force can optimize the human resource allocation, improve the socio-economic structure and promote the sustainable development of the whole society. Therefore, analyzing the factors affecting the rural surplus labor migration has important theoretical significance and practical significance for increasing the income of peasants, narrowing the urban income gap, achieving a new pattern of urban and rural, economic and social integration.

Foreign studies on labor mobility have Lewis model, Ranis—Fei model, Jorgenson model, Todaro model and push-pull theory, etc. Lewis in 1954 proposed the famous

M. Dai (Ed.): ICCIC 2011, Part II, CCIS 232, pp. 518–529, 2011.

dual economic model, one was the traditional sector represented by agriculture, there were infinite surplus labors of zero marginal productivity; the other was modern department represented by industry. Since the industrial sector had higher labor productivity, could get labor supply in order to continuously expand, non-agricultural migration of agricultural surplus labor could reduce dual economic structure gradually [1]. Gustav Ranis and John C.H.Fei in 1960 created Ranis – Fei model based on the dual economy model, revealed linkages of the agricultural sector and industrial sector, accordingly, standed out the importance of agriculture in the process of industrialization, they believed that, only agricultural productivity increased evenly, just ensured that the industrial sector expansion and the smooth migration of labor [2]. Jorgenson's economic model thought that, agricultural surplus was the necessary and sufficient condition of that labor force was transferred from the agricultural sector to the industrial sector, the agricultural surplus was larger, the size of labor force was greater [3]. Todaro's population flow model thought that, the decision-making about migration of rural surplus labor force depended on expected income differences between urban and rural areas and urban unemployment rate, rather than the differences of the actual income [4]. Thomas presented push - pull theory on the migration, the driving force of the migration from rural to urban was come down to two categories, that were, "push" factor and "pull" factor [5]. E·S·Lee introduced the barriers and personal factors lying the middle of the land of turning in and turning out into the framework, and the factors of affecting labor mobility were divided into four categories, namely, the land of turning out, the land of turning in , middle barriers and personal factors [6].

The research on the migration of surplus rural labor in China is mostly based on the foreign theoretical model, combines the actual situation in our country to analyzing. Yaohui Zhao used Sichuan province as a case, studied the impact factors of China's rural labor migration, pointed out the role of education mostly [7]. Shi Li established the labor mobility mode in the economic transition, analyzed labor migration motivation caused by wage gaps of a market-driven sector and government-controlled sector [8]. Xianguo Yao and Xiangmin Liu thought that, the wage gap, employment opportunities and migration of existing networks were three basic factors to determine the flow of rural labor force [9]. Fang Cai believed that migration costs, included transportation costs, living costs, psychological costs, training costs in order to find work and the opportunity cost of missed work, etc [10]. Shouhai Ding by quantitative analysis showed that migrant workers' wages were the main factors of affecting rural labor migration [11]. Xiaoyun Chen used "push-pull theory" to analyze the factors of affecting rural labor migration, the results showed that, increasing the income of peasants, increasing the stock of rural human capital, eliminating the block role of institutional factors, speeding up the development of the second and third industries were the main focus of rural surplus labor migration [12].

Non-agricultural migration of agricultural surplus labor is the necessary choice of increasing farmer incomes and promoting the harmonious development of urban and rural areas, however, the restriction from economy and institution impedes the migration of rural labor force. Based on existing research results, this paper quantifies the factors affecting migration of the rural surplus labor, making an empirical analysis through the establishment of multiple regression model. The second part of this paper analyzes the status of rural surplus labor migration and its role of gaining income for farmers; the third part of this paper selects the variables affecting the labor force migration based on theoretical analysis, makes an empirical analysis through the establishment of multiple regression model; Finally, this paper proposes the conclusions and the suggestions.

2 The Analysis on the Status and Role of Migration of Rural Surplus Labor

According to table 1, in 2009 the total amount of migration of rural labor was 229,780,000, this included migrant workers to go out was 145,330,000, and there were 4,920,000 more than last year, it was an increase of 3.5%.The number of local migrant workers who had worked more than 6 months in the township was 84,450,000, the number reduced 560,000, and the rate declined 0.7%. According to 2009 monitoring survey report of migrant workers, migrant workers at present still go to the eastern region, however, the proportion of workers in the central and western regions has increased, the number of migrant workers to go out of working in the province has increased more, the proportion of outward migrant workers has declined, the main flows of migrant workers to go out are cities above the prefectural level. The migrant workers to go out are mainly masculine youth, the rate of men is 65.1%, the rate of women is 34.9%. Most migrant workers to go out have the junior high school education, and the proportion of high school and higher education has increased. The proportion of migrant workers in the manufacturing sector is the largest, is 39.1%; the second is the construction industry, is 17.3%; the rate of service is 11.8%; the rate of hotel and restaurant industry and the wholesale and retail trade is 7.8% apiece; transportation, warehousing and postal sector accounts for 5.9%.

Table 1. The number of migration of rural labor unit: million, %

	2009	2008	Change of number	Change of rate
The total of migrant workers	22978	22542	436	1.9
1. Outward migrant workers	14533	14041	492	3.5
(1) In households	11567	11182	385	3.4
(2)Whole family out	2966	2859	107	3.7
2. Local migrant workers	8445	8501	-56	-0.7

Data Source: 2009 Monitoring Report of migrant workers.

The migration of rural labor has a significant stimulative role and strategic contribution for economic development and farmers' income. First, the migration of rural labor force helps to optimize the allocation of land resources, to expand the scale of land management. Second, as the number of migrant workers increases, farmers' income pattern is undergoing fundamental changes. Shown in Fig.1, since 90th, wage income represented by migrant workers to go out has been growing, families operating income represented by the agricultural income in the proportion of net income has been decreasing. Farmers' wage income growth is a major force to promote net income growth. In 2009, rural per capita net income was 5153 yuan, of which the wage income was 2527 yuan, the family business net income was 2061 yuan, for the first time, rural per capita wage income was more than 2000 yuan, and exceeded the primary industry net income of the family business.

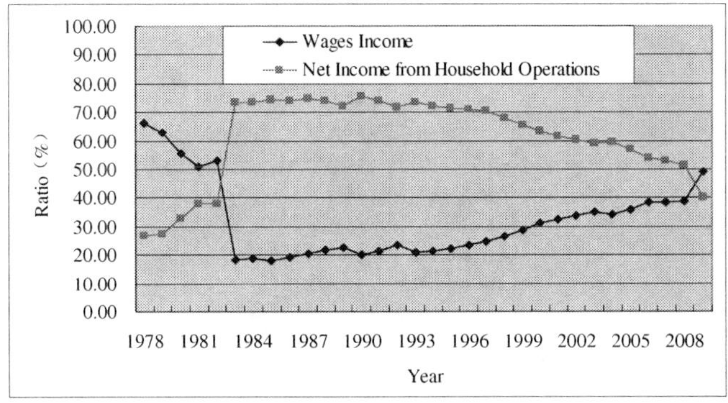

Fig. 1. The proportion of wage income and income from household operation

3 Empirical Analysis

A. Variable selection and basic assumptions

1) Dependent variable

Fig.2 shows, during the reform and opening, China's surplus rural labor has gone through two migration modes, and this is the local migrant from 1978 to 1988, and remote migrant mode after1989. In China, from the late 70's to 80's, township enterprises had a breakthrough development, the migrant of rural surplus labor force mainly characterized "leave the land but not their homes" to implement local migrant in the historical period; remote migrant refers to that, with the development of industrialization, rural surplus labor force gradually shifts to the city, is absorbed by industry and tertiary industry, and it ultimately implements the urban and rural integration.

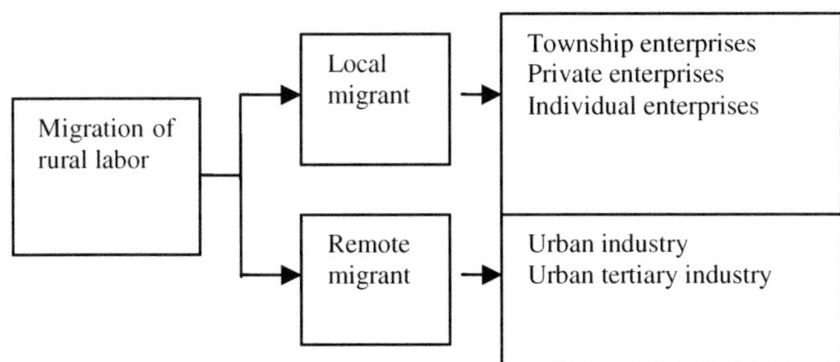

Fig. 2. Model of Rural Labor migrant

The number of migrant of rural labor (Y) is calculated by the Xueyi Lu's way [13], that is, the number of "migrant workers" entering the urban employment= the number of urban practitioners - the number of urban workers, the number of rural non-agricultural labor force= the number of rural employment - the number of agricultural employment, and the number of total rural labor migrant is the summation of both above.

2) Independent variable

Fig.3 shows that, this paper constructs the analytical framework of influence factors of rural labor migration from push, pull, the system influence, personal influence.

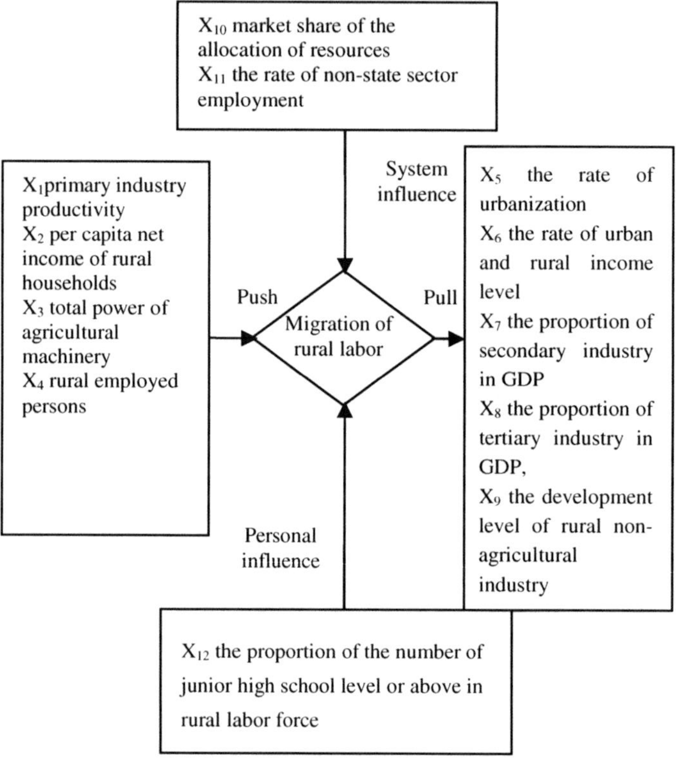

Fig. 3. Analysis framework of migration of rural labor

(1) "Push" factors. The "push" of rural labor migration is from the advance of agriculture productivity, agricultural technology improvement and the level of farmers' income by the development of the rural economy.

Primary industry productivity (X_1) reflects the number of size and speed of the rural labor force by the "release" of the first industry. Higher labor productivity needs the less agricultural labor force, and releases the more labor force. Primary industry productivity is showed by the ratio of output value of primary industry and the number of primary industry employees.

Per capita net income of rural households (X_2) reflects the ability of migration of rural labor.

Total power of agricultural machinery (X_3) reflects the level of modernization of agriculture, the level is higher, technical level of agricultural production and the efficiency is higher, the amount of labor required is less.

Rural employed persons (X_4), reflects the situation of rural labor supply.

(2) "Pull" factors. The "push" of rural labor migration is from the attractiveness of labor resources resulting from the development of industrialization and urbanization.

The rate of urbanization (X_5), reflects the extent of cities and towns to accommodate the population. This indicator reflects a country's growth rate and urbanization level, the larger proportion indicates a higher level of urbanization, and the higher ability to accommodate rural migration labor.

The rate of urban and rural income level(X_6) reflects the inequality of the urban and rural residents' per capita real income levels. With the gradual expansion of urban-rural income gap, the proportion of the rural labor force should be increased.

The proportion of secondary industry in GDP(X_7) and the proportion of tertiary industry in GDP (X_8), reflect the space of migration of rural surplus labor force, the larger proportion can accommodate more rural population.

The development level of rural non-agricultural industry(X_9) reflects the space size of the local migration of rural labor force. The development of rural non-agricultural industries can absorb a large number of rural surplus labor, increase the wage income of farmers. This paper uses the proportion of the rural non-farm employment in all employees as a measure index of the development of rural non-agricultural industries, rural non-farm employment is found through the number of all village labor force minus the number of employees in primary industry.

(3) "System influence" factors. The system factor of affecting migration of rural labor force mainly refers to the household registration system and a series of the urban bias welfare system and employment system attached to the household registration system. It is very difficult or even impossible to quantify these factors directly. This paper selects the following two indicators to investigate system influence indirectly.

Market share of the allocation of resources(X_{10}) approximately reflects marking degree of the allocation of resources. The calculation formula is: (GDP-state revenue) / GDP.

The rate of non-state sector employment(X_{11}) is the proportion of non-state sector employment accounted for total urban employment. Non-state sector is main employment channel of migration of rural labor force, so the non-state sector employment rate can reflect the influence of migration from the changes of economic sectors.

(4) "Personal influence" factors, mainly refers to the cultural quality of rural labor, is showed as the proportion of the number of junior high school level or above in rural labor force (X_{12}). The degree of labor education has a direct impact on accessing to the capacity employment opportunities and choice. High education level of the labor force, not only can get the work of higher knowledge, but also can allocate resources in the broader spatial scale and wider range of industries, so it is easy to get a higher non-farm employment income. Can be assumed, with the education and skill levels increase, the likelihood of rural labor migration is the greater.

(B) Sources and description of the data

China's rural labor migration policies have undergone a process from the inside to outside, from tight to loose, from disorder to the specification, from discrimination to impartiality. Specifically, the process can be divided into control the flow period (1979 ~ 1983), allow the flow period (1984 ~ 1988), blind control flow period (1989 ~ 1991), standard flow period (1992 ~ 2000) and start fair flow period (after 2000) [14]. Rural labor force from 1978 to 1983, thanks to the policy of reform and opening up, mainly migration in agriculture within, due to lack of more data, his paper used the data between 1983 and 2008 to analyze it (see Table 2).

The number of rural labor migration, total agricultural mechanical power, the number of employees of state-owned units are from *China Statistical Yearbook* and *China Compendium of Statistical 1949-2004*; financial income data is from the *China Statistical Abstract 2009*; the registered urban unemployment rate is from the *China Statistical Yearbook 2008* and *China Labour Statistical Yearbook 2009*; cultural conditions of rural households labor force data is from the *China Yearbook of Rural Household Survey 2008* and the *China Rural Statistical Yearbook* 2009; Other data are from *China Statistical Yearbook* of each year.

Table 2. The number of migration of Chinese rural labor and its impact factor data

Year	Y (thousand)	X_1 (Yuan /person)	X_2 (Yuan)	X_3 (thousand kilowatt)	X_4 (thous-and)	X_5 (%)	X_6 (%)	X_7 (%)	X_8 (%)	X_9 (%)	X_{10} (%)	X_{11} (%)	X_{12} (%)
1983	37700	635.10	309.80	180219	346900	21.62	1.82	44.38	22.44	10.20	77.07	25.33	28.37
1984	54390	750.32	355.30	194972	359680	23.01	1.83	43.09	24.78	14.18	77.21	29.37	29.73
1985	63850	823.77	397.60	209125	370650	23.71	1.86	42.89	28.67	16.01	77.76	29.81	35.00
1986	72190	892.27	423.80	229500	379900	24.52	2.12	43.72	29.14	17.73	79.35	29.78	35.84
1987	79060	1021.08	462.60	248360	390000	25.32	2.17	43.55	29.64	18.81	81.76	29.96	36.61
1988	84770	1198.60	544.90	265750	400670	25.81	2.17	43.79	30.51	19.51	84.33	30.02	37.70
1989	83620	1283.95	601.50	280670	409390	26.21	2.29	42.83	32.06	18.84	84.32	29.76	38.76
1990	117760	1300.82	686.30	287077	477080	26.41	2.20	41.34	31.55	18.43	84.27	39.29	40.41
1991	118850	1366.36	708.60	293886	480260	26.94	2.40	41.79	33.69	18.59	85.54	38.94	43.55
1992	126610	1515.96	784.00	303084	482910	27.46	2.58	43.44	34.76	19.86	87.06	39.03	44.75
1993	142790	1848.13	921.60	318166	485460	27.99	2.80	46.57	33.72	22.38	87.69	40.20	46.50
1994	159780	2613.49	1221.00	338025	488020	28.51	2.86	46.57	33.57	24.95	89.17	39.88	48.13
1995	176270	3415.65	1577.70	361181	490250	29.04	2.71	47.18	32.86	27.53	89.73	40.86	49.91
1996	192850	4025.10	1926.10	385469	490280	30.48	2.51	47.54	32.77	28.98	89.59	43.56	53.25
1997	203120	4145.20	2090.10	420156	490390	31.91	2.47	47.54	34.17	28.95	89.05	46.86	54.79
1998	231230	4212.31	2162.00	452077	490210	33.35	2.51	46.21	36.23	28.24	88.30	58.10	55.96
1999	238530	4129.40	2210.30	489961	489820	34.78	2.65	45.76	37.67	26.98	87.24	61.75	57.38
2000	247830	4146.36	2253.40	525736	489340	36.22	2.79	45.92	39.02	26.34	86.50	65.00	59.69
2001	257200	4322.10	2366.40	551721	490850	37.66	2.90	45.05	40.46	25.61	85.06	68.09	60.99
2002	263120	4485.22	2475.60	579299	489600	39.09	3.11	44.79	41.47	24.69	84.29	71.09	61.78
2003	273940	4756.12	2622.20	603865	487930	40.53	3.23	45.97	41.23	25.10	84.01	73.18	62.67
2004	293550	6071.26	2936.40	640279	487240	41.76	3.21	46.23	40.38	27.61	83.49	74.66	63.30
2005	310050	6599.94	3254.90	683979	484940	42.99	3.22	47.70	40.10	29.95	82.73	76.26	65.90
2006	326780	7383.07	3587.00	725221	480900	43.90	3.28	48.70	40.00	32.29	81.71	77.29	67.00
2007	341190	9104.12	4140.40	765896	476400	44.94	3.33	48.50	40.37	34.00	80.05	78.11	67.90
2008	353110	11091.54	4760.62	821904	472700	45.68	3.31	48.62	40.07	35.15	79.60	78.66	68.55

(C) Model building and regression results

Based on the above theoretical analysis, the text uses time series data in China from 1983 to 2008 (see Table 2), to establish multiple linear regression model. Using the number of the rural labor force as the dependent variable Y, X_1, X_2 ..., X_{12} as explanatory variables, model building as follows:

$$Y = \beta_0 + \sum_{j=1}^{12} \beta_j \cdot X_j + \varepsilon \tag{1}$$

Table 3. Regression Analysis Result Using the Method of Enter—Coefficients

Model		Unstandardized Coefficients		Standardized Coefficients	t	Sig.	Collinearity Statistics	
		B	Std. Error	Beta			Tolerance	VIF
1	(Constant)	-10297.667	4439.757		-2.319	0.037		
	Primary industry productivity(X_1)	0.111	0.271	0.031	.411	0.688	0.001	854.093
	Per capita net income of rural households(X_2)	0.600	0.873	0.078	.687	0.504	0.001	1904.158
	Total power of agricultural machinery(X_3)	0.067	0.043	0.130	1.555	0.144	0.001	1043.193
	Rural employed persons (X_4)	0.047	0.038	0.024	1.251	0.233	0.019	53.918
	The rate of urbanization(X_5)	-106.292	100.630	-0.082	-1.056	0.310	0.001	900.156
	The rate of urban and rural income level(X_6)	1183.929	456.075	0.058	2.596	0.022	0.013	74.785
	The proportion of secondary industry in GDP(X_7)	-72.655	79.724	-0.016	-.911	0.379	0.022	45.254
	The proportion of tertiary industry in GDP(X_8)	-278.635	65.764	-0.149	-4.237	0.001	0.005	184.008
	The development level of rural non-agricultural industry (X_9)	256.734	30.446	0.164	8.433	0.000	0.018	56.363
	Market share of the allocation of resources(X_{10})	69.762	29.041	0.028	2.402	0.032	0.051	19.793
	The rate of non-state sector employment (X_{11})	274.892	17.333	0.535	15.859	0.000	0.006	169.573
	the proportion of the number of junior high school level or above in rural labor force(X_{12})	194.715	59.526	0.249	3.271	0.006	0.001	864.873

Among them, ε is the random error term, β_0 is the constant term, $\beta_j(j = 1,2,\cdots,12)$ is the parameter to be estimated.

1) The diagnosis of multicollinearity

Using the statistical software SPSS 18.0 and the Enter method in regression analysis, the results is in Table 3.

As can be seen from Table 3, some regression coefficients can not pass the test of significance, while VIF are much larger than 20 other than X_{10}, it indicates that the model exists multicollinearity.

2) The result of stepwise regression analysis

In econometrics, the methods of eliminating multicollinearity have expanding the sample size, stepwise regression, ridge regression, principal component regression and partial least squares regression method, etc. In this paper, we used stepwise regression to solve the multicollinearity problem, to find the following better regression model estimations, the results are shown in Table 4.

Model 1:

$$\hat{Y} = -10818.010 + 2.333X_2 + 105.410X_{11} + 396.728X_{12} \tag{2}$$

The ample determination coefficient $R^2 = 0.998$, sample multiple correlation coefficient R = 0.999, and F = 3432.651, significant P value ≈ 0.000, F test shows good goodness of fit equation.

Model 2:

$$\hat{Y} = -21869.929 + 1.7309X_2 + 0.168X_4 + 211.6174X_7 + 247.392X_9 + 282.664X_{11} \tag{3}$$

The sample determination coefficient R^2=1.000, sample multiple correlation coefficient R= 1.000, and F = 15070.774, a significant P value ≈ 0.000, F test shows good goodness of fit equation.

Table 4. Regression Analysis Result Using the Method of Stepwise—Coefficients

Model		Unstandardized Coefficients		Standardized Coefficients	t	Sig.
		B	Std. Error	Beta	B	Std. Error
1	Constant	-10818.01	847.261		-12.768	0.000
	X_{12}	396.278	31.710	0.507	12.497	0.000
	X_2	2.333	0.251	0.302	9.300	0.000
	X_{11}	105.410	20.317	0.205	5.188	0.000
2	Constant	-21869.929	1584.017		-13.807	0.000
	X_2	1.730	0.173	0.224	9.995	0.000
	X_{11}	282.664	8.092	0.550	34.929	0.000
	X_9	247.392	25.526	0.158	9.692	0.000
	X_4	0.168	0.016	0.084	10.495	0.000
	X_7	211.617	36.372	0.046	5.818	0.000

From Table 4, the T-statistics of explanatory variables of the two models all pass the test; the result indicates that the regression model is valid.

4 Conclusions and Suggestions

A The main conclusions

(1) Per capita net income of rural households (X_2) and migrant of rural labor (Y) are positive correlation. Computing results by models 1 and 2 all show: the partial regression coefficients of per capita net income of rural households(X_2) are positive, the result suggests that increasing per capita net income of rural households benefits the migrant of rural labor force.

(2) Rural employed persons (X_4) and migrant of rural labor (Y) are positive correlation. A large number of labors gathered in country decline the marginal productivity of the agricultural production and the comparative efficiency of agricultural production, and they become the rural labor's main driving force of migration to non-agricultural industries.

(3) The proportion of secondary industry in GDP (X_7) and migrant of rural labor (Y) are positive correlation. As known by the model 2, the partial regression coefficient of the proportion of industry in GDP (X_7) is 211.617, it indicates that the number of migrant of rural labor will increase 2116.17 million, when the proportion of secondary industry in GDP increases 1 percentage point.

(4) The development level of rural non-agricultural industry (X_9) and migrant of rural labor (Y) are positive correlation. As known by the model 2, the partial regression coefficient of the development level of rural non-agricultural industry (X_9) is 247.392, it indicates that the number of migrant of rural labor will increase 2473.92 million, when the development level of rural non-agricultural industry increases 1 percentage point.

(5) The rate of non-state sector employment (X_{11}) and migrant of rural labor (Y) are positive correlation. As known by the model 2, the partial regression coefficient of the rate of non-state sector employment (X_{11}) is the most, it indicates that non-state sector is the main channel of migrant of rural labor.

(6) the proportion of the number of junior high school level or above in rural labor force (X_{12}) and migrant of rural labor (Y) are positive correlation. As known by the model 1, the number of migrant of rural labor will increase 3962.78 million, when the proportion of the number of junior high school level or above in rural labor force increases 1 percentage point. It indicates that, enhancing the cultural quality and technical skills of the rural labor force, increasing their human capital accumulation, can promote the smooth migrant of rural labor force.

(B) Suggestions

(1) To raise the per capita net income of rural households, in order to create conditions for the smooth migrant of rural labor. The elevation of per capita net income of rural households makes farmers hold more resources to improve human capital and social capital accumulation, increases non-agricultural employment opportunities for success. Meanwhile, the higher the real income of farmers, the more they are able to pay migrant costs.

(2) To speed up the industrialization process, create more jobs and achieve a smooth migrant of rural labor force.

(3) To reform the household registration system and promote the free flow of rural labor force. To establish a system of free movement of people gradually, eliminate a series of urban bias of the welfare system and employment system cling to household registration system, impart equal "citizen" treatment for migrant in employment, housing, wages, health care, education of their children and all aspects, create a good institutional environment in order to speed up the migrant of rural labor.

(4) To develop the rural non-agricultural industries and enhance the absorptive capacity of the rural labor force. Development of rural industry and tertiary industries needs to strengthen the government's policy support and guidance, to use the advantages of rural labor resources and low labor cost, to develop township enterprises and labor-intensive agricultural products processing enterprises actively. Meanwhile, we should encourage and support farmers in rural areas to start their own businesses.

(5) To increase human capital investment and improve the quality of the rural labor force. Currently a major factor of restricting the effective migration of rural labor is that, the quality of the rural labor force in general is relatively low, the percentage of trained skills is low, most migrant workers can only engage in the big dirty work of the poor work environment and big labor intensity, the gap of skilled workers is larger. Therefore, we should develop the rural compulsory education vigorously, improve worker's human capital accumulation, increase their employment opportunities in non-agricultural industries, and enhance employment training of rural surplus labor force and rural workers' competitiveness in urban labor market.

References

[1] Lewis, A.R.: Economic Development with Unlimited Supplies of Labor. Manchester School of Economic and Social Studies 22(2), 139–191 (1954)

[2] Fei, J.C.H., Ranis, G.: Development of the Labor Surplus Economy: Theory and Policy. R.D. Irwin, Homewood (1964)

[3] Jorgenson, D.W.: The Development of a Dual Economy. Economic Journal 71(282), 309–334 (1961)

[4] Todaro, M.P.: A Model of Labor Migration and Urban Unemployment in Less Developed Countries. American Economic Review 59(1), 138–148 (1969)

[5] Thomas, D.: Social Aspects of the Business Cycle. Dutton, New York (1925)

[6] Lee, E.S.: A Theory of Migration. Demography 3(1), 47 (1996)

[7] Zhao, Y.: China Rural Labor Migration and the Role of Education: Based on Sichuan Province. Economic Research Journal (2), 37–42 (1997)

[8] Shi, L.: Labor Force Flow Model in China Economic Transition. Economic Research Journal (1), 23–30 (1997)

[9] Yao, X., Liu, X.: Migration Networks in Labor Mobility Decision-making. Journal of Zhejiang University (Humanities and Social Sciences) (4), 124–130 (2002)

[10] Cai, F.: Analysis of Institutional Barriers about the Flow of Rural Surplus Labor Force–to Explain the Paradox about the Expansibility of Flow and Difference Simultaneity. Economics Dynamic (1), 33–39 (2005)

[11] Ding, S.: The Wages of Migrant Workers and Rural Labor Force Migration: A Empirical Analysis. Chinese Rural Economy (4), 56–62 (2006)
[12] Chen, X.: The Push-pull Model and Empirical Analysis Base on the Migration of Chinese Rural Labor Force. Science Technology and Industry 9(9), 86–89 (2009)
[13] Lu, X.: Social Mobility in Contemporary China, pp. 24–28. Social Sciences Academic Press, Beijing (2004)
[14] Deng, D., Meng, Y.: The Change of History about Migrant of Rural Surplus Labor Force in China: Policy review and Comment. Guizhou Social Science 223(7), 4–11 (2008)

A Novel Real-Time Eye Detection in Human-Computer Interaction

Yan Chao[1], Wang Yuanqing[1], and Zhang Zhaoyang[2]

[1] Stereo Imaging Laboratory, NanJing University
Nan Jing China
[2] School of Comminication and Information Engineering
Shang Hai University
Shang Hai China
yan58569@sina.cn

Abstract. Human eyes detection is one of the critical technologies in free stereoscopic display system. And the eye detection in free stereoscopic display system should be pretty accurate and real-time. To satisfy this demand, bright pupil effect under active infrared illumination is applied to provide the position of human eyes approximately; then the real AdaBoost algorithm is applied to locate human faces preliminarily and detect human eyes precisely; at the same time, the Kalman algorithm is applied to track the eye positions already detected to make sure the precision and speed of the human eyes detection further.On circumstance of Windows XP, PentiumIV, 512Memory, 2.4GHZ, for a video sequence of 640*480-pixel images, eye detection rate is 92.5%; the average processing time for each image is less than 10ms, meeting the need of real-time; this new method is also robust when there is variation of facial expression or a little degree leaning of human face.

Keywords: eye detection, face detection, bright pupil effect, real AdaBoost, Kalman.

1 Introduction

Eye detection means to obtain the location, size and position of all human eyes in an image. In civil field, it could be used in free stereoscopic display system and fatigue driving alarm system; in military field, it could be used in long-distance battlefront command and non-invade human-computer interaction. There are two standards to judge an eye detection algorithm: accuracy rate and speed. For accuracy, the difference in skin color, eye status and illumination will all make influence on the final detection result; for speed, more and more applications demand eye detection algorithm to be real-time.

As a hot issue in pattern recognition, many eye detection algorithms which treat and analyze the topic in different ways have been promoted recently. Such as: Template Matching[1], Hough transform[2], frame-to-frame difference[3], Mean-shift method[4]. Eye detection systems trained based on these algorithms behave good in accuracy and

M. Dai (Ed.): ICCIC 2011, Part II, CCIS 232, pp. 530–538, 2011.

speed. But there obviously is some short-coming about these systems as well, such as: the initial matching position must be pretty accurate; the calculating involved is numerous; the processing speed is slow; the accuracy rate is too low; applicable scope is too narrow.

Firstly, we make use of the bright pupil effect under infrared illumination to get the positions of human eyes which are also called candidate points approximately; then we detect the surrounding area of the candidate points in different scales to get the possible human faces; then according to the candidate points and the geometry features of human face, we detect human eyes in the human faces which have been detected. Human face detection and eye detection all utilize the real AdaBoost algorithm which is pretty precise. With Haar features[5] and Integral image[6], the "human faces—human eyes" detection process consumes very little time. At the same time, we employ Kalman algorithm to track the eyes which have been detected already, to provide priority detection area for the next frame of image.

2 Candidate Points Obtain

A Bright Pupil Effect

Imaging of external world in human eyes is greatly analogous with the pin-hole imaging, except that retina is a winding hold-screen. Part of beams would be reflected in the disperse ways by retina when the beams straightly pass through pupil and image on the retina. If the reflected beams are captured by CCD camera, pupils of human eyes in images will be in high gray. This phenomenon is called bright pupil effect.

Bright pupil effect needs light source to provide near-axle beams, so the light source should be close to the CCD camera. When light source is far away from CCD camera, the beams will be far-axle beams, and there is no bright pupil effect phenomenon. Images of human eyes under near-axle and far-axle illumination are shown in Figure.1 respectively.

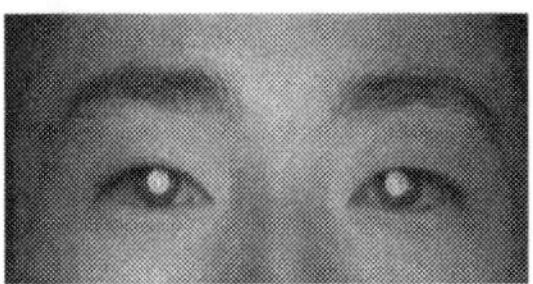

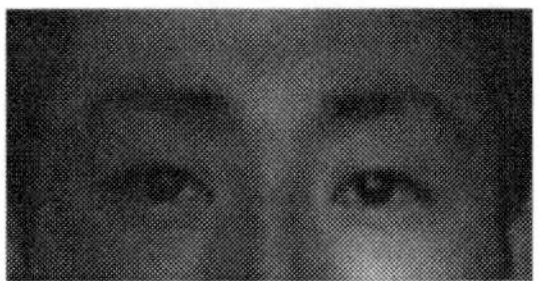

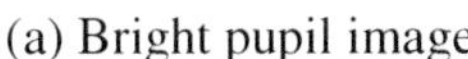

(a) Bright pupil image (b) Dark pupil image

Fig. 1. Bright pupil effect

B. Obtain Candidate Points

According to the principle of bright pupil effect, we use the active infrared illumination which is shown in Figure.2: the infrared LEDs away from CCD camera provide far-axle illumination, and the infrared LEDs around CCD camera provide near-axle illumination. We use the infrared illumination for that in all illumination with different frequency, the infrared illumination makes the bright pupil effect most obvious. We compile programs to control the far-axle and near-axle illumination, making them radiate alternatively[7], so the adjacent images will be bright pupil image and dark pupil image. Then we acquire the difference image of two adjacent images and utilize a threshold to filter the difference image. The pixels in which gray values are larger than the threshold are thought to be the possible pupil positions which are also called eye candidate points.

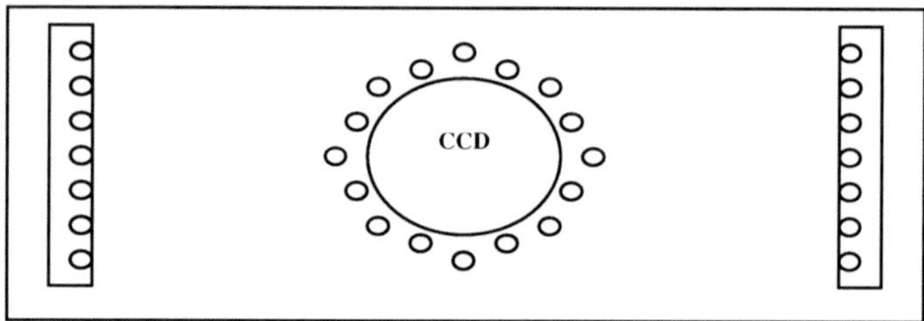

Fig. 2. Active infrared illumination("O"is infrared LED; those LEDs next to CCD camera are near-axe light, and those LEDs away from CCD camera are far-axe light)

Human faces are detected in eight different sizes, so the distance between two adjacent candidate points should shorter than half of the minimum human face size. With this principle, we clear up the candidate points which are too close to each other when we select the eye candidate points, avoiding redundant human face detection and saving detection-consuming time.

3 "Face--Eye" Detection

According to the eye candidate points' position, we save all the "ready-to-detect" human face area in different sizes in different vectors. Then we detect all these area from large size to small size to get real human face area. The detection algorithm we use is real AdaBoost, the calculating involved is finished with Haar features and Integral image.

The core thought of AdaBoost algorithm is to integrate the easy-got weak classifiers of which accuracy rate is approximately fifty percents to a strong classifier of which accuracy rate is greatly surpassing fifty percents. AdaBoost algorithm could self-adaptively adjust the weight distribution of samples, and select the best-performance weak classifiers in different situation of the weight distribution of samples, then make all the weak classifiers selected vote according to their own weight, making a strong classifier. The output of dispersed AdaBoost is one or zero; relatively, the output of real AdaBoost could be any real number, so real AdaBoost could nearly simulate all kinds of probability distribution.

The reason we use the method based on Haar features not the method directly based on gray is that with limited data, the method based on Haar features could code the state of special area, and the system based on Haar features is much faster than the system directly based on gray. For Integral image, every value is the gray sum of top-left pixels, so with Integral image, the calculation of Haar feature value is only related to the feature value of the endpoints of Haar rectangle features. As a result, no matter how large the size of a rectangle feature is, the time consumed in the calculation of feature value is little, and the calculation involved is only addition and subtraction.

Face detection and eye detection both use detectors in cascade structure[8]. By arrangement of strong classifiers reasonably, this kind of detectors could recognize and refuse non-target as much as possible in the front layers, promoting detection speed a lot. The flow path of human face detection in cascade structure is shown in Figure.3. The whole face detection system is composed of several layers, and every layer is a strong classifier trained by real AdaBoost. But each strong classifier contains different numbers of weak classifiers: the strong classifiers in the front of the detection system contain less weak classifiers; the more behind strong classifier lies in, the more weak classifiers it contains. From the structure of this kind of detection system we could know that: the speed of the front strong classifiers which contain less weak classifiers is faster, so they could be used to recognize and refuse the easy-to-recognize non-faces which are majority of all the human faces; the rear strong classifiers contain more weak classifiers, but the non-faces which could arrive at these layers are few, and in the factual human face detection, the human face area takes up a little space in the "ready-to-detect" images, so the rear layers also consume little time.

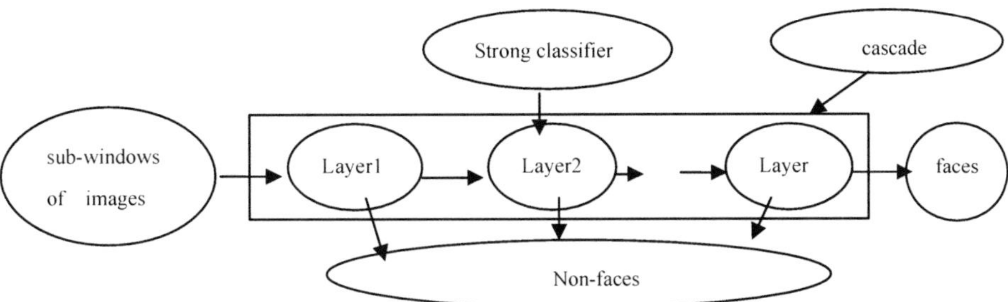

Fig. 3. Cascade structure

Human eye "ready-to-detect" area is composed of two parts: the eye position anticipated by Kalman tracking algorithm combining the eye position detected in the former image and the eye position in the face area newly detected. The Kalman tracking algorithm will be described in detail in part four. We will detect human eyes around the eye position anticipated and in the top half of the human faces newly detected. The detection algorithm is also the real AdaBoost based on Haar features and Integral image.

Because there possibly is some deviation about the eye position anticipated by Kalman tracking algorithm or some noise about the eye candidate points newly got, we not only detect the eye position anticipated and the eye candidate points newly detected, but also detect the area around the eye position anticipated and the eye candidate points newly detected. Detection sequence is shown in Figure 4: area zero is the eye position anticipated or the eye candidate point newly detected, we should firstly detect this area, then we will detect area one, and then we will detect area two and

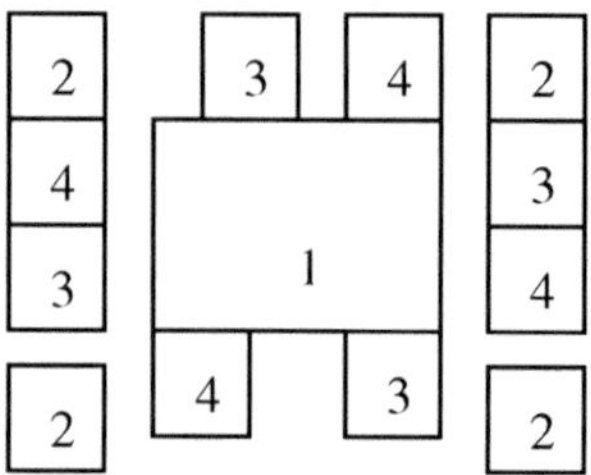

Fig. 4. Procedure of detection sequence

so forth. The area which could pass thorough detection and be given the highest confidence will be thought to be the human eye position, and we will, according to this area, anticipate the eye position in the next image.

If point P(x, y) is the eye position anticipated or the eye candidate point newly detected, the "ready-to-detect" window will be RECT (x, y)=(x-eyesize/2, y-eyesize/2,eyesize); facesize/4<eyesize<facesize/2. Facesize and eyesize are the width of human face window and the width of human eye window in corresponding size respectively; x-eyesize/2 is the Abscissa of the top-left endpoint of the "ready-to-detect" eye window; y-eyesize/2 is the ordinate of the top-left endpoint of the "ready-to-detect" eye window; the human face window and the human eye window are all squares.

4 Eye Position Tracking

To narrow eye "ready-to-detect" area and promote the precision and speed of eye detection, after getting the human eye position in current image, we anticipate the possible eye position in the next image with Kalman algorithm, and then we detect human eyes around the eye position anticipated firstly.

Simulating the motion situation of the "ready-to-detect" target in front of CCD camera, we suppose the motion of the target both in x and y axles are even-speed straight motion which is bothered by a random acceleration α. α is a random variable, $a(t) \sim N(0, \sigma_{\omega}^{2})$ .And we suppose the motion state vector of the "ready-to-detect" target : $X(k)=[X(k),Y(k),Vx(k),Vy(k)]^T$. X(k) and Y(k) are the abscissa and ordinate of the "ready-to-detect" target; Vx(k) and Vy(k) are the speed of the "ready-to-detect" target in x and y axles. The measure matrix is Y(k): $Y(k)=[Xc(k),Yc(k)]^T$. Xc(k) and Yc(k) are the measure abscissa and ordinate of the "ready-to-detect" target, and we suppose they are the same with the abscissa and ordinate of the eye position detected in the former image.

So Kalman anticipation algorithm includes two models:

Motion state vector model:

$$X(k)=A(k-1)X(k-1)+B(k)W(k);$$

Measure vector model:

$$Y(k)=C(k)X(k)+V(k);$$

They can be also described in matrix form:

$$\begin{bmatrix} X(k) \\ Y(k) \\ Vx(k) \\ Vy(k) \end{bmatrix} = \begin{bmatrix} 1,0,t,0 \\ 0,1,0,t \\ 0,0,1,0 \\ 0,0,0,1 \end{bmatrix} \begin{bmatrix} X(k-1) \\ Y(k-1) \\ Vx(k-1) \\ Vy(k-1) \end{bmatrix} + \begin{bmatrix} t^2/2 \\ t^2/2 \\ t \\ t \end{bmatrix} W(k)$$

$$\begin{bmatrix} Xc(k) \\ Yc(k) \end{bmatrix} = \begin{bmatrix} 1,0,0,0 \\ 0,1,0,0 \end{bmatrix} \begin{bmatrix} X(k) \\ Y(k) \\ Vx(k) \\ Vy(k) \end{bmatrix} + \begin{bmatrix} 1 \\ 1 \end{bmatrix} V(k)$$

t is the time interval between adjacent images, t=0.04s; $\sigma_w = 1$.

So far, the detection based on bright pupil effect, AdaBoost algorithm and Kalman algorithm finishes detecting one frame of image, as which the eye detection on the follow-up images will be the same. The flow path of the whole human eye detection algorithm is shown in Figure 5.

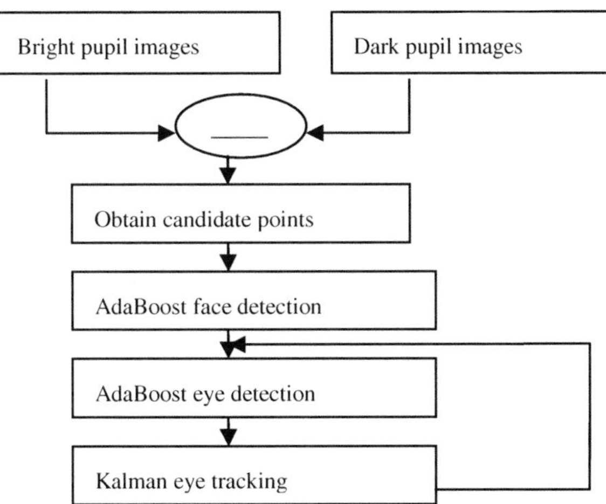

Fig. 5. Procedure of the algorithm

5 Experience and Contrast

Calculating of Haar features in AdaBoost is all based on gray of images, so we should think of all kinds of factors which make influence on gray distribution on images used in detector training. As a result, we gather the samples with different distances from the active infrared illumination and the samples with human faces leaning to different aspects.

Because in realistic application, non-face samples are much more than human face samples, we fix the ratio between face samples and non-face samples 1:8 in each face detection layer; at the same time, the more abundant texture non-faces have, the more mistakes detection makes, so we gather a lot of non-face samples with abundant texture when we disperse the non-face samples. Because one single human eye takes up two-fifteenths of a human face, we fix the ratio between eye samples and non-eye samples 2:13 in each eye detection layer; at the same time, the eye "ready-to-detect" area is all in face area, so we should ensure some proportion of non-eye samples gathered from human faces, according to the mistake-rate which is four percent, we fix the proportion 100:104, approximately ninety-six percents.

In human face detector training, there are 5009 face samples and 41700 non-face samples which are of 20*20-pixel; in human eye detector training, there are 4795 eye samples and 31167 non-eye samples which are all of 15*15-pixel. The final cascade face detection system has eight layers and the final cascade eye detection system has three layers. Some of the samples used in the whole detection system training are shown in Figure 6.

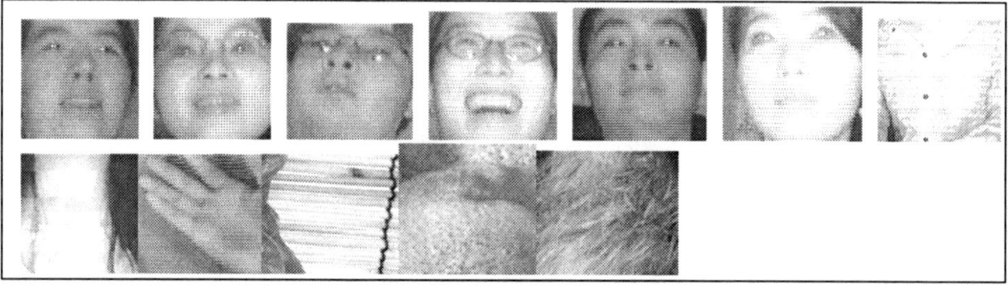

Examples of face samples(including front faces, a little degree leaning faces, faces with glasses, faces with facial expression and so on)&& Examples of non-face samples

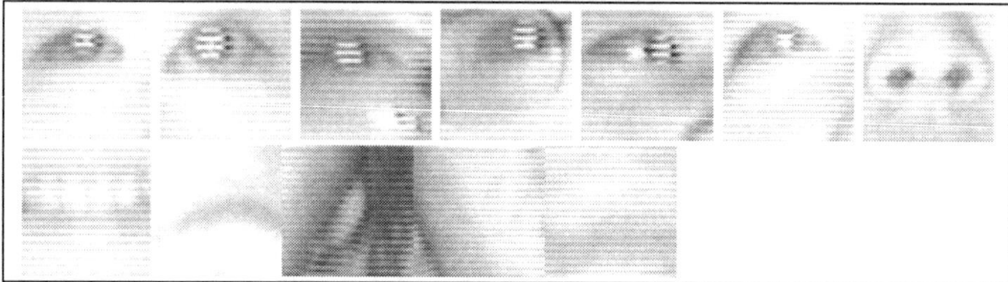

Examples of eye samples(including front eyes, a little degree leaning eyes, eyes with glasses, eyes with different sexes and so on)&& Examples of non-eye samples

Fig. 6. Samples used in training

Compared with other human eye detection algorithms, the detection algorithm based on bright pupil effect, AdaBoost algorithm and Kalman algorithm behaves better in algorithm speed. We compare our method with the Pyramid AdaBoost and the AdaBoost based on motion detection, and the result is shown in Table 1. All the pictures used in our experience are of 20*20-pixel.

Table 1. Speed compare of several eye detection algorithms

Detection algorithm	Pyramid AdaBoost	AdaBoost+Moti on detection	AdaBoost+Bright pupil
Time per-frame(ms)	94	16.7	4

On circumstance of Windows XP, PentiumIV, 512Memory 2.4GHZ, for a video sequence of 640*480-pixel images, eye detection rate is 92.5%; the average processing time for each image is less than 10ms, meeting the need of real-time; this new method is also robust when there is variation of facial expression or a little degree leaning of human face.

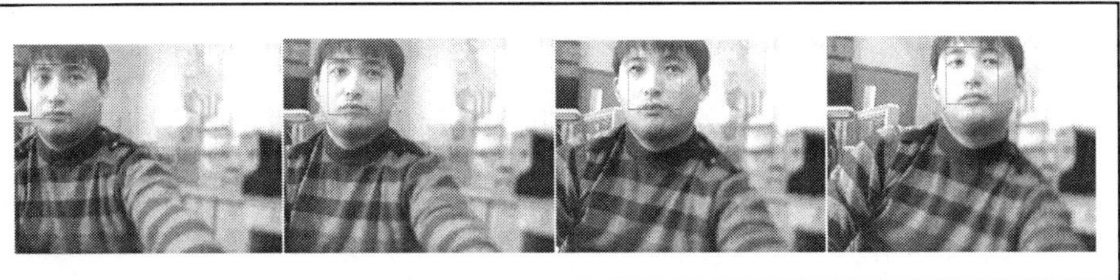

Fig. 7. Eye detection in video sequence(The black frame is the face detected, and the crosses are eyes detected)

6 Conclusion

With active infrared illumination, we could make use of bright pupil effect to speed up eye detection algorithm,; at the same time, all pictures are gathered under the same illumination, as a result, the influence on detection result by illumination variation could be eliminated, and the application range of illumination compensation could be enlarged. Compared with detecting human eyes directly, the "Face-Eye" detection could lower the mistake-rate of detection effectively. The combination of the "Face-Eye" structure and the cascade structure focus on the targets which are more difficult to classify, so the combination could narrow the range of eye detection, speeding up eye detection too. The constant output value of real AdaBoost could depict the border of two different types more precisely, so the "Face-Eye" detection with real AdaBoost could be pretty accurate. Kalman tracking of eye position detected could also narrow the range of eye detection and thereupon cut the mistake-rate down, advancing the precision and speed of human eye detection. But owing to the active infrared illumination, wearing glasses sometimes causes serious light reflection, which will harm the precision and robustness of human eye detection. So in the near future, how to avoid the serious light reflection of wearing glasses will be our research emphasis.

Project Fund: Key Project from National Natural Science Fund Commission, China(608320036)

Key Laboratory of Advanced Display and System Application (Shanghai University), Ministry of Education, China (Project No. P200902).

References

[1] Horng, W.-B., Chen, C.-Y.: Driver Fatigue Detection Based on Eye Tracking and Dynamic Template Matching. In: Proc. of IEEE International Conference on Networking Sensing and Control, Taipei, pp. 7–12. IEEE Press, China (2004)

[2] Zhangjie, Yang, X., Zhao, M.: Eyes detection based on Hough trans—form. Compute Engineering and Application 27, 43–44 (2005)

[3] Yano, K., Ishihara, K., Maikawa, M.: Detection of eye blinking from video camera with dynamic ROI fixation. In: IEEE International Conference on Systems, Man, and Cybernetics, vol. 6, pp. 335–339 (1999)

[4] Peng, N.S., Yang, J., Zhou, D.: Mean-Shift Tracking with Adaptive Model Update Mechanism. Journal of Data Acquisition & Processing 2(20) (2005)

[5] Viola, P., Jones, M.: Rapid object detection using a boosted cascade of simple features. In: IEEE Conf. Computer Vision and Pattern Recognition, Kauai, Hawaii (2001)

[6] Viola, P., Jones, M.: Robust real-time object detection, Cambridge Research Laboratory. Tech.Rep.: CRL (January 2001)

[7] Haro, A., Flickner, M., Essa, I.: Detecting and tracking eyes by using their physiological properties, dynamic and appearance. In: Proceeding of CVPR 2000, pp. 163–168 (2000)

[8] Freund, Y., Schapire, R.E.: Experiments with a new boosting algorithm. In: Proc. The 13th Conf. Machine Learning, pp. 148–156. Morgan Kaufmann, San Francisco (1996)

Author Index

Ai, Shengli VI-480
Aithal, Himajit IV-351
AliHosseinalipour V-36
Anil kumar, A. IV-351
Aslam, Mohammed Zahid IV-260

Babaei, Shahram V-36
Bailong, Liu III-39, III-47
Bangjun, Lu VI-124
Bangyong, Hu II-60
Bao, Liwei IV-93
Bi, Guoan IV-224
Bin, Dai II-436, II-443
Bin, Li III-151
Bing, Hu V-476
Bingxue, Han IV-265
Bo, Qi VI-282
Bo, Sun I-526, II-475
Bo, Wu V-74
Bo, Yang IV-1
Bo, Zhou V-461
Bu, Yingyong I-335

Cai, Nengbin IV-402
Cai, Ning II-87
Cai, Xiaonan I-519
Cai, Xiaoqing VI-166
Cao, An-Jie IV-376
Cao, Fengwen IV-189
Cao, Jianbo VI-398
Cao, Jianshu VI-536
Cao, Qiang VI-417
Cao, Yukun III-232
Chang, Henry Ker-Chang VI-500
Chang, Ling-Wei V-483
Chang, Yinxia IV-427
Chang, Zhengwei IV-167
ChangJie, Hu VI-461
Chang-ping, Zhao VI-290
Changxi, Ma VI-282
Changyuan, He V-211
Chao, Hu IV-42
Chao, Yan II-530
Chaoshi, Cai I-395, III-321
Chen, Bin V-170, V-175
Chen, Cheng II-157
Chen, Chuan IV-369
Chen, Chun IV-376
Chen, Haijian III-508
Chen, Haiyuan III-9
Chen, Hong-Ren III-407
Chen, Huiying V-201
Chen, Lingling V-125
Chen, Weiping III-508
Chen, Xiaodong V-175
Chen, Xinglin VI-110
Chen, Yan VI-152
Chen, Yanhui VI-84, VI-89
Chen, Yu-Jui V-10
Cheng, Jiaji IV-280
Cheng, Li V-321
Cheng, Shih-Chuan VI-436
Cheng, Yingjie III-74
Chengcheng, Jiang I-288
Chenguang, Zhao IV-136, IV-144, IV-151
Chi, Xiaoni I-143
Chiang, Yea-Lih III-407
Chong, Guo VI-50
Chuan, Tang I-29
Chuang, Li VI-404
Chujian, Wang I-191, I-366
Chun, Huang I-36
Chun, Yang Chang VI-511
Chunhong, Zhang II-326
ChunJin, Tian III-207
Chunling, Zhang V-381
Chunqin, Zhang III-369
Congdong, Li I-288
Congmei, Wan V-321
Cui, Kang IV-59
Cui, Yanqiu I-550
Cui-lin, Zhang V-461

Da, Zheng V-94
Dai, Minli VI-424, VI-430
Dai, Wei-min V-100
Danxia, Bi V-105

Dasen, Li II-405
Deng, Fang II-294
Deng, Hui V-201
Deng, Jianping IV-189
Deng, Nan IV-402
Deng, Xianhe II-396
Deng, Xiaoyun VI-343
Deng, Xubin VI-26
Deng, Yibing V-316
Deqian, Xue VI-383
Ding, Feng II-350
Dong, Hao VI-1
Dong, Liu III-292
Dong, Xu III-39, III-47
Dong, Yu VI-50
Dong-Ping, Liu II-303
Du, Jiang V-523
Du, Maobao V-365
Du, Wencai III-1

E., Shiju VI-398

Fan, Hongda VI-1
Fan, Jihua III-515
Fan, Tongliang IV-433
Fan, Zhao IV-441
Fang, He II-172
Fang, Ligang VI-430
Fang, Qiang VI-166
Fang, Sun IV-242
Fang, Yuan II-274
Fanjie, Bu II-382
Fei, Zhou II-281
Feng, Lei V-304
Feng, Lou III-312
Feng, Lv II-101
Feng, Pengxiao IV-172
Feng, Wenlong III-1
Feng, Yuan II-194
Fengling, Wang I-262
Fengxiang, Chen V-234
Fu, Wenzhi IV-172
Fu, Xixu V-43
Fu, Yizhe VI-179
Fuhua, Xuan I-275
Furong, Wang VI-445, V-511

Gaijuan, Tan V-234
Gai-ning, Han VI-39
Gan, Jing III-427
Gang, Chen I-492
Gao, Cheng I-359
Gao, Fei III-427
Gao, Haiyan III-433
Gao, Jin IV-306
Gao, Junli VI-166
Gao, Li VI-357
Gao, Shuli V-226
Gao, Wei VI-188, VI-197
Gao, Xin II-391
Gao, Xiuju V-365
Gao, Zhijie III-17
Gong, Jun V-529
Gong, Xiaoyan II-194
Gong, Xizhang V-43
Gu, Caidong VI-424, VI-430
Guan, Xianjun I-21
Guangyu, Zhai IV-503
Guilin, Lu VI-232
Guo, Changgeng III-442
Guo, Fachang IV-382
Guo, Lejiang II-194
Guo, Lina III-494
Guo, Lu VI-452
Guo, Shuting V-288
Guo, Wei V-428, V-435
Guo, Wenping III-488
Guo, Xinbao I-403, I-409
Guo, Yanli V-226
Guo, Zhiyun III-284
Guo, Zirui I-359
Guohong V-64
Guohong, Li I-248
Guojin, Chen III-299, III-305
Guojing, Xiong II-267
Guo-song, Jiang I-320, I-328

Haicheng, Xu IV-10
Hailong, Sun I-161
Hai-qi, Feng V-374
Haitao, Hong VI-50
Haiwen, Li IV-335
Haixia, Wan I-484
Haixia, Yu VI-522
HamidehJafarian V-36
Han, Baoyuan IV-450
Han, Dong IV-464
Han, Hua I-478
Han, Xinchao III-401
Han, Xu V-100

Hang, Ling-li V-268
Hantian, Wei VI-445, V-511
Hao, Fei Lin V-304
Hao, Hong VI-551
Hao, Yitong II-143
Hau, Chuan-Shou V-239
He, Jilin V-137
He, Juan III-103
He, Li III-174
He, Lijuan III-337
He, Siqi II-420
He, Weisong VI-94, VI-100
He, Xiangguang VI-188, VI-197
He, Yang II-312
He, Yinghao IV-32
He, Yong V-304
He, Zhuzhu II-458
Heng, Chen III-89
Hengkai, Li I-213
Hong, Liang IV-181
Hong, Lu I-465
Hongbing, Zhang VI-551
Hongjun, Liu I-533
Hong-li, Zhang I-302
Hongmei, Jiang IV-159
Hongmei, Tang III-345, III-355, III-363
Hongwei, Luo III-183
Hou, Shouming III-337
Hou, Xuefeng IV-369
Hu, Caimei IV-81
Hu, Jianfeng IV-456
Hu, Jun V-409
Hu, Wenfa V-281, V-288
Hu, YongHong VI-452
Hu, Zhigang V-246
Hu, Zhiwei IV-392
Hu, Zong IV-54
Hua, Wang Guo VI-157
Huan, Wang V-518
Huang, Changqin V-258
Huang, De-Fa V-239
Huang, Haifeng I-428
Huang, Hanmin I-94
Huang, Hexiao III-508
Huang, Jun V-268
Huang, Qiong II-287
Huang, Tao III-174
Huang, Weitong V-117
Huang, Xiaodi V-468
Huang, Yu-Chun V-239
Huang, Zhiqiu V-409
Huanhuai, Zhou V-334
Huijuan, Ying V-334
Hui-li, Wang VI-370
Huili, Zhang I-161
Huixia, Wang II-150, II-172
Huixin, Jin I-248

Jangamshetti, D.S. IV-351
Jen, Yen-Huai V-483
Ji, Jia VI-398
Jia, Guangshe V-125
Jia, Zhiyang VI-188, VI-197
Jian, Wang V-374
Jian, Zhou III-143
Jiang, Fuhua II-396
Jiang, Jia VI-398
Jiang, Xuping III-482
Jiang, Yuantao II-17, II-95
Jian-Hao, Xu VI-34
Jianhong, Sun IV-1, IV-10
Jian-Min, Yao III-151
Jianping, Li I-395, III-321
Jianping, Tao III-143
Jianqi, Han VI-50
Jian-tong, He VI-290
Jianwen, Cao IV-503
Jianxin, Gao V-518
Jianzheng, Yi IV-342
Jiao, Linan V-189
Jia-xin, Lin VI-224
Jie, Jin II-303
Jie, Quan I-413
Jie, Xu V-82
Jie, Yu VI-467
Jieping, Han I-132
Jin, Haiyi V-328
Jin, Min II-73
Jin, Wang V-82
Jinfa, Shi III-453, III-465
Jinfang, Zhang VI-467
Jing, Liang V-207
Jing, Tu I-184
Jing, Zhao III-292
Jing, Zhou I-66, I-71
Jing-xin, Chen I-343, I-351
Jingzhong, Liu II-318
Jin-hai, Wang VI-319
Jinhui, Lei III-207
Jinwei, Fu IV-10

Jinwu, Yuan III-420
Jiuzhi, Mao I-313
Jou, Shyh-Jye V-10
Jun, Li VI-148
Jun, Song V-137
Jun, Wang V-82
Jun, Zhang VI-45
Jun-qi, Yang VI-297
Junsheng, Li IV-1
Jyothi, N.M. III-328

Kai, Zhang V-133
Ke, Xiaoyu II-73
Kebin, Huang II-150
Kewen, Geng VI-124
Kun, Shi VI-66

Lai, Herbert Hsuan Heng VI-500
Lan, Jingli II-518
Lee, Xuetao II-226
Lei, Xu VI-232
Lei, Yang II-109
Lei, Yu V-193
Li, Chen II-303
Li, Cungui II-499
Li, Deyang III-263
Li, Dou Hui VI-157
Li, Fengri VI-20
Li, Fengying IV-101, IV-110
Li, Guanglei III-433
Li, Guangzheng III-81
Li, Haibin I-115
Li, Haiyan IV-233
Li, Hongli VI-424
Li, Houjie I-550
Li, Hua I-380
Li, Hui III-174
Li, Jia-Hui IV-316
Li, Jianfeng IV-297
Li, Jianling IV-233
Li, Jinglin III-502
Li, Jinxiang VI-430
Li, Kuang-Yao V-239
Li, Li VI-458
Li, Liwei III-241
Li, Luyi III-192, III-394
Li, Mingzhe IV-172
Li, Na II-202
Li, Peng V-56
Li, Qi I-359
Li, RuZhang V-18
Li, Shaokun VI-335
Li, Shenghong IV-441
Li, Shijun IV-233
Li, Wan V-416
Li, Wang V-346
Li, Wenbin IV-392
Li, WenSheng I-101
Li, Xiangdong III-401
Li, Xiumei IV-224
Li, Yang IV-42
Li, Yanlai IV-297
Li, Ying V-443, V-449, V-455
Li, Yu II-128
Li, YuJing V-18
Li, Zhenlong III-488
Lian, Jianbo I-451
Lianbo, Jiang VI-551
Liang, Wen-Qian II-450
Liang, Yuechen III-232
Liang-feng, Shen I-255
Liangtao, Sun I-492
Liao, GaoHua VI-7, V-498, V-504
Liao, Jiaping III-174
Lieya, Gu I-8
Lifen, Xie II-34
Li-jia, Chen VI-297
Lijun, Shao V-105
Li Jun, Sun II-428, II-436, II-443
Liminzhi I-513
Lin, Chien-Yu V-483
Lin, Haibo II-414
Lin, Ho-Hsiu V-483
Lin, Jing VI-179
Lina, Wang IV-59
Ling, Chen I-29, IV-59
Ling, Shen Xiao VI-511
Lingrong, Da II-373
Li-ping, Li V-221
Liping, Pang V-82
Lisheng, Wang V-234
Liu, An-Ta VI-500
Liu, Bao IV-427
Liu, Bingwu I-437
Liu, Bojia V-111
Liu, Bosong IV-32
Liu, Chunli III-255
Liu, Daohua V-491
Liu, Deli II-181
Liu, Gui-Ying II-342

Liu, Hong VI-74
Liu, Hongming III-116
Liu, Hongzhi VI-335, VI-343, VI-357
Liu, Jia V-504
Liu, Jiayi II-1
Liu, Jingwei IV-491
Liu, Jixin IV-360
Liu, June I-143
Liu, Jun-Min II-493
Liu, Li V-258
Liu, Lianchen III-158
Liu, Lianzhong II-164
Liu, LinTao V-18
Liu, Linyuan V-409
Liu, Shiwang II-181
Liu, Tao III-442
Liu, Wenbai V-316
Liu, Xiaojing V-117
Liu, Xiaojun I-59, II-164
Liu, Xin V-491
Liu, XingLi IV-181
Liu, Yang VI-110
Liu, Yanzhong II-235
Liu, Yongsheng I-471
Liu, Yongxian III-337
Liu, Yuewen II-458
Liu, Zhaotian IV-233
Liu, Zhi-qiang III-112
Liu, Zhixin I-177
Liurong, Hong V-389
Liuxiaoning V-64
Lixia, Wang VI-267
Lixing, Ding V-50
Li'yan II-22
Li-yan, Chen I-76, I-83
Liyu, Chen I-166, I-172
Liyulong I-513
Long, Chen VI-50
Long, Hai IV-25
Long, Lifang II-181
Long, Shun II-450
Long, Xingwu IV-252
Lu, Hong V-428, V-435
Lu, Hongtao IV-392, IV-402
Lu, Jing I-519
Lu, Ling V-258
Lu, Xiaocheng II-294
Lu, Y.M. V-353, V-359
Lu, Zhijian II-47
Luo, Rong I-222
Luo, Yumei II-414
Lv, Qingchu IV-93
Lv, Rongsheng II-211
Lv, Xiafu IV-280

Ma, Chunlei I-471
Ma, Jian V-164
Ma, Lixin V-328
Ma, Qing-Xun II-116, II-122
Ma, Sen IV-369
Ma, Yuan V-189
Ma, Zengjun IV-93
Ma, Zhonghua III-103
Mai, Yonghao VI-417
Mamaghani, Nasrin Dastranj III-22
Maotao, Zhu VI-210, V-211
Maoxing, Shen VI-148
Masud, Md. Anwar Hossain V-468
Meilin, Wang V-181
Meng, Hua V-69
Meng, Yi-Le V-10
Mengmeng, Gong V-82
Mi, Chao VI-492
Miao, J. V-353
Milong, Li I-457
Min, Ye Zhi VI-511
Ming qiang, Zhu I-150, I-206
Mingqiang, Zhu II-81
Mingquan, Zhou VI-528

Na, Wang I-233
Naifei, Ren V-133
Nan, Li I-533
Nan, Shizong IV-476
Nie, GuoXin V-523
Nie, Zhanglong VI-138
Ning, Ai V-334
Ning, Cai I-36
Ning, Yuan V-416
Nirmala, C.R. III-328
Niu, Huizhuo IV-369
Niu, Xiaoke IV-289

Pan, Dongming V-43
Pan, Min I-446
Pan, Rong II-1
Pan, Yingchun V-170
Pan, Zhifang IV-392
Pei, Xudong VI-105

Peng, Fenglin III-482
Peng, Hao IV-335
Peng, Jianhan III-508
Peng, Jian-Liang II-136
Peng, Yan V-309
Pengcheng, Fan VI-528
Pengcheng, Zhao II-405
Piao, Linhua VI-239, VI-246, VI-253, VI-261
Ping, Li VI-273
Pinxin, Fu V-181

Qi, Lixia I-124
Qi, Zhang IV-219
Qian, Minping IV-491
Qiaolian, Cheng V-370
Qin, G.H. V-89
Qin, Zhou I-302
Qingguo, Liu III-130
Qinghai, Chen IV-335
Qingjia, Geng V-105
Qingling, Liu IV-273, V-24
Qingyun, Dai V-181
Qinhai, Ma I-238
Qiong, Long VI-467
Qiu, Biao VI-179
Qiu, YunJie IV-402
Qiuhe, Yang VI-267
Qiyi, Zhang VI-124
Qu, Baozhong III-255
Qun, Zhai III-143
Qun, Zhang III-377, III-386

Ramaswamy, V. III-328
Rao, Shuibing V-137
Ren, Chunyu VI-218
Ren, Hai Jun V-56
Ren, Honge VI-131
Ren, Jianfeng III-494
Ren, Mingming I-115
Ren, Qiang III-276
Ren, Shengbing V-246
Ren, Wei III-81
RenJie VI-376
Rijie, Cong I-132
Rubo, Zhang III-39, III-47
Rui, Chen II-303
Rui, Zhao I-248, I-313
Ruihong, Zhang II-253
Ruirui, Zhang IV-204, IV-212
Runyang, Zhong V-181
Ru'yuan, Li II-22

Saghafi, Fatemeh III-22
Samizadeh, Reza III-22
San-ping, Zhao VI-13, VI-410
Sha, Hu IV-470
Shan, Shimin IV-32
Shang, Jiaxing III-158
Shang, Yuanyuan IV-369, IV-450
Shangchun, Fan V-321
Shao, Qiang I-109
Shaojun, Qin VI-210
Shen, Ming Wei V-304
Shen, Qiqiang III-95
Shen, Yiwen II-47
Shen, Zhang VI-370
Sheng, Ye VI-232
Shi, Danda V-316
Shi, Guoliang IV-48
Shi, Li IV-289
Shi, Ming-wang V-143
Shi, Wang V-105
Shi, Yan II-414
Shi, Yi VI-131
Shidong, Li V-296
Shou-Yong, Zhang II-428, II-436, II-443
Shu, Xiaohao III-95
Shu, Xin V-164
Shuai, Wang V-221
Shuang, Pan III-30
Song, Haitao VI-166
Song, Meina III-284
Song, Yichen IV-73
Song, Yu IV-73
Sreedevi, A IV-351
Su, Donghai V-404
Sun, Qibo III-502
Sun, Zhaoyun V-189
Sun, Zhong-qiang V-100
Sunqi I-513
Sunxu I-484
Suozhu, Wang I-14

Tan, Liguo VI-110
Tang, Dejun V-328
Tang, Fang Fang V-56
Tang, Fei I-478
Tang, Hengyao II-274
Tang, Peng II-1

Tang, Xin II-17
Tang, Xinhuai V-1
Tang, Yong V-258
Tanming, Liu II-331
Tao, Li IV-204, IV-212
Tao, Zedan II-357
Tian, Fengbo IV-280
Tian, Fengqiu VI-430
Tian, Ling III-241
Tianqing, Xiao IV-10
Ting, Chen I-387
Tong, Guangji II-499, II-510, II-518
Tong, Ruo-feng IV-198
Tu, Chunxia I-46, I-59

Wan, Hong IV-289
Wan, Wei VI-452
Wan, Zhenkai III-9, IV-484
Wang, Bing II-484
Wang, Chen V-328
Wang, Chengxi I-451
Wang, Chonglu I-222
Wang, Chunhui I-500
Wang, Dan IV-433
Wang, Dongxue IV-297
Wang, Fei I-88
Wang, Feng V-201
Wang, Fengling II-128
Wang, Fumin I-198
Wang, Haiping III-224
Wang, Hongli VI-315
Wang, Huasheng II-350
Wang, Hui-Jin II-450
Wang, JiaLian V-252, V-422
Wang, Jian II-211
Wang, Jianhua IV-48
Wang, Jianqing V-111
Wang, Jie V-404
Wang, Jing V-100
Wang, Jinyu I-335
Wang, Li-Chih V-483
Wang, Lijie V-529
Wang, Linlin V-275
Wang, Luzhuang IV-93
Wang, Min VI-424
Wang, Qian III-166, III-284
Wang, Ruoyang VI-398
Wang, Ruo-Yun IV-376
Wang, Shangguang III-502
Wang, Shanshan II-458
Wang, Shijun IV-464
Wang, Shi-Lin IV-376, IV-441
Wang, Shimei I-428
Wang, Shuyan II-10
Wang, Tiankuo II-510
Wang, Ting V-449, V-455
Wang, Weiliang VI-544
Wang, Xia I-21
Wang, Xiaohong III-241
Wang, Xiaohui I-269
Wang, Xiaoya II-420
Wang, Xiaoying V-117
Wang, Xing VI-239, VI-246, VI-253, VI-261
Wang, Yan IV-508
Wang, Y.C. V-359
Wang, Yiran III-247
Wang, Yongping III-276
Wang, YouHua V-18
Wang, Yu IV-252
Wang, Yude VI-480
Wang, Yuqiang V-170
Wang, Zhenxing III-166
Wang, Zhizhong IV-289
Wei, Cai II-150, II-172
Wei, Cheng-Wen V-10
Wei, Fengjuan II-235
Wei, Guo IV-252
Wei, Li III-30
Wei, Lin VI-79
Wei, Ling-ling III-212, III-218
Wei, Liu I-351
Wei, Ou V-409
Wei, Xianmin IV-418, IV-422
Wei, Yang II-253
Wei, Yu-Ting III-407
Wei, Zhou VI-305
Weihong, Chen III-89
Weihua, Liu III-183, III-369
Weihua, Xie V-30
Weimin, Wu IV-242
Weiqiong, He IV-219
Weiwei, Fang III-321
Weixi, Han I-465
Wen, Chengyu I-177
Wen, Jun Hao V-56
Wendi, Ma II-364
Wenping, Zhang I-184
Wu, Bin V-246

Wu, Caiyan VI-424
Wu, Di II-143
WU, Guoshi III-247
Wu, Hao I-380
Wu, Kaijun V-43
Wu, Peng VI-452
Wu, Xiaofang IV-32
Wu, Xiwei II-357
Wu, Xue-li V-69
Wu, Yanqiang IV-470
Wu, Yong II-493
Wu, Zhongbing I-109

Xi, Ba IV-325
Xi, JunMei VI-7
-xia, Gao VI-297
Xia, Li IV-273, V-24
Xiang, Hongmei VI-94, VI-100
Xiang, Jun II-181
Xiang, Qian V-215
Xiang, Song VI-305
Xiang_Li, Wang II-428
Xianzhang, Feng III-453, III-465
Xiao, Weng III-130
Xiao-hong, Zhang IV-411
Xiaolin, Chen II-281
Xiao-ling, He I-320, I-328
Xiaona, Zhou I-313
XiaoPing, Hu VI-350
Xiaosai, Li V-340
Xiaosheng, Liu I-213
Xiaowei, Wei VI-391
Xiaoxia, Zhao III-207
Xiaoya, He II-259
Xiaoyan, Xu VI-528
Xiao-ying, Wang I-343
Xiaoyong, Li II-364, II-382
Xie, Dong IV-25
Xie, Hualong III-337
Xie, Li V-1
Xie, Lihui II-218
Xie, Luning III-122
Xie, Qiang-lai III-212, III-218
Xie, Xiaona IV-167
Xie, Xing-Zhe IV-316
Xie, Zhengxiang IV-280
Xie, Zhimin I-21
Xifeng, Xue VI-148
Xijun, Liu V-476
Xilan, Feng III-453, III-465
Xiliang, Dai VI-124
Xilong, Jiang IV-219
Xin, Xiao IV-204, IV-212
Xin, Zhanhong I-222
Xing, GuiLin VI-357
Xing, Wang V-461
Xing, Xu VI-210
Xinhua, An II-40
Xinling, Wen VI-66, VI-474
Xinzhong, Xiong II-52
Xinzhong, Zhang I-373
Xi ping, Zhang I-150, I-206
Xiucheng, Dong V-340
Xu, Dawei IV-450
Xu, Jing III-166
Xu, Kaiquan II-458
Xu, Li VI-305
Xu, Ming III-95
Xu, Shuang I-550
Xu, Wanlu VI-398
xu, Wenke VI-20
Xu, Zhifeng II-17
Xu, Zhou III-64
Xuan, Dong VI-305
Xue, Qingshui IV-101, IV-110
Xuemei, Hou V-193
Xuemei, Li V-50
Xuemei, Tang V-158
Xuhua, Chen IV-342
Xuhua, Shi V-148, V-153
Xuhui, Wang II-22
Xun, Jin IV-252
Xuxiu IV-521
Xu-yang, Liu V-207

YaChao, Huang V-30
Yachun, Dai V-133
Yamin, Qin I-373
Yan, Fu I-14
Yan, Jun I-115
Yan, Peng V-74
Yan, Qingyou II-420
Yan, Shou III-158
Yan, Yunyang IV-120
Yan, Zhang IV-325
Yanbin, Shi VI-517, VI-522
Yang, Chen VI-210
Yang, Fangchun III-502

Yang, Fei IV-88
Yang, Hao III-122
Yang, Lianhe IV-476
Yang, Li Chen III-292
Yang, Liming V-365
Yang, Qian II-164
Yang, Qin VI-458
Yang, Renfa II-287
Yang, Song I-238, I-395
Yang, Wei III-112
Yang, Xinhua IV-450
Yang, Xue I-101, I-124
Yang, You-dong V-164
Yang, Yue II-87
Yanli, Shi VI-517, VI-522
Yanli, Xu IV-136, IV-144, IV-151, IV-159
Yanping, Liu III-369
Yan-yuan, Zhang VI-79
Yanzhen, Guo I-248
Yao, Lei-Yue III-218
Yaqiong, Wei I-132
Yazhou, Chen V-211
Ye, H.C. V-89
Yi, Cui V-82
Yi, Jing-bing III-54
Yi, Ru VI-474
Yifan, Shen III-312
Yihui, Wu IV-335
Yin, Jinghai IV-456
Yin, Qiuju IV-66
Yin, Zhang I-313
Yinfang, Jiang V-133
Ying, Mai I-280
Yingfang, Li IV-1
Yingjun, Feng IV-144, IV-151
Yingying, Ding III-89
Ying-ying, Zhang IV-42
Yixin, Guo VI-282
Yong, Wu I-156
Yong-feng, Li VI-39
Yongqiang, He III-413, III-420
Yongsheng, Huang V-518
Yong-tao, Zhao VI-224
Yongzheng, Kang I-161
You, Mingqing III-200
Youmei, Wang IV-18
Youqu, Lin II-326
Yu, Chen VI-66, VI-474
Yu, Cheng III-377, III-386
Yu, Chuanchun IV-120
Yu, Deng I-8
Yu, Jie VI-398
Yu, Liangguo VI-488
Yu, Quangang VI-239, VI-246, VI-253, VI-261
Yu, Shuxiu II-226
Yu, Siqin II-95
Yu, Tao I-244
Yu, Tingting V-281
Yu, Yan IV-48
Yu, Yao II-143
Yu, Zhichao I-52
Yuan, Fang I-76, I-83
Yuan, Feng III-473
Yuan, Qi III-312
Yuan, Xin-wei III-54
Yuanqing, Wang II-530
Yuanquan, Shi IV-204, IV-212
Yuanyuan, Zhang V-374
Yue, Wang VI-328
Yue, Xi VI-204
Yu-han, Zhang VI-319
Yuhong, Li I-465
Yuhua, He I-1
Yujuan, Liang VI-173
Yun, Wang V-133
Yun-an, Hu VI-224
Yunfang, Chen IV-242
YunFeng, Lin VI-350
Yunna, Wu IV-325
Yuxia, Hu VI-364
Yuxiang, Li V-105
Yuxiang, Yang VI-267

zelong, Xu VI-551
Zeng, Jie III-433
Zeng, Zhiyuan VI-152
Zhai, Ju-huai V-143
Zhan, Yulong II-143
Zhan, Yunjun I-421
Zhang, Bo I-437
Zhang, David IV-297
Zhang, Fan IV-32
Zhang, Fulin III-200
Zhang, Haijun I-437
Zhang, Haohan IV-172
Zhang, Hongjing II-10
Zhang, Hongzhi IV-297

Zhang, Huaping VI-1
Zhang, Huiying V-416
Zhang, Jian VI-131
Zhang, Jianhua V-69
Zhang, Jie IV-93
Zhang, Kai V-404
Zhang, Kuai-Juan II-136
Zhang, Laishun IV-464
Zhang, Liancheng III-166
Zhang, Liang IV-484
Zhang, Liguo IV-508
Zhang, Ling II-466
Zhang, Minghong III-135
Zhang, Minghua I-451
Zhang, Qimin VI-376
Zhang, RuiTao V-18
Zhang, Sen V-529
Zhang, Shu V-43
Zhang, Shuang-Cai II-342
Zhang, Sixiang IV-427
Zhang, Tao VI-179
Zhang, Tingxian IV-360
Zhang, Wei II-350
Zhang, Wuyi III-64, III-74
Zhang, Xianzhi II-194
Zhang, Xiaolin I-500
Zhang, Xiuhong V-404
Zhang, Yi III-268
Zhang, Yingqian II-414
Zhang, Yong I-269
Zhang, Yu IV-189
Zhang, Yuanliang VI-117
Zhang, Yujin IV-441
Zhang, Yun II-66
Zhang, Zaichen IV-382
Zhang, Zhiyuan III-135
Zhangyanpeng I-513
Zhanqing, Ma V-399
Zhao, Hong V-275
Zhao, Huifeng II-244
Zhao, Jiyin I-550
Zhao, Liu V-321
Zhao, Min IV-306
Zhao, Xiaoming III-488
Zhao, Xiuhong III-433
Zhao, Ying III-276
Zhaochun, Wu II-26
Zhaoyang, Zhang II-530
Zhe, Yan VI-273
Zhen, Lu II-187
Zhen, Ran V-69
Zhen, Zhang VI-232
Zhen-fu, Li VI-290
Zheng, Chuiyong II-202
Zheng, Fanglin III-394
Zheng, Jun V-409
Zheng, Lin-tao IV-198
Zheng, Qian V-321
Zheng, Qiusheng III-401
Zheng, Xianyong I-94
Zheng, Yanlin III-192, III-394
Zheng, Yongliang II-181
Zhenying, Xu V-133
Zhi, Kun IV-66
Zhi'an, Wang II-22
Zhiben, Jie II-259
Zhibing, Liu II-172
Zhibo, Li V-193
Zhi-gang, Gan I-295
Zhi-guang, Zhang IV-411
Zhijun, Zhang II-109
Zhiqiang, Duan IV-342
Zhiqiang, Jiang III-453, III-465
Zhiqiang, Wang I-262
Zhisuo, Xu V-346
Zhiwen, Zhang II-101
Zhixiang, Tian II-373
Zhiyuan, Kang I-543
Zhong, Luo III-442
Zhong, Shaochun III-192
Zhong, Yuling II-181
Zhongji, Tan VI-517
Zhongjing, Liu VI-370
Zhonglin, He I-1, I-166
Zhongyan, Wang III-130
Zhou, Defu VI-430
Zhou, De-Qun II-466
Zhou, Fang II-493
Zhou, Fanzhao I-507
Zhou, Feng I-109
Zhou, Gang VI-417
Zhou, Hong IV-120
Zhou, Jing-Jing VI-58
Zhou, Lijuan V-309
Zhou, Wei IV-427
Zhou, Yonghua VI-492
Zhou, Zheng I-507
Zhu, JieBin V-498
Zhu, Jingwei III-508
Zhu, Libin I-335

Zhu, Lili II-420
Zhu, Linlin III-135
Zhu, Quanyin IV-120, IV-189
Zhu, Xi VI-152
Zhuanghua, Lu V-389
Zhuping, Du V-193
Zou, Qiong IV-129
Zunfeng, Liu V-381
ZuoMing IV-514
Zuxu, Zou II-81